THE UNRAVELING OF AMERICA

The

New American Nation Series

EDITED BY

HENRY STEELE COMMAGER

AND

RICHARD B. MORRIS

THE UNRAVELING OF AMERICA

OF AMERICA

*A History of Liberalism
in the 1960s*

ALLEN J. MATUSOW

1817

HARPER & ROW, PUBLISHERS, New York
Cambridge, Philadelphia, San Francisco, London
Mexico City, São Paulo, Sydney

Grateful acknowledgment is made to the following publishers for permission to reprint:

Selection from "Howl" from *Howl and Other Poems* by Allen Ginsberg. Copyright © 1956 by Allen Ginsberg. Selection from "Change" from *Planet News* by Allen Ginsberg. Copyright © 1968 by Allen Ginsberg. Reprinted by permission of City Lights Books.

Selection from "Roland Hayes Beaten" by Langston Hughes. Copyright 1948 by Alfred A. Knopf, Inc. Reprinted from *Selected Poems of Langston Hughes*, by Langston Hughes, by permission of the publisher.

Lyrics from "We Can Be Together" by Jefferson Airplane © 1969 Icebag Corp. All rights reserved. Reprinted by permission of the publisher.

Selection from "The March 1" from *History* by Robert Lowell. Copyright © 1967, 1968, 1969, 1970, 1973 by Robert Lowell. Selection from "Waking Early Sunday Morning" from *Near the Ocean* by Robert Lowell. Copyright © 1963, 1965, 1966, 1967 by Robert Lowell. Reprinted by permission of Farrar, Straus and Giroux, Inc.

Selection from *DO iT!* by Jerry Rubin. Copyright © 1970 by the Social Education Foundation. Reprinted by permission of Simon & Schuster, Inc.

FIRST EDITION

Library of Congress Cataloging in Publication Data

Matusow, Allen J.
  The unraveling of America.

  (The New American Nation series)
  Includes index.
  1. United States—Politics and government—1961–1963.
  2. United States—Politics and government—1963–1969.
  3. Liberalism—United States—History—20th century.
  I. Title. II. Series.
  E841.M33 1984   973.92   83-48019
  ISBN 0-06-015224-9   84 85 86 87 88 10 9 8 7 6 5 4 3 2 1
  ISBN 0-06-091086-0 (pbk.)   84 85 86 87 88 10 9 8 7 6 5 4 3 2 1

For Rosie

Contents

PART III

Editors' Introduction

I T is the special virtue of this significant book that its assessment of the Kennedy-Johnson presidencies never permits the reader to lose sight of the impact of both men and measures on American society. The story Professor Matusow narrates is one of both triumph and tragedy. Lyndon Baines Johnson had Congress adopt the major socio-political legislation initiated in the Kennedy years, and in his quest for social justice went beyond those goals. Notable among the author's assessments are the Civil Rights Act of 1964 and the Voting Rights Act of 1965, the valiant enforcement of which not only finished off Jim Crow but achieved a minor revolution in the balance of political power by enfranchising the blacks in the South. The Medicare-Medicaid legislation imposed huge responsibilities upon the federal government and the states for the health of its citizenry, although at the expense of inflated hospital and medical costs.

Such statutes, as the author recognizes, marked the crowning achievements of Lyndon Johnson's administration. The author proceeds to show how the dedication to the welfare state concept by the Kennedy-Johnson administrations, sustained by Keynesian economics, was to be extended into areas which previous administrations never touched, in part because, with World War II, F.D.R. turned from reform to the business of winning a global war, and in part because of the relative indifference to such issues evidenced in the eight years of Republican rule that preceded the presidency of John Fitzgerald Kennedy.

The Kennedy-Johnson years sought to expand liberalism's dedication to the welfare state, to end poverty, both white and black, and to eradicate racial discrimination in voting, housing, jobs, and schooling, in the last of which the Supreme Court had taken the initiative. Professor Matusow finds that on balance educational desegregation, despite the phenomenon of "white flight," paid off in improved education for black children. While segregation collapsed in the urban South, the efforts to end it encountered unanticipated resistance in the North. Yet the War Against Poverty grinds to an end without solving the problem of equal opportunity for blacks, and with liberals themselves sharply divided over issues of quotas and reverse discrimination.

The author attributes much of the economic woes of the period —inflation and unbalanced budgets—to reliance on then accepted Keynesian economics, although Lyndon Johnson's stubborn insistence on guns *and* butter indubitably was a major contributory factor in creeping inflation and out-of-control deficits. In turn, as we have since seen, monetarism would bring down inflation at the cost of a degree of high unemployment which Keynesians would regard as unacceptable.

If the economists were in disarray, the sociologists emerge heavily battle-scarred. Idealistic though their motivations might have been, the various social action programs they too often espoused encompassed naive, unworkable, and ever more bureaucratic solutions. How the War Against Poverty was impacted by the assassinations of President Kennedy, Martin Luther King, and Robert F. Kennedy are appropriate subjects for speculation, for no leaders with their charisma replaced them.

Overshadowing the ambitious effort on the domestic front was an unpopular war in faraway Vietnam, seen in retrospect to have been an imprudent and tragic entrapment for the United States, and one that brought about the greatest division in American society since the Civil War. It was, so the author argues, the launching in 1965 of the ground war in Vietnam, after years of lesser involvement, that diverted energies and resources that otherwise might have been expended to rehabilitate the ghettos and deal with the larger and more complex issues of the War Against Poverty. It was Vietnam that disclosed the "generation gap" and contributed to what the author sees as the "unraveling" of Lyndon Johnson's hopes for America by way of liberal formulas.

The author provides an analysis in depth of the counterculture of the "beat," "hip," and "New Left" generation. He brings us face-to-face with its leaders, with Herbert Marcuse, Norman O. Brown, Allen Ginsberg, Jack Kerouac, Carl Snyder, Timothy Leary, Bob Dylan, and many other colorful or bizarre nonconformists. He finds this era marked by rock and roll, ghetto riots, peace demonstrations, college seizures, draft-card burnings, the psychedelic style, sex communes, and bombings. Its most significant confrontation occurred at the Democratic National Convention in Chicago, the mishandling of which by Mayor Richard J. Daley contributed so much to the disaffection of the younger generation from Hubert H. Humphrey's presidential candidacy. Matusow pursues this generation's aims and antics, analyzes its impact, and explains its cultural collapse under Weathermen and Black Panther leadership.

This volume is part of the *New American Nation* series, a comprehensive, cooperative history of the area now embraced in the United States, from the days of discovery to the present. In chronological terms it is preceded by a volume on the New Deal by William E. Leuchtenberg, another in preparation on the Truman-Eisenhower years by Robert Griffith, while foreign affairs and the Vietnam involvement are to be treated in a forthcoming volume by Kenneth W. Thompson and Norman A. Graebner. Many of the constitutional issues earlier faced by the Warren Court and raised in this book are considered in Paul L. Murphy's *The Constitution in Crisis Times, 1918–69*, a volume also in this series.

HENRY STEELE COMMAGER
RICHARD B. MORRIS

Preface

IN retrospect, the distinguishing feature of the post–World War II era was its remarkable affluence. From 1950 through 1970, by fits and starts, the American Gross National Product grew at an average annual rate of 3.9 percent, perhaps the best performance in the nation's history. Autos, chemicals, and electrically-powered consumer durables were the leading sectors driving the economy forward in the 1950s; housing, aerospace, and the computer industry, in the 1960s.[1] In consequence the average American commanded 50 percent more real income at the end of the period than at the beginning. Exuberant growth and dramatic increases in the standard of living were hardly novel in the American experience, and it was possible to view postwar economic developments as a mere extension of historic trends. But in one crucial respect the era was indeed different. Past increases in real income had mainly purchased improvements in the necessities of life—more and better food, clothing, shelter. After 1950 rising income meant that the mass of Americans, including many blue-collar workers, could, for the first time, enjoy substantial amounts of discretionary income— i.e., income spent not for essentials but for amenities.

That fact decisively determined the character of the era. Sociologically, increased discretionary income blurred class lines and eased class antagonisms. Culturally, it undermined the self-denying ethic, now inappropriate to economies of high consumption. And politically it underlay the celebration of American life in the Eisenhower years and the optimistic conviction of liberals in the decade following that most American problems could and would be solved.

This book is a history of domestic liberalism in the 1960s. More specifically, it tells the story of how liberals attained political power and attempted to use it for extending the blessings of American life to excluded citizens. Liberals came to identify the main problems confronting the country as unemployment, racism, and poverty. The solutions they sponsored were Keynesian management of the economy, civil rights laws, and special measures to bring the poor into the economic mainstream—measures that came to be called the War on Poverty. While I have tried to convey some of the sound and fury of the attending political struggles, I have been even more concerned with issues of policy. Above all, I have tried to answer this question: What were the concrete consequences of liberal reforms? It is currently the fashion to pronounce the liberal effort to improve America a failure. Reared in the liberal tradition myself, I take no pleasure in having written a book that, in the main, documents the conventional wisdom. Like the premise of abundance that nourished the decade's idealism, the premises of its liberalism proved far more fragile than they seemed at the time.

The history of liberalism's rise and fall, as I write it here, has three parts. Beginning with the election of John F. Kennedy in 1960, Part I traces the conversion of his administration to liberal programs and the emergence of a national consensus in favor of their enactment. In Part II the liberals win resounding endorsement with the landslide election of Lyndon B. Johnson, pass more laws, and then suffer disappointment as the high hopes invested in reform fail of fulfillment. Part III examines the great uprising against liberalism in the decade's waning years by hippies, new leftists, black nationalists, and the antiwar movement—an uprising that convulsed the nation and assured the repudiation of the Democrats in the 1968 election. Thus, in a few short years, optimism vanished, fundamental differences in values emerged to divide the country, social cohesion rapidly declined, and the unraveling of America began.

I am deeply grateful to the people who stole time from their own valuable work to read all or part of my manuscript and to improve it with their criticism. Among them are Barton Bernstein, William Ballew, John Boles, Bob Brito, William Broyles, Chandler Davidson, Louis Galambos, Allen Ginsberg, Alan Grob, Julie Jeffrey, Donald Matusow, Michael Miller, Kathleen Much, Jerry Myers, James P.

O'Brien, Gordon Smith, Martin Wiener, and Herbert Yoskowitz. I owe a special debt to my colleagues Charles Garside and Richard J. Smith for their criticism and encouragement, to William Lewis for his editorial assistance, and to my sister, Barbara Matusow Nelson, for her invaluable help and advice. The American Philosophical Society and the National Endowment for the Humanities provided support for my research in the early days, and I spent a fruitful year at Harvard's Charles Warren Center for American History, whose director at that time, Oscar Handlin, extended me many courtesies. Linda Quaidy heroically bore the brunt of the typing. Most of all, I want to thank my wife, Rosie, who saw many of the deadlines I set myself for completion of this book come and go and for some reason continued to believe that I would, after all, someday actually finish the task.

ALLEN J. MATUSOW

Rice University
August 1, 1983

PART I

CHAPTER 1

The Liberals, the Candidate, and the Election of 1960

I

THE election of 1960 became a classic of American political history. It attracted the highest rate of voter participation in half a century (64 percent), marked the emergence of a glamorous new personality (John F. Kennedy), and restored to power, after an eight-year lapse, the normal majority party (the Democrats). More important than the fate of men and parties, the election initiated the resurgence of American liberalism, which had not commanded the political landscape since the first term of Franklin D. Roosevelt. No one knew it at the time, but with the 1960 presidential campaign a new age of liberal reform was dawning.

Broadly speaking, contemporary liberalism could claim legitimate descent from historic bourgeois liberalism, with its affirmation of reason, progress, order, and the rights of the individual within the context of capitalism. But liberals long ago had cut loose from the original faith in the invisible hand and the limited state. Confronted by the problems of twentieth-century industrial society, liberalism had experimented with so many programs and intellectual reformulations that it seemed less a creature of the past than of mere mood. The liberal mood of 1960 was largely defined by elite intellectuals residing on the East Coast, principally in New York City and Cambridge, Massachusetts. Constituting an intense subculture at the center of the nation's communication network, these intellectuals— nearly all of them liberals—shared a world view that profoundly

3

influenced the political climate in this election year.

The mood of the elite intellectuals originated after World War II, when revulsion against Stalinism inspired a major reappraisal of belief. Liberal revulsion had little in common with popular anti-Communism because it was revulsion born of guilt, the revulsion of the sinner in the throes of confession. The alleged sin, committed in the Great Depression, was the sin of romantic delusion. As the intellectuals remembered the 1930s, too many of them had flirted with Marxism, dreamed of utopias, idealized common folk, joined popular front groups manipulated by Communists, and praised Russia as a progressive state. Because it was not wholly false, this caricature acutely embarrassed the intellectuals in the early years of the Cold War, and for it they did penance by eventually rallying to Harry Truman's ideological crusade against Soviet communism. Living in the shadow not only of Stalin's purges but of Hitler's death camps, those intellectuals who had once harbored chiliastic hopes and radical illusions abandoned them.

The world now seemed grim, intractable, menaced on all sides by the forces of unreason. As the appeal of Marxism waned, Sigmund Freud's pessimistic speculations on the human condition became the indispensable text. Neo-orthodox theology, which dominated the seminaries after the war, also enjoyed a symptomatic vogue among secular liberals, who found in its rehabilitated doctrine of Original Sin a powerful metaphor to express their own disillusionment with human possibility. "More and more of us have come to feel, with Melville, Hawthorne, and Dostoevsky," wrote Robert Nisbet of his fellow intellectuals, "that in men's souls lie deep and unpredictable potentialities for evil that no human institutions can control."[1]

The manifesto of postwar liberalism was Arthur Schlesinger's *The Vital Center*, published in 1949. At thirty-two already a famous Harvard professor and winner of a Pulitzer prize in history, Schlesinger took aim in this book at those "progressives" who, he said, were still clinging to the dreams of the thirties, still believing in the perfectibility of man, still blind to Soviet imperialism and the malevolence of the American Communist party. In particular he meant former Vice President Henry A. Wallace and the benighted citizens who had supported his candidacy for president on a third-party ticket in 1948. Thanks to a "restoration of radical nerve,"[2] he wrote, the vogue of the fellow traveler was diminishing. Liberalism was prepared now to reject all forms of totalitarianism unequivocably and to affirm a realistic democratic creed. As Schlesinger described it, this liberalism inspired the formation of the anti-Communist Americans for Democratic Action (ADA) in 1947. It favored containing Communism in Europe and aiding progressive regimes in former colonial areas. It relied on piecemeal reforms to solve the remaining problems of capitalist society. And it recognized the complexity of reality, the ineradicable sinfulness of human nature, the corruption of power, the virtues of pragmatism and gradualism, and the narrow possibilities of all human endeavor. Schlesinger's was a liberalism in retreat, and as such satisfied most intellectuals as they entered the decade of the 1950s.

Prominent intellectuals not only declared for the West in the Cold War; they volunteered to be foot soldiers in the ideological battle. In 1950 a former Army colonel connected with the U.S. occupation in Germany organized the Congress for Cultural Freedom and invited intellectuals from Western countries to attend an inaugural session in West Berlin. The purpose of the Congress, which became a Cold War fixture, was to extol the virtues of intellectual life in the West.[3] In the United States the affiliate of the Congress was called the American Committee for Cultural Freedom, and its membership included some of the brightest liberal stars in the nation's intellectual firmament: Schlesinger, David Riesman Daniel Bell, Reinhold Niebuhr, Sidney Hook, Dwight Macdonald, Richard Rovere, Lionel Trilling, James Wechsler, and the coeditors of the *Partisan Review,* Philip Rahv and William Phillips. The American Committee had an active life sponsoring conferences, attacking the excesses of McCarthyism, and policing the intellectual community for signs of weakening will in the anti-Communist struggle. Most of the Americans affiliated with the Congress presumably did not know that its activities were partly subsidized by CIA funds laundered through dummy foundations.[4]

As the intellectuals rallied to the defense of America in the early fifties, they retreated from their role as critics of society. For one thing, there no longer seemed much to criticize. After the war the crisis of capitalism had failed to make its expected reappearance, and unprecedented prosperity began eroding the old antagonism toward big business. Here the representative figure was the Harvard economist John Kenneth Galbraith, whose book *American Capitalism* (1952) codified the terms of the truce. Galbraith's message was that liberals should quit worrying about contemporary capitalism. Governments knew enough Keynesian economics to prevent another depression. Large corporations were not the enemies of economic efficiency but the promoters of technological progress. And concentrated corporate power was now "held in check by the countervailing power of those who are subject to it,"[5] by big unions, cooperative buying organizations, and government actions to increase the market power of the economically vulnerable. Galbraith described a self-regulating economy nearly as flawless in fact as the classical model had been in theory. Liberals heeded Galbraith's message and relaxed.

The intellectuals also stopped worrying about economic inequality. Indeed, the condition of the masses in the 1950s occasioned more celebration than regret. The historian Richard Hofstadter observed, ". . . the jobless, distracted and bewildered men of 1933 have in the course of the years found substantial places in society for themselves, have become homeowners, suburbanites, and solid citizens." The New Deal having apparently purged the system of its inhumanities, old liberals could envision nothing more than "simply to defend as much as possible of the old achievements."[6] Hofstadter's view was not strictly accurate. ADA, for example, annually endorsed a laundry list of improvements in the welfare state.[7] But in so doing it was performing not a serious political act but merely a ritual. Though belief in reform survived, only the reemerging issue of legal and political equality for southern blacks engendered any passion.

Gone with the old issues was the old feeling of kinship with the masses. In the thirties intellectuals had expected politics to be the battleground of ideologies, the focal point of class conflict, the medium for translating the will of the people into policy. In the fifties "the people" were transformed into that scourge of the age—"mass man." In *Quest for Community* Columbia's Robert Nisbet typically explained mass man as the end result of historical forces which, since the Middle Ages, had ground down the primary associations of family, village, church, and guild, reducing individuals to social atoms and depriving them of community. Here was the clue to contemporary totalitarian movements, to Nazism and Communism, Hitler and Stalin. Demagogues achieved power in this century, Nisbet explained, by promising to lead the alienated and lonely masses "to the Promised Land of the absolute, redemptive state."[8] When Joe McCarthy rose to prominence in the early fifties by conducting an unscrupulous red hunt, the liberal opposition fit him neatly into its facile categories. He was only the latest totalitarian demagogue, mobilizing the masses by voicing their resentments and fears. In contrast, conservative elites, which had once borne the brunt of earlier liberal attack, seemed now the last principled defenders of liberty left in America—except, of course, for the intellectuals themselves. Sociologists David Riesman and Nathan Glazer observed, "Wall Street was closer to the liberal intellectuals on the two issues that were still alive—civil rights and civil liberties . . . than were the former allies of the liberal intellectuals, the farmers and lower classes of the city."[9] The problem of democracy, it now appeared, was how to save it from the people.

The problem had a solution which almost all the intellectuals advanced. It was called pluralism, defined as a multiplicity of autonomous associations responsive to the genuine needs of individuals and strong enough to resist both the state and the destructive impulses of the mass.[10] Curiously, among the political philosophers most admired by liberal intellectuals at midcentury were such conservative critics of majority rule as Edmund Burke, James Madison, Alexis de Tocqueville, and even John C. Calhoun. Intellectuals found in their writings not only a description of the ideal polity but, happily, of contemporary American realities as well. For, despite the aberration of McCarthyism, most of the intellectuals believed that America had already done a tolerable job of creating a pluralistic society and containing the masses. Pluralist theory, therefore, turned out to be one more form of the American celebration. Politics in contemporary America was seen as a beneficent competition among interest groups, not as a struggle among ideologies with their pernicious tendency to arouse mass man. Ideology had been the mistake of the 1930s; it must not be repeated now. "The tendency to convert concrete issues into ideological problems, to color them with moral fervor and high emotional charge, is to invite conflicts which can only damage a society," wrote Daniel Bell.[11] Fear of excited electorates was one reason why Bell hailed "the end of ideology" in the 1950s.

Though contained politically, mass man dominated culture, the lone realm where the intellectuals continued to despise America. The trouble with the masses, they agreed, was their deplorable taste. *The Democratic Vista,* a book by the well-regarded Columbia literary critic Richard Chase, was characteristic. On politics Chase was brief: "For the moment, American politics and economics, on the domestic scene, appear impenetrable, mysterious, and roughly successful. A revolutionary politics or economics makes no sense to contemporary America. What does make sense is the liberal virtues: moderation, compromise, countervailing forces, the vital center, the mixed economy."[12] Though the middle way was acceptable in politics, Chase said, in culture it fostered complacency, orthodoxy, and conformism. The danger in America was that mass culture would boil all taste and opinion into a sort of middle brow mush. Thus, while they no longer attacked big business, intellectuals like Chase railed endlessly against the organization man, Madison Avenue, hidden persuaders, television, tail fins on cars, and the grosser evidence of American materialism. Because the intellectuals linked bad taste to the rise of mass man rather than to values fostered by capitalism, their critique was elitist, not radical, and increased their political isolation.

As the decade began to wane, the intellectuals grew restless. They liked to think of themselves historically as the friends of progress and justice, but found themselves now in uncomfortable alliance with regnant classes and institutions. Schlesinger noted the widespread feeling "that liberalism in America has not for thirty years been so homeless, baffled, irrelevant, and impotent as it is today."[13] Attempting to recapture a mission for liberals in an article for the *Reporter* in May 1956 he wrote that liberals must move beyond the "quantitative liberalism" of the New Deal. Poverty still existed, of course, but "the central problems of our time are no longer problems of want and privation." The times called for a " 'qualitative liberalism' dedicated to bettering the quality of people's lives and opportunities." The first requirement of a qualitative liberalism would be "the rehabilitation of a sense of the public interest." "While private wealth heaps up in our shops and homes, we refuse to undertake adequate programs to improve our schools, our hospitals, our cities, our natural resources, our public domain," he said. So long as we rely on the pursuit of private profit to guarantee the public welfare, "we can expect that while we privately grow richer, our nation will grow in proportion poorer."[14] Schlesinger's piece was an early intimation of a changing mood.

In the end it was the Russians who inspired a revival of liberal purpose. On October 4, 1957, the Soviet Union launched into orbit a 184-pound artificial satellite called Sputnik—and incidentally struck a devastating blow at America's self-regard and sense of security. If the Russians had Sputnik, a host of commentators concluded, they probably had intercontinental ballistic missiles. If they beat us into space, they must be forging ahead in science, technology, education. If they were capable of concentrating resources inferior to America's to launch Sputnik, their will to prevail in the Cold War just might be firmer than ours. The conservative New Hampshire Republican Senator Styles Bridges, for once catching the national mood, declared, "The time has come clearly to be less concerned with the depth of pile on the new broadloom rug or the height of the tail fin on the new car and to be more prepared to shed blood, sweat, and tears."[15] Concern about the nation's purpose found its chief spokesmen among the liberal intellectuals. Sputnik gave point to their invocations against complacency and hedonism. It lent urgency to their preference for community well-being over narrow personal pursuits. And it made social criticism fashionable again.

John Kenneth Galbraith was writing another book in 1957. He had no high hopes for its reception until the launching of Sputnik. Then, he recalled, "I knew I was home."[16] A best-seller in 1958, The Affluent Society took exception to what it claimed to be the preeminent social goal of the American people—the perpetual increase of production for private use. In a society where the real wants of most people were already satisfied, it made no sense to keep producing more consumer goods. Indeed, disposal of new products depended on creating synthetic wants primarily through advertising and emulation. More private consumption meant less production for the public sector, social imbalance, and public squalor amid private opulence. Accordingly, Galbraith advocated higher taxes to divert wealth from private consumption into schools, parks, police departments, hospitals, slum clearance, and scientific research. He conceded that some poverty still existed in America, but, he said, "it can no longer be presented as a universal or massive affliction. It is more nearly an afterthought."[17] One benefit of spending more on schools and slum clearance would be the reduction of such poverty as still existed. As he knew it would, Galbraith's call for less materialism and more attention to the public welfare perfectly suited the nation's post-Sputnik temper.

The attacks on Galbraith's book were as important as the book itself. Leon Keyserling, once chairman of the Council of Economic Advisers under Truman and Galbraith's chief liberal critic, took aim at the heart of his argument by denying that the U.S. was an affluent society. Not only did most families not live in luxury, a huge minority—25 percent—were actually poor. Poverty on this scale could be diminished neither by spending more on public services, as Galbraith argued, nor by redistributing the wealth, as Galbraith emphatically did not argue. Poverty could be reduced in the future mainly as it had been in the past—by large increases in production for private use and hence in general living standards. Thus, while Galbraith ridiculed growth, Keyserling sang its praises. Keyserling did agree with Galbraith on one important point, however: the public sector was in sorry disrepair. But, said Keyserling, as private production increased, tax yields would also rise, thus providing the revenue to make Galbraithian improvements. Keyserling blamed the Eisenhower administration for an annual growth rate in gross national product of only 2 percent in 1953–1957 and advocated policies to increase it to 5 percent a year.[18] Thanks in large measure to Keyserling, the issue of faster economic growth became a deepening liberal concern as the decade neared its end.

Galbraith's case was open to amendment on still other grounds. He had said relatively little about the Cold War and showed no disposition to enlarge public spending to win it. For once he was as heretical as he liked to imagine. In the view of most liberal intellectuals President Eisenhower's failed quest for a balanced budget had not only starved the public sector at home but crippled the nation abroad. After Sputnik, liberal concern over national security became obsessive. When liberal intellectuals talked about reviving the public sector, they usually included building missiles, improving conventional military forces, and increasing foreign aid.

The Yale economist James Tobin, a liberal, a Keynesian, and a future member of Kennedy's Council of Economic Advisers, warned in 1958 that Eisenhower's fallacious economic theories "have cost the United States its world leadership and gravely threatened its survival as a nation." What did Eisenhower's past reductions of military spending accomplish? Tobin asked. For what purpose were productive resources diverted from defense production to private production? "For research and development of new consumer luxuries," he answered, "for new plants in which to produce more consumers' goods, old and new, all to be marketed by the most advanced techniques of mass persuasion to a people who already enjoy the highest and most frivolous standard of living in history." If the nation's leadership would only inform the people of the dangers, they would willingly "pay the taxes necessary to keep the Western World ahead in basic science, in weapons research and development, in armaments in being."[19] Those intellectuals less concerned with weaponry than Tobin still had plenty to worry about in the growing challenge of the Russians for influence in the Third World. Liberals strongly advocated increased economic aid to strengthen progressive non-Communist regimes in Latin America, Asia, and Africa. Better weapons and more aid would, of course, cost more money—money currently squandered on hair dryers, deodorants, and motorboats.

The liberal intellectuals, who had entered the fifties in retreat, were departing them in a fighting mood. Inspired by Galbraith, they summoned the nation to higher purpose than mere production for private consumption. Persuaded by Keyserling, they demanded a national commitment to an increased rate of economic growth. They urged the nation to repair the public sector, and they pleaded with it to spend more to win the Cold War. But though more aggressive than in the early 1950s, they had amended none of the premises with which they began the decade. Their program contained no hint of radicalism, no disposition to revive the old crusade against concentrated economic power, no desire to stir up class passions, redistribute the wealth, or restructure existing institutions. Ideology was still dead, except in the struggle against world Communism. The reforms they advocated were piecemeal and implied no basic dissatisfaction with the existing capitalist system. Above all, liberals remained dedicated to that Pax Americana whose benefits to mankind would seem less evident later than at the time. At the end of the decade as at the beginning, the intellectuals were holding fast to the vital center.

Thanks to the anxieties provoked by Sputnik, the elite intellectuals found the public increasingly attentive to their exhortations. Committed Democrats were especially receptive, since the critique of the intellectuals lent itself readily to partisan purposes. The nation was threatened by a missile gap, the Democrats said, but Eisenhower was more worried about the budget. The nation needed spiritual inspiration, but Eisenhower was playing golf. The nation needed strong leadership and an activist government, but Eisenhower was old, tired, and increasingly dominated by reactionary advisers. In contrast, the Democrats were prepared by history and by preference to use the state for great public ends and to lead the people out of danger.

In the first half of 1960, a presidential election year, American self-esteem suffered its worst setbacks since Sputnik, making prophets of the intellectuals and issues for the Democrats. In January Soviet Premier Nikita Khrushchev alarmed the gullible by boasting again that he had nuclear rockets capable of wiping any country "off the face of the earth." In May the Russians shot down an American U-2 spy plane and captured its pilot. In Paris for a summit meeting, Eisenhower endured Khrushchev's denunciations of the spy flights, refused to apologize, and finally left deeply depressed. In June as Eisenhower was preparing to depart for Japan, anti-American riots in Tokyo forced his hosts to cancel their invitation. Communist influence, meanwhile, was increasing in the Middle East and Africa, the military situation was deteriorating in Southeast Asia, and Castro was rapidly leading Cuba into the Soviet bloc. The American decline, of which the intellectuals had warned, was apparently well advanced.

Liberal intellectuals and Democrats led the nation in an orgy of self-flagellation. "If I wanted to destroy a nation, I would give it too much and I would have it on its knees, miserable, greedy, and sick" —so wrote the novelist John Steinbeck.[20] "With the supermarket as our temple and the singing commercial as our litany, are we likely to fire the world with an irresistible vision of America's exalted purposes and inspiring way of life?"[21] The quotation was from Adlai Stevenson, ingenious as always at restating his favorite theme. Senator J. William Fulbright, fearful that the Russians would use ICBMs to win the world in thirty minutes, compared the U.S. to "a miserly recluse found starving"—wealthy enough to have security but unwilling to commit the necessary resources.[22] Senator Frank Church foresaw America becoming "a kind of modern Babylon of private plenty in the midst of public poverty."[23] Senator Mike Mansfield warned that the U.S. was like a ship in stormy seas, "frozen in a dangerous course and with a hull in pressing need of repair."[24] One evidence of the spreading malaise was the search in 1960 for the national purpose. President Eisenhower appointed a commission to define it. *Life* magazine engaged distinguished Americans to recover it. The Junior Chamber of Commerce exhorted its 200,000 members to discuss it. The national purpose eluded all pursuers, but of one thing the people could be sure. Whoever was the Democratic presidential candidate in 1960 would insist on its restoration. As it turned out, that candidate was John Fitzgerald Kennedy.

I I

The intense national interest in the campaign of 1960 owed as much to the personality of John Kennedy as to the somber character of the issues. The man intrigued nearly everybody, including the novelist Norman Mailer, who wrote the year's most interesting appraisal of the candidate for *Esquire* magazine. Mailer dismissed Kennedy's public mind as "too conventional" but hailed him nonetheless as "a great box office actor," a character of genuine mystery and heroic dimension. Mailer sensed that Kennedy as hero would have a more profound impact on America than Kennedy as statesman, that a Kennedy presidency might give "unwilling charge" to energies now confined to the American underground. Kennedy, Mailer thought, might rescue mass man from the supermarket of contemporary culture by reviving the myth that every American is potentially extraordinary. Mailer entitled his piece "Superman Comes to the Supermarket" and later advanced the immodest thesis that it had elected Kennedy president.[25]

Was Kennedy really extraordinary? To some extent Mailer was the victim of supermarket advertising in buying Kennedy's Superman image. Kennedy was hailed as a naval hero of World War II for rescuing his crew after a Japanese destroyer rammed a PT boat he commanded in the Pacific in 1943. But his fatally bad judgment at moments during this episode might have earned him a court-martial as easily as the Navy Cross. He nearly died in 1954 after an operation to repair a back injury supposedly incurred while winning his medal. In fact, he suffered from a congenitally bad back and came near death following surgery because of complications resulting from Addison's disease, which his family always denied he had.[26] Kennedy wrote a Pulitzer-prize-winning book in 1955, *Profiles in Courage*, about courage in the Senate, but he himself demonstrated precious little of it in his eight years as a member of that body. He was, as advertised, an extraordinarily intelligent man, but his was an intelligence concerned with process and technique, not with ends and values. He was an expert practitioner of the cool style so much in vogue in his time—detached, ironic, self-mocking, graceful under pressure. But the cool style made a virtue of stunted feelings, in Kennedy's case not only for people, women especially, but for the causes that stirred other men. In truth, legions would follow Kennedy not because he was extraordinary but because he might be —not for his achievement but for his promise. The man had mysterious recesses of character that hinted of great deeds someday to be performed. If not Superman yet, he might become Superman, and this was the secret of his personal and political magnetism.

Mailer found the political Kennedy uninteresting, but it was only as a practical politician that Kennedy might truly be described as extraordinary. "Kennedy became a statesman," his close political aide Lawrence F. O'Brien has written, "but he was a politician first, a tough and resourceful one, the best of his time."[27] Here was an aspect of the man of which there had been no early hint. Kennedy won election from Massachusetts to the U.S. House in 1946 and to the Senate in 1952 on no more than his good looks, his father's money, and his war record. In Congress he attempted neither to gather power nor to wield influence, content to remain on the fringes and play the loner. But in the mid-1950s he emerged as something of a Washington matinee idol, author and war hero, husband of a beautiful socialite, a millionaire who knew and enjoyed the pleasures of the world. This was enough to bring him within a few votes of winning the nomination for vice president at the 1956 Democratic convention. Only then did Kennedy determine his true vocation, which was to secure the top spot for himself in 1960.

His mission set, Kennedy rapidly developed into the complete politician. In 1957 he began crisscrossing the country, sizing up local politicians, learning the terrain in strange regions, charming audiences, making friends. To set the stage for his presidential bid, he sought and won a massive majority in his campaign for reelection to the Senate from Massachusetts in 1958. The following April Kennedy met with his closest advisers at his father's house in Palm Beach and between dips in the pool planned the most effective national machine in the history of presidential politics. Two weeks later Larry O'Brien began touring the primary states to gather intelligence and seek alliances. "I kept waiting for the opposition to show up, but it never did," O'Brien recalled.[28] The opposition consisted of Senator Stuart Symington of Missouri, a political lightweight with the advantage of having few enemies; Lyndon B. Johnson of Texas, the Senate strong man who nurtured the fantasy that influence in Washington could produce delegates at the convention; Adlai Stevenson, the darling of the liberals and two-time party nominee, longing to be drafted for one more try; and Senator Hubert Horatio Humphrey, the talkative liberal from Minnesota with a legislative record that put Kennedy's to shame.

After he announced his candidacy in January, 1960, Kennedy plunged into the primaries.[29] He had to enter several and win each one to convince the party managers that a Catholic at the head of the ticket would not bring ruin in November. Only Humphrey was willing to contest the primaries with him. Kennedy hoped to finish off Humphrey with a crushing victory in Wisconsin in April and then march through the rest of the primaries unopposed. But, when Kennedy scored a less impressive victory in Wisconsin than anticipated, the dogged Humphrey pursued him into West Virginia, a Bible-belt state not famous for charity toward the Catholic Church. For the first and only time of the campaign, gloom descended on the Kennedy camp. But Kennedy's people blitzed the state, and the candidate himself, never more effective, disarmed bigots by forthrightly discussing the religious issue. Kennedy's victory in the West Virginia primary in May was a dazzling achievement that assured his nomination at the July convention in Los Angeles. He had defeated men with better claims than his because he was a better politician than any of them. None of his rivals could match him in managing men, attracting talented subordinates, mastering the details of a thousand local political situations, and using the media to personal advantage.

Kennedy was not equally successful with all groups. Notably resistant to his embrace and hostile to his heroic poses were the liberals, especially the intellectuals among them. They remembered that the candidate's father, Joseph P. Kennedy, American ambassador to Great Britain before the U.S. entered World War II, had supported the appeasement of Hitler. They remembered Jack Kennedy's irresponsible charge from the floor of the House in 1949 that pro-Communists were influencing America's Far Eastern policy.[30] They remembered Kennedy's comment to an interviewer in 1953 that he was not a true liberal and did not feel comfortable with people who were.[31] They remembered, indeed could not forget, that the entire Kennedy family had regarded Senator Joe McCarthy as one hell of a fellow, that Robert Kennedy had served as minority counsel of McCarthy's investigating committee, and that Jack Kennedy had maintained a discreet silence on the whole subject of McCarthyism. As late as 1957 Kennedy outraged liberals by siding with the South on some peripheral issues regarding the civil rights bill passed that year. Kennedy's standing among liberal intellectuals was so low in the mid-1950s that his only conspicuous supporter on the Harvard faculty was the law professor Abram Chayes.[32]

But Kennedy needed the liberal intellectuals, the soul of the party, the guardians of its ideals; and in 1959 he set out to win them too. He began making occasional trips to Boston to meet with Cambridge academics, soliciting their advice, sometimes even taking it. Some of the professors agreed to write position papers for his developing campaign. In 1960 Kennedy flooded the intellectual community with copies of his campaign tract *Strategy for Peace.* In primary states he made contact with groups of local intellectuals, flattering them with his attentions.[33] Most of all, that spring, Kennedy's speeches reflected the concerns of liberal intellectuals with such fidelity that he was indistinguishable on the issues from his major liberal rivals, Humphrey and Stevenson. Though still sentimentally attached to Stevenson, most liberals were preparing for a realistic switch of allegiance to the new power in the party, as the national convention convened in Los Angeles, July 11, 1960.

Kennedy nearly lost the liberals again, when after his first-ballot nomination he chose Lyndon Johnson as his vice president. The conservative Texan was a man whom liberals could not abide. Before the balloting, they rejoiced at the deft way Kennedy had dispatched Johnson's bitter challenge for control of the convention. Now Kennedy was cynically resurrecting Johnson to buy the loyalty of Southern Democrats. Though liberal threats to resist Johnson's nomination on the convention floor never materialized, the liberals went home mad and stayed mad into the next month.

On the eve of the campaign against the Republicans, late in August 1960, the national board of the Americans for Democratic Action met in secret to endorse candidates at the Congressional Hotel in Washington, D.C. The most important voice of independent liberalism in the United States, the organization's national leadership urged unqualified support for Kennedy and Johnson. But as Arthur Schlesinger reported in a letter to Kennedy, delegates from the local chapters either opposed endorsement or favored it with "utmost tepidity." Schlesinger had expected to find apathy for

the ticket at the meeting but not the hostility he actually encountered. At one point a majority of the ADA board voted to excise
from an endorsement motion a paragraph praising Kennedy as "an
aggressive champion of creative liberalism." In the end, the ADA
endorsed Kennedy but not Johnson.

Schlesinger warned Kennedy that he was in danger of losing the
liberals and the intellectuals, "the kinetic people" who "have traditionally provided the spark in Democratic campaigns." He advised
the candidate to get his campaign off the ground by activating "the
political crusaders in the Democratic party—the issue-oriented people who would ordinarily by this time be covering their cars with
Kennedy stickers, arguing with their friends, sending letters to the
papers, manning local organizations, canvassing their neighborhoods, and, in general, charging the campaign with emotion and
zeal (and incidentally knocking down all efforts to insert the religious issue into the discussion)."[34] Schlesinger urged Kennedy to
make use of liberals in the campaign and to run as a liberal himself.
He need not have worried. Kennedy had been running as a liberal
for some time and did not intend to change course now. When that
became clear, as it soon did, most of the ADA types, the liberals and
the intellectuals who cursed the candidate in August, would find him
no less extraordinary, no less heroic, than did Norman Mailer.

III

From the opening address of his campaign in Detroit's Cadillac
Square on Labor Day to his tumultuous homecoming in Boston on
election eve, across thousands of miles, in hundreds of speeches,
and to millions of people, Kennedy appealed for votes using the
issues developed by the intellectuals in the late 1950s. They saw
complacency, lethargy, imminent decline and decay. So did he.
They called for national sacrifice, for energetic executive leadership, for the will to repel Communism abroad and repair the public
sector at home. So did he. Early in the campaign Harvard law
professor Archibald Cox moved into Kennedy headquarters in
Washington to act as a conduit between intellectuals writing
speeches and position papers in Cambridge and the candidate on
the road. Cox soon discovered he was wasting his time.[35] The candidate's speeches were written on the campaign train chiefly by Richard Goodwin and Theodore Sorensen of his senatorial staff. Those

speeches were the general ideas of the liberal intellectuals stripped to their essentials and simplified for a mass audience. Their purpose was not to elaborate or document the liberal case but to suit it to the national mood. This Kennedy did brilliantly by reducing the liberal critique to a single theme. It was time, he proclaimed, to get the country moving again.

Kennedy's main issue was the Cold War and how to stop losing it. "My campaign for the Presidency," he reiterated, "is founded on a single assumption, the assumption that the American people are tired of the drift in our national course, that they are weary of the continual decline in our national prestige . . . and that they are ready to move again."[36] To discourage Russia from launching a surprise attack, he pledged to build more missiles. To stamp out "brush fire wars," he promised to procure more conventional weapons.[37] He would never be content with second place in the space race, with producing fewer scientists than the Russians, or with an economy that grew only one-third as fast as Russia's. Lamenting Communist inroads in the Middle East, Africa, and ninety miles off our shores in Cuba, he described the uncommitted nations as standing "on the razor edge of decision" between our system and Russia's, with the fate of the world hinging on our ability to demonstrate our youth, vigor, and superiority.[38] He was certain that "the people of this country are willing to give, are willing to sacrifice, and will spare no effort" to meet their responsibilities.[39] He had no doubt that America was the greatest country, that she would commit herself to great ends, that she would insist on being "First, period."[40] The rhetoric was a bit chauvinistic for the intellectuals, but Kennedy accurately conveyed their perception of the world in an era when American hegemony was easily equated with the good of the human race.

Second only to the Cold War as an issue in Kennedy's campaign was economic growth and how to increase it. Faster growth would keep us ahead of the Russians, impress the uncommitted peoples, cure unemployment, and pay for improvements in the public sector. Too busy to learn much about the growth issue before his nomination, Kennedy sought expert guidance soon after he won it. On August 3, 1960, the candidate spent several hours on his yacht off Cape Cod conferring with liberal economists J. K. Galbraith, Paul Samuelson, Seymour Harris, and Richard Lester. (Galbraith was there mainly for the sunshine and Bloody Marys since growth was hardly his issue.) The economists told Kennedy that faster growth depended on getting businessmen to increase their rate of investment in new plants and equipment. How could the government induce business to invest more? Simply by lowering interest rates to reduce the cost of borrowing investment capital, the professors explained. But nothing is really simple in the arcane world of economics. Cheap money posed dangers of its own, Samuelson warned, because it could trigger an investment boom and, hence, inflation. To avoid inflation, Kennedy would have to offset increased business spending with decreased spending either by the government or private consumers; that is, he would have either to put a brake on the federal budget or raise taxes on individuals. In his summary of the meeting Samuelson wrote, "Thus an overbalanced budget or one with a lower deficit would be the counterpart of the investment-inducing easy-credit policy."[41] Seymour Harris, who had advised Senator Kennedy on Massachusetts problems, said later, "I think this was the first real education he had in modern fiscal policy."[42]

Kennedy found the advice of Samuelson and company to his taste. He personally preferred easy money and a tight budget to Eisenhower's policy of high interest rates, and by all indications so did the voters. In his campaign he promised to reverse the disastrous Republican policy of tight money and to run a budget surplus in good times, thereby achieving faster growth without inflation.[43] Exactly how fast the economy should grow he was careful not to say. He knew now that the 5 percent growth rate endorsed by the Democratic platform and made famous by Keyserling would either generate inflation or require politically unacceptable cuts in consumption. He contented himself, therefore, with promising some unspecified "more."

Repair of the public sector was Kennedy's other variation on the theme of getting the country moving again. This had originally been Galbraith's issue, but Kennedy studiously avoided giving him credit, since a substantial number of citizens considered the economist a crackpot. But Kennedy left no doubt that he too was disturbed by Republican neglect of community well-being. Kennedy promised to clear the slums, wipe out poverty, bring prosperity to depressed areas, provide a decent education to every school child, restore dignity to the aged, and remove the hardships attendant on automation. A large gap separated these goals from Kennedy's specific proposals, which turned out to be merely the piecemeal reforms advanced by the Democrats unsuccessfully in recent Congresses. They included more urban renewal, federal loans to businessmen locating in depressed areas, Medicare, federal aid to help build classrooms and pay teachers, and higher minimum wages. Mere extensions of the welfare state perhaps, but sufficient to permit the candidate to run in the tradition of Wilson, Roosevelt, and Truman. Most liberals asked no more.

Finally, there was the issue of civil rights, fast becoming the most emotionally charged topic in American politics. It posed an apparently insoluble dilemma for Kennedy. To win he needed the black vote and would have to support the cause of civil rights to get it. But he also needed white southern votes, which he might lose if he pressed the issue too hard. Liberals urged Kennedy to champion vigorously the cause of the black man. Party pros, including some close to Kennedy, were not so sure. For one thing, it was not clear that Kennedy could capture the black vote. In 1956 Eisenhower had made significant inroads among blacks, many of whom were disgusted by the power of southern segregationists in the Democratic party. The GOP entered the 1960 campaign determined to do even better. Moreover, Kennedy's personal standing among blacks was low. Marjorie Lawson, a black Washington lawyer and a Kennedy adviser before the convention, had explained to Kennedy in June the causes of his problem. Blacks regarded him as "an intellectual liberal," hence lacking "in real understanding of Negro problems and goals," she said. They did not like some of his votes on civil rights in 1957 and worried about the early endorsement of his candidacy by Alabama's racist governor, John Patterson. They noted his failure to campaign in black wards during the Wisconsin primary, virtually conceding the black vote to Humphrey. And they were still waiting for him to make "a strong civil rights statement from a national stage."[44]

Throughout August Kennedy wrestled with the political dilemmas of the civil rights issue. Among those in his camp urging Kennedy to go all out for the Negro vote was Harris Wofford. A friend of Martin Luther King and a former staff member of the U.S. Civil Rights Commission, Wofford left a post at the University of Notre Dame Law School in the spring of 1960 to join the Kennedy staff. By August he had emerged as a key figure in the campaign's civil rights division. Wofford found his candidate neither knowledgeable about the civil rights problem nor committed to a position on it. Kennedy regarded discrimination as "irrational," Wofford thought, but "alien to most of his experience." One morning during the August congressional session, Kennedy spotted Wofford looking for a cab and gave him a lift to the Senate Office Building. Kennedy was driving his red convertible fast, Wofford recalled, "and his left hand was tapping on the door. . . . And he said, 'Now, in five minutes, tick off the ten things that a President ought to do to clear up this goddamn civil rights mess.' "[45]

By the time the campaign opened in September, Kennedy had decided to heed the liberals and run as the civil rights candidate, leaving the South to LBJ. His rhetoric, at least, was uncompromising. "If a Negro baby is born here," he told a Harlem audience, "and a white baby is born next door, that Negro baby's chance of finishing high school is about 60 percent of the white baby. This baby's chance of getting through college is about a third of that baby's. His chance of being unemployed is four times that baby's."[46] Kennedy's program was appropriately liberal. He promised to offer a bill early in the next session of Congress to implement the pledges of the Democratic platform. He said that with "a stroke of the Presidential pen" he would do what Eisenhower had not done—end discrimination in federally supported housing.[47] He even gave oblique sanction to the growing campaign of civil disobedience against segregation. The president, he said, had to exert moral leadership "to help bring equal access to facilities from churches to lunch counters, and to support the right of every American to stand up for his rights, even if on occasion he must sit down for them."[48] Whether Kennedy was promising blacks enough to improve his image among them remained to be seen.

When the campaign began in early September, the polls rated the contest a tossup, but seasoned observers gave the edge to the Republican nominee, Vice President Richard M. Nixon. On the surface this was surprising. Nixon was the candidate of the minority party, which had won in 1952 and 1956 only because Eisenhower was a national hero with a nonpartisan image. In 1960 Nixon was stuck with the record of the last eight years and the profitless duty of defending it. Moreover, he lacked magnetism, was a mediocre orator, and was the politician most despised by the liberals, who had watched him since his days as a neophyte redbaiter and who were unshakably convinced that he was a bad man. But the general public had a more generous opinion of Richard Nixon. He had, after all, braved mobs in Latin America in 1958 and stood up to Khrushchev during an impromptu TV debate in an American kitchen exhibit in Moscow in 1959. He had assiduously cultivated the image of a "new Nixon" in recent years, a moderate Nixon, the advocate of Keynesian economics in the Eisenhower administration and a strong supporter of civil rights. In the campaign he countered Kennedy's charges of American decline by insisting that things had never been better. "If you think the United States has stood still," Nixon said in Portland, Oregon, "who built the largest shopping center in the world, the Lloyd Shopping Center right here?"[49] Not for sallies such as this was he the early favorite, but for two advantages he had over Kennedy. He seemed the more experienced candidate, and he was Protestant.

In order to get a hearing on the issues of his choosing, Kennedy had to quiet the growing clamor about his religion and dispel the widespread impression that he was a callow youth. Before September was gone, he established his credentials as the Superman of American politics by doing both. The religious issue was clearly his biggest problem. Not only was the Southern Baptist Convention, with its 9.6 million members and 31,000 preachers, mobilizing against Rome; Protestants in the North were also restless. On September 7 Norman Vincent Peale, the famous salesman of positive thinking, joined other Protestant clergy and laymen to organize the National Conference of Citizens for Religious Freedom. "Is it reasonable to assume that a Roman Catholic President would be able to withstand the determined efforts of the hierarchy of his church to gain further funds and favors for its schools and institutions, and otherwise break the wall of separation of church and state?" they asked.[50]

Early in September the Greater Houston Ministerial Association, a group of not altogether friendly clergymen, invited Kennedy to meet them and defend the right of a Catholic to be president. Though Kennedy had so far failed to dampen the religious issue by ignoring it, many in his camp feared that open confrontation would only make matters worse. Among those counseling silence were his campaign manager, Robert Kennedy; his closest political aide on the campaign train, Kenneth O'Donnell; and veteran Texas politicians Lyndon Johnson and House speaker Sam Rayburn. The candidate overruled them all.[51] In the Rice Hotel in Houston on September 12, 1960, before a hostile crowd, Kennedy delivered the best speech of the campaign. "I believe in an America," he said, "where the separation of church and state is absolute—where no Catholic prelate would tell the President (should he be Catholic) how to act, and no Protestant minister would tell his parishioners for whom to vote."[52] "By God . . . ," said Rayburn, watching on television elsewhere in the hotel, "he's eating 'em blood raw!"[53] Nixon agreed next day that the religious issue should be eliminated from the campaign, Peale soon backed down, and the furor subsided. Though bigotry continued to thrive underground, Kennedy's performance in Houston kept it from destroying his campaign.

Kennedy buried the issue of his alleged inexperience in a single hour on September 25. On invitation from the networks the two candidates met in a Chicago television studio to answer questions from newsmen in the first of four historic debates. Seventy million viewers watched the candidates rehearse their campaign arguments and dispute whether or not the national performance had deteriorated since 1952. Judged by the printed text, the debate was a draw. But on TV image counts more than argument. Grim and confident, Kennedy delivered his message of imminent danger. Nixon smiled nervously and dabbed at the perspiration on his forehead. He looked tired, gaunt, even sickly, the camera detecting the fatigue he felt after a month spent first in the hospital for treatment of a knee infection, then in furious campaigning to make up for lost time. Kennedy's image bested Nixon's image, with the result that thereafter few would dispute the claim of the Democrats that their man was a bona-fide contender, heavyweight division.[54]

Kennedy emerged from the first debate a celebrity. His crowds got larger, his delivery improved with his confidence, and he inspired receptions usually reserved for romantic leads in the movies. Women shrieked when they saw him, and young girls grabbed at his clothing.[55] Among reporters traveling with Kennedy the suspicion grew that the momentum was shifting his way. Kennedy's aides thought so too, and so did Nixon's.[56]

Late-breaking developments seemed to confirm the Kennedy trend. Providentially, and at the last minute, the economy faltered. Nixon and Arthur Burns, former chairman of the Council of Economic Advisors, had pleaded with Eisenhower in March, 1960, to ease credit and increase federal spending to forestall a recession before the election. But Ike turned them down.[57] The economy showed signs of anemia by the summer, and in the last week in

October Kennedy was able to proclaim the third Republican recession in six years.[58] Unemployment, which stood at 5.7 percent in
September rose to 6.3 percent in November.[59] It is axiomatic in
politics that recessions hurt the party in power. Kennedy aide Theodore Sorensen wrote later, "The votes of newly unemployed workers alone in Illinois, New Jersey, Michigan, Minnesota, Missouri,
and South Carolina were greater than Kennedy's margins in those
states."[60]

Kennedy had similar good luck with the civil rights issue. Nixon
had begun the campaign ready to compete with Kennedy for every
black vote—until he took a swing through Greensboro, Atlanta, and
Birmingham in August. His tremendous receptions in these cities
fired his hopes for big gains among white voters in the South and
kept him teetering thereafter between black and white voters.
Though he forthrightly supported equal rights during the campaign, his rhetoric was muted compared to Kennedy's. The issue
was more personal than legal, more moral than governmental,
Nixon said.[61] He was less than pleased when on October 12 his
running mate, Henry Cabot Lodge, pledged in Harlem that, if
elected, Nixon would appoint a Negro to the Cabinet. (Lodge actually made his pledge in East Harlem to a predominantly Puerto
Rican audience that could not have cared less.) "With respect to any
appointments to the Cabinet," Nixon said in disowning Lodge, "I
will attempt to appoint the best man possible without regard to race,
color, or creed."[62]

In the last week of October an unanticipated development put
both candidates to the test. A Georgia judge sentenced Martin Luther King on a technicality to four months in jail deep in cracker
country. It seemed entirely probable that King would not get out
alive. Through an aide, Nixon said he would make no comment.[63]
To keep the Democrats from exploiting the case, he privately urged
the White House to announce that the Justice Department was
going to look into it. To no avail. Once again Eisenhower ignored
him.[64]

John Kennedy did not hesitate. At Wofford's instigation,
Kennedy called the distraught and pregnant Mrs. King on October
26 to express sympathy and pledge help. Robert Kennedy at first
feared his brother's gesture would hurt the ticket in the South, but
the more he considered the danger to King, the more concerned he
became. The next morning Bobby phoned the local judge on King's

behalf. When on October 27 the judge released King, the Kennedys got the credit, though in truth legal developments in the case made King's release mandatory.[65] The Reverend Martin Luther King, Sr., announced that he had intended to vote for Nixon on religious grounds but would now vote for Kennedy. "Imagine Martin Luther King having a bigot for a father," Kennedy said privately, adding, "Well, we all have fathers, don't we?"[66] King himself did not endorse candidates, but he left no doubt how he felt. "It took a lot of courage for Senator Kennedy to do this especially in Georgia," King said. "For him to be that courageous shows that he is really acting upon principle and not expedience. . . . I am convinced he will seek to exercise the power of his office to fully implement the civil rights plank of his party's platform." Outside Negro churches on the Sunday before the election, the Democrats distributed two million copies of a brochure quoting the praise of various members of the King family for John Kennedy. How much the Kennedy phone calls affected the election was a moot question, but no one argued that they hurt the candidate.[67]

As the campaign entered the final two weeks the press acted as if it was over. James Reston reported in the *New York Times* on October 23, "In the last few days a strong feeling has developed that more people are going to vote against Nixon than are going to vote against Kennedy."[68] But in the final days Nixon staged a furious rally. At last he took the wraps off Eisenhower, who spoke to great ovations and derided Kennedy as "this young genius."[69] Nixon himself, seizing the offensive, struck at Kennedy with the hardest blow of his campaign. The Gallup poll, which had Kennedy leading by four percentage points in the third week of October, found his lead cut to one point in the first week of November.[70] The race was ending in a virtual dead heat.

As it turned out the election was the closest in history. Kennedy won 49.7 percent of the popular vote to his opponent's 49.5 percent, and his plurality was only 118,550 votes. Of the eight large industrial states, which he considered the prize of the contest, Kennedy won easily in New York and Massachusetts, managed narrow but firm majorities in Pennsylvania and Michigan, and barely squeezed by in New Jersey and Illinois. Only Ohio and California got away. The six big states gave Kennedy 156 of the necessary 269 electoral votes. As planned, he picked up most of what he still needed in the South. Seven of the eleven states of the Old Confederacy gave him 81 of their 128 electoral votes, and the border states of Maryland, Delaware, Missouri, and West Virginia secured his majority. In the South Kennedy lost only Florida, Virginia, and Tennessee to Nixon, while Mississippi and 6 of Alabama's 11 electors went for Virginia's Senator Harry Byrd. For good measure, Kennedy carried Connecticut, Minnesota, and a scattering of smaller states to give him a total of 303 electoral votes to Nixon's 219.[71]

Republicans rather doubted that it was an honest tally, especially in Illinois, where Kennedy's margin was a mere 8,856 votes out of 4.75 million cast. On election night, when he was sweating out the returns, Kennedy called Mayor Richard J. Daley of Chicago, the last of the great American machine politicians, who told him, "Mr. President, with a little bit of luck and the help of a few close friends, you're going to carry Illinois."[72] Because Kennedy received a remarkable plurality—in excess of 450,000 votes—in Chicago, the mayor was right. Local Republicans alleged that Kennedy's friends in the Daley machine had inflated his total through bribes, floaters, cemetery voters, uncounted absentee ballots, doctored registration lists, stuffed ballot boxes, and other assorted acts of fraud. How, other than fraud, for example, could the Democrats explain precinct 50, ward 2, where 22 registered voters somehow cast 74 votes for Kennedy and 3 votes for Nixon?[73] Indeed, to judge by the available evidence, Daley probably did steal the state for Kennedy.[74] Illinois Democrats defended themselves by asserting that irregularities in Chicago merely canceled out Republican cheating downstate.[75] If so, the Democrats made no effort to prove it. They did not have to. Republican attempts to contest the results in Illinois fizzled in the face of Nixon's indifference and insurmountable legal and political obstacles.

But Illinois's 27 electoral votes would have been insufficient to produce a Nixon majority in the Electoral College. He also had to have Texas, with its 24 electoral votes, the other state where Republicans alleged foul play. Kennedy carried Texas by 46,233 votes out of 2.3 million cast—at least according to official returns. Those returns were tainted, Republican leaders charged, because county election officials, almost all of whom were Democrats, inconsistently applied the state's 1957 election law, which required voters casting paper ballots to indicate their candidate by scratching out the names they did not want. In 1960 the names of four presidential candidates appeared on the Texas ballot. Mass voter confusion inevitably resulted. Some election judges threw away more than 40 percent of the ballots cast in their counties because of illegal markings. Other judges counted almost all ballots, no matter how marked.[76] Republican partisans claimed that most of the 100,000 thrown-away votes had been cast in Republican areas, while illegal ballots were routinely accepted in areas heavily populated by illiterate Democrats.[77] All they wanted, the Republicans contended, was an honest recount in which *all* illegal ballots would be discarded. But in argument before a federal judge, the Republicans backed off. Did Republicans and Democrats suffer the same loss from inconsistent application of the law? the judge asked. Counsel for the GOP gave away his case by conceding that they had.[78] The judge dismissed the suit for lack of jurisdiction. And the Democrats quite properly could now assert that they had carried Texas, and therefore the nation, fair and square.

The main puzzle of the election was why it was so close. Eisenhower was off the ballot, the nation was in the mood for a change, the Democrats were the normal majority party, and Kennedy had been a great campaigner. In popular voting for seats in the U.S. House, the Democrats won an impressive 54.7 percent of all ballots cast, a good indication of the party's real strength and 5 percent better than Kennedy had run against Nixon.[79] Kennedy's weak showing was really no mystery. The most important issue in the campaign was not the Cold War, economic growth, civil rights, or social welfare. It was Kennedy's Catholic religion, which stirred fears among strongly Protestant voters of a popish plot.[80] The religious issue hurt most in the South, where, according to the best analysis, Protestant defectors cost Kennedy an estimated 17 percent of the normal Democratic vote. The issue also cut deeply in the Protestant farm states of the Midwest. This geographical concentration of bigotry was fortunate from Kennedy's point of view. The South was still so overwhelmingly Democratic that Kennedy won it despite defections of perhaps one million Protestant voters. In the traditionally Republican farm states of the Midwest, Kennedy figured to lose anyway. Indeed, despite the large number of Protestant voters whom he lost nationwide, the religious issue clearly defeated Kennedy in only two states—Tennessee and Oklahoma.[81]

The religious issue worked two ways, of course. Kennedy proved especially attractive to Catholic voters, winning approximately 80 percent of them, compared to an estimated normal Democratic vote of 63 percent. Once again demography helped Kennedy. While Kennedy did lose some Protestant Democrats in northern industrial states, the extra Catholic votes he attracted there more than offset them.[82] His net gain was small, but in closely contested states like New Jersey, Illinois, and Michigan, it was indispensable. In short, religion hurt Kennedy in the popular vote but helped him win his majority in the electoral college.

Aside from religion the most interesting facet of the election was the contest for the South. Kennedy lost few white votes by having spoken louder for civil rights than had Nixon. Southern whites still tended to view both national parties as hopeless on this issue and to cast their votes instead for reasons of class or tradition. But for southern blacks civil rights was by far the salient issue. Kennedy's aggressive campaigning for civil equality in 1960 practically erased Eisenhower's 1956 inroads into the southern black vote.[83] Blacks returning to the party gave Kennedy his 10,000-vote margin in South Carolina and were probably necessary to his victory in North Carolina and Texas as well. Without these three states Kennedy would have fallen short of a majority in the Electoral College.[84] Johnson, meanwhile, traversed the South, seeking to keep conservative white Protestants loyal to the ancestral party. The tug of tradition proved strong. Thus in the campaign's closing days Senator Richard B. Russell of Georgia, the pride of the South's states-rights Democrats, stumped Texas for the ticket.[85] Without Johnson's exertions Kennedy would certainly have failed in Texas and probably fared much less well than he did elsewhere in the region. To bag a majority of both black and white southerners in 1960 was a neat trick, and in part because they performed it, Kennedy and Johnson won the election.

In a close election, of course, every stratagem, every accident, the contribution of every voting bloc can be made to seem decisive. From hindsight, not the least of the causes of Kennedy's victory were Kennedy himself and the issues which he raised. In his long march to the White House, he had made scarcely a false step and at the critical moments always made the winning move. Moreover, he had convinced millions of voters that he was not just another ambitious senator, but a national leader capable of firing men with his political vision. Herein lay the significance of the issues. By appropriating the critique of the liberal intellectuals, Kennedy acquired a political identity, gave contour and content to his candidacy, and invested his campaign with a sense of historic purpose. No one, in the end, was more impressed by the performance than the liberals themselves, imitation being the highest form of flattery. It remained to be seen in the months and years ahead whether Kennedy's liberalism in 1960 was a matter of convenience or conviction, whether indeed Superman had come to the Supermarket.

CHAPTER 2

Kennedy, Keynes, and the Corporations

I

AS the complete politician, John Kennedy understood that image
was power. Hence, from the outset, he sought to create glitter-
ing images of himself and his presidency. These images, painstakingly crafted, were arguably the greatest achievement of his administration. None among them was more brilliant than the image
of his inauguration, carried by television into the homes of millions
and lingering long in the collective memory of his people. Tanned
and coatless in subfreezing temperatures, Kennedy radiated vitality
in contrast to the departing Eisenhower, who, at age seventy, was
the oldest man ever to occupy the White House and on this occasion
looked it. On the program by Kennedy's invitation, Robert Frost
read one of his poems, prefaced by a few lines in praise of a president who would bestow such honor on an artist.[1]

The inaugural address itself was the best campaign speech
Kennedy ever gave. Masterfully distilling his recent themes, he said,
"Let every nation know, whether it wishes us well or ill, that we shall
pay any price, bear any burden, meet any hardship, support any
friend, oppose any foe to assure the survival and the success of
liberty."[2] Americans who would later find this martial rhetoric repellent cheered at the time along with everybody else. "Reaction to
the speech was immediate," *Time* reported. "From all shades of
political outlook, from people who had voted for Kennedy in November and people who had voted against him, came a surge of
congratulations."[3] So luminous was the image created by Kennedy

that day that for countless of his countrymen no disaster of policy, no paucity of achievement, would ever dim it.

Abetted by the media, Kennedy mass-produced flattering images of himself for a public whose appetite for them proved insatiable. Images of Kennedy in command, dominating his press conferences by information, skilled evasion, and sheer presence. ("That camera angle murders me," he moaned on reviewing one of his taped performances.)[4] Images of Kennedy as idealist, summoning America to alleviate world suffering through the Peace Corps or to conquer space for the good of mankind. ("But why, some say, the moon?" he asked at Rice University. ". . . Why does Rice play Texas?")[5] Images of Kennedy as intellectual, devouring books, quoting poetry, populating his administration with professors and Rhodes scholars. ("There's nothing like brains," he said. "You can't beat brains.")[6] Images of Kennedy as First Host, serving vintage wines and cracking jokes to the gifted and the celebrated. ("This is the most extraordinary collection of talent, of human knowledge, that has ever been gathered together at the White House, with the possible exception of when Thomas Jefferson dined alone," he told a group of Nobel laureates.)[7] Images of Kennedy as father and husband, permitting his little son John to disrupt high councils and showing off his wife to admiring heads of state. ("I am the man who accompanied Jacqueline Kennedy to Paris," he quipped after she had charmed de Gaulle.)[8] Conductor Leonard Bernstein, who attended Kennedy's famous party for cellist Pablo Casals and never got over it, summed up the perception of Kennedy's adoring partisans when he described his administration as "a remarkable combination of informality and stateliness . . . casualness and majesty."[9]

But the shining surface obscured some shabby realities. Only later, for example, did the public learn of Kennedy's unscrupulous vendetta against Castro, undertaken to avenge his personal humiliation at the Bay of Pigs. American agents clandestinely contaminated sugar exports out of Cuba, damaged imports into Cuba, sabotaged sugar mills and oil refineries, ran guns to guerrilla groups, and even undertook to kill Castro.[10] J. Edgar Hoover had the delicate task of informing Kennedy in 1962 that one of the ladies he entertained in the White House bedroom happened also to be the mistress of Mafioso Sam Giancana, a dubious patriot who had agreed to help dispose of Castro for the CIA.[11] The Kennedys, meantime, snooped into the tax returns of private citizens;[12] wiretapped distinguished reporters, a congressman, Martin Luther King, and perhaps others;[13] and prodded the Internal Revenue Service to investigate the tax-exempt status of groups they viewed as ideologically obnoxious.[14] In citing Kennedy as precedent for their own abuse of power, later presidents had a point.

Liberals cared less for images than most citizens and were just as ignorant of life behind the scenes of the White House. Their concern was issues, particularly the domestic issues raised so compellingly by Kennedy in 1960—the economy, civil rights, and social welfare. Though the new president moved swiftly, as promised, to escalate the Cold War, he initially disappointed liberals on the home front. Political considerations and a conventional turn of mind made him slow to substantiate the liberal image he had so carefully fashioned in the campaign. But most liberals never lost faith, and in the end Kennedy became the president they always hoped he would be. Whether Kennedy's liberalism in the realm of economic policy, best described as corporate liberalism, deserved the encomiums it eventually brought him remains problematical.

II

The concept "corporate liberalism" was the contribution of new left intellectuals, who emerged in the early 1960s to formulate a radical critique of the American political economy, mainly in the pages of a journal called *Studies on the Left*. [15] The old left was wrong to identify right-wingers as the major obstacle to a truly democratic society, the new left said. The real enemy was liberalism, corporate liberalism—liberals in service to the large business corporations. Most corporate leaders were not reactionary champions of laissez-faire, as myth would have it, but sophisticated managers seeking to secure their hegemony with governmental assistance. Most political liberals were not champions of the people against the special interests, but pseudo-reformers who did the bidding of big business. Ever since the days of Teddy Roosevelt—new left historians asserted—liberals had sought a stable environment for the corporations, helped insulate them from the competitive rigors of the market, and offered just enough concessions to labor and the middle classes to stave off real reform.[16] In his 1963 study, *The Triumph of Conservatism*, an examination of early twentieth-century "progressivism," Gabriel Kolko defined terms. "I use the attempt to preserve existing power and social relationships as the criterion for conservatism because none other has any practical meaning," he wrote.[17] Using this criterion, the new left attempted to reveal the conservative reality behind liberalism's façade.

Whatever its merits for understanding the past, the concept of corporate liberalism cut to the heart of the post-1945 American political economy. Intellectual liberals unashamedly asserted the benevolence of large corporations and defended the existing distribution of wealth and power in America. Political liberals assumed corporate hegemony and pursued policies to strengthen it. The quintessential corporate liberal was John F. Kennedy, who never pretended to be otherwise and for whom the good opinion of big business was the highest political priority. The president's economic policies—some defensible, some not—would be framed above all to create a stable environment for corporate prosperity and corporate expansion. What was good for the corporate system would be good for the country. Even his reforms were the minimum necessary for buying off traditional Democratic interest groups or forestalling radicalism. Three weeks into his presidency, Kennedy set forth the conception of corporate-government relations that would guide him in the years ahead. Speaking to a big-business audience, he said that the government's revenues and "thus our success are dependent upon your profits and your success—and . . . far from being natural enemies, Government and business are necessary allies."[18]

That Kennedy sought this alliance was less remarkable than the determination of the corporations to resist it. Most big businessmen preferred corporate Republicans to corporate Democrats and initially insisted on viewing Kennedy through the distorted lense of partisanship. As Robert Kennedy once remarked, "The business community always has a greater distrust of any Democratic President than of a Republican Administration. It is an ideological reflex —obsolete in my opinion—but that's one of the facts of life."[19] Every action, every statement of the administration was scrutinized for anti-business nuance.

Indeed, those arguing the thesis of Kennedy's hostility could find scraps of evidence to support it. In 1961 Commerce Secretary Luther Hodges and the Business Advisory Council—a quasi-governmental consulting group of the nation's biggest businessmen—got into a quarrel over whether to open Council meetings to the public and include small businessmen as members.[20] Some Kennedy appointees to the regulatory commissions actually threatened to regulate. And Attorney General Robert Kennedy alarmed business by stating his intention to enforce the laws against price fixing.[21] The president spared no effort in trying to persuade business that these were mere details in his larger policy of serving corporate needs, and he sent his lieutenants ranging far and wide in search of business audiences to mollify. After one such encounter with the U.S. Chamber of Commerce, administration economist Walter Heller reported to Kennedy, "I had a good meeting with its president, Richard ('call me Siegfried') Wagner. . . . We went round the Nibelungen Ring, the cost-price spiral, and the growth merry-go-round. It was a dizzying experience, but well worth it in terms of better communications and relations with business."[22]

Despite difficult relations, Kennedy's policies on taxes, trade, and the all-important matter of antitrust could hardly have been more to corporate taste. The nation's antitrust laws were potentially a powerful weapon against economic concentration, and as such filled big businessmen with fear and loathing. Indeed, their first requirement of any administration was that it refrain from busting up old "trusts" or blocking new mergers. As the Kennedy administration entered office, the conglomerate merger era was just beginning, an era in which giant holding companies acquired firms in noncompeting industries. But trusts—conglomerate or otherwise—did not much trouble the Kennedy brothers, which made all the more puzzling their choice of Lee Loevinger as chief of the Justice Department's antitrust division. A Minnesota judge close to Hubert Humphrey, Loevinger once called antitrust his "secular religion" and entered office hoping to take on some of the Goliaths of American enterprise.[23] But, as he soon learned, his intentions were not Bobby Kennedy's. Loevinger aggressively prosecuted the anticompetitive practices of some major corporations, but he hardly laid a hand on monopoly itself. After a few months on the job, he confessed to a reporter, "It is probably true that we are affected by business uncertainties to the point where we are holding up cases with a novel or uncertain legal approach. We are sticking pretty much to the predictable, to the established lines."[24] In 1963 Loevinger, who never did hit it off with Robert Kennedy, departed for the Federal Communications Commission. Enforcement of the antitrust laws, meanwhile, proceeded with the same vigor under Kennedy as it had under Eisenhower, which is to say not vigorously at all.[25]

President Kennedy rendered tangible benefits to business on the matter of taxes. In April 1961, long before he considered lowering taxes for others, he proposed an investment tax credit, which, as finally enacted, permitted business to deduct from taxes 7 percent of the cost of new investment. The administration defended the credit as a spur to greater investment, hence to growth. Critics attacked the credit as an unwarranted business subsidy that would affect investment decisions much less than would business expectations of market demand. Among those who viewed the tax credit with skepticism were, surprisingly, most businessmen.[26] For years the corporations had urged the Treasury to liberalize tax guidelines for writing off losses due to depreciation of plant and equipment. Their fear was that the administration intended to substitute the investment tax credit for essential depreciation revision. Business misjudged the administration, as usual. In July 1962 the Treasury issued new depreciation guidelines, permitting write-offs 30 to 40 percent faster than before. "It could have been done in the past," said Treasury Secretary Douglas Dillon, "but it fell to this Administration to actually do it."[27] After that, business became noticeably more enthusiastic about the tax credit, which passed in October 1962. The combined effect of the investment tax credit and liberalized depreciation was a generous corporate tax cut the first year of $2.5 billion or approximately 10 percent.[28]

As the political manager of the corporate system, Kennedy energetically pursued foreign markets for American business and agriculture. This meant free trade—one Kennedy policy in which the interests of the corporations clearly converged with the public good. The nation needed freer trade, the president argued, to achieve national prosperity, reduction in the balance-of-payments deficit, and continuing leadership of the free world. In 1962, adopting the slogan "trade or fade,"[29] he introduced the Trade Expansion Act and proclaimed it his number-one legislative priority. This act was America's response to the threat and promise of the Common Market. If Britain's pending application for membership was accepted, the Common Market loomed as a vast internal free trade area that would either hide from American competition behind high tariffs or join with America in mutual tariff reduction. Kennedy asked Congress for authority (1) to reduce existing American tariffs up to 50 percent in return for similar concessions by foreign nations and (2) to negotiate total elimination of tariffs on goods for which the U.S. and the Common Market accounted for 80 percent or more of world trade.[30] With Britain in the Market, the free list could be extensive and significant. The bill passed with a handsome majority for two reasons: Bowing to political realities, Kennedy compromised his free trade principles to appease powerful protectionist industries, notably textiles and domestic oil production. And export-minded corporations lobbied hard for the heart of the measure, whose intent was to expand their foreign markets. Working closely with the administration for passage was the Committee for a National Trade Policy, chaired by Carl Gilbert of the Gillette Company and including members from IBM, the Ford Motor Company, H. J. Heinz, Crown Zellerbach, and Pillsbury. Among other business voices speaking up persuasively for freer trade were Standard Oil, the American Iron and Steel Institute, and the Chamber of Commerce.[31] Unfortunately, the Trade Expansion Act never realized the high hopes invested in it. French President Charles de Gaulle vetoed Britain's admission into the Common Market, rendering meaningless the act's authority to eliminate many tariffs. In 1967, at the end of the so-called Kennedy round of tariff talks, tariffs were cut an average of 35 percent on 6,300 products, a forward step considerably less dramatic than the corporate liberals and the corporate leaders had originally envisioned.[32]

The administration did more than tend to the health of the system; it also bestowed special favor on individual corporations. For example, there was the matter of AT&T's desire for control over communications space satellites, a revolutionary new technology making possible the transmission of TV signals, telephone messages, and computer data across the oceans and continents. Having developed the technology, the United States government had to determine who would put it to civilian use. In 1961, AT&T and lesser carriers already in intercontinental communications backed legislation authorizing them to form a consortium for exploiting space satellites commercially. A small group of antimonopoly senators, however, adamantly opposed any measure that would augment the power of the world's biggest monopoly. If it got hold of space technology, they charged, AT&T would sabotage it to protect the company's investment in existing technologies, notably undersea cables. Let the government own space satellites and use them to force competition on AT&T,[33] antimonopolists urged.

In 1962 the Kennedy administration proposed a compromise that would create a new company—the Communications Satellite Corporation (Comsat)—for developing space communications. Half of Comsat's stock would be sold to the public, half to private companies, with AT&T obtaining 29 percent. Charging a sellout, antimonopolists described Kennedy's bill as an insidious device to turn over control of space to AT&T. It did nothing to lessen their fears of the measure that AT&T labored mightily for its passage. Lacking votes to defeat it when it came up for Senate debate in June 1962, the antimonopolists tried to kill the bill by filibuster.

AT&T was nothing if not resourceful. On July 10, 1962, with the assistance of a rocket furnished by the government at cost, it launched an experimental satellite called Telstar.[34] A brilliant bit of lobbying, Telstar enthralled millions by transmitting the first TV images from Europe into American living rooms—incidentally generating widespread public support for congressional action on the satellite bill. The Senate broke the filibuster, and Kennedy's measure passed easily. In subsequent years, with a little help from its friends on the Federal Communications Commission, AT&T so successfully defended its investments in antiquated systems against the new space technology that one critic was moved to accuse the company of "corporate Luddism."[35]

The drug companies similarly benefited from Kennedy's indifference to monopoly. Tennessee Senator Estes Kefauver had conducted a devastating investigation of the drug industry in 1960, following it up a year later with a bill whose purposes were twofold: to grant the Food and Drug Administration new powers to protect consumer health, and to increase price competition in drugs by amending the patent laws.[36] Kefauver asked the White House for support[37] and seemed to get some in March 1962, when Kennedy proposed drug legislation which, though ignoring price, strengthened the FDA's police power over quality.[38] But Kefauver soon had grounds to question Kennedy's commitment to stronger regulation. Administration emissaries, meeting with drug lobbyists and staff members of a Senate committee, rewrote pending drug legislation, emasculating health provisions deemed essential by Kefauver.[39] When he learned of the secret meeting, the Tennessean concluded that the White House had betrayed him and said as much in an angry speech before an unusually crowded and attentive Senate.[40] Kefauver had a trick of his own to play. His staff had been collecting material on Thalidomide, a sedative that had caused a ghastly outbreak of fetal malformations in Europe but that a suspicious doctor in the Food and Drug Administration single-handedly kept off the American market. The story, passed on to the Washington *Post* in July 1962, created precisely the national outcry for stronger drug laws that Kefauver anticipated.[41] Hastening to rejoin the senator as a champion of consumer health, Kennedy proposed another series of changes in the drug bill to protect the health of drug consumers.[42] During debate, Kefauver offered an amendment that would have struck at monopoly pricing in drugs as well. On orders from the White House, Senate Majority Leader Mike Mansfield successfully moved its defeat.[43] Not surprisingly the Pharmaceutical Manufacturers Association found the final version of the bill, which helped revive lagging confidence in drug products, perfectly acceptable.[44]

Kennedy further antagonized antimonopolists by coming to the aid of the Du Pont Company, the world's largest producer of chemicals. In a landmark antitrust decision in 1957, the Supreme Court had ordered Du Pont to divest itself of ownership of 63 million shares of General Motors stock. Du Pont elected to get rid of its GM shares by distributing them as dividends to its own shareholders. Friends of Du Pont in Congress wept tears over the plight of the widows and orphans who would have to pay income taxes on these dividends, and legislation was introduced to cut taxes on the distributed GM stock.[45] Antimonopolists protested that the proposed legislation would cost the Treasury $700 million in taxes; reduce the penalty for violating the antitrust laws; give special assistance worth $100 million to the Christiana Securities Corporation, a holding company owned mainly by the Du Pont family; and allow GM shares to pass through Christiana into the hands of individual Du Ponts, undoing the Court's decision.[46] Within the administration, the Justice Department opposed the Du Pont relief bill and the Treasury Department favored it—forcing President Kennedy himself to break the impasse in September 1961. On condition that the bill be limited to the Du Pont case, Kennedy decided to support the company. At the president's request Treasury Secretary Douglas Dillon called Du Pont president Crawford H. Greenewalt to give him the good news that he would get a special tax break for stockholders. Dillon reported back, "Mr. Greenewalt expressed great appreciation for your interest and your action. He said that duPont, of course, did not have any objection to a bill applying solely to duPont."[47] During debate prior to the bill's passage in March 1962, Senator Stuart Symington underscored the obvious: "The administration is not opposed to business . . ." he said. "I believe the proposed legislation would be further proof of that fact."[48]

Kennedy's devotion to the corporate system did not mean that he always saw eye to eye with individual corporations. He was obliged to look to the health of the system, they to the prosperity of their stockholders. On the issue of prices, these differing perspectives produced genuine antagonism. Prices must remain stable, Kennedy believed, if American exports were to remain competitive and the international payments balance to be corrected. Theoretically, businessmen agreed—except where their own prices were concerned. When the administration moved to apply pressure on corporations and labor unions to hold down prices and wages, conflict inevitably resulted.

In the view of the president's Council of Economic Advisers, the major threat to price stability was monopoly, though that particular word appeared nowhere in its public utterances. Giant corporations and big unions enjoyed discretionary power over wages and prices, the Council argued—power that they would be tempted to abuse whenever demand pushed against supply. In the absence of price and wage controls, the Council sought some other way to restrain business and labor from triggering an inflationary spiral. The Council's solution, proposed in its 1962 annual report, was to mobilize public opinion on behalf of responsible price and wage behavior. To gauge whether a price or wage decision was socially responsible, all the public had to do was to measure it against the Council's wage-price guideposts. The premise of the guideposts was simple. Allowing for exceptions, if wage increases throughout the economy rose no faster than output per worker (productivity), wage costs per unit would remain constant, and business would not have to raise prices. Over the long run labor productivity had been rising approximately 3 percent a year. Individual wages should, therefore, rise no faster.[49]

The price of steel especially worried the administration. "Steel bulks so large in the manufacturing sector of the economy," Heller wrote Kennedy, "that it can upset the price applecart all by itself."[50] In the winter of 1962 Kennedy and Labor Secretary Arthur Goldberg, a former lawyer for the United Steel Workers of America, exerted extraordinary pressure on the unions to agree to a new wage contract within the Council's guideposts. When the union did so, Kennedy assumed that the steel companies would keep an implicit bargain and hold the price line. But on April 10, less than two weeks after steel wage negotiations were concluded, Roger Blough, president of U.S. Steel, walked into the White House and handed Kennedy a press release. U.S. Steel was raising its average price six dollars or 3.5 percent a ton. Bethlehem Steel, Republic Steel, and other big companies immediately followed suit.[51]

Kennedy felt personally betrayed by Blough's action. He had used the power of the presidency to keep labor costs down for the companies, and they had slapped his face for his trouble. The next day the president went on television to deliver a furious tongue lashing to the steel industry: "The American people will find it hard, as I do, to accept a situation in which a tiny handful of steel executives whose pursuit of private power and profit exceeds their sense of public responsibility can show such utter contempt for the interests of 185 million Americans."[52] To force a reversal, the administration initiated a grand jury investigation into price fixing, hinted at a reconsideration of planned revisions in depreciation guidelines for the steel industry, persuaded Congress to launch an investigation, aroused the Federal Trade Commission, and announced Pentagon intentions to divert steel purchases away from the offending companies. FBI agents even awakened newsmen in the middle of the night to verify remarks reportedly made before the crisis by the president of Bethlehem Steel opposing any price increase.[53]

In the end the administration divided to conquer. A number of smaller steel companies had hesitated to increase prices, and administration officials privately urged them not to do so. On April 13, 1962, Inland Steel wrecked industry hopes for a united front by announcing that it would hold the price line. Bethlehem Steel, which competed with Inland for the Chicago market, then rescinded its own increase. That very day, at a secret meeting with administration emissaries in New York, Blough himself surrendered.[54]

The puzzle was why Blough raised prices in the first place. The industry needed higher prices to increase profits, Blough explained in his own TV address, and it needed higher profits to finance modernization, without which it could not meet the competition of foreign steel producers.[55] But the administration pointed out that American steel was suffering competitively precisely because its price was already 30 percent higher than European prices. Raising the American price still higher simply made no economic sense. (The logical way to finance modernization was to borrow from the banks or sell new stock.)[56] Events in the short run bore out the administration's analysis. Weak markets as well as strong competition from foreign steel actually forced prices on selected steel products below the pre-crisis level by the end of 1962.[57] Blough's general price increase could probably not have stuck, therefore, even if Kennedy had done nothing. Some observers speculated that Blough's motives were political rather than economic. As an industrial statesman and leader of his industry, he had raised prices to assert the autonomy of private corporations against the encroachments of the state.[58] If this was Blough's intent, then Kennedy taught him that he possessed rather less autonomy than he thought.

Kennedy's assault on Big Steel undid more than a year of painstaking effort to win business favor. The dark suspicions that Democrats were hostile to the private sector had, it seemed, been confirmed. It especially rankled to learn that Kennedy had reportedly called businessmen "sons of bitches" in a private tirade following Blough's visit. Government-business relations deteriorated so badly that they attained the status of a national crisis. Kennedy tried to soothe corporate anxieties with a conciliatory speech before the Chamber of Commerce on April 30, 1962. Following him, Chamber president Richard Wagner declared, "We should remember that dictators in other lands usually come to power under accepted constitutional procedures."[59]

While businessmen were still reeling from Kennedy's humiliation of Roger Blough, the bottom fell out of the stock market. On Monday, May 28, 1962, after months of irregular decline, panic selling drove the Dow Jones average down 35 points. It was the largest one-day drop since October 1929. When the market finally hit bottom on June 25, the value of all stock on the New York Stock Exchange was 27 percent less than it had been in December. Corporate leaders blamed it all on Kennedy. The steel fight, they claimed, had destroyed business confidence.[60] Actually, according to an authoritative report by the Securities and Exchange Commission, investors themselves were responsible because they had driven the market to unrealistic heights in 1961.[61]

The administration did its best to ease the crisis of confidence. Publicly and privately, before large and small gatherings, Kennedy's men assured business of the administration's good will. The president even had his chief domestic counselor, Theodore Sorensen, lead a Cabinet meeting on the care and feeding of businessmen. But events of the spring were not without their effects on the administration's political perceptions. Kennedy and Sorensen were now convinced that no matter what they did business would remain irrationally, illogically, unshakably against them. Though the administration should make every effort to dissipate the climate of distrust, Sorensen advised the president, it would be folly to jeopardize public support "by policies designed to appease those who will never support us."[62] In this mood Kennedy undertook a major reassessment of his economic policies. Perhaps, for example, the time had come to adopt the Keynesian measures urged on him by his economic advisers but so far resisted because business might disapprove. Ironically, it was these measures that would make possible the eventual rapprochement with the corporations he had so far pursued with so little reward.

III

John Maynard Keynes was the British economist who argued brilliantly during the Great Depression that governments do not have to sit idly by while imperfect markets visit misery on mankind. Governments had at their disposal two tools for submitting the economy to rational control, Keynes maintained: regulation of the money supply (monetary policy) and the power to tax and spend (fiscal policy). Using these tools to manipulate aggregate demand, political leaders could make capitalism work properly. Keynesian ideas, suitably modified to suit new circumstances, swept most university economics departments after World War II, becoming the new academic orthodoxy. To convert the national economy into a Keynesian laboratory, however, the professors had first to gain the ear of the politicians. President Kennedy was one politician who was willing to listen—skeptically at first, attentively by the end. It helped that, like him, Keynes had sought not the reform or reconstruction of the existing system, only its more efficient operation. Indeed, an alliance between Keynesian economists and corporate liberals was a natural.

As a matter of fact, Keynesian economics appealed only to liberals. Traditional conservatives in the main tended to distrust academic theory, governmental meddling in the market, and the Keynesian propensity for deficit spending, which they feared risked inflation. Liberals, on the other hand, relied on government to correct market imperfections and were less concerned by inflation than by unemployment, an abhorrence of which they shared with academic economists. It was precisely because Keynesians promised to create permanent full employment that their doctrines eventually became part of liberal policy in the 1960s.

Kennedy first sought Keynesian advice in August 1960 and then fashioned his presidential campaign to suit it. Faster economic growth rather than unemployment was then on his mind. If you want faster growth, MIT's Paul Samuelson had told him, run on a platform of low interest rates (i.e., "easy money") to spur invest-ment and a tight budget to prevent inflation. But even before elec-tion day events rendered both the growth problem and the easy-money solution obsolete. Kennedy's promise to expand the nation's productive capacity faster than the usual 3½ percent a year assumed that existing men and machines were already fully employed. With the onset of recession in October 1960, the assumption of full employment no longer held. Indeed, complete recovery from the 1958 recession had yet to be achieved when this latest downturn began. Economists gloomily concluded that the economy could not generate sufficient steam to reach full employment even at the peak of the business cycle. Suddenly, the main problem looming for policy was not how to increase capacity faster, but how to achieve full employment at existing capacity. Increased long-term growth rates were a luxury that would have to await this accomplishment.

A gold panic during the campaign did to easy money what reces-sion did to the growth issue. In October 1960, rumors surfaced in the London press that the Democratic nominee privately favored devaluing the dollar and would do so if elected. Speculators in the free London gold market began buying gold in anticipation of devaluation, and the gold price soared to the then unheard-of price of $40 an ounce. The rush into gold was an early symptom of the developing crisis in the international monetary system. For ten years the United States had been paying out more dollars for im-ports, foreign aid, tourism, and foreign investments than it earned back by exports.[63] In 1958, foreigners began exercising their right to exchange excess dollars for American gold at the fixed price of $35 an ounce, and the gold hoard at Fort Knox rapidly dwindled.

In truth, the dollar was overvalued at the fixed price and could not in the long run be defended. Devaluation would have been a rational response to world monetary realities. But Kennedy personally believed that countries were only as strong as their currencies (whatever that meant). And he deemed it essential for his election prospects to quiet the panic now threatening the monetary system.[64] On October 31, 1960, the candidate issued one promise he was never tempted to break: "If elected President, I shall not devalue the dollar from the present rate," he said.[65] Money markets calmed immediately.

Kennedy's pledge to defend the dollar was bad news for the Keynesians. Not only did it violate economic common sense; it made attainment of domestic objectives like faster growth and full employment more difficult. There was, for example, the matter of easy money. If the government lowered American interest rates for domestic reasons, dollars would flee the country in search of higher interest rates elsewhere, and the deficit in the balance of payments would worsen. The health of the dollar, therefore, required the quiet interment of the easy-money panacea.

After the election the president-elect sought Samuelson's advice again, appointing him chairman of his pre-inaugural task force on the economy. The problem now was recession, not growth, and it required a new remedy since easy money was out. Fiscal policy was the other weapon in the Keynesian arsenal, and the task force intended to recommend a healthy dose of it to put the economy back on track.[66] Samuelson had in mind a quick and temporary tax cut of, say, $5 billion to revive lagging demand. But when Myer Feldman of Kennedy's staff visited a task force meeting before Christmas 1960 and got the drift of the discussion, he was, recalled Samuelson, "absolutely horror struck."[67] And so was Kennedy.

Kennedy rejected advice to cut taxes for several reasons. First, the departing Eisenhower had spent his last years warning against the inflationary danger of deficit spending, the corollary of a Keynesian tax cut, and his message had registered with Congress and the public. Kennedy lacked heart to defy Eisenhower's homilies. Second, Federal Reserve Chairman William McChesney Martin argued that unemployment arose not from inadequate demand but from structural causes like lack of marketable skills or worker refusal to move from declining regions. If he was right, fiscal stimulation would only inflate prices and aggravate the payments deficit without reducing unemployment. And, finally, Kennedy and his advisers, knowing little economics themselves, were simply not persuaded that the professors were right. "If you have 7 percent unemployment," Sorensen was fond of saying in this period, "you're getting a grade of 93. Why on earth should the administration make great efforts with all the fiscal dangers and the political dangers too to raise the grade from 93 to 96?"[68] Clearly, the Keynesians had a hard row to hoe.

The Keynesian stronghold in the new administration was the Council of Economic Advisers, whose chairman was Walter Heller. Kennedy had appointed Heller on the recommendation of Samuelson, who could have had the job himself but did not want it. A solid economist with a gift for writing witty and concise memos, Heller had shuttled between the University of Minnesota and the government throughout his career and had been an adviser to prominent Democrats, notably Hubert Humphrey, in the 1950s. For Kennedy's purposes, Heller was the ideal economist—loyal, sensitive to political realities, and an engaging salesman for administration policies. No old pol in the Kennedy entourage was more devoted to the re-election of his chief than he. Serving with Heller were Yale's James Tobin, whose professional reputation among Keynesians was matched only by Samuelson, and Kermit Gordon of Williams College, whose political savvy so impressed Kennedy that he made him director of the Budget Bureau in 1962. Lacking a political constituency of their own, Council members could influence policy only by relying on patient pedagogy. They had a simple point to make. If the government temporarily spent more than it collected in taxes, aggregate demand would increase and the economy would revive.

In the beginning everything went against them. The new president stunned Heller in his January 1961 State of the Union Message by promising to submit a balanced budget for the fiscal year beginning in July. It helped only a little that he hedged the pledge with a half-dozen carefully crafted loopholes.[69] A few days later the president proposed an anti-recession program consisting not of a temporary tax cut but only of gimmicks cooked up as a substitute for a real policy.[70] "You might say we are in the midst of 'a placebo program for recovery,'" Samuelson ruefully commented.[71] When Kennedy got lucky in February 1961 and the economy turned around, his interest in the dismal science and those who practiced it waned noticeably.

Still, in an endless stream of memos, reports, and public appearances, Heller stated his case. Even at the peak of the next recovery, he said, the economy would suffer from "chronic slack."[72] Chronic slack meant a gross national product that grew at a rate of 2.5 percent a year instead of the 3.5 percent historic average, an unemployment rate that had dipped below 5 percent in only three months since 1957, and a $30 billion gap between what the economy could produce and what it would actually be producing at the top of the business cycle. The task of government was to restore full employment and close this gap. The Council defined full employment as an unemployment rate of 4 percent because this was the lowest figure attainable without generating too much inflation—or so it hoped.

The cause of the $30 billion gap was insufficient demand for the economy's potential product, the Council argued, a deficiency that could be corrected, for example, by a temporary $10 billion tax cut. How could $10 billion in tax reduction close a $30 billion gap? By the magic of the Keynesian multiplier, the Council explained. If a taxpayer spent a dollar he received from a tax cut, it became someone else's income, part of which would be saved, part returned to the government in taxes, but most spent again, becoming someone else's income. In that way $10 billion in fiscal stimulus would eventually generate $20 billion in additional GNP. Most of the remaining gap would close as business investment increased in response to rising consumer demand. Such thinking was familiar to countless college freshmen, but in 1961 it was viewed with a mixture of incomprehension and political skepticism at the highest levels of the Kennedy administration. At a White House meeting in March, when Heller formally proposed a $9.5 billion fiscal package to stimulate the economy, he got nowhere. "I was universally complimented on the cogency and clarity of the memo and clobbered by the assemblage," he reported to his Council colleagues. "It was done on the basis of political unacceptability of the tax cut." Heller's ideas might be worthy, but Congress, conservatives, and the corporations would not buy them.[73]

Nevertheless, through 1961 Kennedy moved inadvertently in the direction the Council was urging. Resorting to the escape hatches in his January pledge, he began adding billions to the budget: $2.3 billion for new domestic programs; $3.7 billion for "urgent" national security needs; and in July $3.5 billion to finance his martial response to Khrushchev's menacing gestures toward West Berlin.[74]

Except for the Council, all Kennedy's advisers wanted to finance the Berlin crisis by raising taxes rather than by more deficit spending. As Robert Kennedy forcefully argued at a White House meeting on Thursday, July 10, 1961, here at last was the administration's chance to summon the people to sacrifice. Apparently persuaded, the president told Sorensen to draft a Berlin speech that included a recommendation for a 1 percent across-the-board increase in personal income taxes.[75] But the Council mounted a furious counterattack over the weekend, culminating on Monday morning when Samuelson hitched a plane ride with Kennedy from Cape Cod to Washington and filled the presidential ear with Keynesian argument. Increased defense spending without a corresponding tax rise was one way to pump fiscal fuel into a laggard economy, Samuelson explained. Reconvening his advisers, Kennedy gave Heller his first victory: Berlin spending was not to be accompanied by a tax increase.[76]

Owing to increased expenditures, the budget deficit for the fiscal year ending mid-1962 was $6.3 billion—closer to the Council's $10 billion hope than to Kennedy's early promise to balance the budget. The Council termed the deficit "probably the principal driving force" in the 1961 recovery.[77] Unemployment, which had been 7 percent in April 1961, was down to 5.6 percent one year later.[78] It was still too high, and Kennedy remained unpersuaded by Keynesian argument. But Heller had made progress. John Kenneth Galbraith, whom Kennedy had appointed ambassador to India, found the president's economic policies somewhat mystifying. On the one hand, deficit spending was lifting the economy toward full recovery. On the other, administration officials kept saying that a balanced budget would be the ultimate test of economic achievement. Writing to Heller and Dillon, he said, "I am reminded of a courtesan whose conquests have made her the cynosure of all men and the envy of all women and who at any critical moment in the conversation insists on the absolute importance of chastity."[79]

It took the twin shocks of the steel crisis and the stock-market collapse to prod Kennedy into reappraising his economic policies. As long as the economy continued to mend, he had been content to ignore it. But as soon as the economic indicators threatened to plunge, he regarded them with near morbid fascination. Meeting with his top advisers on May 29, 1962, one day after the stock panic,

Kennedy expressed fear that the rest of the economy might go down too. Heller was not so gloomy, estimating the chance of a recession at only one in five. Nevertheless, he took advantage of the president's mood to push again for his favorite cure-all: a $5 to $10 billion temporary tax cut to keep the economy moving toward full employment.[80] For once, Kennedy did not turn him down out of hand. If the economy worsened in the weeks ahead, he was finally prepared to ask Congress for a shot of Heller's medicine. But by midsummer it was clear that there was no emergency. Much to his own relief, Kennedy was able to announce in August that he would not seek a temporary tax cut in 1962.[81]

But Kennedy was clearly a changed man. He had entered office virtually an economic illiterate, committed to policies which he thought would win approval of the corporations. Now he was practically a Keynesian, willing to contemplate policies that would be good for business whether business knew it or not. Indeed, the time had come to stop pandering to business ignorance and to start talking straight about economic reality. This was his intention when, resplendent in a purple-trimmed LL.D. hood, he delivered the commencement address on the lawn of Yale's Old Campus on June 11, 1962.

"The dialog . . . between business and government . . ." he said on this occasion, "is clogged by illusion and platitude and fails to reflect the true realities of contemporary American society." The first task, then, was to disenthrall ourselves from myth—myth that the federal debt was growing larger when as a proportion of GNP it was growing smaller; myth that government was getting bigger when its civilian agencies had grown "less than any other major sector of our national life" since World War II; myth that budget deficits generated inflation when, in fact, persistent deficits in recent years had not upset price stability. Declaring that political rhetoric bore little relation to our actual problems, the president summed up in a single line the premise of postwar American liberalism: "What is at stake in our economic decisions today is not some grand warfare of rival ideologies which will sweep the country with passion but the practical management of a modern economy." Kennedy proposed the initiation of a government-business dialogue— "sober, dispassionate, and careful"—that would seek "technical answers" to the nation's difficulties. The speech, rhetorically one of Kennedy's best, was not a political success.[82] "The old Elis had listened with acute discomfort," Arthur Schlesinger wrote.[83] As for business, memories of the steel crisis were still too fresh to admit of dispassionate conversation with John F. Kennedy.

Despite its perception that the corporations would be opposed, the administration was now moving rapidly toward adoption of Keynesian policies. Treasury Secretary Dillon ironically played the key role. Son of a self-made Wall Street banker and himself no mean figure in the world of high finance, Dillon had been ambassador to France and an assistant secretary of state under Eisenhower. As a Republican emissary from the corporate world to the Kennedy administration, he enjoyed rare entrée into the president's social circle and exercised singular influence on matters of economic policy. Whenever Heller had argued for a tax cut, Dillon was always there to thwart him. But Dillon had his own cherished project. To crown his tenure, he was preparing tax-reform legislation to close inequitable loopholes and eliminate the special preferences that distorted the flow of private investment. Closing loopholes would increase federal revenue and thereby make possible a cut in income tax rates. Indeed, to make unpopular reforms politically palatable, Dillon was prepared to return to taxpayers more in reduction than he took in with reforms. Net tax reduction of $2 or $3 billion might "sweeten" reform enough to get it through Congress.

Early in June 1962, while the president was still worrying about a possible "Kennedy recession," Dillon suggested giving the country a peek at the Treasury's plan, which would be ready for Congress early in 1963. The prospect of a small tax cut might "restore business confidence," he said.[84] The next day Kennedy discussed his forthcoming tax-reform bill with the press. Reform would make possible "an across the board reduction in personal and corporate income tax rates which will not be wholly offset by other reforms—in other words, a net tax reduction," he explained.[85] This was an announcement whose true significance Kennedy himself did not yet know.

Heller's long pedagogical effort finally paid off in the summer of 1962 when Dillon at last saw the Keynesian light. Converting his tax cut from a mere sweetener into a massive stimulant for a slack economy, Dillon agreed to net tax reductions of approximately $10 billion. This was precisely what Heller had wanted all along, with the crucial exception that Dillon's cut would be permanent rather than temporary. In August, deploying charts and telling homely anecdotes, Kennedy went on TV to announce a major departure in his economic policies and to unveil its Keynesian rationale. Existing high tax rates, he said, were a drag on the economy, cutting into consumption, discouraging enterprise, and preventing the economy from climbing all the way back to full employment. The remedy was significant and permanent tax reduction. This he would ask Congress to enact when it convened in January 1963. Though tax reduction would temporarily enlarge the deficit, it would "prevent the even greater budget deficit that a lagging economy would otherwise surely produce." His forthcoming bill, he emphasized, was not intended to combat a temporary recession but to remove a serious barrier to the attainment of full employment. Though it was a brave effort to bring Keynes to the masses, Kennedy graded his performance only "C minus."[86]

Though Kennedy's commitment to a tax cut was now irrevocable, the whole subject made him profoundly uneasy. He virtually ignored it during the 1962 congressional campaign and did not focus on it again until December, when decisions on the next budget could no longer be postponed.[87] In the second week of the month he found lots of reasons to regret his Keynesian conversion. Galbraith dropped by to ridicule tax cutting and urge higher expenditures. Senate strong man Robert Kerr of Oklahoma phoned to report his skepticism. Members of the Cabinet expressed a decided preference for spending more money rather than reducing revenue. And, worst of all, the president learned that his economic advisers expected the tax cut to produce a budget deficit considerably in excess of Eisenhower's 1958 peacetime record of $12.4 billion.[88] For political reasons, he now insisted that under no circumstances could his deficit exceed Eisenhower's. As a result, the tax cut he proposed would not be concentrated in one or even two years, as Heller had hoped; tax rates would be lowered in stages over three years, considerably diluting the expansionary impact.[89] On December 14 Heller noted, "As of the moment, the President is shaken on the question of the tax cut. . . . I have never seen the President so anguished and uncertain about the correctness of his course on a domestic matter in the two years that I have served with him."[90]

That very night Kennedy was scheduled to address the Economic Club of New York, the sort of group whose opposition he had come to believe was implacable. How this audience would react to his speech—on the forthcoming fiscal package—was a matter of intense concern to him. As he was putting the finishing touches on his text, he told Sorensen, "If I can convince them, I can convince anybody."[91]

Kennedy went to great lengths in this speech to sound like some-body other than the liberal Democrat he was supposed to be. Our tax system, he declared, "siphons out of the private economy too large a share of personal and business purchasing power . . . it reduces the financial incentives for personal effort, investment, and risk-taking." His tax bill would increase profits, keep the deficit in bounds, eventually generate budget surpluses, and avoid inflation. Going the last mile, Kennedy pledged to keep spending on civilian domestic programs next year "at approximately its current level."[92] *Time* thought that Kennedy sounded like an officer of the National Association of Manufacturers.[93] So apparently did the New York Economic Club. Their response was so warm that Kennedy re-turned to Washington in exuberant spirits. The next day he called the chairman of his Council of Economic Advisers. "I gave them straight Keynes and Heller," he said, "and they loved it."[94] From then on Kennedy's enthusiasm for the tax cut grew steadily.

Kennedy's encounter with the New York Economic Club was a turning point in his relations with the corporations. The veil of myth that had distorted the image each had of the other now began to fall away. Kennedy discovered that not all businessmen were pre-Keynesian reactionaries and, indeed, that sophisticated members of the managerial elite had long been ready for a judicious application of Keynesian principles. Kennedy received the cheers of the New York businessmen not because he persuaded them but because they were already persuaded.[95] For their part, businessmen were begin-ning to realize that Kennedy's anger against them during the steel crisis was an aberration and that he sincerely wished to serve their interests and enhance their profits. The tax cut he proposed would clearly have that effect. Ironically, then, the corporate liberal in the White House and the corporate managers in business were brought close to reconciliation by the very Keynesian measures that Kennedy, partially in deference to supposed business prejudices, had hesitated so long to embrace.

IV

"I am convinced that the enactment this year of tax reduction and tax reform overshadows all other domestic problems in this Con-gress," Kennedy said in January 1963.[96] But, when he sent up his bill, it got caught in a crossfire between liberals and conservatives and bogged down in committee. Ironically, among the bill's severest critics were some of the nation's leading Keynesians, including John Kenneth Galbraith, James Tobin, and Leon Keyserling, all of whom praised the administration's endorsement of Keynesian theory but not the purpose for which it was now to be employed.

Impatient with the intrusion of politics into policy, James Tobin had never been happy during his stay on the Council of Economic Advisers. In mid-1962 he returned to Yale. During the 1963 tax debate, Tobin sent Heller a memo from his ivory tower, explaining why he did not share the enthusiasm of his former colleague for the tax program. Tobin had long supported a quick, temporary tax cut to nudge the economy back to full employment; permanent tax cutting was another matter. Permanent reduction, he pointed out, was incompatible with a faster rate of economic growth, which liberals had only recently proclaimed to be the prime objective of enlightened policy. Tobin reminded Heller that the trick to achieving faster growth was to decrease the proportion of GNP going into consumption and to increase the proportion for savings and investment. Once a temporary tax cut restored full employment, existing high tax rates would generate a budget surplus. Surpluses were a form of forced savings, which could be invested directly by the government, lent to private investors, or used to pay off the national debt, freeing private capital for private investment. But, if existing rates were now permanently slashed, consumption would increase at the expense of investment, and surpluses would vanish, blocking the surest route to faster long-run growth. Tobin implicitly condemned the tax program as a betrayal of fifties liberalism, which indeed it was.[97]

Measuring the tax program by the standards of *The Affluent Society*, Ambassador Galbraith, too, found it wanting. Fiscal policy offered two paths to full employment, he pointed out: more consumer spending, achieved by a Kennedy-type tax cut; or more government spending, without a corresponding tax increase. More government spending could achieve that repair of the public sector—better schools, parks, and welfare programs—which he had urged in the fifties and Kennedy had endorsed in the campaign. Writing from New Delhi, Galbraith congratulated the president on his recent conversion to the still-controversial Keynes, suggesting that "he put a picture of the Master in your bedroom or some other suitably secluded place." But the choice of Keynesian remedies grieved him: "Needless to say, the addition of more and better depilatories has nothing to do with national health and vigor."[98] Socialist Michael Harrington more bluntly, if less elegantly, attacked Kennedy's tax cut for the same reasons. He called it "reactionary Keynesianism."[99]

Leon Keyserling, former CEA chairman under Truman, objected to the tax cut on grounds of equity—an unfashionable concern for a Keynesian in these years. While offering tax reduction from top to bottom, the president's program provided disproportionate benefits for the wealthy, Keyserling asserted. According to his calculations, the richest 12 percent of the nation's taxpayers would obtain 45 percent of the cut. That, in his view, was not only unfair but economically unsound. Keyserling contended that the underlying cause for the past decade's sluggishness was maldistribution of income, which left the mass of consumers with insufficient purchasing power to buy the economy's potential product. Concentrate tax reduction in the upper brackets, he said, and much of it would become savings, which were already in oversupply. Concentrate it in the lower brackets, and all of it would be spent for consumption, which was precisely what the economy needed. Regardless of its merits, Keyserling's critique had political significance, for it became the rationale for the AFL-CIO's resistance to Kennedy's tax program.[100]

Kennedy could handle labor and the liberals. It was the conservatives he worried about. Citizens still clinging to the "puritan ethic,"[101] as Heller once called it in a moment of despair, found it offensive both to common sense and morals that the president wished to increase spending by $4 billion while cutting taxes a net $11.4 billion. A *New York Times* survey of public opinion reported "a deep worry about the size of the national debt."[102] Congressmen found amazing reluctance among their constituents for lower taxes, if the consequence was a bigger deficit.[103] And Harry Truman, speaking for millions of other common men, remarked, "I am old fashioned. I believe you should pay in more than you spend."[104]

But the conservative case rested on more than popular intuition. A small band of renegade anti-Keynesians led by Chicago's Milton Friedman logically assaulted the theory of the tax cut at its critical point. The multiplier, they said, would not work. Suppose the government cut taxes without cutting expenditures, producing a deficit of $10 billion. Taxpayers indeed would have more to spend, as Walter Heller said. But where would the government obtain $10 billion to make up the deficit and pay its bills? Assuming no change in money supply, the government would have to borrow from private citizens. As a result, $10 billion would be sucked out of the private economy—$10 billion that would have been lent and spent. In short, though the tax cut would add to private demand, government borrowing to finance the deficit would depress private demand—and the fiscal multiplier would prove a dud.[105]

Economists subsequently described this "crowding out" process more technically in terms of the demand for money. To facilitate transactions, the public holds a certain proportion of its income as money (currency plus checking accounts), which does not earn interest. When the government finances a deficit (again assuming no change in the money supply), it must persuade people to reduce their money holdings and buy its bonds. The inducement, of course, is an offer to pay a higher rate of interest than the one prevailing. But higher interest rates discourage private borrowing and dampen the economy. The stimulating effects of a tax cut will, therefore, be "crowded out" by the depressing side effect of financing the deficit. The real question is, how much crowding out will occur? Because Friedman believed that people were extraordinarily stubborn about the amount of money they wished to hold, he thought interest rates would have to climb high indeed before people would part with money for bonds. If so, crowding out would be nearly complete.[106] Friedman co-authored a controversial study in 1963 purporting to show that, historically, one dollar in fiscal stimulus generated not two or three dollars of GNP, as Keynesians believed, but approximately one dollar.[107]

But, said Friedman, there was another possible tax-cutting scenario. This time, when the Treasury enters the credit markets to borrow, the Federal Reserve eases the way by increasing the rate of growth of the money supply. Now the public holds more money than it wants, facilitating bond sales and holding down the interest rate. In this case, public borrowing does not reduce private spending, and aggregate demand temporarily increases. Friedman made two points: First, in his view, the real cause of the expansion would not be the tax cut but increased monetary growth, which could have taken place without a tax cut. Second, printing up money faster than normal, if continued for very long, would eventually push up prices. One of the curiosities of the period was the indifference of Keynesian economists to Friedman's two scenarios—"crowding out" on the one hand, inflation on the other.

While debate swirled around it, the president's tax bill languished through the summer in the House Ways and Means Committee, not so much because of its tax-reduction features but because of the tax reforms that, at Dillon's insistence, had been included with them. An army of lobbyists descended on the committee to rescue cherished loopholes. In the end, none of the major reforms survived. Heller could not resist saying, I told you so. "As you know," he wrote Kennedy, "I opposed cluttering up the 1963 tax cut by inclusion of tax reforms—and I never bought the argument that the vested interests, just because we fed them a high protein diet of tax cuts, would be any less venal or voracious when we kicked them in their private parts. And they're not."[108]

By the time the tax bill reached the House floor, in September 1963, its prospects had brightened considerably. Many of those who, for differing reasons, had expressed strong reservations about the bill in the spring now backed it as the best tax cut they were ever likely to get. Labor still grumbled about its inequities, and many liberals would have preferred more spending; but both accepted the cut because it promised full employment. Moreover, it was now clear that conservative taxpayers had become as greedy for tax relief as everybody else. House Democrats easily beat back a Republican attempt to link tax reduction to mandatory spending limits,[109] and the bill proceeded to the Senate, where the only issue was not whether it would pass, but when.

One constituency that had been unswerving in its support of Kennedy's tax-reduction proposal, and lobbied for it with genuine enthusiasm, was the corporate community. In April, as a result of discussions with Douglas Dillon, key business leaders formed the Business Committee for Tax Reduction in 1963. Co-chaired by Pennsylvania Railroad president Stuart Saunders and Henry Ford II, the committee's executive board included representatives of AT&T, Standard Oil, the Chase Manhattan Bank, Westinghouse, American Can, and Consolidated Edison. The Business Committee raised $160,000 to finance the activities of a full-time lobbyist, and its members used personal contacts in Congress to excellent effect. Though professing great fear of government spending, the Committee opposed Republican efforts to link tax cuts to an expenditure ceiling.[110] Reporting to Kennedy, a Treasury official said that the Business Committee was "of immeasurable assistance in marshalling support among the various established trade organizations and

avoiding the 'knee jerk' type of opposition that normally character-
izes response to any initiative from a Democratic president."[111]
Whatever their partisan affiliations, few businessmen could resist a
program that promised higher profits and a reduction of the corporate income tax from 52 percent to 47 percent. A late-blooming love
affair between Wall Street and the White House was entering its first
stage.

On November 23, 1963, two months after House passage of the
tax bill and one day after John Kennedy's assassination in Dallas, a
grieving Walter Heller had a talk with President Lyndon B. Johnson.
After promising to stay in the administration and briefing his new
chief on a variety of topics, he was about to take his leave when
Johnson called him back. "Now, I want to say something about all
this talk that I'm a conservative who is likely to go back to the
Eisenhower ways or give in to the economy bloc in Congress," he
said. "It's just not so, and I want you to tell your friends—Arthur
Schlesinger, Galbraith, and other liberals—that it is not so. I'm not
a budget slasher. I understand that expenditures have to keep rising
to keep pace with the population and to help the economy. If you
looked at my record, you would know I'm a Roosevelt New Dealer,
As a matter of fact, to tell the truth, John F. Kennedy was a little too
conservative to suit my taste."[112]

Just two days later, over Heller's strenuous objections, Johnson
began slashing the budget being prepared for submission to Congress in January, 1964. Siding with the Treasury, the president
agreed to appease the economy bloc in the Senate by setting the
ceiling on expenditures at no more than $100 billion, rather than
the $102 billion ceiling approved earlier by Kennedy.[113] Otherwise,
the nation's chief executive remarked to Heller, "you won't pee one
drop."[114] In January, Johnson astonished nearly everybody by submitting a final budget that cut spending to only $97.9 billion,
slightly *below* the limit proposed unsuccessfully by House Republicans in September.[115] But at the same time he asked Congress to
shift more of the tax cut than originally planned into calendar 1964,
assuring no loss of overall stimulus in the first year.[116] (In its final
form, the tax bill provided $10 billion in tax reduction over two
years—1964 and 1965.) With this package, the president robbed
Republicans of the economy issue, kept faith with the Keynesians,
and secured approval of the bill in February 1964, a few weeks,
perhaps even months, earlier than it otherwise would have passed.

All that remained was to determine whether the tax cut actually worked. No one knew for sure whether consumers would really spend 92 to 94 percent of the tax cut, whether the multiplier would change one dollar of tax reduction into two dollars of GNP, whether unused capacity would disappear and unemployment shrink to 4 percent. In mid-1964, about five months after enactment, with the nation's cash registers ringing up record sales, Heller cautiously told Johnson, "Though I cannot and do not suggest that we now have test-tube evidence of the success of the tax cut, it is hard to explain the continued strong advance to date—and the budget prospects ahead—except in terms of fresh confidence, the expanded purchasing power, and the new incentives created by the Revenue Act of 1964."[117] By the time Heller retired from the Council in November 1964, Keynesians were incautiously jubilant. The Council had said in January that, given a tax cut, GNP would increase approximately 6½ percent in 1964, and unemployment would fall from 5.5 percent to 5 percent by the end of the year. This actually happened.[118]

But then the Council was suddenly assailed by doubt. In December 1964, it concluded that the second stage of tax reduction, due to take place the following month, would not be sufficient to drive the economy all the way to full employment after all. The Council privately pleaded with the president to cut taxes again or else spend more money.[119] But Johnson, in no mood to antagonize conservatives, refused to do either. His inaction proved fortunate. The Council was way off the mark the rest of the year. GNP for 1965 overshot the Council's prediction by $9 billion, and in December unemployment sank to 4.1 percent, virtually the Council's definition of full employment.[120] Nobody was more surprised than the Council, but everybody insisted on giving it the credit. The once skeptical *U.S. News and World Report* commented, "Tax relief, in massive doses, appears to have achieved something like magic."[121] The final apotheosis of the "new economics" occurred in December 1965, when *Time* put a picture of the master on its cover and ran a story called "We Are All Keynesians Now."[122]

V

Whether the tax cut deserved all this praise is no easy matter to determine. The classic Keynesian analysis of the tax cut was performed in 1965 by Arthur Okun, a member of the Council of Economic Advisers and later its chairman. Assuming Keynesian premises, Okun devised equations to estimate the amount of consumption and investment that the $10 billion cut should theoretically have generated. Okun's equations predicted an increase in GNP from the start of 1964 to mid-1965 close to the actual gain. This congruence of prediction and reality did not "prove" the validity of the Keynesian model but without it, Okun observed, the tremendous surge in consumer spending was "an insoluble mystery."[123]

Milton Friedman and his fellow anti-Keynesians believed they could explain the mystery without recourse to the tax cut. Friedman was a so-called monetarist, who believed that short-run fluctuations in economic activity were determined by changes in the quantity of money.[124] The Federal Reserve controlled the money supply by expanding and contracting bank reserves, causing the economy to go up and down. When the Fed speeded up the printing presses, the public held more money than it desired and proceeded to spend its unwanted balances. The result was increased aggregate demand with a multiplier effect.

In Friedman's version of recent history, the origins of the 1964–1965 expansion dated not from the 1964 tax cut but from the decision of the Federal Reserve, late in 1962, to reverse course and increase the rate of growth of the money supply. Said Friedman, "Lo and behold, about six or nine or ten months later, before the tax cut had taken effect, income started to rise at a more rapid rate."[125] In the period following enactment of the tax cut, the Federal Reserve, attempting to hold down interest rates, continued its easy-money policy. That was why the economy was booming at mid-decade, and that was why in October 1965 Friedman wrote a letter to the Federal Reserve predicting trouble ahead. Recent large increases in monetary growth were "not indefinitely sustainable without a price rise," he said.[126] Given his model, Friedman could hardly have predicted otherwise. Given their relative indifference to the quantity of money, it is not surprising that inflation would catch the Council of Economic Advisers by surprise. In the fiscal year 1965–1966 prices, which had been relatively stable, jumped 3 percent. The congruence of Friedman's prediction with reality did not "prove" the validity of his model either; but when inflation actually materialized, his influence began to grow rapidly.

VI

The 1964 tax-reduction act was one of the major liberal measures of the decade. In one sense, of course, it represented a retreat from the liberalism of the fifties, with its concern for faster growth and increased public spending. But, despite early qualms, liberals were glad enough to claim the act as their own. It not only delivered full employment—or seemed to; it appeared to vindicate liberal belief that the technical problems of a modern economy were best managed by enlightened politicians advised by the experts. Moreover, the tax cut perfectly suited the postwar liberal temper, with its implicit acquiescence in corporate domination of the economy. As a good corporate liberal, Kennedy proposed tax reduction that sought no redistribution of wealth and power. Lubrication of the system, not its reform, was his only purpose. His tax cut—"reactionary Keynesianism"—underwrote demand and enhanced profits without infringing on corporate autonomy or augmenting the public sector.

Johnson reaped the political rewards of what Kennedy had sown. During the 1964 presidential election, Wall Street was Johnson country, and most of the corporate contributions went to him. It is not the least of the era's ironies that the Keynesian policy which brought corporate leaders and corporate liberals together may have helped cause the price inflation subsequently so harmful to both. That depressing story awaited the administration's second term.

CHAPTER 3

Politics and Principle: The Issue of Civil Rights

F ROM the beginning, President Kennedy knew that his most difficult domestic problem would be civil rights for southern blacks. Here was an issue that, mismanaged, could split the Democratic party, menace the civil peace, and endanger his re-election. Lacking a personal commitment, Kennedy approached civil rights as he did any other issue—as a matter of politics, not of morals. By deft maneuver he hoped to deflate racial passions and delay a showdown between oppressor and oppressed. Only then could he avoid choosing sides. But not even John Kennedy could deflect the forces of history. Currents of change sweeping through the South for a generation were rendering segregation a mere anachronism. Only the time and manner of its demise remained to be ascertained. As it turned out, the time arrived during Kennedy's brief tenure, and the manner ultimately became his to determine.

The economic foundation of white supremacy in the South had been cotton agriculture. As long as most blacks were landless tenants on cotton farms or domestic servants, it was an easy matter to police them, keep them semiliterate, and humiliate them by enforcing racial separation. But beginning in the 1930s the cotton kingdom suffered a series of reverses that led to its rapid overthrow. New Deal farm policies cut back cotton acreage. Synthetic fibers slashed demand for cotton products. Foreign producers aggressively entered world markets, causing a drastic decline in American cotton exports. Cotton acreage in the United States, which had stood at 43 million in 1929, shrank to less than 15 million acres in 1959, even as cotton farming shifted out of the South into states west of the Mississippi.[1] Millions of southern acres once planted in cotton now grew corn, soybeans, peanuts, and grass for cattle. Millions of southern tenants, black and white, once trapped on the land to pick cotton, now of necessity were free to go.

Between 1930 and 1960 the South's farm population fell from 16.2 million to 5.9 million, setting in train one of the great migrations of American history.[2] Some of the superfluous millions moved into the South's cities, where they became cheap labor for the region's post-1940 industrial boom. For blacks, the consequences of urban migration were extraordinary. In the cities they earned more money, received better schooling, and escaped surveillance by virtue of anonymity. While southern blacks growing to maturity after World War II still knew fear, its sharp edge cut less deep. Even in rural areas tremors of change shook the old foundations. At last there arrived a black generation that might bid farewell to Uncle Tom and bury Jim Crow.

The social and political dislocations caused by the overthrow of cotton were by no means confined to the former states of the Old Confederacy. Three million blacks were among the uprooted southerners who migrated northward from 1940 to 1960,[3] swarming mainly into the ghetto neighborhoods of the nation's dozen largest cities. In the decade of the 1950s, for example, as a result of migration and natural increase, the black population of Chicago grew from 14 percent to 23 percent, Detroit from 16 percent to 29 percent, Washington from 35 percent to 54 percent.[4] Since blacks in the North could vote, their political influence grew apace with their numbers. The result was a crisis for the Democratic party. On the one hand, machine Democrats in the urban North increasingly depended on black support and were willing to seek it by promising civil rights in the South. On the other hand, southern Democrats stood unflinchingly for states' rights and white supremacy. At the 1948 Democratic convention the party broke decisively with its past when big-city bosses waged a successful floor fight for a strong civil rights platform. That year, while Harry Truman was winning the black vote, four traditionally Deep South states supported the renegade Dixiecrat, Strom Thurmond.

But the tilt of the Democratic party toward civil rights was not simply a matter of politics. The Democrats were the liberal party, and postwar liberalism regarded civil rights as the preeminent issue. It had not always been so. For more than half a century, most liberals had either acquiesced in segregation or treated it as a secondary problem. But, having recently waged World War II against demonic racism abroad, liberals could no longer ignore the domestic variety. After the war, for the first time since Reconstruction, a significant body of white opinion was willing to confront the contradiction between American principle and black reality. The principle had been stated by the founders in the Declaration of Independence: All men are created equal. Whatever else these words meant, they at least meant this: All citizens are equal before the law. But southern reality was a legal system that made invidious distinctions on the basis of race and imposed the humiliation of segregation on blacks. As the Old South crumbled, a civil-rights movement emerged to purge the contradiction from the New South arising.

Year by year the pace of racial change quickened. In 1954 the Supreme Court in *Brown v. Board of Education of Topeka* ruled that legally enforced school segregation was unconstitutional. In 1956 Martin Luther King, Jr., preaching a philosophy of Christian nonviolence that he said would conquer evil and save America, led the black people of Montgomery, Alabama, in a successful boycott of the city's segregated buses. In 1957 President Eisenhower sent the U.S. Army to Little Rock, Arkansas, to enforce a court order desegregating Central High School; and Congress passed the first civil rights act since Reconstruction. In 1960 militant black students led a sit-in movement that in less than one year enlisted 50,000 people and desegregated public facilities in 140 cities and towns, mainly in the upper South. And in January 1961 John F. Kennedy, who had campaigned as a champion of civil rights, was inaugurated president of the United States.

I

President Kennedy's initial civil rights strategy derived not from the promises he had made but from the arithmetic of his victory. Needing the votes of blacks and of white southerners, he had received enough of both to win. His object now would be to keep these disparate constituencies in delicate balance and attached to his electoral base. That meant finding a civil rights position sufficiently strong to appease blacks but not so strong that it would alienate the white South. The first obstacle was his own campaign promises. In 1960 Kennedy had said that a president should move against racial discrimination on two fronts. He should use his executive authority to wipe out bias "in every field of Federal activity";[5] and he should lead the fight for new civil rights legislation. During the campaign, to prove his sincerity, the candidate had asked leading Democratic congressmen to draft a bill based on the civil rights plank of the party platform. That plank, shaped to fit liberal specifications, called for creating a Fair Employment Practices Commission, empowering the attorney general to file suits to protect individuals deprived of their constitutional rights, and requiring southern school districts to submit plans for first-step desegregation by 1963.[6]

On January 6, 1961, the president-elect met privately with Roy Wilkins, executive director of the NAACP, to explain why he would not sponsor a civil rights bill after all. If he did, southern congressmen would not only defeat it but reject his other measures, many of them beneficial to blacks. Wilkins would have none of the argument. Southern congressmen would vote against his programs no matter what he did on civil rights, Wilkins insisted. Kennedy parried with what would become the official administration line: Why emphasize civil rights legislation when the president could accomplish just as much by issuing executive orders? Wilkins had not spent years around Washington for nothing. Fine, he said; but don't issue a lot of little orders, each addressed to a single area of discrimination. "You ought to issue a sweeping Executive Order taking in the whole business." Barely masking his skepticism, Kennedy told Wilkins to prepare a memo on the subject for his chief adviser on domestic matters, Theodore Sorensen.[7]

The memo Wilkins submitted in February 1961 forced the new administration to determine early just how far it was willing to go on civil rights. Wilkins proposed a single executive order to accomplish three purposes: end discrimination in the federal civil service, require federal contractors to provide equal job opportunity, and make nondiscrimination a condition of federally-aided programs.[8] The last of these demands was the crucial one. If Kennedy used federal money as a club against discriminatory programs, he would be undertaking nothing less than a full-scale assault on southern segregation. Federal funds subsidized segregation as well as other

forms of racial bias in southern hospitals, colleges, housing programs, job training programs, National Guard units, and public
schools adjacent to federal installations. Dismayed by the implications of Wilkins's memo, Sorensen warned Kennedy of "severe"
political problems if he moved in the South against "customs which
are very deeply rooted."[9] He meant segregation. At the outset,
then, the administration determined neither to sponsor a civil rights
law, issue a sweeping executive order, nor endorse a frontal assault
against the segregation system. Still, blacks would have to get something. Off the record in March 1961 the White House summed up
its program for blacks—find them jobs and get them the vote.[10]
Here was a package that would please neither white racists nor the
civil rights lobby but keep both from declaring war on Kennedy.

To obtain the jobs, Kennedy issued an executive order in March
1961—the only civil rights order he issued that year—creating the
President's Committee on Equal Employment Opportunity.[11] He
appointed Vice President Lyndon B. Johnson as the committee's
chairman, gave it more power than similar committees had enjoyed
in the past, and charged it with eliminating job discrimination in the
civil service and among government contractors. The committee
attacked its task with considerable energy and a certain flair for
publicity. But even within the federal civil service, where it hoped
to crack the white monopoly on the good jobs, the committee could
not overcome the inertial force of custom. Its report on November
1963 buried the information that after two years black employment
in the middle grades (GS 5 through 11) had risen from 4.9 percent
to only 6 percent, and in the upper grades (GS 12 through 18) from
0.7 percent to 1 percent.[12]

The main target of the employment committee was private businesses holding government contracts. Every federal contract already contained a clause requiring recipients to practice nondiscrimination in employment. Armed with the power to terminate
contracts, the committee set out to give this clause life. But Lyndon
Johnson, who disliked coercion, never did cancel a contract. Instead, his committee devised a program called "Plans for Progress"
that relied on voluntary pledges by private corporations to take
specified actions for reducing job discrimination. By 1963, 115 companies with 5½ million workers had signed a plan for progress.

Civil rights groups put little stock in voluntary programs generally and none at all in Plans for Progress. It was a hoax, they said,

which actually protected participants from real compliance with the nondiscrimination clause of their contracts.[13] This was partly true. In the program's early period, companies enrolled in Plans for Progress were the only government contractors not required to provide the government with information on steps taken to fulfill the nondiscrimination clause. As a result, the employment committee's special counsel noted in 1962, there was "no way to ascertain from a plans for progress report whether the company had complied with any of its specific undertakings."[14] It hardly surprised the knowledgeable, therefore, that from May 1961 through January 1963 black employment in Plans for Progress companies rose from 5.0 percent to 5.1 percent, while the Negro share of white-collar jobs increased from 1.5 percent to 1.6 percent.[15] Nor did performance improve notably with time. A 1967 study of companies headquartered in New York compared 30 companies enrolled in Plans for Progress with 30 randomly selected companies that were not. The companies not enrolled actually employed a higher proportion of blacks in white-collar jobs.[16]

Among the committee's severest critics was the attorney general. Perusing a list of 35,000 government contractors in 1963, Robert Kennedy noticed that "there was just pages of companies" that had still never hired even a single Negro. Since the public considered the employment committee not Lyndon Johnson's creature but John Kennedy's, RFK shuddered at the political implications: "I could just see going into the election of 1964 with this great buildup . . ." he later remarked, "and, eventually, these statistics or figures would get out; and . . . there would just be a public scandal." The sole cause of the committee's lame performance, in Kennedy's view, was Johnson's inept leadership.[17]

At a meeting of the employment committee on May 29, 1963, the attorney general humiliated the vice president by submitting vague claims of the committee's accomplishment to pitiless cross-examination. As Johnson sank deeper in his chair and everybody else—in the words of one witness—was "sweating under the armpits,"[18] the attorney general cut short a biting interrogation of NASA director James Webb by saying, "I am trying to ask some questions. I don't think I am able to get the answers, to tell you the truth."[19] Later that year Robert Kennedy showed his brother statistics exposing the failure of Johnson's committee. The president, said Bobby, "almost had a fit. . . . He said, 'That man can't run this Committee.

Can you think of anything more deplorable than him trying to run the United States? That's why he can't ever be President.' "[20] By then John Kennedy knew that he had failed to deliver on his promise of jobs for blacks.

He was no more successful in redeeming the other half of his promise to the civil rights movement—votes for disfranchised southern blacks. The administration's chief weapon in its drive to enfranchise blacks was the 1957 Civil Rights Act, which empowered the attorney general to sue in federal court for injunctive relief of citizens whose right to vote was denied or threatened by reason of race. The target of the act was the one hundred counties in eight southern states where voting discrimination was systematically practiced. For the Kennedys the benefit of a voting campaign was obvious. It would help southern Negroes secure their other rights, inflame the passions of southern whites less than would a direct attack against segregation, and no doubt add loyal Democrats to the South's voting lists. In three years the Justice Department's Civil Rights Division filed a remarkable fifty voting-rights cases.[21]

But existing voting legislation proved too feeble for Kennedy's purpose. The government had to proceed case by case, county by county, and expend vast quantities of man hours in preparation of briefs to prove "patterns of discrimination."[22] Even when it won a case, local and state officials often raised new obstacles, forcing the government's lawyers back to court again. Not the least of the problems was racist judges, some of whom Kennedy himself appointed to the bench. As one of Robert Kennedy's deputies aptly put it, presidents did not appoint federal district judges with the advice and consent of the Senate; senators appointed them from their own states "with the advice and consent of the President."[23] Thus Kennedy's first judicial appointment was William Harold Cox, college roommate of Mississippi Senator James O. Eastland. Judge Cox once referred to black litigants in his courtroom as "niggers" and compared them to "chimpanzees."[24] Kennedy also appointed E. Gordon West, a former law partner of Senator Russell Long of Louisiana, who observed in one opinion that *Brown v. Board of Education* was "one of the truly regrettable decisions of all time."[25] Though Kennedy also put some good judges on the southern bench, the fact remains that four of the eight district judges whom he appointed in the Deep South willfully obstructed the efforts of the Justice Department to enforce the law.[26] That was one reason why, in 1963, seven years after passage of the first voting rights act, total Negro registration in the hundred target counties had increased from 5 percent to only 8.3 percent.[27]

By early 1962 Robert Kennedy and Burke Marshall, head of the Civil Rights Division, realized that they needed a stronger voting law. Literacy tests, often unfairly administered, were the most popular device for denying the vote to southern blacks. Accordingly, Marshall drafted a bill to make a sixth-grade education proof of literacy in states where literacy was a test for voting. Though Senate Majority Leader Mike Mansfield sponsored it, President Kennedy, who did not much like backing a loser, kept his distance from the whole enterprise. The day after the bill was introduced, he called Marshall and asked skeptically, "What's this bill of yours and Bobby's?"[28] Senate liberals failed badly in their attempt to save the bill from a southern filibuster. Neither the White House nor the civil rights lobby gave them much help. Roy Wilkins ungenerously called the bill "but a token offering on the full civil rights program pledged by the administration's party platform in 1960."[29]

Even if Kennedy could have produced votes and jobs, he would not have satisfied civil rights lobbyists. Segregation was their target, and federal help in smashing it their rising and insistent demand. In 1961 Martin Luther King accused the federal government of being "the nation's highest investor in segregation." "It is no exaggeration to say," he wrote, "that the President could give segregation its death blow through a stroke of a pen."[30] On August 29, 1961, on behalf of thirty-five liberal organizations belonging to the Leadership Conference on Civil Rights, Roy Wilkins presented the White House with a sixty-page paper called *Federally Supported Discrimination,* documenting the use of federal funds to nourish segregation and renewing the demand that Kennedy cut those funds off.[31]

Whether Kennedy had the power was legally arguable. The Supreme Court had ruled publicly supported segregation unconstitutional but permitted school segregation to continue under its dictum of "all deliberate speed." Congress, meanwhile, was still providing financial assistance to programs whether or not they were segregated. The Kennedy administration characteristically equivocated. The Pentagon ordered desegregation of military reserve units but left untouched racial segregation in the National Guard.[32] The Labor Department told state employment agencies to stop filling discriminatory job orders, and the Office of Education said that federally aided libraries must be open to all citizens, but neither agency cut off funds to defiant recipients.[33] HEW took effective steps to end discrimination by southern colleges in programs funded by the National Defense Education Act,[34] but continued to subsidize segregated local public-school districts adjacent to federal installations. The Justice Department in 1962 initiated suit to desegregate the federally aided schools of Prince George County, Virginia,[35] but suits were a less drastic and more time-consuming remedy than cutting off funds.

The civil rights lobby was most aggrieved by Kennedy's reluctance to issue an executive order barring discrimination in federally aided housing programs. The Civil Rights Commission had first recommended its issuance in 1959. During the 1960 campaign Kennedy had lightly remarked several times that, if Eisenhower did not end housing discrimination by "a stroke of the presidential pen," he would.[36] Once in office, however, the president kept finding reasons of his own to procrastinate. First he feared that a housing order would jeopardize his nomination of Robert Weaver, a Negro and president of the NAACP, as head of the Housing and Home Finance Agency (HHFA). (Weaver was approved.) Then he worried about the effect of such an order on congressional consideration of his 1961 Omnibus Housing bill.[37] Even though his civil rights aide, Harris Wofford, warned him in the fall of 1961 that delay was jeopardizing all his political gains among Negroes to date, Kennedy found still new reasons to hesitate.[38] Soon, pens to help the president make that promised stroke began flooding the White House. Where was the troublemaker who put that line about pens into his campaign speeches? Kennedy jokingly inquired.[39] The troublemaker was Wofford, who never did take hold on the White House staff and found himself over at the Peace Corps in 1962.

Kennedy waited until Congress adjourned, the midterm elections were safely past, and public attention was riveted on China's incursion into India before issuing his housing order on Thanksgiving eve, 1962.[40] It was hardly a great victory for the rights of man. The heart of the order was a provision forbidding the Federal Housing Authority to insure mortgages for builders who refused to sell to minorities. Unfortunately, the FHA insured only 20 percent of newly built homes. To cover most of the rest, Robert Weaver had urged Kennedy to enjoin banks and savings and loans associations from lending to discriminatory builders. Justice Department lawyers questioned the president's authority over savings and loan associations;[41] and panicky congressional Democrats in big-city districts emphasized the political risks of an order that might actually accomplish its object.[42] Kennedy accordingly declined to cover financial institutions.

Among its other flaws, the order depended for enforcement on complaints initiated by victims of discrimination, a method that had never worked under state and local fair-housing laws. It forced only marginal changes in the biased policies of local public-housing authorities. And it exempted the nearly two million existing in-construction units still receiving federal assistance.[43] Looking back in 1966, Robert Weaver judged the order to have been virtually null. It covered less than 3 percent of existing housing; and "since the total new construction in any one year adds perhaps 2.5 percent to the total supply, of which one-fifth is covered by our present nondiscrimination requirements, it follows that the rate at which we are increasing nondiscrimination coverage is only one-half of one percent annually."[44] Kennedy's housing order, in short, was an empty gesture toward the principle of open housing, a necessary move in the complex game he was playing on the civil rights issue.

Kennedy's failure to produce much in the way of concrete benefits for Negroes in 1961–1962 hardly affected his standing among them. Accustomed so long to political invisibility, most blacks were grateful even for symbolic acts. Kennedy might shrink from confronting segregation in the South, but at least he confronted it in the Coast Guard. His Employment Committee might flounder, but he himself was showering prominent blacks with presidential appointments. He had broken his promise on legislation, but rare was the prominent black who had not received at least one invitation to a White House social function. Even the leadership of the NAACP was not immune to the Kennedy blarney. In July 1961 a trainload of delegates from the NAACP's annual convention in Philadelphia came to Washington to push for civil-rights legislation of the sort promised in the 1960 Democratic platform. Kennedy himself received a delegation of sixty-five of the group's top leaders. He set up chairs for the ladies, listened intently to a brief appeal for "an enduring law,"[45] and then took everyone on a tour of the White House that included a look at Lincoln's bed. Charmed by the man and flattered by his attention, the delegates hardly noticed his unequivocal rejection of their petition.[46]

Occasionally the president's performance was too cute for a

tough professional like Roy Wilkins. In a 1961 letter to Harris Wofford, Wilkins wrote, "The Kennedy administration has done with Negro citizens what it has done with a vast number of Americans: it has charmed them. It has intrigued them. Every seventy-two hours it has delighted them. On the Negro question it has smothered Unguentine on a stinging burn even though for a moment (or for perhaps a year) it cannot do anything about a broken pelvis. It has patted a head even though it could not bind up a joint."[47] Significantly, Wilkins kept his complaints private. Because he was a professional, he understood the president's problems. And he had a sufficiently good memory to know that Kennedy was right in claiming that he was doing more for black people than any of his predecessors. Thus, like the mass of his fellow blacks, even Roy Wilkins counted himself a Kennedy man.

If he could have confined the civil rights issue to Washington, Kennedy could probably have managed it. He had disappointed but not finally alienated the civil rights lobby. At the same time southern congressmen appreciated the president's sensitivity to the prejudices of their region and realized that what he did to secure the Negro vote he had to do. But civil rights was not an ordinary problem. Nor were its parameters defined by civil rights lobbyists and southern congressmen in Washington. Down South, both among those who believed in freedom now and those who believed in segregation forever, passions were rising that would wreck the president's political calculations and confront him with the racial crises he wanted so desperately to avoid.

II

Robert Kennedy was the administration official who had to grapple day by day with the developing race crisis. This was ironic. As one of the attorney general's admiring aides later remarked in a masterpiece of understatement, he began his tenure without regarding "the incipient black rebellion as the gravest threat to American society."[48] Crime busting was his real interest. But Robert Kennedy was his brother's chief political adviser, and civil rights proved to be the administration's toughest political problem. He was also the nation's top law-enforcement officer, and civil rights became increasingly a matter of how to enforce the law. Civil rights activists brandishing the Constitution were meeting white violence in their attempts to overthrow segregation. What, if any, were the legal responsibilities of the attorney general? And what were the political costs of deciding to intervene and protect the activists or deciding to stay aloof from their plight?

Robert Kennedy approached the problem of racial violence concerned more with its political than its legal aspects. It helped that he had in Burke Marshall, chief of his Civil Rights Division, a legal mind honed by years of practicing corporate law and capable of producing a good brief to justify any reasonable posture. Guided by his brother's general civil rights strategy, RFK wished to avoid choosing sides in the confrontation between violent white racists and nonviolent integrationists. To avoid a choice, he and Marshall worked tirelessly behind the scenes to defuse potential explosions. Sometimes they were successful but on occasion, when they were not, choice was thrust upon them. Then they had to either intervene, outraging the white South, or stay out, infuriating the civil rights movement. On this dilemma the administration's civil rights strategy ultimately foundered.

The problem attained stark clarity with the advent of the Freedom Riders. James Farmer, national director of the nonviolent Congress of Racial Equality, conceived the Freedom Rides as a means to test a recent Supreme Court decision forbidding racial discrimination in terminals serving interstate travelers. On May 4, 1961, Farmer led a carefully selected biracial group onto a bus in Washington, D.C., and headed south for New Orleans. Under no illusions about the hospitality awaiting them, the Riders, recalled Farmer, were "prepared for anything, even death." When the bus stopped at Rock Hill, South Carolina, John Lewis, a black theology student, tried to enter a waiting room reserved for whites only. A gang of hoods blocked his path. "I have every right to enter this waiting room according to the Supreme Court of the United States in the Boynton case," he said. "Shit on that," the hoods replied, and beat him to the floor.[49] On May 14, the Freedom Riders having split into two bands, one group was mobbed outside Anniston, Alabama, and the other was set upon by club-wielding whites in Birmingham. CORE promptly called off the Rides.

At once Nashville members of the Student Nonviolent Coordinating Committee rushed to finish what CORE had begun.[50] SNCC (pronounced Snick), had been organized during the 1960 sit-in movement and had since established itself as the most militant of all civil rights organizations. In the third week of May 1961, while a mob milled around outside, SNCC members waited in the Birmingham terminal for a bus to take them to Montgomery. Speaking for all the drivers, one of them declared, "I only have one life to give and I'm not going to give it to CORE or the NAACP."[51]

President Kennedy met with the attorney general and other top Justice Department officials on Wednesday, May 17, to discuss the crisis. The president accepted without question his constitutional responsibility to assure safe passage of all interstate passengers through Alabama. But he hoped privately to persuade state officials to keep order and so spare himself the political embarrassment of deploying federal force. Kennedy tried to phone Alabama Governor John Patterson, his strongest supporter among southern governors in 1960, to obtain protection for the Freedom Riders. Patterson would not receive Kennedy's calls. Finally, on May 19, Patterson sent word that he would see a representative of the president. Meeting with John Seigenthaler of the Justice Department later that day, Patterson declared that he had "the will, the force, the men and the equipment to protect everyone in Alabama." Robert Kennedy told the Greyhound Bus Company to take the Freedom Riders on to Montgomery.[52]

But if Patterson had promised protection for the Riders, as Kennedy believed, he reneged. The Freedom Riders arrived in Montgomery on Saturday morning, May 20, to confront a mob of some one thousand. On the phone in a federal building across from the bus terminal, John Doar, Marshall's chief assistant in the Civil Rights Division, described the unfolding scene to the attorney general in Washington. "Now the passengers are coming off," Doar said. "They're standing on a corner of the platform. Oh, there are fists, punching. A bunch of men led by a guy with a bleeding face are beating them. There are no cops. It's terrible. It's terrible. There's not a cop in sight. People are yelling, 'Get 'em, get 'em.' It's awful."[53] Among those beaten up was John Seigenthaler, hit from behind when he tried to help a young white woman who had been on the bus.

That blow galvanized Robert Kennedy. A journalist who saw him immediately after he heard about Seigenthaler recalled that the attorney general "looked like he'd just been poleaxed *himself*. He took it as if he had been down in Montgomery himself and been hit."[54] For the Kennedys, the moment of decision had arrived. John

Doar rented a car and drove fifty miles in search of a sympathetic judge to issue a temporary restraining order against the forces of violence, including the Ku Klux Klan. Citing the 1895 case of *In Re Debs* as precedent, Doar argued that the federal government had inherent authority to keep interstate commerce free of obstruction.[55] Even before the restraining order was issued, Robert Kennedy dispatched four hundred U.S. marshals to Montgomery for the purpose, as he said in a telegram to Patterson, of assisting "state and local authorities in the protection of persons and property and vehicles in Alabama."[56]

The marshals had no easy time of it that weekend. By coincidence, Martin Luther King had a speaking engagement in Montgomery. His arrival poured oil on the fires of white hatred raging through the city. On Sunday, May 21, fifteen hundred blacks sat in a church praying with King for the Freedom Riders, while outside a mob of whites edged toward incendiary violence.[57] James Farmer, who was there, recalled, "The mob kicked open the door . . . and they just *poured* in. And people were screaming, backed up against the wall. I don't know where they came from or how they did it, but the marshals materialized. . . . It seemed almost fictional."[58] For hours thereafter, with diminishing success, the marshals held the mob at bay. His nerves frazzled, King berated Robert Kennedy over a phone in the church for the continuing breakdown of law and order. "I said," Kennedy recalled, "that we were doing the best that we could and that he'd be as dead as Kelsey's nuts if it hadn't been for the marshals and the efforts that we made."[59] Forces beyond his control had made Kennedy the protector of Martin Luther King and the adversary of the one southern governor well-disposed to his brother. "You are destroying us politically," Patterson told Robert Kennedy in another call that night. "John," replied Kennedy, "it's more important that these people in the church survive physically than for us to survive politically."[60] Patterson decided at the last minute to dispatch the Alabama National Guard. Order was restored by morning.

Having been provoked into precisely the kind of action he most wanted to avoid, Robert Kennedy now tried to get the militants off the buses. Let us have a "cooling-off period," he urged.[61] But the Riders, who spent three days in Montgomery nursing their wounds, had already resolved to risk death again and proceed to the next stop, which was Jackson, Mississippi.[62] The Riders asked Martin

Luther King to join them, but he declined on the grounds that to do so would violate his parole on a previous civil rights conviction. That finished him with SNCC for good. James Farmer, who had departed from the bus in Atlanta to attend his father's funeral, did not want to go either. He had work to do back at the office, he said. But when a girl who was going pleaded, "Jim, *please*," he knew he could not run. "Get my luggage out of the car and put it on the goddam bus," he said.[63] Meanwhile, Mississippi Senator James Eastland gave Robert Kennedy his private guarantee for the safety of the passengers.[64] All that awaited them in Mississippi was arrest in Jackson for violating local segregation ordinances.

Though the Kennedys had intervened in the South to protect integrationists, they had done so with carefully calculated circumspection. Hoping to cushion the blow, they used marshals instead of soldiers, kept the president in the background, and stressed the need to uphold the law, rather than the moral right of blacks to use desegregated facilities. Administration restraint did not go unappreciated. Southern senators, including the region's most noted constitutional lawyer, Sam Ervin of North Carolina, admitted the legality of the president's intervention.[65] And even Governor Patterson said he still considered John Kennedy a friend.[66] But to countless southern racists unlearned in the law, the meaning of the federal marshals in Montgomery seemed clear: the president had joined forces with the outside agitators and race mixers. A wound had opened in the relations of the Kennedys and the white South that would never heal.

Through the summer of 1961 the Riders kept coming. The roads were safe now, and so were the terminals, but in Jackson those who tried to integrate terminal facilities continued to go to jail. The Justice Department decided that the only way to end the current Freedom Rides and prevent new ones was to seek implementation of the court's decision barring discrimination in interstate travel facilities. The department petitioned the Interstate Commerce Commission to issue nondiscrimination rules binding on the bus companies; and acting with unwonted speed, the ICC obliged in September 1961. The administration also negotiated with southern railroads and airports to desegregate their facilities. In January 1963 RFK told the president, "I can report to you that in the past year, segregation in interstate commerce has ceased to exist."[67]

Robert Kennedy emerged from the Freedom Rides confirmed in

his conviction that he must keep the racial conflict off the streets. In particular, he needed some way to deflect SNCC militants from direct confrontations with segregation. Meeting privately with representatives of the civil rights groups in June 1961, the attorney general offered a suggestion: Why not move away from confrontation in favor of a voter-registration campaign? "I felt nobody could really oppose voting," Kennedy recalled. It was not like school desegregation with people saying, "We don't want our little blond daughter going to school with a Negro."[68] At follow-up meetings the Taconic, Field, and Stern foundations offered to provide financial assistance for a voting drive; civil rights groups agreed to unite in conducting a Voter Education Project; and Burke Marshall and Harris Wofford, representing the administration, promised federal cooperation.[69]

The precise nature of the cooperation promised became an issue of no small historical consequence. SNCC's representatives came away from the meetings believing that they had been promised quite a lot. Timothy Jenkins recalled one administration representative, perhaps Wofford, saying that "if necessary in the course of protecting people's right to vote . . . the Kennedy administration would fill every jail in the South." According to Lonnie King, "Bobby pledged marshals and what have you to help us out."[70] But Harold Flemming of the Southern Regional Council, who also attended the meetings, said later, "I never heard anybody from the Justice Department say, 'Sure you fellows go out there and we'll give you all the protection you need.' "[71] Most likely, SNCC read into the promise of cooperation implications the administration had not intended. It simply never occurred to the militants soon to embark on a southern invasion that the administration that had encouraged them to go would abandon them to the Ku Klux Klan.

The Voter Education Project was formally launched in March 1962. Though all the major civil rights groups participated, SNCC provided most of those who risked their lives to man voting projects in the Deep South. By 1963, 180 full-time SNCC "field secretaries," the majority of them black, were working principally in southwest Georgia and the state of Mississippi.[72] This was one Kennedy idea that backfired. SNCC workers met intransigent and often violent white opposition. They responded by organizing local black communities to resist. The result was the very confrontations Robert Kennedy had hoped to avoid.

In the fall of 1961, even before the Voter Education Project officially commenced, the first SNCC workers straggled into Albany, Georgia, a city of fifty thousand, to organize a voting project. In a few weeks they turned this sleepy bastion of segregation into a cockpit of racial strife. First, SNCC workers got arrested trying to integrate the Trailways Bus Terminal. Then local blacks, forming the Albany Movement, took to the streets by the hundreds to protest. When the authorities responded by filling the jails with hymn-singing demonstrators, Martin Luther King rushed to town to get arrested too. Albany was now the hottest civil rights story since the Freedom Rides.[73] At the end of December, with the Justice Department exerting pressure behind the scenes for a peaceful resolution, Albany city fathers and the Albany Movement negotiated a compromise that permitted King to leave jail and moved the story off the front pages.[74] Once the reporters were gone, city officials failed to honor the agreement, and the struggle resumed.

For the SNCC workers who stayed to fight it out, life in southwest Georgia was hard indeed. In the summer of 1962 an Albany court convicted Martin Luther King on charges stemming from the previous year's demonstrations, briefly returning him to jail. The Albany Movement again took to the streets, and white violence in surrounding rural counties escalated. Churches were bombed, meetings harassed. In one two-week period in July, a deputy sheriff of Mitchell County beat and kicked the pregnant wife of a local black leader (her child was born dead); a sheriff of Dougherty County caned Albany's only black lawyer about the head; and a prison trusty beat a SNCC worker senseless.[75] One night while SNCC's Charles Sherrod and other project workers were getting ready for bed, unknown assailants fired on them from the darkness. "We were all on the floor," Sherrod reported to SNCC headquarters. "We were working together on Voter Registration. We had been shot at. Some were hit. There was blood. We were afraid. Where was the Federal Government?"[76]

Sherrod's question reverberated through the civil rights movement in the summer of 1962. Engulfed in terror and losing local support, SNCC and the Albany Movement pleaded with the administration to redeem its supposed promises of protection. The president himself was not unmoved. One weekend in July 1962 he bombarded Burke Marshall with telephone calls, asking if there was not something that could be done about Albany.[77] And in his August 1 press conference he said he could not understand why the Albany City Council refused to negotiate with the city's black citizens.[78] Meanwhile, the Justice Department sought an injunction to prevent intimidation of voting workers in one county, opposed issuance of an injunction to stop protest demonstrations in Albany, and sought to prevent prosecution of two black leaders on trumped-up charges.

But in the eyes of the civil rights workers this was not enough. They urged the Justice Department to break the back of white resistance by seeking injunctions to compel desegregation of public facilities and to prevent public officials from violating the civil rights of black citizens. Above all, the workers demanded physical protection from white violence. When the Kennedys did not deliver, the embittered Albany Movement turned against them. In December 1962 W. G. Anderson, leader of the Albany Movement, sent President Kennedy a telegram: ". . . Ignoring the acts of demagogs and tyrants perpetuating segregation and discrimination is tantamount to aiding and abetting. You cannot continue to ignore the cries of these oppressed people."[79] Anderson received a reply of sorts in August 1963 when Robert Kennedy personally announced indictments against nine Albany civil rights activists, including Anderson, on charges of obstructing justice and perjury. The accused had allegedly picketed a white juror for voting to acquit a sheriff accused of shooting a black prisoner.[80]

Mississippi was even tougher for SNCC to crack than Georgia. In the summer of 1961 Robert Moses, a Harlem schoolteacher with an M.A. degree in philosophy from Harvard, became the first SNCC worker in the state. Soon joined by others, Moses opened a voter-education project in McComb and endured the determined effort of Klansmen and others to break him. In August 1961 Moses led a small group of Negroes in Liberty, Mississippi, to the voter-registration office. One block from the courthouse, a prominent citizen attacked Moses on the street and beat him with the butt end of a knife. Two weeks later, other SNCC workers were beaten up in Liberty, this time on the courthouse lawn. In September Herbert Lee, a local black activist in the voting campaign, was shot and killed by a member of the Mississippi legislature.[81] But SNCC would not break. In a letter from the Magnolia County jail on November 1, 1961, Moses wrote, "This is Mississippi, the middle of the iceberg. Hollis is leading off with his tenor, 'Michael row the boat ashore,

Alleluia. Christian brothers don't be slow, Alleluia; Mississippi next to go, Alleluia.' This is a tremor in the middle of the iceberg."[82]

In 1962 SNCC workers spread over a large portion of the state, attempting to tear down the walls of fear in local black communities and establish indigenous organizations. They spent months mostly talking to people on porches or in churches, proving to them that no matter how hard it got, they were staying.[83] Fannie Lou Hamer, a timekeeper on a cotton plantation who became a leader in the Mississippi movement, recalled, "Nobody never come out into the country and talked to real farmers and things. . . . They treated us like we were special and we loved 'em. . . . We trusted 'em, and I can tell the world those kids done their share in Mississippi."[84] Amzie Moore of the state NAACP remembered with awe how SNCC workers would lead a march up against a phalanx of armed rednecks, *"How they stood . . . how gladly they got in front of that line . . . and went to jail. It didn't seem to bother 'em."*[85]

But it did bother them. In Leflore County, for example, project workers were beaten and jailed. Officials retaliated against their influence by cutting off surplus food for needy blacks. Jimmy Travis was shot in the neck as he was driving on the highway. Late one night, while a group of project workers was meeting in their Greenwood office, men with guns gathered outside. When the workers hurriedly placed a call to Burke Marshall in Washington, he told them he could do nothing until a crime had been committed. They escaped with their lives by climbing to the roof and sliding down a TV antenna.[86]

As the terror mounted, so did demands for federal intervention. "We ran through that a dozen times over the period of a thousand days," Robert Kennedy remembered, "because there were always things arising, where people would say, 'Why don't you provide protection? Why don't you send marshals? Why don't you send the troops in?' "[87] It fell to Marshall to provide the legal justification for his department's policy of steadfast inaction.[88] Federal attorneys could not, he explained, seek injunctions to prevent violations of constitutional rights, unless, as in the 1957 Voting Rights Act, Congress specifically provided statutory authority. In a federal system, Marshall declared, civil rights "are individual and personal, to be asserted by private citizens as they choose, in court, speaking through their chosen counsel."[89] Moreover, it was pointless for the Justice Department to prosecute those who violated the civil rights of others, using statutes passed during Reconstruction. The Supreme Court had so narrowly construed these statutes that convictions would be difficult to obtain under the best of circumstances and nearly impossible before southern juries. As for physical protection, the government could neither provide it nor authorize on-the-spot arrests when federal rights were being violated. In a federal system local governments alone must preserve law and order and protect citizens from unlawful conduct. The alternative was a national police force, which did not exist and was not desirable. Marshall offered SNCC only an occasional suit of limited scope and his own honest sympathy.

Lawyers for the civil rights movement disputed every point in Marshall's brief. The Justice Department could seek injunctions without a specific statute, they said, and in fact had done so to stop violence during the Montgomery Freedom Rides crisis. Government lawyers in that case had correctly cited the precedent of *In Re Debs* (1895), in which the Supreme Court had granted a Justice Department request for an injunction, in the absence of a statute to halt a railroad strike on the basis of the commerce clause of the Constitution. Civil rights lawyers also demanded vigorous federal prosecution, under the Reconstruction acts, of local officials who violated the civil rights of others. Juries might fail to convict, they said, but trials would educate the public and induce caution on the part of the police.[90] As for a national police force, the United States already had one. The U.S. Code empowered the Federal Bureau of Investigation to make arrests without warrant for offenses against the laws of the United States committed in the presence of its agents. A law student active in the movement wrote, "The FBI makes arrests for Federal bank robberies, espionage, kidnapping, narcotics violations, and other crimes. There is no legitimate reason why it cannot make on-the-spot arrests for violations of the Federal civil rights statutes." If all else failed, there was always Title 10, Section 333 of the U.S. Code, which empowered the president to use force to protect the constitutional rights of citizens and uphold the laws in any state where local authority was unwilling or unable to do so. President Eisenhower had invoked this section in sending the U.S. Army into Little Rock to enforce court-ordered school desegregation in 1957. President Kennedy had used it to dispatch marshals to Alabama during the Freedom Rides. Civil rights workers called on Kennedy to invoke Section 333 to protect them in the wake of the breakdown of law and order in Mississippi.[91]

The most visible representatives of the federal government in the

Deep South were local FBI agents. That fact alone placed a tremendous strain on the relations between civil rights workers and the federal government. FBI Director J. Edgar Hoover had no sympathy with the civil rights movement and used his every resource to limit his responsibility in this area.[92] The FBI might boast of gunning down Dillinger and apprehending bank robbers, but in cases of alleged violations of the civil rights laws, it claimed only the legal authority to investigate, a point on which Robert F. Kennedy and J. Edgar Hoover were in rare harmony. FBI methods infuriated civil rights workers almost as much as the narrow definition of FBI responsibilities. Time and again in these years SNCC workers would suffer violence at the hands of racist officials, while Bureau agents impassively stood by taking notes. Agents investigated SNCC's complaints of civil rights violations, but nothing ever seemed to happen. Agents interviewed the victims of police brutality and then passed what they heard on to local police departments. Martin Luther King said in 1962, "Every time I saw FBI men in Albany, they were with the local police force."[93]

This attack on the FBI confirmed Bureau Director Hoover in his determination to get King, whose race, cause, and character he could not abide and even whose loyalty to the United States he had come to question.[94] Early in January 1962 the FBI made the startling discovery that one of King's closest advisers was a New York lawyer, Stanley Levison, key administrator in the early 1950s of the secret funds of the American Communist party. Though Levison had become alienated from the party sometime in 1955 and ceased thereafter to participate in its activities, the FBI reflexively concluded that he was now exploiting his considerable influence on King to advance the world Communist conspiracy. Levison's failure ever to admit his past role in Communist party affairs strengthened the Bureau in this fanciful hypothesis.[95] Hoover described Levison to Robert Kennedy in 1962 as "a secret member of the Communist Party,"[96] and Bureau officials once told Burke Marshall that Levison was an important Soviet espionage agent.[97] Evidence in the FBI's possession casting serious doubt on these characterizations was ignored.[98] Trusting Hoover's estimate of Levison, Robert Kennedy tried repeatedly—in person and through intermediaries—to persuade King to break off the relationship. Because Kennedy refused to document his charges against Levison, King refused.

By 1963 the issue of Stanley Levison had come to color all King's dealings with the administration. Noticeably cool to the nation's foremost black leader, the Kennedys feared that public disclosure of the King-Levison connection would damage not only the civil rights movement but the administration that was widely perceived as its ally.[99] On June 22, 1963, the president himself took advantage of a visit by King to the White House to escort him into the Rose Garden for a private chat. Repeating FBI charges against Levison, Kennedy said, "If they shoot *you* down, they'll shoot us down too."[100] Maybe, King thought, noting the president's reluctance to converse in his own office, he was afraid of Hoover himself.[101]

In July King ostensibly severed relations with Levison but actually kept in touch with him through a third party. Suspecting as much, Robert Kennedy raised the possibility with the FBI of tapping King's phones. Intercepting phone messages was illegal, but since 1940 attorneys general had claimed exceptions in national security cases. By the time the Bureau submitted a formal request on July 26, 1963, to tap King, Kennedy had decided the risks were too great. Meanwhile the Bureau, which had been tapping Levison for years, gathered evidence that the King-Levison relationship continued to flourish and, moreover, that Jack O'Dell, a Southern Christian Leadership Conference employee with a Communist background, had not been excommunicated from the organization as King had publicly claimed. The next time Hoover sought authority to tap King—October 7, 1963—Kennedy signed on.[102] Not terminated until June 1966, the FBI's phone taps on King yielded no evidence of Communist subversion, but they did generate political intelligence on the civil rights movement useful to both the Justice Department and the White House.

Hoover was not content merely to wiretap King. On December 23, 1963, relevant FBI officials met at Washington headquarters to explore ways, as Assistant Director William C. Sullivan put it, of "neutralizing King as an effective Negro leader." At the proper time, Sullivan promised, the Bureau would expose King for the "clerical fraud and Marxist he is."[103] Taking note shortly after the new year that King had reservations at Washington's Willard Hotel, Sullivan authorized the first microphone surveillance of King's rooms. Bugging was not illegal, but the necessary trespass to plant a bug was. Recorded highlights of a party in King's suite at the Willard so titillated Hoover that he immediately sent a transcript to the White House.[104] "King is a 'tom cat' with obsessive degenerate sexual urges," Hoover wrote Sullivan.[105]

In succeeding months FBI agents pursued King across the country in an effort to record him in compromising situations. They leaked damaging tapes to newsmen in the vain hope their contents would be published. And on November 21, 1964, thirty-four days before Christmas, a Bureau agent mailed a tape of some of King's indiscretions to SCLC's office in Atlanta. The accompanying anonymous note, composed by Sullivan himself, said in part,

> King, look into your heart. . . . You even at an early age have turned out to be not a leader but a dissolute, abnormal moral imbecile. . . . King, there is only one thing left for you to do. You know what it is. You have just 34 days in which to do (this exact number has been selected for a specific reason, it has definite practical significant [sic]). You are done. There is but one way out for you. You better take it before your filthy, abnormal fraudulent self is bared to the nation.[106]

Weeks later Mrs. King, thinking it contained one of her husband's speeches, began playing the tape.[107] King himself never doubted who had sent it. In a phone call duly tapped by the FBI, he told one friend, "They are out to break me," and another, "They are out to get me, harass me, break my spirit."[108] Robert Kennedy and White House officials were reasonably well informed about the FBI's vendetta against King. They did little to stop it. Thus, while King was summoning the liberal state to bestow civil rights upon his people, he himself was the victim of its sinister underside.

King was sophisticated enough to distinguish between Robert Kennedy and the virtually autonomous Hoover. SNCC workers, however, knew only that FBI agents worked for Kennedy's department. Increasingly they came to regard the FBI, and therefore Kennedy, as indistinguishable from their racist enemies closer at hand. A sign in SNCC's Jackson office caught the spirit of SNCC's growing alienation:

> There is a place in Mississippi called Liberty
> There is a department in Washington called Justice.[109]

In January 1963 SNCC initiated an unsuccessful suit in federal court to force the Justice Department to protect civil rights workers. The very name of the case told volumes about the history of the civil rights movement in the early 1960s. It was *Moses v. Kennedy*.[110]

Though Robert Kennedy was not ordinarily disposed to inaction, Marshall's doctrine of federalism afforded him a refuge from the racial strife so threatening to his brother's political fortunes. But federalism was not proof against every call upon the president's authority in civil rights matters. In the fall of 1962 administration strategy met its most difficult test when James Meredith, a black man, sought admittance to the all-white University of Mississippi. A federal court in June 1962 had ordered Meredith's admission. On September 13, one week before registration for the fall semester, Mississippi Governor Ross Barnett announced that the state was taking over operation of the university and interposing its sovereignty between the federal government and the people of the state. "No school will be integrated in Mississippi while I am your Governor," Barnett said.[111] The Kennedys had not been party to Meredith's suit, and at no time in the coming weeks would they comment on its merits. But their obligation to uphold the orders of the federal courts could not be shirked. Thus there loomed that September the worst of all prospects from the Kennedy point of view—an insurrection in defense of segregation that only the president had the force to subdue.

Robert Kennedy frequently phoned Governor Barnett that month, seeking some way to avoid sending the army against citizens of Mississippi.[112] Yield to the courts, he pleaded; and if not that, at least keep order and peacefully accede to superior force. A weak man whose word was no better than his judgment, Barnett proved unwilling to resist the mood of defiance gripping white Mississippi. Sometimes he took an uncompromising line with the attorney general; sometimes he flirted with schemes that would save face and also avoid the ultimate clash. But when Meredith, protected by U.S. marshals, came to the Oxford campus on registration day, September 20, 1962, Barnett personally turned him away. Five days later (Tuesday, September 25) Barnett defied a federal court order by physically preventing the university trustees from registering Meredith in Jackson.[113] On Friday, September 28, the U.S. Court of Appeals for the Fifth Circuit ordered Barnett to purge himself of contempt within four days or face arrest and a fine of $10,000 a day.

Barnett seemed ready on Friday to lead a reincarnated Confederacy in one last stand. "What appeared to be going to happen," Burke Marshall recalled, "was Barnett was intending to put state patrols and a whole civilian army up there and we would have to send troops in and fight their way through these people." President Kennedy himself got on the phone with Barnett on Saturday for a series of conversations to dissuade him from this mad course. The governor, in one of his conciliatory moods, proposed a scheme that would save both lives and his own political skin. On Monday Barnett would go with his army to Oxford, while the marshals secretly took Meredith to Jackson to be registered. He would announce that the government had surprised him, that Meredith was now in the university, and that he could do nothing more to prevent Meredith's admittance. Seeing this proposal as a way to avoid sending troops, the president bought it. But, after the benefit of a few hours' reflection, Barnett phoned the White House Saturday night to call off the deal.[114]

Barnett and Robert Kennedy were back on the phone early the next afternoon. It was Sunday, September 30, 1962. Bobby was not above a little blackmail to bring the crisis to a satisfactory issue. The president, he told Barnett, intended to go on TV that night and, in the course of explaining why force was needed in Mississippi, he would unmask the secret deal to which Barnett had agreed the day before and which he then had canceled. This disclosure of collaboration would have finished Barnett in Mississippi.[115] According to Marshall, "that was the only thing at any time that made an impression on the governor. And he pleaded in a childish, whining sort of way that the president not do that." Barnett and his legal adviser then proposed another face-saving script. The marshals should take advantage of the Sabbath calm to whisk Meredith into the university that very evening. Barnett would see that the state police kept order and at the same time feign surprise at the government's maneuver. The crisis would end without the army having to be used. Kennedy was satisfied.[116]

That night several hundred federal marshals quietly installed Meredith in a dormitory on the Oxford campus and then took up positions around the university's main administration building. At 8 P.M. the president went on TV to announce that Meredith was on the campus and, invoking the great tradition of the state and the school, he urged students to uphold the law.[117] Kennedy apparently did not know that a large crowd, including rednecks from all over Mississippi, was already surrounding the administration building, throwing rocks and bottles and occasionally firing rifles. The state police, which Barnett had assured Kennedy would keep the peace, disappeared into the darkness. The marshals tried to control the mob with tear gas, but their position was dangerously exposed. Reporting to the White House over a pay phone inside the embattled building, Deputy Attorney General Nicholas Katzenbach asked whether his men could defend themselves with live ammunition. Hold your fire no matter how dire the circumstances, the president commanded.[118]

Finally around midnight, with the situation worsening by the minute, Kennedy moved to save the marshals. Taking the one action he most hoped to avoid, he ordered the army to Oxford. Troops arrived on the campus at 5 A.M. The mob set a fire in their path, but as one Justice Department man in the building remembered it, "the troops came to the flames, and they marched right through without breaking step. And there was a kind of visceral, almost physical impact on the mob. They fell back a couple of steps, and there was a kind of exhalation of breath, as if they had each been punched by the troops marching through the flames, and that was really the end right there. . . . The mob just melted away."[119] The toll of battle included two persons (one a foreign newsman) killed, and 375 others, including 166 marshals, wounded.[120] But Meredith was in the university to stay, and the federal court orders had been upheld.

One of the casualties of the battle of Oxford was Kennedy's civil rights strategy. Having already alienated the SNCC militants, he had been forced into bloody confrontation with the segregationists. The Gallup poll recorded only a temporary slip in Kennedy's rating in the South after federal troops invaded Mississippi, but his hold on the region was clearly slipping. Knowledgeable observers believed that if the Republicans nominated the conservative Barry Goldwater in 1964 Kennedy would lose the South. The president's efforts to straddle the civil rights issue were failing. Events beyond his control made it unlikely that he could long postpone an answer to the question posed by a song that rights workers had appropriated from the labor movement of a generation before: "Which Side Are You On?"

III

In 1960 civil rights had been just one among many tough political issues that candidate John Kennedy had to manipulate. By the beginning of 1963 it was a movement capable of delivering thousands of black demonstrators to the streets and summoning moral support from millions of white northerners. Eighty-nine members of the House submitted civil rights bills at the beginning of the new congressional session.[121] Though manipulation of the issue was now beyond his capacity, Kennedy kept trying. His major civil rights proposal that winter was a bill to strengthen existing voting rights legislation. The staff of the Civil Rights Commission warned the White House that civil rights groups would greet it "with massive indifference or actual opposition."[122] And they did.

The Kennedys in fact, could not even manage the Civil Rights Commission. The attorney general somehow dissuaded the commissioners from holding hearings in Mississippi;[123] but John Kennedy failed to deter them from issuing a special report in April 1963, indicting Mississippi for wanton lawlessness and calling on the president to consider withholding federal funds from the state, pending compliance with the Constitution.[124] Here was fresh evidence, if any was needed, that among those most engaged the time was ripe for a showdown with segregation.

The showdown took place in Birmingham, Alabama. In response to an invitation from local black leaders, Martin Luther King initiated a carefully prepared campaign on April 3, 1963, to smash segregation in that grim, raw industrial city. King was aware of the stakes. "We believed that while a campaign in Birmingham would surely be the toughest fight of our civil rights careers, it could, if successful, break the back of segregation all over the nation," he wrote later.[125] Demonstrations grew daily in size and intensity, until on April 10 a local judge issued an injunction banning further protests. King, who had never defied a court order, decided this time to take his Gandhian philosophy to its logical conclusion and keep on marching. On Good Friday, April 12, he was arrested and jailed.[126] One consequence was his famous "Letter from the Birmingham Jail"—an eloquent defense of demonstrations, civil disobedience, and nonviolent protest. If nonviolence had not emerged, King lectured whites, the streets of the South would "be flowing with blood," and millions of Negroes would have already turned for solace, and might yet, to "black nationalist ideologies."[127]

After eight days King departed from his cell and resumed leadership of the demonstrations. When secret talks between white and black leaders broke down, he dramatically escalated tactics on May 2 by recruiting thousands of schoolchildren to join the protests and fill up the jails. The appearance of the children threw Bull Connor, Birmingham's Commissioner of Public Safety, into a rage.[128] So far,

Connor had handled the demonstrations with relative restraint. But on May 3 he set upon the marchers with dogs, clubs, and fire hoses, making martyrs of his victims and assuring their triumph.[129] The very caricature of a southern bully and perfect foil for King, Connor remarked after one civil rights leader, injured by water from a fire hose, was hospitalized, "I wish he'd been carried away in a hearse."[130]

Connor's repressive tactics generated a massive outpouring of national sympathy for King's campaign. On the morning of May 4 Yankee newspapers featured a photograph of a police dog lunging at a demonstrator. Outrages were hardly a novelty in the South, and the North had seen many pictures of racist brutality over the years. But the conscience of northern liberalism was sensitized in 1963 as it had not been before. This fact transformed Birmingham into an extraordinary historical event. The pictures out of Birmingham helped create a mass constituency for civil rights for the first time since Reconstruction.

The administration remained unmoved. The president told a delegation from the Americans for Democratic Action on May 4 that, though the pictures in the paper made him "sick," he had no power to take action.[131] The attorney general called for redress of "just grievances," but also suggested an end of demonstrations.[132] Burke Marshall flew to Birmingham to mediate the conflict and get it off the streets. On May 7, when 125 white businessmen of the Senior Citizens Committee met downtown to consider King's demands, their mood was so intransigent that Marshall despaired of a settlement. But, on breaking for lunch, the senior citizens went into the streets and confronted an extraordinary sight. King described it in his book, *Why We Can't Wait:*

On that day several thousand Negroes had marched on the town, the jails were so full that the police could only arrest a handful. There were Negroes on the sidewalks, in the streets, standing, sitting in the aisles of downtown stores. There were square blocks of Negroes, a veritable sea of black faces. They were committing no violence; they were just present and singing. Downtown Birmingham echoed to the strains of the freedom songs.[133]

That afternoon business leaders sent word to King that they were ready to negotiate. Three days later, truce terms were announced: the big department stores agreed to desegregate within 90 days and promote and hire Negroes; Negro leaders canceled demonstrations and called off the boycott of the stores. The crisis had apparently ended without the Kennedys having to choose.

But on Saturday night, May 11, two bombs exploded in Birmingham—one at the home of Dr. King's brother and the other at a motel used by black leaders. Word of the explosions quickly spread through the Birmingham ghetto, where the subtleties of King's nonviolent philosophy had never been much appreciated. More than 2,500 Birmingham blacks took to the streets that night and pioneered a form of social protest new to the 1960s: the urban riot. Rampaging for three hours, the rioters attacked police and firemen, wrecked cars, and burned stores. By the time order was restored, nine blocks of the ghetto were in ruins. On Sunday President Kennedy put the Alabama National Guard on the alert and sent federal troops to stations near Birmingham. But by then the spasm of black rage had passed.[134]

The riot at Birmingham provoked a major reappraisal of policy inside the Kennedy administration. John Kennedy had long been worried by the violent possibilities of the black revolution. He knew of Robert F. Williams's recent call for black self-defense in *Negroes with Guns,* of the growing influence of Malcolm X in the northern ghetto, and of the fading appeal of nonviolence among young blacks. That night in Birmingham Negroes shed white blood and put the torch to private property. In the space of a few violent hours civil rights for Negroes came to seem no longer the program of zealots, but a policy for moderate men. Two days after the riot Kennedy confided his fears at a private meeting with Alabama editors. If moderation and nonviolence failed, he said, Negroes might turn to violence and the black Muslims.[135]

As the embers of the Birmingham ghetto were cooling, Kennedy decided at last to honor his 1960 campaign pledge of major civil rights legislation. Burke Marshall recalled that, except for the attorney general, "every single person who spoke about it in the White House—every single one of them—was against President Kennedy sending up that bill."[136] The bill would not pass. It would destroy Kennedy in the South. It might stir up a white backlash in the North. Possessing a surer sense of the moment than any of those who counseled him, John F. Kennedy brushed aside all objections and bid for command of the civil rights movement. He did so even though he feared that his advisers might be right, that this bill was

—as RFK phrased it—"maybe going to be his political swan song."[137]

The Kennedys were right to fear for the civil peace that spring. Inspired by the example of Birmingham, demonstrators were marching in streets all over America. In southern cities like Jackson, Raleigh, and Tallahassee, marchers protested segregated accommodations. In Los Angeles, Philadelphia, and St. Louis, the issues were jobs and schools. One estimate put the number of Americans participating in racial demonstrations in May alone at 75,000.[138] To better comprehend this social earthquake, Robert Kennedy met privately in New York on May 24, 1963, with a group of blacks assembled for him by novelist James Baldwin. Among those present were social psychologist Kenneth Clark, singer Harry Belafonte, actress Lena Horne, and playwright Lorraine Hansberry. Beginning with a civil rights worker saying that being in the same room with the attorney general made him feel like vomiting, the meeting degenerated into an emotional, sometimes tearful, three-hour denunciation of administration policy. Kennedy endured most of it sitting in angry silence. In despair he said afterward, "We seem to be shut out everywhere."[139]

There seemed no escape from crisis in the spring of 1963. George Wallace had won election as governor of Alabama the previous year, vowing to defend segregation by standing "in the schoolhouse door." When two black students arrived on the University of Alabama campus on June 11 with a federal court order requiring their admittance, there he stood, blocking the entrance.[140] Assistant Attorney General Nicholas Katzenbach stepped forward with a presidential proclamation commanding Wallace to desist "in unlawful obstructions."[141] The governor read a proclamation of his own and refused to move. Wallace, however, was no Ross Barnett. Having had his hour on national TV, he yielded to superior force later in the day after the president nationalized the Alabama National Guard. Kennedy had planned to address the nation that night in case of trouble at the university. Now that there was no trouble, he decided to speak anyway.

The speech Kennedy gave was the speech the civil rights movement had been awaiting for nearly three years—the most moving speech of his presidency. Ted Sorensen finished writing it only a few minutes before delivery, and Kennedy extemporized the conclusion on the air.[142]

We are confronted primarily with a moral issue. It is as old as the scriptures and is as clear as the American Constitution. . . . If an American, because his skin is dark, cannot eat lunch in a restaurant open to the public, if he cannot send his children to the best public school available, if he cannot vote for the public officials who represent him, if, in short, he cannot enjoy the full and free life which all of us want, then who among us would be content to have the color of his skin changed and stand in his place? Who among us would then be content with the counsels of patience and delay? . . .

Are we to say to the world, and much more importantly, to each other that this is a land of the free except for Negroes; that we have no second-class citizens except Negroes; that we have no class or caste system, no ghettoes, no master race except with respect to Negroes?

Kennedy informed the nation of the legislation he intended to send to Congress, called upon individuals to fight race prejudice in their homes and communities, and asked for help in making equality of opportunity a reality for Negro Americans.[143] The President, noted the *New York Times*, delivered his speech with unaccustomed "fervor."[144] Later that same night, a white sniper shot and killed Medgar Evers, leader of the Mississippi NAACP, in Jackson.[145]

On June 19, 1963, Kennedy sent Congress a civil rights bill embodying most of the movement's urgent demands. The best efforts of the Justice Department having failed to enfranchise blacks in the Deep South, Kennedy's bill further strengthened the voting rights laws. Massive resistance had practically nullified the Supreme Court's 1954 *Brown* decision; his bill empowered the attorney general to initiate school desegregation suits. Roy Wilkins and Martin Luther King were demanding termination of federal support for discriminatory state programs; Kennedy's bill granted the president discretionary authority to cut off funds. Blacks in Birmingham had marched by the thousands to petition for equal treatment in public places; the president's bill outlawed discrimination in such places of public accommodation as hotels, motels, movie theaters, sports arenas, retail stores, gas stations, restaurants, and lunch counters.[146]

But the civil rights lobby, determined to exploit this unique moment, pressed not merely for most of its objectives, but for all of them.[147] That meant a civil rights bill even more far-reaching than Kennedy's. Specifically, civil rights spokesmen demanded a ban on job discrimination, enforced by a fair employment commission; statutory authority for the attorney general to initiate suits protecting the constitutional rights of private citizens against deprivation by state and local officials; and stronger voting provisions than Kennedy was proposing.

Kennedy's bill contained less than the movement wanted because his top priority was enactment. Senate Majority Leader Mike Mansfield had told him the votes in Congress to pass any bill were not there.[148] The only way Kennedy might find them was by converting Republicans not ordinarily sympathetic to him or civil rights. Accordingly, before submitting the bill, the president draped the flag around it, consulted with Republican leaders, and urged the parties to join together, as in wartime, to deal with a national crisis. Only by fending off demands for a stronger bill could he hope to secure necessary bipartisan support.

Kennedy also tried to fend off the March on Washington, which was planned that summer by civil rights leaders as a giant demonstration in support of civil rights legislation. Kennedy warned black leaders at a meeting late in June that key congressmen might interpret the march as intimidation and turn against the bill. "Frankly," Martin Luther King replied, "I have never engaged in any direct action movement which did not seem ill-timed." Once the March became inevitable, the administration virtually took over its management to assure success.[149] Kennedy remained nervous, nevertheless. As the March approached, he privately expressed fears of violence, a small turnout, a backlash in Congress. He declined to speak to the crowd, though he did agree to meet with its leaders at the conclusion. On the day of the March, in case the worst happened, he had four thousand soldiers stationed nearby to defend the capital.[150]

The March on Washington, August 28, 1963, was the great day of the civil rights movement. Nearly 200,000 Americans, most of them black, gathered at the Lincoln Memorial in the largest assembly for redress of grievances ever seen in Washington. The good-humored crowd, dressed in their Sunday best, "had come," said the New York Times, "in the spirit of a church outing."[151] Many on the fringes could not hear entertainers Bob Dylan, Joan Baez, and Dick Gregory. And no one heard the militant speech that SNCC's John Lewis had prepared but that nervous moderates in the March persuaded him to rewrite. Concluding a slashing attack on Kennedy's bill, Lewis had intended to say, "We will march through the South, through the heart of Dixie, the way Sherman did. We shall pursue our own 'scorched earth' policy and burn Jim Crow to the ground —nonviolently. We shall fragment the South into a thousand pieces and put them back together in the image of democracy."[152]

Those who heard Martin Luther King's speech learned, if they did not already know, why this black man had become the unrivaled leader of his people. Eloquently distilling the liberal faith on which the movement had been built, King said, "When the architects of our great republic wrote the magnificent words of the Constitution and the Declaration of Independence, they were signing a promissory note to which every American was to fall heir. This note was a promise that all men, yes, black men as well as white men, would be guaranteed the inalienable rights of life, liberty, and the pursuit of happiness." King's critics in the movement might accuse him of failure as an organizer, hit-and-run tactics in the South, monopoly of civil rights funds, and willingness to compromise at critical moments. But on this occasion, as on so many others, declaiming in the cadence of the southern pulpit his dream that the sons of slaveholders and the sons of slaves might "sit down together at the table of brotherhood,"[153] he elevated the March from a mere political tactic into a spiritual event.

In September 1963 Congress began serious work on the bill that so many were so earnestly pressing upon it. Administration strategy paid off in the form of working relations with Representative William McCulloch, Republican of Ohio, the key minority member of the Judiciary Committee. McCulloch, it seemed, would support Kennedy's bill and carry enough Republicans with him to assure House passage. These calculations were nearly wrecked when Emanuel Celler, the aging chairman of the committee, yielded to pressure from civil rights lobbyists and joined with other liberals to force a bill through the civil rights subcommittee containing the full menu of militant demands.[154] McCulloch threatened to mutiny, and the committee's southern Democrats moved in for the kill.[155] The southerners decided to join with liberals in the full committee to report out the strongest possible bill and then vote with Republicans on the House floor to defeat it. The episode confirmed the belief of the Kennedys that their father's judgment on businessmen applied just as well to liberals. Said RFK, "They're sons of bitches."[156]

It took the president's personal intervention to undo the subcommittee's liberal mischief and restore the bipartisan alliance on which passage of a civil rights bill realistically depended. As a result of meetings he held with Democratic liberals and House Republican leaders, the administration's original bill was revised to contain a section outlawing discrimination in employment. Conservatively drafted, the new employment section strengthened the bill sufficiently to appease most liberals but not enough to alienate McCulloch.[157] In the meantime, McCulloch extracted a promise from the administration not to sacrifice any part of the bill to obtain passage in the Senate without his permission.[158] Rejecting the militant bill previously approved by its subcommittee, the full Judiciary Committee voted 23 to 11, on October 23, 1963, to report out the administration's amended measure.[159]

By November 1963 John Kennedy had cause to be satisfied with his recent civil rights performance. His pending bill had made him a hero to most liberals and won him respect from all but the militant fringe of the civil rights movement. His parliamentary strategy had assured early passage in the House and given him an even chance in the Senate. In addition, the white backlash was drawing less blood than he had feared. Pollster Louis Harris reported that fall that Kennedy had lost 6.5 million voters who had supported him in 1960 —4.5 million because of his civil rights stand. But he had also attracted 11 million Nixon voters, giving him a substantial lead over all his likely Republican challengers in 1964.[160] The civil rights issue might well cost Kennedy the South, and, as he learned in October on a tour of deserted Italian neighborhoods in Philadelphia, was doing him no good in white ethnic neighborhoods in the North.[161] But 63 percent of the American people backed his civil rights bill and 60 percent continued to approve his conduct of the presidency.[162] Prepared to concede nothing to the Republicans, Kennedy took his fateful trip to Texas to lay the groundwork for his forthcoming presidential campaign in that southern state.

After the president's assassination in Dallas, millions of Americans felt bereft of a truly great leader in large measure because Kennedy had cast his lot with civil rights. Comparisons with Abraham Lincoln, another president martyred before completing the work of liberation, were immediate. Especially among blacks, grief was tinged with anxiety. The first Emancipator had been succeeded by a southern president named Johnson, who shattered the dream of a racially reconstructed South. At an overflow memorial service for Kennedy in Harlem, a minister spoke the fear of his race when he said, "Let us pray that what happened 100 years ago will not repeat itself."[163]

But, as civil rights leaders who knew him understood, Lyndon Johnson would finish Kennedy's work, not destroy it. As a Texas senator, he had broken with the South in 1957 to pilot through Congress the first civil rights bill since Reconstruction. As chairman of the President's Committee on Equal Employment Opportunity, he had revealed an honest, if ineffective, commitment to a color-blind labor market. In the spring of 1963 he had counseled Kennedy against sending a civil rights bill to Congress because he expected its defeat, but in meetings of prominent citizens at the White House that summer he had been the most eloquent and emotional advocate for its passage. Indeed, he had privately urged Kennedy to tour every southern state to tell white people in person that segregation was morally wrong, utterly unjustifiable, and in violation of the tenets of Christianity.[164] A complex man notorious for ideological insincerity, Johnson's simple motive on this issue was to make the Constitution a living document in his native region.

Civil rights leaders required of Johnson only that he reaffirm Kennedy's commitment to trade away none of the civil rights bill in the Senate. Meeting with them one by one in the days following the assassination, Johnson pledged to stand by the bill as written. Indeed, he had even less freedom to compromise than Kennedy, for only by proving himself on the civil rights issue could he allay the skepticism about him so long nourished in liberal circles. Georgia's Richard B. Russell, the leader of the southern contingent in the Senate and an old friend of Johnson's, grasped this point early. There was less chance of compromise now, he said, "than there would have been had President Kennedy not met his tragic fate."[165]

The civil rights bill passed the House in February 1964 and proceeded to the Senate. Southerners promptly mounted a determined filibuster to prevent the bill from ever coming to a vote. The Senate had never before produced the two-thirds majority to vote cloture on a civil rights debate, and success was by no means assured now. If all 100 Senators were present, the bill's managers could count on only 42 Democratic votes for cloture. That meant that 25 of the 33 Senate Republicans would have to supply the winning margin. Again and again in early 1964, Johnson would ask Robert Kennedy, to whom he had delegated complete authority for managing the bill,

"Where are we going to get the votes?"[166] Only one Republican commanded enough prestige to produce the requisite number, but that man, Minority Leader Everett McKinley Dirksen, seemed something less than a champion of the rights of man.[167]

Dirksen, whom Richard Russell called "the most accomplished thespian who has ever trod" the Senate floor,[168] reveled in the spotlight now focused on him. Carefully cloaking his ultimate intentions, he had few kind words to say about the bill, especially its public-accommodations and fair-employment sections. On May 5, 1964, after months of doleful comment, Dirksen finally sat down with Robert Kennedy for the first of a series of meetings to spell out the amendments he would require as the price of his support. They turned out to be mainly technical.[169] The ritual of doubt, agonizing appraisal, and eventual conversion that Dirksen had so publicly enacted had merely been contrived to make it easier for other Republicans to join him in voting to close debate and enact the bill. Quoting a line he said was the last in Victor Hugo's diary but actually came from Hugo's *Histoire d'un crime,* the unlikely hero of this parliamentary drama declaimed, "No army can withstand the strength of an idea whose time has come."[170]

The Civil Rights Act that Johnson signed in July 1964 was the great liberal achievement of the decade, though at the time not every liberal thought so. Critics belittled the act because it did not attack de facto segregation or because it left untouched vast areas of subtle discrimination or because it was irrelevant to the scandal of black poverty. None of these were its purpose. The act's main intent, limited but indispensable, was the accomplishment of legal equality in a region where it did not exist. Because the act passed and was eventually enforced, the southern segregation system soon vanished into history. The southern black men and women who lived through this attempt to reconcile American principle and black reality knew best what it had cost and what had been gained. Hartman Turnbow, a black farmer in the Mississippi delta, was one of those who had gone to a SNCC freedom school and risked his life to register. Looking back a decade later, he rendered his judgment:

Anybody hada jus told me 'fore it happened that conditions would make this much change between the white and the black in Holmes County here where I live, why I'da just said, "You're lyin'. It won't happen." I just wouldn't have believed it. I didn't dream of it. I didn't see no way. But it got to workin' just like the citizenship class teacher told us—that if we would redish to vote and just stick with it. He says it's gon' be some difficults. He told us that when we started. We was looking for it. He said we gon' have difficults, gon' have troubles, folks gon' lose their homes, folks gon' lose their lives, peoples gon' lose all their money, and just like he said, all of that happened. He didn't miss it. He hit it ka-dap on the head, and it's workin' now. It won't never go back where it was.[171]

CHAPTER 4

Origins of the War on Poverty

P RESIDENT Kennedy began by handling social-welfare policy as he did the economy and civil rights—with caution. Most of the welfare measures he proposed in 1961 had been advanced unsuccessfully by Democrats in recent Congresses and derived ultimately from the complacent assumptions of the corporate liberalism of the 1950s. With social problems seemingly few and manageable, minor reforms would suffice to prevent discontent. In time, like other liberals, Kennedy would grasp the true dimensions of poverty in America, the linkage between joblessness and race, and the dangerous discontent festering in big-city slums. Goaded by powerful constituencies, he would become convinced near the end of his life that to defend and perfect the existing order more of the same would no longer do, that what the country needed now was a brand-new War on Poverty.

I

Meeting with Democratic leaders at his father's house in Palm Beach, December 20, 1960, the president-elect determined to give top legislative priority in the coming session to five "must" welfare bills: increased minimum wages, aid to depressed areas, housing legislation, federal assistance for public schools, and hospital insurance for the aged.[1] Soon after, he added a measure to retrain the unemployed. Some liberals, disturbed by the modest scope of the "must" list, agreed with Oscar Gass, when he wrote in *Commentary*, "How small a gap separates these critics of the Affluent Society from the most devoted spokesmen for the affluence."[2] But the best critics proved to be the conservatives. Committed in principle to free markets and local government, they endeavored to expose the flawed logic underlying Kennedy's 1961 social-welfare programs. Indeed, those programs remain interesting mainly because of the telling illustrations they provided for the conservative case against the American welfare state.

No issue better illustrated the contrasting assumptions of liberals and conservatives than Kennedy's proposal to raise the minimum wage from $1 to $1.25 over three years and extend coverage to four million new workers. Congress had passed the first minimum-wage law in 1938 at the insistence of liberals who wished to help the poor by placing a floor under the wage rate for certain classes of employees. Conservatives had argued ever since that tampering with the free market in this way actually did more harm than good. By raising wage costs in low-wage industries, they said, minimum-wage legislation induced employers to economize on labor—either by accomplishing the same amount of work with fewer employees, substituting machines for workers, or closing down.[3] The unintended consequence of the minimum wage, then, was to increase unemployment among the poor. In company with most other liberals, President Kennedy ignored the argument. "I find it difficult to know why anyone would oppose seeing somebody, by 1963, paid $1.25," he said.[4]

Passage of Kennedy's minimum-wage bill hinged on winning the support of unenthusiastic southern congressmen. This the president accomplished by trading away some of the bill's substance.[5] First, he agreed to reduce the number of newly covered workers by half a million. And when this concession proved insufficient, his lieutenants reluctantly acquiesced in an amendment proposed by Carl Vinson, a Georgia congressman deemed sufficiently influential to be worth buying off. "Let me say merely that this amendment takes out of the bill the provisions with respect to laundries," Vinson explained, as the House chuckled. "We are washing laundries clean out of the bill."[6] Removing laundry workers from the bill's protection was a heavy price for Kennedy to pay. During the 1960 campaign, he had said in Buffalo, "As long as the average wage for laundrywomen in the five largest cities of this country is 65 cents

[sic] for a 48 hour week . . . there is need for our party."[7]

When the bill passed in May 1961, liberals hailed it as a great victory for the poor and downtrodden. Almost certainly, they were wrong. Most professional economists, both liberals and conservatives, agreed that insofar as the minimum wage actually lifted the floor under the wage rate, it did, indeed, increase unemployment. This would have been its certain effect, for example, in the laundry business. Professional laundries had long been losing business to automatic home washers, self-service launderettes, and wash-and-wear garments. One consequence was that the number of laundry workers had fallen by 16 percent since 1947. Already operating on the narrowest of profit margins, laundries would have had to pass on increased wage costs to consumers in the form of higher prices. Historically, higher prices had reduced the volume of poundage. Less volume meant even fewer employees.[8] Most of the laundry workers who would lose their jobs as a result of minimum-wage coverage were unskilled workers earning money to supplement family income. Presumably they preferred to work for low wages rather than not to work at all. It may have been that the real friend of the laundry workers was not President Kennedy, who wished to include them in his bill, but Carl Vinson, who cut them out.

Though the 1961 minimum-wage law did not cover laundries, it did, for the first time, extend protection to employees of retail stores doing a substantial business in interstate commerce. Within the retail industry, variety stores in the South paid the lowest wages and therefore were most affected by the legislation—providing an ideal test case to determine the effects of minimum wages on employment. After passage of Kennedy's wage law, employment in the southern variety stores it covered declined by 20 percent. At the same time, employment in exempt variety stores increased 30 percent. Total employment in all variety stores in the region fell by 4 percent.[9] Throughout the retail industry, the effects of the 1961 law on unemployment generally conformed to conservative expectations, offering fresh evidence that the minimum wage was bad policy.

Among those economists who opposed minimum-wage laws were the liberal Keynesians on the Council of Economic Advisers. The Council muted its objections in 1961, since Kennedy had irrevocably committed himself in the campaign to an increase. But in 1965, when the issue surfaced again, the Council attacked minimum-wage laws in a series of hard-hitting memos to President Lyndon B. Johnson. The minimum wage would make it "harder for teenagers, unskilled, uneducated workers to find jobs," the Council wrote. "It would hurt many of those it was supposed to help." Labor unions, especially textile unions in the Northeast, were the real force behind the wage law, the Council explained. Their motive was not to help the poor, as the gullible supposed, but "to stop the movement of industry to the South by raising labor costs there." Why? Because unions were strong in the North, weak in the South. The Council pointed out that, by retarding the South's industrial development, a higher minimum wage would slow down the exodus of the region's rural poor into industrial jobs.[10] Johnson knew the economics and the politics of the minimum wage at least as well as the Council, but Democratic presidents need the support of big labor. With Johnson's blessing, therefore, Congress raised the minimum wage in 1966 to $1.65.[11]

The virtues of the free market were at issue again in debate over Kennedy's bill to aid depressed areas. Kennedy had become interested in this problem when, during the 1960 West Virginia primary, he toured regions devastated by a depression in coal. By all accounts he was moved by what he saw. In the fall campaign he promised to send Congress, within sixty days of his election, "a complete program to restore and revive the economy of West Virginia—to bring new industry and new jobs to your state, and all other neglected areas of our country."[12]

The president's Area Redevelopment bill, which honored this pledge, had actually been kicking around Congress in one form or another since 1956. Compassionate liberals had taken note of the many American communities that had thrived once but been victimized by capricious market forces or by depleted resources—hollows in the Appalachian coal country, New England textile towns, Alaskan villages dependent on the vanishing salmon, mined-out counties along the Great Lakes. These communities should not be left to wither, the liberals said. Too much social capital would go to waste; too many families with deep attachments to their region would be forced to endure the pain of uprooting. The answer was federal aid that would move jobs in, not people out. Kennedy's bill offered two kinds of inducement to attract private industry into depressed regions: $175 million to help needy communities improve public facilities and $200 million in cheap loans for businesses willing to locate in eligible areas. Illinois Senator Paul

Douglas, a professional economist who should have known better, predicted that the bill would provide "seed capital" to revive growth in America's neglected communities.[13]

The bill's chief opponent was Republican Senator Wallace Bennett of Utah, past president of the National Association of Manufacturers and an ideologue committed to the free market. In dynamic capitalist societies, he said, regions rose and fell all the time. If the government diverted resources to retard this inevitable process, it would impair the efficient flow of labor and capital, slowing down economic growth. Workers in depressed areas should solve their problems now as they always had before—by moving from where they were not needed to where they were. Bennett attacked the bill as much for inability to accomplish its purpose as for violation of sound principle. He cited evidence that businessmen rated many factors more important than the cost of borrowed capital in choosing a location—availability of markets, access to transportation and raw materials, the local business climate. He pointed out that, if cheap plants were enough to attract new investors, New England towns with their deserted mills would have returned to prosperity long ago. He predicted that only two types of businesses would apply for the below-the-market-interest-rate loans provided in the bill—businesses that planned to relocate in depressed areas anyway and marginal businesses that could not raise private capital and would not create many jobs.[14] Bennett's arguments notwithstanding, the president signed the bill into law in May 1961, and shortly afterward the Area Redevelopment Agency (ARA) opened for business.

Republican conservatives hounded the fledgling agency unmercifully. Keeping it under constant surveillance, they soon assembled a serviceable list of its bureaucratic blunders, such as the motel it helped finance in Detroit, where half the hotel rooms were ordinarily vacant, and the shoe factory in Indiana that refused to hire blacks, kept out unions, and added to competitive pressures in a domestic industry already near ruin.[15] When 78 of ARA's first 100 projects went to Democratic districts, Republicans rechristened it the Administration's Reelection Agency.[16] In 1963 Bennett took malicious pleasure in announcing that so far the program had produced a grand total of 350 jobs for the entire state of West Virginia.[17] That year Congress stunned the administration by refusing to replenish the Agency's nearly depleted loan fund.

By the time it closed shop in 1965, the Area Redevelopment

Agency had largely been discredited. Attempting to broaden its political support, the Agency had generously declared 1,061 counties with 37 million people eligible for aid. Spread so thin, it could neither catalyze growth nor reduce unemployment anywhere.[18] To make matters worse, it had made too many loans to marginal enterprises, especially tourist businesses that employ mostly seasonal labor.[19] Even its meager boast of having directly created 34,168 jobs did not survive a General Accounting Office investigation that sampled 80 percent of the Agency's completed projects and cut the claim by nearly half.[20] In a rare display of bureaucratic candor, the Agency's last report conceded, "results were limited."[21] Whether or not it was wise policy to discourage the mobility of labor, this program failed to do so. Nevertheless, in 1965, Congress created the Economic Development Administration to do the same job in much the same way.

The third of Kennedy's 1961 "must" measures was his Omnibus Housing Act, whose most important section authorized an additional $2 billion for urban renewal. Here again liberals attempted to improve on the results of the market forces. Though the private housing market was rapidly upgrading the nation's housing stock, millions of Americans continued to live in substandard structures. The liberal solution to slum neighborhoods was to eradicate them, which is what liberals had tried to accomplish with passage in 1949 of the urban-renewal program.[22] The result was one more example of liberal benevolence gone haywire.

Urban renewal worked this way: Local authorities condemned blighted neighborhoods, leveled them, and collected from the federal government two-thirds of the cost of acquiring the land and razing the buildings. The cleared land, often improved at public expense, was then sold to private developers for redevelopment at an average cost of 30 percent of its market value. Liberal sponsors of the program had assumed that one consequence of knocking down the housing of the poor would be to supply them with better. Developers, however, typically built middle-class housing, luxury apartments, commercial establishments, or civic monuments. For the poor they built almost nothing. From 1949 to 1961 urban renewal had demolished 148,000 buildings, causing the involuntary removal of an estimated 500,000 people, most of them poor blacks and Puerto Ricans.[23]

As critics pointed out, the irony of the carnage was that it reduced the quantity of slum housing only temporarily. Destruction of low-cost housing did not reduce the demand for it. Displaced families would continue in the low-cost housing market, putting upward pressure on slum rents and inducing landlords with properties slightly above slum level to filter them down—by subdividing into smaller apartments, for example, or cheating on maintenance. In time, the consequence of displacing poor people without either building new housing for them or increasing their income would be to convert some sound housing into slums. Urban renewal did not eliminate slums, it only relocated them.[24]

All this was reasonably well known in 1961. In that year Jane Jacobs wrote of urban renewal in her influential *The Death and Life of Great American Cities,* "At best it merely shifts slums from here to there adding its own tincture of extra hardship and disruption. At worst it destroys neighborhoods where constructive and improving communities exist."[25] That year, too, Jack Wood of the NAACP told a Senate committee, "Urban renewal has displaced many thousands of Negro families en masse. Entire Negro neighborhoods have been cleared to make way for housing restricted to white families."[26] Still, urban renewal ("Negro removal" to some) was the least controversial part of Kennedy's housing bill. Big-city Democrats were allied with mayors who favored the program; and Republicans were sympathetic to the business interest that stood to gain from it. Virtually no one in Congress spoke for the poor. Fueled by ever larger appropriations in the 1960s, the federal bulldozer savaged cities at an ever accelerating rate. By 1967 the number of demolished buildings had climbed to 400,000 and the estimated number of displaced persons exceeded 1.4 million.[27]

Kennedy's most popular welfare measure in 1961 was his Manpower Development and Training Act to retrain workers displaced by automation. Automation was a topic of widespread concern in the early 1960s. Unleashed by blind market forces, new machines seemed suddenly to be destroying jobs so fast that manual labor might one day become obsolete. Everybody knew a frightening example. Automation in Ford's Cleveland plant permitted 48 workers to make an engine block where once it had taken 400. Two men instead of 200 were assembling 1,000 radios a day in Chicago. Oil workers, clerks, engineers, and railroad employees were all threatened by newly automated processes of production.[28] "The displaced wage earner of today is in a position comparable to that of the migrant Oklahomans of the 1930's," Representative James Roosevelt told the House. "He is the victim of the industrial dust bowls created by automation and technological advances."[29]

Fortunately, the problem admitted of a solution. The same machines that displaced old skills were creating unmet demand for highly trained technical workers. Labor Secretary Arthur Goldberg noted chronic shortages of "persons engaged in transistorized circuitry, inertial guidance, ferret reconnaissance, human factors science, gyrodynamics and data telemetry."[30] To reduce unemployment, the government had only to train displaced workers for the good jobs going begging. This is what President Kennedy's manpower bill proposed to do. Visions of displaced clerks and oil workers learning in midlife to be data telemeters and human-factors scientists proved irresistible to a large bipartisan majority in Congress, which passed the measure early in 1962. Only a small band of diehard Republican conservatives dissented. "The hard, cold truth of the matter," they said, was that most displaced workers lacked the educational background for advanced technical training.[31]

Kennedy's manpower program proved to be a cure for a disease that did not exist. The French economist J. B. Say had remarked to Malthus in the 1820s, "I have always found, practically, that new machines produce more alarm than injury."[32] Nearly all contemporary economists rejected the thesis that machines were displacing workers at historically unusual rates.[33] Unemployment was high in 1961 because demand was weak. Indeed, when the economy picked up in 1963, unemployment among experienced workers would diminish rapidly and along with it fears of automation. Of course, there were other workers without jobs, workers who never had displaceable skills—the poor, the uneducated, the black. Of only peripheral interest when the manpower program began, the disadvantaged became, by default, its main clientele.[34]

The 1962 Manpower Development and Training Act became one of the most important programs of the decade. In the first six years it spent $1.5 billion to provide vocational training for one million persons, of whom 600,000 completed a course of study.[35] The Labor Department argued insistently that this investment paid off. Though unemployment among graduates was high, it was higher still among control groups. And graduates earned a better wage after training than before. The typical trainee had made modest gains, and this was enough to satisfy the program's many friends.[36]

But in 1968 doubts about the program began to surface. A Senate committee visiting a training center in Kentucky was shocked to learn that training was for "dead end jobs."[37] Meanwhile, an independent evaluation commissioned by Congress reported, "Even among the most disadvantaged trainees, there was resentment about the low level of the jobs for which training is being given."[38] "The hard, cold truth of the matter" *was* that nineteen-year-old dropouts lacked the educational background for advanced technical training. Indeed, given the existing level of pedagogical knowledge, the manpower program provided the only training it could—training for jobs mainly near the bottom of the labor barrel.[39] But no shortage of workers to fill low-skill jobs existed,[40] and employers were perfectly capable of providing on-the-job training themselves. All the manpower program accomplished, therefore, was to give its graduates an advantage over other disadvantaged workers competing for the same jobs. Just as urban renewal shifted slums from one part of a city to another, so the manpower program shifted unemployment from one group of disadvantaged workers to another. In the damning words of the program's leading authority, "There is no evidence that the unemployment rate is appreciably lower than it would have been had the program never existed."[41] Nevertheless, in 1968, when Congress extended the manpower program for three years, one senator accurately remarked, "as far as I know it is not controversial."[42]

Kennedy's most bitterly debated welfare measure in 1961 was his proposal to provide federal aid to every school district in America.[43] During the 1960 campaign Kennedy had argued the thesis that schools faced a crisis so grave that only federal dollars could rescue them. Classrooms were overcrowded, teachers were underpaid, and the Russians were outspending Americans on education as a percentage of national income. Kennedy's stand won his candidacy the endorsement of the National Education Association, main spokesman for the nation's public school teachers. But it also incurred the special wrath of conservatives, who regarded education as a responsibility of local governments and federal aid as a euphemism for federal control. In the end, however, the bill that President Kennedy sent Congress went down to defeat primarily because the bishops of the Catholic Church decided to kill it rather than accept exclusion from its benefits.

Though the religious controversy got the headlines, the liberal-conservative debate over the bill's merits was no less interesting. The main issue was whether an education crisis really existed. Arguing that it did, Health, Education and Welfare Secretary Abraham Ribicoff explained to Congress why the administration was proposing $2.3 billion over three years to help local school districts build classrooms and pay teachers' salaries. Public school districts were currently short 142,000 classrooms and employed 90,000 unqualified teachers, he said. This was bad enough, but in the decade ahead the crisis would actually worsen, as the school-age population jumped from 36 to 44 million. Having nearly exhausted their capacity to levy new taxes or issue new bonds, local districts could not, unaided, meet the crush of these additional students. Unless the federal government came to the rescue, Ribicoff suggested, the nation would break faith with its children and risk loss of world leadership.[44]

Arizona Senator Barry Goldwater, the emerging hero of the Republican right, answered Ribicoff point for point. The real education crisis had occurred in the 1950s, Goldwater explained, when the influx of war babies had swollen enrollments by 46 percent—compared to a projected increase of only 20 percent in the 1960s. Local school districts had handled their problems with such success in the last decade that the number of students per classroom had actually declined substantially and so had the number of pupils per teacher. Looking ahead, Goldwater saw no grounds for concern. So many college students were enrolling in education courses that qualified teachers would become a glut on the market. Voters were approving new school bonds at record rates. No school board in the United States had asked Congress for federal aid, and the National School Board Association was on record against it. The real reason liberals were trumpeting an education crisis that no longer existed, Goldwater said, was to scratch their itch for federal control of local schools—the best reason of all to defeat Kennedy's aid bill.[45]

Whether Ribicoff was right in predicting a crisis or Goldwater in denying one was an empirical matter that awaited only the passage of time to determine. As it turned out, Goldwater proved incomparably the better prophet. Without federal aid, Ribicoff had said, local districts could not build the 60,000 classrooms annually that would be needed in the 1960s; unaided, the districts actually built an average of 69,000 classrooms a year.[46] Without aid, school districts could not hire the necessary 437,000 additional teachers, Ribicoff had claimed. They hired 600,000[47] and raised their salaries faster than average compensation in the economy as a whole.[48] Local districts had exhausted their financial resources and could not meet the coming financial challenge alone, Ribicoff had predicted. In fact, public school expenditures were a remarkable 2½ times greater at the end of the decade than at the beginning.[49] Scattered districts, as always, needed help. But it hardly made sense to bestow aid on all districts to reach those few in true distress. Despite liberal hand-wringing, Kennedy's proposal deserved the oblivion to which Congress had consigned it.

Kennedy's 1961 "must" measures illustrated the flaws that conservatives had long argued inhered in liberal programs—violation of market logic, covert service to special interests, and perversion by bureaucrats. No less vindicated were those leftist critics who dismissed liberals as pseudo-reformers unwilling to address the only real issue—the maldistribution of wealth and power in America. But there was one administration measure in 1961, absent from the "must" list, which did not fit the critique by either the right or the left. It was the Juvenile Delinquency and Youth Offenses Control Act. This measure funded an obscure program that was irrelevant to markets and bent on reforming powerful institutions. Indeed, though no one knew it, Kennedy's juvenile-delinquency program foreshadowed—indeed, inspired—the radical aspects of the later War on Poverty.

II

When Robert F. Kennedy became attorney general–designate in November 1960, he decided that he should do something about juvenile delinquency, one of the few social problems of widespread concern in the 1950s. Kennedy had little knowledge of the problem, and so he delegated it to his friend and campaign aide David Hackett. Hackett's charge, in effect, was to do whatever he wanted. The result was a social experiment that ultimately attempted nothing less than the reorientation of liberalism in the direction of real reform.

Hackett and Kennedy had been close since their adolescent years together at patrician Milton Academy, where Bobby had been an Irish intruder and Hackett a legendary athlete. Hackett had gone on to McGill University in Canada, twice to the U.S. Olympic hockey team, and to a publishing career in Montreal. A year before the 1960 Los Angeles convention, Hackett, then thirty-four, answered Bobby's call to join the biggest game of all. Before the convention Hackett kept tabs on delegates and afterward ran the campaign's "boiler room" or correspondence-information section.[50] As befitted the man on whom John Knowles modeled the hero of his novel *A Separate Peace,* Hackett had no qualms in accepting appointment as a special assistant to the attorney general with responsibility for juvenile delinquency. Knowles's novel begins with Phineas, the matchless athlete of Devon Academy, confronting a tree that no one in his class had climbed before. "Naturally Finny was going to be the first to try," the narrator says, "and just as naturally he was going to inveigle others, us, into trying it with him."[51]

A can-do man in the Kennedy mold, Hackett decided early to find the best ideas about juvenile delinquency and translate them into national policy. Hackett spent months just talking to people— professors, police officials, bureaucrats, and Ford Foundation executives dabbling in urban reform. Finally, in May 1961, he took three important steps to create a program of his own. First, at Hackett's instigation, President Kennedy issued an executive order creating the President's Committee on Juvenile Delinquency, whose members were the attorney general, the secretary of HEW, and the secretary of Labor.[52] Robert Kennedy was chairman; Hackett, executive director. Charged, among other things, with coordinating the youth programs of the various federal agencies, the committee proved a fiction, its members never coordinating anything—indeed, never even meeting. But the president's committee did provide Hackett with an indispensable base from which to operate in the government. Second, on the same day he created the president's committee, John Kennedy sent Congress the Juvenile Delinquency and Youth Offenses Control Act. When signed in September, this act authorized $30 million over three years for grants to finance local delinquency projects. HEW was formally charged with administering the money, but everybody knew it belonged to Hackett.[53] Third, that May, Hackett recruited the professor who practically everyone told him was the best in the field. He was Lloyd Ohlin, research director of the Columbia School of Social Work.[54]

A modest but persuasive academic in his mid-forties, Ohlin was the bearer of a brilliant tradition in criminal sociology which had been flourishing at the University of Chicago since the 1920s. The Chicago school dissented from the prevailing view of the juvenile delinquent as a psychiatric case in need of individual treatment. Delinquents were normal boys seeking viable roles in a slum context, the Chicago school said. Prevention and cure lay not in more or better case work but in restoring to slum dwellers a sense of social competence so that they could control their own young. In the 1930s sociologists from the University helped found the Chicago Area Project, which hired community organizers to locate the natural leaders of the poor and help them mount their own youth programs.[55]

In 1960 Ohlin and his collaborator Richard Cloward updated the Chicago view in their book *Delinquency and Opportunity: A Theory of Delinquent Gangs.* Society encouraged slum kids to have high aspirations but provided few legitimate opportunities to satisfy them, Ohlin and Cloward contended. Temptation was great, therefore, to exploit "illegitimate opportunities"—i.e., crime—to achieve material and status ambitions. Where slum neighborhoods were stable, profitable opportunities in crime abounded. But in the disintegrating slums of contemporary big cities even illegitimate opportunities were few. There, teenagers tended to band together in gangs, seeking status by violent display of "heart" or "guts." Ohlin and Cloward's so-called opportunity theory had decidedly reformist implications. Delinquency, they said, was a property of social systems. "It is our view, in other words, that the major effort of those who wish to eliminate delinquency should be directed to the reorganization of slum communities."[56] By slum communities, Ohlin and Cloward meant black ghettos. To eliminate delinquency, they advocated opening up new opportunities for the children of the poor.

Ohlin brought Hackett not only a theory but the outlines of a program. Since 1959 he and Cloward had been engaged in a complex social experiment to test the opportunity theory on New York's Lower East Side, a predominantly black and Puerto Rican slum. The experiment, called Mobilization for Youth, was currently in the planning stage. Columbia professors, social workers, and representatives of institutions affecting the lives of the East Side poor were fashioning a comprehensive design to expand opportunity. When operational, the plan would test the theory that more opportunity meant less delinquency.[57] The plan had yet to be completed —or his theory validated—when Ohlin departed for Washington in

May 1961. Nevertheless, Hackett arranged for Ohlin's appointment as director of the Office of Juvenile Delinquency, the agency in HEW that would dispense grants under the administration's juvenile delinquency act. Whatever Bobby wanted was fine with HEW secretary Abraham Ribicoff. Ohlin stayed one year, long enough to set Hackett's course. "Ohlin was the leader," said Hackett. "He developed our program."[58]

But, of course, the indispensable man was really Robert Kennedy. In 1961 Hackett took Kennedy on trips to Harlem, arranged meetings with angry gang members, and exposed his chief to a slice of American life of which he had hitherto been innocent. Kennedy came away profoundly disturbed and totally committed to Hackett's work. Later that year, when Hackett's delinquency bill got stuck in the creaky machinery of the House, it was Robert Kennedy who eased it through to final passage. The attorney general became so involved with the local delinquency program in Washington, D.C., that no detail was too small to escape his notice. Once he visited a ghetto school to inspect a swimming pool repaired with $30,000 he himself had raised. After rebuking an official because the shallow end was too deep, he moved slowly among hundreds of black children—an aide recalled—"smiling, rubbing their heads, squeezing their hands, reaching out to the smaller ones who could not get near him. This was not done for show—there were no reporters or photographers along—but because he loved those slum children, loved them as much as he disdained the fool of a bureaucrat who could not give him the answers he wanted."[59] Said Hackett, "RFK would go anywhere. Do anything we wanted."[60]

In October 1961, as Hackett and Ohlin were gearing up in Washington, Mobilization for Youth completed its long-awaited planning document for the East Side. Hackett sent Kennedy a summary of Mobilization's plan along with a note saying, "I think if you read this, it would be the best way to bring you up to date on the current thinking and type of program we are envisioning."[61] Similarities between Mobilization for Youth and later nationwide antipoverty programs were not coincidental. A comprehensive attempt to prevent delinquency by unlocking opportunity, the plan included, among other things, public service jobs for teenagers, neighborhood service centers offering a variety of welfare services in one convenient place, employment of neighborhood people as subprofessionals in service institutions, and organizing residents into groups to solve their own problems. In May 1962, at a ceremony in the White House Rose Garden, President Kennedy presented Mobilization for Youth with a $2.1 million delinquency grant to help pay for its programs.[62] Hackett and Ohlin, meanwhile, had already begun promoting the opportunity theory and the Mobilization model in cities across America.

But how could they accomplish their purpose, given the delinquency program's paltry appropriation and the almost total ignorance of the Mobilization experience outside New York? Ohlin and Hackett hit on the expedient of planning grants to solve their problem. By parceling out money in relatively small sums to finance a year or two of planning, the president's committee could gain access to a large number of cities and provide them time to absorb both the opportunity theory and the Mobilization model.[63] When local plans were eventually complete, the five or six best would be selected for funding in the action stage. During the spring of 1962 Ohlin and Hackett toured American cities looking for sympathetic mayors and power elites prepared to sponsor social change. Of the sixty-five communities applying for planning grants, sixteen met the criteria and got the funds.[64]

Pity the poor cities that had really only wanted to get their hands on a few federal dollars and now had to fathom the esoteric intent of Lloyd Ohlin! They grappled with the program's abstract vocabulary, carefully scrutinized the Mobilization planning document, and sought hidden meanings in the sometimes contradictory directives emanating from Washington. Eventually, they got the message. Most cities created nonprofit private corporations, bringing together professors, social workers, and powerholders. Planners were expected to design scientific experiments to test either the opportunity or some other delinquency theory. Plans, when operational, must not fritter away scarce resources on unconnected programs but mount a comprehensive, coordinated attack on all the causes of delinquency simultaneously. And participating institutions must be willing to reorient their services to the real needs of the poor.

Of all its goals, the president's committee came most to cherish institutional reform. "Be not unaware of the implications of this—," one of them wrote, "*a major function of planning* becomes one of inducing change and adaptation in prevailing social services, and educational institutions, employment services, even political structures."[65] According to the reformers, the prime cause of slum delinquency was blocked opportunity, and those doing much of the blocking were the very institutions supposedly serving the poor and their children. The schools, permeated by middle-class values, shaped curricula irrelevant to slum students and expected them to fail. Private welfare agencies had gradually disengaged from the poor to serve prestigious middle-class clients. Public welfare departments robbed poor families of dignity and often undermined family stability. Vocational educators provided job training for jobs that did not exist. City halls contributed to the deterioration of poor neighborhoods by providing inferior services. Police departments patrolled ghetto neighborhoods like armies of occupation in a hostile foreign country. The driving purpose of the president's committee was to change these institutions. Bring them together to plan for poor youths, the reformers reasoned, and they would at last see their complicity in the plight of poor families. "We thought that once the authorities were shown the needs, they would be reasonable men. Or, if they were tough, we thought we could buy them off," said one program official.[66] Here at last, in the guise of fighting delinquency, was a Kennedy program with reformist, even radical implications.

As local planning bodies got down to work, a sense of high excitement gripped program personnel in Washington. Morale was high, the hours long, the dedication total. One reason for the group élan was David Hackett—an easy man to underrate. Not notably articulate, certainly no deep thinker, a person of eminence only by the accident of friendship, he nonetheless possessed tenacity of purpose and the ability to attract and lead capable men. He conceived his job as political—to push his program at all levels of government and to get things done. Working out of the attorney general's office, he recruited a staff of twelve young men, most of whom knew little about delinquency but had some connection with Kennedy's 1960 campaign.[67] In part because Hackett kept them in a state of high tension, they took the bare bones of Ohlin's program and gave it life.

One other leader who imparted his spirit to the program was Leonard Cottrell. Cottrell, executive director of the Russell Sage Foundation, was a surviving pioneer of the Chicago school of sociology and sometime mentor to Lloyd Ohlin. As chairman of the delinquency program's Demonstration Review Panel, Cottrell headed a group of distinguished social-work professionals who advised Hackett's staff on awarding grants. In time, he became the program's intellectual anchor and a vital source of its reform impulse. "Cottrell loved being part of the New Frontier," a staff member said. ". . . All the staff adored him. He played the role of papa."[68] Because of who he was and all that he had done, Cottrell lent the program credibility, not least in the eyes of the staff itself.

But the alliance of Cottrell and Hackett—of knowledge and power—had serious deficiencies. Hackett, who had access to power, knew little of social science and uncritically deferred to its practitioners. "Dave had an awe of a Ph.D.," said a staff member who had one.[69] Whatever Ohlin and Cottrell wanted to do, Hackett was willing to try. On the other hand, Ohlin and Cottrell, though not without experience in the corridors of power, became intoxicated by their proximity to the Kennedys, who they seemed to believe could accomplish anything, even the realization of their complex plans to reform America. In short, Hackett had an unreasonable faith in sociology, Ohlin and Cottrell in politicians. The result was that both sides of the alliance—Hackett and Cottrell, staff and panel —entertained a fanciful conception of the possible. They were revolutionaries, they imagined, on a mission to root out the causes of delinquency and reshape complex institutions according to the specifications of science. What's more, they believed, they were fated to succeed. It seemed never to have occurred either to Hackett or to Cottrell that they might not overcome the resistance which their labors were bound to encounter.

Resistance quickly developed in Congress, where Representative Edith Green, Democrat of Oregon, conceived a deep dislike for both Hackett and his program. Mrs. Green had been one of the sponsors of the 1961 delinquency bill. But, once she grasped how Hackett intended to spend the people's money, she was appalled. "What I had in mind, and what I believe is in the record," she said later, "is a number of experimental projects, such as . . . the early identification of potential delinquents, the increased study of biochemical factors that may influence behavior in the adolescent stage, the anchoring of a ship near slum areas for recreation purposes, and so forth. I surely wasn't thinking of what they refer to in the profession today as the 'thirty million dollar test of Ohlin's opportunity theory'." Like most members of Congress, Mrs. Green distrusted social scientists, disliked planning, and wanted quick and tangible results from social programs. Her hostility forced Hackett to cancel tentative plans for expanding the number of planning grants from sixteen to twenty-three. Though Congress would extend the juvenile delinquency act in 1963 for two more years, it soon became clear that Hackett would have to look elsewhere to fund his projects in the expensive action stage.[70]

The only other place where Hackett might find big money was in the budgets of the regular departments. But they proved no more sympathetic than Congress. The problem of bureaucracy fascinated and frustrated Hackett, who considered the determination of jealous federal agencies to guard their own turf as a principal cause of ineffective government. That was why he had conceived the president's committee in the first place. If three key Cabinet officers worked together on youth problems, would not interagency coordination follow? Hackett soon learned that Cabinet officers, being politicians on limited tenure, were no match for entrenched bureaucrats. So he experimented with other schemes to subvert the defenses of the regular departments and get his hands on their money. He placed members of his staff in other agencies, cultivated influential civil servants, located sympathetic mavericks. Those drawn into his orbit became known as "Hackett's guerrillas"—conspirators within the government committed to changing ossified bureaucracies and finding funds for Hackett's projects.[71]

But despite their considerable esprit, the guerrillas could not deliver the goods. One staff member said, "In retrospect they were not very key people. We probably ended up with the Kennedy guys in agencies."[72] Daniel P. Moynihan, then executive assistant to the secretary of Labor and himself on the fringe of Hackett's circle, thought Hackett's experiment in "anti-bureaucracy" failed for deeper reasons. "The concept of the 'guerrillas'—living off the administrative countryside, invisible to the bureaucratic enemy but known to one another, hitting and running and making off with the riches of the established departments—was attractive, but also romantic," Moynihan wrote. "Simply as a matter of fire power, God was on the side of the big battalions."[73] The guerrillas did, however, receive a valuable education in the ways of bureaucracy, which would well serve many of them later, when they resurfaced to play a major role in the War on Poverty.

The most disheartening resistance of all came from the local projects. Circumstances varied widely, but in one major respect the projects all yielded a common result. Planning proved to be a political, not a scientific process. Without money to buy change or a constituency to force change, the reformers lacked sufficient leverage to induce reform in local institutions. The president's committee confronted hard reality in December 1962, when Cleveland became the first of Hackett's cities to complete a draft of a delinquency plan. David Austin, the director of the Cleveland project and a social planner with a national reputation, came to Washington to present his plan to Cottrell's Demonstration Review Panel.

As the Review Panel saw it, the elaborate design of the president's committee had become garbled in the Cleveland translation. Research was shoddy, the opportunity theory insufficiently appreciated, and provisions for scientific evaluation of programs sadly inadequate. Worse, local institutions had participated in the planning process mainly to protect themselves from harebrained reform schemes. Even by Cleveland's primitive standards there was nothing innovative about nursery classes for preschool children, special classes for potential delinquents, and smaller caseloads for parole officers. Measured by the standards of institutional reform, the plan was a failure. Nevertheless, after Austin made a few cosmetic changes, the president's committee awarded Cleveland a $1 million action grant in March 1963. It had little choice. Mrs. Green was clamoring for action, and the program had to use up its unexpended funds by the end of the fiscal year on June 30. Besides, Cottrell mused, maybe the process of change had to begin imperceptibly in Cleveland to begin at all.[74]

The arrival of federal money in the spring of 1963 plunged the Cleveland delinquency project (Cleveland Action for Youth) into crisis. The sponsoring agencies had paid little attention to the project when it seemed the plaything of social workers. Suddenly it commanded the means to advance or threaten vital institutional interests. Cleveland was a nervous city anyway in 1963. Black militancy in Hough, the delinquency project's target neighborhood, was rapidly rising, causing anger among whites and fear among dominant institutions, especially the school system. David Austin won the confidence of Hough, but he had failed to cultivate Cleveland's politicians and public institutions. The school superintendent executed a coup against Austin in June, replacing him with a reliable school administrator. By fall Hough had turned against Cleveland Action for Youth, and the project's staff pined for Austin.[75] Local agencies had failed to contribute promised funds, and whole sections of the Cleveland plan lay unimplemented. Mel Moguloff of the federal staff wrote, "Does anybody feel loyalty to the project as an entity apart from its instrumental use in funding or personal ambitions?"[76] Viewed from Washington late in 1963, the Cleveland project was a shambles.

Details varied from city to city but basically the Cleveland pattern held. In Philadelphia the delinquency project occasioned a tug of war between reform-minded social scientists at Temple University and hack politicians in the administration of Mayor James Tate, finally succumbing to attack from the local NAACP for ignoring the target neighborhood.[77] In Minneapolis the project staff simply asked the service agencies to write their own programs and then devised a theory to rationalize them.[78] In New Haven the project functioned practically as a satellite of the mayor's office, where the goals of the president's committee were treated with a casualness bordering on contempt.[79] In Boston the project's staff was devoted to the goals of research, science, and institutional reform but ultimately submitted a plan shaped by the conservatism of the city's service institutions.[80] In every city the planning project either accepted the cooperation of participating institutions on their own terms or risked extermination. None of the plans emerging from the projects late in 1963 was, by federal standards, comprehensive, scientific, or rich with the promise of new opportunities for poor youth.

By 1963 the federal staff was reassessing its original model. That model had been elitist, envisioning an alliance of professors and power holders, planning *for* the poor, not *with* them. Power holders were expected to emerge from the planning period eager to reorient their services for the poor. Those expectations having failed, it dawned on Hackett's guerrillas that they needed a new lever to move institutions in the direction of reform, a new constituency to compel change where persuasion had failed. That lever, that constituency, could only be the poor themselves. No consensus emerged within the president's committee in 1963 on the precise role that the poor might play in the committee's scheme of things. But influential voices within the delinquency program had begun to articulate the possibilities.

Leonard Cottrell, a founder of the Chicago school, located the root cause of delinquency in the disorganization of slum communities. When blacks, for example, migrated to northern cities, their old culture disintegrated, social controls broke down, and apathy became a characteristic refuge. Amid such conditions, community resistance to delinquency was bound to be low. Preventing delinquency, then, became a matter of restoring competence to slum communities, of empowering the poor to take over their own neighborhoods, of enabling adults to reimpose authority over the young.[81] Poor people had to learn "how to speak, how to use the law, how to approach city hall," Cottrell said.[82] Hackett's projects could only succeed, therefore, if they developed "community competence." This they could do by putting residents on advisory boards, using them to carry out programs, teaching them their legal rights, and organizing them for political action. Cottrell did not believe that delinquency projects should foster conflict between the poor and power holders, but if the poor chose conflict, so be it. (Once we uncorked the bottle, Cottrell said later, there was "so much pent up deprivation that the thing just blew.")[83] Cottrell's concept of the competent community seeped into the collective consciousness of the president's committee and undermined its elite model. Indeed, there was a latent anti-professionalism in Cottrell's ideas. When communities gained competence, he said, social workers should go home.[84]

Richard Boone was also a persuasive voice urging participation of the poor. Another product of the Chicago school of sociology, he had worked on prison research in the 1950s with Lloyd Ohlin and served as a police captain in Cook County. Boone was a heretic in his own profession. When he needed to hire gang workers, he looked for ex–gang leaders to do the job. Psychiatric social work, he said, was "a big fraud."[85] In 1962 Hackett brought Boone to Washington and put him in charge of a Cabinet-level committee to plan a National Service Corps. This was a pet project of Robert Kennedy, who envisioned it as the domestic equivalent of the highly successful Peace Corps. Idealistic Americans would receive a brief period of training and then work for a year in areas where human services were in critically short supply.[86] Boone's committee set up task forces to study not only the urban poor but also the rural poor, migrant workers, Indians, and the institutionalized. The task forces did more than read books. They made direct contact with the poor, flew their leaders to Washington, even arranged three Cabinet meetings where the poor could speak their minds. From the start, Boone recalled, "They began to hit us, saying, 'For God's sake, quit planning for us. If you really want us involved, then don't play games with us.' "[87] In Boone's conception of the Service Corps, volunteers would work on projects conceived by local people and leave behind men and women capable of carrying on by themselves. In 1963 President Kennedy's bill to create a National Service Corps died in the House. But in the meantime, Boone became a radicalizing influence on the president's delinquency committee—"a Mau Mau,"[88] as he said, on the issue of involving poor people.

In 1963 Mobilization for Youth was evolving uses for the poor rather different from Cottrell's or Boone's. As usual, its activities on the East Side commanded avid attention in Washington. The elite model had originated in Mobilization. Participating institutions were supposed to emerge from the planning process committed to self-reform. But in its action phase the project also hired community workers to organize the poor for political action—that is, to apply pressure on those with power. Therein lay a potential dilemma. What if residents whom Mobilization organized attacked the very institutions with which Mobilization was cooperating? This happened in 1963. Groups organized by Mobilization employees protested against the schools, the welfare department, the police. Led by irate politicians, the city's institutions counterattacked, embroiling Mobilization in bitter controversy.[89] The social-work intellectuals who ran Mobilization supported their community organizers, and the president's committee supported Mobilization. The elite model having failed to achieve institutional reform, Hackett and company were willing to countenance political action by the poor as one possible way to get it. And, if confrontations between power and the poor resulted, the president's committee was prepared not to flinch. Defending Mobilization's organizing tactics to an assistant secretary of HEW, one delinquency-program official said, "Nothing could be more truly democratic than what is happening now."[90]

It was all very exciting, no doubt, but to what purpose? The president's committee operated as a virtual conspiracy within the nether regions of the Kennedy administration. It functioned without a mandate from the people, the approval of Congress, or the knowledge of most of its co-workers in the executive branch. Those federal agencies that could not ignore the committee refused it resources and quarantined its influence. The cities it had stirred up had no special interest in juvenile delinquency or institutional reform, only in gaining access to the committee's appropriation. Most of these cities were putting the finishing touches on their planning documents by the fall of 1963 and would soon be in Washington seeking their reward. But the coffers were nearly bare, and most would have to return home empty-handed, no doubt embittered by the waste of their efforts. The attorney general might remind Mrs. Green, Hackett wrote Kennedy in August 1963, that "abandonment of programs with staunch community support in major cities in July 1964, will have adverse effect in the 1964 elections."[91]

Yet Hackett was not so far from the mainstream as it appeared. Administration officials closer to the White House even than he had also begun, in 1963, to focus on the poverty problem. Eventually these officials would stumble across Hackett and the President's Committee on Juvenile Delinquency. When they did, Hackett would bid to make his delinquency projects the basis of a War on Poverty.

III

President Kennedy had grown dissatisfied with his domestic program by the end of 1962. "I want to go beyond the things that have already been accomplished," he told Walter Heller. "Give me facts and figures on the things we still have to do. For example, what about the poverty problem in the United States?"[92] Kennedy did not pluck the subject of poverty out of thin air. With social criticism returning to fashion, a spate of books appeared that year announcing that one-fifth of the nation was still ill-housed, ill-clad, ill-nourished. The best of these, Michael Harrington's *The Other America*, painted a stark portrait of America's disinherited and summoned government to solve the problem. Revelations that poverty remained a mass affliction in the United States shocked liberals, most of whom only recently had thought that, since they could not see it, poverty did not exist. One liberal who read Harrington was John F. Kennedy.

But the government did not undertake a War on Poverty because Michael Harrington wrote a book. A constituency both aggrieved and vocal had first to demand it. In the spring of 1963 the civil rights movement took on mass dimensions, creating that constituency overnight. Migrating rapidly northward, the movement provided ghetto blacks with a vehicle for protesting not only discrimination but unemployment and low wages. That spring, black demonstrations took on ominous, even violent overtones in Philadelphia, St.

Louis, Chicago, and other big cities. That summer, national attention focused on the March on Washington, which turned out nearly 250,000 Americans, most of them black, to demand jobs as well as freedom. The war on poverty began, in short, because the civil rights movement was educating whites to the realities of black deprivation and because deprived blacks were mute no longer. Indeed, few Americans knew that three of every four poor people were white.

It was not till June 1963, while the civil rights bill was being drafted, that Walter Heller accepted Kennedy's challenge to take a serious look at poverty. Heller began by delegating the problem to two staff members of the Council of Economic Advisers—William Capron of Stanford and Ralph Lampman of the University of Wisconsin. Conducting an interagency seminar or "Saturday morning club," these economists quickly encountered three obstacles that would vex planners until the end: knowledge, bureaucracy, and money. So little was known about poverty that the experts could neither define it nor propose a cure. Federal bureaucrats were barren of ideas unrelated to their own aggrandizement. And no money to fight poverty was available, since President Kennedy had put a lid on domestic spending for the next fiscal year. By summer's end poverty planning had gone nowhere.[93]

Unaware of these frustrations, the White House was rapidly concluding that it wanted a poverty bill in its 1964 legislative package. Indeed, in September, Theodore Sorensen commissioned the Council of Economic Advisers and the Budget Bureau to form a special poverty task force and draw up a program. Running day-to-day operations were economist Capron of the Council and the Budget Bureau's William Cannon, a political scientist who had once worked on ghetto relations as assistant vice president of the University of Chicago. October was spent sorting out ideas from the departments. "They were awful," Cannon recalled.[94] Not knowing what else to do, Heller sent the departments a memo on November 5, asking for final suggestions. He got back "garbage," Capron remembered.[95] On November 19, 1963, Heller reported on the state of poverty planning to President Kennedy, who was not pleased but who was by now determined to unveil a poverty bill in January. That left Heller only six weeks to come up with a program. Less time than that, it turned out, remained to Kennedy. On November 23, 1963, Heller sought guidance from President Lyndon

B. Johnson, who told him that, so far as poverty was concerned, "push ahead full tilt."[96] Like Kennedy, Johnson wanted a program by January.

During the frantic autumn of 1963, the poverty task force had encountered only two men in the government who had anything useful to say. One was David Hackett, and the other was Richard Boone. "I was . . . sort of swept off my feet," Capron recalled, "because these guys were really way ahead of and had tremendous impact on the thinking of the Council."[97] Cannon and Capron treated Hackett and Boone as raw recruits treat battle-hardened veterans, listening in fascination to their stories of the wars. Hackett, for his part, put his staff to work full-time on poverty. In response to Heller's November 5 memo, Hackett submitted a preliminary program outline and on December 1 followed it up with a thirty-nine-page memo, fleshing out his ideas.[98] This memo was Hackett's bid for control of the emerging War on Poverty—a phrase, incidentally, he detested.

The great virtue of Hackett's proposal was that it confronted head-on the problems of knowledge, bureaucracy, and money that had dogged planners for months. "I would never recommend to Robert Kennedy or the president of the United States that you get up and announce to anybody that we're going to solve poverty," Hackett recalled. "The number of people who really had any real knowledge of it, you could put in this room."[99] The first job, therefore, was to deepen knowledge. Poverty having many faces, Hackett proposed a series of task forces to study the problem in urban areas, in rural areas, and among Indians, Alaskans, Mexican Americans, and "others." Each task force would go into the field and look at the world from the perspective of poor people themselves. Their work completed, task forces would then choose communities suitable for mounting "federally-supported comprehensive demonstration projects"—each to apply local solutions to local poverty problems. Years from now, after these experiments yielded usable knowledge, an all-out attack on poverty might perhaps be declared. Hackett warned, however, that even a modest demonstration program would fail unless the problem of the federal bureaucracy was solved first. His remedy was a Cabinet Committee on Poverty, closely resembling the President's Committee on Juvenile Delinquency, except that this one would command the active interest of the president himself. Money would then cease to be a problem. Demonstration projects were relatively cheap, and if the president compelled coordination, sufficient funds would be forthcoming from regular departmental budgets to pay the whole bill. Like the cavalry in a grade-B Western, Hackett was riding to the rescue of the poverty task force just as all hope appeared lost.

In advancing his proposals, Hackett had purposes of his own to serve. Conveniently, he said, experimental comprehensive demonstrations appropriate for fighting poverty already existed. These were Hackett's delinquency projects, the best half-dozen of which he proposed to refurbish for poverty duty. In other words, Hackett's demonstrations would save the planners from coming up blank, and the planners, in turn, would save his delinquency projects from fiscal starvation. It was a bargain neither side could resist.[100]

Within a day of receiving Hackett's long memo, Cannon and Capron embraced it as their own. Unfortunately, things were moving so fast that neither man had time to acquaint himself with the complex history of the delinquency program and so did not entirely grasp all that Hackett intended. "We were going on faith," Capron admitted.[101] We seized on an idea "without really knowing what it would mean when it got translated."[102] Cannon and Capron were drawn to Hackett primarily because they shared his obsession with coordinating federal programs, especially in local communities. More and more federal money was flowing into local communities, Capron believed, but "nothing much seemed to be happening." Hackett's comprehensive projects seemed to offer a "handle that would help to shake up the bureaucracies, pull things together so that you got coherent programs at the delivery level, where . . . we were getting nonsense."[103] It dawned on neither Capron nor Cannon that beyond improved governmental efficiency, Hackett was aiming to reform local institutions in part by involving the poor. It was not that Hackett intentionally hid anything. It was just that institutional reform seemed to him so obvious an objective that its articulation was not necessary. Thus Capron and Cannon were playing with political dynamite and did not even know it. Neither did Walter Heller, who on December 20, 1963, formally submitted to Sorensen a poverty program framed by the task force in just three weeks. It called for five urban and five rural local demonstration projects to test a comprehensive anti-poverty strategy, and it endorsed a Cabinet-level committee to coordinate the federal effort. Heller called his proposal "the Community Action Program."[104]

During Christmas week 1963, Heller and Budget Director Kermit Gordon flew to the LBJ ranch to sell community action to President Johnson. His first impulse was to scrap it forthwith. No man to be satisfied with a modest admission of ignorance or a few demonstration projects, he wanted something, he said, that would "be big and bold and hit the whole nation with real impact."[105] In the end Johnson would accept the program only if it was drastically amended. Any locality that wanted one could have its own community action program, could have it now, and could use it to mount instant programs—with the federal government picking up most of the bill. In one stroke Johnson escalated community action from an experimental program to precede the War on Poverty into the very war itself. No one at the Texas White House told the president that Hackett's delinquency projects—community action's model—had so far yielded no promising results, that a major purpose of the projects was institutional reform, and that at least one project was dreaming up ways to enlist the poor in a struggle against entrenched local power. No one told Johnson because no one who knew was there.

By January 1964 Hackett had been shunted to the sidelines, where he watched in dismay as philistines mutilated his cautious design. Even his cherished Cabinet Committee on Poverty had by then got lost in the bureaucratic shuffle, foreclosing any chance of real federal coordination. If John Kennedy had lived, Robert Kennedy could have rescued Hackett's scheme and based the poverty program upon it. But Johnson was president now, and Robert Kennedy's power was gone. Even so, in January, Kennedy roused himself from his grief long enough to send Johnson a warning. "In my opinion," the attorney general wrote the president, "the anti-poverty program could actually retard the solution of these problems," unless Hackett's basic approach was used.[106] Though their entreaties went unheeded, Hackett and Kennedy continued to regard community action as their offspring, even if illegitimate, and worked for its eventual enactment.

January was a chaotic month for the planners. Once the regular departments got wind of the poverty program being cooked up in the White House, they counterattacked. The Labor Department wanted to fight poverty with jobs, HEW wanted to do it with education,[107] and a variety of conflicting views on who should administer community action surfaced. In his State of the Union address, January 8, 1964, Johnson announced, "This administration today, here and now, declares unconditional war on poverty in America."[108] But, given the bickering within his own house, the president had to defer the details. Two weeks later, in his budget message, he finally unveiled the community action concept, describing it rather fully and proposing to spend $500 million the first year for its implementation.[109] By the end of the month the poverty task force was finishing work on a poverty bill which had community action as its centerpiece. Then on February 1, 1964, Johnson sprang one of his little surprises. Annoyed by interagency disharmony over the poverty program, he removed responsibility from the Cannon-Capron task force and gave it to R. Sargent Shriver, the Kennedy brother-in-law who had made such a success of the Peace Corps. Johnson charged Shriver, in effect, to start from scratch.[110] Everyone understood that the program Shriver finally composed would be his to administer.

One night after his dramatic appointment as "poverty czar," Shriver received a briefing on community action. "It'll never fly," he said.[111] Shriver wanted a program he could sell—something simple, clean, capable of producing fast results. Moreover, having once headed the Chicago Board of Education, he knew only too well how hard it was to coordinate local institutions.[112] Community action had acquired too much momentum simply to be discarded; so Shriver demoted the program to just one among many, fastening on the Job Corps as the approach most likely to cover him with quick glory. Community action was relegated to secondary status, and its development turned over to a group dominated by Hackett's guerrillas. Hackett himself was given no responsibility, since he and Shriver did not get along. But Richard Boone was there to advance their common interests. At a large brainstorming meeting called by Shriver on February 4, Boone spoke of "maximum feasible participation" of poor people so often that Shriver's deputy, Adam Yarmolinsky, said to him, "You have used that phrase four or five times now." "Yes, I know," Boone replied. "How many more times do I have to use it before it becomes part of the program?"[113] It was Hackett's guerrillas who wrote the community action title of Shriver's bill, and it was they who made sure it contained its one immortal line. A community action program, the bill said, is one "developed, conducted, and administered with maximum feasible participation of residents. . . ."[114] In other words, poor people themselves.

To anyone familiar with the history of Hackett's delinquency program, the reform implications of this language were clear. Participation by the poor meant keeping programs "honest" to their purpose, developing competence so that poor people could take control of their own neighborhoods, or organizing the poor politically to demand institutional change. Remarkably, through the entire process of drawing up the poverty program, no outsider divined that one consequence of community action might be to ignite, at the local level, political and social conflict. One of those who did not understand was Lyndon Johnson. He persisted in thinking of community action as the contemporary equivalent of the National Youth Administration, which he had headed in Texas during the Depression.[115] Community action seemed to him merely a convenient device for funneling an expanded flow of traditional services into Democratic neighborhoods in the big cities. Only too late did he realize that loyalists of Robert Kennedy had planted a time bomb in *his* antipoverty program. By then Hackett's guerrillas were ensconced in the new Office of Economic Opportunity, administering community action and stirring up the poor.

Johnson's Economic Opportunity Act, which he sent to Congress on March 16, 1964, proposed creation of an Office of Economic Opportunity with two principal functions—administering the community action program and running the Job Corps. Lesser programs were distributed to the regular departments as part of the poverty spoils.[116] It was a highly controversial measure, and many of its proposals were intensely debated. Community action was not one of them. Like the White House, Congress regarded the program essentially as a way to dispense services to the poor through local governments, though the bill explicitly authorized private community action agencies as well. On behalf of his fellow mayors, Chicago's Richard Daley summarized the prevailing view. "We think the local officials should have control of this program," he said.[117] No congressman disagreed. And yet Robert Kennedy tried to tell them.[118] In his testimony on the bill, Kennedy began by noting the similarity between CAP and Hackett's delinquency program. And then he got to the point, which was, of course, institutional reform and how to get it.

The institutions which affect the poor—education, welfare, recreation, business, labor—are huge, complex structures, operating far outside their control. They plan programs for the poor, not with them. Part of the sense of helplessness and futility comes from the feeling of powerlessness to affect the operation of these organizations. The community action program must basically change these organizations by building into the program real representation for the poor. This bill calls for "maximum feasible participation of residents." This means the involvement of the poor in planning and implementing programs; giving them a real voice in their institutions.

No congressman thought to probe the meaning of "maximum feasible participation," and none noted the differing interpretations of community action offered by Mayor Daley and Robert Kennedy. Thus in August 1964, when the Economic Opportunity Act was enacted, neither the president who sponsored it, the director-designate who would administer it, nor the congressmen who passed it really knew what they had done. Indeed, a history of the legislation might well be entitled "How Not to Pass a Law."

Or better, "How Not to Fight Poverty." The main task, Hackett had said, was "to think it over,"[119] and that task had gone undone. Haste had precluded serious thought, but so too did political reality. Poverty was a condition characterized by insufficiency of money, and its surest remedy was redistribution of income. That was radicalism, and no politician in America would dare embrace it—not David Hackett, not Robert Kennedy. Poverty planners, therefore, could devise programs, like community action, that at best nibbled at the edge of the problem. But alone among the social-welfare programs of the 1960s, community action at least attempted to redistribute power, if only on the local level and in limited ways. By the standards of American politics, that was radicalism too. Of course, Lyndon Johnson had become the sponsor of this experiment in social change not by choice—only by sheerest accident.

IV

That the administration begun by John F. Kennedy should have become the sponsor of liberal reform was one of the decade's ironies, for he was transparently a conventional politician of conservative inclination. But Kennedy was also a politician keenly sensitive to shifts in the political climate, and that climate altered perceptibly during his years in the White House. Diminishing obsession with the Cold War permitted intellectuals to look critically at their own country once again. The era's affluence spawned both social optimism and the revenues to pay for modest new welfare measures. The civil rights movement touched the nation's conscience and illuminated the squalid underside of American life.

Not least among the causes of the new mood was Kennedy himself, whose Superman persona, as Norman Mailer had predicted in 1960, gave "unwilling charge" to energies previously confined to the underground—though resurrection of political liberalism was hardly what Mailer had in mind. By his heroic poses, his urgent rhetoric, his appeal to idealism and the nation's great traditions, Kennedy inadvertently helped arouse among millions a dormant desire to perfect America. Ironically, therefore, forces he himself helped generate had moved Kennedy to become the reluctant champion of John Maynard Keynes, Martin Luther King, and Michael Harrington. Only later, during Lyndon Johnson's term as president, would the limits of liberal good will become apparent and the flaws of liberal reform be exposed.

PART II

CHAPTER 5

The Election of 1964

I

AFTER Kennedy's assassination the outcome of the 1964 presidential election was never seriously in doubt. A grief-stricken public insisted on perceiving the fallen president as a martyr to the hatreds polluting American life and demanded that his sacrifice not have been in vain. All that Kennedy had tried to do, all that he stood for, became in some sense sanctified. Lyndon Johnson, the accidental president, had only to execute his predecessor's political estate to attain legitimacy and claim succession in his own right.

Johnson exploited every opportunity to wrap himself in Kennedy's mantle. When he took the oath of office aboard Air Force One in Dallas, he made sure to have Mrs. Kennedy, the bloodstains on her suit not yet dry, photographed at his side. In the next weeks he persuaded Kennedy's aides to remain in the White House, assured foreign leaders that Kennedy's policies were his also, and urged in his first speech, "Let us continue."[1] Then, one by one, he guided to passage the main legislative items of Kennedy's program —the tax cut, the civil rights bill, the War on Poverty. "We would be untrue to the trust he reposed in us, if we did not remain true to the tasks he relinquished when God summoned him," Johnson said.[2] Because his performance in the months of national mourning was nearly flawless, he achieved stature as a true national leader.

The public acquiesced but did not rejoice in Johnson's ascendance. As it perceived them, neither his character nor his career inspired unalloyed admiration. Johnson had been a noted power broker in his Senate days, but did he possess a core of firmly-held beliefs? He had amassed a fortune in the broadcasting business, but was it ethical for a member of Congress to invest in a government-regulated industry? He possessed a quick and keen intelligence, but could a man whose knowledge of history began with the New Deal and whose conception of patriotism derived from the Alamo meet the demands of the modern presidency? Stories began filtering from the White House of Johnson's mercurial moods, his meanness to servants, his abuse of aides, the slights he inflicted on reporters who incurred his wrath. (Johnson once gave a gold-filled tie clasp to every reporter who covered his 1964 campaign, except Frank Cormier of the Associated Press, who received a gift-wrapped box, delivered by a White House chauffeur, with nothing in it.)[3] To make matters worse, Johnson cultivated a TV personality wildly at odds with his true self. The unctuous, sentimental, magnanimous Johnson whom he created for mass consumption was something less than a work of art, and the public recognized its essential insincerity. Even while basking in the nation's appreciation of his early perform-ance, Johnson knew he was not loved. "Why don't people like me?" he asked visitors in 1964. "Because Mr. President," an intrepid elder statesman replied, "you are not a very likeable man."[4]

Insecurity was Johnson's great flaw. "I am the king!" he declared in a private moment of exhilaration,[5] but the need to say it revealed the inner doubt. Reared in the Texas hill country and educated at Southwest Texas State Teacher's College, Johnson was convinced that men of distinguished family, old money, and Ivy League educa-tion would always scorn him. Other rough-hewn politicians had come to the capital and learned the manners of gentlemen in the drawing rooms of Georgetown. But Johnson avoided Washington society, rejected its pretensions, and clung defiantly to his frontier manners. He no doubt knew that he would shock a woman reporter visiting his ranch with his graphic dissertation on the sex life of bulls, that the fastidious would gasp when he wiped salty hands on the tuxedoed backs of his guests at a State Department reception, that reporters would snicker at the belches he delivered between gulps of his highball or recoil when he paused to urinate on his grave site during a tour of the LBJ ranch.[6] Indeed, Johnson flaunted his crudeness, even exaggerated it, as if belligerently denying some secret hurt. ("Georgetown," he said when once informed that black militants were marching to burn it down, "I've waited thirty-five years for this day.'"[7]) Insecurity helped poison his relations with the press corps, which found his thin skin and obsessive secrecy remarkable even in Washington. And insecurity fed his jealousy of the Kennedys, adulation for whom he thought was undeserved.

Still, there existed in this man the possibility of greatness. Though he had compromised his beliefs on racial equality and social justice in the past, Johnson's commitment to act on those beliefs was now firm. He would confound his critics by doing good, employ his talents for manipulation to pass more bills than FDR, and escape the shadow of John Kennedy by being the better president. The more he heard of Kennedy's greatness, the more determined he was to become, as he said, "the greatest of them all, the whole bunch of them."[8] But to attain greatness Johnson had first to win the 1964 election, win it by a bigger margin than Kennedy had won in 1960, bigger even than Roosevelt in 1936, so big that his legitimacy would be unassailable and his mandate to complete the liberal program of the 1960s beyond dispute.

II

It was Johnson's good fortune to have as his opponent in 1964 the improbable Barry Goldwater, an Arizona senator espousing a brand of conservatism with distinctly limited appeal. In the months before the Republican convention Goldwater had voted no on the tax cut, no on civil rights, and no on the War on Poverty. As he had explained in his best-selling *The Conscience of a Conservative* (1960), the conservative "looks upon politics as the art of achieving the maximum amount of freedom for individuals that is consistent with the maintenance of the social order."[9] It followed that the federal government had no business enforcing school desegregation, paying subsidies to farmers, funding urban renewal, taxing incomes progressively, or aiding education.

Goldwater, however, was a Jeffersonian only to the water's edge, summing up his foreign policy in the title of his 1962 book, *Why Not Victory?* The enemy whom this major general in the Air Force Reserve wished to smite was, of course, Communism. Eliminate Castro, he said. Quit disarmament negotiations. Give a freer hand to the military, use foreign aid only to promote free enterprise, and discourage decolonization wherever it plays into the hands of the reds. "Our job, first and foremost, is to persuade the enemy that we would rather follow the world to Kingdom Come than consign it to Hell under communism," he wrote.[10] Goldwater spoke no words critical of the military service, the CIA, the FBI, or any other arm of the expanding national security bureaucracy. Indeed, it seems never to have occurred to him, or to the conservative movement he led, that his urge to mobilize the country for Armageddon contradicted his preference for small government—that, in the name of liberty, he was merely proposing to replace the welfare state with the garrison state.

Goldwater emerged as the chief political spokesman for the conservative movement by dint of personality, not intellect. As befitted a successful dry-goods merchant from Phoenix, Arizona, he was glad-handing, gregarious, and free of pretension. Authentically Western, he loved nature and flew jet planes, seeming to embody the rugged virtues he so often celebrated in his oratory. Conservatives appreciated the simple way he preached their gospel. Women admired his good looks. And shrewd professionals recognized in Goldwater the charisma that might at last attract converts to conservatism's depleted ranks.

The Goldwater movement began at the 1960 Republican convention when, in angry protest against Nixon's capitulation to the liberals on the issue of the platform, the senator took the podium and told conservatives "to grow up" and "take this party back."[11] The man who took Goldwater's injunction seriously was F. Clifton White. A professional who had learned his trade fighting the conservative fight in the Byzantine world of New York politics, White was prominent enough to head Citizens for Nixon-Lodge in the 1960 campaign. In 1961 he began covertly plotting a conservative coup at the next Republican convention. Recruiting like-minded party pros to the cause, he divided the country into nine regions, appointed regional directors, and set about organizing at the precinct level.[12] White knew that hundreds of thousands of grassroots conservatives were out there waiting to be mobilized and that party organizations in many states were vulnerable for a putsch. What he could not know was that the early front-runner, New York Governor Nelson Rockefeller, would wreck his own chances in May 1962, by marrying a divorcee amid circumstances deemed scandalous by the public. White's candidate—Goldwater, of course—darted ahead in the polls.[13]

As he did, the Machiavellis of the right explained why Goldwater was the Republican with the best chance of defeating John Kennedy. Alone among Republican hopefuls, they said, he could run as the candidate of states' rights, not civil rights, assuring a sweep of the South and the border states, with perhaps 165 electoral votes. Add to these the approximately 140 votes in GOP strongholds elsewhere, and the result would be a clear majority in the electoral college. If the southern strategy stirred up an anti-Negro, anti-Kennedy backlash among ethnic white voters in the North—and it might—who knew the possible dimensions of a Goldwater victory?[14]

The only problem was that Goldwater did not want to run. Better than those who were entreating him to be their leader, the senator sensed how unequal he was to the ordeal being thrust upon him. "You know," he told a reporter in 1963, "I haven't got a really first-class brain."[15] Kennedy's assassination not only upset the southern strategy; it so depressed Goldwater that for a few weeks he came close to washing his hands of what he called "this president thing." But sometime in December 1963 he concluded that the movement to nominate him had gone too far. Having become the hero of American conservatives, he could not honorably desert them now. Without lust for the fight ahead, Goldwater announced his candidacy in January 1964.

The senator's self-doubts were vindicated in the New Hampshire primary, the first of the campaign. At the outset, polls showed him leading Rockefeller four to one. But the more Goldwater campaigned, the faster his lead dwindled. As long as his romantic pleas for self-reliance remained unattached to concrete issues, they had a certain appeal. But when he got specific, when he called for a social security system financed by voluntary contributions or a Marine assault on Cuba or repeal of the progressive income tax, as he did in off-the-cuff remarks in New Hampshire, he got into trouble.[16] Rockefeller seized on these casual pronouncements to label Goldwater an extremist and declare him outside the mainstream of the Republican party. Audiences, however, were noticeably cool to the governor, who campaigned with the new Mrs. Rockefeller at his side. On March 10, 1964, the voters of New Hampshire rebuffed both Goldwater and Rockefeller by giving a substantial plurality to Henry Cabot Lodge, a write-in candidate and the U.S. ambassador to South Vietnam.[17] "A lot of people may not be ready to be conservative yet," Goldwater said the next day.[18]

Entering several primaries in April and May, Goldwater scored no notable victories and suffered several humiliating defeats. But in the non-primary states, Clifton White's organization was quietly corralling the delegates, so many, in fact, that White felt certain of victory even if his man lost the climactic California primary, June 2, 1964. Goldwater himself adhered to the conventional view that without one big primary win he was finished.[19] The California primary was a head-to-head, winner-take-all contest between Goldwater and Rockefeller. No one else was on the ballot; no write-ins were permitted. Goldwater entered the primary as the underdog, but closed strong. For one thing, in the last days of the campaign Mrs. Rockefeller gave birth to a son, a blessed event that revived memories of the governor's complicated domestic life. For another, 40,000 Goldwater volunteers blanketed the state, contacting in Los Angeles County alone some 300,000 voters in the weekend before the election. Goldwater defeated Rockefeller by 68,000 votes out of more than two million cast. Despite a desperate, last-minute challenge from Pennsylvania governor William W. Scranton, F. Clifton White had pulled off his coup.[20]

Goldwater's was a victory of a minority faction in a minority party. Gallup reported that, even as late as July 1964, Republican voters favored Scranton over Goldwater by 60 percent to 34 percent.[21] With Rockefeller unacceptable, other moderates unwilling, and the nomination not worth much anyway, Goldwater won partly by default, partly by organizing at the grassroots. The nature of his following was one of the most fascinating puzzles of the campaign. Poll data showed that throughout the spring of 1964 Goldwater was the first choice of only 13 percent of white voters, spread evenly across occupational, income, and party lines. The major factor differentiating support for Goldwater was regional. While a mere 7 percent of the East and 11 percent of the Midwest preferred Goldwater, the senator was the first choice of 15 percent of the West and 21 percent of the South.[22]

Journalists covering the Goldwater story reported that his most fanatic following in the South and West belonged to the newly affluent middle classes. Here were the people most likely to believe that the welfare state promoted moral decay, that an Eastern Seaboard establishment exercised undemocratic authority over American institutions, and that Wall Street bankers had bought the Republican party for crypto–New Dealers every four years since 1940. Behind the Goldwater movement, wrote Stewart Alsop, "new money, boom money," was asserting its independence of eastern bankers.[23] There was "general agreement," wrote Norman Mailer, "that the basic war was between Main Street and Wall Street."[24] The core of Goldwater's support, wrote I. F. Stone, "is from a section which likes to think of itself as rugged and frontier because Western and Southwestern. But the covered wagons in which it travels are Cadillacs and its wide open spaces have been air-conditioned."[25] In proposing that the East Coast be "sliced off and cut adrift,"[26] as he once did, Goldwater was the authentic voice of this sectional resentment.

The Republican convention, held in San Francisco's Cow Palace in mid-July 1964, was a watershed in the history of the party, marking, as it did, the transference of power from moderates to conservatives, from Northeast to Sun Belt. Unfortunately for Goldwater, his troops made no effort to curb their rancor in this, their moment of triumph. When Dwight Eisenhower criticized "sensation-seeking columnists and commentators," the delegates directed a chorus of jeers at the press tables and TV booths. Convention guards shoved NBC reporter John Chancellor off the convention floor in full view of a national TV audience.[27] The Goldwater galleries booed so loudly when Nelson Rockefeller rose in defense of a minority plank condemning by name the Communist party, the John Birch Society, and the Ku Klux Klan that he could not be heard.[28]

No one, it turned out, was in a more rancorous mood than Goldwater himself. The moderates had abused him without mercy, read him out of the party, painted him as an extremist and a warmonger. His charity exhausted, he rubbed salt in their wounds by picking as his running mate William E. Miller, an obscure upstate New York congressman at least as conservative as he was. Goldwater's speech accepting the nomination was a deliberate effort to taunt his moderate foes, with whom, by every rule of politics, he should now have made peace. "I would remind you that extremism in defense of liberty is no vice," he said in its most memorable lines. "And let me remind you also that moderation in pursuit of justice is no virtue."[29] Senator Kenneth Keating, up for re-election in liberal New York and no friend of extremism, immediately led forty members of his delegation from the convention. In a trailer nearby, Clifton White watched Goldwater's performance in stunned silence. The speech, White knew, turned sour the taste of victory and assured disaster in November.[30]

III

Or did it? On the day the Republican convention convened, Henry Hall Wilson, who worked on congressional relations in Johnson's White House, wrote his chief, Lawrence F. O'Brien, "I suggest it is time someone said to the President what apparently no one has yet said to him—that he could lose this election."[31] Prominent among the reasons for Wilson's foreboding was the great imponderable of the campaign—the so-called white backlash against civil rights.

The man responsible for exposing the backlash was the governor of Alabama, George Corley Wallace.[32] Wallace became a hero to the white South when, in June 1963, he literally stood in "the school house door" to block court-ordered integration of the state university. He proved no one-day wonder. What separated Wallace from ordinary politicians was his extraordinary comprehension of "common folk," among whose number he counted himself and whose prejudices he faithfully served. It was his genius to intuit that there were people all over America just like people in Alabama and that they were waiting for him to articulate their desperation and their resentments. So Wallace announced in the spring of 1964 that he was coming north to enter a few Democratic primaries, ostensibly to send a message to the U.S. Senate, which was then debating the civil rights bill, but really because Alabama was just too small to contain his ambition.

Wallace began his campaign in Wisconsin. He had no organization, little money, and the opposition of every respectable institution in the state. But the more hostile the environment, the more this former bantamweight boxing champion of Alabama enjoyed himself. There was no doubt that he was an electric presence on the platform. When he was really charged up, he was venomous, even suggestive of barely controlled violence. And, despite his country manners and slicked-down hair, he was a nimble debater with a talent for laying bare the hypocrisies of white liberalism. He was not a racist, he said, only a segregationist. He had come north not to preach segregation but states' rights. It was not Negroes he opposed, but a tyrannical government that was trying to take away the freedom of people to run their own schools, businesses, and homes.[33] Governor John W. Reynolds, Johnson's stand-in on the Wisconsin ballot, said that if Wallace won 100,000 votes, Wisconsin would be disgraced. On April 7, 1964, Wallace shocked the nation by winning 264,000 votes, 34 percent of all those cast in the Democratic primary.[34] Wallace followed this feat by winning 29.8 percent of the Democratic vote in the Indiana primary and 42.7 percent in Maryland. "If it hadn't been for the nigger bloc vote," Wallace said of Maryland, "we'd have won it all."[35] Commentators blamed Wallace's strong showing on working-class ethnic Democrats in Milwaukee and Gary.[36] If Goldwater could attract these Wallace voters in the fall, the pundits said, he could cut into the heart of the Democratic coalition. In fact, both Indiana and Wisconsin permitted cross-over voting in primary elections, and Wallace had run at least as strong in the Republican suburbs as in working-class neighborhoods. The backlash, in short, touched a large number of conservative Republicans who planned to vote for Goldwater anyway.[37]

Exhilarated by his successes, Wallace announced in June that he was going to run for president on a third-party ticket. In July he got on the ballot in sixteen states and was forecasting enough electoral votes to force the contest into the House. But southern conservative leaders preferred Goldwater to Wallace because they thought Goldwater had a better chance to beat Johnson. Wallace might hurt Johnson in the North; he would kill Goldwater in the South. After Goldwater asked him to withdraw, Wallace reluctantly quit the race on July 19, 1964.[38]

The night before, the first northern ghetto riot of the decade erupted in Harlem.[39] It started, as so many others would, in a police incident—a white patrolman shooting a fifteen-year-old black boy in the course of a routine arrest. A protest march degenerated into a pitched battle between blacks and police, and mobs began rampaging through the streets, burning, looting, and attacking whites. After a week black rage ran its course in Harlem and then exploded upstate in Rochester. Suddenly the foundations of the social order seemed to tremble. The riots quickened white fears, increased the possibility of voter backlash, and bestowed on Goldwater's candidacy temporary plausibility. Declaring that the first priority was to register black voters and defeat the Arizona senator, civil rights leaders Martin Luther King, Whitney Young, Roy Wilkins, and A.

Philip Randolph issued a plea on July 29 for "a moratorium" on demonstrations until after the election.[40] But the riots continued into August, scarring Paterson, New Jersey; Elizabeth, New Jersey; and, at the end of the month, Philadelphia. Then, as suddenly as they had begun, the riots stopped. Whether Goldwater could exploit the racist fears uncovered by Wallace and fed by the riots remained to be seen.

IV

In matters great and small, Lyndon Johnson dominated the Democratic convention, which met in the last days of August on the tawdry boardwalk of Atlantic City. The president chose the convention theme song ("Hello, Lyndon"), the convention motto ("Let us continue"), the convention speakers, and the two forty-foot portraits of himself looming over the convention rostrum.[41] It cost delegates thirty cents for a small LBJ button, and big corporations $15,000 for a page of advertising in the convention program. (Twenty-seven major defense contractors, among others, prudently bought space.)[42] The delegates had come not so much to nominate Johnson as to pay him court, their pleasure in the occasion being enhanced by the latest Gallup poll, which showed the president leading Goldwater 65 percent to 29 percent.[43] Still, for Johnson, the convention was not without annoyances.

The chief of these was the Mississippi Freedom Democratic party, brainchild of the Student Nonviolent Coordinating Committee.[44] Assisted by some eight hundred white student volunteers, SNCC workers walked the back roads of Mississippi in the Freedom Summer of 1964, selling the idea of an extralegal political party for disfranchised blacks. The idea caught on. The Freedom Democratic party enrolled 60,000 Negro members, held local and state conventions, and selected 68 delegates, four of them white, to attend the Democratic National Convention. Freedom delegates came to Atlantic City demanding the ouster of the racist Mississippi regulars and recognition of themselves as the only morally legitimate political party in the state. "I will tell you a tale of terrors," the Freedom party's counsel, Joseph Rauh, promised the convention's credentials committee. His witnesses, black Mississippians all, gave graphic descriptions of the brutality they had endured merely for attempting to register. Liberals on the credentials committee immediately rallied to the Freedom Democrats. The convention, they said, should acknowledge their legitimacy by giving them half of Mississippi's seats, the other half going to the Mississippi regulars. Though the liberals could not carry their proposal in the credentials committee, they had enough votes to assure a minority report to the full convention. SNCC would then get what it wanted above all else —a floor debate before a national TV audience that would expose the racist violence engulfing Mississippi.

Johnson was not pleased. If the convention backed the Freedom Democrats, not only would the Mississippi regulars bolt, but so might delegations from other southern states he had a better chance to carry in November. The president was so concerned by the challenge that he enlisted the FBI to help him subvert it. Cartha DeLoach, the Bureau's liaison to the White House, secretly ensconced a team of fifty FBI agents in Atlantic City, officially to gather intelligence on possible violence at the convention but really to spy on the civil rights movement.[45] DeLoach's men wiretapped Martin Luther King, bugged the storefront headquarters of SNCC and CORE, and infiltrated the Freedom party command post in the Gem Motel. They even posed as newsmen, using NBC press credentials to obtain confidential information from civil rights workers "on background." DeLoach himself kept the White House up-to-the-minute on convention developments. Summarizing the results of his assignment in a FBI memo, he said, "Through our counter intelligence efforts, Jenkins, et al., were able to advise the President in advance regarding major plans for the MFDP [Mississippi Freedom Democratic Party] delegates. The White House considered this of prime importance."[46] If the nation had known of DeLoach's possibly illegal operation, it might have been more sympathetic to Goldwater's campaign charges of Big Brother in the White House.

Meanwhile, Johnson dispatched Hubert Humphrey to Atlantic City to prevent, if possible, a floor fight on Mississippi and a southern walkout. A leading contender for the vice-presidential nomination, Humphrey's chances were widely regarded to hinge on the success of this mission. He proposed a three-part compromise: the white Mississippians would have to take an oath to support the ticket before being seated; the Freedom Democrats would be granted two seats at the convention, not to represent Mississippi but to vote at large; and no delegation chosen by racially discriminatory means could sit at future conventions. "Crumbs" from the table,[47] said

Freedom Democrats, who would accept nothing less than the minority report that the liberals on the credentials committee had promised to support. But one by one the liberals on the committee deserted that report for the Humphrey compromise. In the end there would be no minority report, no floor debate, and no Freedom party delegates in Mississippi's seats—unless the Freedom delegates walked onto the convention floor and seized them, which, briefly they did. SNCC and the Freedom delegation got back on their buses and headed home, convinced that white liberals on the committee had betrayed them to bail out Humphrey. Indeed, the major consequence of this episode was to propel the militant wing of the civil rights movement further and faster down the path of black separatism. As for Lyndon Johnson, he got what he wanted. The Alabama delegation left the convention over a credentials fight, and most of the white Mississippians left too, but the rest of the South swallowed the Humphrey compromise and stayed put.

LBJ's other problem was Robert Kennedy. Bitter enmity had marked the relations between these two men since the 1960 Los Angeles convention when John Kennedy offered the vice presidency to Johnson in the expectation he would decline, and Robert Kennedy tried to dissuade him after he accepted. Subsequently, whenever the attorney general and the vice president crossed paths in the Kennedy White House, the atmosphere crackled with hostility. Though RFK remained in the Cabinet for the first nine months of Johnson's administration, relations between the two top Democrats, if anything, worsened. Kennedy regarded Johnson as a usurper, and Johnson regarded Kennedy as his most dangerous rival in the party. When a groundswell among Democrats began building for a Johnson-Kennedy ticket in 1964, Kennedy was interested but Johnson was not. On July 29, certain now that he could trounce Goldwater without any help from Robert Kennedy, Johnson summoned him to the Oval Office and ruled him out of contention. Kennedy decided to run for the Senate from New York, and Johnson groomed Humphrey to be his running mate.

But what if the convention veered out of Johnson's control? What if the pent-up grief of the delegates for JFK expressed itself in a vice-presidential boom for RFK? To forestall this possibility, Johnson ordered a filmed tribute to John Kennedy, which Bobby was to introduce at the convention, moved from before the balloting for candidates to after it. Humphrey had safely been nominated for vice president when Kennedy finally stood before the convention on its last day. He was greeted by one of the great ovations in party history. "Let it go on . . ." said Senator Henry Jackson when Kennedy tried to stop it. "Just let them do it Bob. . . . Let them get it out of their system."[48] So exuberant was Johnson as he savored his own nomination by acclamation that this evidence of the party's true affections dampened his spirits only a trifle.

V

Comparing the personalities of the candidates, the Very Reverend Francis B. Sayre, Jr., of Washington's Episcopal Cathedral spoke for many concerned Americans when he said that the electorate faced a "sterile choice" between "a man of dangerous ignorance and devastating uncertainty" and "a man whose public house is splendid in its every appearance, but whose private lack of ethic must inevitably introduce termites at the very foundation."[49] Beyond personality, however, there was ideology, and here the choice was hardly sterile. True, Johnson would seek to blur the issues, and Goldwater would blunder in trying to raise them. But the public knew the true significance of the 1964 election. Johnson was the liberal, Goldwater the conservative, and the election was a referendum on the policies of the past four years—indeed, the liberal policies of the past generation.

The campaign's central figure was Goldwater. It was his personality that aroused the deepest passions, his unflinching conservatism that gave the contest its distinctive flavor. "There is a stir in the land," he said in early September. "There is a mood of uneasiness. We feel adrift in an uncharted and stormy sea." A power-hungry Big Brother occupied the White House. Corruption had penetrated to the highest levels of American life. The moral character of the people was showing evidence of deterioration. As Goldwater saw it, the root problem was the welfare state. "If it is entirely proper for government to take from some to give to others, then won't some be led to believe that they can rightfully take from anyone who has more than they?" No wonder law and order had broken down, mob violence had engulfed great American cities, and "our wives, all women, feel unsafe in the streets." The time had come for the "forgotten American," who pays his taxes and stays out of trouble, to restore to their rightful eminence the values of "private property, free enterprise, and hard work."[50]

Since the welfare state was the source of American evils, Goldwater proposed its virtual abandonment. Instead of Keynesian tax cuts, he suggested automatic tax cuts every year for five years to deny the government revenue for new welfare measures.[51] Instead of federal grants for purposes deemed worthy in Washington, he proposed consolidating grants into one lump sum, which localities could use as they pleased.[52] He told voters in Knoxville, the administrative center of the Tennessee Valley Authority, that he would like to sell TVA to private enterprise.[53] At the National Plowing Contest in North Dakota, he called agricultural price supports "absurd" and said their "gradual decline" would be good for farmers.[54] He chose to attack Medicare in Florida, despite the large colony of retired citizens living there.[55] And he went to impoverished West Virginia to denounce the poverty program.[56] When he asked, "What place does politics have in a campaign for the presidency?" he had already given his answer.[57]

On foreign affairs, Goldwater defied current fashion no less fearlessly. An administration "soft on communism,"[58] he said, had accepted the "silly"[59] theory that the Communist bloc was splitting apart and that the Russians were mellowing. It had been wrong to pledge no invasion of Cuba, to negotiate a ban on nuclear tests in the atmosphere, to sell wheat to the Russians. Not coexistence but victory was the proper objective of U.S. policy. Not appeasement but the mightiest weapons arsenal in history was the sole path to American security.[60] Among his more celebrated proposals, Goldwater recommended giving the NATO commander "authority over the *tactical* nuclear weapons appropriate to NATO's defenses."[61]

Potentially, Goldwater's best issue was the moral character of Lyndon Johnson. Johnson was vulnerable on three counts: his success in making money in a government-regulated industry; his limited association with Billy Sol Estes, an entrepreneurial crook who gave campaign contributions to Texas politicians; and above all, his involvement in the sensational case of Bobby Baker.

Robert G. Baker was a good ole boy from Pickins, South Carolina, who rose from Senate page to secretary of the Senate majority, acquiring along the way more power than many senators. Baker was Johnson's boy, the son he never had, the indispensable "fixer" in the years of Johnson's Senate dominance. Idolizing those whom he served, Baker mindlessly adopted the moral standards prevailing among them. "Little Lyndon," as he was called, acted as a bag man for illegal political contributors, introduced senators to eager young ladies, and sought to make his fortune by selling influence and exploiting his political connections. In October 1963 the world of Bobby Baker suddenly came unglued when charges of financial impropriety forced his resignation and the Senate prepared to investigate his activities.[62]

Meanwhile, Attorney General Robert Kennedy dipped into FBI files on Baker and discovered the existence of call-girl operations, not directly related to Baker, involving numerous senators of both parties, including southern senators with Negro mistresses. "I thought that it would just destroy the confidence that people in the United States had in their government and really make us a laughing stock around the world," Kennedy recalled. After conferring with President Kennedy, the attorney general initiated a cover-up, sending J. Edgar Hoover to brief Senate leaders Mike Mansfield and Everett Dirksen on the sordid details that might emerge from a wide-open Baker probe. Shocked by Hoover's revelations, the two senators took pains to steer the investigation into safer waters. "I don't know how they handled it," Robert Kennedy said. "But in any case, they handled it."[63]

Only weeks after the Baker scandal broke, Johnson became president. The mere fact that Baker had been his protégé was bad enough. But in January 1964 insurance agent Don Reynolds told the Senate that Baker had helped him sell Johnson $200,000 in life insurance from 1957 to 1961, but that Johnson's aide Walter Jenkins had pressured him, Reynolds, into kicking back part of the commission for advertising on Johnson's Austin TV station and an expensive stereo for Johnson's family.[64] On January 23, 1964, Johnson made a brief and not altogether convincing reply to Reynolds's charges and then lapsed into silence.[65] Privately, he tried to destroy Reynolds's credibility by leaking derogatory FBI and Pentagon reports about him to select newsmen.[66] In March 1964 the Democratic majority of the Senate investigating committee managed to terminate the Baker hearings amid Republican cries of whitewash.[67] But fresh charges against Baker kept the case in the headlines throughout the summer. That fall a day scarcely passed without Goldwater mentioning Baker at least once. "You've got a new nursery rhyme in Washington . . ." Goldwater said. "The butcher, the Baker, and the stereo-taker." Goldwater defined a Baker dozen this way: "You get thirteen, but you have to kick back two."[68]

On October 14, when the press broke the sad story of Walter Jenkins, the morality issue took a new turn. Jenkins, forty-six-year-old father of six, had been Johnson's most trusted employee for twenty-five years. In the White House, he was Johnson's chief of staff, the one subordinate who could speak with unquestioned authority in Johnson's name. On October 7 this self-effacing man, target of so many of Johnson's tantrums, broke under the strain of his crushing workload. Police arrested him in the men's room of a YMCA near the White House and charged him with "indecent gestures."[69] Johnson learned of Jenkins's indiscretion only one day before the public did. His first impulse was to slash at the Republicans for their own sins. Campaigning in New York when the furor hit, he showed Robert Kennedy a statement he intended to release, indirectly linking Jenkins to Goldwater, since Goldwater was his commanding officer in the Air Force Reserve. Johnson also told Kennedy that he had spent the previous night reading FBI files (apparently the same ones RFK had seen at the start of the Baker case) and that he might, in Kennedy's words, "try to develop information on Republican senators and to develop information on Barry Goldwater." Kennedy advised him to meet the Jenkins crisis by talking foreign policy.[70] Fortunately, Johnson took the advice. Meantime, Goldwater's references to Johnson's "curious crew" took on new innuendo.

Some Republicans saw in the fall of Walter Jenkins a unique opportunity for exploiting the morality issue. Citizens for Goldwater paid $65,000 for a half-hour TV film, picturing America as a modern Sodom and Gomorrah. The film included shots of a girl in a topless bathing suit, pornographic magazine covers, strip-tease joints, blacks rioting in the streets, teenagers on a rampage, and even Billy Sol Estes and Bobby Baker. Goldwater insisted on viewing the film before it was shown. Calling it racist, he banned it from the campaign.[71] The morality issue had fallen flat anyway. The public had shown little interest in the Baker case and soon grew bored reading about Jenkins. Polls showed that the voters gave higher marks for personal integrity to Goldwater than to Johnson but considered other issues more important.

Compared to Goldwater's quixotic, not to say suicidal, efforts to challenge the spirit of the age, Johnson's campaign was mostly a bore. Since Goldwater occupied the right flank of American politics, Johnson muted ideology and moved into the vacated center. This he accomplished by sticking to platitudes and preaching unity, love, and brotherhood. Goldwater warned of impending calamity. Johnson told his audiences how happy they looked. Goldwater emphasized military might. Johnson stressed his horror at the prospect of atomic holocaust. Goldwater said that Americans were losing their freedom. "Every day," Johnson said, ". . . I see by the hundreds of thousands, men, women, and children who love freedom and know they have it."[72] Goldwater wanted to repeal the welfare state. So Johnson promised that farmers would keep their price supports. Old people would continue receiving their social security checks. Nobody would sell TVA.[73] "A man who loves his country" can build a house, he told the steelworkers' convention, but "a ranting, raving demagog" just might tear it down.[74] "We have so much to be thankful for," he said in Dayton. "We have so much to preserve and so much to protect."[75]

To fix the image of Goldwater the Trigger Happy, the Democrats seized on his loose talk about giving the NATO commander authority over nuclear weapons. No one but the president should control nuclear weapons, they said, because dispersing authority increased the risks of annihilation. Actually, the NATO commander already had advance authority to employ nuclear weaponry in certain circumstances, as Goldwater himself well knew. Nothing better illustrated his ineptitude than that he had opened himself to charges of nuclear irresponsibility for a proposal that either was superfluous or was too sensitive for security reasons to be discussed candidly.[76] The Democrats ran a one-minute TV ad showing a young girl plucking petals from a daisy, while in the background a voice counted down. "Ten, nine, eight . . ." At zero, a mushroom cloud exploded on screen, and Johnson's voice said, "These are the stakes. To make a world in which all of God's children can live, or go into the dark. We must either love each other or we must die." He did not mention Goldwater's name. By then, he did not have to.[77]

To dramatize their differences with Goldwater on the welfare state, the Democrats chose to make their stand on social security, the most venerated of their achievements. Ironically, this was one program that Goldwater did not challenge. After musing aloud in New Hampshire about a voluntary social security system, he had retreated to safer ground and endorsed social security as it was. But the damage was done. The Democrats ran an ad showing disembodied hands ripping up a social security card. Said an announcer, "On at least seven occasions Senator Barry Goldwater said that he would change the present social security system. But even his running mate, William Miller, admits that Senator Goldwater's voluntary plan would destroy the social security system. President Johnson is working to strengthen social security."[78] It was a dishonest way to highlight a genuine philosophical difference—and further bury Goldwater's candidacy.

The big surprise of the campaign was the inconsequence of the civil rights issues, which had once seemed likely to dominate the autumn debate. Memories of the summer's riots dimmed quickly, white working-class Democrats worried more about Goldwater's economics than about race, and a "front lash" of moderate Republicans favoring Johnson promised to offset any losses he might suffer because of civil rights. In the spring the president's ad agency, Doyle Dane Bernbach, Inc., had prepared a series of TV spots on the race issue. In the fall, with the black vote in Johnson's pocket and white fears easing, the agency canceled the spots.[79] Except for a brave speech in New Orleans, Johnson himself generally stayed clear of the subject. Goldwater was only slightly less circumspect, his efforts to exploit the possible backlash being confined to half-hearted innuendo. "Choose the way of the present administration," he said, "and you have the way of mobs in the streets, restrained only by the plea that they wait until after election time to ignite violence once again."[80] Only once, at Chicago in October, did he offer a full statement of his views. State-enforced school segregation was wrong, he now contended, but so was forced busing. For, while government should assure freedom of association, "it cannot and should not ensure association itself." The goal of public policy should be neither a segregated society nor an integrated society, but a free society. And a free man had the right to practice unfair discrimination, however regrettable, in his private affairs.[81] By the time he made this speech, few were any longer paying much attention to anything he said.

In retrospect, the campaign's most interesting issue was Vietnam. Contemptuous of a policy he regarded as pusillanimous, Goldwater explained in a TV interview in May 1964 how he would fight a war to which, so far, only American "advisers" had been committed.

Bomb the supply routes in North Vietnam, he suggested, to stem the flow of supplies southward. What would he do about supply trails hidden in dense jungle? a reporter asked. "There have been several suggestions made," Goldwater replied. "I don't think we would use any of them. But defoliation of the forests by low-yield atomic weapons could well be done. When you remove the foliage, you remove the cover." To still the international tempest that followed this remark, Goldwater had to issue the usual denials and clarifications.[82] But on one essential point he remained steadfast. Give the generals a free hand, he said in July, and they will bring victory in Vietnam.[83]

If he had been privy to its secret deliberations, Goldwater would have perceived his differences with the administration to be less than he imagined. In the spring of 1964 Johnson's advisers were reluctantly concluding that sooner or later, to save South Vietnam, the U.S. would have to bomb North Vietnam. The Joint Chiefs preferred sooner; civilian officials preferred later. But all agreed on one point: the time had come for the president to ask Congress for a Southeast Asia resolution authorizing escalation in advance. Johnson was not yet ready to go even this far. On June 15, 1964, National Security Adviser McGeorge Bundy circulated a White House memo calling only for vigorous application of current policy. It concluded, "Defense of U.S. interests is possible, within these limits, over the next six months." In six months, of course, the election would be over.[84]

As a political issue, Vietnam had, for Johnson, both its uses and its dangers. On the one hand, Goldwater's warlike talk enabled the president to run as the peace candidate. On the other, the inconclusive character of the war lent point to the senator's charges of timidity. The dilemma was inconvenient but, thanks to unanticipated events in the war theater, not insoluble. Shortly after 10 A.M., Washington time, August 4, 1964, the destroyer *U.S.S. Maddox* reported from the Gulf of Tonkin that she, along with the *C. Turner Joy*, was under North Vietnamese torpedo attack. Seeing his opportunity, Johnson wasted no time in grasping it. By noon, he had decided to retaliate against North Vietnam with a one-shot air raid which would accomplish a variety of purposes. It would constitute that warning blow favored by his civilian advisers in the spring, provide an occasion to send Congress a Southeast Asia resolution, and refute Goldwater's accusation of weakness. Late that night, grim-faced on TV, Johnson announced that American planes were heading for North Vietnamese military targets. The next day he submitted to Congress the famous Gulf of Tonkin Resolution, later described by the administration, not without reason, as "the functional equivalent" of a declaration of war. Only two senators, Wayne Morse and Ernest Gruening, voted against it.[85]

The administration was less than candid in portraying the Tonkin Gulf incident to Congress and the public.[86] Johnson described the *Maddox* as being on routine patrol in international waters. In fact, the *Maddox* was a spy ship that had violated the twelve-mile limit claimed by Communist countries. Johnson characterized the attack on the *Maddox* and *Turner Joy* as unprovoked. In fact, these ships had become enmeshed in a covert operation to bombard North Vietnamese coastal targets, an operation orchestrated by the U.S. but carried out by the South Vietnamese. Johnson gave no hint of doubt that attacks on the American ships had actually occurred. In fact, messages from the *Maddox* in midafternoon discounted much of the evidence on which the first attack reports were based. Johnson had proceeded with his retaliatory strikes despite a shaky case because they suited his immediate purpose, not the least of which was to land a blow on Barry Goldwater.

After passage of the Gulf of Tonkin Resolution, Johnson's war policy commanded a temporary national consensus, and Goldwater discussed Vietnam only infrequently. Goldwater did create a minor stir in October when he said that if elected he would ask General Eisenhower "to go to South Vietnam and report back to me on the situation." Not even Eisenhower thought much of that idea.[87] Johnson, too, would have been better off to remain silent. On September 7, 1964, he again rejected secret military recommendations for immediate air attacks against North Vietnam. But, as the Pentagon Papers later revealed, top officials were now firmly convinced "that some form of additional and continuous pressure should be exerted against North Vietnam" in the near future.[88] Knowing that he might have to escalate, Johnson nonetheless found the temptation to run as the peace candidate irresistible. "There are those that may say you ought to go north and drop bombs, to try to wipe out the supply lines, and they think that would escalate the war," he said in Eufaula, Oklahoma. "We don't want our American boys to do the fighting for Asian boys. We don't want to get involved in a nation with 700 million people and get tied down in a land war in Asia."[89] In Kentucky two weeks later he said, "If . . . you seek no larger war, and you don't want to pull out and run home, the only thing you can do is what we are doing."[90] And before an audience of editors in New Hampshire: "We are not going north and we are not going south."[91] The price in future credibility that Johnson paid to win the nondebate on Vietnam would prove, in the long run, absurdly high.

All that counted in November was that Johnson, who had begun the campaign determined to pull off a historic landslide, actually did it. Thanks in good part to Barry Goldwater, Johnson polled 61 percent of the popular vote and carried 44 states. The voters rejected Goldwater personally, viewing him as a dangerous and shallow man; and they rejected him ideologically, finding his conservatism merely cranky in an era of so many liberal good works. "To the extent that Goldwater was interpreted along the lines that he wished to be understood—that is ideologically—he suffered considerably as a consequence," one public opinion survey reported.[92] The only states Goldwater carried, besides Arizona, were states deep in the heart of Dixie—Mississippi, Louisiana, Alabama, Georgia, and South Carolina. Seven other states of the Old Confederacy, with the majority of the region's electoral votes, went for LBJ.

To achieve so crushing a victory, Johnson had to carry not only the traditional Democratic constituencies but Republican ones as well. A majority of white Protestants, suburbanites, and Midwest farmers went for the Democrats in 1964.[93] For Johnson, the sweetest returns of all came from Wall Street. The nation's corporate elite, abandoning its traditional preference for the GOP, voted for the party that had stimulated sales, fueled profits, and lowered corporate taxes. An estimated 60 percent or more of the Business Council—the semi-official link between the corporations and the government—favored LBJ.[94] The lion's share of the big contributions flowed into his campaign coffers.[95] And on September 3 a group of corporate leaders met in the White House to organize a business committee for Johnson's re-election. Its forty-five founding members included Henry Ford II, Edgar Kaiser of Kaiser Aluminum, Joseph Block of Inland Steel, two members of Eisenhower's Cabinet, and several New York bankers.[96] Corporate liberalism paid big dividends for the Democrats at last.

As a result of the all-embracing coalition he had fashioned, Johnson's legitimacy was established beyond dispute, his majorities in Congress were now overwhelming, and his mandate to proceed with the work of liberalism was clear. It was Johnson's intention, as he prepared for his own term, fully to realize the opportunity now his. He would be the champion of the poor and the black, the president who made the free-enterprise system hum as it never had before, and the prophet who would usher in an era when the quality of life would transcend the Gross National Product as a source of national concern. No one, least of all Johnson himself, could have foretold his true fate—which was to preside over the unraveling of America.

CHAPTER 6

War, Inflation, and Farewell to Keynes

I

PRESIDENT Johnson's inaugural address, January 20, 1965, was hardly a great state paper. Critics variously described it as flat, bland, muddy, and dull, and wondered how a speech so short could seem so interminable in delivery. Still, in its optimistic appraisal of American possibilities the inaugural faithfully reflected the mood of the time. "Is our world gone?" the president asked. "We say farewell. Is a new world coming? We welcome it, and we will bend it to the hopes of man."[1] Liberals, in particular, were afflicted with euphoria. Johnson's programs had received thunderous endorsement at the polls. Keynesian management had apparently propelled sales, profits, and wages to delirious heights. The Democratic party had increased its majority by thirty-eight seats in the House, and the machinery of Congress was the president's to command. "Don't stay up late," Johnson told revelers as he departed from the Inaugural Ball. "There's work to be done. We're on our way to The Great Society."[2]

In the remarkable year that followed, Johnson confirmed his reputation for parliamentary genius. Reform measures in profusion emanated from the White House, and one by one the president coaxed, wheedled, or rammed them through Congress. According to the tally of Eric Goldman, the Princeton historian who served as Johnson's liaison with the intellectuals, it took just 87 days to pass the education bill, 204 days for Medicare, 142 days for the Voting Rights Act.[3] Passing bills became an end in itself, and as the list grew, the president took immense pride in its sheer length. "Working in the White House during this period produced on occasion an almost eerie feeling," Goldman recalled. "The legislation rolled through the House and Senate in such profusion and so methodically that you seemed part of some vast, overpowering machinery, oiled to purr."[4]

But the legislative achievements did not produce presidential peace of mind. Johnson was haunted by the knowledge that the reform fad would soon end, that his accomplishments did not ignite the same wild enthusiasm in the country that FDR's had thirty years before, and worst of all, that his programs were more admired than he was.[5] Widespread distrust of his character was mainly Johnson's own fault, since so much of it originated in his inability to speak the simple truth. By 1965 everybody in America, it seemed, was talking about Johnson's "credibility gap."[6] On the president's orders, his doctor had reported that he drank only bourbon, when all Washington knew he drank only scotch. He insisted before his gall-bladder operation that he had no other medical problems, though he had a kidney stone which also had to be removed. He justified his military intervention in the Dominican Republic in April 1965 partly on grounds that innocent people had been beheaded by insurgents and that the U.S. ambassador had phoned him from under an embassy desk, bullets whizzing through the windows. There were no beheadings and no bullets.[7] And in June 1965, columnist Arthur Krock expressed the prevailing view when he accused Johnson of cloaking each of his escalatory moves in Vietnam with intentionally "evasive rhetoric."[8]

Vietnam—this was the main reason for the president's anxious mood at the apparent zenith of his political career. The worsening crisis in this small country 10,000 miles away was becoming his obsession. In January 1965, 20,000 American military personnel were serving in Vietnam, advising the South Vietnamese Army on how to fight the war. The Vietcong were winning anyway. In February, Johnson initiated air attacks against North Vietnam on the theory that pressure on the North would restrain the Vietcong in the South. Rolling Thunder, as the air campaign was called, failed badly. In March, Johnson began sending combat troops to South Vietnam, principally to guard military bases but also to serve as a reserve in case of emergency. The Vietcong were not intimidated, and the South Vietnamese did less fighting than before.

By early June 1965 the military and political situations in South Vietnam were rapidly deteriorating.[9] On the 7th day of the month General William Westmoreland, U.S. military commander in South Vietnam, privately asked for large ground reinforcements to "take the fight to the V.C."[10] Recognizing that to honor this request would be to transform Vietnam into an American war, senior officials debated options for more than a month. On July 28, 1965, at a tense news conference, Johnson said, "We did not choose to be the guardians at the gate, but there is no one else." Consequently, he was ordering an immediate increase in U.S. troop strength in Vietnam from 75,000 to 125,000, with additional men to be sent as requested.[11] Responding to a reporter's question, Johnson refused to acknowledge that the mission of American forces was changing.[12] It was another of his deliberately misleading replies.

There is no doubt that one of the war's casualties was Lyndon Johnson. Vietnam cut short the rush to the Great Society, smashed his consensus, widened the credibility gap, and made him one of the most hated chief executives in a hundred years. Not the least of the war's consequences for the nation Johnson struggled to govern was the Great Inflation, which intensified as the war proceeded and endured long after it was over. The public feared inflation more than the economists did, feared it enough by 1966 to rate it behind only the war and the race crisis among the nation's problems, feared it so much that any politician associated with its ravages was bound to suffer stern rebuke. At the beginning of 1965, Johnson had promised to bend the world to the hopes of man. Not too much later he discovered that he could not even bend the economy to the hopes of the voters.

II

The Great Inflation damaged not only the economy but the reputation of the economists who presumed to manage it. They had come to Washington in 1961, seeking converts to Keynes. They had seen their labors of persuasion crowned by passage of the 1964 tax cut, which wrote the Keynesian multiplier into national policy. And they had conquered most unbelief by mid-decade when the prosperity they prophesied actually materialized. But, as it says in Proverbs, "Pride goeth before destruction, and an haughty spirit before a fall."

The turning point for the economy, as for so much else in the decade, occurred during the fiscal year coinciding with Year One of Johnson's ground war—July 1, 1965 to June 30, 1966. As this year approached, most Americans were bullish. Unemployment stood at 4.5 percent, prices were rising at the politically acceptable rate of 1.6 percent annually, and private investment was advancing briskly. When, in May 1965, J. K. Galbraith described the Keynesian Revolution as one of the "great modern accomplishments in social design,"[13] he was merely retailing the latest conventional wisdom. But privately Gardner Ackley, the chief Keynesian in the White House, was not rejoicing. A University of Michigan economist noted for unflappable calm and professional caution, Ackley had joined the Council of Economic Advisers in 1962 and become its chairman when Walter Heller resigned after the 1964 election. Though he lacked Heller's ingratiating public personality, Ackley, too, possessed qualities esteemed by presidents—brains, loyalty, conciseness, and political savvy. And he, no less than Heller, regarded full employment as the ultimate end of policy, which was why his mood was somber in the spring of 1965. The true state of things was being obscured "by an artificial glow," Ackley told the president in May. The effects of the 1964 tax cut were wearing off, the economy was going to stall out short of full employment, and the unemployment rate might climb back to 5.5 percent within a year. The time had come, he urged, to begin considering a new round of tax cuts in 1966.[14]

Pessimism remained Ackley's mood until July 28, 1965, when Johnson announced his decision to dispatch ground troops to Vietnam. The president offered no estimates of the costs of escalation on this occasion, and he skillfully dodged a question about whether "down the road a piece the American people may have to face the problem of guns or butter."[15] Evasion suited Johnson's political purpose, but he could not have knowledgeably answered the question even if he had wanted to. Concerned as always with secrecy, he had proceeded into the Vietnam quagmire without taking his economic advisers into his confidence. Ackley immediately sought his own sources of information and within two days of Johnson's announcement submitted his unsolicited view of the new situation.

"The current thinking in DOD [Department of Defense], as relayed to me by Bob McNamara on a super-confidential basis," Ackley wrote Johnson on July 30, 1965, "points to a gradual and modest build-up of expenditures and manpower." Ackley could scarcely contain his pleasure at this intelligence. He had wanted a dose of fiscal stimulus, and thanks to the war, he was going to get it. "We are certainly not saying that a Vietnam crisis is just what the doctor ordered for the American economy in the next 12 months. But on a coldly objective analysis, the over-all effects are most likely to be favorable to our prosperity." The upward creep of prices might accelerate a bit during the next year, Ackley admitted, but the Council's wage-price guideposts could help contain inflationary pressures. No tax increase to finance the war would be needed unless costs got "into the $10 billion range"—a possibility that he termed "remote." In view of the economy's rapid growth in productive capacity, Ackley foresaw ample room "for both more butter, and if needed, more guns."[16]

Ackley's buoyant forecast derived from McNamara's assurances that the costs of the war over the next year would be modest. In a way, they were. The United States had a large standing army in 1965 and a vast store of military supplies. The cost of shifting part of this existing force to Vietnam, which principally occupied the military in the war's early stages, was relatively small. Indeed, actual federal expenditures for Vietnam in Year One of the war totaled only $6 billion,[17] approximately the fiscal stimulus deemed appropriate by the Council to resume the march to full employment.

The great imponderable, as the buildup got underway, was prices. In view of prevailing economic doctrine, Ackley had to take the problem seriously. In 1958 an economist named A. W. Phillips had demonstrated a statistical relationship between unemployment and wages. When unemployment fell, wages—hence prices— rose.[18] This relationship, enshrined in the textbooks as the Phillips Curve, described only too well the nation's last inflationary episode. In the mid-1950s when unemployment had fallen to almost 4 percent, prices increased 3 percent annually, enough to send shivers of fear through the body politic. The task of policy, as the Council saw it in the early sixties, was to achieve a more favorable trade-off between unemployment and prices—namely, 4 percent unemployment with a 2 percent inflation rate.[19]

Gearing up in the fall of 1965 to reshape the Phillips Curve, the Council located the probable source of inflationary danger not in excess demand fueled by the war, but in monopoly. When markets tightened, big unions and corporations could exploit their discretionary power over wages and prices by raising them. This was "cost-push" inflation, which most economists blamed for the upward trend of prices in the mid-fifties. In 1962, anticipating future cost-push outbreaks, the Council had devised a handy standard for measuring the social responsibility of wage and price decisions. According to the Council's famed guideposts, if wages rose no faster than output per worker, labor costs per unit would remain constant, and corporations would ordinarily have no excuse to raise prices. Since long-run output had been rising by 3.2 percent a year, the Council implicitly argued that wages too should rise no more than 3.2 percent. Even before the war's escalation, the administration had begun rigorously applying "moral suasion" to obtain guidepost compliance from business and labor. Immediately after the war's escalation in mid-1965, the guideposts became the main weapon in Ackley's battle with the Phillips Curve.[20]

The big test for the guideposts that year, as in 1962, was steel. Ackley wrote Johnson in June that even though the deadline for current wage bargaining in the industry was not until September 1, the administration should begin developing a strategy. "If the steel settlement is close to guideposts, and the companies hold the price line, then industrial prices generally can't move up very much," he said.[21] When steel talks broke down on August 29, 1965, the Council met the crisis by deploying its ultimate weapon—the president himself. In a virtuoso display of the "Johnson treatment," Johnson summoned both sides to Washington, virtually held them prisoner in the White House, appealed in person for a noninflationary settlement on behalf of our boys in Vietnam, sent in his own proposal for a settlement, and paced the alley outside the Executive Office Building, waiting for the final word. At 6:30 P.M. on September 3, an exultant president appeared on TV to announce a wage increase for steel workers estimated by the Council to be exactly 3.2 percent.[22] After following up this success with equally dramatic tactics against an aluminum price rise in November, the Council pursued the policy of moral suasion far into 1966.

"As long as total demand in the economy remains clearly within our overall production potential, guideposts can make a useful contribution to price stability," Ackley told Johnson on November 13, 1965.[23] The qualification was crucial. Moral suasion might restrain the greed of unions and corporations; it could not repeal the law of supply and demand. If aggregate demand outstripped supply, prices would rise, in which case workers would inevitably smash the guideposts. For to accept a wage increase of, say, 3 percent when the inflation rate was 3 percent, would be to receive no wage increase at all. The guideposts were obviously only as good as the Council's belief that demand still had a way to go to catch up with supply—Vietnam spending notwithstanding.

Throughout the fall of 1965 the Council clung to its optimistic assessment. When Federal Reserve chairman William McChesney Martin argued for higher interest rates to slow expansion, Ackley wrote the president, "We see no need for sedatives."[24] In late November Ackley thought that price rises in the next twelve months "could well be smaller" than in the past twelve.[25] It would be "premature," he said, "to conclude that even our interim goal of 4 percent unemployment is just around the corner."[26] On December 2 Ackley dismissed fears of a runaway boom by telling the president, "We remain determined to make policy on the basis of facts not nightmares."[27]

One day later, December 3, 1965, when the Council got an advance look at the government's survey of business investment, nightmare became fact. Businessmen had substantially revised upward their investment plans, throwing the administration's expectations into disarray.[28] On December 4 Johnson's advisers finally told him, "We are in danger of too much steam."[29] Indeed, a tremendous boom had been gathering force for months—as the economic statistics for December were to establish beyond any doubt. Unemployment that month fell to 4.1 percent, virtually the Council's goal; consumer prices rose 0.4 percent, the highest December increase since the Korean War; and GNP was galloping out of control.[30] The genie of inflation had escaped the bottle.

Once it caught the economy's true drift, the Council attempted to switch course. Johnson was already at work on the budget for the next fiscal year, beginning July 1, 1966. In mid-December 1965, he asked his economists a question. Given that spending this fiscal year, as measured by the conventional administrative budget, would be $100 billion, what would happen if next year's expenditures reached $110 billion or $115 billion? Ackley replied, "If the budget is $115 billion, there is little question in my mind that a significant tax increase will be needed to prevent an intolerable degree of inflationary pressure." Even if the budget was $110 billion, he still thought "a tax increase would probably be necessary."[31] That same day, another of Johnson's Keynesian advisers, Budget Director Charles Schultze, urged a tax increase of $5 billion.[32] Less spending by taxpayers would mean less overall demand and a reduction in inflationary pressure. If fiscal policy could revive an economy in the doldrums, it could just as successfully restore calm in an episode of hyperactivity. Or so Johnson's Keynesian advisers reasoned.

Johnson now confronted one of the most difficult decisions of his presidency. To squeeze an unpopular tax increase from a reluctant Congress, he would have to wrap himself in the flag and frankly ask for a war tax. But, if he did so, conservatives would enforce austerity on his Great Society programs, and liberals would have additional evidence that the war was hurting America.[33] In his notorious guns and butter budget submitted to Congress on January 24, 1966, Johnson resolved the dilemma by a combination of wish projection and deceit. Johnson estimated total expenditures for the coming fiscal year at $112.8 billion, with $10.3 billion earmarked for Vietnam. Except for a temporary reinstatement of some excise taxes, he refrained from requesting a tax increase. And he unblushingly described his budget as consistent with "an environment of strong but noninflationary economic growth."[34] Johnson did not say that his own economists disagreed with him. And he left to Secretary McNamara the disagreeable task of informing Congress that official estimates of Vietnam costs assumed the war's end by June 30, 1967.[35] No one expected that, least of all McNamara. In fact, in the fiscal year beginning July 1, 1966, budgetary expenditures would be not $112.8 but in excess of $126 billion, with Vietnam costing not $10 billion but almost $20 billion.[36] In the Keynesian version of history, this budget, with its refusal to raise taxes, opened the floodgates to the Great Inflation.

Throughout the winter of 1966 the tremendous boom, first detected in December, kept accelerating. Real growth, termed "phenomenal" by the Council, exceeded an annual rate of 7 percent, and unemployment dropped to 3.8 percent, the lowest rate since Korea.[37] By March Johnson was besieged by Keynesians, columnists, and some congressmen demanding that he raise taxes. It was a topic that could be counted on to turn him surly. In the 1950s he said, you couldn't walk in any hostess's home without them saying,

" 'What do you think about McCarthy?' . . . Now it is, 'What do you think about inflation?' "[38]

But once again the economy fooled the economists. In the spring of 1966 growth in GNP slowed down, unemployment stopped falling, and industrial production no longer increased faster than capacity. Thanks to unexpected restraint in consumer spending, the temperature of the economy had cooled. The reason: taxes had increased substantially after all. A previously scheduled rise in social security taxes had taken place in January; and in March Congress passed the "bits and pieces" tax program that Johnson had submitted earlier in the year—higher excise taxes, improved withholding on personal income tax, and accelerated collection of corporate taxes.[39] Though the investment boom proceeded, the saner pace of activity elsewhere eased the worst fears of Johnson's economists. Their pleas for higher taxes continued, but not their sense of urgency.[40] Nevertheless, as the new fiscal year began in July 1966—Year Two of Johnson's ground war—one statistic dominated all the others. The consumer price index had risen 2.5 percent in the past twelve months.[41] Low by later standards, this rate signaled to the public the end of several years of price stability and awakened widespread anxieties.

It had been a hard year for the president's economists. Their forecasts had been off the mark, their advice had been ignored, and prices had risen more than they had gambled on. Still, after the fact, they could plausibly account for events. Year One of Johnson's war had generated too much demand in relation to supply, and prices had gone up. The $6 billion direct cost of Vietnam did not, by itself, trigger inflation. In fact, according to the national income accounts budget, which gave a better picture of the government's fiscal impact on the economy than did the conventional administrative budget,[42] government revenue had risen just as fast as defense expenditures. The national income accounts budget showed not a deficit but a $1 billion surplus for the fiscal year, compared to $2 billion the previous year.[43] It was the indirect effects of war spending, the Council argued, that propelled the economy out of control. Businessmen, interpreting escalation to mean that good times would roll on, had gone on an investment binge.[44] If Johnson had raised taxes in time, the inflationary effects of war spending and booming investment would have been offset, aborting the Great Inflation. This was the Keynesian story, which, though consistent with events, was not the only story possible.

III

In the late 1960s Milton Friedman emerged as one of the most influential intellectuals in the United States. Diminutive, combative, and brilliant enough to win a Nobel Prize for economics, Friedman spent most of his academic life dueling with liberals and Keynesians. In a sense Friedman's economics were incidental to his philosophy. Valuing individual liberty as the highest good, he cherished the free market as its best defense. Accordingly, Friedman was bound to dispute two of Keynes's central doctrines—that economic instability originated in the private sector and that government should manage aggregate demand to cure the problem. To refute the Keynesians, Friedman not only attacked the logic of their system; he championed a rival explanation of reality. Rehabilitating and revising the ancient quantity theory of money, he used it to argue that economic instability originated in the public sector and that government could best serve the economy by remaining neutral. Friedman's remarkable success in popularizing the quantity theory in the Johnson years had three causes: his skills as an advocate, the simplicity of his theory, and the stumbling performance of his Keynesian adversaries.

Friedman's position was often misstated as "only money matters." In the long run, he said, the only factors that really mattered in determining output were real ones, like technological change, the rate of savings, and relations among nations.[45] But in the short run, money possessed a unique power to throw smoothly running economies out of gear. In the United States the Federal Reserve, familiarly known as the Fed, regulated the money supply. When the Fed decided to increase the rate of growth of money, output and then prices rose. When the Fed decided to put on the monetary brakes, recession inevitably followed. It took anywhere from six to eighteen months for a change in money to affect the business cycle; but despite the long and variable lags Friedman never doubted the causal short-run relationship between money and output.[46]

Why was money so potent? Friedman's answer to this question hinged on his empirical claim that "people seem to be extraordinarily stubborn about the real amount of money that they want to hold."[47] For example, say the public wishes to hold money (narrowly defined here as currency plus checking accounts) equivalent to seven months' income. For any one of a number of reasons, the Fed decides to expand the money supply by purchasing bonds from dealers with checks drawn on itself and subsequently deposited in the banking system. As the banks spend or lend these additions to their reserves, the public comes to hold more money—equivalent, say, to eight months' income. To restore their money holdings to the desired level, individuals begin spending their excess balances —on consumer goods or equities or by paying off debts. Some of the increased spending will translate initially into increased output; but if monetary growth is prolonged and significant, all of it will eventually translate into higher prices. For no matter how hard individuals try to reduce their money balances, collectively they cannot possibly succeed, since one person's expenditures are another's receipts. But, as prices rise, the real value of money falls— until finally the public finds itself once again holding money balances whose purchasing power is equivalent to seven months' income. In the end, then, the only lasting consequence of an increased rate of monetary growth is price inflation. Friedman believed that if only the Fed would permit the money supply to grow at about the same rate as output, without starts and stops, the main source of economic instability would be eliminated and so would the main excuse for government intervention.

Keynesian giants including James Tobin, Paul Samuelson, and Walter Heller entered the lists to joust with Friedman. They did not believe, as he did, that the demand for money was stable. They denied that the money supply was determined solely by the monetary authorities, stressed the failure of quantity theorists (also called monetarists) to agree on which of the various definitions of money was the important one, and scoffed at a model that could not account for wide variations in lags between money and output. As scientists, they were particularly offended that Friedman's theorizing was so "casual." Indeed, even his disciples referred to his "black box." Money went in, and income and prices came out, but what happened inside remained a mystery.[48]

In truth, both the Keynesians and the quantity theorists were less like scientists than they were akin to religious prophets. The competing models of reality they advanced in the 1960s relied mainly on unproved premises and lacked satisfactory validation. Despite the passionate loyalty each side felt for its own system of belief, events would, in time, damage the credibility of both. Only as critics of one another did they prove entirely sound. But in the Johnson years Friedman had the advantage. Because Keynesians controlled policy, he could act as gadfly, pointing out the logical errors of his opponents and winning converts as their policies failed. In addition, his model proved more successful, at least for a while, in accounting for events. Not the least telling of his points was that the quantity of money mattered a whole lot more than Johnson's economists, for example, had once believed.

Predictably, Friedman's account of the Great Inflation differed from that of the Council. "Inflation is always and everywhere a monetary phenomenon, resulting from and accompanied by a rise in the quantity of money relative to output," he said.[49] Friedman traced the origins of inflation not to Johnson's 1965 escalation or to the accompanying investment boom, but to the decisions of the Fed some years before to step up monetary growth. In his famous letter of October 1965 to the Federal Reserve Board Friedman surveyed recent monetary history and predicted its consequences. From August 1962 through August 1965, he said, money growth had increased significantly faster than the historic average. Printing money faster had so far translated into higher output because people had been expecting stable prices and because excess capacity in the economy existed. But, he warned, "past experience suggests that a continuation of the present rate of [monetary growth] . . . is not indefinitely sustainable without a price rise."[50]

The villain in Friedman's story, then, was the Fed. This was ironic. No man in public life had spoken more frequently and emotionally against inflation than the Fed's chairman, William McChesney Martin, Jr. Past president of the New York Stock Exchange, Martin was a Democrat appointed by Harry Truman in 1951. He liked to play his daily game of tennis, keep in personal touch with financial markets, and make policy according to his intuitive feel of conditions.[51] In Friedman's view Martin was the classic example of the misguided money manager who regarded interest rates, not the quantity of money, as the proper measure of whether money was easy or tight. Interest rates were inching up in 1965, so Martin concluded that money was tightening. Actually, rising rates stemmed from the brisk demand by business borrowers for investment loans, a demand that the Fed's metaphorical printing presses all too willingly accommodated.[52]

On December 5, 1965, two days after the government's survey of current business investment had confirmed his premonitions of inflation, Martin took what seemed to him to be the logical step. To discourage borrowing he announced a rise in the discount rate (the interest rate the Fed charges on loans to member banks) from 4 percent to 4½ percent. Martin's action infuriated both Lyndon Johnson, who opposed high interest rates on populist principle, and Gardner Ackley, who resented the Fed's failure to consult the administration beforehand. In fact, all that Martin did was ratify the upward movement of interest rates originating in the market.[53] While skirmishing with the Fed over interest rates, the White House ignored the recent ominous trend in the money supply. From June 1965 to May 1966, money would grow at the exuberant annual rate of more than 6 percent—compared to a 2.8 percent historic average. In Friedman's view, the Fed was the true engine of inflation and did not even know it.[54]

If Friedman was right about inflation, then not only Martin but the president's economists were wrong. Friedman thought the Keynesians were wrong, for example, to take seriously the threat of cost-push inflation. No such phenomenon could logically exist, he declared. Suppose the steel workers exact a wage increase that forces steel companies to raise prices. Two outcomes are possible. Demand for steel declines at the higher price, leading to unemployment in the industry; or steel consumers pay the higher prices, leaving them less to spend for other goods. Either way, the inflationary effects of higher steel prices are offset by increased unemployment or perhaps by lower prices in competitive sectors. A rise in steel prices could nudge up the price indexes only temporarily—unless, said Friedman, the Fed stepped in to restore the former level of output and employment by printing more money. Then, as always, the true cause of inflation would be an increase in money relative to output.[55]

Whether or not Friedman was right about cost-plus inflation, all economists agreed that it was not the cause of the initial inflationary spurt of 1965–1966. Price increases began in raw materials, services, and non-unionized industries, not in sectors characterized by concentrated economic power. "Market pressures—not monopoly power—made the difference between the good price record of the early sixties and its deterioration in 1966," wrote Council member Arthur Okun later.[56]

And if Friedman was right about inflation, then the president's economists were also wrong in believing that fiscal policy could counter it. As good Keynesians, they had advocated a tax increase in December 1965, theorizing that reduced spending by taxpayers would reduce pressure on prices. More bad logic, said Friedman. If taxes rose, taxpayers would, indeed, have less to spend. But increased federal revenue would also reduce the need of government to borrow from the public. Funds that would otherwise have been lent to the Treasury would now be available for more lending or spending in the private economy, offsetting the deflationary effect of higher taxes. Friedman conceded one possible deflationary consequence of a tax increase. Reduced borrowing by the government would lower interest rates; and lower rates in turn might induce people to lend less and hold more of their income in the form of idle cash. To the extent this happened, aggregate demand in fact would fall. But, believing as he did that people's desire to hold money was stable, Friedman expected the impact of lower interest rates on lending to be slight.[57] There was only one way to reduce inflation, Friedman said, and that was to slow down the rate of growth of the money supply.

The curious thing was how little attention the quantity theory attracted during the initial phase of the Great Inflation. The financial press virtually ignored money growth. The Fed conducted policy with blithe unconcern for its rate of increase. And the Council of Economic Advisers, though theoretically committed to the view that monetary policy could affect aggregate demand through interest rates, treated money as a distinctly secondary topic. Friedman noted that in the chapter on prices in its 1966 *Annual Report,* the Council referred only twice to monetary policy and managed to avoid using the word "money" at all. This, he said is "strictly comparable to the way a rigid Puritan writing a book about love might have handled 'sex.' "[58]

I V

The quantity theory came into its own in the fiscal year beginning July 1, 1966, and ending June 30, 1967—Year Two of Johnson's ground war. As the year began, Keynesians were once again gloomy about prices. Though the economy was straining against capacity, fiscal policy would be expansionary, showing a $7 billion deficit in the national income accounts budget, the largest in years.[59] Given their premises, Johnson's economists produced an inevitable fore-cast, namely, excess demand and 4 percent inflation by mid-1967.[60] The Council took no note that over at the Fed Chairman Martin had turned off the money spigot.

Deeply worried by deficit spending and feverish business invest-ment, Martin switched course in the spring of 1966 and decided to kill the boom himself. Specifically, he curbed credit by drastically reducing the supply of new reserves to the commercial banks. For quantity theorists the chief consequence of Martin's tough new line was this: the money supply, which had been growing at a 6 percent annual rate for almost a year, grew not at all from May through December 1966.[61] If money was as important as Friedman said, the economy faced dangers quite different from those anticipated by the budget-conscious Keynesians. As it turned out, danger took the form of the famous Credit Crunch of 1966, the first in a series of crunches that periodically racked the economy over the next dec-ade.

The shortage of credit, created by the Fed, sent ever-widening shock waves through the financial world in the summer of 1966, nearly causing its ruin.[62] First hit were the thrift institutions (savings and loan associations and mutual savings banks), which provided the major source of money for the home-building industry. In April 1966, for the first time in the post–World War II era, commercial banks began paying higher interest rates (5½ percent) on savings deposits than did the thrifts. Because their funds were tied up in long-term, low-interest-rate mortgages, the thrifts were not earning enough to pay their own depositors competitive rates. Net deposits in thrift institutions stopped growing, and for a while it appeared that a large segment of the industry would go under. When the thrifts get squeezed, the home-building industry feels the pain. Mortgage money dried up, private nonfarm housing starts in the last half of 1966 fell to approximately 60 percent of what they had been in the similar period of 1965, and depression gripped the home-building industry.

By August 1966 the shortage of money was driving interest rates to levels unknown since the 1920s. The stock market went into a severe slump, and insurance companies were besieged by customers taking advantage of their legal right to borrow against their policies at interest rates now below the market. The commercial banks, desperate for money to lend their favorite customers and unable to replenish their reserves at the Fed, began selling off their large holdings of state and municipal bonds. As the price of municipals plummeted, state and local governments found it nearly impossible to find buyers for their long-term securities. By mid-August the commercial banks themselves had reached a crisis. Market rates edged above 5½ percent—the legal limit they could pay their depositors—and corporations began threatening to withdraw their large certificates of deposit. The banks had no choice except to curtail their loans. Now it was the turn of business to scream. For a few days it appeared that credit to finance American business might not be available at any rate of interest. The head of the New York Federal Reserve Bank reported that at the end of August "the financial community was experiencing growing and genuine fear of a financial panic."[63]

The resolution of the crisis came on September 1, 1966, in the form of an unprecedented letter from the Fed to its member banks.[64] The Fed called on the banks to moderate their business loans and to stop selling municipals. In return the Fed would re-open its discount window to cooperating banks. In other words, if banks would voluntarily ration credit, the Fed would ease up. Tension in financial markets diminished immediately.

In the fall of 1966, the volume of bank loans fell, interest rates eased, the market for municipals firmed, and thrift institutions foresaw brighter days. The pace of GNP growth slowed down, and the inflation rate did not speed up. Heaving a sigh of relief, Johnson's economists privately admitted in November 1966, "Monetary policy has done more than some of us expected it would or could."[65] The Council estimated that tight money had had about the same effect on the economy as the tax increase it had unsuccessfully urged on the president earlier in the year.[66] Reducing the quantity of money had, after a fashion, worked.

Among those critical of the Fed's performance was Milton Friedman. He had always said that too little was known about how monetary policy actually worked to use it for purposes of short-run stabilization. The Credit Crunch only confirmed his view. Though the Fed had jammed on the brakes to curb business investment, businessmen proved ingenious in finding new sources of credit outside the banks. Investment did slow down, but only because of bottlenecks in industrial construction and the producers' goods industry.[67] While the bludgeon of tight money missed business investment, it landed a nearly lethal blow on housing, whose depressed state had chiefly caused economic activity to moderate in the last half of 1966. This consequence of tight money the Fed had neither expected nor desired.

Once they were past the Credit Crunch, economists debated the effects of tight money in 1966 on output in 1967. In September 1966 Gardner Ackley, who was more impressed by the growing budget deficit than by the Fed's stringency, predicted resumption of excess demand and accelerating inflation.[68] Friedman, disregarding the budget and looking only at money, predicted a recession.[69] As money grew scarce, Friedman believed, individuals would hoard it to maintain their desired cash balances, thereby spending less and reducing output. The economy now became not merely a source of goods and services but a grand experiment to test the rival models of Keynesian and quantity theorists.

Friedman almost got his recession (defined as declining output in two successive quarters), but not quite. In the first quarter of calendar 1967, real GNP did not grow at all, and in the second quarter it rose slightly. For the full six months, output increased by only 1 percent. Friedman found consolation in the decline of industrial production over both quarters.[70] The "mini-recession" of 1967, as the press called it, embarrassed the Keynesians more than Friedman. Back in September 1966 they had been so worried about inflation that they had persuaded Congress to repeal the investment tax credit. In April 1967, fearful of a slump, they sheepishly asked for its immediate restoration.[71] In the midst of war, a big deficit, and 4 percent unemployment, the economy trod water for half a year. Prices, meanwhile, rose in Year Two of Johnson's ground war not by 4 percent, as Johnson's economists had predicted, but by 2.7 percent, approximately the same rate as the year before. Wholesale prices did not rise at all.[72] The quantity of money suddenly emerged as the hottest topic in the economics profession.

V

Secretary McNamara once budgeted the war in Vietnam to end by June 30, 1967. Instead, in July 1967, Year Three of Johnson's ground war began, with the United States sinking ever deeper into the quagmire. That same month the economy began reheating, and along with it White House fears of galloping inflation. Vietnam would cost $26.5 billion in the fiscal year just beginning. Unemployment would get down below 4 percent and stay there. And the national income accounts budget would show a huge $11.3 billion deficit.[73] At long last President Johnson decided he had to bite the fiscal bullet. He would request a tax increase, he informed his advisers in June, and if Congress refused to oblige him, he would ax to the bone his health and education programs.[74] In short, Johnson was in a mood to trade the Great Society, whose merits he hoped would assure him the good opinion of history, for a war that a growing number of his fellow citizens thought mad. Only more revenue from higher taxes could enable him to sustain, simultaneously, both Vietnam and reform.

On August 3, 1967, two years and five days after he launched the ground war, Johnson sent Congress a special message warning that the deficit ahead could ignite "a spiral of ruinous inflation." To curb private spending, ease pressure on prices, and incidentally restore his good standing among Keynesians, Johnson proposed a temporary 10 percent tax surcharge. Corporations and individuals would compute their income taxes under existing tax schedules and then add 10 percent. Johnson estimated that the surcharge would raise $6.3 billion in additional revenue for the current fiscal year—ending June 30, 1968.[75]

Friedman agreed with the administration's forecast of accelerating inflation, but not with its diagnosis or cure. As always in Friedman's world, the real problem was the blundering Fed. After having kept money too tight for the last eight months of 1966, Chairman Martin overreacted to the mini-recession by generously pumping reserves back into the banking system. From January through September 1967, the money supply (cash plus checking accounts) grew at the truly alarming rate of 8.2 percent. More inflation was bound to follow, Friedman said, unless the Fed came quickly to its senses.[76] As for the tax increase, Friedman stated once again the grounds for his opposition. Its result would be not only to decrease spending by taxpayers, but, by reducing government borrowing, to increase lendable funds available to private borrowers. More private borrowing would offset less taxpayer spending, and the net effect of the tax increase on aggregate demand would be inconsequential.

The administration's real problem was not Friedman but Wilbur Mills, the conservative Arkansas Democrat who chaired the House Ways and Means Committee, where all tax legislation must originate. In certain moods Johnson regarded the surcharge as essential to the survival of Western civilization. Mills was skeptical. Who really knew if the boom predicted by the economists would occur? And why was Johnson attacking the problem of the budget primarily from the revenue side, when expenditures were running wild? "It just seems to me like we are going to have to find some way to bring about reductions on the spending side to coincide . . . with increases in revenues if we are to . . . get any acceptance by the American people of a tax increase," Mills said.[77] In September 1967, while hearings on the surcharge were in progress, Mills offered the administration some private advice. Johnson should go on TV, explain that the nation had to choose between guns and butter, and announce he was choosing guns. If the administration cut domestic spending, Johnson could count on him to back a tax increase "all the way."[78]

This was hardly what Johnson had in mind. The point of raising taxes was to save his domestic reforms if he could, not to starve them. Urging Johnson to stand firm, Budget Director Charles Schultze told him in September 1967 that budget cuts to satisfy Mills "would have to be very heavy in education, health, housing, pollution, and poverty . . . reducing some programs to a shambles." Mills and his committee, said Schultze, "are playing 'chicken' in an eyeball-to-eyeball confrontation. . . . I think that if we are willing to take a strong and unyielding stand, they will blink first."[79] Johnson agreed. A few days later, when Treasury Secretary Henry Fowler conveyed the desire of leading committee members for a meeting, Johnson refused to see them. He knew what they would say, and he was not interested.[80]

But Mills did not blink either. On October 3, 1967, his committee shocked Johnson by voting twenty to five to lay aside the tax bill until both sides reached "an understanding on a means of implementing more effective expenditure reduction and controls."[81] There the matter rested until November 18, 1967, when the British devalued the pound, touching off a run on the dollar in international financial markets. Besides saving America from inflation, the tax surcharge now seemed vital to the dollar's rescue. Without the surcharge, Secretary Fowler argued, the price of American goods would continue to rise, exports would suffer, the balance-of-payments deficit would worsen, and foreigners holding dollars would rush to exchange them for American gold. On November 30, 1967,

Secretary Fowler returned to the Ways and Means Committee to offer a deal. The administration would cut spending by $4 billion this fiscal year if Mills would raise taxes.[82] Unimpressed, Mills recessed the hearings for the rest of the session.

When Mills reopened hearings in January 1968, the economy was lurching out of control. Growth in real GNP would soon reach an unsustainable 6½ percent (annual rate) and prices were rising 4 percent a year.[83] Still, according to Gallup, 80 percent of the public opposed paying more taxes. Mills listened attentively, even sympathetically, as administration witnesses testified to the lean and austere character of Johnson's new budget. But in the end he was still against them. Go back, he admonished the witnesses, and see if you can cut expenditures some more.[84] According to the *New York Times,* on hearing Mills deny them again, "Mr. Schultze clenched his jaw and softly threw his pencil down on the witness table. For just an instant, Secretary of the Treasury Henry H. Fowler buried his face in his hands."[85]

It was the Senate that moved to end the impasse. On April 2, 1968, that chamber took a minor tax bill sent over from the House and amended it to include both the 10 percent surcharge, which pleased Johnson, and a mandatory $6 billion cut in planned spending next fiscal year, which pleased Mills.[86] The bill then went to a House-Senate conference committee, where it languished for weeks, as the principals sought grounds for compromise. The main obstacle proved to be Johnson. He preferred no budget cuts next year, would sorrowfully accept a $4 billion cut if he had to, but was dead set against the Senate's $6 billion figure because he thought it would cripple the Great Society.[87]

Meanwhile, the economic boom was gathering force, and the weakness of the dollar was again threatening to bring the international monetary system down in ruins. William McChesney Martin told a meeting of newspaper editors on April 19, 1968, "The nation is in the midst of the worst financial crisis since 1931." On the 30th, Secretary Fowler told the U.S. Chamber of Commerce, "We are facing nothing less than a test of representative government in economic and financial affairs."[88] More weeks dragged by until Johnson, conceding he did not have the votes, ran up the white flag on expenditures. On June 28, 1968, too late to do any good in the fiscal year just ending and ten months after he proposed it, the president signed the Revenue and Expenditure Control Act, which enacted the 10 percent tax surcharge for one year and required the executive to slash planned expenditures by $6 billion—the sum Mills had desired all along.

In mid-1968, as Year Four of Johnson's war began, the revenue act inspired little joy in the White House. The mandatory spending cut was a blow not only to the president and his programs, but to the Keynesian economists who had for so long urged the tax increase. Fiscal restraint was one thing, fiscal overkill another. The combination of higher taxes and lower spending would cause one of the most dramatic swings in fiscal history—from an $11.3 billion deficit to a $2.7 billion surplus in one year.[89] The main burden of forecasting the consequences fell on Arthur Okun, who had become chairman of the Council of Economic Advisers after Johnson appointed Ackley ambassador to Italy in February 1968. Okun thought the revenue act would flatten the economy as well as inflation. In August 1968 he joined with the Secretary of the Treasury and the Budget Director to give the president some good news. The inflation rate would probably fall to 2 or 2½ percent next year, he said. Okun also had some bad news. GNP would grow by only 1 percent in the last half of 1968 and not at all during the six months following —with the result that unemployment might climb to 5 percent by December 1968. Only a continuing trend toward monetary ease "could prevent the expected pause from turning into a full-fledged recession."[90]

Fortunately, from Okun's point of view, the Fed was in an accommodating mood. Sharing the Council's fear that the revenue act was too much of a good thing, William McChesney Martin abandoned several months of sensible moderation and speeded up the presses to stimulate demand. From April to December 1968, the money supply grew at an annual rate of 8.5 percent. Once again, fiscal and monetary policy were pulling on opposite ends of the policy rope. Looking at the tight budget, Keynesians forecast a near recession and declining inflation. Looking at easy money, Friedman predicted rising prices.[91]

Okun waited through the summer of 1968 for the surcharge to weaken demand. Consumers ignored higher withholding rates and actually spent more. Okun admitted surprise.[92] In October Okun thought the economy had "embarked on a slowdown" decisive enough to improve "our price performance markedly over time."[93] Consumer spending did slow down in the last quarter of 1968 but not enough to flatten GNP. At the end of the year the economy was clearly in defiance of Okun's well-known expectations. He had predicted that by December 1968 growth in GNP would fall to 1 percent (annual rate), unemployment would rise to 5 percent, and inflation would come down toward 2½ percent. Instead, GNP was growing by 4 percent; unemployment dropped to 3.3 percent, the lowest point in the Vietnam era; and inflation, at 4.7 percent, was soaring.[94] Extended for an additional year, the tax surcharge never did work. The pace of GNP moderated in 1969 but unemployment remained low. When the surcharge finally expired in mid-1970, the inflation rate had climbed to 6½ percent.[95] Thanks to the surcharge fiasco, Johnson's economists left the government in January 1969 considerably more deflated than the economy.

Okun had plenty of leisure to ponder the surcharge episode during his exile at the Brookings Institution. Running his data through an econometric exercise in 1971, he obtained the surprising result that the surcharge had curbed consumption of nondurables just about as much as could reasonably be expected. Unfortunately, for reasons he neglected to explain, expenditures on autos, housing, and business investment had shown more strength than most economists had anticipated, canceling out the good effects of the surcharge. "Don't blame the medicine," Okun said, but the diagnosticians who had misread the "feverish" condition of the patient. Keynesians, take heart; fiscal policy worked after all.[96]

If the character of aggregate demand in 1968–1969 surprised Okun, it made a prophet out of Friedman. He had agreed with Okun that the surtax would indeed curb consumption by taxpayers. But he pointed out that by increasing federal revenues the surcharge would also reduce the need of the government to borrow. As a result, lendable funds available to private borrowers would increase, resulting in more spending on "construction, business investment, and the like."[97] The expenditures which had so confounded Okun were, for Friedman, the logical outcome of the surtax itself. Why, then, had inflation accelerated despite the massive shift of fiscal policy toward restraint? Because, said Friedman, the Fed was printing too much money. This was Friedman's story, and, not surprisingly, a growing number of concerned citizens were beginning to believe it.

Though Friedman's case against fiscal policy scored points, he overstated it. Fiscal policy did not matter much, he said. In fact,

Johnson's failure to raise taxes at the beginning of the war had been a mistake. The deficits he ran up had confronted the Fed with a painful dilemma: either it printed up money to finance the war, causing inflation; or it refused, risking credit crunches. No doubt the Fed's poor judgment at critical moments made a bad situation worse, and no doubt the Fed created serious problems as well as reacted to them. But its job would have been immeasurably easier, and its errors fewer, if the budget had been more nearly in balance and less subject to violent swings. The Keynesians had been right in pressing for an early tax increase—though not necessarily for the right reasons.

VI

It was among the public's most firmly held beliefs that inflation was a bad thing. When Gallup asked Americans in the fall of 1967 to name "the most urgent problem facing you and your family," an astounding 60 percent answered the "high cost of living."[98] At that time the inflation rate was still around 3 percent. Some economists shared the public's anxieties, arguing that inflation was a cruel tax that arbitrarily and unfairly robbed some and enriched others. Other economists, especially of the Keynesian variety, failed to understand why so many were so afraid.

Who had been helped by the inflation in the Johnson years and who hurt? Old people living on private pensions were clear losers. So were small savers, less because of inflation than because of the government's refusal to let banks pay competitive interest rates. And so, too, were steadily employed factory workers, whose real wages had stagnated.[99] But there were winners also, most notably poor Americans for whom the war in Vietnam was an inefficient but highly successful antipoverty program, the only one in the Johnson years that actually worked.

The war helped the poor, at least temporarily, mainly by increasing the demand for labor. The defense budget was $30 billion higher in 1968 than when the war began, an increase almost entirely attributable to Vietnam. These extra billions directly paid for 767,-000 more soldiers, 185,000 civilian government employees, and 1,472,000 jobs in defense production.[100] War spending, financed by the Fed, also unleashed excess demand for the products of the private sector and so indirectly generated further demand for labor.

Tight labor markets meant more rapid promotion for the working poor, new jobs for the unemployed poor, and more wage earners in the families of the poor. As employers scraped the bottom of the labor barrel, they bid up the wages of marginal workers—bid them up faster than the wages of skilled workers. Blacks made exceptionally large relative gains in these years. Median family income for blacks was 52 percent that of whites in 1959, 54 percent in 1965, and 60 percent in 1968. The war not only shoved millions above Johnson's fixed poverty line, it even temporarily reduced income inequality.[101]

Among the war's losers might be counted the nation's businessmen. The war brought an end to the spectacular profits of the decade's first half, as rising costs, especially labor costs, cut into profit margins. Labor's share of aftertax national income grew from 72.2 percent in 1966 to 77.5 percent in 1970; the share going to corporate profits fell from 10.6 percent to 7.2 percent.[102] Louis B. Lundborg, chairman of the board of the Bank of America, the largest bank in the world, said in 1970, "protestations of the new left to the contrary, the fact is that an end to the war would be good, not bad, for American business."[103] Lundborg was right.

"What's so bad about inflation?" a reviewer in the *New Republic* asked, after reading an essay on the subject by Arthur Okun. "Prices go up, but so do incomes. The nickel candy bar is no longer, but neither is the $1.25-an-hour hospital orderly or the $5000 per year teacher."[104] No less an authority than James Tobin was of similar mind. The Phillips Curve taught that the cost of reducing unemployment would be some degree of inflation. Because he, along with most liberals, had no policy objective higher than full employment, this was a cost Tobin was willing to pay. Once, the Council of Economic Advisers had hoped to achieve 4 percent unemployment with a 2 percent inflation rate. Toward the end of the Vietnam era Tobin admitted that the price of "full employment" might be a 4 or 5 percent annual inflation rate. But any attempt to reduce inflation would only wring out the economy and hurt the poor. "So," he concluded, "let us aim at the 4 percent unemployment rate . . . and accept the 4 percent inflation that comes with it."[105]

Friedman rejected this logic because he rejected the Phillips Curve. Phillips and Tobin believed that the trade-off between unemployment and inflation was permanent, that if unemployment fell to 4 percent and stayed there, prices would rise at a constant rate, say 4 percent annually. In his 1967 presidential address before the American Economic Association, Friedman introduced the concept of the "natural rate of unemployment," which he defined as the rate of unemployment that would exist if supply and demand were in balance at stable prices. Governments could attempt to peg the unemployment rate below the natural rate by pumping up aggregate demand, Friedman said. He conceded that for a while the policy would succeed: Prices would rise, and because workers did not anticipate inflation, wages would lag behind. As real wages fell, employers would have an incentive to hire more workers, lowering unemployment. Temporarily, the Phillips Curve described reality: prices rose, unemployment fell. But eventually workers would wise up to the higher price level and demand compensating wage increases. As real wages rose to their original level, unemployment would fall back to the natural rate. Everything would be the same as before, except that the price level would be higher. To reduce unemployment again, the government would have to inflate still more, which would work only until employees anticipated the new inflation rate. Contrary to the Phillips Curve—argued Friedman— the cost of pegging unemployment below the natural rate was not a constant, but an accelerating rate of inflation.[106]

Laymen had intuited from the beginning that a little inflation would lead to more, and that the higher the price level, the worse off they would be. Time proved them right. Inflation made winners of some, but society was one of the losers. By the late 1970s accelerating inflation discouraged savings, added to the risks of long-term investment, cut real transfer payments to the poor, destabilized financial markets, automatically siphoned off a growing proportion of national income to the federal government, and eroded social stability. By then, even Keynesians began to concede that inflation might be a bad thing after all.

VII

In the 1960s Keynesian economists went back to school. Testing their theories in the laboratory of the nation's economy, they obtained results that were something less than vindication. When the period ended, they had to rewrite their textbooks, taking account of recent experience and Friedman's critique. Calling themselves post-Keynesians, mainstream economists developed models so sophisticated that Heller's 1961 version of orthodoxy came to seem both archaic and naïve.[107] Even a partial list of revisions conveys some sense of the intellectual distance traveled.

On unemployment: Friedman's concept of "the natural unemployment rate" became widely accepted, replacing the older notion of "full employment." Retrospective calculations estimated the natural rate in the 1960s above 5 percent. Pegging unemployment at 4 percent, therefore, was bound to generate inflation.

On the Phillips Curve: Friedman was right in denying any permanent trade-offs between prices and unemployment. The cost of pegging unemployment below the natural rate would be accelerating inflation. For an illustrative case, the 1960s would do.

On the Keynesian multiplier: In its 1963 Annual Report the Council of Economic Advisers explained how one dollar of a tax cut (with no cut in federal spending) would generate two dollars of GNP. Friedman countered that, unless the Fed financed the deficit by printing money faster, the Treasury would have to borrow from the public, driving up interest rates. Higher interest rates were prominent among the reasons why Friedman believed that the stimulating effects of a pure fiscal policy would be "crowded out." Post-Keynesians, repudiating the Council's simple version of the multiplier, conceded that some crowding out would occur. It would be partial, however, and fiscal policy still contained some kick.

On the business cycle: In the sixties Keynesians on the Council had paid scant attention to the quantity of money as a determinant of output. Though denying money the potency ascribed to it by Friedman, post-Keynesians developed a healthy respect for its short-run influence on the business cycle. The quantity of money mattered after all.

On inflation: Post-Keynesians regarded Friedman's simple explanation of inflation as extreme. Inflations were *not* always and everywhere a monetary phenomenon. Supply shocks—for example, an oil embargo or bad harvests—could cause cost-push inflations and drive up the price indexes for considerable periods. But the textbooks now taught that eventually cost-push inflations would have deflationary side effects and could not be sustained without printing up more money. Friedman's simple definition was not refuted but amended. No one was likely ever again to write about inflation, as the Council did in 1966, without mentioning the word "money."

On the role of government in economic stabilization: Post-Keynesians continued to believe that the private economy was inherently unstable and that government policy could steady it. But they knew now that fiscal policy was a less effective and more erratic tool than they had once supposed and that monetary policy performed in mysterious ways. They also conceded that government was the prime source of recent instability. While not abandoning Walter Heller's old faith, post-Keynesians advanced their claims with considerably more humility.

The fate of Keynesian ideas had relevance for politics. In the 1960s liberals and Keynesians, sharing abhorrence of unemployment and trust in government, struck up a natural alliance. Keynesian professors supplied the brains, and liberal politicians supplied the power, their fates intertwining as the decade proceeded. When the Keynesians were riding high, as they were midway through, the liberals rode with them. When they hit the skids in the war years, the liberals did too. If 4 percent unemployment was the wrong goal, if fiscal policy was the wrong tool, if inflation was underrated and the forces governing the economy misunderstood, the liberals paid the political price for Keynesian error. Keynesian ideas played no small role in the unraveling of both liberalism and the economy—and no small role, therefore, in the unraveling of America.

CHAPTER 7

Civil Rights: Triumph and Retreat

L YNDON Johnson had a story he liked to tell when explaining why, late in life, he had become an enthusiast for civil rights. Not many years ago, he had asked his black cook and her husband to drive his car south from Washington to the LBJ ranch. Passing through Alabama, Mississippi, and Louisiana, the travelers searched for accommodations to serve them, but finding none that would, had to stop by the side of the road to eat or to answer a call of nature. "Two people who worked for the Vice President of the United States peeing in a ditch . . . that's not right," he said.[1] The story neatly illustrated Johnson's initial conception of the race problem—humble Negroes, victimized by southern-style discrimination, in need of federal laws to defend their dignity. But there turned out to be more to the civil rights movement than that. Racial discrimination, subtler but no less insidious, existed in the North as well, and, beginning in 1965, the civil rights movement pressed Johnson hard to challenge it. Tempted, he would count his divisions and then ingloriously quit the battle. President Kennedy had treated civil rights as a political annoyance until his northern constituency took up the cause. President Johnson treated civil rights as a moral imperative until the North, now the target, abruptly lost interest. Still, though mainly confined to the South, Johnson's contributions to civil rights were the greatest achievement of his tenure.

I

Johnson was not content with the acclaim he had received for helping to pass the historic Civil Rights Act of 1964. Later that year, following his triumph over Barry Goldwater, he turned to the major unfinished task confronting the southern movement. Despite passage of three laws in eight years dealing in some way with the problem, hundreds of thousands of Deep South blacks still could not vote, primarily because of their color. To cite the worst cases, only 6 percent of voting-age blacks were registered in Mississippi, 19 percent in Alabama, and 32 percent in Louisiana.[2] Justice Department lawyers, acting under the 1957 Civil Rights Act, had fought hard in the courts for equal voting rights, but local resistance and the glacial pace of judicial change had thwarted their best efforts. Late in 1964 Johnson directed Attorney General Nicholas Katzenbach to draft voting legislation that would work,[3] and in his January 1965 State of the Union Message proposed to eliminate "every remaining obstacle to the right and the opportunity to vote."[4] If Johnson did submit voting legislation in the coming congressional session—and he made no promises—passage was hardly assured, since the country was in a mood to digest the 1964 Civil Rights Act before considering more. The man who eventually determined the timing of a voting bill and nurtured a climate favorable for enactment was Martin Luther King.

Having also selected voting as the next item in the civil rights agenda, King laid careful plans for a campaign of nonviolent resistance to secure passage of a law. King's views on nonviolence had changed over the years. Once he had employed it to persuade racial oppressors of their guilt and to change their hearts. Many broken heads later—in fact, by Birmingham, 1963—he had come to direct his campaigns not at the heart of the South but at the conscience of the North, seeking primarily to enlist the coercive power of the federal government against racial injustice. Success now hinged on the readiness of southern whites to meet nonviolence with fists and clubs—or else the North would not be moved. That was why King chose to stage his voting campaign in the city of Selma, county seat of Dallas County, in the heart of the Alabama black belt.[5] Selma had a voting-age black population of 15,000, of whom only 383 were registered to vote in 1965.[6] But Selma's main appeal was Sheriff Jim

Clark, who, as members of the Student Nonviolent Coordinating Committee working there since 1963 could testify, habitually lost his self-control at the sight of a marching Negro.

Shortly before King arrived, the new mayor of Selma nearly wrecked King's scenario by appointing as director of public safety a shrewd segregationist named Wilson Baker, who understood King's tactics and intended to frustrate them by acting legally and without violence.[7] On January 18, 1965, King and SNCC chairman John Lewis opened the Selma campaign by leading four hundred disfranchised blacks from movement headquarters at Brown's Chapel to register at the county courthouse. The courthouse was under Sheriff Clark's jurisdiction, but yielding to pressure from Baker and the mayor, Clark refrained from violence and made no arrests. Baker, meantime, had obtained inside information from King's camp that, if Sheriff Clark did not live up to his mad-dog reputation by the next day, King was prepared to move his campaign elsewhere. But the following morning, egged on by Klansmen in his informal posse, Clark flew into one of his rages, roughed up a local black leader, and arrested sixty-seven marchers. Meeting later at Brown's Chapel, Baker recalled, demonstrators voted Clark "an honorary member of SNCC, SCLC, CORE, the N-Double A-C-P. . . . And from then on they played him just like an expert playing a violin."[8]

Over the next weeks Clark stoked the fires of moral outrage in black Selma, and King steadily heated up the tempo of protest. On the 1st of February, 1965, King attracted national attention by getting himself arrested by a reluctant Wilson Baker, whose jail he preferred to Clark's. On the fifth day of the month King conferred with a delegation of sympathetic congressmen visiting Selma to investigate the need for a voting law. On the 9th he flew to Washington, where President Johnson promised to send a voting rights message to Congress "very soon." Throughout the next week the national news media reported a series of violent racial incidents in Dallas County, culminating on the night of February 17 when a state trooper in the town of Marion chased a twenty-six-year-old demonstrator named Jimmy Lee Jackson into a café and shot him in the stomach. The day of Jackson's funeral, March 3, King announced the climax of his campaign—a fifty-four-mile protest march from Selma to the state capital of Montgomery.[9]

On March 6, 1965, one day before the march was scheduled,

Governor George Wallace banned it on grounds that it would impede traffic on the highways. Nonetheless, the next day, Sunday, King's aide Hosea Williams and SNCC's John Lewis led nearly 600 marchers across the Edmund Pettus Bridge onto U.S. Highway 80, the road to Montgomery. Alabama state troopers halted the marchers, gave them two minutes to disperse, and then set upon them with tear gas and clubs. First to fall was John Lewis, hit on the head exactly where he had been struck during the Freedom Rides four years before.[10] Fleeing in panic back into Selma, the marchers met the furies of Jim Clark's posse, urged on by their leader's command, "Get those god-damned niggers." Bloody Sunday, filmed for the evening news, appalled the North and created an instant constituency for a new voting law. King's tactics had worked to perfection.[11]

But King himself was not on the Pettus Bridge. Warned by Attorney General Katzenbach of a plot on his life, he had spent Bloody Sunday in Atlanta, tending to his duties as pastor of the Ebenezer Baptist Church.[12] That night, shaken by the reports of violence, he vowed personally to lead a second march two days later and sent telegrams to two hundred religious leaders, asking them to join him.[13] But things got complicated on Monday when word arrived that federal district judge Frank M. Johnson, Jr., intended to issue a temporary order barring all marches, including Tuesday's, pending a full hearing later in the week. King suddenly confronted one of the most difficult dilemmas of his career. Clergymen were pouring into Selma expecting to march, and SNCC militants were urging him to defy the judge. But it was precisely to federal authority that King was appealing for redress, which was why he had never before violated a federal court order. Resisting intense pressure from Washington, King announced that night that the march would proceed next day—court order or no.

But sometime before dawn former Florida Governor LeRoy Collins, Johnson's personal emissary, visited King and informed him of the president's personal wish that no march take place. Sensing that King wanted a way out, Collins then negotiated a secret deal with Alabama authorities to avoid a showdown. King would lead the marchers onto the bridge, halt on orders of the state police (now tightly leashed by Governor Wallace), offer a prayer—and then turn back. A few hours later that is what happened.[14] Most of the two thousand marchers, who had set off singing "Ain't Gonna Let Nobody Turn Me Round,"[15] were no doubt pleased by their unanticipated reprieve from martyrdom. One who attained it nonetheless was the Reverend James Reeb, a white minister from Boston, whom toughs found walking in the streets of Selma that night and beat to death.[16]

King's decision to turn back on the Edmund Pettus Bridge proved a momentous event in the history of the civil rights movement, for it strained to the breaking point his relations with SNCC. When King first arrived in Selma, SNCC workers complained that he was infringing on their territory. He would only stage pointless parades, drain away energy from local projects, and then depart, leaving SNCC to pick up the pieces, they said.[17] When King announced the first Montgomery march, every SNCC leader, except John Lewis, opposed it. By forbidding self-defense, the militants argued, King was risking a needless slaughter of the innocent.[18] When Jim Clark's posse did in fact bloody heads, SNCC was incensed as much by King's absence in Atlanta as by Clark's sadism. The next day SNCC's Willie Ricks demonstrated contempt for King's teachings by attempting to incite local kids against the police.[19] And when King turned back on that bridge on the second march, SNCC accused him of betrayal, cowardice, and deflating the militance of the people. Even as King touched the nation's conscience at Selma, the movement he led was crumbling beneath him. At Selma, King spoke for the last time as the undisputed leader of the civil rights movement, the façade of black unity shattered, and ominous indications of the new direction of black protest unmistakably emerged.

President Johnson, meanwhile, moved to exploit the national mood that King had so skillfully manipulated. Working closely with Senate Minority Leader Everett McKinley Dirksen, as in 1964, the president's lieutenants put the finishing touches on a voting rights bill in the days after Bloody Sunday. On March 15, 1965, Johnson appeared before Congress on prime time TV to preview its contents and plead for passage. Direct, simple, and delivered with obvious emotion, his speech moved the nation as none of his others ever did. "Should we defeat every enemy," he told a cheering Congress, "should we double our wealth and conquer the stars," and still deny equal rights to Negro Americans, "we will have failed as a people and as a nation." At its climax, this man of the South, still sentimentally tied to the region and enveloped in its myths, embraced the slogan of the civil rights movement. Not just Negroes but all of us, he exhorted, must work to "overcome the crippling legacy of bigotry and injustice. And . . . we shall . . . overcome." Even the justices of the Supreme Court joined in the standing ovation that greeted these words.[20]

All that remained now for Martin Luther King was to finish that march so far twice attempted and twice halted. When Governor Wallace refused to provide protection, President Johnson secured the highway by federalizing the Alabama National Guard, and on March 21, 1965, the procession safely departed.[21] Four days later, their numbers swollen to 25,000, the marchers heard King deliver a brilliant address from the steps of the state capitol. No one knew it at the time, but it was the valedictory of the southern movement. Declaring that they had come a long way but still had far to go, King said,[22]

I know you are asking today, "How long will it take?" I come to say to you this afternoon, however difficult the moment, however frustrating the hour, it will not be long, because truth pressed to earth will rise again. How long? Not long, because no lie can live forever.

How long? Not long, because you still reap what you sow.

How long? Not long. Because the arm of the moral universe is long but it bends toward justice.

How long? Not long, cause mine eyes have seen the glory of the coming of the Lord. . . .

That night, Viola Liuzzo, a white mother of five from Detroit and a member of the march's transportation committee, was driving with a black passenger on Highway 80 when she was overtaken by four Klansmen and shot through the head. Thirteen years later, Gary Thomas Rowe, Jr., a paid FBI informer whose testimony helped send three others in the Klan car to jail, was himself indicted for the fatal shooting.[23] How long indeed!

Unveiling the administration's voting bill in late March 1965, Attorney General Katzenbach found ample constitutional justification in the Fifteenth Amendment, which forbade any state to deny the right to vote for reasons of race or color.[24] The target of his bill was literacy tests—the principal device, often unfairly administered —to disfranchise Deep South blacks. Unfortunately, Katzenbach told Congress, reliable statistics on black political participation in the South did not exist. He therefore proposed an indirect formula for defining and locating racial discrimination in the application of literacy tests. If a state or any of its political subdivisions employed literacy or other similar tests for voting, and if less than 50 percent of *all* its voting-age citizens voted or were registered to vote in 1964, racial discrimination would be presumed. A finding of discrimination would automatically suspend literacy tests in the offending jurisdictions. If local officials persisted in discriminatory behavior even after tests were suspended, the attorney general was authorized to dispatch examiners to process applications and place eligible voters directly on the voting rolls. Thus in Mississippi, where less than half the state's voting-age population was registered, either local officials would enroll blacks—literate or not—or the Johnson administration would do it for them. The bill's formula would automatically suspend literacy tests not only in Mississippi but in five other southern states (Louisiana, Alabama, Georgia, South Carolina, and Virginia), plus thirty-nine counties in North Carolina. It also covered Alaska, which had both a literacy test and less than half its citizens registered, as well as one county each in Arizona, Maine, and Idaho.

Southerners who thought the bill went too far and northern liberals who thought it did not go far enough found numerous anomalies in the triggering formula. North Carolina Senator Sam Ervin noted that 51.8 percent of the voting-age population of his state voted in the last election, but if the percentage had fallen below half, literacy tests would have been suspended in every one of the state's counties, including the senator's own, "notwithstanding the fact that . . . the Civil Rights Commission reported that 104.1 percent of all Negroes of voting age in my county are registered."[25] Texas, Florida, and Arkansas did not have literacy tests and so did not fall within the bill's scope, though voting discrimination was hardly unknown in those states. Liberals pointed to Crittenden County, Arkansas, for example, where only 14 percent of 12,800 blacks were registered, and to Gadsden County, Florida, where only 12 percent of 12,200 were.[26] Designed for the relief of southern blacks, the bill did nothing for the hundreds of thousands of Spanish-speaking Puerto Ricans in New York, disfranchised by English-language literacy tests for voting. Since more than half of New York's voting-age population was registered and voted in 1964, the triggering formula did not apply.[27] Alaska's literacy test, on the other hand, *was* suspended, though the cause of low voter participation was not racial discrimination but cold weather.[28]

Taking liberal criticism to heart, Congress accepted the triggering formula only after strengthening the bill in two major respects. The attorney general now had discretionary authority—never used, as it turned out—to send examiners into places like Crittenden and Gadsden counties, where voting discrimination existed in the absence of literacy tests. And in New York registrars would henceforth have to accept a sixth-grade education in a Spanish-language school under the U.S. flag as evidence of literacy. Compared to past struggles, southern opposition to the Voting Rights Act was half-hearted and easily turned aside. On August 5, 1965, at a ceremony in the rotunda of the Capitol, President Johnson proudly signed the last of the great laws to secure legal and political equality for southern blacks.

II

Because Johnson was president, the 1964 Civil Rights Act and the 1965 Voting Rights Act were enforced—not always wisely or aggressively but with sufficient determination to finish off Jim Crow. Least resisted was Title II of the 1964 act, outlawing discrimination in such places of public accommodation as restaurants, motels, theaters, and gas stations. Immediately upon its passage, businessmen in the South's cities and larger towns—even in bulwarks of the old order like Albany, Georgia, and Birmingham, Alabama—complied with the law. Surveying the touchy problem of gas-station accommodations in twenty urban areas, a government survey in 1965 reported continuing discrimination only in Savannah and Jackson. The old ways died hardest in rural areas, where significant resistance lingered for years and where even the long arm of the Justice Department seldom reached.[29] But the remarkable collapse of segregation in the urban South, the ease with which white waitresses learned to be polite to black patrons, the routine mixing of the races at lunch counters and theaters—all this confirmed the liberal faith that law, at least sometimes, could help change custom.

Results of the Voting Rights Act were no less impressive. By 1968, in the six fully covered states where the act triggered suspension of literacy tests black registration had increased by 740,000 in three years—from 31 percent of the eligible black population to 57 percent. The worst offenders underwent the most far-reaching change —black registration increasing from 19 percent to 53 percent in Alabama, 32 percent to 60 percent in Louisiana, and 6 percent to

44 percent in Mississippi. Election officials in most of the 556 counties whose literacy tests had been suspended voluntarily enrolled black voters themselves. Federal examiners invaded only 62 counties, there to enroll approximately 150,000 of the previously disfranchised, including many illiterates, who would not have been registered under the suspended laws, even if the statutes had been fairly administered.[30] Indeed, examiners reported rates of black illiteracy ranging from 15 percent in urban areas to 65 percent in rural counties—reason enough to explain why the Second Reconstruction of the South was so necessary.[31]

Despite these voting gains, the civil rights lobby in Washington was not satisfied. According to the Civil Rights Commission, in many counties covered by the law "a generalized climate of intimidation" continued to keep blacks from exercising their political rights. Rights leaders urged Johnson to send examiners into the 185 counties where literacy tests had been suspended, but where, as late as 1968, more than half of the voting-age blacks still had not registered. The Justice Department inaccurately countered that, without local voting drives to accompany their efforts, federal examiners could accomplish little.[32] Doubtless, Johnson refused to send more examiners because it suited his political purposes to minimize the federal coercive presence.

Though cautious enforcement robbed the act of some of its potential, even the Civil Rights Commission attributed to it "unprecedented progress."[33] Its effects on Selma, Alabama, illustrated its potency. Four days after the act passed, Johnson sent examiners into Dallas County, where in two months they increased the number of black voters from 320 to 6,789. The following spring these voters provided the margin for Wilson Baker's successful bid to capture the office of county sheriff from Jim Clark. Two years after that, six blacks were running for city council, another was running for mayor, and two more served the county as deputy sheriffs.[34] Overall, in the six affected states the number of elected black officials increased from 70 to nearly 400 in four years. Racist demagoguery in political contests declined markedly.[35] And a new generation of moderate governors, putting aside the ancient obsession with race, gave the South enlightened leadership. The act, then, did nothing less than cleanse the poisoned atmosphere of southern politics.

The most bitterly defended citadel of the old regime was its dual school systems—one for blacks, one for whites. As late as 1964, ten years after *Brown v. Board of Education,* a mere 2 percent of black students in the eleven states of the Old Confederacy attended schools with whites. Judges, it turned out, were not suitable instruments to effect a social revolution—at least not by themselves.[36] As a U.S. circuit court later observed, among the most important reasons for the poor performance of the courts was "the lack, until 1964, of effective congressional statutory recognition of school desegregation as the law of the land."[37]

The 1964 Civil Rights Act contained two sections relevant to school desegregation. One lifted some of the burden of litigation from aggrieved black parents by empowering the attorney general to initiate school desegregation suits. More important, Title VI required nondiscrimination in any federally aided program. Invoking Title VI on December 31, 1964, HEW's Office of Education laid down this condition for future receipt of federal funds by southern schools: Dual school districts would have to furnish the U.S. Education Commissioner either an acceptable desegregation plan—contents unspecified—or a copy of a federal court order mandating school desegregation.[38] (Only 164 of the South's 2,000 dual school districts were under court orders, but these included most of the region's big cities and approximately half its public school pupils.) Title VI was the noose which, placed around the South's segregated schools, would be pulled tighter year by year until no life in them remained.

The winter of 1965 was a season of confusion, uncertainty, and near panic for many southern school officials. On the one hand, the Education Office had imposed a requirement that was both politically explosive and maddeningly vague. On the other hand, southern districts hungered for the federal funds—amounting, in some cases, to 20–30 percent of their budgets—that they expected to receive under Johnson's 1965 Elementary and Secondary Education Act—money HEW was now threatening to withhold. Desperate for clarification, southern districts demanded to know precisely what the government was requiring of them in the matter of desegregation.[39] The response was the Office of Education's famous "General Statement of Policies under Title VI," issued in April 1965 and popularly called the Guidelines.[40]

The Guidelines were welcome news for white supremacists. Among desegregation plans deemed acceptable by the education commissioner were so-called freedom-of-choice plans—the South's favorite device for minimizing school integration. Freedom of choice meant that individual black students in dual systems had the option of crossing over into white schools. Though free choice sounded democratic, it placed the entire burden of desegregation on a few courageous blacks, assuring minimal integration in some southern districts, none in many.

Early in May 1965 Johnson aide Douglas Cater, obviously relieved, reported to his chief that southern reaction to the Guidelines "has been far more restrained than we could have hoped."[41] Meanwhile, Education Commissioner Francis Keppel was deep in negotiations with southern districts, hoping to obtain the required desegregation plans from all 2,000 of them before schools opened in September. Johnson personally kept daily tabs on Keppel's efforts, summoning him to the White House every few days that summer for a report. Keppel recalled, "We finally got down to a hundred of them, or something, and the President would wander in and out saying, 'Get 'em! Get 'em! Get the last ones.' "[42] By September, Keppel had got desegregation plans from all but 110 of the South's dual districts. Accordingly, the percentage of southern black students attending school with whites rose from 2 percent in 1964 to 6 percent in 1965.[43] This was the year when many districts in the Deep South made the critical psychological leap from intransigent defiance to token compliance via freedom of choice. If that was all Johnson was asking, the South could live with it.

The civil rights groups, however, could not. Bitterly attacking the Office of Education for its timid enforcement efforts, they pointed out that 102 districts with approved plans had undergone no actual desegregation. Moreover, HEW had failed to mount an inspection effort to monitor implementation. And finally, only 38 of 51 districts failing to submit plans by December 1965 had had federal funds cut off. The time for tokenism, they declared, was over.[44]

The anonymous bureaucrats in HEW agreed. Supported by Attorney General Katzenbach[45] and, presumably, by Johnson, the Office of Education issued revised Guidelines in March 1966, further tightening the noose.[46] Henceforth, freedom-of-choice plans would not be considered ends in themselves but mere steps toward dismantling dual school systems. The test of a plan's effectiveness would be how much desegregation it actually promoted. The Guidelines suggested standards for measuring the adequacy of freedom-of-choice plans for the school year beginning September 1966.

Districts in which 8 or 9 percent of black students were desegregated in 1965 should at least double this rate next year; districts with 4 or 5 percent should triple their rate; and districts with no desegregation should make a "very substantial start." Meanwhile, the Office of Education was assembling effective enforcement machinery to monitor the compliance process.

The revised Guidelines threw the South into a fury and had a sobering effect on some northern politicians as well. Eighteen southern senators pleaded with Johnson by letter to put an end to "unfair and unrealistic" abuse of bureaucratic power.[47] Education Commissioner, Harold Howe II was denounced on the floor of the House as a man who "talks like a Communist," rants like an "idiot," and is "so ignorant he should incorporate."[48] A Senate committee slashed HEW's civil rights enforcement budget.[49] Senate Majority Leader Mike Mansfield confessed in an unguarded moment that he thought the Guidelines had gone "too far."[50] And at a press conference in October 1966, even President Johnson conceded "harassment," "mistakes," and bureaucratic enthusiasm in HEW's enforcement effort.[51]

The Office of Education bent under the pressure but did not break. In the school year beginning 1966, it accepted less from the South than its Guidelines seemed to require, but it also invoked Title VI to defer federal funds for new activities in 122 school districts, most of them with less than 2 percent of their black students in desegregated schools. The percentage of southern black students attending school with whites rose from 6 percent in 1965–1966 to 16 percent in 1966–1967. Only in Alabama, where Governor George Wallace urged school officials to resist, was no progress recorded.[52]

It was the courts that ultimately cut the heart out of the South's opposition. In December 1966, at a time when the Guidelines were staggering under six months' accumulated blows, the U.S. Court of Appeals for the Fifth Circuit decided the case of *United States v. Jefferson County Board of Education.* The majority upheld the Guidelines, including their controversial percentage requirements, and ruled free-choice plans permissible only when promoting a system-wide policy of integration.[53] The judges called on federal district courts to bring court-ordered school desegregation plans up to the standards of the Guidelines. Sitting *en banc,* the judges of the Fifth Circuit reaffirmed the *Jefferson County* decision in March 1967. "Officials administering public schools . . . ," said the Court, "have the affirmative duty . . . to bring about an integrated, unitary system in which there are no Negro schools and no white schools—just schools."[54]

The *Jefferson County* case was the beginning of the end for the South's dual school districts. The federal courts were emboldened by the Guidelines to require real desegregation, and the Guidelines received needed legitimacy from the decisions of the federal courts. Working together to enforce the law, the executive and judiciary branches would prove invincible. Segregated districts now had a choice of desegregating voluntarily and receiving federal aid, or of defying the Office of Education, losing federal aid, and desegregating involuntarily under court order.

The school year beginning September 1967 was the third under HEW's searching gaze and the first since Title VI's enactment in which no discernible progress toward desegregation occurred. Freedom-of-choice plans, it was now abundantly clear, were inherently incapable of promoting unitary school districts. But failure had its uses. As the head of HEW's new Office of Civil Rights explained, "We had to follow the freedom of choice plan to prove its ineffectiveness, and this was the year that it did prove its ineffectiveness, so that now we're ready to move into the next phase."[55]

The next phase began in March 1968 with publication of the third version of the Guidelines. No percentage requirements appeared in this edition, not only because they had not worked well, but because —in the words of the Southern Regional Council—they "perhaps unwittingly allowed attention to shift from the illegitimacy of dual schools" to haggling "over whether 'ten percent is too much.' "[56] Southern school officials, the new Guidelines said, now had to act promptly to bring about an integrated, unitary system, and they had only until September 1969 to finish the job.[57] The deadline was later moved back to September 1970 for districts with black student majorities and for districts in the midst of new construction.

In May 1968 the Supreme Court finished with tokenism, too, unanimously striking down a freedom-of-choice plan in New Kent County, Virginia, because it failed to eliminate racial discrimination "root and branch." Delays toward that end were "no longer tolerable," the Court declared. "The burden on a school board today is to come forward with a plan that promises realistically to work and promises realistically to work *now*."[58] The NAACP Legal Defense fund immediately announced that it would ask federal district courts to strengthen existing court-ordered school desegregation plans.[59] In the following months judges began replacing free choice with geographical zoning and school-pairing plans and imposing deadlines similar to HEW's. When schools opened in September 1968, the forward thrust of desegregation resumed. The percentage of black students in desegregated schools rose that year to 32 percent, double what it had been two years before.[60]

In 1969 and 1970, when the deadlines fell due, the South capitulated. The most dramatic gains occurred in rural areas and small towns, rather than big cities, where the slow process of updating court orders was just beginning. How much desegregation actually took place was a matter of definition. In the 1960s HEW had counted as desegregated all blacks in a school if even a single white child was enrolled with them. By that standard 86 percent of the South's black schoolchildren were desegregated by 1970. Thereafter HEW switched to a more exacting measure. A black student was counted as desegregated only if he attended a school in which whites were the majority. In 1968, by this definition, 18 percent of southern black students were desegregated; in 1970, 39 percent; in 1972, 46 percent. By contrast, in 1972 only 28 percent of black students in the North and West attended integrated schools.[61]

On balance, the result was worth the effort. True, in districts above 35 percent black, desegregation typically caused the flight of 8 to 10 percent of white students the first year; and in some communities desegregation, mismanaged, produced dangerous racial animosities and impaired the educational mission of schools. But desegregation also improved the achievement of blacks without hurting the achievement of whites. If assigned to a typical desegregated school in kindergarten or the first grade when effects on cognitive development were the most dramatic, the average black student could eventually expect to achieve at a level one grade higher than if he had attended a segregated school. No less significant, his IQ score would rise by an estimated 4 points, meaning that instead of the 91 IQ with which he began, he would have a 95, reducing by nearly half the distance that separated him from the norm of 100. But of course schools are not mere knowledge factories, and higher test scores were hardly the sole purpose of desegre-

gation. Schools are, after all, the purveyors of the nation's ideals and
the prime focus of a community's hopes.[62] As long as schools were
segregated by law, southern blacks lived in a society whose public
authority defined them as inferior and where, for them, democratic
principles were a mockery. Insistence on unitary school systems
meant that for blacks and whites there was now one law, one standard of democracy, and one community.

Johnson's role in all this was quiet but critical. Commissioner
Howe, who kept his job despite pressure on Johnson to get rid of
him, knew this better than most. Howe recalled, "When you get
right down to the bite of the thing as to whether you were going to
do something that had to be done or not to enforce the law, the
President was always on the right side. He or his staff would make
you run all the way round the barn and try to have people happy
with the decision and have it explained to them ahead of time
. . . and in some way insulate the administration from the public
reaction. But when you had taken all the time and gotten everything
done that could be done . . . and there still was a question of pushing
ahead and antagonizing some powerful people in the Senate and the
House, he was there saying, 'Let's go.' "[63] Doomed in any case, the
South's caste system disappeared as rapidly and completely as it did
in large measure because Johnson was president. Not until the civil
rights movement migrated north did his commitment falter.

III

Black protest, northern-style, gathered force for two years before
white liberals fully grasped its significance. First there had been the
1963 school boycotts in New York, Chicago, and Boston, then the
1964 summer riots in a handful of East Coast ghettos, and now in
the spring of 1965 angry demands by local black leaders for control
of antipoverty programs. It did not take long to locate the sources
of this discontent—de facto segregation, poverty, social decay.
Fresh from their southern successes, liberals were initially eager to
redress northern grievances too. The question—on which the national tranquillity seemed increasingly to hinge—was, what to do?
Among liberals seeking answers that spring was Lyndon Johnson.

The man who appointed himself to instruct the president was
Daniel Patrick Moynihan, an assistant secretary of Labor with a
Ph.D. in political science, a penchant for ambitious hypothesis, and

a talent for cultivating the right political connections. In 1965 Moynihan sensed the arrival of a historic moment in American race relations. But, as he told White House assistant Harry McPherson, "The worst part of the Negro problem is, it's being tended by you southern liberals."[64] To educate the White House, Moynihan spent most of the winter of 1965 setting forth his analysis of the ghetto crisis in a paper entitled, *The Negro Family: The Case for National Action.* In April, carrying a bottle of scotch in one hand and a copy of his secret report in the other, he paid a hospital call on his friend McPherson, recuperating from minor surgery. "For the next four hours we talked and read and drank,"[65] recalled the patient, who found in the so-called Moynihan Report the key to the ghetto puzzle that he—and the president—had been looking for.

Moynihan's report began by saluting the civil rights movement for breaking through artificial barriers to equal opportunity.[66] But, he warned, in the next phase of the Negro Revolution mere opportunity would not be enough. Blacks would demand equality as a fact —equality defined as "a distribution of achievements among Negroes roughly comparable to that among whites." What good was mere opportunity, after all, if blacks finished behind whites even in a fair race? Moynihan's grim message was not only that blacks were still losing, but that in some ways the gap between whites and blacks was actually widening. To explain why, he chose to emphasize the condition of the lower-class black family, so unstable in many urban areas that it was "approaching complete breakdown." As male desertion increased, so too did the percentage of families headed by women, welfare dependency, failure in school, and youth crime. Ascribing some family weakness to slavery and some to rapid urbanization, Moynihan laid the primary blame on thirty-five years of depression-level unemployment among black men. Humiliated by their failure as providers, fathers disappeared. Concluding with a call for national action to strengthen the black family, Moynihan omitted his policy recommendations in order not to detract from his analysis. In any case, he thought they were obvious. Jobs and money hold families together. Therefore, the government should provide jobs for the unemployed and family allowances for all parents who lived with their children.[67]

On May 4, 1965, Moynihan's boss, Labor Secretary Willard Wirtz, sent the White House a memo summarizing the report and including recommendations. The timing was perfect. Johnson, too, believed that the moment to achieve racial justice—North as well as South—might be at hand. After all, the nation was at peace. Confidence in the therapeutic power of reform had never been higher. Sympathy for the cause of black people, in the aftermath of Selma, was running deep. Docile majorities in Congress awaited the president's bidding, and budget surpluses to pay for new programs apparently loomed just ahead. Now, providentially, came Moynihan, daring to shatter the liberal silence on the disorganization of ghetto life and proposing a way out. Within days of its receipt, Johnson decided to make the Moynihan Report the basis of his commencement address at Howard University, the nation's leading black institution of higher learning. Moynihan himself helped write the speech and hours before delivery on June 4, 1965, Martin Luther King, Whitney Young, and Roy Wilkins all personally cleared it.[68]

Like Moynihan in his report, Johnson at Howard declared that the task ahead for civil rights was to achieve "equality as a fact," argued that blacks were actually falling further behind, and suggested Negro family breakdown as the most important source of the problem. Measures to fight poverty would help relieve the crisis, he said, but other answers had to be found. To help find them, Johnson announced that he would summon scholars, experts, and outstanding Negroes to the White House in the fall for a conference to be entitled "To Fulfill These Rights." Though he did not say so, he hoped that the conference would focus on the black family and produce consensus on ways to secure "equality as a fact and equality as a result."[69]

But that summer the moment was lost. In July 1965, responding to the entreaties of General Westmoreland, Johnson launched the ground war in Vietnam, which soon absorbed energies and resources that might otherwise have been devoted to ghetto rehabilitation. Then in August the Watts riot erupted in Los Angeles—five days of furious civil insurrection that unmasked black hatred and required the California National Guard to quell. After Watts, the legions of moderate whites who had so recently demanded justice for the meek, Christ-like demonstrators of Selma began melting away. No white man in America was more stunned by Watts than the president himself. "He just wouldn't accept it," recalled aide Joseph Califano. "He refused to look at the cables from Los Angeles. . . . He refused to take calls from the generals who were requesting government planes to fly in the National Guard. . . . We needed decisions from him. But he simply wouldn't respond."[70] Despite all that he had done for them, the ingrates of Watts, with an assist from the Vietcong, were wrecking his dream to go down in history as the great reformer.

One other event blocked new departures in civil rights that summer. When the government finally released the Moynihan Report in August 1965, thunderous denunciation greeted it. Catching the new mood of self-assertion and black pride taking hold on the streets, many civil rights spokesmen decided that white liberals had no business poking around in the sexual mores of the ghetto. And, in the process of making this point, they willfully distorted what Moynihan had said—easy to do, given his rather casual argumentation and the omission of his policy recommendations. CORE's James Farmer accused him of "taking the real tragedy of black poverty and serving it up as an essentially salacious 'discovery' suggesting that Negro mental health should be the first order of business in a civil rights revolution."[71] Other writers accused Moynihan of failing to appreciate the strength of the matriarchal family, of imposing middle-class values on lower-class blacks,[72] and of misusing statistics, which to an extent he did. It remained for a white critic in the *Nation* to strike the lowest blow. The Moynihan Report, he said, was another example of the "new ideology" that blamed the plight of the victim on his own supposed defects and legitimized the popular sport of savage discovery. "The all-time favorite 'savage' is the promiscuous mother who produces a litter of illegitimate brats in order to profit from AFDC."[73] On November 9 a civil rights meeting in New York, called by religious groups, petitioned the president to strike the Negro family from the agenda of the White House Conference.[74]

In fact, there was no conference that fall. Jolted by the reaction to the Moynihan Report and never quite recovering, the White House opted for a small planning session in November and postponement of the conference until the following spring. From Johnson's viewpoint, the whole affair was turning into a political nightmare. The director of the planning session confided to the two hundred invited participants, "I have been reliably informed that no such person as Daniel Patrick Moynihan exists."[75] The conferees produced no worthy new ideas and managed to attain consensus only on a single point—the dereliction of the Johnson administration in enforcing civil rights legislation.[76]

Having committed himself to a conference, Johnson had no choice but to go on with it. To prevent it from becoming a forum for militants, the White House appointed railroad executive Ben Heineman as conference director and packed the board of directors with big businessmen.[77] When the 2,500 invited delegates, representing every point of view except the Ku Klux Klan and the Black Muslims, showed up at the Sheraton-Park Hotel on June 2–3, 1966, they discovered that their sole function was to offer individual views on prepackaged recommendations. CORE's Floyd McKissick had to threaten rebellion before the delegates won the right at least to vote on resolutions.[78] Only after it became apparent that militance had been contained did Johnson decide to make an unscheduled appearance at the conference dinner. The ovation he received was a tribute both to his real contributions to civil rights and to the care with which his lieutenants had picked the delegates.[79] Indeed, they picked so well that Johnson achieved his main purpose at the conference—defeat of resolutions condemning the war in Vietnam.[80] The real meaning of the conference was this: so far as the president was concerned, the civil rights movement was over.

IV

But the movement went north anyway. After Selma, there were those like Moynihan who said that it had finished its work, that artificial racial barriers to equal opportunity had been successfully razed, that the need now was less to push harder for civil rights than to lift Negroes out of poverty or enhance their racial pride or strengthen their families. This view of the matter missed the point. North and South, racial discrimination not only persisted; it remained the fundamental problem of black Americans. As in the South, so in the North—the first task of the civil rights movement was to tear down the walls. Less flagrant than in the South but no less vicious and even harder to reach, northern discrimination took three mutually enforcing forms. Segregated housing led to segregated schools, and these together handicapped lower-class black workers in a job market increasingly located in the white suburbs and requiring quality education. And, too, the job market inflicted a discrimination all its own. Facing problems of this magnitude in the North, the movement soon came to view the old southern struggles with a certain nostalgia.

Civil rights in the North was a drama in three parts—schools, housing, and jobs—played out in Chicago and featuring Mayor Richard J. Daley, Lyndon Johnson, and Martin Luther King. From the black perspective, there was little to choose between Chicago, Illinois, and Selma, Alabama. Daley was no less a segregationist than Jim Clark, except that he would combat the movement with smiles, patronage, promises, and cynical duplicity. And Chicago, no less than Selma, was a thoroughly segregated city. For example, there was the white, lower-middle-class neighborhood of Bridgeport, where Daley was born and still lived in a modest bungalow. In 1962, when a five-year-old black child enrolled in a local kindergarten, white threats forced her withdrawal. In 1964, when a black student from Loyola University briefly broke the color line by moving into a Bridgeport flat, his neighbors threw rocks, and his possessions mysteriously turned up at the local district police station. And in the racially tense summer of 1965, at a playground four blocks from the mayor's house, little girls jumped rope to a new chant:

> I'd like to be an Alabama trooper,
> That's what I would truly like to be,
> Cause if I were an Alabama trooper,
> I could kill the niggers legally.[81]

Lyndon Johnson was a far more sympathetic character than Mayor Daley. No segregationist, he would have used his powers to attack discrimination, if he could. But forced to choose between Daley and King—between the black minority in the ghetto and the white majority whom Daley represented—he did what any politician concerned with survival would do. He chose Daley. This failure of nerve was a reflection less on Johnson than on a hypocritical northern public, which applied one standard of racial conduct to the South and quite a different one to itself.

And, finally, there was Martin Luther King, who became, in Chicago, a tragic hero. After Selma King could have retired with his Nobel prize to his church in Atlanta, there to live out a life as one of the nation's most esteemed and honored citizens. But the messianic impulse in him ran too deep. Once he had believed that northern blacks would "benefit derivatively from the southern struggle"; by 1965 he had taken a hard look at what he called "the Negro's repellent slum life" and knew he was wrong.[82] So he would go to Chicago, live among the wretched poor, and mount still another crusade against racial injustice—this one, as he must have known, doomed from the start. When a child, he had loved to sing "I Want to Be More and More like Jesus."[83] In the last years of his life, he was never closer to the goal.

The civil rights battle in Chicago began over the issue of segregated public schools. As in most other northern big-city districts—and for many of the same reasons—90 percent of Chicago's black students attended all-black classes. Superintendent Benjamin Willis explained that unlike schools in the South, where segregation arose from governmental action, schools in Chicago were segregated de facto—that is, because blacks and whites happened to live in separate neighborhoods.

Beginning in 1962, local rights groups angrily countered that the distinction was false—that Chicago's black children attended schools that were not only racially separate but also unequal because Ben Willis schemed to achieve this result. Their brief in support of this contention was devastating. Though schools in the ghetto were overcrowded, hundreds of white classrooms stood empty; rather than transfer black students out, Willis moved mobile classrooms in. Zonal boundaries were gerrymandered to keep blacks in changing neighborhoods from entering white schools. And the best vocational school in the city was 98 percent white. Moreover, compared to white schools, black schools had more pupils per teacher, twice as many noncertified teachers, fewer libraries, and anemic curricula. In protest, blacks had staged massive school boycotts in October 1963 and February 1964, but the real showdown began in the spring of 1965 when, after weeks of controversy, the school board voted to renew Willis's contract.[84]

Civil rights groups did not doubt the cause of the board's action. Mayor Daley had the board majority in his pocket, and Daley wanted Willis.[85] On June 10, 1965, the Coordinating Council of Community Organizations, a coalition of civil rights, religious, and neighborhood groups, retaliated against the mayor by launching a nonviolent campaign to force Willis out and begin school desegregation in Chicago. Marching on City Hall almost daily for more than a month, many of the demonstrators tried to tie up the city by sitting down at major intersections. More than seven hundred arrests eventually resulted.[86] But, despite the fact that one million blacks lived in Chicago, the average demonstration attracted only one hundred to two hundred people, hardly enough even to inconvenience the city. Most of Chicago's poor blacks were either apathetic, scornful of nonviolence, or unwilling to challenge the Daley machine, self-proclaimed source of jobs, housing, and welfare in the ghetto.[87]

Casting about for a way to build support, local leaders hit on the idea of inviting King to lead a demonstration. Accordingly, in Chicago in the last week of July 1965, King made his northern debut. Crisscrossing the South and West sides, he spent three days speaking at housing projects and churches, trying to drum up support for a climactic march. "We want a number that no man can number," he said.[88] On July 26, 1965, 15,000 people, the largest civil rights demonstration in Chicago history, followed King down State Street to City Hall.[89] But the next day King was gone—for a while, at least. In August, when protests shifted to the mayor's house in Bridgeport, the number of demonstrators dwindled again to a mere handful. By refraining from provocative action and creating no martyrs, Daley had kept his hold on his black constituents and turned back the challenge.

Still, local civil rights groups were hopeful. After all, this was the summer when HEW was invoking Title VI of the 1964 Civil Rights Act against dual school systems in the South. If Tupelo, why not Chicago? It was a good question. On July 4, 1965, rights groups formally submitted a complaint to Commissioner Keppel, charging Chicago school officials with fostering segregation.[90] Similar complaints from other cities now confronted HEW with the delicate task of formulating a policy for the North.

HEW lawyers took the view that the department could go no further than the courts in attacking segregation. That meant that segregated schools in the North could not be considered illegal unless a school board intentionally acted to keep the races separate.[91] Intent was notoriously hard to prove. Still, if there was one city in the North where intent might be established, that city was Chicago. While HEW was still wrestling with the legal problem and before its investigators reported from Chicago, Congress passed the first appropriation for the 1965 Elementary and Secondary Education Act. Keppel received reports that Willis intended to spend some of the $32 million earmarked for Chicago, not on the children of the poor who were the act's intended beneficiaries, but on non-poor whites. When Keppel made inquiries, Willis brushed him off.

That was the last straw. To defend the integrity of his new education program, Keppel sent State School Superintendent Ray Page a letter on September 30, 1965, informing him that Chicago was in probable noncompliance with Title VI and temporarily deferring program funds.[92]

Before he dispatched his letter, Keppel informed Douglas Cater, Johnson's man on the White House staff in charge of education. Cater could have stopped it but did not. Only on the next day, October 1, 1965, did Johnson learn what his subordinates were doing in his name. Cater alerted Johnson by memo, "There may be some news by the end of the day regarding action taken by Commissioner Keppel in deferring commitment of Federal funds for the Chicago school system. . . . He has arranged to keep Mayor Daley informed through a mutual friend. Keppel believes this whole matter can be worked out swiftly."[93] Indeed it was.

Keppel had made a terrible mistake. The terrain he chose for a stand against northern school segregation was politically indefensible. He had challenged not only Willis but Daley, boss of the strongest political machine in America. Willis, Page, and Mayor Daley's mouthpiece in Congress, Roman Pucinski, immediately denounced Keppel for having acted arbitrarily and without cause. Unfortunately for Keppel, his investigators in Chicago not yet having reported, he lacked the clinching evidence he needed for self-defense.

Lyndon Johnson was not happy. Nobody in the bureaucratic chain of command had understood the political dangers, and now a baron of the party was threatening to rebel. On October 3, 1965, after issuing an order banning comment on Keppel's letter, Johnson flew to New York to sign his immigration reform law at the Statue of Liberty. Also in New York for the occasion was Mayor Daley. The president and the mayor had a little chat.[94] Back in Washington on the 4th, Johnson received a note from his appointments secretary, inquiring when he wished to meet with HEW officials to discuss Chicago. Johnson scribbled back, "To-day."[95]

Later that afternoon, in the presence of HEW Secretary John Gardner and Assistant Secretary Wilbur Cohen, Johnson permitted the unfortunate Keppel to glimpse his wrath. The president did not order Keppel to reverse himself, but he indicated he wanted the controversy to end quickly. The next day Cohen flew to Chicago to negotiate a truce with the Chicago school board.[96] Though advertised as a compromise, the result was a repudiation of Keppel. HEW turned the spigot of federal aid back on and withdrew its investigators from Chicago. In return the school board agreed to a few small concessions[97]—as it turned out, never implemented. Investigators returned to Chicago later in the year and eventually filed a report charging the school system with Title VI violations.[98] Harold Howe, Keppel's successor, confined himself to pious hopes that Chicago would voluntarily obey the law.[99]

Chicago was off the hook, and because Chicago was, so was the rest of the North—at least until 1973, when judges, with a gentle assist from HEW, began applying the same legal logic to northern school districts that had been applied to those in the South. Still, as late as 1979, the Civil Rights Commission reported that schools in the Northeast and North Central states remained the most segregated in the country, with two out of three black students attending "at least moderately segregated school districts."[100] In refusing to challenge school segregation northern-style, Johnson had been less than valorous, though politically realistic.

V

In 1966 the issue switched from schools to housing, with King moving center stage. King's organization—the Southern Christian Leadership Conference—had by now chosen Chicago as the testing ground for nonviolent resistance in the North. Operating on a budget of $10,000 a month, members of his staff opened an office on the West Side in October 1965 and began planning a major campaign, whose slogan would be "end slums." In January 1966 King himself came to town, moved part-time into a dingy $90-a-month flat in the heart of the ghetto, and took over the so-called Chicago Movement.[101] In truth, he had no more idea how to end slums than did the army of social workers and reformers who had preceded him. Months drifted by while he and his aides—southerners in a strange land—groped for a workable strategy. By June, time had about run out. Black radicals were electrifying the ghetto with the new cry of "black power." King's doctrine of nonviolence had been thrown on the ideological defensive. And another summer of rioting appeared imminent. Either King delivered in Chicago, or nonviolence was finished in the North. Needing to begin somewhere, King decided on a campaign for open housing.[102]

On July 10, 1966, Freedom Sunday, King launched his drive with a rally that only half filled the 85,000 seats in Soldier's Field. "Our power does not reside in Molotov cocktails, knives and bricks," he told a crowd, whose members included the notorious Blackstone Rangers and other of the city's street gangs. Afterward, like his namesake at Wittenberg four centuries before, he marched to City Hall and placed on the door a list of his movement's demands.[103] Chief among them was open housing. "As of July 11, we shall cease to be accomplices to a housing system of discrimination, segregation, and degradation," he declared. "We shall begin to act as if Chicago were an open city."[104]

Two days later, after police tried to shut off the cooling waters of a fire hydrant, the nation's first big riot of the summer broke out in King's own neighborhood. Roaming the riot area for most of the next seventy-two hours, King confronted gang leaders on street corners, in churches, and at barbecue restaurants, trying desperately to open a dialogue on nonviolence.[105] It was tough going. Late one night, Assistant Attorney General Roger Wilkins—dispatched by the president to scout the riot scene—climbed four flights of stairs to King's ghetto apartment and found forty or fifty people crowded in a hot, airless room. Wilkins, who had before dismissed King as nothing but a showman, movingly recalled the scene:

In the middle of this, here is this Nobel Prize laureate, sitting on the floor, having a dialogue with semiarticulate gang kids. He was holding a seminar in nonviolence, trying to convince these kids that rioting was destructive; that the way to change a society was to approach it with love of yourself and of mankind and dignity in your own heart.

For hours this went on; and there were no photographers there, no newspaper men. There was no glory in it. He also kept two assistant attorney generals of the United States waiting for hours while he did this. And when we did talk to him, it was four o'clock in the morning. We had to walk through the bedroom—it was a railroad flat—to get to the kitchen. His children were sleeping in the bedroom.

He got Mrs. King up, and she gave us coffee. We sat and we talked. He was a great man, a great man![106]

The riot past, King began demonstrations against the conspiracy of bankers, builders, real-estate brokers, and home owners to keep Chicago's black population penned up in the ghetto. Never in the history of the movement had he attempted a harder task. For one thing, he called for thousands to follow him, but only hundreds came. For another, the descendants of the Irish, Italians, and Poles who resided in neighborhoods like Gage Park, Bogan, and Marquette Park had already fled the black invasion once—sometimes twice—and would not run again. On July 29, 1966, King led the first group of forty demonstrators into Gage Park for an all-night prayer vigil at the office of a white real-estate broker. Only the police prevented two hundred jeering whites from assaulting them.[107] On succeeding days, in one or another of Chicago's neighborhoods, white mobs greeted demonstrators by overturning cars, throwing rocks, or chanting, "Go back to Africa. We don't want you here."[108] On August 5, as police struggled to control four thousand infuriated whites, King told six hundred marchers in Marquette Park, "We are bound for the promised land."[109] Minutes later a stone bloodied his head and knocked him to the ground. Staggering to his feet, he managed to walk another hour past whites screaming, "We want Martin Luther Coon," whites waving Confederate flags, whites wearing Nazi-style helmets. "I think the people from Mississippi ought to come to Chicago to learn how to hate," he said at the end.[110]

During the next three weeks, as King's demonstrations continued, tension built toward a climax. On the 19th, the city obtained an injunction to prevent King from holding more than one march at a time. That same day black testers visited 110 real-estate brokers, finding all of them either closed or uncooperative.[111] On the 20th, King made the riveting announcement that one week hence he would lead a march into the nearby suburb of Cicero, where 11,000 blacks worked by day but not a single one lived at night. No one expected Cicero's tiny police force to cope any more successfully with white violence now than it had in 1951 when a terrible riot drove a black home buyer out of town.[112] Prudently the governor announced on August 24 that he was calling up the National Guard as a preventive measure.[113] Fearful that Negro blood would flow in Cicero—creating martyrs and igniting a race war—Mayor Daley decided the time had come to execute a tactical retreat.

The result was a treaty, negotiated at a dramatic summit meeting of civil rights and civic leaders on August 26, 1966. By its terms every relevant institution in the city—from the public-housing authority to the real-estate board—was pledged to uphold the principle of fair housing and to promote the dispersal of the black population throughout the city. King hailed it as a great victory and called off his demonstrators, promising, however, to return next spring if,

by then, no progress toward open housing had been made.[114] Of
course, once King left, Daley reneged. And, when King came back,
it was not to resume leadership of the moribund Chicago Movement, but to make a major address denouncing the war in Vietnam.[115] As with schools, so with housing: nonviolence having failed,
federal intervention was the only hope.

Civil rights leaders had been pressing Johnson to act against
housing discrimination since 1964. By himself, they said, he had the
authority to kick the financial props from under the dual housing
market and open the suburbs for blacks. All he had to do was amend
Kennedy's 1962 housing order by forbidding banks and savings and
loans associations to lend mortgage money to biased builders and
developers.[116] Johnson hesitated for two reasons. The Justice Department doubted he had the requisite authority,[117] and the political risks of such an order were enormous. Vice President Humphrey
wrote him in May 1965, "There will be substantial criticism if the
Order is not extended. . . . At the same time, I know I need not
belabor the potentially explosive nature of any attempt by the Federal government to extend its regulations of private housing in this
sensitive area."[118]

Johnson solved his housing dilemma by shirking responsibility
while appearing to fulfill it. In his January 1966 State of the Union
Message he called on Congress to enact a fair-housing measure and
in April submitted appropriate legislation.[119] Of course, as civil
rights leaders knew only too well, Congress was unlikely to enact it
—which was why they had favored an executive order in the first
place. Joseph Rauh, counsel for the Leadership Conference on Civil
Rights, commented sourly, "I think it is a means of getting off the
hook on an issue they don't want to face."[120]

The heart of Johnson's 1966 omnibus civil rights bill was Title IV,
outlawing housing discrimination by "property owners, tract developers, real estate brokers, lending institutions and all others engaged in the sale, rental, or financing of housing."[121] The prohibi-
tion could hardly have been more sweeping—or provision for
enforcement more feeble. Under the act, aggrieved parties could
obtain effective redress only by initiating costly and time-consuming
court suits.

Congress greeted the measure with a notable lack of enthusiasm.
To get it through a reluctant House, Johnson had to acquiesce in

amendments exempting 60 percent of the nation's housing units from coverage.[122] In the Senate, passage of even this truncated measure depended, as usual, on Minority Leader Everett Dirksen, who had expressed opposition to past civil rights legislation, only to ride to the rescue in the end. This time he announced his opposition and did not budge.[123] On September 14, 1966, the crucial effort to cut off an incipient southern filibuster fell ten votes short of the necessary two-thirds. Expressing a widely held view, Martin Luther King remarked, "I don't think the President has done battle for the bill or given enough leadership to get it through."[124] Remaining optimistic, however, Attorney General Katzenbach predicted, "I will live to see the day when Senator Dirksen votes for a fair housing section."[125]

In 1967, facing a Congress with fewer Democrats than before and a civil rights climate that could only be described as sullen, Johnson tried again. To enhance the chances of his less controversial civil rights proposals, he broke the 1966 omnibus bill into its various titles and submitted each separately. The House this time refused to vote on the administration's housing measure unless the Senate acted first. But the House did pass Johnson's proposal to protect civil rights workers. When this bill came up for Senate debate in January 1968, Minnesota Democrat Walter Mondale, playing a long shot, proposed to amend it by adding on a version of Johnson's fair-housing legislation.[126] Meanwhile, "Old Switcheroo," as some reporters fondly called Dirksen,[127] took note of the surprising support among Senate Republicans not only for the housing measure but for limiting debate and executed another of his remarkable shifts. Producing a fair-housing bill of his own, covering 80 percent of the nation's housing stock, he said, "One would be a strange creature indeed in this world of mutation if in the face of reality he did not change his mind." Mondale considered this turn of events "a miracle."[128] In March 1968 the Senate voted cloture and passed a stronger fair-housing bill than the one that had died in that chamber eighteen months before.

In the House the question was not whether fair housing would pass but whether the Senate's version would be accepted without change. If altered in any respect, the bill would have to go to a House-Senate conference committee and certain emasculation. Among those lobbying for passage intact was Lyndon Johnson. The issue was still in doubt on April 4, 1968, when Martin Luther King was murdered in Memphis, Tennessee. The resulting wave of remorse that swept the country helped carry the bill through the House unamended.[129] Thus, almost by accident, the civil rights lobby and its liberal allies scored their last victory of the decade.

A great victory for civil rights it was not. Without an enforcement agency to issue cease and desist orders against violators, the act was little more than a gesture toward the principle of fair housing. For example, it charged the Department of Housing and Urban Development to seek voluntary compliance with fair-housing complaints but denied it any power to impose remedies. The Justice Department received authority to initiate housing discrimination suits where "patterns and practices of discrimination" existed, but in practice chose cases that ducked difficult and sensitive issues like exclusionary zoning and "redlining" (i.e., refusal by mortgage lenders to provide home financing because of a neighborhood's minority composition).[130] Finally, though required by the law to take affirmative action on behalf of fair housing, the financial regulating bodies were slow to issue rules requiring nondiscrimination in mortgage lending and then derelict in enforcing them.[131] Still, the act had beneficial consequences, its mere existence serving to drive underground forms of discrimination that had once been flagrantly practiced. "This, in itself, is a measure of progress," one authority commented, "because resort to elaborate concealment makes discrimination less effective."[132]

Law or no law, did America move any closer in the sixties to Martin Luther King's goal of an open housing market? Apparently, she did. On the basis of data in the 1970 census, demographers detected a slight trend toward residential desegregation in the nation's larger cities.[133] One expert estimated that at the beginning of the decade "seven out of every eight nonwhite families living in nonwhite blocks of central cities would have had to move to a white block to attain a random racial pattern." By 1970, it was six out of seven.[134] Optimists felt heartened; pessimists pointed out that at this rate of change residential desegregation might be centuries away. One fact was not in dispute—thanks in part to an authoritative study of housing discrimination commissioned by HUD and published in 1978:[135] ten years after passage of Johnson's toothless fair-housing law, "a vast residue of discrimination"[136] in the housing market still remained—one reason why vast black ghettos continued to survive in the heart of metropolitan America. Johnson might have done more than he did for fair housing, but as no one knew better than he, the political cost would have been enormous and the benefits rendered aggrieved blacks problematic.

VI

The northern movement's last target was employment discrimination. As the sixties began, the situation of black Americans in the job market could only be described as appalling. Nearly half of black workers not on farms had unskilled jobs; only 13 percent of employed blacks in 1959 had white-collar positions; and the median income of black families was a mere 52 percent that of whites.[137] Blacks who were educated and blacks who were not knew it was a white man's world. Among carpenters, factory operators, and truck drivers with less than an eighth-grade education, the average black received only two-thirds the lifetime income of the average white. And black college graduates had less lifetime earnings than white workers who had not gone beyond grade school.[138] Experts advanced a variety of reasons to explain why blacks lagged behind so badly—inferior schooling, cultural disadvantage, disproportionate residence in the underdeveloped South. But, as numerous studies established beyond doubt, blacks were also the victims of corporations, craft unions, and even governments that refused to hire, pay, or promote without regard to race.[139]

Martin Luther King had a nonviolent solution to this problem, too. He called it Operation Breadbasket.[140] Originating in Philadelphia in 1959 and adopted for Atlanta by SCLC in 1962, Operation Breadbasket took root in Chicago on February 1, 1966, when King sold the idea to a group of local ministers. With recruits drawn from their congregations, he explained, the black clergy could organize picket lines and consumer boycotts to hit biased employers where it hurt—in their cash registers. To direct Operation Breadbasket in Chicago, King chose one of his more flamboyant staff aides, a twenty-four-year-old seminarian named Jesse Jackson. Jackson's first target was a local dairy called Country Delight. When its management rebuffed his efforts to negotiate in March 1966, Jackson put pickets in front of 40 of the 90 area stores selling Country Delight products and issued a demand for a fair-employment agreement. Four days later, having suffered losses of $500,000, the com-

pany capitulated, and subsequently so did all the other major dairies
in the city. Next, Jackson tackled local soft-drink-bottling plants,
including Pepsi Cola, which held out against a boycott for ten days
and then agreed to hire thirty-two black workers. Jackson chose
dairies because their products spoiled rapidly, and soft drinks because by now it was summer, the weather was hot, and the average
black drank 9 percent more soda than the average white. Climaxing
Operation Breadbasket in May 1967 with a dramatic victory over
local A&P stores, Jackson had apparently demonstrated the power
of nonviolence to achieve justice in the job market. At least Martin
Luther King thought so, for he announced in March 1967 that
Operation Breadbasket was graduating from a local to a national
program, that it was recruiting ministers in major cities across
America, and that it would challenge national corporations.

Actually, the program's well-publicized successes in Chicago were
illusory. Jackson himself claimed to have produced only 4,000 jobs
for blacks, but because he failed to follow up fair-employment
agreements, the actual number was not even close. In time, Jackson
became less the champion of lower-class black workers than of
middle-class black manufacturers, for whom he secured shelf space
in the white-owned stores of Chicago. As for Operation Breadbasket nationwide, Jackson was too busy cultivating his local following
to give it more than passing attention, and it never got off the
ground. Thus did flawed leadership, hit-and-run tactics, and the
usual difficulty of organizing poor blacks turn Breadbasket into
another of King's broken dreams.

Theoretically at least, Lyndon Johnson had considerably more
power to promote equal employment opportunity than did King.
After all, he headed a government that was itself the largest em-
ployer in the country, that required nondiscrimination of its contractors, and that was armed with Title VII of the 1964 Civil Rights
Act, outlawing discrimination in employment. But to transform
pious declarations of racial principle into living policy, Johnson
would have had to flog the lethargic bureaucracy into determined
action. This he was not prepared to do, not because he was indiffer-
ent to fair employment, but because he would not antagonize corporations and unions on this issue when he needed their support for
so many others.[141] In February 1965 Johnson appointed Vice President Humphrey chairman of the President's Committee on Equal
Employment Opportunity and designated him the administration's

civil rights coordinator. Rights leaders knew they were in trouble when, seven months later, the president abruptly and without explanation disbanded the committee and stripped Humphrey—a liberal on racial matters—of his civil rights responsibilities. "Well," said Humphrey, "I'm still Vice President."[142] Thereafter, agencies with fair-employment responsibilities were left to drift listlessly on their own rudders.

None of them acquitted themselves with distinction during Johnson's tenure. For example, the Civil Service Commission did help increase the percentage of black employees in the government, but one-third of them still worked in the Post Office, and only a tiny handful made it to the top grades. The Labor Department, taking over the task of enforcing the nondiscrimination clause in government contracts, performed so timidly that the Civil Rights Commission could find little difference between firms with government contracts and firms without. And the Equal Employment Opportunity Commission, created by Title VII of the 1964 Civil Rights Act, but given no power to enforce it, floundered around searching for an identity.[143] Nevertheless, enforcement efforts—begun in the 1960s—gathered considerable momentum and some force through the next decade. Thus in 1972 the Equal Employment Opportunity Commission finally obtained congressional authority to initiate court suits and was soon racking up fair-employment victories against some major corporations. But, even in the 1970s, the direct effects of federal enforcement on the vast and complex American job market were small.[144] Indirectly, of course, the effort helped raise the consciousness of some employers and coaxed others into voluntary compliance with the law.

Despite Johnson's lame performance in this area, blacks made major employment gains during the 1960s. They did so for several reasons. First, white opinion underwent a seismic shift in favor of nondiscrimination. In 1944 only 45 percent of whites polled believed that "Negroes should have as good a chance as whites to get any kind of job"; in 1963, it was 80 percent.[145] Second, blacks had begun rapidly to acquire more education—indeed to acquire it at a faster rate than whites. Third, as the result of severe labor shortages in the late 1960s, when the big breakthrough occurred, employers had to hire more blacks and promote them faster whether they wanted to or not. And fourth, the 1964 Civil Rights Act, not because it was enforced but merely because it existed, provided employers with an excuse to hire the black workers they now needed.[146] Pessimists who predicted that the end of the boom times would wipe out black progress proved wrong. Despite severe recessions and slower growth in the 1970s, blacks not only kept the gains they had made; they actually further closed the black-white education, earnings, and employment gaps—an achievement not possible without further decline in job market discrimination. Consider these facts:

- Technological change upgraded the entire labor force, but blacks moved up faster than whites.[147]

	Employment in White-Collar Jobs		
	1960	1970	1979
Black male labor force	11%	17%	28%
White male labor force	37%	40%	43%
Black female labor force	17%	32%	50%
White female labor force	59%	61%	67%

- One consequence of the especially rapid gains for black women was that white women found it ever more difficult to find maids. In 1960, 36 percent of black women were in household service; in 1970, 15 percent, in 1979, 6.5 percent.[148]

- As the employment gap narrowed, so did the income gap. The median income of black male employees was 59 percent that of white male employees in 1959, 67 percent in 1969, and 69 percent in 1977. Among women, the racial differential was nearly obliterated. The median income of black women was 64 percent that of white women in 1959, 82 percent in 1969, and 93 percent in 1977. Of course, both black and white women labored under the common burden of sex discrimination.[149]

- Increasing educational attainments helped open opportunities for blacks, and increasing opportunity encouraged blacks to improve their educational attainments. In 1960 approximately one of every three blacks aged 25–29 had a high school diploma; in 1972, it was two out of three. More whites had diplomas too, but the rate of increase was slower. As for college, 10 percent of college-age blacks attended in 1965, 21 percent in 1977. White enrollment in these years rose slightly from 26 percent to 26.5 percent.[150]

- Statisticians even found one category in which blacks had caught up by 1970. If a black family living in the North or West had a male head under 35 and both husband and wife working, its income, on the average, exceeded that of similarly situated white families by 4 percent.[151]

What, then, of Moynihan's famous assertion back in 1965 that "the gap between the Negro and most other groups in American society is widening"?[152] He was right, and he was wrong. It became a convention of analysis in the 1970s to view the black population as divided into two classes—those who were making it and those who were not.[153] Thanks to falling barriers in the job market, a growing proportion of the black population had climbed onto at least the lower rungs of the middle class. The result was a large step toward equality, defined by Moynihan himself as "a distribution of achievements among blacks comparable to that among whites."

But there remained a vast black underclass—perhaps one-third of the whole—still mired in the decaying heart of the ghetto and indeed worse off than before. These were, primarily, the blacks who dropped out of school, found themselves increasingly irrelevant in the complex modern economy, and often took advantage of the growing availability of welfare[154] to quit the job market altogether. Among black males with an eighth-grade education or less, labor-force participation rates declined alarmingly from 74 percent in 1965 to 53 percent in 1978; for high school dropouts, the rate declined from 87 percent to 62 percent.[155] It came as no surprise to Moynihan that, as employment performance declined, the pace of family breakdown dramatically quickened. Families headed by women without husbands increased from 22 percent in 1960, to 28 percent in 1970, to 39 percent in 1978.[156] The percentage of illegitimate black births rose from 22 percent in 1960 to 52 percent in 1977.[157] And drug abuse, venereal disease, and crime rates among black youths attained epidemic dimensions.[158]

After the Civil War the first Reconstruction undertook to ensure newly freed black citizens in the South legal and political equality. A hundred years later, in the Second Reconstruction, the civil rights movement successfully achieved this goal and in addition attempted to level artificial barriers, nationwide, against black achievement. Perhaps a century hence, a Third Reconstruction will accept the hardest challenge of all—final destruction of the ghetto's walls and integration of the black underclass into the mainstream of American life.

VII

After Watts, many liberal politicians, like President Johnson, found their close identification with the cause of black Americans a political liability. By the time of the 1966 congressional elections, the trend toward racial conservatism was unmistakable. "I call it an underriding issue," said one Republican state chairman, referring to the white backlash whose existence few politicians openly acknowledged but all had to reckon with.[159] That fall Gallup reported that 52 percent of white respondents thought the administration was pushing too hard on civil rights (up 20 points since 1962), while only 10 percent said not fast enough.[160] Many Republican candidates campaigned against "crime in the streets"—a frequent euphemism for black riots—and denounced the administration for sponsoring open-housing legislation.[161] Democrat George Mahoney won the Maryland gubernatorial primary on the slogan, "Your Home Is Your Castle—Protect It" (he lost to the moderate Republican Spiro Agnew in November).[162] "Go . . . into any home, any bar, any barber shop and you will find people are not talking about Vietnam or rising prices or prosperity," observed Chicago Congressman Roman Pucinski. "They are talking about Martin Luther King and how they are moving in on us and what's going to happen to our neighborhoods."[163]

The backlash cut less deep on election day, 1966, than many liberals had feared, but cut it did. Backlash voters helped reduce the Democratic House majority by forty-seven seats, ending the brief era of liberal dominance in Congress.[164] In Illinois, the old liberal stalwart Paul Douglas failed in his bid for a fourth Senate term partly because traditional Democrats in Chicago's ethnic neighborhoods would not forgive his unflinching support of open housing.[165] And in California conservative Republican Ronald Reagan amassed nearly one million more votes than incumbent Governor Pat Brown, partly because of white reaction against black rioting.[166] Surveying the wreckage of his campaign, Brown remarked, "Whether we like it or not, the people want separation of the races."[167]

In 1967, buffeted by the violence of blacks at home and the Vietcong abroad, Johnson's ship began to sink. This was the year when the racist demagogue H. Rap Brown preached black hate on the evening news, when 164 racial disturbances flared in communities across America, and when National Guard units, at one time or another, occupied parts of eight major cities.[168] Attacked on the left for not sponsoring a Marshall Plan for the cities and on the right for coddling rioters, Johnson found his leadership paralyzed. Nevertheless, he was not without compassion for the desperate people whose rage was destroying him. Indeed, in an effort to better understand the black dispossessed, he sent seven of his staff members for brief forays into fourteen of the nation's ghetto neighborhoods, anonymously, to act as his eyes and ears. To a man, these innocents were moved, even shocked, by what they saw. "Ways and means must be found to clean up the streets and vacant lots," Harry McPherson wrote the president. "It breaks the spirit, the ugliness everywhere."[169]

But compassion was not the mood of Congress, whose members cast about indiscriminately for ways to show the folks back home that they loathed rioters too. On July 19, 1967, only days after the Newark ghetto exploded, the House shouted through a bill making it a federal crime to cross state lines for the purpose of inciting a riot.[170] Never mind that the administration doubted the bill's utility or that civil libertarians doubted its constitutionality.[171] One day after this attempt to outlaw H. Rap Brown, the House took up Johnson's measure providing $40 million to assist local communities in exterminating rats. On the grounds that passage would reward rioters, conservatives laughed this "civil rats" bill off the floor. Predicting the eventual appointment of a rats commissioner, they said that the "rat smart thing for us to do is vote down this rat bill rat now"—which is what the House did.[172] Less than one week later the Detroit ghetto had to be pacified by the U.S. Army. Faced with the greatest domestic crisis of the century, Johnson could only create a commission to study the riots and designate a day of prayer for "order and reconciliation among men."[173]

By the autumn of 1967 Johnson stood lower in the polls than any president since Truman during the Korean War. Political analyst and demographer Richard Scammon suggested to Harry McPherson that the best thing Johnson could do was to have his picture taken with a policeman. The president had already figured that out for himself. In September he flew to Kansas City to deliver a speech, written by McPherson, before the International Association of Chiefs of Police. The only showstopper was a line he extemporized. "We cannot," he said, "tolerate behavior that destroys what generations of men and women have built here in America—no matter what stimulates that behavior, and no matter what is offered to try to justify it."[174] Thus Lyndon Johnson, who had once told his staff that civil rights leaders would have to wear sneakers to keep up with him, entered the twilight of his presidency in retreat from the liberal hope of racial justice and ingratiating himself with the police.

CHAPTER 8

War on Poverty I: The Failure of the Welfare State

I

PRESIDENT Johnson's 1964 declaration of war on poverty precipitated instant controversy. On the right Barry Goldwater attacked the "Santa Claus of the free lunch" and implied that the "attitude or actions" of the poor themselves might be the cause of their problem. On the left socialist Michael Harrington predicted that the likely result of the war would be not to abolish poverty but to enrich the politicians. Skepticism permeated even the great amorphous public, 83 percent of whom, according to Gallup, doubted that the war could ever be won.[1] Nonetheless, Johnson's declaration seemed at the time a master stroke. As policy, it perfectly suited the nation's post-assassination mood of idealism. And, as politics, it embarrassed the Republicans in the midst of the presidential campaign, since to oppose the war seemed tantamount to approving poverty. In the spring of 1964 the Republican Congressional Campaign Committee was reduced to sending two congressmen to Alabama to snoop around 3,600 acres of Lady Bird Johnson's land, where they triumphantly uncovered five black tenant farm families crowded into unpainted shacks without plumbing. "I want to stay here until the Good Lord takes me away," said Mrs. Charles Cutler, a tenant since 1914. "But I do wish that Mrs. Johnson would fix the roof. This old house leaks bad."[2] The blow was a glancing one, smudging Johnson's new image as champion of the Other American only slightly.

Johnson knew, of course, that he was running grave political risk by attacking poverty. There were far more affluent than impoverished voters, which meant that whatever he did for the poor must not impinge on the perceived interests of the middle classes—or else they would destroy him. Accordingly, he went to extraordinary lengths to convince well-heeled voters that his poverty programs conformed to traditional American values, would turn tax eaters into taxpayers, and were designed to forestall radicalism. "What you have and what you own . . ." the president told the Chamber of Commerce, "is not secure when there are men that are idle in their homes and there are young people that are adrift in the streets."[3]

Johnson's commitment to class harmony decisively influenced the administration's answer to the crucial question—what is poverty? In its 1964 annual report the Council of Economic Advisers defined poverty, sensibly enough, as lack of income. If a family of four received $3,000 or less annually it could not maintain "a decent standard of living," hence it was poor.[4] The arresting feature of the Council's definition was its treatment of poverty as a fixed condition with a permanent boundary. Any family able to purchase more than $3,000 worth of goods and service (in constant dollars) was then and thereafter to be considered nonpoor. One corollary of this definition was that, even if the government took no special measures to help the poor, the percentage of people living below the poverty line could be expected to decrease—since economic growth by itself would raise the real income of all classes. This conception of poverty had two political benefits from Lyndon Johnson's point of view: It virtually guaranteed that so long as the economy remained strong his promise to reduce poverty would be kept—regardless of the efficacy of his poverty programs. And, even more important, it meant that fighting poverty did not necessarily require the rich to be cast down, only that the poor be raised up.

Though politically serviceable, the Council's definition of poverty was intellectually indefensible. The concept of poverty as a fixed or absolute condition made sense only for past ages or for developing continents, in which to be poor meant command of resources— food, clothing, shelter—so meager that life itself was threatened. But poverty of this character hardly existed anymore in advanced industrial countries. Though undernourished children did exist in the United States, even among the poor they were the exception.

Compared to poor people in Bangladesh or the poor in Western countries only a century ago, most of the American poor enjoyed a living standard that far removed them from the margin of existence. Indeed, poverty in advanced societies differed so radically from other forms that it required a definition quite different from the one advanced by Johnson and his advisers.

The clue to the meaning of modern poverty was embedded in a paradox: real income for all classes of Americans in this century kept growing; yet estimates of the size of the poor population have rarely varied. In 1904 Robert Hunter's classic study estimated that "in all probability, no less than 20 percent" of the population in industrial states was poor "in ordinarily prosperous years."[5] In 1925 economist (later U.S. senator) Paul Douglas established a poverty standard for larger cities that translated into about 20 percent of their population.[6] And in 1964 the Council of Economic Advisers estimated that 20 percent of American families were poor.[7] The poverty line in each of these periods approximated half of median family income. In the mid-1920s when median income was roughly $2,000,[8] the 20 percent of families considered poor by Douglas received $1,000 or less. And in 1963, when median income was $6,000, the poverty line set by the Council of Economic Advisers was $3,000. The bottom 20 percent of American families kept getting richer, thanks to economic growth, but they lagged just as far behind everybody else as before. They were, in short, chasing a moving poverty line—and not gaining.[9]

Contrary to the Council, then, modern poverty was a relative, not a fixed, condition, for the concept of a "decent standard of living" expanded along with the Gross National Product. "Solely as a result of growing affluence," a presidential commission said in 1969, "a society will elevate its notions of what constitutes poverty."[10] Expectations about consumption rose, and so too did the quantity of goods actually required to become a participating member of society. Yesterday's luxuries became today's necessities. At the beginning of the century only wealthy Americans had cars, central heating, or refrigeration.[11] In 1970, 41 percent of *poor* families had cars, 62 percent had central heating, and 99 percent had refrigerators. But by the standards of the 1960s it did not matter that children fighting off rats in the Bronx or coal miners living in shacks in Appalachia or Mrs. Johnson's tenants in Alabama were better off than people living in other times and places or even that some of them drove old cars and had TV sets. What mattered was that they enjoyed so much less of a good life than other contemporary Americans that their condition was generally regarded as pitiable.

If poverty was not a matter of absolute want but of relative deprivation, then its cause was simple enough to grasp. It could only be income inequality. It followed that, to attack poverty, the government would have to reduce inequality, to redistribute income, in short, to raise up the poor by casting down the rich. By American standards, this was radicalism, and nobody in the Johnson White House ever considered it. As Ralph Lampham, staff member of the Council of Economic Advisers, wrote Walter Heller during the earliest phase of planning for the poverty program, "Most people see no political dynamite in the fact that our income distribution at the low end is about the same as it has always been"—the bottom fifth receiving about 5 percent of national income. "Probably a politically acceptable program must avoid completely the use of the term 'inequality' or of the term 'redistribution' of income or wealth."[12] It was not only the terms that were spurned, but the policies they implied. So Johnson went off to fight his war declaring that there would be no casualties. As in other wars, of course, so in this one —no casualties, no victories.

In fact, the War on Poverty was destined to be one of the great failures of twentieth-century liberalism. Most of its programs could be grouped under two strategies. One of these emphasized opening new opportunities for poor people either by investing in their education or by investing in areas, like Appalachia, where they were heavily concentrated. The other strategy, recognizing that mere opportunity would not be enough for many of the poor, provided subsidies to increase their consumption of food, shelter, and medical care. The administration hastened to assure that the cost of the new subsidies would be paid painlessly from expanding federal revenues generated by existing tax rates. Taken together, the programs spawned by these two strategies did little to diminish inequality and therefore, by definition, failed measurably to reduce poverty. Examined individually, moreover, each program turned out to be seriously flawed, not only because its conception was shoddy but because it sought to appease vested interests that had resisted reform or occasioned the need for it in the first place. (The one exception—an accidental anomaly—was the Community Action Program, whose treatment awaits the next chapter.) As illustrations of why the War on Poverty failed, four case histories will do: the Elementary and Secondary Education Act, Medicare-Medicaid, the 1968 housing act, and the Job Corps. The lesson to be learned was that appeasing the haves and helping the have-nots were incompatible policy goals—the fond hopes of Lyndon Johnson notwithstanding.

I I

Once President Johnson paused in an Appalachian hollow to chat with a bona-fide poor person, a father of eight with an annual income of $400. On taking his leave, the president paused to offer some implausible but earnest advice. "Don't forget now!" the president said. "I want you to keep those kids in school."[13] Whenever he looked at a ragged child, Johnson pretended to see himself. Schooling had rescued him from poverty, he claimed, and if possible, he would see that it rescued other poor children as well. In 1964, sensing the time was right, he delegated to Education Commissioner Francis Keppel, a former Harvard dean, the delicate task of framing appropriate legislation. The result was the most important education measure since the 1862 Morrill Act and the basis of Johnson's hopes that he would go down in history as "the education president."[14]

Keppel unveiled the Elementary and Secondary Education Act before Congress in 1965. Its heart was Title I, which proposed a nationwide program of compensatory education to improve the academic achievement of students from low-income families. Advancing a few simple propositions, which he regarded as practically self-evident, Keppel explained the bill's rationale. Students from poor families lacked the cultural advantages of the affluent and therefore tended, on the average, to fall behind academically, he argued. Schools could and should promote equality of academic achievement among social classes by devoting more resources to the poor than to the nonpoor, overcoming inequality originating in the home. If poor children performed better, they would stay in school longer; and, said Keppel, clinching his case, "We know that income correlates highly with the number of years of schooling completed." Thus a billion or two of federal dollars annually invested in educating poor children "could interrupt the cycle of poverty where we have a fighting chance."[15]

Of more pressing concern to Keppel than the bill's rationale was the politics of passage. As recently as 1961 a bitter church-state controversy had killed a federal school-aid measure. This time around Keppel applied his remarkable skills as a negotiator to arrange an ingenious truce among the contending parties. Deferring to the constitutional scruples of the National Education Association and organized Protestants, his bill provided no aid to parochial *schools*. But, to appease the Catholic bishops, it offered assistance to poor parochial school*children*. Public school districts were obliged to make Title I programs available to underprivileged private school students through expedients such as dual enrollment, educational television, and mobile equipment. As it turned out, the bishops were not well rewarded for their pliancy in this matter. Only 4 percent of private school students ever participated in Title I programs, compared to 19 percent of public school students.[16]

No less necessary to passage than solving the religious problem was appeasing the principal vested interest in public education— local school districts. To win their approval, the bill granted local districts primary responsibility for conceiving and administering compensatory programs. At the hearings the junior senator from New York, Robert F. Kennedy, questioned this surrender to localism. Did not local school districts themselves create educational deprivation? Kennedy asked Keppel. "I am sorry to say that is true," Keppel candidly replied. If Congress put funds "into a school system which itself creates this problem," Kennedy pushed on, "or helps create it, or does nothing, very little to alleviate it, are we not just in fact wasting the money of the Federal Government . . . ?" Keppel assured Kennedy that educators were undergoing "a rapid change in attitude," and would conscientiously use Title I money for social reform.[17] Keppel did not say that, unless local districts were appeased by being granted program control, they would never permit the bill to pass. And, for Lyndon Johnson at least, passage was everything.

"You take it from me," the president said, "I worked harder and longer on this measure than on any measure I ever worked on since I came to Washington in 1931." After he induced Congress, in April 1965, to pass the bill virtually as he submitted it, Johnson flew to Johnson City, Texas, to sign it on the site of the one-room schoolhouse where he began his own education. "As a son of a tenant farmer," he said, invoking a favorite myth about himself, "I know that education is the only valid passport from poverty."[18]

Soon after federal funds for compensatory education began flowing, it became clear that Johnson's faith would not receive a fair test—for the reasons Robert Kennedy had anticipated at the hearings. Most of the local districts charged with administering Title I were singularly lacking in sympathy for its objectives. Power in most local systems resided either in school boards dominated by middle-class conservatives or in bureaucrats wedded to routine and the status quo. For them, reorienting schools to the needs of the poor meant losing middle-class support, disrupting established procedures, and summoning imagination for which they were hardly famous.[19] Seventy percent of district superintendents polled in 1966 opposed allocating Title I funds on the basis of poverty.[20] Accordingly, in the early years, local districts siphoned off uncounted millions of program dollars into regular school budgets and away from compensatory education.[21] In Waukegan, for example, Title I paid for an assistant principal who performed routine administrative duties. In Cairo, Illinois, it supported general overhead costs. In Fresno it bought an educational TV system for all students in the county. In Camden, New Jersey, it subsidized physical education classes for students regardless of family income.[22] Illegal expenditures diminished by the early 1970s, but vested educational interests had other ways to subvert the program's reform intent.

The critical issue was targeting. As the law required, the Office of Education apportioned Title I funds to districts on the basis of the number of poor children residing in them. But it was up to the districts to chose recipient schools, and the schools to select Title I students. In 1965 Keppel's office issued tentative guidelines to assure that only schools with high concentrations of needy students would receive funds. When local officials and some congressmen protested, Keppel backed down. "That is when we gave away the ball game," one federal official commented. In eligible districts local school officials selected seven of every ten schools for Title I benefits. Within schools, officials exploited an anomaly in the act to blur targeting even further. The law mandated expenditures for the "educational needs of educationally deprived children."[23] "What is an educationally deprived child?" Robert Kennedy asked Keppel at the hearings. Keppel's reply implied that educational deprivation meant cultural deprivation and that cultural deprivation was the special handicap of students from low-income families.[24] But school administrators generally chose to define educational deprivation as low achievement, which can afflict the poor and nonpoor alike. Lyndon Johnson thought Title I was an antipoverty program. Local officials made sure it never was. A 1977 sample survey revealed that nearly two-thirds of the students in programs funded by Title I were not poor; more than half were not even low achievers; and 40 percent were neither poor nor low achieving.[25]

If properly administered, as it was in some districts, how likely was Title I to succeed? Did good compensatory education programs hold real promise of equalizing educational attainments among social classes? At the hearings only Congressman John Brademas had raised serious questions about the capacity of compensatory programs to improve the relative academic performance of the poor. "How can we be sure that if we spend more money on education for low-income children we will in fact improve the quality of their education?" he asked.[26] Despite Keppel's confident assurances, good evidence in support of compensatory education was lacking. The real test would have to be Title I itself.

But in the summer of 1966, just as the first Title I programs were gearing up, the Office of Education published a study called *Equality of Educational Opportunity*, which cast the pessimistic shadow of social science over the whole enterprise.[27] Authorized by the 1964 Civil Rights Act and carried out by a team of researchers under James S. Coleman of Johns Hopkins University, the survey tested 567,000 students, elicited questionnaires from 70,000 principals and teachers, and obtained information on facilities in some 4,000 schools. Though the Coleman Report primarily addressed the problem of equal educational opportunity by race, its conclusions dealt the whole edifice of received thinking about schools a shattering blow.

Coleman found that school factors did not explain much about why some students performed better than others. Physical plant, curriculum, and expenditures per child had little explanatory power. Teacher quality made only a small, though measurable difference. More important than any and all school factors in determining academic achievement was the student's family background. Schools, it seemed, could not overcome inequalities of achievement originating in unequal home environments. As the report put it, "Taking all these results together, one implication stands out above all: That schools bring little influence to bear on a child's achievement that is independent of his background and general social context; and that this very lack of an independent effect means that the inequalities imposed on children by their home, neighborhood, and peer environment are carried along to become the inequalities with which they confront adult life at the end of school."[28] These findings did not mean that schooling did not matter, only that beyond certain levels, additional inputs did not pay off. Nor did they mean that schools must always remain impotent to redress social inequalities. Said Coleman, "It is not, I suggest, that schools cannot have a powerful effect in reducing inequality. It is rather that they have not yet learned how to do so."[29] If Coleman was right (it would take more than a decade to undermine his authority[30]), then Title I, even if conscientiously administered, would not work.

Whether it worked or not became a matter of intense interest to educators and politicians. Enthusiasm for Title I might not have been overflowing in the local districts, but they did accept the money and in time acquiesced in spending most of it for instruction in reading and mathematics. Evaluations of Title I did not ask whether it assisted the poor but whether it helped "educationally deprived students" in compensatory programs to improve their academic performance relative to other students. Early surveys, all flawed, yielded mostly negative results.[31] But, as time went on, local projects began to report occasional successes, and educators professed to see cause for hope.[32] A 1977 study sponsored by the National Institute of Education surveyed 400 classes in 100 schools and reported the good news that Title I worked. Third graders in compensatory programs, for example, began the school year twelve months behind grade level in reading but ended the year only five months behind. The Institute concluded, "What happens in the classroom does have a strong effect on student learning."[33] Unfortunately, another study, also funded by the Institute, found that gains made during the school year were not maintained over the summer and that students entered the new grade as far behind as they would have been without special instruction. Indeed, studies of target populations over a period of years failed to detect any lasting impact of Title I on achievement.[34] The liberal hope that compensatory education could promote equality of opportunity had so far proved false.

Radicals who wished to reduce poverty by reducing income inequality also had reason to hope for Title I's success. Though no one in the Johnson administration ever acknowledged it, human-capital theorists predicted that one consequence of raising the educational attainments of the poor relative to the nonpoor would be to make incomes more equal. As the supply of highly skilled labor increased, the supply of unskilled labor would decrease, lowering wages at the top and raising them at the bottom. But, by the end of the decade, human-capital theory was in retreat and with it radical faith in the equalizing potential of formal schooling. For, as economist Lester Thurow observed, while the number of years of school among social classes had grown more equal since 1950, incomes had not.[35] Thus, even if Title I had worked, it might not have had much effect on poverty. In his 1972 polemic, *Inequality,* debunking the capacity of schools to do much of anything, Christopher Jencks drew the logical conclusion. Radicals, of whom he was one, should give up the effort to reduce inequality indirectly through education and agitate instead for efficient mechanisms to take money from the rich and give it to the poor.[36]

III

The most ambitious effort ever made by the government to furnish in-kind income to some of its citizens was popularly known as Medicare.[37] Climaxing nearly a decade of debate, President Johnson asked Congress in January 1965 to enact compulsory hospital insurance for nearly all persons over sixty-five, financed by contributions to the social security system. After all, advocates argued, old people used hospitals three times as frequently as the non-aged, had average incomes only half as large, and possessed inadequate health insurance.[38] Given the overwhelming liberal majority in the 89th Congress, there was no doubt that this case would prevail. What no one foresaw was that Congress would take Johnson's bill, rewrite it, and legislate a program dramatically more generous.

It was Wilbur Mills, chairman of the House Ways and Means Committee and a Medicare opponent, who took note of the nation's liberal mood and presided over the bill's expansion. Many old persons incorrectly believed that Johnson was proposing to pay all their medical costs, not just hospitalization, and few Congressmen cared to risk the consequence of their disappointment. At a committee session in March, Mills suddenly suggested that some elements of a Republican substitute be reworked and added to the administration's measure. Medicare now would provide not only compulsory hospital insurance for the aged under social security; it would offer voluntary insurance covering doctors and surgical fees, the premiums to be split between the government and the beneficiary.[39] Elated, assistant Health, Education, and Welfare secretary Wilbur Cohen rushed to the White House to seek Johnson's approval. "Just tell them to snip off that name 'Republican' and slip those little old changes into the bill," Johnson said.[40]

So far the Medicare bill was not strictly speaking an antipoverty measure. One had only to be old to receive benefits. Almost casually, Mills tacked on a new program that would benefit not the old primarily, but the poor, regardless of age. This was Medicaid, a real antipoverty program that could potentially affect as many people and cost as much money as Medicare, but which received only cursory attention from the Congress enacting it. Medicaid was an appendage of the welfare, not the social security, system. States electing to participate would receive matching grants from the federal government to pay medical bills for two classes of citizens— welfare recipients and the medically indigent. Medically indigent persons were those in certain categories (the blind, the disabled, the aged, or children in single-parent families), who were ineligible for welfare but could not afford to pay for medical care. Conspicuously absent from Medicaid coverage were the working poor.

When it came time to sign the bill, Johnson flew to Independence, Missouri, home of Harry Truman, who had proposed national health insurance twenty years before. There, in the presence of the grateful elder statesman, Johnson hailed the arrival of a new medical era. "No longer will older Americans be denied the healing miracle of modern medicine," he said. "No longer will illness crush and destroy the savings that they have so carefully put away." Johnson was even moved by the occasion to invent an appropriate passage of scripture. "Thou shalt open thine hand wide unto thy brother, to thy poor, to thy needy, in thy land," he said.[41]

The government did indeed open wide its hand in distributing benefits under the new programs. Nearly all aged persons in the country qualified for Medicare's hospitalization benefits, and 96 percent elected to buy supplementary physician's insurance as well. Costs quickly outstripped estimates, rising from $3.4 billion to nearly $18 billion in ten years. Medicaid caught on more slowly, since its implementation was up to the states. But in time Medicaid nearly matched Medicare's scope, the number of recipients growing from 4 to 24 million in a decade and costs reaching $14 billion.[42] In sum, by 1976, Medicare and Medicaid financed medical services for one-fifth of the population at a cost of $32 billion.

Like so many other welfare programs, Medicare-Medicaid represented a ruinous accommodation between reformers and vested interests, in this case the organized doctors. So desperate was the American Medical Association to exorcise the specter of socialized medicine that in the climactic final days of congressional debate it paid twenty-three lobbyists a total of $5,000 a day to prevent passage.[43] Though the doctors were no longer strong enough to defeat Medicare, they nevertheless extracted their pound of flesh. HEW's Wilbur Cohen recalled that he had had to pledge to the Ways and Means Committee "that there would be no real controls over hospitals or physicians. . . . I promised very conscientiously that I would see to it there was no change in the basic health delivery system because so far as the AMA and Congress were concerned, this was sacred."[44] The law, therefore, provided that hospitals would be reimbursed for their reasonable costs and physicians for customary fees. As it turned out, this formula not only guaranteed that the medical profession could continue as before; it guaranteed galloping medical price inflation as well.

The major cause of medical price inflation was health insurance, of which Medicare was only one example.[45] Private health insurance had begun to spread after 1950, and as it did, medical prices spurted upward, especially hospital prices, which account for 40 percent of the nation's health bill. Most hospitals were nonprofit organizations. Before the widespread availability of insurance, hospital administrators had every incentive to keep costs down, because customers (i.e., patients) had to bear most of them. But insurance reduced the net price of hospital services for the patient at the time he consumed them and thereby removed the chief motive for cost restraint. Patients and doctors typically responded to lower net prices by demanding the best or, more accurately, the most expensive care that other people's money could buy. In other words, patients demanded more expensive care than they would elect if they paid all of the bill directly. Administrators could now please doctors by buying the latest equipment, patients by adding amenities, workers by raising wages, trustees with grandiose visions by adding beds—and pass on the added costs in the form of higher prices, increasingly paid through the painless mechanism of insurance. The process fed on itself. "People spend more on health because they are insured and buy more insurance because of the high cost of health care," one economist explained.[46] Insurance was the main reason why, between 1950 and 1965, hospital prices rose 7 percent annually, while the general price level went up less than 2 percent a year.

Doctor's fees, accounting for 20 percent of medical expenditures, also rose in response to the spread of private health insurance. Unlike most hospitals, most doctors were in business for a profit. Insurance reduced the net price of physician services for covered patients, causing demand to increase. Doctors exploited the favorable market by raising fees. Insurance caught on more quickly for hospital than for doctor care; so inflation in doctors' fees was less acute, rising at 3 percent annually from 1950 to 1965.[47] Insurance was not the only reason for medical price inflation, but it was the most important.

With passage of Medicare-Medicaid in 1965, the quantity of insurable services stood on the verge of significant increase. By the logic of medical economics, inflationary pressure on medical prices was bound to mount. The new programs, after all, imposed no cost controls and did not alter the way hospitals and doctors ordinarily conducted their business. Hospital prices, which had risen 7 percent in the year before Medicare, jumped by 14 percent in the year after and continued to rise, on the average, 14 percent annually over the next decade. Physicians' fees rose 7 percent a year.

Medicare not only increased the cost of medicine for society as a whole; it provided far fewer financial benefits for most recipients than was commonly believed. For that small minority of old people who had both long periods of hospitalization and small savings, Medicare was everything it was cracked up to be.[48] But the average aged person was little better off. True, he paid only 29 percent of his medical bills directly out of pocket in 1975, compared to 53 percent before Medicare; but his total bill was also much higher. The average beneficiary spent $237 out of pocket in the year before Medicare and $390 ten years later—in constant dollars almost exactly the same.[49] Aged persons not only had to buy drugs, eye glasses, and dental care, which Medicare did not cover; they expended increasing out-of-pocket sums for physicians' and hospital bills, part of which Medicare did cover. For example, in 1975 beneficiaries paid a deductible for each stay in a hospital, reaching $104 (up from $40 when the program began); and they paid, on the average, $156 for physician services (up from $66).[50] Some additional expenditure could be explained by increased consumption of medical services and by better services. But, ironically, medical price inflation fueled by Medicare itself helped erode much of Medicare's benefits. So many gaps existed in Medicare's coverage that 24 percent of health care expenditures for the aged in 1970 had to be covered by state and local government, mainly in the form of Medicaid payments.[51]

Medicaid helped states pay for a wide assortment of medical expenses for welfare recipients and the medically indigent. What prompted this generosity on the part of the government is not entirely clear. Most likely, Congress theorized that lack of income was a barrier to treatment. Actually, the poor had not fared all that badly prior to Medicaid, thanks to the willingness of doctors and hospitals to dispense charity medicine. In the last year before Medicaid the hospital admission rate for families with incomes below $3,000 was 107 per 1,000 families; for families with incomes $10,-000 and above, it was only 89 per 1,000 families. Before Medicaid, the average low-income person visited a doctor 4.3 times a year—not dramatically less than the 5.1 visits made by high-income persons. Granted that the poor are more frequently ill, these figures do not sustain a thesis of gross inequality. Still, if its purpose was to increase access to medical services, Medicaid succeeded. By 1968 the hospital admission rate for poor families had climbed from 107 to 123 per 1,000, while the admission rate for the affluent fell slightly. And low-income persons now actually saw doctors more frequently than high-income persons (5.6 visits compared to 4.9 visits).[52] The question is, were the benefits worth the cost?

For one thing, Medicaid did not buy a better brand of service than charity medicine had dispensed. The typical doctor shunned Medicaid patients not only from considerations of status and paperwork, but also from income—state governments usually setting fees far below customary charges. In New York City only an estimated 8 percent of the city's 12,000 doctors, often the least capable, accepted Medicaid patients.[53] Dr. John Knowles, director of the Massachusetts General Hospital and a medical reformer, said in 1969, "Medicaid has degenerated into merely a financing mechanism for the existing system of welfare medicine which is not adequate and must be changed. . . . It perpetuates . . . the very costly, highly inefficient, inhuman and undignified means tests in the stale atmosphere of charity medicine carried out in many instances by marginal practitioners in marginal facilities."[54] Nothing happened subsequently to invalidate this judgment.

Medicaid had other problems as well. While it reduced some inequalities, it created others: annual benefits in 1974 varied from $214 per recipient in Missouri to $911 in Minnesota; 40 percent of the poor were not on welfare and so received no benefits; 30 percent of Medicaid recipients were not poor at all.[55] Fraud haunted the program. Medical entrepreneurs, often in so-called Medicare mills, bilked the government by dispensing unnecessary services or charging for nonexistent services, abuses that cost the state of New York an estimated $250 million annually.[56] And finally, it was absurd on the face of it that nearly $6 of every $10 spent on public assistance in 1975 took the form of Medicaid payments.[57] Undoubtedly, most poor people would have preferred the cash.

In the end Medicare-Medicaid relied on a simple equation: more medicine equals better health. After 1965 death rates resulting from the major diseases dropped sharply, and so did infant mortality rates.[58] Friends of these programs hailed these trends as evidence that increased utilization of medical services by the poor and the aged had paid off. Skeptics had their doubts.[59] After Medicare, old people saw doctors more frequently and stayed in hospitals more days per admission (though their admission rate did not rise). Still, according to one prominent medical economist, "there is no evidence that Medicare has had a significant effect on the mortality rate of the aged."[60] As for the rapidly declining infant mortality rate, it may be linked to the increasing proportion of poor pregnant women who visit doctors in the first trimester,[61] or just as plausibly, to improved birth control techniques that have reduced the number of unwanted births.[62]

Equalitarians had their own standards for judging Medicare and Medicaid. Since some Medicare benefits and all Medicaid benefits aided poor and near-poor persons, these programs appeared to reduce income inequality. Taxpayers lost money income, and the needy gained income in kind. But, as so often happens in the world of welfare, appearances can be deceiving. Most of the government's medical payments on behalf of the poor compensated doctors and hospitals for services once rendered free of charge or at reduced prices. Only that small fraction of Medicare-Medicaid payments purchasing additional services for the poor constituted real additions to their income. Aside from middle-class old persons protected from the financial ravages of long illness, the clearest beneficiaries of Medicare and Medicaid were doctors, who, according to one estimate, enjoyed an average income gain of $3,900 in 1968 as a result of these programs.[63] Medicare-Medicaid, then, primarily transferred income from middle-class taxpayers to middle-class health-care professionals. In this way, once again, the politics of consensus prevailed over the policy of redistribution.[64]

IV

Johnson did not submit major housing legislation until February 1968, by which time ardor for reform had practically vanished. But the previous summer rampaging blacks had set fire to slum neighborhoods in Newark, Detroit, and a hundred other American communities. Since most liberals equated slums with bad housing, Johnson responded to the ghetto crisis by sending Congress the most ambitious housing program in American history.[65] Its purpose—to replace bad housing with good. The housing census having counted 6 million substandard units in the United States, the president proposed building 600,000 federally subsidized housing units for lower-income families every year for the next ten years. By contrast, federal programs had subsidized an annual average of only 40,000 units over the preceding twenty years.

As novel as the goal were the tactics Johnson proposed to achieve it. Since public housing had become mired in controversy, the president decided to rely on "the genius of American business"[66] to meet the housing needs of lower-income families. In other words, the same vested interests—bankers and builders—who had hitherto ignored or failed the poor were to become the instruments of the Great Society's housing reform. Recognizing a good thing when they saw it, the bankers and builders immediately took up the reform cause and helped lobby Johnson's housing measure through Congress in six months. The 1968 housing act authorized 1.7 million subsidized units over the next three years—the first installment on Johnson's ten-year goal. The president characteristically hailed the measure as a potential "Magna Carta to liberate our cities."[67]

The law created two new programs, which became sections 235 and 236 of the National Housing Act. Both programs depended on the private housing market for implementation and used the same bait—government-subsidized mortgages. Section 235 had the remarkable purpose of bringing home ownership within the reach of lower-income families. For as little as $200 down and 20 percent of monthly income, a needy family could obtain mortgage money from a bank, at the market interest rate, for a modestly priced house. Bankers would lend the money since the Federal Housing Authority had to insure "235" mortgages. Developers would supply the homes, since they were allowed to charge whatever the market would bear. And eligible poor citizens would line up to participate, since they might pay as little as 1 percent interest on the mortgage (depending on income), with the government paying the rest. In this way, it was hoped, sullen slum dwellers would be transformed into responsible, property-owning citizens.

The worthy purpose of the second program—section 236—was to increase the supply of rental housing available to the needy. The program worked this way: Developers borrowed mortgage money from bankers at market rates to build a "236" project; obtained a government mortgage subsidy, which lowered their interest payments to 1 percent; and passed the subsidy benefit on to low-income tenants in the form of lower rates. The sponsor-developers could be nonprofit community groups or, more commonly, limited dividend corporations. It seemed unlikely that private investors would be attracted to the program, since profits were limited by the law to an unattractive 6 percent. But in 1969 Congress solved this problem by providing special tax treatment for rental housing in the form of accelerated depreciation allowances not available to other kinds of investment. The ironic result was to turn section 236 into a tax shelter for the rich.

As it turned out, implementation of the Great Society housing law fell to President Richard Nixon and his Secretary of Housing and Urban Development, George Romney. Elected in 1968 not to repeal social programs but make them work, these Republicans exerted pressure on the HUD bureaucracy to produce subsidized housing fast. As a result, Nixon built more units for lower-income families (1.3 million) in three years than all previous administrations combined. The new programs accounted for most of this production. Through 1972 section 235 was providing mortgage subsidies for 398,000 housing units, and section 236 was either assisting or was scheduled to assist 593,000 more—committing the government to an estimated $16.5 billion in mortgage payments over the next forty years.[68] At last, it seemed, a social-welfare program was working. Large numbers of needy families actually obtained better housing than they had before at prices they could afford.[69]

But almost from the beginning the smell of scandal hovered over the new programs. Profit seekers were attracted by the bait, as Johnson hoped, but with results he had not anticipated. In January 1971 a House committee investigating complaints from families that had purchased 235 homes declared that the Federal Housing Administration "may be well on its way toward insuring itself into a national housing scandal."[70] Eight days after labeling the House report "inaccurate, misleading, and very incomplete," Secretary Romney changed his mind and briefly suspended that part of section 235 initially permitting 30 percent of subsidized homes to be supplied from existing rather than newly built homes.[71]

Fast-buck speculators had responded to this provision in 235 by purchasing cheap homes in deteriorating ghetto neighborhoods, making cosmetic repairs, and reselling them at inflated prices to buyers with government subsidized mortgages. Theoretically, appraisers from the FHA, which insured 235 mortgages for the banks, could block the sale of shoddy homes by refusing to certify them as sound. In fact, FHA appraisers had always been in bed with realtors and bankers and lived by the motto "caveat emptor." Thousands of lower-income families, many on relief, bought homes with leaky plumbing, cracked plaster, flooded basements, faulty heating, and rotted roofs.[72] In 1971 HUD's own auditors sampled 235 homes supplied from the existing housing stock and reported that 43 percent had been unsuitable for certification at the time of sale. HUD's sample of *newly* built section 235 homes was only somewhat more encouraging, 26 percent of them being judged unfit for sale, pending repair.[73] Saddled with maintenance costs they had not expected, many owners simply walked away from section 235 homes, leaving the federal government to pay off the banks and take over the property. As HUD's inventory of foreclosed homes mounted, journalists began to describe the department as the nation's number one slumlord.[74]

The problems that plagued the section 236 rental housing program stemmed from the bizarre incentive system used to attract builders and investors.[75] With HUD approval, a builder-developer could obtain an FHA-insured mortgage sufficient to cover 90 percent of estimated costs of constructing a low-cost rental housing project. The builder's incentive for undertaking construction was the right to a fee, which, in practice, he collected by selling shares in the project. The only buyers for these shares were wealthy investors interested not in the project's limited profitability but in the tax dodge available to owners of rental property. The developer usually sold shares—that is, obtained a fee—equivalent to 15 percent of the mortgage; and shareholders usually received an aftertax return on their investment of 15–20 percent.[76] This incentive system produced two regrettable consequences. First, it encouraged builders to proliferate construction costs, since a more expensive project meant bigger fees for developers and tax write-offs for investors (as well as higher rents for tenants).[77] Second, neither the builder nor the investor had an interest in the long-term viability of the project. The developer's interest essentially ended when he obtained his fee; and investors were concerned mainly with taking paper depreciation losses, which were exhausted after ten years. No one but the tenants had a stake in sound maintenance and management for the full forty years of the mortgage. Primarily because of weak management, 20 percent of all section 236 projects were projected to fail within the first ten years.[78]

As information on these programs accumulated, congressmen, scholars, and housing officials were afflicted with a growing sense of unease. Like other in-kind programs, sections 235 and 236 were supposed to redistribute income from affluent taxpayers to the needy. But it turned out that the subsidies did not reach deep enough to help many poor families. Of home owners subsidized under 235, only 13 percent were poor. Of renters subsidized under 236, less than half (43 percent) were poor, and many of these could afford the rent only because, in addition to the mortgage subsidy, they also received rent supplement payments under a different federal program.[79] What social purpose was served by a program most of whose beneficiaries were moderate-income families of unproved need? Was it equitable to provide a subsidy of approximately $900 annually to a small fraction of eligible families and nothing to the rest? And how could the government justify expending $1,050 in tax dollars to provide the $900 subsidy, when most of the assisted families would have settled for some lesser sum in cash to spend as they pleased?[80]

Not only did sections 235 and 236 provide few direct benefits to real poor people; indirect effects in some cities actually aggravated the slum problem. Like all subsidized housing programs since the Depression, sections 235 and 236 were intended not only to help the needy but to stimulate the construction industry. As a result, 90 percent of all units subsidized under the 1968 housing law were newly built. But for many cities, especially older cities, new housing was a curse. As every newspaper reader in the 1960s knew, white middle-class families were fleeing older central cities even faster than lower-class black families moved in, causing population declines of 17 percent in St. Louis, 16 percent in Boston, 14 percent in Cleveland and Pittsburgh, 10 percent in Detroit, and lesser declines elsewhere.[81] One result was a chronic oversupply of housing in older cities. Lower-class families with rising incomes could exploit slack housing markets by moving into recently vacated homes in good neighborhoods. But the hard-core poor could not afford to move, unless landlords in marginal neighborhoods, desperate for tenants, converted their properties for low-income occupancy by subdividing them or economizing on maintenance—in short, by creating new slums.[82]

As poor tenants moved into new slum neighborhoods, population in older slums thinned out, leaving some landlords no choice but to abandon unwanted properties. Abandoned housing—100,000 units in New York, 30,000 in Philadelphia, 10,000 in St. Louis[83]— became a cause as well as a consequence of decay, a haven for winos, the breeding ground for rats, an invitation to vandals and pyromaniacs. Into this urban quagmire stepped HUD, spending millions for new homes that aggravated the problem of oversupply. New construction under 235 and 236, often in the suburbs, promoted migration from old neighborhoods, further depressed inner-city rents, and hastened the process of disinvestment and abandonment.[84] The mayor of Seattle, which had a temporary glut of housing in the early 1970s, could just as well have spoken for older cities with a permanent glut when he said, "The last thing I want is money for new housing."[85]

In January 1973 President Nixon infuriated liberals by suspending all federally subsidized housing programs. Doubtful as a matter of law, Nixon's action was eminently sensible as a matter of policy. It had by now begun to dawn on housing officials that the real housing problem of the poor was not the physical condition of their dwellings but lack of money to afford better. The government began to experiment with housing allowances, which poor people could spend as they wished for housing of their choice. Housing allowances had problems of their own but nonetheless represented a major conceptual advance over past programs. As a way to redistribute income, sections 235 and 236 had hardly proved efficacious, unless one happened to be a mortgage lender, a builder, or a wealthy tax dodger who had seen his chance and taken it.

V

No aspect of poverty worried liberals more than the one million young men, ages sixteen through twenty-one, who were unemployed or out of the work force in 1963.[86] As superfluous labor, this population stood as a threat to the social peace and an indictment of the social system. Years of agitation by reformers to offer these young people special vocational education finally paid off in 1964 when Congress created the Job Corps as part of the Economic Opportunity Act. The Job Corps intended annually to recruit 100,-000 unemployed young men and women, remove them far from slum environments, and provide them skills to exploit the abundant opportunities of the American economy. Training would take place either in "urban centers" (most of which were actually abandoned military bases) or, at the insistence of the conservation lobby, in rural conservation camps where the least literate would receive basic education and work experience. Sargent Shriver, director of the Office of Economic Opportunity, waged fierce warfare with the Labor Department to win control of the Job Corps, hoping that it would yield instant results and cover him with quick glory. He never made a greater mistake.

Shriver launched the Job Corps with a major promotional drive to attract recruits, a drive so successful that by mid-1965 the Corps had received 300,000 applications for the available 10,000 slots.[87] Most of the thousands turned away never returned. Shriver tapped some of the most prestigious corporations in America, including General Electric, IBM, Litton Industries, RCA, and Westinghouse to run the urban centers, convinced they would provide the most efficient but innovative training programs possible. The corporations pioneered no pedagogical breakthroughs, and the cost-plus contracts under which they operated offered no incentives for efficiency.[88] Shriver launched the Job Corps, excited by the therapeutic possibilities of residential training centers far from the slum neighborhoods of the recruits. But this experiment never paid off, creating so many problems and generating so much bad publicity at the beginning that the Job Corps never really recovered.

The first recruits typically found themselves 1,200 miles away from home, isolated from members of the opposite sex, subjected to unaccustomed discipline, and disappointed in the Corps's facilities and programs. The first year—1965—troubles abounded. Several corpsmen were arrested at the Atterbury center in Indiana for forcing a fellow trainee to commit sodomy. In Austin, Texas, a trainee on leave from Camp Gary got stabbed in a fight. At Camp Breckinridge in western Kentucky a food riot had to be quelled by federal marshals. Corpsmen were charged with burglaries in Laredo, promiscuity in St. Petersburg, and window smashing in Kalamazoo.[89] Meanwhile congressmen expressed shock on learning that the average cost per enrollee at a residential center in 1966 exceeded $8,000 and debated whether a Harvard education cost as much.[90] In 1966 Shriver was disappointed when Congress limited Job Corps slots to 45,000, though applicants to fill even this number would soon prove exceedingly difficult to find.

During the second year, the Job Corps solved its worst problems and settled down to dispense vocational education. To its everlasting credit, it recruited from a clientele that nearly every other institution in America had abandoned. One of every four corpsmen had an eighth-grade education or less; more than half were black; all came from poor families.[91] But, while many no doubt benefited from the experience, only a minority emerged notably more employable than before they began. Throughout the first decade, two-thirds of enrollees quit before completing the typical six-to-nine-month course, and nearly half were gone in three months or less.[92] Those who did graduate received better wages and had lower unemployment rates than Corps dropouts but, according to surveys made in 1966 and 1967, did no better in the labor market than "no-shows" (applicants who had been accepted by the Job Corps but had not shown up). Six months after leaving the Corps, 28 percent of *graduates* were unemployed and only one-third had jobs related to their training.[93]

At root, the problem of the Job Corps, as with other government manpower programs, was the nature of the training. It was simply unrealistic to expect any educational institution to take young men and women as culturally handicapped as Job Corps recruits and train them for really good jobs. Corps courses prepared trainees only for entry-level proficiency in occupations such as cook, baker, janitor, welder, construction worker, meat cutter, and auto-body repairer.[94] These were jobs for which employers could easily hire workers from the existing labor pool and provide simple on-the-job training. The probable effect of the Job Corps, therefore, was to give its graduates a slight advantage over other similarly disadvantaged youths competing for the same openings. Because jobs obtained by corpsmen would have gone to someone else, the program had little or no effect on the overall unemployment rate,[95] nor did it achieve much income redistribution, except perhaps from one group of the disadvantaged to another.

Among those who questioned the wisdom of expanding training opportunities without expanding the supply of jobs was Labor Secretary Willard Wirtz. In the hectic early weeks of 1964, while poverty legislation was still being drafted, Wirtz persuaded Shriver, Johnson's chief poverty planner, that training alone was not enough. On February 18 Shriver presented the Cabinet a proposal to levy a five-cent tax on cigarettes to raise $1.25 billion annually for a public employment program.[96] Adam Yarmolinsky, present at the meeting as Shriver's deputy, recalled, "I have never seen a colder reception from the president. He just—absolute blank stare —implied even without opening his mouth that Shriver should move on to the next proposal. We weren't even going to discuss that one. Whereupon Bill Wirtz, being the original proponent of jobs as a solution chimed in and made the impassioned speech for jobs which the president completely ignored."[97]

Johnson had the best of reasons for turning Shriver down, as Shriver might already have known. That very day Gardner Ackley, acting chairman of the Council of Economic Advisers, had sent Shriver a memo explaining why it was not good policy to tax a dollar away from the private economy to spend it on a public employment program.[98] Tax plus spending "is unlikely to produce much if any net increase in the total number of jobs," Ackley explained. The government would merely remove a dollar from the private economy, thereby lessening private demand and private employment, in order to add to public demand and public employment. Employment would shift from the private to the public sector, with little or no net change. So the Job Corps dispensed training which its clients frequently did not appreciate and for which there existed less than pressing need.

VI

In October 1968, during the gloomy twilight of his presidency, Lyndon Johnson entertained a group of regional OEO directors at the White House. "Here are the campaign ribbons that you and I have earned during the past 5 years," he said, whereupon he rattled off figures showing that his administration had moved people out of poverty at "the fastest rate in all of our history." Updated, these figures were his consolation and his vindication. Federal spending on the poor had risen from nearly $12 billion to more than $27 billion in six years. The incidence of poverty had gone down from 20 percent of the population to 12 percent. And 12 million people had moved across the official poverty line. He had had failures along with successes, Johnson admitted, but he could say at the end, as he had at the beginning, "we must continue."[99]

That the war on poverty had much to do with reducing poverty is doubtful. Its programs were too recent to make much difference and too misconceived ever to do so. Indeed, those who most directly benefited were the middle-class doctors, teachers, social workers, builders, and bankers who provided federally subsidized goods and services of sometimes suspect value. The principal cause of the mass migration across the administration's fixed poverty boundary was not the war on poverty but the war in Vietnam. That war helped overheat the economy, generated rapid increases in GNP, and moved the poor up with everybody else, temporarily even a little faster.

Johnson's boast that poverty had diminished was, in any case, only as good as the official definition of the problem. Those who regarded poverty not as a fixed but a relative condition could argue that no progress at all had occurred. As confirmed by recent opinion surveys, the public continued to regard half of median family income as a realistic poverty line.[100] In 1963, when median income was $6,000 and the poverty line $3,000, 20 percent lived beneath it. In 1976, more than a decade after Johnson launched his poverty war, the median had risen to $15,000, and 20 percent still received less than half.[101] By this view of the matter, income inequality had not been reduced and therefore the extent of poverty had remained constant.

Agreeing that the reduction of inequality was the test of success, some defenders of Johnson's war eventually argued that merely looking at the distribution of money income was not enough. Great Society programs to provide in-kind income to the poor—food stamps, Medicare-Medicaid, housing subsidies—were just as good as money, they said. If the dollar value of in-kind income was added to the money income, the poor received a larger share of national income than if money income alone was considered. Inequality, hence poverty, had diminished after all. The argument was as ingenious as it was spurious.[102] Approximately 85 percent of in-kind income took the form of medical services provided by Medicare-Medicaid.[103] But, since most payments under these programs compensated doctors and hospitals for services previously rendered free of charge or for reduced charges, Medicare-Medicaid added little to the real income of poor people. Of the government's in-kind expenditures, only food stamps were income as good as cash for the poor.

While Great Society programs accomplished little redistribution, older government measures did. Cash transfer programs originating in the New Deal—public assistance, social security, unemployment insurance—provided disproportionate benefits to poor people. In 1972 the bottom 20 percent had only 1.7 percent of national income before transfers but 5.4 percent afterward[104]—not enough to raise them above half the median but a significant addition to income nonetheless. Many reformers came increasingly to advocate more generous cash transfer programs as the way to move families at the bottom of the income scale above the poverty line, no matter how defined.

But, even from the point of view of equalitarians, these schemes posed problems. A reasonable program to lift most American families above even the official, fixed poverty line in 1972 would have required additional tax transfers of $30 to $40 billion. Since there were not all that many rich people, and tax rates at the top were already steep, much of the burden of redistribution would have fallen on families with incomes between $15,000 and $25,000, families not so very affluent.[105] Moreover, redistribution of that magnitude might seriously inhibit the incentive to work. High taxes had not yet encouraged a taste for leisure among earners in the top brackets, but at some undetermined higher level they almost certainly would. The effects of generous cash transfers on the work incentives of low-wage workers were easier to measure. A painstak-

ing experiment in 1971–1972 tested a variety of income-mainte-
nance schemes to aid poor families in Denver and Seattle. Testifying
before a dismayed congressional committee in 1978, the director of
the study reported a significant work disincentive. "On the average," he said, "we found that the experiments caused a reduction
in annual hours of work of about 5 percent for the male heads of
families, about 22 percent for wives and 11 percent for female heads
of families."[106]

Finally there remained the perennial puzzle of what effect higher
taxes would have on the willingness to save and invest.[107] Progressive tax rates had not so far affected the rate of investment, but if
high enough would undoubtedly do so. By inducing less work and
less investment, more drastic income redistribution would result in
less economic growth. Less growth would mean fewer jobs and a
slower rise in living standards, important to poor people above all.
It was indeed a hard world when redistribution, which alone could
reduce the extent of poverty, might in the long run hurt the poor.

But inequality was not merely a matter of income. The poor also
lacked political power and all that it commands in the way of essential community services. The War on Poverty did sponsor one program that challenged this form of inequality. It was the Community
Action Program, whose brief but raucous history confirmed anew
the instinct of discreet politicians to shun the issue of equality altogether.

CHAPTER 9

War on Poverty II: The Strange History of Community Action

I

THOUGH priding himself on his mastery of legislative detail, President Johnson had been curiously inattentive to the contents of his most important antipoverty measure—the 1964 Economic Opportunity Act. Among other things, that act created the Office of Economic Opportunity (OEO) and delegated to it the Job Corps, VISTA, and the highly controversial Community Action Program. Somehow Johnson's usually reliable antennae failed to sense in community action a threat to that social harmony and political consensus he so valued. Somehow it eluded him that here was a measure capable of provoking bare-knuckle brawls between the classes and the races in communities across America. According to a tale oft-told in the corridors of OEO, Johnson issued a single instruction to Sargent Shriver on appointing him agency director: Keep out "crooks, Communists, and cocksuckers."[1] It never occurred to him that the real problem might be the closet radicals who would infiltrate the agency and attempt to use it for promoting social change.

The choice of Shriver as director of OEO seemed at the time an inspired one. A devout Catholic from an old Maryland family, husband of Eunice Kennedy, Shriver had a patrician's sense of obligation so profound that he was known within the Kennedy family as the "house Communist."[2] Assigned by his brother-in-law to launch the Peace Corps in 1961, Shriver soon dazzled Washington with his energy, enthusiasm, and creative contempt for bureaucratic routine. It was he who translated the Peace Corps from a risky concept into the greatest public-relations triumph of the Kennedy years. When Johnson put him in charge of the emerging poverty program in February 1964, Shriver was hailed as the ideal man to get it through Congress and make it work. But techniques that succeeded at the Peace Corps were not necessarily appropriate to OEO, and Shriver's easy triumph with one proved poor preparation for the immense political problems that would beset the other. His emphasis on quick results would wear out OEO's employees, preclude rational planning, and contribute to the administrative chaos of the agency's early years. His penchant for the hard sell would antagonize Republicans and erode his credibility with the public at large. And his conviction that social reform and class collaboration were somehow reconcilable would not withstand the test of reality. Buffeted by critics on the left and right, he would get in quick trouble with Congress and soon fall out of favor with Lyndon Johnson, who contrived for long periods to pretend he did not exist.

Community action seemed simple enough in 1964 when Shriver's task force planned it. The Community Action Program (CAP) would invite local communities to establish new organizations or designate old ones as community action agencies, called CAAs. Modeled after David Hackett's delinquency projects, CAAs were charged with mobilizing local resources for a comprehensive attack on poverty, an attack that was to have three objectives: to provide new services to the poor; to coordinate all federal, state, and local programs dealing with the poor; and to promote institutional change in the interests of the poor. Passionate commitment to change animated the eager idealists at the helm in OEO's early days. And the struggle for change made CAP the most fascinating of all Lyndon Johnson's domestic programs.

A good many of the program's idealists had acquired their education with David Hackett's delinquency program, graduated in 1964 to Shriver's task force, and then surfaced in key positions at CAP. Notable among Hackett's guerrillas taking this route were Richard Boone, Sanford Kravitz, and Fred O'Reilly Hayes. Experience had taught these men to despise local schools, police, welfare departments, and private charity institutions for dispensing demeaning, fragmented services to the poor. As Boone expressed it, service institutions were "oppressive bureaucracies" staffed by people chiefly concerned with reinforcing "professional prerogatives and the status quo."[3] Like the Columbia professors Lloyd Ohlin and Richard Cloward, co-authors of a book on delinquent gangs that had deeply influenced President Kennedy's Committee on Juvenile Delinquency, Boone and his friends believed that local institutions held the keys to opportunity and meant now to unlock the doors.

Of course, as veterans of Hackett's delinquency experiments, OEO's reformers knew how resistant local institutions would be to real reform. That was why they wrote into the Economic Opportunity Act the historic requirement that a community action agency must be "developed, conducted, and administered with the maximum feasible participation of residents of the areas and members of the groups served."[4] Other Great Society programs sought reform by appeasing institutions; community action would seek to reform institutions by empowering the poor.

While the poverty bill was still being debated by Congress in 1964, a group under Boone's leadership grappled with the concept of "maximum feasible participation." Three major strategies for involving the poor were considered—each soon to be tried. First, poor people might be directly represented on the governing boards of local CAAs, where they could plan and oversee programs. Second, the poor might be employed as "subprofessionals" to help carry out programs in schools, hospitals, and welfare agencies, acting as a bridge between institutions and clients. And third, CAAs might hire workers to organize the poor into groups capable—in the words of Fred O'Reilly Hayes—"of pressing their needs upon the political officials and the bureaucracies of the community."[5] Boone's planners were not unaware of the latent contradictions in their model. Community action was supposed both to elicit the cooperation of local institutions and to reform them—to promote community consensus and to risk conflict. Naïvely, the planners hoped for a creative synthesis in which the institutions would respond positively to protest, and the protesting poor would accept the necessity of compromise. These hopes were soon blasted.

On October 3, 1964, six weeks after Johnson signed the Economic Opportunity Act, Congress appropriated $800 million to launch OEO, including $300 million for community action. Thus began the wild scramble of local communities to create community action agencies and get the money. By June 1965, 415 CAAs were already in existence; a year later, more than 1,000.[6] Though 80 percent of the CAAs were private nonprofit corporations, elected officials took the initiative in forming most of them. The bulk of CAP's money went to the 100 or so biggest cities, which possessed more than their share of the poor and the technical knowhow to get grants. The mayors of these cities were guided by their own convenient conceptions of what community action should be. To them, it was merely a new mechanism to provide an expanded flow of conventional services to restless (i.e., black) neighborhoods, with city hall garnering the credit. Insofar as poor people participated at all, the mayors expected them to be passive beneficiaries of governmental largess. Few mayors understood that CAP intended to improve services by changing the institutions dispensing them. Fewer still would have found this goal at all appealing.

The first year of the program saw a tug-of-war between the mayors and OEO reformers to determine the character of community action. At their disposal the reformers had two weapons: control of the purse strings and the legal requirement for maximum feasible participation. The struggle began in October 1964, when Philadelphia's Mayor James Tate brought to Washington an antipoverty plan written by a task force of city officials and designating as the city's CAA a delinquency project notorious for unresponsiveness to the poor. Holding up funds, OEO told Tate to go home and get the poor involved.[7] Cleveland's poverty plan received a similarly cold reception, as in succeeding months did those of New York, Los Angeles, and San Francisco.[8]

Angered by OEO's rebukes, the mayors counterattacked. On January 20, 1965, President Johnson received from Baltimore mayor Theodore McKeldin a report on a recent closed-door session of the Board of Advisers of the U.S. Conference of Mayors. There was an "almost unanimous feeling," wrote McKeldin, that the poverty program was being administered by people "who do not understand the problems and operations of local governments." The president should know that, if the situation is not soon corrected, the program "might well obtain an unfavorable image which could hurt it immensely." A few days later Shriver and Vice President Hubert Humphrey received a note from presidential aide Bill Moyers. "The President was disturbed by the attached letter," it said. "He asked that you and Sarge get together and work out the problem. Would you let me know how it turns out?"[9]

It would take more than the president's furrowed brow to stay the forces in OEO at work for social change. In February 1965 CAP issued its *Community Action Program Guide,* making clear that mayors could not pack CAA governing boards with political hacks and that the poor must be accorded a measure of power in the new program. CAA boards, said the *Program Guide,* should include representatives of three groups—public and private institutions dealing with the poor; community elements like churches, unions, and minority groups; and poor people themselves.[10] Later CAP directives sought further to assure the poor a voice by mandating decentralization of local poverty programs.[11] Community action agencies were to identify target neighborhoods with heavy concentrations of poor people, authorize residents in them to choose neighborhood advisory councils, and empower the councils not only to influence programs on their own turf but ideally to choose the representatives of the poor for citywide CAA boards.

In March 1965 CAP followed the *Program Guide* with its notorious *Community Action Workbook.* [12] Somehow, despite the year-long effort in 1964 to plan and pass the poverty program, neither Congress, the president, nor the public had understood the purposes of CAP, at least as conceived by its theoreticians. Appearance of the *Workbook* exposed these purposes with reckless clarity. Written in part by Richard Boone and intended as a series of suggestions for involving the poor, the *Workbook* addressed the problem of how to make institutions responsive to poor people rather than to the more "politically effective sectors of society." Reform would require power, the *Workbook* said—power the poor did not yet have, but which community action should help them acquire. One way proposed in the *Workbook* to empower the poor was community organizing—that is, the use of trained workers to help the poor form "autonomous and self-managed organizations which are competent to exert political influence on behalf of their own self-interest." These organizations might engage in protest demonstrations to help the poor "enhance their confidence" and "improve their circumstances." Here, vividly expressed, was CAP's intention of forging the disinherited into a political instrument capable of compelling the reconstruction of local communities.

Class struggle was not something Boone particularly desired, but to achieve change he would not shrink from it either. Boone, it happened, directed CAP's Program Policy and Planning Division, with Sanford Kravitz as his supervisor of experimental demonstrations. The Economic Opportunity Act permitted CAP to spend up to 15 percent of its appropriations for research and demonstration projects, which could be mounted without permission of local governments or their designated CAAs. Whenever Kravitz—known around OEO as "Dr. Strangegrant"—and Boone presented one of their proposals, Shriver would ask only half in jest, "Well, what have you nuts got cooked up for me now?"[13] Quite often they had some scheme or other for experimenting with maximum feasible participation. In February 1965 Boone bypassed the local government of Syracuse, New York, to fund a high-risk experiment testing the theories of Saul David Alinsky, the self-styled professional radical who had spent twenty-five years organizing the poor by rubbing raw, as he liked to say, the sores of their discontent.[14]

With a grant of $314,000 from Kravitz and Boone, Syracuse University established a center in 1965 to train twenty community organizers in Alinsky's techniques and contracted with another agency, newly formed for the purpose, to undertake the actual organizing.[15] Alinsky was hired as a part-time consultant for the program. The appearance in Syracuse of Lenin himself could hardly have aroused more local antagonism. Soon the fledgling organizers were forming tenant unions in public-housing projects, spending public money to bail out protesting welfare mothers, and conducting a voter-registration drive whose purpose could only be to defeat Republican Mayor William Walsh in the city's upcoming elections. "I'm not going to take this lying down," the angry Walsh warned one OEO inspector.[16] Said the director of the Syracuse Housing Authority, "We are experiencing a class struggle in the traditional Karl Marx style in Syracuse, and I do not like it."[17] Mayors everywhere that spring nervously took note.

Community action created embarrassment even for mayors who never lost control. With customary efficiency, Mayor Daley quickly turned the Chicago program into an extension of his political machine, appointing himself head of his CAA and overloading its governing board with city officials.[18] The mayor's idea of comprehensive planning was to send OEO a two-foot box containing every antipoverty proposal submitted by the city's service institutions, along with a request for nearly half of CAP's entire budget.[19] Given Daley's clout—and Shriver's long-standing ambition to run for governor of Illinois—OEO moved with utmost circumspection early in 1965 to improve matters. Grudgingly, Dr. Deton Brooks, the Negro educator and civil servant appointed by Daley as the program's executive director, agreed to pare down his applications to reasonable proportions. And in a gesture meant either to appease or defy OEO—it was hard to tell which—Daley added two middle-class Negroes to the previously all-white board and designated them as representatives of the poor.[20] Meantime, Dr. Brooks moved skillfully to keep any semblance of real power out of the target neighborhoods. Brooks personally appointed the directors of the program's dozen neighborhood service centers; and these directors appointed the poor who sat on the neighborhood advisory councils. Troublemakers were screened out.[21] Meantime, the program began hiring a thousand poor Chicagoans at $4,070 a year to serve in the nebulous capacity of "community representatives." Critics alleged, not without evidence, that job applicants with letters of recommendation from precinct captains and aldermen had the inside track.[22] In Chicago, then, Daley converted the poverty program into a virtual conspiracy to block institutional change and achieve the minimal feasible participation of the poor.

But Daley's tactics provoked criticism both locally and nationally, and Daley hated criticism. Chief critic was The Woodlawn Organization (TWO), a coalition of more than a hundred groups formed a few years before in one of the city's black slums by none other than Saul Alinsky. Though TWO's crusades against price gougers, slumlords, and segregated schools inspired journalist Charles Silberman to call the group "the most important and the most impressive experiment affecting Negroes anywhere in the United States,"[23] Daley despised its tactics and froze it out of the poverty action. TWO got a measure of revenge in April 1965, when its president made national headlines with a blistering attack on Daley's poverty program before a congressional committee. "In Chicago," said the Reverend Lynwood Stevenson, "there is no war on poverty, there is only more of the ancient galling war against the poor."[24] Alinsky himself further damaged Daley's image by using Chicago to illustrate his well-publicized attacks on the poverty program as "a prize piece of political pornography."[25] Stung by the rash of hostile comment and infuriated by OEO's gentle pleas that he reform his program, Daley arrived in St. Louis on June 1, 1965, to attend the annual meeting of the U.S. Conference of Mayors.

Daley was not the only mayor in a dyspeptic mood. The main business of the conference was a resolution co-sponsored by Los

Angeles Mayor Sam Yorty and San Francisco Mayor John Shelley, both Democrats, attacking the Community Action Program for its implicit endorsement of "class struggle." Local programs should be controlled by local officials, the resolution said.[26] To keep from embarrassing President Johnson, the conference managers kept the resolution bottled up in committee and arranged a private meeting between a group of ten mayors and Vice President Humphrey. Daley, naturally, led the mayors. According to a summary of the ensuing conversation, the mayors "expressed their concern that OEO seems to be operating on the theory that existing institutions in society are antagonistic to the poor or unwilling to make changes necessary in their own structures to effectively lead the war against poverty."[27] Reported a spokesman for the mayors, the vice president agreed "that the success of the program depends on very extensive leadership by local government and that's what they are going to get."[28]

After that, the influence of OEO's reformers began fading rapidly, though it would not be entirely eliminated for some years. Boone left in August 1965 to become executive director of the Citizens Crusade against Poverty, a recently formed organization bankrolled by Walter Reuther's United Auto Workers, and others of like mind soon drifted away too. In the fall the White House itself got tough with OEO. Budget Director Charles L. Schultze sent Johnson a memo in September criticizing OEO for failing to promote local coordination and comprehensive planning. Instead, said Schultze, OEO had got off on the wrong foot by "organizing the poor politically" and arousing fears among the mayors that it was "setting up competing political organizations in their own backyards." OEO should be told to "soft-pedal its conflicts with local officials over heavy representation of the poor on the poverty planning boards." In a scribbled response that hardly conveyed the depth of his own irritation with CAP, Johnson replied, "OK. I agree."[29]

I I

During OEO's first year the idealists Shriver had recruited nourished the happy illusion that they were the cutting edge of social change in America. Sober reality dawned in the fall of 1965. There was, for example, the crucial matter of money. That summer, when all things had still seemed possible, OEO's Office of Plans, Progress, and Evaluations produced a long-range plan for ending poverty. Dominated by economists who scoffed at Boone's theories, the Office of Plans called for a massive job-creation program, more social services for the poor, and a negative income tax to assist unemployables. Shriver embraced this package with characteristic enthusiasm—though it bore scant resemblance to anything his agency was currently doing—and forwarded it to the president, along with a recommendation for a $10 billion expenditure next year to get it started. Of this amount, $4 billion would go to OEO. Johnson thought enough of the plan to ask the Budget Bureau to do an analysis.[30] But in December 1965 the true costs of the recent Vietnam escalation became evident, and the reign of austerity commenced. OEO's long-range plan went on the shelf for the duration, and the agency's budget for the next year inched up from $1.5 billion to only $1.8 billion. Once the poverty warriors realized how small would be the resources at their disposal, a pall descended on the agency that never lifted.[31]

No less disheartening were the early returns on maximum feasible participation. Thanks to OEO's efforts, approximately 30 percent of CAA board members represented the poor. But it was hard to see what difference it made.[32] The voice of the poor on the boards was typically drowned out by articulate professionals and politicians, while real power belonged mainly to executive committees, which contained few poor people. Employing the poor as subprofessionals in social service programs proved only slightly less disappointing. Employment was provided by local CAAs for 125,000 poor people trained as community organizers, family counselors, day-care workers, and teachers' aides.[33] But the real point of this application of maximum feasible participation was not to create jobs but to promote institutional change. Subprofessionals would break down the distrust of the poor for the agencies and by educating middle-class professionals to the real needs of their clients. Unfortunately, the institutions played it safe by hiring not the hard-core but the upwardly mobile poor, who too often lacked empathy with those they were leaving behind. And middle-class professionals demonstrated little interest in learning whatever it was the subprofessionals were supposed to teach.[34]

That left community organizing. Whether this version of maximum feasible participation was effective was debatable. That it entailed unacceptable political costs was not. In the first year Shriver permitted the "nuts" to have their way, alienating the mayors. In his second year he reined in the nuts, earning the enmity of the organized poor. On December 6, 1965, Shriver ate crow before an audience in Chicago triumphantly assembled for the occasion by Mayor Daley. "The establishment is not a bunch of guys in black hats against good guys in white hats," Shriver said. Outside, as he spoke, picketers from TWO carried signs reading, "The War on Poverty Is a Big Fraud."[35]

Shriver's retreat from maximum feasible participation began December 1965 when he cut loose from the controversial Alinsky demonstration in Syracuse by refusing to fund the action arm of the project. Carloads of the city's poor descended on OEO headquarters to engage Shriver in acrimonious debate.[36] Boone wrote his former chief to warn of the wrath of the mobilizing dispossessed.[37] And Alinsky—asked how he felt at being summarily sacked from the program—merely shrugged, "Have you ever been to Syracuse?"[38]

OEO's standing among reformers was further damaged by the shoddy treatment it accorded James Farmer, director of CORE. In August 1965 Farmer had applied to OEO for seed money to launch an adult literacy program that would rely heavily on civil rights activists as instructors. Farmer made no effort to discourage widespread belief that one of the purposes of his proposed program was to mobilize the poor for political action.[39] In December 1965, his application having passed every hurdle in OEO and news of an impending grant having leaked, Farmer announced his forthcoming resignation from CORE to head a new group called Center for Community Action Education.[40] Shriver believed Farmer's group was controllable, White House counsel Harry McPherson recommended his literacy proposal to the president,[41] and all the civil rights groups urged approval of Farmer's grant application.[42] But in the end the president himself turned thumbs down. Johnson had distrusted Farmer ever since 1964 when he had refused to join other black leaders in a pre-election call for a moratorium on racial demonstrations.[43] If Farmer intended to stir up the ghettos, he would have to do it without Johnson's help. Taking the heat for the White House, OEO suddenly began to find all sorts of insubstantial reasons to delay Farmer's grant. Unable to get through to Shriver and disgusted by OEO's feeble excuses, Farmer withdrew his application in July 1966. "They want the rain without the thunder and lightning," he said, "the ocean without the terrible roar."[44]

Among advocates of social change, Shriver lost his white hat for good during the long controversy over the Child Development Group of Mississippi (CDGM). This was a Head Start project for disadvantaged Mississippi preschoolers, first funded by OEO in the summer of 1965. Remnants of Mississippi's civil rights movement saw in Child Development a new means of organizing poor black communities—a way to pursue the movement's old goals by new means.[45] Thus CDGM's job application, item 12, asked potential employees to "outline the civil rights activities in which you have been involved."[46] And the site of CDGM's headquarters was an abandoned campus leased by the Delta Ministry—the civil rights arm of the National Council of Churches. Distrustful of professionals, CDGM's central staff thought Head Start would work only if poor people developed their own educational system and taught their own children. Late in the spring of 1965, movement veterans fanned out over the state looking for sharecroppers, domestics, and other of the black poor who would plan and operate Head Start summer programs. Miraculously in July, 83 Head Start centers in 40 communities opened their doors for 5,800 kids.[47] Though it got high marks from visiting educators, white Mississippians feared CDGM because it provided poor blacks with an independent source of income and a measure of self-determination.[48] In August 1965 Mississippi Senator John Stennis, a figure of towering influence in Washington, declared war on CDGM by charging it with civil rights activity and sloppy bookkeeping—charges of which it was not entirely innocent.

Shriver would have been happy to bury CDGM at the end of the summer of 1965, but bowing to liberal pressure, he belatedly funded the project the following February for another six months.[49] That hardly ended matters. In July 1966 CDGM submitted a wholly unrealistic request for $41 million for a year-round program. Convinced that CDGM would never keep orderly books and that it had been corrupted by black power ideologues, OEO announced in September that, so far as it was concerned, CDGM was on it own.[50]

All hell immediately broke loose as reform-minded liberals rallied to CDGM's cause. The Citizens Crusade against Poverty sent a friendly team of investigators into Mississippi to exonerate it, the National Council of Churches accused Shriver of appeasing Stennis by sacrificing it, and housewives and clergymen picketed OEO headquarters demanding the agency refund it.[51] The campaign to save CDGM reached its climax on October 19, 1966, with a full-page ad in the *New York Times*—"Say It Isn't So Sargent Shriver"—signed by scores of distinguished liberals and clerics.[52] Falling back under the barrage, the White House opted for compromise: CDGM agreed to add whites to its board and reform its administration, and OEO agreed to fund a scaled-down CDGM program for 6,000 children.[53] The big loser was Shriver, who had seemed all too willing to act as Stennis's patsy.

Shriver already knew how low his stock had fallen among those who were supposed to be his constituency. On April 13, 1966, a poor people's convention gathered in Washington under the sponsorship of the Citizens Crusade against Poverty. Present as delegates were not only the usual clergymen and liberals but bona-fide poor people from such regions of despair as Harlem, Watts, Appalachia, and Mississippi. Though Shriver had been warned that the grassroots delegates were in an ugly humor, he nonetheless went ahead with his scheduled speech. Halfway through, as if on cue, three dozen people drifted toward him down the aisles and began hurling insults. "Looking strained and upset," he rushed through the rest of his text and exited through a jostling mob. Moments later the convention dissolved into chaos. Remarked the Reverend Eugene Carson Blake to the delegates on taking his leave, "There won't be anything to take over after you've taken over."[54]

It was a low moment for Shriver in a year marked by few satisfactions. Concluding in December 1965 that the program needed a new face, he submitted his handwritten resignation to the White House.[55] But Johnson feared that Shriver's departure would be bad for public relations and would not let him go. Like the good soldier that he was, Shriver reluctantly returned to the front lines and a war he now knew was lost.

III

Press and public naturally focused on the highly visible events in Washington to form their impressions of community action. But the real story of CAP was the story of the CAAs operating in one thousand communities across the country. Though OEO ceased aggressively to champion maximum feasible participation after the fall of 1965, it continued to assert the principle and insist on its observance in some form. The fate of maximum feasible participation, in fact, came to hinge less on OEO than on widely varying local circumstances. Power elites had firm control over some cities, a feeble grip in others; some CAAs served established institutions, others fomented class and racial strife. And between these poles an array of other possibilities played themselves out. Since remarkably little is known about CAAs in the great majority of communities, no final judgment on CAP will be possible until an army of local historians recovers the program's lost fragments. The best-documented cases come from the biggest cities, which had special problems and were probably not representative. Nonetheless, a survey of some of these may convey CAP's variety and bring the elusive reality of community action into better focus.

Atlanta

Atlanta's story, short but hardly sweet, illustrated the fate of community action when local elites took control. The white businessmen who ruled the city were quite willing to tolerate community action, provided it did not rile the placid waters of civic life. To make sure that it did not, Boisfeuillet "Bo" Jones was made chairman of Economic Opportunity, Atlanta. A well-connected Democrat and president of the wealthy Woodruff Foundation, Jones ran a top-down poverty program brooking no interference from the poor. His board contained no poor people; an advisory committee recruited from the target neighborhoods had no function; and the community organizers attached to the neighborhood service centers were diverted from organizing to rendering short-term services for individual poor people.[56]

Though OEO's staff persuaded a reluctant Shriver to require reform of the Atlanta program as a condition of a large grant awarded in the fall of 1965, Bo Jones continued to do business as usual.[57] The following spring the head of OEO's Office of Inspection wrote Shriver, "Ugly as the implication may be, there is a clear undercurrent in the community that the only reason OEO permits Atlanta to disregard the CAP Guidelines is that Boisfeuillet Jones has a close personal relation to the Director of this Agency."[58] A team of OEO investigators, summing up the prevailing view, said that Atlanta's CAA "has developed into a large, cumbersome bureaucracy whose major achievement to date appears to have been the attraction of federal money into the city."[59] In April 1966, when OEO staff people recommended withholding funds from Atlanta, Shriver overruled them. His view, as summarized by a program official, was that "Atlanta is a good program, and he didn't want any dallying so far as providing funds."[60]

Philadelphia

In Philadelphia, politicians, not businessmen, killed community action. In October 1964 OEO tried to thwart Mayor Tate's attempt to exclude the poor from his preliminary board and convert the program into a source of political patronage. The following February, Tate started fresh by creating a brand-new CAA—the Philadelphia Antipoverty Action Committee—reserving twelve of the thirty seats on its governing board for representatives of the poor. In May 1965 Philadelphia became the first city in America to experiment with formal elections for choosing the representatives of the poor. Residents in each of twelve target neighborhoods elected members to a neighborhood advisory council, and each of the twelve councils chose one member to sit on the citywide CAA board.[61] Though only 2.5 percent of the eligible population voted, OEO bravely hailed the election as an example of grassroots democracy and subsequently repeated the experiment in eight other cities—until Shriver, embarrassed by a 0.7 percent turnout in Los Angeles, called a halt.[62] In August 1965, impressed by the façade of democracy Tate had created in Philadelphia, an OEO inspector reported, "ultimate power rests with the neighborhood councils. . . . So far, so good."[63]

But in reality the poverty program in Philadelphia belonged not to the poor but to one man, a wealthy sixty-four-year-old impresario named Samuel L. Evans. One of the most powerful blacks in the city, Sam Evans was closely allied with Mayor Tate, who appointed him vice chairman of the city's CAA, with power to pick key staff members. Evans set out to insulate the program from the influence of the poor and run it in Tate's political interest. His first task was to nullify the potential power of the twelve board members chosen in the target areas. This he did by ruling that they were not bound in voting by their neighborhood councils and by personally courting them with lunches, dinners, and private caucuses—"an expensive proposition," he admitted.[64] Next, he isolated and undercut the neighborhood councils by forbidding them to consult with each other, by ignoring their advice, and by buying off their members with jobs. Of the 144 poor people who sat on area councils in 1966, 118 had obtained employment either with the poverty program or the city government.[65] By shrewd maneuver and sometimes even threat, Evans succeeded in turning community action, Philadelphia-style, into "the maximum feasible participation of Sam Evans."[66]

The consequences were devastating for the city's poverty program. "The heavy bulk of the programs are delegated to old line agencies, a very heavy percentage going to the board of education," reported an OEO inspector. "Many programs are extensions or modifications of existing programs."[67] There was, of course, no community organizing, either to bring the disaffiliated in touch with service programs or to mobilize the poor for political action. Institutional reform attributable to community action in Philadelphia was nonexistent. In the spring of 1967 an OEO investigation found that Evans had discredited community action "with every responsible agency and group in the city and has hurt OEO's image nationally."[68] OEO decided to stop paying the administrative expenses of Evans's agency and force a cleanup. Among those whom Tate appointed to the blue-ribbon panel overseeing reorganizing of the program was Sam Evans.[69]

Harlem

As the experience of Harlem proved, black politicians could sabotage community action no less effectively than white politicians. This dismal story began in 1962, when the President's Committee on Juvenile Delinquency awarded a planning grant to Harlem Youth Opportunities Unlimited (HARYOU), whose director was the distinguished black psychologist Kenneth Clark. Himself a product of a Harlem boyhood, Clark assembled a staff of twenty-five and spent eighteen months preparing a comprehensive delinquency plan, completed in 1964 and called *Youth in the Ghetto.* [70] Black ghettos like Harlem were colonies, Clark said, whose inhabitants were subject peoples and whose pathology derived from their powerlessness. Clark's delinquency plan called, therefore, not only for more youth services but for neighborhood boards that would empower the poor to deal with their own problems and press for institutional change.

No one was more interested in Clark's plan than Congressman Adam Clayton Powell, the high-living cleric who was Harlem's most powerful politician. David Hackett had tried to keep Powell off Clark's back in 1962 by giving Powell his own delinquency grant for something called Associated Community Teams (ACT),[71] an experimental domestic service corps that quickly degenerated into an appendage of Powell's machine. Powell soon cast covetous eyes at HARYOU as well. Beginning in early 1964, he looked for ways to horn in on Clark's operation, finally demanding in the spring that Livingston Wingate—his man at ACT—be made HARYOU's executive director. Clark knew that Powell's influence would wreck HARYOU, and he prepared to fight.[72] As it turned out, he fought alone, since nobody on whom he counted—not Mayor Robert Wagner, the civil rights groups, Harlem leaders, or even David Hackett—dared defy Powell. Hurt and embittered, Clark resigned from HARYOU in July 1964.[73] A few months later the recently combined board of HARYOU-ACT named Wingate executive director, and HARYOU-ACT graduated from Harlem's delinquency project to its community action agency.

A former porter at Grand Central Station, Wingate had earned a law degree studying nights before becoming one of Powell's congressional aides. Though he possessed many talents, it was HARYOU's great misfortune that administration was not one of them. Despite $5 million annual budgets in HARYOU's first years, programs either did not get started, floundered, or provided the poor with only routine services. The Labor Department, for example, uncovered the interesting fact that its $141,781 grant to HARYOU for an apprenticeship program had employed only five youths.[74] And despite Wingate's eloquent affirmation of maximum feasible participation he made no progress toward activating the grassroots neighborhood boards provided for in Kenneth Clark's original plan. Noting that these boards might evolve into a political force independent of Powell, few observers expected ever to see their formation.[75]

The pivotal event in Wingate's tenure was Project Up-Lift, conceived hurriedly in the spring of 1965 to keep malcontented teenagers from burning down Harlem. Working in a crisis atmosphere, Up-Lift's staff began in June to let contracts that eventually provided 5,000 of Harlem's 71,000 teenagers with summer jobs. But the project quickly spun out of Wingate's control, even Up-Lift's payroll becoming a thing of chance. When marauding gangs began demanding their pay checks and otherwise causing trouble, the embattled agency had to hire a local protective agency at a cost of $15,000 a week.[76] By September 1965 the profligate Wingate had overspent his budget by $400,000. OEO not only bailed him out but gave him $400,000 more to keep Up-Lift afloat through November. Either that or Wingate threatened to tell the enraged young of Harlem that OEO—i.e., "whitey"—was trying to starve them.[77] Who knew what might happen then?

Worse than overspending his budget, in OEO's view, Wingate used Up-Lift funds to subsidize the Black Arts Theater, creature of poet and playwright LeRoi Jones (not yet reborn Imamu Amiri Baraka), who once declared that America should be stormed "by 20 million spooks . . . with furious cries and unstoppable weapons."[78] Jones got his money simply by barging into Wingate's office one day and emphatically demanding it.[79] That summer Jones spent $100,-000 and employed 242 people to stage plays nightly on the streets of Harlem. Blending racism with Marxism, the plays included one by Jones himself—*Jello*—in which Jack Benny's valet, Rochester, rises up and kills his white oppressors.[80] When the public learned how Jones was using public money, OEO suffered yet another public-relations disaster, though it had never been consulted by Wingate about the grant or even been informed when it was made.

That fall, despite OEO's desire for Wingate's ouster, HARYOU's board merely suspended him with pay until he straightened out the agency's books. Back on the job in the spring of 1966, Wingate found his support on the board to be weakening so rapidly that intimidation became his last defense. In July a gang of toughs, including Wingate supporters on the HARYOU staff, invaded a meeting of the board, "slugging board chairman Andrew Tyler on the head and chasing president Ed Lewis out of the room."[81] Wingate held on to his $25,000 job until November and then resigned.

Subsequently reorganized, HARYOU quit administering its own programs and merely dispensed grants to neighborhood boards, now finally activated. Grave problems continued nonetheless. At a HARYOU board meeting in 1968, it took a pistol shot and a canister of tear gas to block a resolution that would have shut HARYOU down until the staff provided information necessary for a program evaluation. Afterward, board chairman Marshall England, announcing that he would seek a federal investigation of his own agency, said, "I just don't think the programs are useful."[82] Kenneth Marshall, who had worked with Kenneth Clark on HARYOU's original plan, agreed. "None of it worked," he said, "and the $20 million that went into it has disappeared without a trace."[83]

San Francisco

San Francisco learned, to its sorrow, that black militants could kill community action as easily as black politicians. Community action began in San Francisco in September 1964, when Mayor John F. Shelley created the Economic Opportunity Council and appointed all fifty of its members, none of whom were poor. Shelley expected his new agency merely to fund traditional employment and education programs through existing institutions. Local civil rights leaders had other ideas. Organizing a coalition of ethnic and neighborhood groups, they advanced the most radical interpretation of maximum feasible participation extant. The poor, they said, should control community action in San Francisco, with power over programs residing in the target neighborhoods. Though the mayor's own hand-picked CAA board proved sympathetic to the dissidents, he held his ground—until the Watts riot erupted down the road in Los Angeles in August 1965. When the board met a few weeks later, thirty-nine organizations testified in favor of the dissident program, and every mention of Shelley's name occasioned a chorus of boos. Shelley capitulated on the spot. San Francisco shortly enjoyed the distinction of having the only CAA in America whose board contained a majority representing the poor and whose target areas possessed total program autonomy. Two of the city's five target areas provided most of the subsequent action—the Western Addition and Hunter's Point, both predominantly black.[84]

The key man in Western Addition was area director Wilfred Ussery, who happened also to be national chairman of CORE. Having masterminded the struggle against Mayor Shelley, Ussery collected his reward in the form of $400,000 to run a program for Western Addition's 62,000 people. He chose to use the money almost exclusively to organize the poor for neighborhood self-government, a strategy he believed would cure powerlessness and enhance self-respect. By the time his organizers completed the arduous task of building representative structures in all thirty-two Western Addi-

tion neighborhoods, it was April 1966, and Ussery was under heavy
fire for monopolizing patronage, ignoring services, and promoting
black-power ideology. Ussery's community organizers not only sol-
icited memberships for civil rights groups, they preached hatred of
whites and organized racial demonstrations.[85] One of Ussery's close
aides was quoted as saying, "This is not a poverty program. It is a
civil rights program and anybody who thinks differently is mis-
led."[86]

Ussery's attempt to build a black-power machine with federal
funds came to OEO's attention when one of his organizers, the
Reverend Robert Gardley, sent secret letters of protest to Shriver,
J. Edgar Hoover, and President Johnson. Someone in OEO's regional office leaked the letters to Ussery. On September 28, 1966,
while the worst riot in San Francisco history raged a few miles away
at Hunter's Point, Ussery told a staff meeting, "Old Whitey's got to
go. We're going to raise hell tonight. We've got a nigger here who's
got to go. . . . I got some letters here he wrote." Defending himself
with a chair, Gardley retreated from the meeting and called federal
authorities for protection.[87] Ussery soon had to contend not only
with OEO, which launched an investigation, but with his own area
board, which twice tried to fire him. In January 1967 the board was
dissolved and Ussery was permitted to resign. Except for a lucky few
who had obtained jobs in the program—mainly CORE members—
the poverty program had had virtually no impact on the Western
Addition.[88]

Located three miles from downtown San Francisco, Hunter's
Point was an isolated, disintegrating ghetto on a hill jutting into the
bay. In 1965 a mass meeting of its residents elected an area poverty
board that subsequently sponsored community organizing to improve the neighborhood and force change. But the payoff from
organizing proved too small to maintain resident enthusiasm, and
by 1967 the area board had become paralyzed by internal strife.[89]
That summer, however, the citywide CAA designed and funded a
program that Hunter's Point, along with the other target areas,
appeared really to need—summer jobs for unemployed teenagers.

The official in charge of the city program developed a novel
concept for reaching really hard-core kids. Bad dudes, he said,
should run the program in the target areas. That was how Charles
Sizemore—large, bearded, and mean—became chief supervisor of

the summer program on Hunter's Point. A militant closely associated with the Black Student Union of San Francisco State, Sizemore's forte was intimidating whites.[90]

Sizemore had no sooner settled into the job in June 1967 than he learned of budget cuts requiring a reduction in the number of the youth supervisors on his payroll from sixty to forty. A few days later some thirty hoods, led by one of Sizemore's aides, marched to City Hall and confronted Mayor Shelley in his office. The hoods berated the mayor, interrupted him, and finally told him that if he did not come up with the money to restore the jobs by 5 P.M., "this goddam town's gonna blow."[91] Visibly shaken, the mayor produced $45,000 by the deadline. Thus was invented the tactic of "mau-mauing"[92]— the least appealing application of maximum feasible participation and one all too common in San Francisco that summer.

Sizemore was not particularly interested in lining up jobs for the two hundred kids in his program, keeping them busy instead with cultural-enrichment classes featuring black-power luminaries like Bobby Seale. Seale told the teenagers of Hunter's Point, "And while we are surviving every day in our struggle, remember, when you . . . steal from the white man . . . you are dealing with real politics."[93] A group of teenagers whom Sizemore took to the theater one day got really political by looting two stores on Geary Street and beating up a bartender. When Sizemore's budget ran out in August, some of his boys invaded a CAA board meeting and extorted another $30,000 from its frightened members to keep the program going.[94] By then, community action had become an object of contempt in San Francisco, not least among the black militants who had so cynically exploited it.

Mobilization for Youth

If any CAA in America had a chance to succeed, it was Mobilization for Youth—the model for all the others and the purest case. It was run neither by politicians nor by black militants but by social scientists and social workers who had pioneered community action and were dedicated to its goals. Those goals were hardly static. Opening for business in 1962, Mobilization had expected to test Ohlin and Cloward's opportunity theory in sixty square blocks of New York City's Lower East Side—a test involving a comprehensive plan, coordination of local resources, scientific evaluation of programs, and institutional change. Little of this design was realized. Mobilization created too few opportunities to test the theory, offered services piecemeal rather than comprehensively, failed to coordinate participating agencies, and compromised scientific evaluation by tinkering with programs in the midst of their operation. The one goal that Mobilization would not surrender, and indeed pursued with intensifying zeal, was institutional change. Mobilization's 350-member staff spent most of their days, after all, dealing with the problems of the poor, seeing the world as the poor saw it, and experiencing vicariously the callous behavior of service institutions. When Mobilization's leaders realized late in 1963 that job training and education programs were producing little real change, they switched emphasis to organizing the poor for political action.

Results were mixed. Organizers promoted voter-registration drives but ironically concluded that the best way to involve poor people politically was to end the poverty which was the chief cause of their alienation.[95] Mobilization supported the 1964 East Side rent strike and organized tenant unions to obtain enforcement of the building codes—only belatedly to discover that slumlords would abandon their properties rather than make uneconomic repairs and that the only way to end bad housing was to provide the poor with the means to afford better.[96] Indeed, organizers obtained their best results when they mobilized the poor to get the one thing they needed most—cold, hard cash.

From the day its neighborhood service centers first opened, Mobilization had been flooded by poor people with complaints about welfare—late checks, snooping case workers, arbitrary termination of benefits, illegal intimidation.[97] Admitting the futility of handling complaints individually, staff began in 1965 to organize welfare rights groups on the East Side and to seek alliance with similar organizations in other parts of the city. Pressure tactics against the Welfare Department rapidly escalated. In the summer of 1966 the welfare groups, adopting an idea of Richard Cloward's, actually tried to wreck the whole mad system by swamping it with formal complaints.[98] Though Mobilization for Youth broke off connections with the welfare rights movement at this point, the movement rolled on under its own momentum. During the next two years welfare rights groups in New York routinely occupied welfare offices, damaged furniture, and clashed with police. Shaken by these confrontations, the Welfare Department used its discretionary authority to increase payments of supplemental special grants from $3.1 million in April 1967 to $11.5 million in May 1968.[99] Thereafter, the Welfare Department shored up its defenses, and the movement, at least in New York City, went into decline. The movement nonetheless could boast that because of its militance clients now had the right to telephones, bank accounts, automatic school clothing allowances, and burial expenses, not to speak of new respect from case workers.[100]

In the end, Mobilization's efforts to change institutions merely provoked the institutions to castrate Mobilization. The agency first grasped how tenuous its position really was in 1964. Then, school principals on the East Side attacked Mobilization for employing "full-time paid agitators and organizers for extremist groups."[101] The FBI infiltrated the agency to hunt evidence of financial impropriety and political disloyalty. The mayor of New York phoned Mobilization's board chairman to pass on reports that the agency was "filled with communists from top to bottom."[102] And in August 1964 the New York *Daily News* took lethal aim at Mobilization with a series of articles accusing it of harboring scores of "leftists" and subversives—charges implicitly endorsed by City Council President Paul Screvane, who announced that, unless Mobilization was cleared of the charges, the city would not renew its contract with the agency. During the ensuing crisis, most of the local institutions that were supposed to be Mobilization's collaborators on the East Side lifted not a finger in its defense. Mobilization nevertheless survived attack because Screvane failed to win the Democratic nomination for mayor, Lyndon Johnson won his election as president, and the charges against the agency had almost no foundation.

Though Mobilization did not immediately call off its community organizers in the wake of the crisis, Bertram Beck, nationally known leader of the social-work profession who took over the agency in 1965, knew that the price of survival was accommodation with established institutions.[103] In November 1966, after public officials scolded Mobilization for organizing welfare clients, Beck withdrew his agency from the welfare rights movement.[104] By the end of the decade community organizing ceased entirely to be a component of the agency's program. Mobilization by then was concentrating on vocational education, with stress on changing the poor to suit the job market rather than changing the market to suit the poor.[105] As a bureaucratic agency bearing a distinct resemblance to the type it had once set out to reform, Mobilization appropriately became a favorite target for militant demonstrations on the East Side.[106] Here, writ small, was the history of CAP.

IV

No overall assessment of the decade's liberalism is possible without at least tentative evaluation of community action. At issue is how well the program achieved its three main purposes—coordination of relevant agencies, provision of new services, and institutional change. Easiest to assess is coordination. Describing the goal of coordination, the political scientist James Sundquist explained, "Community action was repeatedly described as a device that would draw federal, state, and local programs together and meld them into an integrated assault upon the problems of poverty."[107] This, the recurring dream of the Budget Bureau, never came to pass. Coordination required planning, but Congresswoman Edith Green had stricken the planning requirement from the administration's 1964 poverty bill; and Shriver himself, anxious for quick results, decided at the outset to fund individual and unconnected programs prior to completion of local poverty plans. Piecemeal and uncoordinated services were the result. Moreover, CAP's service programs tended to compete with ones already in existence, further undermining coordination. And to the extent that CAP attempted to change the institutions it was supposed to coordinate, it inspired mainly unremitting hostility. CAP, in short, increased the very fragmentation and bureaucratic rivalry it was designed to remedy.

Judged by its expenditures, CAP's principal function was dispensing services. Despite the agency's formal commitment to localism, most CAP service programs were not originated by local CAAs to suit local circumstances, but were so-called "national emphasis programs," prepackaged in Washington and administered according to federal guidelines. Popular from the start, national programs quickly developed constituencies of their own. CAP sponsored 70 Comprehensive Community Health Centers—one-stop clinics—located in target areas. In 1971 these centers treated an estimated one million patients.[108] CAP's Upward Bound program attempted to provide low-income teenagers with the skills and motivation they needed to attend college. Though many of Upward Bound's clients were already well-motivated, and some were not even poor, 80 percent of the 70,000 who participated in the first four years entered college and had retention rates exceeding the national average.[109] CAP funded birth control programs for 320 CAAs, which dispensed information and supplies in 1970 to 300,000–400,000 women.[110] And CAP conceived two national emphasis programs that ranked among the most imaginative and useful antipoverty programs of the decade—Head Start and Legal Services.

Begun in the summer of 1965 as a crash program for preschoolers from poor families, Head Start matured into a year-round program eventually serving 400,000 children annually.[111] Improving the cognitive activities of its students was one of Head Start's purposes, of course, but more than that, it was a comprehensive child development program, providing among other things nourishing meals and medical examinations. Head Start's immense popularity dimmed a bit in 1969 when a well-publicized evaluation showed that cognitive gains achieved by its children were not maintained in elementary school.[112] But later studies partially revived Head Start's reputation for educational effectiveness by showing that graduates were less likely to require special classes or to be retained in grade than children in control groups.[113] There was even evidence that in communities where Head Start stressed parent involvement, established institutions became more sensitive to the special educational and health needs of poor children.[114] Though falling short of early expectations, Head Start was nonetheless one Great Society program that worked.

CAP's Legal Services Program eventually opened law offices staffed by 2,000 lawyers in slum communities throughout the nation. Envisioned by its theoreticians as an agent of law reform, Legal Services lawyers were expected by OEO planners to initiate class-action suits to compel equitable treatment of the poor by public and private institutions. Legal Services lawyers challenged public-housing authorities, urban-renewal agencies, welfare departments, the police, slumlords—now and again winning a signal victory. Legal Services lawyers forced the state of California to restore medical benefits to 1.5 million persons who were poor or old; won a case in a U.S. circuit court to allow tenants to withhold rent from landlords who refused to correct dangerous or unsanitary conditions; and persuaded the Supreme Court to throw out the notorious "man-in-the-house" regulation that deprived 400,000 children of welfare benefits.

But, as a strategy for change, law reform encountered two big obstacles. First, at the insistence of the American Bar Association, local legal establishments—never noted for reforming zeal—obtained extensive influence over local Legal Services programs.[115] Second, law proved to be an inherently limited tool for achieving social change. Judges might mandate higher welfare benefits, for example, or the enforcement of building codes, but they could not force legislatures to appropriate more welfare money or prevent landlords from abandoning properties. As one study concluded, "The most that can be said for legal change is that it may be used in conjunction with a host of other policy instruments if directed social change is desired. And until other forces can be brought into play, law alone can usually achieve only very modest results."[116] Nonetheless, Legal Services yielded real benefits to the poor—not so much from its occasional class-action victories but by providing a remarkable quantity of routine services, which the poor needed as much as other groups and obtained far less often. In 1971 the program's overworked lawyers handled considerably more than one million cases. Just as no other defense of Legal Services was really required, so CAP itself required none other than this—that cheaply and effectively it provided a host of services to deprived groups who badly needed them.

But it was not mere services, after all, that had been the major concern of CAP's founders or had stirred the deepest commitment of OEO's staff. It was institutional change. How seriously did local CAAs pursue the goal, and in any case, how could success be measured? Two notable studies, both funded by OEO, wrestled with these problems. Brandeis University's Florence Heller School investigated a sample of twenty CAAs in cities with populations ranging from 50,000 to 800,000.[117] Most of them, this study found, employed strategies to co-opt the poor rather than to empower them, and merely provided traditional services through established institutions. Only in three of the twenty cities—Durham, Cincinnati, and Hartford—did CAAs seek to mobilize the poor for political action. There, newly organized groups of poor people "became involved in controversies involving the school board, city hall, housing authorities, police department, and other major community institutions." The depressing conclusion of the Brandeis study was that though some beneficial changes in the three cities did occur, "At best, these were few in number and in most cases limited in scope."[118]

Barss, Reitzel and Associates, a think tank in Cambridge, Massachusetts, undertook an ambitious evaluation of CAP that entailed interviews with three thousand relevant persons in one hundred cities.[119] It found that measured by such criteria as the number of remedial teachers employed in target-area schools and the quantity of services rendered by private social-welfare agencies, some institutional change did indeed occur between 1964 and 1968. Furthermore, CAP seemed to contribute to change, especially if the local CAA emphasized community organizing. Unfortunately, only twenty-eight of the one hundred neighborhood service centers in the sample spent any appreciable resources for this purpose. Moreover the payoff, even when community organizing was stressed, was not large. Barss, Reitzel concluded, "Relative to the fundamental overhaul of our institutional system many would like to see, there has been little change."[120] Judged by the standard of institutional change, then, CAP did not exactly fail, but neither did it vindicate the theories of Richard Boone and his fellow reformers.

But, beyond coordination, services, and institutional change, CAP had an implicit goal that transcended all the others. It was supposed to help reduce poverty in America. Few of those who planned, enacted, or administered CAP ever took the time to consider exactly how CAP might contribute to that end. Only a tiny band of initiates knew that community action had originated in Ohlin and Cloward's opportunity theory, which held that, in order for poor youths to escape poverty, local opportunity structures had to be reformed. This perspective on the problem of poverty appealed to social-work intellectuals because it focused primarily on the world they knew so well—the world of social service. But, even if community action had succeeded in reforming this world, the end result would merely be better services, and services could help few escape from poverty. Poverty was a problem not of services but of unequal income distribution; and the solutions, if any, depended on national, not local, action. Changing local institutions was a worthy objective, and to the limited extent that CAAs achieved it, the poor were better off. But in a real war on poverty CAP would have been a mere skirmish, not the main theater of battle. Mobilization's Bertram Beck was one social worker who understood this. "Had the nation been genuinely interested in abolishing poverty," he wrote, "the War on Poverty would have had an economic base and would have led to some redistribution of wealth."[121]

V

OEO's adventures as an agent of change were short-lived. The institutions it antagonized forced OEO's retreat to safer ground by the end of 1965, and local CAAs were not far behind. In 1967 the question was not whether CAP would continue to promote change but whether it would even be permitted to exist. As the year began, congressional conservatives had enough votes to kill off OEO, and the White House hardly seemed to care. Turning day-to-day administration of OEO over to his deputy, Bertram Harding, Shriver devoted himself full time to lobbying for the life of his agency. In the end, thanks to a deft maneuver by the steel-jawed lady from Oregon, Edith Green, and support from an unexpected quarter, he prevailed.

In October 1967 the House Committee on Education and Labor took up consideration of a Senate measure to extend OEO for two years. Southern Democrats and Republicans had forged an alliance to carve the bill up, and Shriver's position appeared desperate. But midway through weeks of acrimonious committee debate Mrs. Green introduced an amendment that radically altered the parliamentary situation. Dubbed the "bossism and boll weevil" amendment by unfriendly Republicans,[122] it gave local governments the option, in effect, of taking over and operating private CAAs. Convinced by the amendment's adoption that aggrieved mayors could now control obstreperous CAAs, southern conservatives softened toward OEO, and the Dixiecrat-Republican alliance began to crack. Whether Mrs. Green, who had detested community action since the days of David Hackett, acted to emasculate the program or save the bill was her secret. As for Shriver, he had to pretend to oppose the Green amendment while privately supporting it as a necessary evil.[123]

Surprisingly, the mayors were in OEO's camp even before the Green amendment was proposed. Much had transpired in the two years since Mayor Daley urged Vice President Humphrey to put a leash on the agency. In cities where tensions had once marked relations between private CAA's and local governments, terms of accommodation had been negotiated. In all but a few of the cities where all-out war had once raged, the mayors had emerged victorious. Instincts for self-preservation having prevailed over formal commitments to change, once-militant CAAs rapidly evolved into tame dispensers of services. In this form they served—not threatened—local authority. In October 1967 twenty-one *Republican* mayors telegraphed their party's congressional leadership praising OEO as a "positive force in lessening social tensions."[124] In the end Congress extended OEO for two more years and even increased its appropriation by $100 million. Indeed, the mayors had become so comfortable with their CAAs that in 1968 only nineteen local governments in the entire country exercised their prerogative under the Green amendment to take them over.[125]

OEO's dreary last years were devoted to the twin goals of service and survival. Sargent Shriver left the agency in March 1968 to become ambassador to France. Bertram Harding, his successor, specialized in routine administration. Richard Nixon, elected president in November 1968, first tried to disperse OEO's programs to other agencies and then proposed its total elimination. Congress finally did abolish OEO in 1974, but, as a sop to the mayors, permitted CAP to live on under the newly created Community Services Administration. It hardly mattered, since by now community action had become nothing more than a white elephant of reform.

History will remember community action not only for the turmoil it created and the good that it did, but because its radicalism was the exception that proved the rule of the Great Society. Men of good will, Johnsonian liberals were constrained to act within a political culture that imposed severe limits on the extent of permissible change. To accomplish social reform, they had to buy off vested interests and call it consensus. Once Johnson understood the real intent of those in CAP whom he called the "kooks and sociologists,"[126] he had no choice but to squelch them. By attempting redistribution, even if only redistribution of local power, CAP's reformers had transgressed the limits. As for redistribution of income, Johnson never considered it. This then may serve as the epitaph of the famous War on Poverty—"Declared but Never Fought."

VI

Radicalism did, however, exist in the 1960s. When the liberals undertook to extend the blessings of American life to excluded people, they had expected to encounter opposition primarily from conservatives. As it turned out, radicals would give them far more grief. Two different sources fed the decade's radical impulse: disillusion with liberal reform and the flowering of utopian visions among the children of affluence. While liberals sought to improve American capitalism and American democracy, radicals condemned each as repressive and sought liberation from both. Hippies would seek liberation from repressive American culture. New leftists would seek to liberate themselves and the world from the rapacity of American capitalism. Black nationalists would seek to liberate their ghettos from white racism. And antiwar intellectuals would seek to liberate Vietnam from the American military juggernaut. Though most of these radicalisms were mutually incompatible, all of them tended in the late 1960s toward the same result, namely the unraveling of LBJ's hopes for a liberal reconstruction of America.

PART III

CHAPTER 10

Rise and Fall of a Counterculture

I

A MERICA discovered hippies at the world's first Human Be-In, Golden Gate Park, San Francisco, January 14, 1967. The occasion was something special, even in a Bay Area underground long accustomed to spectacle. Political activists from Berkeley mingled with dropouts from Haight-Ashbury, ending their feud and initiating a "new epoch" in the history of man. "In unity we shall shower the country with waves of ecstasy and purification," sponsors of the Be-In prophesied. "Fear will be washed away; ignorance will be exposed to sunlight; profits and empire will lie drying on deserted beaches."[1] Preparations for the Be-In were casual but appropriate. A hippie newspaper called the *Oracle* invited everyone "to bring costumes, blankets, bells, flags, symbols, cymbals, drums, beads, feathers, flowers."[2] A local painter named Michael Bowen arranged with his guru in Mexico to exchange weather for the day. The Hell's Angels motorcycle gang agreed to guard the electronic equipment of the rock bands, which would play this gig for free.[3] And poets Allen Ginsberg and Gary Snyder arrived two hours early to perform a "purificatory circumambulation" of the field, a ritual they had observed in 1963 in Sarnath, India, to drive out demons.[4]

By early afternoon a crowd estimated at twenty thousand gathered in the park to enjoy the unseasonably warm sun and commune with the hip notables on the makeshift stage. Timothy Leary was there, dressed in white and wearing flowers in his hair. "Turn on to the scene, tune in to what is happening, and drop out—of high school, college, grad school, junior executive—and follow me, the hard way," said Leary, reciting his famous commercial for the synthetic hallucinogen LSD.[5] Ginsberg, in a white Khader suit and blue rubber sandals, chanted a Buddhist mantra as Snyder blew a conchshell he had obtained in Kyoto while studying Zen Buddhism.[6] "We are primitives of an unknown culture . . ." Snyder had said on the eve of the Be-In, "with new ethics and new states of mind."[7] Music for the occasion was acid rock, performed by Quicksilver Messenger Service, Jefferson Airplane, and the Grateful Dead. Already an underground legend, the Dead had played Ken Kesey's notorious "acid tests," which had done so much to spread LSD and the psychedelic style throughout California a year or so before. Representing the new left was Jerry Rubin, released that very morning from jail, but not yet hip enough for this occasion. "Tune-In—Drop-Out—Take-Over," Rubin had said at a press conference prior to the event.[8] But few at the Be-In were in a mood (or condition) to take over anything.

The real show was the crowd. "The costumes were a designer's dream," wrote music critic Ralph Gleason in the San Francisco *Chronicle*, "a wild polyglot mixture of Mod, Palladin, Ringling Brothers, Cochise, and Hells Angel's Formal." Bells tinkled, balloons floated, people on the grass played harmonicas, guitars, recorders, flutes. Beautiful girls handed out sticks of incense. A young man in a paisley parachute drifted from the sky, though no plane was in sight. An old man gave away his poems.[9] A mysterious group called the Diggers had obtained seventy-five turkeys from a drug chemist named Owsley and supplied sandwiches, homemade bread, and oranges, free, to anyone who was hungry.[10] When a sulfur bomb exploded under the stage, people on the grass thought it was a large cloud of yellow incense and broke into appreciative applause.[11] Finally, after poets Michael McClure, Lenore Kandell, Snyder and Ginsberg read in the silent presence of Zen Master Suzuki Roshi who was seated on the stage, and the hours of tripping, dancing, and hugging had wound down, Ginsberg turned toward the setting sun, led a chant "om gri maitreya" (Salutations to Buddha of Futurity), and asked the people to practice "a little kitchen Yoga" by picking up their trash. Officials said that no gathering had left so little litter in the park in a generation.[12]

Newsweek was on hand to photograph the Be-In in gorgeous color and report that "it was a love feast, a psychedelic picnic, a hippie happening."[13] Images of hip quickly began to seep into the public consciousness, provoking intense curiosity and endless analysis in the straight world. Most of the pop sociology deserved the rebuke of Bob Dylan's "Ballad of a Thin Man": "Something is happening here but you don't know what it is. Do you, Mr. Jones?" Yet understanding was imperative, for the hippie impulse that was spreading through a generation of the young challenged the traditional values of bourgeois culture, values still underpinning the liberal movement of the 1960s—reason, progress, order, achievement, social responsibility. Hippies mocked liberal politicians, scorned efforts to repair the social order, and repudiated bourgeois society. In so doing, they became cultural radicals opposed to established authority. Among the movements arrayed against him toward the end of his tenure, none baffled Lyndon Johnson more than these hippies. Somehow, in the name of liberation, they rejected everything he stood for, including his strenuous efforts to liberate the poor and the black. Clearly, liberation meant something different to liberals like him from what it meant to radicals like them.

II

Few hippies read much, but those who did found their purpose strikingly described and anticipated in the strange books of Norman O. Brown. A classical scholar at Wesleyan University, whose underground explorations began in middle age and never strayed beyond the library, Brown published a book in 1959 called *Life Against Death.* A manifesto of cultural radicalism, this book established Brown as a prophet of the counterculture and its preeminent intellectual. Those seeking the meaning of the hippie movement could do no better than begin with him.

Brown was a Freudian who reshaped the ideas of the master to provide a happy ending; no mean feat, given Freud's pessimism. Man was unhappy, Freud argued, because his instincts were repressed. The realm of instinct was the id, wherein resided emotion, desire—above all, Eros, the sexual instinct, which sought bodily pleasure. But to accomplish the survival of the individual, Eros had to be controlled. Thus in childhood there emerged from the id the ego, which mediated between the individual and the outside world and attempted to repress the raging instincts. Eros could not be repressed entirely, however, and the ego was forced to admit it into consciousness—transformed, sublimated, desexualized. Sublimated Eros provided the energy for work, art, and culture. Hence the irony and tragedy of man: he can know happiness only in gratifying his instinctual need for bodily pleasure; but to preserve life and create civilization, that need must be denied. Freud had still other grounds for pessimism. In the id he had discovered, alongside Eros and warring against it, a second instinct, which he called the death instinct, or Thanatos. As civilization advances, Eros weakens, and the death instinct gains force. Directed outward, Thanatos becomes aggression, threatening other men with harm and civilization with extinction. "Men have gained control over the forces of nature to such an extent," Freud concluded, "that with their help they would have no difficulty in exterminating one another to the last man."[14]

Against Freud, Brown intended to show that man could achieve his infantile dream of eternal bodily pleasure. Brown began his reconstruction of Freud by denying that there existed an instinctual dualism—life and death, Eros *vs.* Thanatos—rooted in biology. The pre-Oedipal infant at his mother's breast experiences "union of the self with a whole world of love and pleasure."[15] In this blissful state there are no dualism, no self and other, no subject-object, no life against death, only timeless experience of being one with the world, only instinctual fusion and undifferentiated unity. Bliss ends when the infant experiences separation from the mother, producing anxiety, a sense of loss, and fear of death. According to Brown's argument, it is the infant's attempt to flee death that initiates instinctual de-fusion. Eros emerges, seeking actively to reunite with the mother, the source of bodily pleasure; Thanatos emerges, seeking the peace known at her breast. The ensuing sublimations of the instincts produce the spiritual life of man and propel history, but they cannot make man happy. The flight from death, then, is the critical event in psychic life, condemning man to sickness and removing him from nature. Brown's prescription for health was simple: If man can accept death, he can accept life, achieve instinctual re-fusion, abolish repression, and find happiness through "the resurrection of the body."

There was much in *Life Against Death* that anticipated and expressed the hippie impulse. Like the hippies, Brown was resolutely nonpolitical. Man was the animal who repressed himself; his salvation lay not in social reorganization but in self-reconstruction. Like the hippies, Brown affirmed instinctual freedom against the rational, disciplined, puritanic life that had been the life of man in Western civilization. Like the hippies, Brown was in revolt against civilized sex—exclusively genital, exclusively heterosexual, exclusively monogamous—affirming instead pan-sexualism, "polymorphous perversity," the union of many bodies: in short, erotic life based on the pre-Oedipal Eden. And finally Brown gave definition to the cultural project on which the hippies were soon to embark. Rejecting descent into the id as mere regression, Brown wished to make the unconscious conscious, incorporate the content of the id into the ego—to create, in other words, a new ego, a body ego, which Brown called the "Dionysian ego," overflowing with love, knowing no limits, affirming life. "Dionysus reunifies male and female, Self and Other, life and death," Brown wrote.[16] The creation of the Dionysian ego, the ego in service of liberated Eros—this was a project millions of mothers would soon understand implicitly and fear with good reason.

But Dionysian ecstasy might do more than command the ego; it might overflow the ego's limits until the very self is obliterated. In *Love's Body,* published in 1966, Brown used poetic implication, non-linear argument, and outrageous paradox to develop certain mystical implications in his earlier book. "Dionysus, the mad god, breaks down the boundaries; releases the prisoners; abolishes repression; and abolishes the *principium individuationis,* substituting for it the unity of man and the unity of man with nature," Brown wrote. The body was still there, but as a body in union with other bodies, the body lost. "The solution to the problem of identity is, get lost." The body was still there but now as universal body. "And the resurrection is the resurrection of the body"; Brown said, "but not the separate body of the individual, but the body of mankind as one body." Body existed, not as location or flesh, but as a field of energy; ego, character, personality were mere illusion. Id was now the impersonal energy embracing all mankind in "one mystical symbolical body." Indeed, knowledge of the Unity could be attained only by breaking the bonds of the ego, by having "no self."[17] Illumination, therefore, was consciousness of void, nothingness. This was the language of the satori of the Buddha, of Oriental religion, of mysticism—and the promise of the sixties drug prophets, especially the prophets of LSD.

If Brown's books forecast the hippie projects—Dionysian ecstasies, bodily and mystic—the Human Be-In proclaimed the existence of a hippie culture, or counterculture, committed to realizing those projects through drugs, sex, and rock and roll. But just as Brown did not invent the projects, hippies did not invent their culture from scratch. Hip explorers in the realm of the Dionysian had spent a generation developing rituals and a life style from which hippies freely borrowed. Indeed, without pioneers to point the way, hippies might never have emerged to fascinate and outrage America.

III

The history of hip began with the black hipsters of the 1930s. Black folk had always constituted something of a counterculture in America, representing, at least in the white imagination, pure id. Migrating into northern ghettos after World War I, young black men used their new freedom to improvise a new variation on black deviance—the hipster—who was not only hedonistic, sensual, and sexually uninhibited, but openly contemptuous of the white world that continued to exclude him. The language that hipsters invented on Harlem street corners was jive, an action language honed in verbal duels and inaccessible to most whites. Some jive words that became part of the permanent hip lexicon were *cat, solid, chick, Big Apple, square, tea, gas, dip, flip. Ofay,* the jive word for white, meant foe in pig Latin. The hipster costume was the zoot suit, designed, as hip garb always would be, to defy and outrage conventional taste. For kicks, the hipster smoked marijuana, which heightened his sense of immediacy and helped him soar above his mean surroundings. The only bigger kick was sex.[18]

Vital to the hipster experience was the uninhibited black music called jazz. In 1922 a writer in the *Atlantic Monthly* described jazz as the result of "an unloosing of instincts that nature wisely has taught us to hold in check, but which, every now and then, for cryptic reasons, are allowed to break the bonds of civilization."[19] Indeed, Louis Armstrong, playing his "hot," sensual, raunchy improvisations on trumpet, was the first hipster hero. As jazz changed, the hipster persona changed with it. In the early 1940s a group of rebel black jazzmen, hostile to the commercialization of the big bands, created bebop. Bebop relied on small groups and improvisation, as before, but the sound was cool, the rhythm variable, the volume low, and the technical virtuosity of its leading performers legend.[20] The genius of bebop was Charlie "The Bird" Parker, who lived at "the level of total spontaneity,"[21] whether he was playing alto sax or getting kicks from booze, sex, or heroin. By the mid-1940s, partly because of heroin, hot was out and cool was in. Hipster dress had become more conservative; noise and brash behavior, a breach of taste; detachment, a required pose.[22] By then, too, the hipster had ceased to be a type restricted to blacks only. In New York and other big cities, some disaffiliates among the white young found the hipster persona so expressive of their own alienation that they adopted it as their own. Thus was born, in Norman Mailer's phrase, "the white Negro,"[23] living outside the law for sex, pot, jazz, kicks —in short, for Dionysian ecstasy.

Herbert Huncke was a white hipster who first heard the language and the music on Chicago's South Side in the thirties. Before moving to New York before World War II, he had become a junkie, a habitué of the underworld, and a petty criminal so notorious that the police would name him the Creep and bar him from Times Square. An experimenter with forbidden experience, Huncke took drugs to derange the senses and expand consciousness, and he provided rich source material for Dr. Alfred Kinsey's study of American sexual mores. When wearied of the streets, he sought refuge in a detachment so complete that he was beyond feeling. Huncke had a word to describe his weariness. He said he was "beat."[24]

One day in 1945 Huncke encountered William Burroughs, not yet a famous writer, trying to get rid of a sawed-off shotgun and some morphine. Through Burroughs, Huncke met Allen Ginsberg, Jack Kerouac, John Clellon Holmes, and others in a circle of rebel writers and intellectuals who later became known as the beat generation. Living on the fringes of Columbia University as students or dropouts, the beats engaged in obscure resistance to the "Syndrome of Shutdown" (Ginsberg's later phrase)[25]—the movement toward a totalitarian America based on mass consumption and mass acquiescence. They were rebels too against the official culture purveyed in academic classrooms and celebrated in the lifeless literary quarterlies. In reaction they created their literature from raw experience, which they consumed with reckless and undiscriminating abandon. When Herbert Huncke introduced the proto-beats to the hipster underground, its jive, jazz, drugs, and unconventional sex, they plunged right in. Ginsberg wrote, "As far as I know the ethos of what's charmingly Hip, and the first pronunciation of the word itself to my fellow ears first came consciously from Huncke's lips; and the first information and ritual of the emergent hip subculture passed through Huncke's person."[26]

What the beats added to hip was the mystic quest. In the summer of 1948, living alone in East Harlem and grieving for his departed lover Neal Cassady, Allen Ginsberg had the defining experience of his life. As he lay in bed gazing at tenement roofs with a book of William Blake's *Songs of Innocence* before him, he heard the deep voice of the poet himself reciting the "Sunflower," and he knew it was the voice of God. "Looking out the window, . . ." Ginsberg remembered, "suddenly it seemed that I saw into the depths of the universe, by looking simply into the ancient sky." Ginsberg had auditory experience of other poems that evening, and there were other visions in the days that followed, until, a week later, standing in the athletic field at Columbia, Ginsberg invoked the spirit and experienced the cosmos as monster. "The sky was not a blue hand anymore but like a hand of death coming down on me." It was years before Ginsberg would seek that void again, but in the meantime he did not forget those moments when the ego had overflowed the bounds of the self and illumination had been his.[27] A year later Huncke moved in with Ginsberg, thoughtfully stashing his stolen goods elsewhere. Arrested as an accessory, Ginsberg was committed and stayed eight months in the Columbia-affiliated New York Psychiatric Institute.

After graduating from Columbia in 1949, Ginsberg worked at straight jobs and tried to master his real vocation, which was poetry. In 1954, forsaking New York, he moved to San Francisco to visit Cassady. There a brilliant circle of poets had gathered around Lawrence Ferlinghetti's City Lights Book Store in a neighborhood called North Beach. North Beach provided the cultural soil where the beat seed, originally planted in New York, took root and flowered.[28] With its narrow streets, high walls, and cheap houses overlooking the bay, North Beach reminded Gary Snyder of "ancient terraced fertile crescent pueblos."[29] The beats were hipsters a decade later, explorers in the realm of the Dionysian, searching for ecstasies, bodily and mystic.

For Ginsberg San Francisco was liberation. He found a psychiatrist who told him to do what he wanted, namely write poetry and love men; and he met his "life long sex-soul union" in Peter Orlovsky.[30] Maturing rapidly, Ginsberg also found his authentic voice as a poet. One weekend in 1955 he stayed in his apartment and wrote a poem, with little revision, which one part of him believed he could not publish out of respect for his father and another part believed would change America. In September, at an artists' co-op called the Six Gallery, with his friend Jack Kerouac there to pass around the jug and shout encouragement, Ginsberg read his astounding "Howl." Taking as its subject the life of the poet and his beat friends, "Howl" became a manifesto for the scattered disaffiliates of fifties America.

> I saw the best minds of my generation destroyed
>   by madness, starving hysterical naked,
> dragging themselves through the negro streets at dawn
>   looking for an angry fix,
> angelheaded hipsters burning for the ancient heavenly connection to
>   the starry dynamo in the machinery of night
> who poverty and tatters and hollow-eyed and high sat up smoking in
>   the supernatural darkness of cold-water flats floating across the
>   tops of cities contemplating jazz
> who bared their brains to Heaven under the El and saw Mohammedan
>   angels staggering on tenement roofs illuminated. . . .[31]

When the authorities brought Ferlinghetti to trial for publishing "Howl," on the grounds of obscenity, the poem attained more than literary celebrity. "Howl" sold 100,000 copies in ten years, making it perhaps the most popular serious poem of the century.[32]

Fame did not deflect Ginsberg from his Dionysian projects. Experimenting with psychedelic drugs, he deepened both his understanding of "the female principle" and his desire for women; and he tried again to transcend "this familiar rotting ginsberg" by grasping the Void.[33] In 1961, frightened by visions of the "serpent monster," he set forth on two years of travel to the East, seeking spiritual wisdom from holy men,—from Martin Buber in Israel to Tibetan lamas in India. The holy men had a message Ginsberg had already anticipated. Get back into the body, they told him. Stop trying to "melt into the universe," stop trying to merge with the nonhuman unknown. Riding the train from Kyoto to Tokyo in 1963, Ginsberg had an ecstatic experience as crucial to him as his Blake vision years before. The burden of his cosmic quest was instantly lifted, and he felt "suddenly free to love myself again and therefore love the people around me."[34] Weeping with joy, still on the train, he wrote "The Change."[35]

> Come, sweet lovely Spirit, back
> to your bodies, come great God,
> back to your only image. . . .

Ginsberg returned to America, all his demons exorcised at last, in time to become bard and shaman for the next hip generation. To the hippies, Ginsberg was a new kind of American hero-saint. He had penetrated far enough into the dark recesses of self to risk sanity, and he had returned purified, with reverence for all living things. Norman Mailer once wrote lovingly of him,[36]

> I sometimes think
> that little Jew bastard
> that queer ugly kike
> is the bravest man
> in America.

Jack Kerouac, the beat writer who shared so many of Ginsberg's adventures, also shared his mystic quest.[37] Kerouac had gone to Columbia to play football but rebelled against the discipline, deciding instead to write novels and probe the cultural underground. Recalling the 1940s, he wrote, "Anyway, the hipsters, whose music was bop, they looked like criminals but they kept talking about the same things I liked, long outlines of personal experience and vision, nightlong confessions full of hope that became illicit and repressed by War. . . . And so Huncke appeared to us and said, 'I'm beat' with radiant light shining out of his despairing eyes . . . a word perhaps brought from some midwest carnival or junk cafeteria. It was a new language, actually spade (Negro) jargon but you soon learned it."[38]

Kerouac made his artistic breakthrough when he decided to write a semi-fictional account of his road experiences with Neal Cassady. Some people might have regarded Cassady as a bum. Reared on the streets of Denver by his wino father, in and out of jails mostly for stealing cars,[39] Cassady possessed so much energy and lived so completely in the moment that the beat circle could not resist him. In April 1951 Kerouac fed a roll of teletype paper into a typewriter and let tales of Cassady flow spontaneously from his mind, in one paragraph 120 feet long. It took three weeks to write *On the Road*, six years to get it published.[40]

On the Road portrayed Kerouac, Cassady, Ginsberg, and their hipster friends speeding across the continent in the late forties, consuming pot, jazz, and sex, envying the Negro his spontaneity, his soul, his cool. Cassady (Dean Moriarty in the book) was the natural man, the Dionysian ego, joyfully slaking his unquenchable thirst for food, sex, and life. But Kerouac saw Cassady as more than a glutton. He was "a holy con-man," "the HOLY GOOF," "Angel Dean," questing for "IT," the moment "when you know all and everything is decided forever,"—that moment in jazz, Dean explained, when the man making the music "rises to his fate and has to blow equal to it." In San Francisco, deserted by Cassady and delirious from hunger, Kerouac himself (Sal Paradise) had a mystic vision, reaching "the point of ecstasy that I always wanted to reach." Eventually, as Cassady became ensnared in complication, accusation, wounds of the body, he becomes, in Kerouac's view, "BEAT—the root, the soul of Beatific."[41] A bestseller in 1957, *On the Road* became a literary inspiration for the restless young even then preparing to scale the walls of American suburbia in search of Dionysus.

In 1955 Kerouac, still an obscure writer, bummed his way across the country to visit Ginsberg in San Francisco. Kerouac was by then deep into Buddhism. Recognizing that the beat quest for satori had more in common with Oriental than Western religion, he vowed to end suffering and achieve nirvana by overcoming desire.[42] In California he found that in turning East he was not alone. A pinch of Zen had by now been added to the witch's brew boiling over in North Beach. Zen's chief popularizer in the Bay Area was Alan Watts, a sometime Episcopal clergyman from England who had attained local celebrity in the early 1950s as dean of San Francisco's American Academy of Asian Studies.[43] Watts's was an easygoing brand of Zen, based on the teachings of the Chinese founders, liberally interpreted. Zen taught, Watts explained, that it is absurd to desire the end of desire, to grasp for nirvana, which is nongrasping, to seek to liberate the nonexistent self. Let go of the passions, do not fight them; neither repress passion nor indulge it. Live naturally and spontaneously, and when satori comes, it will come without effort, as a sudden turn of consciousness. To the vast relief of the sympathetic young, Watts stressed that one of the passions that definitely did not have to be denied was sexual passion. Man was both animal and angel, Watts maintained, and can be both sexualist and mystic.[44] Thus was born the strangest of religions—Dionysian Zen.

Kerouac met not only Watts in San Francisco but Gary Snyder. Snyder, said Watts, *"is just exactly what I have been trying to say."*[45] Snyder had felt estranged from industrial civilization since, as a child growing up in backwoods Oregon, he had experienced "an undefinable awe before the natural world."[46] He became fascinated by Indian myths at Reed College and later gave up on white civilization entirely when he discovered the East. In 1953 he began two years of study of Oriental languages at Berkeley in preparation for Zen training in Japan. Among his other accomplishments, he was a poet good enough to share the stage at the Six Gallery the night Ginsberg read "Howl."[47]

Kerouac recounted his adventures with Snyder in *Dharma Bums,* mythologizing him as he had Cassady. When Kerouac first visited Snyder in his twenty-by-twelve shack in Berkeley, Snyder (Japhy Rider in the book) was sitting cross-legged on the floor, translating the poems of the Chinese Zen lunatic Han-shan. Kerouac's admiration for the tough, wiry little Buddhist was instantaneous and complete. A pioneer dropout, Snyder was living a new kind of American life in the interstices of technological civilization. If he needed money, he shipped out on a commercial freighter; if he needed clothes, he bought them at the Goodwill store; if he was thirsty, he brewed tea of intoxicating purity, and if hungry, he could produce a delicious meal from dried vegetables, grains, and herbs. When he wanted women, which was often, he reached out and took them. "I distrust any kind of Buddhism or any kind of philosophy or social system that puts down sex," he told Kerouac. The climax of *Dharma Bums* was a climb up the Matterhorn, with Kerouac the tenderfoot learning the art from the master. Improvising haiku, leaping boulders, meditating by the campfire, the two bodhisattvas experienced ecstatic union with Nature. A thousand feet from the top of the mountain, Kerouac panicked and took refuge under a ledge. But Snyder, defying the terrifying height and wind, darted to the top, shouting "his triumphant mountain-conquering Buddha Mountain Smashing song of joy." Back on the ground Snyder delivered himself of a Zen koan. "When you get to the top of the mountain keep climbing."[48]

And Snyder kept climbing. For most of the next ten years, while publication of his poems nourished his legend in America, Snyder studied Zen in a Japanese monastery. In 1961 he visited India to help guide Ginsberg on a mutual Buddhist pilgrimage to holy places. Five years after that he was back in America to guide a new hip generation in its own revolt against the nature-destroying civilization of the West.

By the late 1950s, a fully developed beat subculture had emerged not only in North Beach but also in Venice West (near Los Angeles), New York's Greenwich Village, and a few other hip resorts in between. The beats possessed deviant tastes in language, literature, music, drugs, and religion. Profoundly alienated from dominant American values, practicing voluntary poverty and spade cool, they rejected materialism, competition, the work ethic, hygiene, sexual repression, monogamy, and the Faustian quest to subdue nature. There were, to be sure, never more than a few thousand fulltime beats, but thanks to the scandalized media, images of beat penetrated and disconcerted the middle classes. Beats, like hula hoops, were a fad. Indeed, by the early 1960s the San Francisco poets had scattered, and cops and tourists had driven the rest of the beats from their old haunts in North Beach. A remnant survived, however, and found convenient shelter in another congenial San Francisco neighborhood. It was Haight-Ashbury, a racially integrated community, forty square blocks, bordering magnificent Golden Gate Park. There, beat old-timers kept alive the hip style and the Dionysian projects, until hippies moved in and appropriated both.

I V

In the metamorphosis from beat to hippie, hallucinogenic drugs played an indispensable part. Indians had been using peyote and magic mushrooms for sacramental purposes since before the rise of the Aztec civilization. But in industrial civilizations, knowledge of mind-altering substances had virtually disappeared. In the 1920s chemists synthesized the active ingredient in peyote, calling it mescaline, and did the same thing in 1958 for the sacred mushrooms, producing psilocybin.[49] Science even outdid nature in 1938 when Dr. Albert Hoffman of the Sandoz Chemical Works in Switzerland fabricated a compound many times more potent than anything imbibed by the most ecstatic Indian. Searching for a respiratory stimulant, Hoffman produced the diethylamide of lysergic acid, a color-less, odorless, apparently useless substance that he called LSD. Five years later, in the course of an experiment on animals, Hoffman accidentally ingested an "unmeasurable trace" of LSD and took the world's first acid trip. (It was, incidentally, a bummer.)[50] Hoffman kept experimenting, and Sandoz began supplying LSD to psychiatric researchers trying to cure schizophrenia. By 1960 LSD was seeping out of the laboratory into the cultural underground.

The herald of the psychedelic revolution was the British author Aldous Huxley. Swallowing some mescaline in 1953, Huxley accidentally triggered a profound mystical experience, in which he watched "a slow dance of golden lights," discovered "Eternity in a flower" and even approached the "Pure Light of the Void," before fleeing in terror from "the burning brightness of unmitigated Reality." In *The Doors of Perception* (1954), which recounted his journey, Huxley lamented that the rich and highly educated white people of the earth were so wedded to words and reason that they had cut themselves off from mystic knowledge. Western man, he said, should accept the "gratuitous grace" of mind-expanding drugs, thus "to be shaken out of the ruts of ordinary perception, to be shown for a few timeless hours the outer and the inner world, not as they appear to an animal obsessed with survival or to a human being obsessed with words and notions, but as they are apprehended, directly and unconditionally, by Mind at Large."[51]

The man who purveyed Huxley's holy message to the millions was Timothy Leary. Possessor of a Ph.D. in psychology, Leary quit his job as director of the Kaiser Foundation Hospital in Oakland, California, in 1958, convinced that conventional psychiatry did not work. Accepting a post at Harvard to pursue his unorthodox ideas, Leary was on his way to a productive scientific career until, one day in Mexico, he discovered the magic mushrooms.[52]

Leary had retreated to a villa in Cuernavaca in the summer of 1960 to write a paper that he hoped would win him points in the academic game. He had never smoked marijuana and knew nothing about mind-altering drugs. But, when a friend procured the mushrooms from a local Indian, Leary thought it might be fun to try some. On a hot afternoon sitting around a pool, Leary and a few companions choked down a bowl of filthy, foul-tasting *crudos*. The game for Leary ended right there. "Five hours after eating the mushrooms it was all changed," he wrote. "The revelation had come. The veil had been pulled back. The classic vision. The full-blown conversion experience. The prophetic call. The works. God had spoken."[53]

Back at Harvard in the fall, Leary secured Huxley's help in designing a scientific experiment to investigate the behavioral effects of psilocybin (synthesized magic mushrooms). Soon Leary was turning on graduate students, ministers, convicts, and stray seekers showing up at his rented mansion in suburban Boston. In truth, Leary was using science to cloak his real purpose, which was to give away the keys to paradise. And he did grow in spiritual knowledge. He learned that drugs alone could not produce a state of blessedness, that they "had no specific effect on consciousness, except to expand it."[54] God and the Devil resided together in the nervous system. Which of these was summoned depended on one's state of mind. Leary, therefore, emphasized the importance of proper "set and setting" (candles, incense, music, art, quiet) to help the seeker experience God.

In December 1960 Leary made the connection with the hip underground in the person of Allen Ginsberg. Having met him in New York, Ginsberg spent a week at Leary's home to enlist the professor in his own crusade for mind expansion. The two hit it off from the start. On Sunday, with dogs, children, and hangers-on scattered about, Leary gave Ginsberg and Peter Orlovsky the sacred mushrooms. The poets repaired to their room, stripped naked, and played Wagner on the record player. Lying in bed, Ginsberg began to succumb to hellish visions, until Leary came in, looked in his eyes, and pronounced him a great man. Ginsberg arose, and with Orlovsky padding behind, descended to the kitchen to proclaim himself the Messiah. We will go into the streets and call the people to peace and love, Leary reports him as saying. And we will get on the phone and hook up Burroughs, Kerouac, Mailer, Kennedy, and Khrushchev and "settle all this warfare bit." Hello operator, Ginsberg said. This is God. Get me Kerouac. And eventually she did. Sitting in the kitchen after the drug had worn off, Ginsberg plotted the psychedelic revolution. Everybody ought to have the mushrooms, he said, beginning with the influentials. They would not listen to him, a crazy beatnik poet, but they might listen to a Harvard professor. Leary must come to New York on weekends and turn on the likes of Kerouac, Robert Lowell, LeRoi Jones, Dizzy Gillespie, Thelonious Monk, and other creative people in Ginsberg's personal telephone book. Leary was willing. "From this evening on," he wrote, "my energies were offered to the ancient underground society of alchemists, artists, mystics, alienated visionaries, dropouts and the disenchanted young, the sons arising."[55]

Not until late 1961 did Leary try LSD—"the most shattering experience of my life."[56] Taking him far beyond psilocybin, LSD enabled Leary to accomplish the projects of the counterculture—Dionysian ecstasies, mystic and bodily. He journeyed down the DNA ladder of evolution to the single cell at the beginning of life and then outward to the cosmic vibrations where he merged with pure energy, "the white light," nothingness.[57] He also experienced the resurrection of the body. "Blow the mind and you are left with God and life—and life is sex," he said. Leary called LSD "a powerful aphrodisiac, probably the most powerful sexual releaser known to man. . . . The union was not just your body and her body but all of your racial and evolutionary entities with all of hers. It was mythic mating."[58] Playboy asked Leary if it was true that women could have multiple orgasms under LSD. He replied with a straight face, "In a carefully prepared, loving LSD session, a woman can have several hundred orgasms."[59]

Huxley had warned Leary that those in authority would oppose him. In April 1963, with LSD selling for a dollar a dose in Harvard Square, the university fired Leary, ostensibly because he cut classes, but really because his work had become an academic scandal. A month later, Richard Alpert, his colleague and collaborator, was fired too. After Mexico bounced the pair as well, a young millionaire came to Leary's rescue by renting him an estate in Millbrook, New York, complete with a musty sixty-four-room Victorian mansion and imitation Bavarian chalets. For the next two years Leary quit proselytizing and presided quietly over a religious commune based on drugs.[60] The atmosphere at Millbrook was distinctly Oriental, for Leary too had discovered the East. Indeed, in 1965 Leary traveled to India where, high enough on LSD to overlook the Himalayas, he translated (from English, of course) Lao Tzu's The Way of Life. He called this ancient Chinese classic a "time-tested psychedelic manual."[61]

Things began to go wrong for Leary in December 1965. On his way to Mexico with his family for a holiday, he was detained at the border and arrested with his daughter for possession of two ounces of marijuana.[62] (Leary said he was probably the first person ever caught trying to smuggle pot *into* Mexico.) There followed more arrests, trials, convictions, appeals. The Millbrook idyll over, Leary again went public, playing to the hilt his role of unrepentant felon and high priest of the psychedelic movement. In 1966 he announced formation of a new religious organization called the League for Spiritual Discovery (LSD). That fall he conducted services in the Village Theatre in New York, where for three dollars a ticket observers could enjoy a multimedia show and a sermon by Leary.[63] After a successful three-month run, Leary took his show on the college circuit, telling audiences to turn on, tune in, drop out. Few lines of the sixties wore so badly.

LSD was a big story in 1966. Congress outlawed it. *Newsweek, Life,* and the *Saturday Evening Post* all did cover stories on it.[64] Sandoz stopped selling it. And the Food and Drug Administration sent a letter to two thousand colleges warning of its "widespread availability" and "profound effects on the mental processes."[65] Years before, Leary had estimated that one million Americans would take LSD by 1967.[66] According to *Life,* the nation had reached the million-dose mark in 1966.[67] As for Leary himself, his reputation among heads declined rapidly after he went show biz. Many of them were already too young to know that he had once been a serious man and that at the dawn of the Aquarian Age Timothy Leary had been the Johnny Appleseed of acid.

If Leary spread the psychedelic revolution, Ken Kesey created the psychedelic style, West Coast version. In 1959, three years before publication of his modern classic *One Flew Over the Cuckoo's Nest,* Kesey took LSD as a subject in a medical experiment, and for him, then and there, the doors of perception blew wide open. In 1964, with a group of disciples called the Merry Pranksters, he established a drug commune in rural La Honda, an hour's drive from San Francisco. One of the Pranksters was Neal Cassady. On acid, Kesey and friends experienced the illusion of self, the All-in-One, the energy field of which we are all an extension. They tried to break down psychic barriers, attain intersubjectivity or group mind, and achieve synchronization with the Cosmos. And they committed themselves to a life of Dionysian ecstasy.[68]

The Pranksters were hip, but in a new way. They were not beaten disaffiliates, warring against technology land, cursing their fate that they had not been born black. In *The Electric Kool-Aid Acid Test,* a history of Kesey in the underground, Tom Wolfe described this new hip generation, these hippies, as products of postwar affluence. Their teen years were spent driving big cars through the California suburbs, believing, like the superheroes in their Marvel comics, that anything was possible. No spade cool for them, no Zen detachment, none of Leary's "set and setting." The Pranksters used LSD to propel themselves out of their skulls toward the outer edge of Western experience. Their style was the wacko style: lurid costumes, Day-Glo paint, crazy trips in Kesey's 1939 multicolored International Harvester school bus, complete with speakers, tapes, and microphones. It was lots of kicks, of course, but it was more than kicks. For Kesey was a religious prophet whose ultimate goal was to turn America, as Michael Bowen put it, into an "electric Tibet."[69]

Toward the end of 1965 Kesey conceived a ritual appropriate for spreading his version of cosmic consciousness. He called it the acid test. Hooking up with the rock group the Grateful Dead, he experimented with multimedia shows so noisy and frenzied that, by themselves, they menaced reason. To make sure that no one missed the point, lots of free LSD was distributed, a legal act, since California did not get around to outlawing the drug until October 1966. The purpose of the acid test was to create an experience so Dionysian that revelers would overflow the bounds of ego and plug directly into the Cosmos. After Kesey tried out the acid tests in a dozen or so road shows on the West Coast, he headed for the big time.[70]

On January 21–23, 1966, Kesey and the Merry Pranksters produced and directed the Trips Festival at Longshoremen's Hall, San Francisco. The timing was perfect. For more than a year teenage dropouts and disillusioned campus radicals had been drifting into the beat haven of Haight-Ashbury. They were on the verge of community, but not quite there, acid freaks in search of identity. At Kesey's festival the heads of the Bay Area discovered their numbers, came out in the open, and confirmed the wacko style. The estimated twenty thousand people who attended wore every variety of wild costume, including Victorian dresses, Civil War uniforms, four-inch eyelashes, serapes, Indian headbands. Live rock propelled dancers through an electronic chaos of strobe lights, movies, tape machines, and slide projectors. High above the hall, dressed in a silver space suit, directing the whole to get the parts into sync, was Kesey himself. A few days later he took off for Mexico rather than face the consequences of a second drug bust.[71] But Kesey's place in the history of hip was secure, no one having done more to create the hippie style that he had now to leave behind.

V

The Dionysian impulse in the hippie counterculture was made up in equal measures of drugs, sex, and music—not jazz music but rock and roll. When hippies moved in, the black jazz bars on Haight Street moved out. Spade jazz was now as irrelevant to hip as spade soul. Rock had once been black music too, but was so thoroughly appropriated by whites that many hip kids never knew its origins. Rock originated in the 1940s as "rhythm and blues," an urban-based blues music played with electric instruments, pounding beat, and raunchy lyrics—music by blacks for blacks. In 1952 the legendary Cleveland disc jockey Alan Freed hosted the first rhythm and blues record show for a white audience, calling the music "rock and roll." The music caught on among teenagers tired of sexless, sentimental ballads, and soon white performers fused pop and country styles with rhythm and blues to create white rock and roll. That's what Elvis Presley sang when he emerged in 1956 to become the biggest star in pop history. From the beginning, rock and roll was protest music, protest against Tin Pan Alley, protest against parental taste, protest against instinctual repression. Music of the id, fifties rock and roll helped create a generation of cultural subversives who would in time heed the siren song of hip.[72]

In 1958, when Elvis went into the Army, rock entered a period of decline. Meanwhile, the black sound that had inspired it was being assimilated anew by other talented musicians, this time in England, and it would return to America, bigger than before, with the Beatles. During their long years of apprenticeship, playing lower-class clubs in Liverpool and Hamburg, John Lennon, Paul McCartney, and George Harrison explored the roots of rock and roll, even as they slowly fashioned a style of their own.[73] By 1963 that style had fully matured. No longer just another scruffy group of Teddy Boys playing electronic guitars, they had become well-tailored professionals with a distinctive hair style (Eton long), immense stage presence, the best song-writing team in pop history (Lennon and McCartney), a fluid sound, contagious vitality, and, above all, the irrepressible beat of rock and roll. That beat helped propel the Beatles to stardom in Britain in 1963 and created Beatlemania.

Within days of its release in the United States in January 1964, "I Want to Hold Your Hand" climbed to the top of the charts, to be followed quickly by "She Loves You" and "Please, Please Me." In February the Beatles themselves arrived for a tour that began with a sensational TV performance on the *Ed Sullivan Show* and continued before hysterical teen mobs in New York, Washington, and Miami. In April all five top singles in the United States were Beatles songs and the two top albums were Beatles albums. In July the first Beatles movie, *A Hard Day's Night,* amazed critics and delighted audiences with its wit and verve. Meanwhile that year Beatles merchandise—everything from dolls to dishcloths—was grossing over $50 million.[74] Nothing comparable to Beatlemania had ever happened in the history of pop culture.

Unlike Presley or their British rivals, the Rolling Stones, the Beatles did not menace society. They mocked it. Insouciant, irreverent, flip, they took seriously no institution or person, themselves included. "What do you think of Beethoven?" a reporter asked at the Beatles' first American press conference. "I love him," replied Ringo. "Especially his poems."[75] Treating the adult world as absurd, they told their fans to kick off their shoes, heed their hormones, and have fun. However harmless initially, the Beatles phenomenon contained the possibility of danger. The frenzied loyalty they inspired endowed the Fab Four with immense potential power —power to alter life styles, change values, and create a new sensibility, a new way of perceiving the world. But in the early days, as they sang their songs of teen love, that power lay dormant. When Ken Kesey attended the 1965 Beatles concert in San Francisco, he was astonished by the "concentration and power" focused on the performers. He was just as astonished by their inability to exploit them. "They could have taken this roomful of kids and snapped them," said Kesey, "and they would have left that place enlightened, mature people that would never have been quite the same again. . . . They had the power to bring off this new consciousness to people, but they couldn't do it."[76]

The artist who first seized the power of rock and used it to change consciousness was Bob Dylan. Born Robert Zimmerman, Dylan tried on every style of teen alienation available during the fifties in Hibbing, Minnesota. Though he wanted to be a rock and roll star, he discovered on enrolling at the University of Minnesota in 1959 that folk music was the rage on campus. In 1961 Dylan arrived in Greenwich Village, the folk capital of America, determined to become the biggest folkie of them all. A little over a year later, he was. Audiences responded to his vulnerability, the nasal whine with which he delivered his songs, and lyrics so riveting they transformed the folk art. Immersing himself in the left-liberal-civil-rights ethos permeating the Village in the early 1960s, Dylan wrote folk songs as protest. He did not compose from the headlines, as other protest singers did. He used figurative language and elusive imagery to distill the political mood of his time and place. Gambling that a poet could become a star, he won big. Two weeks after Peter, Paul, and Mary recorded his song "Blowin' in the Wind," it sold more than 300,000 copies. Songs like "A Hard Rain's Gonna Fall" were hailed as true art. And his "Times They Are A-Changin' " became a generational anthem. It was no less appropriate for Dylan to sing at the 1963 March on Washington than for Martin Luther King to deliver a sermon there.[77]

Meanwhile, the Beatles arrived and Dylan was listening. "Everybody else thought they were for the teenyboppers, that they were gonna pass right away," Dylan said. "But it was obvious to me that they had staying power. I knew they were pointing the direction of where music had to go."[78] In July 1965 Dylan outraged the folk world by appearing at the Newport Folk Festival, no longer the ragged waif with acoustic guitar, but as a rock and roll singer, outfitted in black leather jacket and backed by an electric band. That summer his rock single, "Like a Rolling Stone," perhaps the greatest song he ever wrote, made it all the way to number one.[79]

Dylan took rock and made it the medium for cultural statement —folk-rock, the critics quickly labeled it. As his music changed, so did the message. Moving with his generation, Dylan now abandoned liberal politics for cultural radicalism. The lyrics he sang in the mid-sixties were intensely personal and frequently obscure, but taken together, they formed a stunning mosaic of a corrupt and chaotic America. It is a fact of no small social consequence that in 1965 millions of radios and record players were daily pounding Dylan's message, subliminally or otherwise, into the skulls of a generation. There was, for example, "Highway 61," which depicted America as a junkyard road heading for war; "Maggie's Farm," a dropout's contemptuous farewell to the straight world; "Desolation Row," which portrayed an insane society, governed by insane men, teetering on the brink of apocalypse; "Ballad of a Thin Man," using homosexual imagery to describe an intellectual's confusion in a world bereft of reason; and "Gates of Eden," a mystical evocation of a realm beyond the senses, beyond ego, wherein resides the timeless Real.[80] After Dylan, a host of other rock prophets arose to preach sex, love, peace, or revolution. After Dylan rock and roll became a music that both expressed the sixties counterculture and shaped it.

Among those acknowledging their debt to Dylan were the Beatles. After Dylan, they too began writing songs for the cultural opposition, to which they became increasingly committed. The Beatles induced mystic ecstasies with LSD, discovered the music and religion of the East, even took an abortive pilgrimage to India to study Transcendental Meditation with the Maharishi Mahesh Yogi. In June 1967 they released *Sergeant Pepper's Lonely Hearts Club Band*, a musically innovative album placing them at the head of the psychedelic parade.[81] ("I'd love to turn you on," John Lennon sang on the record's best cut.) Timothy Leary, after *Sergeant Pepper*, proclaimed the Beatles "evolutionary agents sent by God, endowed with a mysterious power to create a new human species."[82]

In the view of some, this new human species had already emerged with the San Francisco hippies, who played their own brand of rock and roll. Literally hundreds of bands had formed in the Bay Area by the mid-1960s, but because no major company recorded there, they developed in isolation from the commercial mainstream. Hippie musicians were freaks who played for freaks, having no other purpose than creation of Dionysian art. They were contemptuous of the star system, top forty stations, giant concerts for idolatrous audiences, Madison Avenue hype. They played their music live in dance halls where the musicians could jam as long as they wanted, and the dancers dressed like rock stars. The songs they wrote celebrated drugs and sex, and the music they played was music to trip on.[83] One rock critic described the San Francisco Sound as "revelatory roaring, chills of ecstasy, hallucinated wandering, mystico-psychotic wonder."[84]

San Francisco's dance-hall craze began in the fall of 1965 when local promoters rented seedy halls to feature hippie bands like the Jefferson Airplane, Big Brother and the Holding Company, Quicksilver Messenger Service, and the Grateful Dead. After Kesey's Trips Festival in January 1966, the acid tests merged with the dances, institutionalized at weekend freakouts at the Fillmore and the Avalon Ballroom. The quintessential San Francisco band was the Grateful Dead, who had been on Kesey's trip and never got over it. "It wasn't a *gig*, it was the Acid Tests where anything was OK," the Dead's Jerry Garcia recalled. "Thousands of people, man, all helplessly stoned, all finding themselves in a roomful of other thousands of people, none of whom any of them were afraid of. It was magic, far out, beautiful magic." In June 1966 the Dead moved into a house in Haight-Ashbury, where they lived together, jammed free for the people, got stoned, got busted, and continued to seek that magic moment in their music when performers, audience, and Cosmos were One.[85]

By the time of the Monterey International Pop Festival, June 1967, the musical energies that had been gathering in San Francisco for two years could no longer be locally contained. Some of the hippie bands performing at the festival got their first national exposure there; others had already succumbed to the lure of fat recording contracts. By summer the San Francisco Sound was making the city the new rock mecca and its performers the newest rock superstars. The big song on the top forty stations that season was the Airplane's "White Rabbit," psychedelic variations on a theme from *Alice in Wonderland,* ending with the command to "feed a head, feed a head." That summer, too, thousands of teenagers took literally Scott McKenzie's musical invitation, with its implicit promise of Dionysian revels, to come to "San Francisco (Be Sure to Wear Flowers in Your Hair)." Ralph Gleason, San Francisco's hip music critic, understood well the cultural significance of rock. "At no time in American history has youth possessed the strength it possesses now," he wrote. "Trained by music and linked by music, it has the power for good to change the world." Significantly, he added, "That power for good carries the reverse, the power for evil."[86]

VI

By 1967 Haight-Ashbury had attained a population large enough to merit, at last, the designation "counterculture." The question was, where was this culture tending? A few days after the famous Human Be-In, the celebrities of the movement met on Alan Watts's houseboat off Sausalito to exchange visions of utopia. Watts summed up for the others the predicament of the West: rational, technological man had lost contact with himself and nature. Fortunately, Timothy Leary said, automation could now liberate man from work and enable him to live a simpler life. Feasting off technology, dropouts from megalopolis could form tribes and move back to the land. Yes, said Gary Snyder. Turn Chicago into a center for cybernetic technology and the rest of America into buffalo pasture. After a while, as life got simpler, "Chicago would rust away." Man's destruction of his natural environment would cease. Nuclear families would give way to communes or tribes, whose members would share food, work, and sex. Like the Comanche and the Sioux, members of these tribes would go off alone to have visions, and all who knew them would know them as men. Already in Big Sur, Snyder continued, kids were using A. L. Kroeber's *Handbook of the California Indians* to learn the art of primitive survival, to learn how to be Indians. Fine, countered Allen Ginsberg, "but where are the people going to buy their Uher tape recorder machines?" which were being used to record the conversation.[87]

Ginsberg's was the authentic voice of Haight-Ashbury. Addicted to electronic amenities, hippies merely played at being Indians, satisfied to wear Navaho jewelry and feathers. They communed with nature by picking Golden Gate Park bare of flowers; their notion of tribal harmony was to let everyone "do their own thing." As love had supposedly done for the Hopi, so it would do for them: it would conquer all. Armed with "flower power," hippies would overwhelm their enemies and live a life of ecstasy on the asphalt pavements of urban America. Real Indians were not much impressed. In the spring of 1967, when Ginsberg and Richard Alpert met Hopi leaders in Santa Fe to propose a Be-In in the Grand Canyon, the tribal spokesman brushed them off, saying according to the *Berkeley Barb*, "No, because you mean well but you are foolish. . . . You are a tribe of strangers to yourselves."[88] If not strangers to one another, the inhabitants of Haight-Ashbury were hardly a tribe. Something of their variety, as well as the contradictory currents swirling through the community, was revealed by the local notables.

Ron Thelin was an early settler who had moved into one of Haight-Ashbury's spacious Victorian homes and founded a commune. It occurred to him that the nascent drug community needed an information center, and so in January 1966, the same month Kesey staged the Trips Festival, he opened the Psychedelic Shop on Haight Street. Beginning with a small stock of books, records, and drug paraphernalia, Ron and his brother Jay built the most famous hippie business in America. Thirty other stores catering to heads opened in the neighborhood, formed a hip proprietors association, and looked to Thelin as their spokesman. Ron, meantime, branched out into journalism, becoming one of the founders of the psychedelic San Francisco *Oracle*. Ron's problem was that he was a capitalist in Bohemia, worse yet, a capitalist who made money. It did not matter that his business returned some of its profits to the people, dispensed vital information, and maintained a free meditation room. Lots of hippies thought everything should be free. Fatally for his peace of mind, Ron Thelin thought so too.[89] To reconcile his ideals with his money, he indulged in fantasies of a Haight Street that would be a "famous dope center." Fine teashops would display large jars of marijuana and even real tea, and fine restaurants would serve organic or macrobiotic food, "all for free or trade."[90] In the meantime, Ron made plans to give it all up and live like an Indian in New Mexico.

Augustus Owsley Stanley III was the legendary chemist who made the acid that made San Francisco famous. Timothy Leary called him "God's Secret Agent." He called himself "Owsley." Grandson of a former U.S. senator from Virginia, Owsley was a thirty-year-old dropout when he set up a lab near the Berkeley campus in 1964 and began mass producing high-quality LSD. Though he made a fortune, he was in it for more than money. It was Owsley who soaked a Bible with acid and smuggled it into a Berkeley jail for the spiritual benefit of the Free Speech Movement. It was Owsley who supplied the LSD for Kesey's acid tests, bought the world's most expensive sound system for the Grateful Dead, and passed out free LSD at San Francisco rock concerts. It was Owsley, most of all, and the estimated ten million doses he marketed that made possible the psychedelic revolution. After Sandoz stopped selling LSD in 1966, Owsley became the world's best source. Still, few could stand his companionship very long. A compulsive talker, he lectured incessantly on meat and showers, which were good, and vegetables and baths, which were bad. Haight-Ashbury tolerated him out of necessity and hoped, for its own selfish reasons, that he could stay out of jail, which for a remarkably long time he did.[91]

Swami A. C. Bhaktivedanta, age seventy-one, was an Indian holy man who arrived in Haight-Ashbury in January 1967 to open the Radha Krishna Temple and recruit disciples. He had been in town only a short time when the leading San Francisco bands, playing "mantra rock," gave him a benefit concert at the Avalon Ballroom. The Swami was something of an oddity in the neighborhood since he frowned on drugs and sex, but he had a solution to human misery that was sufficiently simple and exotic to assure him converts. Were each man to chant the Hare Krishna mantra, the Swami taught, he would find peace in himself and bring peace to the world, for Krishna consciousness was God consciousness. Soon his ecstatic monks, dressed in cotton, shorn of hair, were chanting the Hare Krishna not only in Haight-Ashbury but on city streets across America.[92]

Emmett Grogan was perhaps Haight-Ashbury's most influential citizen. A veteran of gang wars in New York, a student of film in Italy, a draftee who was discharged from the Army in 1966 as a schizophrenic, Grogan found a home in the San Francisco Mime Troupe, which performed radical plays free on the streets. He also plunged into the city's drug culture. Grogan, however, was no ordinary head. During his first LSD session in 1965 it had come to him in a flash of illumination that property was theft. Joined by a few others from the Mime Troupe, Grogan began issuing anonymous mimeographed essays to provide the Haight with some politics. He called his essays "Digger Papers," after the seventeenth-century English radicals who appropriated common land and gave their surplus to the poor. The Digger Papers attacked hip capitalists like Thelin for hypocrisy, the hip *Oracle* for pansyness, and the psychedelic transcendentalism of Swami Bhaktivedanta as "absolute bullshit." But action counted with Grogan more than words, because action was theater, and theater could alter consciousness by altering frame of reference. In October 1966 the Diggers announced that every day at 4 P.M., at the panhandle on Ashbury Street, they would distribute free food to anyone who wanted it. And every day for the next year, serving food they begged and food they stole, the Diggers kept their promise. They also opened a free store, at first called the Free Frame of Reference, and after it was forced to move, the Trip without a Ticket. Anyone could take what he wanted from a free store, and floor space was always available for stray runaways. When liberals gave money, the Diggers burned it. When someone asked who was in charge, he was told he was. The media loved the Diggers and portrayed them as a hip version of the Salvation Army. In truth, there was something sinister about them, especially Grogan. Paranoid, secretive, often violent, Grogan was an anarchist moved less by visions of the beloved community than by hatred of all authority. That, too, was a tendency lurking beneath the surface of Haight-Ashbury.[93]

Chocolate George was the hippies' favorite Hell's Angel. The Angels were the notorious motorcycle gang that had been stomping and raping its way through California for years. Ever since Kesey had invited them to a party in La Honda in 1965 and pacified them with LSD, Angels and hippies had formed an uneasy alliance—outlaw Americans sharing a taste for costumes, drugs, and defying the straights.[94] Indeed, Angels served hippies as a private police force. At free rock concerts in the park, the Angels guarded the stage in exchange for beer. When threatened by black toughs, hippies summoned Angels to the rescue. Sometimes they summoned Chocolate George, whose signature was a large hand forever clasped around a bottle of chocolate milk.[95] Despite his greasy jacket with its death's head insignia, Chocolate George was something of a humanitarian, having worked twelve years as a mechanic at the Recreation Center for the Handicapped. He was also a man of honor. Once when the police arrested a fellow Angel, George tried to drag him from the paddy wagon, getting himself arrested too. Irate hippies marched in protest to the precinct station and raised bail money to get him out. In August 1967 Chocolate George flipped over his Harley-Davidson and cracked open his skull. After his funeral, Angels and hippies held a wake in Golden Gate Park. The Grateful Dead and Big Brother played music, beer flowed, and mourners pelted each other with shaved ice. It was a great party, except for the visiting biker who kicked an Angel's dog and disappeared under a pile of enraged bodies, not to be seen again.[96]

By the summer of 1967 the Haight's bizarre cast of characters was performing for a national audience. This was the summer when *Time* described the neighborhood as "the vibrant epicenter of the hippie movement," hippies estimated their full-time population nationwide at 300,000,[97] imitation Haight-Ashburys bloomed throughout urban America, acid rock dominated the music charts, prestigious museums exhibited psychedelic posters, and doing one's own thing became the national cliché. Once school ended, San Francisco expected one to two hundred thousand kids to flood the city for the Summer of Love. But the real story that summer, unreported by the media, was that few of the thousands who did come stayed very long. Haight-Ashbury was already dying.

Its demise, so similar to the demise of hippie ghettos elsewhere, resulted from official repression, black hostility, and media hype. In San Francisco where city fathers panicked at the prospect of runaway hordes descending upon them, police began routinely roughing up hippies, health officials harassed their communes, and narcotics agents infiltrated the neighborhood. Meanwhile, black hoods from the nearby Fillmore district cruised the streets, threatening rape and violence. Blacks did not like LSD, white kids pretending to be poor, or the fact that Haight-Ashbury was, in the words of a leftover beatnik, "the first segregated Bohemia I've ever seen."[98] Longtime residents began staying home after dark. Finally, the beguiling images of Haight-Ashbury marketed by the media attracted not only an invasion of gawking tourists, but a floating population of the unstable, the psychotic, and the criminal. By the end of the year, *reported* crime in Haight-Ashbury included 17 murders, 100 rapes, and nearly 3,000 burglaries.[99]

In October 1967 community leaders staged a pageant called "Death of Hippie." By then the Free Clinic had closed, the Diggers had stopped serving food, and Ron Thelin had put crepe on the windows of the Psychedelic Shop and headed for Katmandu. While a country fiddler made music, a parade carried an oversized coffin, filled with hippie litter, through "Hashbury." Halting at the panhandle, mourners set the coffin on fire and danced a Dionysian dance. The Diggers bravely proclaimed that the Death of Hippie signaled the "Rebirth of Free Men." In truth, the vision of an acid utopia based on love and flowers was already ashes.[100]

VII

Though Haight-Ashbury died, the counterculture did not. If anything, in the last years of the decade the potent mix of drugs, sex, and rock and roll seduced an even larger proportion of the young. But few of these hip rebels called themselves hippies or talked of flower power any longer. Norman O. Brown had envisioned a cultural revolution in which a Dionysian ego would become the servant of Eros. But in the Freudian metaphor, Eros had to contend with Thanatos. The danger always existed that by liberating one, hip would liberate the other also. Brown himself had warned, "Not only does Dionysus without the Dionysian ego threaten us with dissolution of consciousness; he also threatens us with that 'genuine witches' brew,' 'that horrible mixture of sensuality and cruelty' (Nietzsche again), which is the result of the Dionysian against the Apollonian."[101] After the fall from the Haight-Ashbury paradise, Thanatos, not Eros, prevailed in the counterculture. Confronted by hostile police, hysterical parents, and implacable draft boards, the freaks abandoned the rhetoric of love for the politics of rage. They became willing cannon fodder for the increasingly violent demonstrations of the new left. And they routinely threw rocks at police, rioted at rock concerts, and trashed stores. The nightmare of the Dionysian witches' brew, of Dionysus without the Dionysian ego, had become reality.

As the decade closed, it became clear that drugs, sex, and rock and roll lacked intrinsic moral content. The acid prophets had warned from the beginning that LSD did not inevitably produce the God experience. God and the Devil resided together in the nervous system, Leary had said. LSD could evoke either, depending on set and setting. The streets of Haight-Ashbury, even in the best days, had been littered with kids who deranged their senses on drugs—only to experience spiritual stupor. A fair number ended their trips in hospital emergency rooms, possessed of one or another demon. Satanic cults were not unknown in the Haight. One of them, the Process, apparently influenced Charles Manson, a hippie who lived in the neighborhood in 1967 and recruited confused young girls and a few men into his "family." Manson was an "acid fascist" who somehow found in the lyrics of the Beatles license to commit ritual murder.[102] As violence in the counterculture mounted, LSD became chiefly a means to pierce the false rationality of the hated bourgeois world. The always tenuous link between drugs and love was broken.

Neither was sex itself necessarily the expression of Eros unalloyed with death. Sex in the counterculture did not imply love between two people, but merely gratification of the self—ecstasy through orgasm. Typical encounters in Haight-Ashbury were one-night stands. Rapists prospered, and carriers of venereal disease shared it generously. Janis Joplin, the greatest white blues singer who ever lived and the authentic voice of sexual ecstasy in Haight-Ashbury, sang Dionysian hymns to sexual climax. But for Janis the orgasm was the god that failed. How was your vacation on St. Thomas? a friend asked a year before Janis died of a heroin overdose. "It was just like anywhere else," she said. "I fucked a lot of strangers."[103]

Even orgies in the Haight were charmless. The unsuspecting clergy of the Glide Street Methodist Church once volunteered their sanctuary for an arts festival sponsored by the Diggers, among others. There were art exhibits, a symposium on obscenity, and a rock concert. But, according to Emmett Grogan, there was also a drag queen in the vestibule, Hell's Angels gangbanging a woman dressed as a Carmelite nun, couples copulating on the main altar, and hookers servicing their customers "behind a statue of Christ with blood all over the front of it from a dude who had just got his head cracked during a scuffle."[104] No doubt real love existed somewhere in the Haight. But the case of the sixteen-year-old girl who was shot full of speed and raffled off in the streets was closer to the dominant reality.[105]

Rock and roll was the principal art of the counterculture because of its demonstrable power to liberate the instincts. At the Woodstock Music Festival, held one weekend in August 1969 at Bethel, New York, Eros ran wild. An incredible 400,000 people gathered on a farm to hear the greatest line-up of rock talent ever assembled in one place. Overcoming conditions that could conventionally be described only as disastrous, the crowd created a loving community based on drugs, sex, and rock music.[106] But four months later at the Altamont Raceway near San Francisco, rock revealed an equal affinity for death.

The occasion was a free concert conceived by the Rolling Stones as a fitting climax to their first American tour in three years and the documentary film that was recording it.[107] Altamont was a calamity. Because of a last-minute cancellation elsewhere, concert promoters had only one day to ready the site for a crush of 300,000 kids. Sanitary facilities were inadequate; the sound system, terrible; the setting, cheerless. Lots of bad dope, including inferior acid spiked with speed, circulated through the crowd. Harried medics had to fly in an emergency supply of Thorazine to treat the epidemic of bad trips and were kept busy administering first aid to victims of the random violence. The violence originated with the Hell's Angels. On the advice of the Grateful Dead, the Stones had hired the Angels to guard the stage for $500 worth of beer. Armed with loaded pool cues sawed off to the length of billy clubs, high on bad dope washed down with Red Mountain vin rose, Angels indiscriminately clubbed people for offenses real or imagined. Vibrations of fear and paranoia spread from them outward through the crowd. And yet, when the Jefferson Airplane did their set, they called the Angels on stage to pay them homage. Once a hippie band singing acid rock, the Airplane had moved with the times, expressing in their music the anarchic rage surging through the counterculture. The song they sang to the Angels was "We Can Be Together."[108]

> We should be together.
> All your private property is target for your enemy
> And your enemy is me.
> We are forces of chaos and anarchy.
> Everything they say we are we are.
> And we are proud of ourselves.
> Up against the wall
> Up against the wall motherfucker.

Minutes later, when the Airplane's Marty Balin tried to stop an Angel from beating a fan, he himself was knocked cold.

At nightfall, after keeping the crowd waiting in the cold for more than an hour, the Rolling Stones came on stage. Many critics regarded the Stones as the greatest rock and roll band in the world. Ever since their emergence, they had carefully cultivated an outlaw image—lewd, sneering, surly—to differentiate themselves from their fellow Britons, the Beatles. Their most recent music, including, notably, "Street Fighting Man" and "Sympathy for the Devil," reflected the growing violence of the culture of which they were superstars. Now at Altamont there was Mick Jagger, reveling in his image as rock's prince of evil, prancing on stage while the Angels flailed away with their pool cues below. It was too much even for him. Jagger stopped the music more than once to plead for order; but when the Angels ignored him, he had no choice except to sing on. Midway through "Sympathy for the Devil," only a few feet from the stage, an Angel knifed a black man named Meredith Hunter to death. The moment was captured by camera and made the highlight of the film *Gimme Shelter*, which as much as any counterculture document of the time revealed Thanatos unleashed.

VIII

For a variety of reasons, after 1970 the counterculture faded. Economic recession signaled that affluence could no longer be assumed and induced a certain caution among the young. The Viet-

nam War, which did so much to discredit authority, rapidly de-
escalated. And its own revels brought the hippie movement into
disrepute. Carried to the edge of sanity by their Dionysian revels,
many of the once hip retreated, some to rural communes in New
Mexico or Vermont, most all the way back to the straight world.

Not least among the reasons for the waning of the impulse was
the ease with which the dominant culture absorbed it. Indeed, despite the generational warfare that marked the late 1960s, hippies
were only a spectacular exaggeration of tendencies transforming
the larger society. The root of these tendencies, to borrow a phrase
from Daniel Bell, was a "cultural contradiction of capitalism."[109] By
solving the problems of want, industrial capitalism undermined the
very virtues that made this triumph possible, virtues like hard work,
self-denial, postponement of gratification, submission to social discipline, strong ego mechanisms to control the instincts. As early as
the 1920s the system of mass production depended less on saving
than consumption, not on denial but indulgence. Depression and
war retarded the implications of these changes until the 1950s.

Unprecedented affluence after World War II created a generation
of teenagers who could forgo work to stay in school. Inhabiting a
gilded limbo between childhood and adult responsibility, these kids
had money, leisure, and unprecedented opportunity to test taboos.
For them the Protestant ethic had no relevance, except in the lingering parental effort to enforce it. When Elvis emerged from Memphis, hammering out his beat and exuding sexuality, the teen break-
out from jailhouse America began. The next step in the process of
liberation was hip.

But middle-class teenagers were not alone in kicking over the
traces of Puritanism. Their parents too began reckoning with the
cultural implications of affluence. Critics had attacked the hippies as
hedonistic and narcissistic. By the 1970s social discipline was eroding so rapidly that fashion condemned the whole of middle-class
culture as the "culture of narcissism."[110] Parental discipline declined, sexual promiscuity rose along with the divorce rate, worker
productivity fell, ghetto obscenity insinuated itself into standard
speech, marijuana became almost commonplace, sexual perversions
were no longer deemed so, and traditional institutions like the
Army, the churches, and the government lost authority. At the same
time, the impulse toward ecstasy found increasing expression in
Oriental religion, the New Consciousness Movement, and charis-

matic Christianity. Dionysus had been absorbed into the dominant culture and domesticated, and in the process routed the Protestant ethic.

Cultural change had political implications. While liberals earnestly sought to purge capitalism of traditional problems like unemployment and poverty, a vocal minority of American youth regarded unemployment as a blessing and chose poverty as a way of life. In the short run, hippie scorn was one more problem complicating the life of Lyndon Johnson, who never could understand whatever happened to earnest youth. In the long run, though it proved ephemeral, the hippie movement was profoundly significant, portending as it did the erosion of the liberal values that had sustained bourgeois society, the character type that had been its foundation, and the ethic that had undergirded efforts to accomplish its reform.

CHAPTER 11

Rise and Fall of the New Left

WHILE some young radicals in the 1960s rebelled against liberal culture, others forged a movement—called the "new left"—against liberal politics. New leftists were not dropouts questing after Dionysian ecstasies but, in the main, college students committed to reconstructing the social order. What was wrong with the old one? their baffled elders inquired, and how could a generation so pampered be so ungrateful?—questions that became ever more insistent as the new left moved through the decade from mere disaffection with liberalism to guerrilla warfare against "Amerika."[1]

The phenomenon of the new left could be illumined from a variety of perspectives. The campus perspective focused on the explosive growth in enrollments in institutions of higher learning (from 2 million in 1946 to nearly 8 million in 1970).[2] Here was a vast and volatile population that was largely segregated from the rest of society, freed of adult responsibility, encouraged to think critically, and often hostile to impersonal university bureaucracy—a mix of circumstances volcanic in possibility. The sociological perspective stressed the unprecedented affluence of the era and the upper-middle-class backgrounds of typical protesters. With parents disproportionately employed in well-paying professions, many students could afford the luxury of being political idealists, even utopians. The psychological perspective emphasized the early family life characteristic of new leftists—the permissive discipline, the democratic personal relations, the child-centered ethos. Having

known equality at home, the students demanded instant gratification of their desire for its realization in society.[3] And finally the
religious perspective pointed up the overrepresentation of Jews in
new left ranks. Heirs of a socialist tradition imported from the
ghettos of Eastern Europe, conditioned to distrust authority by the
historical memory of centuries of persecution, brought up by parents respectful of serious ideas, Jewish students played a conspicuous role in the campus left of the 1960s, just as their fathers had
played a conspicuous role in the radical movements of the 1930s.[4]
Taken together, these various perspectives went far to answer the
question—why the new left? A minority of an idealistic and privileged generation confronted the contradiction between American
principles and American realities and would not abide it.

Accurate as far as it went, this view of the matter neglected a
crucial feature of the new left—namely, the specific ideas in the
heads of its adherents, their ever-changing conception of the world.
Shaped by encounter with concrete historical circumstances, those
ideas provided the best perspective from which to view the new
left's development. Like any radical movement, this one, too, required a coherent body of ideas—call them an ideology—that
located the source of current evils and proposed a way out. But
formulation of an ideology for a new American left proved a task
fraught with perplexities. What was the nature of the discrepancy
between American principles and American realities? Who were the
exploited peoples—the poor, the black, and maybe Third World
peasants? Or did they also include middle-class students somehow
thwarted by existing social arrangements from achieving happiness?
Was the reconstruction of America to be undertaken for others or
for the students themselves? The new left would answer these crucial questions in different ways at different times, but it would never
answer them successfully. Without an adequate ideological framework to support its actions, the movement would become increasingly irresponsible, lose touch with social realities, and fade away
with the decade.

I

The new left was wholly innocent of ideology when it spontaneously erupted in 1960, bringing to an end years of political torpor
on campus. As would be true throughout the decade, blacks set the

example. In February four students from North Carolina Agricultural and Technical College touched off a mass sit-in movement in the upper South by refusing to leave a segregated lunch counter at a Woolworth's in Greensboro. In the following months Bay Area students braved fire hoses to protest the appearance of the House Committee on Un-American Activities in San Francisco. Harvard students sponsored a peace walk that attracted a thousand people. The newly formed Student Peace Union sparked demonstrations against ROTC, nuclear testing, and the arms race at Michigan, Chicago, Dartmouth, and Oberlin. And students in a number of northern communities engaged in sympathy picketing to support black students on the front lines of the southern freedom struggle. If anything united the protesters, it was their insistence on "speaking truth to power," on calling America to redeem her democratic values.[5] On May 1 a few hundred opponents of capital punishment, including Berkeley student Abbie Hoffman, stood vigil outside a prison in San Rafael, California, where author and convicted rapist Caryl Chessman was about to lose his twelve-year battle against the executioner. Hoffman recalled that one demonstrator, on the sad ride back to Berkeley after both the governor and the warden had expressed regrets, mused aloud, "How does that work? In a democracy, I mean, no one wants to see him die and the state kills him?"[6]

Sensing they were something new in American politics, the intellectuals among the protesters began immediately to define their distinguishing characteristics. New leftists, they emphasized, were not liberals. Liberals, for example, saw politics as a means to resolve conflicts; early new leftists, as a way to achieve a moral society. Liberals had unlimited faith in the electoral process; new leftists were moving beyond elections to direct action, both as a tactic to achieve justice and as a way to testify to principle. Liberals still believed in America's anti-Communist world mission; most new leftists were trying to detach themselves from the Cold War, and a few were moving with the leadership of the Student Peace Union into a third camp that blamed both great powers for current tensions. And, beyond issues, the early protesters shared a vague feeling, entirely lacking in contemporary liberalism, that somehow the form of existing institutions discouraged authentic personal relations.

If they were not liberals, neither were they the reincarnation of the Marxist old left. The old left consisted of various sects exhausted by pointless intramural feuding and subsisting on an archaic faith in the revolutionary potential of the working class. C. Wright Mills, the intellectual who most influenced the early new left, dismissed the notion of the revolutionary worker as "a legacy from Victorian Marxism . . . now quite unrealistic."[7] In his 1961 "Letter to the New (Young) Left," Tom Hayden wrote, "Marx, especially Marx the humanist, has much to tell us but his conceptual tools are outmoded and his final vision implausible."[8] Impatient with Marxism as a social theory and contemptuous of the parties that treated its texts as sacred, the new left intended to let its ideology emerge from action and chose men of action, not mere thinkers, as its early heroes—Robert Moses walking alone into Mississippi, Fidel Castro in the Sierra Maestra mountains with his tiny rebel band, and Mills himself, the lonely rebel fighting complacency in academe.

The group that undertook the task of comprehending the new student movement and providing it an ideology was Students for a Democratic Society (SDS). SDS was the student arm of the League for Industrial Democracy, which traced its origins back to 1905, when Jack London, Upton Sinclair, and Clarence Darrow had founded a socialist discussion group. By the 1950s the League was a feeble collection of liberals and social democrats subsisting on the charity of a few unions, and its student affiliate, then called the Student League for Industrial Democracy, was a handful of dissenters huddling together for intellectual warmth in the dark days of McCarthyism.[9] But in 1960 the Student League changed its name and acquired vigorous leadership in the person of Robert "Al" Haber, then twenty-four years old and a graduate student at the University of Michigan. A self-described radical, Haber criticized the 1960 student demonstrations for "isolation, narrowness, and shallowness." There was, he said, "no recognition that the various objects of protest are not *sui generis* but are symptomatic of institutional forces with which the movement must ultimately deal." Haber intended to make SDS a radical think-tank that would uncover the interconnection of the issues and formulate "radical alternatives to the inadequate society of today."[10]

In the spring of 1960 Haber looked up a twenty-year-old junior at Michigan named Tom Hayden, then a rising reporter on the student paper. Reared by his Catholic family in a Detroit suburb, Hayden had been a teenage rebel with beat tendencies but no politics, until Haber persuaded him to participate in a sit-in. That summer Hayden hung around with some radicals at Berkeley and then went to Los Angeles to picket the Democratic convention with Martin Luther King. By the fall of 1960, he was hooked on radicalism, dividing his time between the *Michigan Daily*, which he edited, and a new campus political party called VOICE, which he founded. After graduation, Haber hired Hayden to help him transform SDS from an obscure organization of five hundred members into the acknowledged voice of the emerging student movement.[11]

In the fall of 1961 Hayden went south to become SDS's liaison with SNCC. There he got a quick taste of life in the civil rights movement. The Klan beat him up in the streets of McComb, Mississippi, and in Albany, Georgia, the police charged him with Freedom Riding and threw him in jail. In a letter smuggled out of his cell, he wrote that he was glad for the semidarkness because there was much he would rather not see. "For instance, the stained seatless toilet and the rusted tin cup by the water spigot. . . . For instance, the wet patches of water, excretion and spittle that cover the floor where I sleep."[12] Hayden's tribulations in the South and the dispatches he sent from the front lines helped advertise SDS and enhance its reputation on northern campuses.

But his greatest contribution to SDS was a paper he wrote for the organization's 1962 annual convention at a labor resort in Port Huron, Michigan. Revised and released to the world by the fifty-nine persons in attendance, the *Port Huron Statement* seriously attempted to provide the infant new left with an ideology that would analyze the causes of current evils, offer a vision of a better future, and locate the agent of change to effect the social transformation.

The *Port Huron Statement*, which gave form to what hitherto had been mere mood, little resembled radical manifestos of the past. There was in it no analysis of class exploitation or material deprivation. The sickness of America, Hayden maintained, stemmed from the contradiction between democratic principles and actual practice —a sickness that brought spiritual, not economic, misery to the mass of Americans, including students. Elites had perverted democracy by assuming control of major institutions and rendering average citizens isolated, apathetic, and bereft of community. Giant corporations controlled the economy, excluding people from "basic decisions affecting the nature and organization of work."[13] Labor unions were so mired in organizational routine that they were failing the unorganized and the unemployed. The existing system of government thwarted the popular will and permitted business interests to manipulate the state. And universities were run by cumbersome bureaucracies that contributed "to the sense of outer complexity and inner powerlessness that transforms the honest searching of many students to a ratification of convention."[14]

If powerlessness was the evil to be purged, then Hayden's vision of a better future was a society in which the people would take control over their own lives, a society governed by something he called "participatory democracy."[15] This was a concept he only vaguely explained but that was obviously similar to the anarchist dream of inherently good men and women liberated from hierarchic institutions and living in decentralized communities where the individual counted. If students, for example, could manage their own education in true academic communities built by themselves, their alienation would be overcome and their spiritual health restored. Brilliantly expressive of SDS's gut rejection of the form of contemporary institutions, participatory democracy would become the slogan, the rallying cry, and the myth that fused the inchoate protests into a purposive movement.

How would the transformation from corporate to decentralized society be accomplished? Who would be the agent of change? The *Port Huron Statement* nominated students themselves for a crucial role. In complex industrial societies, after all, universities occupied "a permanent position of social influence."[16] If students and faculty would "wrest control of the educational process from the administrative bureaucracy,"[17] they could build bridges to other centers of dissidence—in the civil rights movement, in the peace movement, and among disenchanted liberals in the Democratic party. The result would be a radical movement devoted to nothing less than the reconstruction of American democracy.

One of the most successful radical documents in American history, the *Port Huron Statement* went through four editions and sixty thousand copies in four years. Despite long stretches of arid rhetoric and a regrettable lack of clarity at key points in the analysis, it effectively articulated the felt discontents of the early new left, even as it mirrored its ambiguities. To some, especially later, the statement seemed entirely too liberal, having nothing more to offer in the way of concrete programs than party realignment and enactment of measures like higher minimum wages and better housing programs. Among those who, at the time, regarded the statement as too radical was the League for Industrial Democracy, which was by then highly skeptical of its student affiliate. Shortly after the Port Huron convention, the League temporarily kicked Haber and Hayden off its payroll and locked them out of their New York offices. Though the break was apparently repaired, relations remained strained until mutually agreeable terms of divorce were arranged in 1965.[18]

Whether or not SDS was a success in the year after Port Huron (1962–1963)—Hayden's year as its president—depended on one's choice of criteria. In a sense SDS had become its own justification for being. The inner circle considered the organization to be "a beloved community," a tight-knit group whose members had achieved "intimacy and directness,"[19] and lived according to the principles of participatory democracy. But SDS was also an organization devoted to social change, and as such it had little to show for its efforts that year except a paper endorsed at the 1963 annual convention, entitled *America and the New Era*. This paper clarified current new left thinking about liberals. There were, it turned out, good liberals and bad liberals. The bad liberals were Kennedy liberals, corporate liberals, who managed the problem of the new era so that the "old order of private corporate enterprise shall be preserved and rationalized." The good liberals were the "democratically oriented liberals" who were "trapped by the limitations of the Democratic Party, but afraid of irrelevancy outside." *America and the New Era* predicted that once "the new insurgents" that had gathered around civil rights, peace, and campus issues launched a truly democratic movement, the good liberals would climb aboard.[20] Recalled Hayden, "We accepted the theory for a while that there was a sort of sleeping liberal wing of the Democratic Party that could be energized by moral students taking moral actions."[21]

The episode that dispelled SDS's lingering illusions about "good" liberals was its Economic Research and Action Project (ERAP, pronounced Ē-RAP), funded in 1963 with a $5,000 grant from the United Auto Workers. The question confronting SDS was whether to use the money primarily for education or for action. Bored by his graduate studies at Michigan and losing faith in universities as a base for social change, Hayden led a faction itching to imitate SNCC by dropping out to live amid the grassroots poor. Still committed to organizing students on campuses, Al Haber argued for continuing SDS's emphasis on education. At the SDS National

Council meeting in December 1963 the delegates backed Hayden by voting to make ERAP an instrument for mobilizing the slum poor and replaced Haber as head of ERAP with another Michigan grad student, Rennie Davis.[22]

By endorsing Hayden's version of ERAP, SDS in effect repudiated his *Port Huron Statement.* That statement regarded students as spiritually oppressed, large bureaucracies as the source of the American evil, and universities as crucial agents for social change. ERAP, on the other hand, regarded students as a privileged group, material deprivation of the underclass as the most pressing American problem, and an "interracial movement of the poor" as the main hope for change. The role of middle-class students was no longer to stay on the campus and fight for their own liberation, but to leave campus and organize for the liberation of others. "If poor people are in The Movement because they have nothing to gain in the status system,"[23] Hayden wrote during this period, "students are in it because, in a sense, they have gained too much." Years later Todd Gitlin succinctly stated ERAP's problem. ERAP, he said, "was built on guilt."[24]

Nevertheless, in the summer of 1964, while nearly a thousand northern students went to Mississippi for SNCC, 125 SDS kids organized ERAP projects in the slums of Baltimore, Boston, Chester, Cleveland, Hazard (Kentucky), Louisville, Newark, Philadelphia, and Trenton. It became immediately apparent that Hayden's rationale for the projects was all wrong. Automation, he had argued, was about to swell the ranks of the unemployed and provide the basis for a political alliance of poor blacks and poor whites.[25] In fact, the faddish fear of automation had about run its course, unemployment was rapidly decreasing, and blacks were preparing to expel whites even from the civil rights movement. Those few poor whom ERAP managed to organize were less interested in attacking corporate capitalism than in getting their garbage collected.

Since few of the organizers were willing to subsist for long on peanut butter and jelly, most of the projects folded by the end of the first summer. Hayden stayed on and off in Newark for three years, trying to organize blacks in a neighborhood called Clinton Hill. Richie Rothstein spent three years working with white working-class kids on Chicago's North Side. And Paul Potter stuck it out for two-and-a-half years in Cleveland. As a national project, ERAP actually ended in the spring of 1965 when Rennie Davis closed his office in Chicago and went to live with the local project.[26] In time, even ERAP's fiercest partisans came to regard it as a mistake. Writing of Hayden's paper to justify ERAP, Paul Potter later admitted, "It was not what we believed. It did not represent our political vocabulary or our understanding of words. . . . What we really needed a document for was not to deal with the poor but to deal with us."[27]

In retrospect, ERAP's main benefit was to clarify SDS's position toward liberalism. In Newark Hayden helped found the Newark Community Union Project, whose original sponsors included the local ADA, CORE, a wing of the local NAACP, and a few labor unions. When the project sought to become the voice of the poor rather than a tool of the establishment, the liberals, said Hayden, viewed it "as a problem if not a danger," and bailed out.[28] The same thing happened in Chicago, where the attitude of ERAP organizers toward liberals—in the words of Richie Rothstein—"changed from one of hope to one of the deepest hostility and contempt."[29] Meantime, first-hand experience with the liberal welfare state disabused SDS of the notion, evident in the *Port Huron Statement*, that its extension would benefit the poor. Liberal reform, Hayden now said, was just a way of strengthening "elite rule under the slogan of curbing private enterprise."[30]

ERAP's biggest mistake had been prematurely to write off students on their campuses as a radical force. At the end of the summer of 1964 students from SDS's slum projects and SNCC's Mississippi Freedom Summer returned to school. There were only a thousand of them, but they had broken the bonds tying them to the middle classes, were forging new identities in the crucible of the social struggle, and were utterly certain of their own righteousness. Among those returning from Mississippi to Berkeley was Mario Savio.

At Berkeley that fall the new left rediscovered the relevance of the *Port Huron Statement.* At first the issue was simply free speech on the campus. Students returning from vacation were informed by university administrators that henceforth political activity would be prohibited along a twenty-six-foot strip of brick pavement at Bancroft Way and Telegraph Avenue, the one place on campus where political advocacy and fund raising had previously been permitted. Certain that the ban was directed against them, campus civil rights groups decided to fight oppression at liberal Berkeley as they had fought it in racist Mississippi. On October 1, 1964, when a CORE worker was arrested for setting up a table and soliciting funds on the proscribed strip, hundreds of students spontaneously sat down around the police car and held the arresting officers captive.[31]

Within hours, two thousand students joined the sit-in and, using the car top as a platform, conducted an open forum for anyone who wanted to talk. There was shared danger when the fraternities threatened violence, shared singing to bolster courage, shared discomfort during the long night—and the shared conviction that a new community, better than any they had known before, had sprung into being.[32] Only a last-minute agreement between student spokesmen and university president Clark Kerr ended the thirty-two-hour vigil and prevented the massed phalanx of police from turning the rite of passage into a bloodbath. Concerned student groups, spanning the political spectrum, then formed the Free Speech Movement (FSM) to see the fight through to a successful conclusion. The leading spokesmen were all veteran new leftists.

The leadership exploited the furor over free speech to educate the mass of students about the ways they were oppressed by modern institutions, including Berkeley itself. Their analysis came straight out of the *Port Huron Statement*. "In our free-speech fight," said the fiery Mario Savio, "we have come up against what may emerge as the greatest problem of our nation—depersonalized, unresponsive bureaucracy."[33] Universities are knowledge factories—proclaimed one FSM manifesto—tended by employees called professors and producing "technicians to service society's many bureaucracies."[34] Serious students become engulfed by "a general feeling that the situation is hopeless" and surrender to feelings of "alienation and hostility."[35] FSM spokesmen did not use the phrase "participatory democracy" but that is what they really wanted. Said Jack Weinberg, the nonstudent whose arrest had triggered the crisis, "The students' basic demand is a demand to be heard, to be considered, to be taken into account when decisions concerning their education and their life in the university community are being made."[36] On December 2, 1964, in front of Sproul Hall, Berkeley's main administration building, Savio made a famous speech:

There is a time when the operation of the machine becomes so odious, makes you so sick at heart, that you can't take part; you can't even passively take part, and you've got to put your bodies upon the gears and upon the wheels, upon the levers, upon all the apparatus and you've got to make it stop. And you've got to indicate to the people who run it, to the people who own it, that unless you're free, the machine will be prevented from working at all.[37]

After Savio finished, more than 1,000 students marched into Sproul Hall and staged a sit-in. Acting less to achieve free speech than to protest the oppressiveness of the liberal university, they were the first students of the decade to commit civil disobedience against their own campus. Early the next morning Edmund "Pat" Brown, the liberal Democrat who was governor of the state, sent in the police, who cleared the building and arrested 773 nonviolent demonstrators. Mass arrests of students were a novelty in 1964, and a shocking novelty at that. Moderate students rallied to FSM's call for a strike, the faculty roused itself to endorse the demands of the students, and in due course the administration virtually capitulated.[38] As Jerry Rubin, who was there, later wrote,

> The war against Amerika
>   in the schools
>   and the streets
>   by white middle-class kids
>   thus commenced.[39]

Next step in the rapid radicalization of the new left was Vietnam, which again deflected it away from the campus. At its December 1964 National Council meeting SDS decided to protest the war by organizing a March on Washington the following spring. No one expected the march to attract more than a few thousand participants, until Lyndon Johnson assured its success in February 1965 by launching the air war against North Vietnam. Twenty thousand people turned out at the Washington Monument on April 17 to be entertained by Joan Baez and Judy Collins and edified by notables like Alaska Senator Ernest Gruening, SNCC's Robert Moses, and Yale historian Staughton Lynd.[40] The highlight of the march was the speech by SDS president Paul Potter, who, in the best tradition of radicalism, tried to make the connections. "What kind of system is it," he asked, "that justifies the United States or any country seizing the destinies of the Vietnamese people and using them callously for their own purposes? What kind of system is it that disfranchises people in the South, leaves millions of people throughout the country impoverished and excluded . . . that creates faceless and terrible bureaucracies and makes those the place where people spend their lives and do their work, that consistently puts national values before human values? . . . We must name that system, we must name it, describe it, analyze it, understand it, and change it."[41] Potter's speech so excited the protesters that, according to Staughton Lynd, as they headed toward the Capitol to present a petition to Congress, parade marshals only barely restrained them from overflowing the building and "taking possession of the government."[42]

The man who named the system was Carl Oglesby, a thirty-year-old recent recruit to the new left who had given up serious literary aspirations and a secure job to work full-time for the movement. Elected SDS president in June 1965, Oglesby named the system at the next antiwar gathering in Washington, sponsored by SANE on November 27. The name, Oglesby said, was "corporate liberalism," a concept that was not new to the movement, though Oglesby's attempt to connect it to foreign policy was. The men who engineered the war in Vietnam "are not moral monsters," he said. "They are all honorable men. They are all liberals." The American corporate machine they oversee is the "colossus of history," taking the riches of other nations and consuming half the world's goods. "On the *face* of it, it is a crime that so few should have so much at the expense of so many." Being decent men, corporate liberals rationalize their rapacity and their policy of counterrevolution with the ideology of anti-Communism, defining all revolutions as Communist and Communism itself as evil. In the name of this ideology, they ally with right-wing dictators, undermine popular regimes in Iran, Guatemala, Cuba, British Guiana, Brazil, and the Dominican Republic, and they fight now in Vietnam. If this sounds anti-American to some, Oglesby declared, "I say: Don't blame *me* for *that!* Blame those who mouthed my liberal values and broke my American heart."[43] The crowd, which gave the speech a tremendous ovation, did not know that Oglesby had been less than candid. He realized that the real name of the system he was describing was "imperialism," but because the new left was not ready for this old left concept, Oglesby held back.[44] Still the speech crackled with militance, marking as it did a declaration of war against liberals, now irrevocably declared the enemy.

In the school year 1965–1966 the new left began to assume the dimensions of a mass movement. It was, of course, primarily the war that turned college students against their government and made recruits by the thousands for the radical cause. One symptom of the deepening radical impulse was the spurt in SDS membership—from 2,500 in December 1964 to 10,000 the following October.[45] Henceforth, SDS would cease to be a group of comrades in a close community and would become a collection of autonomous campus chapters with only the loosest connections among themselves and with the national office in Chicago. This arrangement conformed to the anarchist tendency of the movement but was unlikely to contribute to its political effectiveness.

The new militance found expression in the new left's evolving protest tactics. On October 15, 1965, for example, during the so-called International Days of Protest, 10,000 students marched from Berkeley to close down the Army's induction center in nearby Oakland. At the Oakland city limits march leaders disappointed the crowd by voting 5 to 4 to turn back rather than challenge cops armed with clubs, dogs, and tear gas. Jerry Rubin, a leader who had wanted to plunge on, drew the moral for the militants. "A movement that isn't willing to risk injuries, even deaths, isn't worth shit," he said.[46] In the spring of 1966 radical students at a number of schools staged sit-ins against universities for acts of complicity in the war—especially furnishing draft boards with class rankings for the purpose of determining deferments.[47]

Another sign of the movement's rapid radicalization in 1965–1966 was its interest in alternative or counter institutions. SNCC as usual had pointed the way by creating, in the previous year, an alternative political party called the Mississippi Freedom Democratic party. Equating Mississippi with America, the new left now decided to build a new society, with its own institutions, inside the shell of the old. "Free" universities sprang up at mid-decade to offer students radical instruction, experimental pedagogy, and participatory democracy. Soon the radicals would have their own newspapers, radio stations, theaters, community organizations, and co-ops. In a particularly utopian flight of fancy, Tom Hayden even envisioned a Continental Congress called by excluded peoples—"a kind of second government, receiving taxes from its supporters, establishing contact with other nations . . . dramatizing the plight of all groups that suffer from the American system."[48] Whatever else they meant, counter institutions meant at least this: young people in alarming numbers were withdrawing allegiance from the United States of America.

Vietnam, which created the favorable climate for radical growth, posed problems as well. The hordes of converts created by the war knew that the government was evil and liberals the enemy, but quite often they knew little else. Denied the years of gradual disillusionment that had educated the new left's founding generation, most of the newcomers were radicals by emotion rather than by reason and possessed an alarming potential for mindless activism. Though there could be no doubt of their alienation, the real source of that alienation remained unclear. Were they alienated primarily because America bombed Vietnam, or because America was a gilded cage in which middle-class students were among the prisoners? Were the radical thousands fighting against the oppression of others or against the oppression of themselves?

II

In the year 1966–1967 leading movement intellectuals made a serious effort to root the radicalism of the student mass in its own grievances. For this task they took ideas from wherever they could find them, but most of all from Herbert Marcuse. An elderly German émigré steeped in Hegel and Marx, Marcuse had established himself as an influential figure on the American left in 1955 with publication of his brilliant if eccentric *Eros and Civilization.* Wrote SDS leader Greg Calvert, "It is no accident that the books of Herbert Marcuse—especially *Eros and Civilization*—were the most exciting works available" to the movement in the early sixties,[49] no accident because Marcuse purported to explain why many of the beneficiaries of post-scarcity civilization felt so unfree.

Marcuse was to the new left what Norman O. Brown was to the counterculture, a philosopher of liberation who used the ideas of Sigmund Freud to show the way. For Marcuse and Brown alike, freedom meant not constitutional guarantees of civil liberties or even industrial democracy, but rather a psychological condition defined by Marcuse as "free gratification of man's instinctual needs."[50] For both Brown and Marcuse, in short, liberation meant the liberation of Eros. The difference was that, while Brown believed that the individual repressed his own instincts and could therefore free himself, Marcuse believed that repression was at least partly imposed by society and could be diminished only by political revolution.

Marcuse agreed with Freud that personal and social survival depended on work and that work depended on the partial repression of Eros—the desire for bodily pleasure—from consciousness. But, quite unlike Freud, Marcuse asserted that repression existed not only because some of it was biologically necessary for survival but also because dominant groups derived selfish benefits from its maximization. Men suffered, in sum, not only from biologically necessary repression but from sociologically imposed "surplus repression." In contemporary civilization surplus repression resulted from the reign of the "performance principle," which required that society "be stratified according to the competitive economic performance of its members."[51] This appeared to be an oblique definition of capitalism, though Marcuse avoided that term. Under the performance principle, the entire body, except for the genitals, was ruthlessly desexualized to make it readily exploitable as an instrument of labor. But, ironically, the performance principle had worked so well in solving the problem of economic scarcity that it had created the conditions for its own abolition. New modes of production now rendered most human labor unnecessary. If the existing system of domination was dethroned, surplus repression would be ended, Eros liberated, the body resexualized, the death instinct weakened, civilization rendered nonrepressive, and man made happy at last. But, as Marcuse made clear with publication of *One Dimensional Man* in 1964, he considered the system of domination to be so total, the manipulated satisfaction of the masses in superfluous abundance so complete, that rebellion was at best a historical long shot. All that was left for radicals like himself was to confront the civilization of which America was the exemplar and issue the "Great Refusal."[52]

The Marcusean image of bureaucratic man performing alienated labor to produce irrational affluence served well the new left prophets of middle-class liberation. The most notable of these was Greg Calvert. A twenty-eight-year-old former instructor of European history at Iowa State University, Calvert was elected SDS national secretary at the organization's August 1966 convention at Clear Lake, Iowa. Like most of the delegates who chose him, he was one of SDS's "new breed," meaning that he had no connection with the SDS of Haber and Hayden. New man though he was, Calvert clearly grasped the ideological challenge that had confronted the movement from the beginning. In a speech at a Princeton conference of leftist intellectuals in February 1967, he asserted his basic premise: "There is only one impulse, one dynamic, which can create and sustain an authentic revolutionary movement," he said. "The revolutionary struggle is always and always must be a struggle for freedom. No individual, no group, no class is genuinely engaged in a revolutionary movement unless their struggle is a struggle for their own liberation." Here then was the difference between liberals and radicals: liberals acted out of guilt to help the oppressed; radical consciousness was "the perception of oneself as unfree, as oppressed—and finally it is the discovery of oneself as *one of the oppressed.*"

The movement's task, Calvert continued, was to raise the consciousness of the new student radicals so that they understood how class oppression produced their "gut level alienation." If the effort misfired, if new leftists failed to see that they were fighting for their own freedom, then, he predicted, they would "orient themselves toward Third World revolutions and develop those methods of activity which will maximize the impact of peasant-based rebellions on the structure of the American imperialist monster."[53] In other words, fight for yourself, or fight for the Vietcong. Fighting for the Vietcong, Calvert implied, would provide a false foundation on which to build a native American radicalism.

Borrowing ideas from European Marxists as well as from Marcuse, Calvert tried his own hand at sketching an ideology for middle-class liberation. His attempt was in the tradition of the *Port Huron Statement,* though far more radical and sympathetic to Marxism. The oppressed group that could make the revolution, he said, was "the new working class." Old leftists had erred in equating the working class with blue-collar workers. In fact, said Calvert, white-collar employees were no less workers in the classical Marxist sense since they "sell their labor power in order to live and have no control whatsoever over the means of production."[54] Materially prosperous, members of the new working class—teachers, engineers, salaried professionals, and other highly trained technical workers—were manipulated, repressed, bureaucratic men, spiritually choking on waste production for false needs. Here was the subsection of the working class that might lead the whole in a revolutionary struggle. Here were workers strategically located to sabotage the system and intellectually equipped to grasp their own unfreedom. The historic task confronting the new left was to help white-collar slaves pierce the mystification of abundance and perceive their slavery.

New working-class theory provided a convenient rationale for the program and tactics of the movement in 1966–1967. At the Iowa convention in August 1966, newly elected vice president Carl Davidson, a twenty-three-year-old philosophy instructor at the University of Nebraska, led SDS back to campus under the slogan "student power."[55] Students were victims, Davidson argued.[56] Acting at the behest of their corporate masters, universities trained them for membership in the working class, reproducing on campus "all the conditions and relations of production in the factories of advanced corporate capitalism—isolation, manipulation, and alienation."[57] Students fighting for control of the universities would soon see that the issues of dorm hours and Vietnam were connected and that corporate liberalism was the system responsible for both. More important, they would be preparing for the postgraduate struggle in the workplace against their corporate oppressors. That year, in the name of student power, SDS chapters coast to coast used a variety of tactics, including civil disobedience, to attack dorm regulations, ROTC, university cooperation with draft boards, and on-campus recruitment by the military and by the Dow Chemical Company, maker of napalm.

New working-class theory also meshed neatly with SDS's new antiwar program. At its December 1966 National Council meeting, SDS denounced the war as genocidal and summoned its chapters to organize draft-resistance unions. As Peter Henig ingeniously demonstrated the following month in the SDS paper *New Left Notes*, students fighting the draft were fighting not only for the Vietnamese but for themselves. This was true even though most students enjoyed the privilege of draft deferment. Quoting from Selective Service documents, Henig showed how the draft was designed to channel young men into school and from there into occupations deemed worthy by the government. Either they conformed to society's wishes—by becoming trainees for the new working class—and were deferred, or they were drafted into the army. "The psychology of granting wide choice under pressure . . . is the American or indirect way of achieving what is done by direction in foreign countries where choice is not permitted," the Selective Service wrote in one of the documents from which Henig gleefully quoted.[58] The draft, then, was not merely an antiwar issue but SDS's perfect illustration of the totalitarian reality behind America's liberal façade.

New working-class theory also validated the new left's decision in 1966–1967 to opt for the Marcusean Great Refusal. For if the system was as dehumanizing as Marcuse and Calvert described, no other response could be appropriate. In a famous article he wrote in the January 1967 issue of *New Left Notes*, Calvert urged radicals to move "From Protest to Resistance," which instantly became the movement's slogan for that year.[59] "No matter what America demands, it does not possess us," Calvert told an interviewer a few months later. "Whenever that demand comes—we resist." The purpose of resistance was not to seize power, for Calvert knew no revolutionary situation existed. The purpose of resistance was to transform lives. "A resistance movement, based on the slogan, 'Not with my life you don't,' is based on helping people break out of their own prison," he said. "People are capable of doing extraordinary things when they are in resistance. . . . In the process of resistance, in struggling against the powerlessness that capitalism imposes on the individual, there is a rediscovery of the self in the midst of a dehumanizing society." Resistance, though not itself revolution, was the precondition of a "revolutionary struggle."[60]

On April 15, 1967, the spirit of resistance manifested itself at the Sheep Meadow in New York's Central Park, where half a million people gathered for an antiwar march called by the Spring Mobilization Committee. Standing on a grassy knoll, sixty people organized by SDS leaders from Cornell defied federal law and burned their draft cards. Some hundred others spontaneously emerged from the crowd to burn their cards too.[61] This was the origin of the Resistance, a coalition of local draft-resistance groups that risked prison rather than submit to a draft which oppressed peasants, draftees, and deferred students alike. Still, it remained uncertain that spring whether the resisting young at the Sheep Meadow and elsewhere in America were acting primarily for themselves or for Third World victims of American imperialism.

III

In the following school year, 1967–1968, the concept of the new working class was consigned to the new left's junk heap of discarded theories. Traditional Marxists skillfully attacked it as a verbal phenomenon lacking in analytic rigor, and most of the movement's rank and file proved uninterested in ideologies of self-liberation. If not for themselves, then for whom would the young radicals fight? If not for themselves, Greg Calvert had predicted, the young radicals would end up fighting out of guilt for the liberation of Third World peoples. This is precisely what happened.

The prophet of the new direction was Carl Oglesby, whose *Containment and Change* (written with Richard Shaull and published in the spring of 1967) provided the movement with an ideological perspective it really wanted. A year and a half before, Oglesby had not dared to use the word "imperialism" to describe American policy. Now he marshaled evidence to prove that America was a greedy imperialist power, driven by the requirements of capitalism to feed on the resources and exploit the markets of Third World nations. For the new left, the image of America the bloodsucker organized the data of politics in a compelling and persuasive new way. But it also deflected the movement onto a disastrous course by fostering a romantic sense of identification with Third World guerrillas, by bringing old left Marxism back into fashion, and by undermining the movement's commitment to democratic values.

By 1967 it was clear that the real prophet of the new left was not Herbert Marcuse but Che Guevara. An Argentine revolutionary who had fought beside Castro in the Sierra Maestra mountains, Che electrified radicals everywhere in March 1967 when, after two years of invisibility, he resurfaced in Bolivia to lead an armed guerrilla movement.[62] SDS posters of Che soon papered the walls of unnumbered dormitories. New leftists increasingly justified their new interest in Marxism by quoting Che's alleged remark, "It is not my fault that reality is Marxist."[63] And when Bolivian soldiers captured and killed Che in October 1967, the entire new left mourned him, dreamed of imitating his heroic example, and made his book on guerrilla warfare a movement bible. The Che of the new left was Jerry Rubin's Che, a Che whom Rubin recalled telling a delegation of young Americans illegally visiting Cuba in 1964, "You North Amerikans are very lucky. You live in the middle of the beast. You are fighting the most important fight of all, in the center of the battle. If I had my wish, I would go back with you to North Amerika to fight there. I envy you."[64] It is doubtful that Che ever said this and regrettable that so few of his American disciples took the trouble actually to read his primer on revolution. "Where a government has come into power through some form of popular vote, fraudulent or not," Che wrote, "and maintains at least an appearance of constitutional legality, the guerrilla outbreak cannot be promoted, since possibilities of peaceful struggle have not yet been exhausted."[65]

The hypothesis of American imperialism attained its immense popularity in part because it seemed so well to describe Vietnam: In defense of its reactionary client regime in Saigon, the U.S. had mobilized half a million men and unprecedented fire power to crush an indigenous movement of revolutionary peasants. Once the new left determined that America was the villain, it shifted from an antiwar movement to a movement favoring victory for the Vietcong. Communist terror was excused or justified, and Communist administration of "liberated areas" was hailed as an example of revolutionary justice. In September 1967 a delegation of forty-one American new leftists, including Hayden and Rennie Davis, met in Czechoslovakia with Vietnamese Communists and declared their allegiance by turning their draft cards over to a representative of the National Liberation Front.[66]

The ascendance of the imperialist perspective in the summer of 1967 owed as much to ghetto rebellions at home as to the Vietcong. While Detroit and Newark burned, black power ideologues offered a powerful metaphor of explanation. Black ghettos, they said, were internal colonies victimized by American imperialism precisely as were the colonies of Africa, Asia, and Latin America. It followed that black rioters were no less revolutionary guerrillas than the Vietcong —urban guerrillas waging war in the belly of the beast. SNCC chairman H. Rap Brown selected August 18, 1965, as the independence day of the internal colony because on that day "the blacks of Watts picked up their guns to fight for their freedom. That was our Declaration of Independence, and we signed it with Molotov cocktails and rifles."[67] In August 1967 Stokely Carmichael, past SNCC chairman, joined revolutionaries from twenty-seven Latin American countries for a conference in Havana to discuss ways of implementing Che's recent call for "two, three, many Vietnams." Carmichael declared the solidarity of American blacks with revolutionary movements everywhere,[68] and the conference passed a resolution calling on "the Negro people of the U.S. to answer the racist violence of the U.S. imperialist government by increasing direct revolutionary action and strengthening their fraternal relations with the people of Africa, Asia, and Latin America that fight against the same hated enemy: U.S. imperialism."[69] Said Huey Newton of the Black Panther party, "We can stop the machinery. We can stop the imperialists from using it against black people all over the world. We are in a strategic position in this country, and we won't be the only group rebelling against the oppressor here."[70]

As usual, whites in the movement let blacks set the style. Tom Hayden, who had witnessed the 1967 Newark riot first-hand, welcomed the emergence of the "conscious guerrilla," capable of keeping alien authority in the ghetto on the defensive, capable in riots of diverting the police from looters, capable—when appropriate— of carrying the torch to white neighborhoods and business districts. "If necessary," he said, in a line that revealed how far the movement had traveled since Port Huron, "he can successfully shoot to kill."[71] If black radicals could use violence against imperialism, then, some asked, why not white radicals?" "Do what John Brown did—," Rap Brown advised the movement, "pick up a gun and go out and shoot our enemy."[72]

The white left took the decisive step toward acting out its guerrilla fantasy during two spectacular demonstrations in the third week of October 1967. The first, called Stop the Draft Week, occurred in Oakland, California, where Bay Area radicals again attempted to close down the Army's induction center. In the planning stage the Resistance argued for nonviolent civil disobedience, even in the face of arrest. But SDS-ers and other militants flatly rejected nonviolence, hoping to move the antiwar movement "from the level of moral protest to a show of power."[73] In the end, no compromise was possible; so it was agreed that the factions would demonstrate on different days of the week.[74]

Monday, October 16, 1967, belonged to the Resistance, 124 of whose supporters were arrested at the doors of the induction center in a classic example of moral witness. Tuesday belonged to the militants. Three thousand showed up, and were charged by police, gassed, and routed. Enraged, the militants waited for the pacifists to sit in again on Wednesday and Thursday, and then on Friday returned ten thousand strong. The battle that ensued was the Bastille Day of the new left. Blockading intersections with parked cars, trash cans, parking meters, and potted trees, the crowd ringed twenty-five square blocks, declared them a liberated area, and attempted to hold them with improvised guerrilla tactics. When police charged, the protesters broke into small groups, retreated, and then reformed elsewhere to set up new barricades. At two intersections demonstrators found themselves superior in force and retook lost positions. After holding the streets for a few hours, the students retreated rather than engage the National Guard and marched in triumph back to Berkeley.[75]

That next day, October 21, 1967, across the country in Washington, D.C., there occurred one of the most remarkable events in American history.[76] After listening to the usual speeches at the Lincoln Memorial, fifty thousand American citizens made their contribution to Stop the Draft Week by marching into Virginia to close down the Pentagon. "We're now in the business of wholesale disruption and widespread resistance and dislocation of the American society," project director Jerry Rubin had declared on the march's eve.[77] Once on the Pentagon grounds, approximately one thousand demonstrators disregarded the agreements their leaders had negotiated with the government on permissible forms of civil disobedience and immediately headed for forbidden areas, some of them shoving through a line of U.S. marshals to establish an illegal beachhead on the asphalt plaza leading to the Pentagon's main entrance. A handful even briefly made it past guards through a side door. Thousands more crowded menacingly onto the steps leading to the plaza and on the grassy mall below. This was resistance, and to direct it SDS leaders, including Greg Calvert, materialized with bullhorns at strategic locations.

There followed several hours of revolutionary theater—girls putting flowers into the gun barrels of soldiers, hippies attempting to levitate the Pentagon, forays across the plaza to break an occasional window, eloquent pleas to the soldiers to "join us," ugly taunting of MPs, bloody encounters with the troops, and early in the evening small bursts of flame as demonstrators burned draft cards. Past midnight, after the press went home, the authorities struck back in force. Forming a wedge, soldiers and marshals proceeded to clear the plaza, which the protesters held in violation of their permit, and the steps, which legally were theirs. And here a curious thing happened. Though the marshals performed their work brutally, the demonstrators locked arms and passively resisted, waiting their turn to be beaten and arrested. Movement tacticians disapproved. "One is misreading Che Guevara," a new left writer said, "by concluding that a guerrilla fighter confronts a superior military force in positional combat. That just doesn't make sense."[78]

Reaction on the new left to the October demonstrations was euphoric. Underground papers exulted over the tactical brilliance of the protesters, the barriers of fear they demolished, their ability to contest the enemy on battlefields of their own choosing. Cathy Wilkerson, editor of *New Left Notes* and one of those who provided leadership at the Pentagon, wrote, "The success of the Pentagon siege lay fundamentally in our determination to finally demand a serious response from the power structure in America and our ability to withstand that response, learn from it and strengthen ourselves to proceed further."[79] Jeff Segal, a West Coast SDS leader, regarded the Oakland demonstration as a watershed in movement history. The action had not been actual guerrilla warfare, he conceded, but it "carried within itself the seeds for all the elements that we will need when, indeed, our time does come."[80] Commented another participant, "imperialism cannot be defeated by cardboard signs and flowers."[81]

With the onset of the guerrilla fantasy, the corruption of the new left commenced. In the early years movement people tried to live their values by practicing participatory democracy in their organizations, cultivating open relationships, and creating their own community. But even as real guerrillas employed inhumane means to achieve the humane ends of revolution so now new leftists began to wonder whether, given their new seriousness, they could any longer afford to indulge their values. Democracy was the first casualty. Shortly after the siege of the Pentagon, Calvert dismissed participatory democracy because it fostered manipulation by elites, "long, formless mass meetings," and sloppy strategic thinking. He favored "responsible collective leadership which can be held accountable to its constituency."[82] In retrospect, this was the first step toward creation of a party based on the Leninist principle of "democratic centralism." In an even more dangerous departure, Carl Davidson explicitly rejected the very norms of democracy itself. The social order we fight against is "totalitarian, manipulative, repressive, and anti-democratic," he said. Since its institutions "are without legitimacy in our eyes, they are without rights." To accord them civil liberties, to debate rather than immobilize them, was to play by the very bourgeois rules designed to enslave us. As a result, "it is the duty of a revolutionary not only to be intolerant of, but to actually suppress the anti-democratic activities of the dominant order."[83] This argument would become a staple of the new left as it descended into its own form of totalitarianism.

Post-Pentagon, young radicals readily conceded that their liberation fight was not for themselves—beneficiaries of American imperialism—but for imperialism's victims, especially American blacks. SNCC's James Forman found a receptive audience among white leftists in February 1968, when he explained what black radicals expected of them. "Since black people in this country are engaged in a protracted warfare against their colonial domination by the United States," he said, black people must lead the struggle. The tasks of white radicals were to fight fascist tendencies in the working class, combat the power structure, and above all commit themselves to defending blacks from government repression. "White America must begin to formulate its plans to deal with the 101st Airborne Cavalry and all other divisions when they occupy the ghettos of the United States trying to exterminate black people," Forman said. When "the Man" kills "uppity niggers" like himself, whites must retaliate. "And," concluded Forman, "I will tell you what I will expect from white revolutionaries for my assassination:

> 10 war factories destroyed.
> 15 police stations blown up.
> 30 power plants demolished.
> No flowers.
> 1 Southern governor, 2 mayors, and 500 racist
> white cops dead."[84]

At Columbia University in the spring of 1968 the implications of the anti-imperialist tendency in the new left became clearer. The crisis at Columbia began in March when the so-called "action-faction" captured control of the local SDS chapter and set out to polarize the university on radical issues, forcing the students to choose sides. The leading spokesman for action was Mark Rudd, newly elected chapter president. A twenty-year-old junior barely known on his own campus when the year began, Rudd would emerge within months as an international celebrity—mainly because the news media chose him as the symbol of the radical student movement now rapidly attaining mass dimension.

It was not a bad choice. A third-generation Jewish American whose grandparents had immigrated from Eastern Europe (the family name had been Rudnitsky), Rudd was reared in comfortable and secure surroundings in the suburb of Maplewood, New Jersey, not far from Newark. His father, a retired Army officer in the real-estate business, supported Mark's extracurricular radicalism, and his doting mother spoke proudly of my son "the rebel." On Mother's Day 1968, while Mark was busy paralyzing Columbia, Mrs. Rudd prepared a home-cooked meal and drove with the family to the campus so he could eat it. "I was a member of the depressed generation, and my greatest concern has always been making a living," his father remarked. "Mark doesn't have to worry about that so much and we're glad he has time to spend on activities like politics. He never cared about material things anyway." Mark himself traced the origins of his radicalism to his early perception of some ugly American realities. "I lived in a middle-class home and I could see the contrast between the environment I grew up in and the slums. My grandmother owned a candy store in the Central Ward of Newark, and I used to visit her all the time. The area was turning black and I was stunned by the poverty." Why did this young man—former Boy Scout, good student—come to rage against America?[85] Perhaps he screamed "motherfuckers" at the authorities because he was conducting some unconscious Freudian vendetta against his father.[86] Or perhaps, more plausibly, he entered Columbia a naïve and idealistic adolescent and discovered there, in the fashionable radicalism of the time, an explanation of the world so compelling that he gave himself to it utterly.

Rudd's real education had little to do with his formal classes. In his sophomore year he became friends with Herbert Marcuse's stepson Mike Neumann, who introduced him to SDS activists as well as to the works of the new left's favorite philosopher. Though Rudd claimed to have been influenced by Marcuse, the real tendency of his thought was better indicated by his March 1968 trip to Cuba, where he confirmed his admiration for Castro's revolution, his hero worship of the martyred Che, and his affinity for the seductive Third World Marxist perspective. Meanwhile, he was emerging as a leader of the tiny Columbia left. Lanky and stoop-shouldered, with black hair, strong jaw, and piercing blue eyes, he had the power to stir people by the passion of his radical commitment. He was not a deep thinker, merely quick; not a notably informed speaker, but one in command of the facile categories of his radicalism. Rather soon he envinced characteristics hardly unknown to revolutionaries of the past—abrasiveness, intolerance, and a capacity to be ruthless. Like others in SDS, he was mastering that fear of violence and of bad manners that was the affliction of the children of his class. Under Rudd's leadership SDS members pushed a lemon meringue pie into the face of a Selective Service officer, disrupted the university's memorial service for Martin Luther King, and in Rudd's name sent a letter to Columbia president Grayson Kirk that concluded, "There is only one thing left to say. It may sound nihilistic to you since it is the opening shot in a war of liberation. I'll use the words of Le Roi Jones, whom I'm sure you don't like a whole lot: 'Up against the wall, motherfucker, this is a stick-up.' "[87]

In the end the university gave Rudd the issue he needed to vindicate the action faction.[88] Brushing aside years of protest by black community groups, the Columbia administration had begun construction of a new gymnasium in Morningside Park, a sloping hill that separates Columbia above from Harlem below. At noon, Tuesday, April 23, 1968, supported for a change by the Students Afro-American Society, SDS called a meeting at the Sundial in the center of the campus to protest the gym and other issues. At one point, part of the assembled crowd of five hundred charged Low Library, only to be repulsed by a line of conservative students. While Rudd stood on a trash can pondering aloud what to do next, the crowd suddenly dashed toward the gym site, where some of its members ripped down a fence, tussled briefly with police, then retreated to campus. Back at the Sundial Rudd was again immobilized by uncertainty—until a black student, William Sales, made a speech that uncannily caught the developing mood of the new left.[89]

I thought up until this stage of the game, white people weren't ready, but I saw something today that suggests that this is not true. . . . Because when the deal hit the fan you were there. . . . If you're talking about revolution, if you're talking about identifying with the Vietnamese struggle, you don't need to go to Rockefeller Center, dig? There's one oppressor—in the White House, in Low Library, in Albany, New York. You strike a blow at the gym, you strike a blow for the Vietnamese people. You strike a blow at Low Library, you strike a blow for the freedom fighters in Angola, Mozambique, Portuguese Guinea, Zimbabwe, South Africa. . . . All we need is some sophistication. . . . Next time we go down there, [the police] will be waiting. An incoherent mob will not be able to deal with them. So we have to be more sophisticated. Need I say more? I don't want to get arrested for sedition.

Galvanized by this expression of the imperialist hypothesis and the guerrilla fantasy, Rudd shouted, "Let's go to Hamilton," a classroom and administration building nearby.[90] Four hundred and fifty people marched into the building, hung a picture of Che over a doorway, and took a dean prisoner. It was great fun at first—live rock, red balloons, Chinese takeout food—until black militants from Harlem, rumored to be carrying guns, began filtering in. At 5:30

A.M., blacks ordered the whites to pick up their blankets and go, which, disappointed and chagrined, they did. Nevertheless, Rudd would say afterward, "We were spurred on by a tremendous push from history, if you will, embodied in the militant black students of Columbia."[91]

Resilient, the whites decided to occupy a building of their own, choosing Low Library, where Grayson Kirk had his offices. Soon students were smoking Kirk's cigars and rifling his files. In the past SDS's antics had left most Columbia students cold, but this time SDS had the right issues. Over the next week, a thousand Columbia students participated in the takeover of three more buildings, including Mathematics Hall, where Tom Hayden himself turned up to provide leadership. At Columbia, as Mark Rudd explained later, the movement learned "that racism and imperialism really are issues that affect people's lives. And it was these things that people moved on, not dorm rules, or democratizing university governance or any of that bullshit."[92] So far had the movement come since Berkeley!

Inside the buildings the students created communes governed by participatory democracy and devoted to the creation of the "new man." Many communards who entered the buildings only vaguely sympathetic to SDS left them convinced radicals. Unfortunately, they did not leave voluntarily. SDS would not compromise its demands, and the administration would not grant amnesty to the demonstrators. The cops came, as they had to, and behaved as Rudd knew they would, wantonly and with violence. Police brutality furthered the radicalization of the student mass, and the inevitable strike received overwhelming undergraduate support. Classes virtually ceased in Columbia College and final exams were canceled. SDS had, in effect, closed down a great American university.[93]

Rudd was not one who saw Columbia as a victory. After the police bust, SDS argued for a radical strike that would destroy the university and replace it with one that was truly free. But the mass of the students, demanding "student power," wanted only to restructure the existing institution. Rudd finally concluded that there could be no free university until revolution put an end to unfree society.[94] Soon a major figure in national SDS, he became a strident voice urging the movement to look away from the campus for allies in the revolutionary task of bringing down the empire.

That spring the slogan "two, three, many Columbias" sounded on campuses across America, and as it did, dozens of colleges and universities experienced various forms of militant protest. The movement had forced its way to center stage, and its possibilities suddenly seemed limitless. Writing in *Ramparts*, Hayden proclaimed Columbia to be "a new tactical stage in the resistance movement that began last fall: from the overnight occupation of buildings to permanent occupations; from mill-ins to the creation of revolutionary committees; from symbolic civil disobedience to barricaded resistance." As support for the movement developed in the cities, Hayden continued, "A crisis is forseeable that would be too massive for police to handle." One thing was certain: "We are moving toward power—the power to stop the machine if it cannot be made to serve humane ends."[95]

In truth, Columbia began the new left's decline into madness. Greg Calvert had once advocated resistance as a way to build revolutionary consciousness. After Columbia, revolutionary consciousness rapidly took hold, and the goal of the movement became the seizure of power. Events worldwide conspired that spring to create the illusion of a revolutionary situation ready for exploitation by the sons of Che. In Vietnam the Tet Offensive seemed to signal the American defeat. In the black ghettos of American cities Martin Luther King's assassination touched off a new wave of bloody rioting. In world money markets the American dollar was taking a beating, and the international monetary system was edging toward collapse. Above all, in France students and workers paralyzed the country in May 1968, by striking against the universities and factories, nearly toppling the regime. Totally misconceiving reality, the new left concluded that the empire was nearing collapse and that the time had come to assist blacks at home and peasants abroad in finishing it off.

IV

By the time of the SDS national convention at East Lansing, Michigan, June 1968, the new left was rapidly coming to resemble the old. Pictures of Mao and Lenin hung on the walls, and copies of Mao's little red book were everywhere. Not long ago Marx had been regarded as an old fogy from the Victorian past. But, once the movement became committed to the revolution, Marxism proved irresistibly seductive, in part because the young radicals had not successfully developed an ideology of their own. Resemblance between old and new left extended beyond ideology. Like the old left before it, the new splintered into Marxist sects that often hated each other more than they hated their capitalist enemies. In addition to anarchists and Wobblies, there were in attendance at East Lansing Spartacists, Trotskyites, International Socialists, and members of the American Communist party.[96] But the main contenders for ideological dominance were, on the one hand, the SDS mainstream, which saw the world through the eyes of Third World Marxists like Ho, Mao, and Che, and, on the other, the Progressive Labor party (PL), which accepted as literal truth the texts of Marx and Lenin.

PL had been organized in 1962 by schismatic youths expelled from the Communist party for ultra-leftism.[97] Though calling itself a Maoist party, PL believed that the industrial working class in America, not peasant guerrillas in the Third World, would destroy the capitalist system. In 1966, having attracted no more than a thousand members, PL disbanded its own youth front and migrated *en masse,* as a disciplined cadre, into SDS to seek recruits. As Marxism grew in influence, so did PL, much to the distress of SDS's leadership. Indeed, PL opposed almost everything the mainstream believed in. PL opposed Castro because he was a lackey of the hated revisionist regime in the Soviet Union; the National Liberation Front, especially after it entered into negotiations with the United States in April 1968; rock music and drugs because they antagonized the workers; resistance and confrontations for the same reason; and any role for students except as dropouts in the factories helping to spread the revolutionary message. Short of hair, neat of dress, PL members had a Puritan style repellent to most young radicals, even as their skill in dialectics impressed them. At SDS conventions PL enjoyed a special advantage because its members turned out in large numbers and voted as a bloc.

By the time of the 1968 East Lansing convention, SDS leaders in the national office regarded PL as so dangerous and disruptive that open war was inevitable. Frustrated by PL's successes in floor debate, Tom Bell, a longtime SDS leader, rose to accuse PL of dishonestly manipulating the delegates. PL countered by accusing Bell of redbaiting. Bell shook with rage. "Red-baiting!" he shouted. "I'm the communist here, not PLP." Taking their cue from Bell, hundreds of delegates turned to the PL section of the convention floor and began shouting, "PL out! PL out! PL out!"[98] PL was not moved. In the end the national office had only the satisfaction of electing its slate of national officers, one of whom was Bernardine Dohrn, a young lawyer attracted to SDS during the Columbia uprising. "Do you consider yourself a socialist?" someone asked her from the convention floor. Dohrn replied, "I consider myself a revolutionary communist."[99]

Revolutionaries, of course, accepted the necessity of violence; and in the months after the East Lansing meeting, violence emerged as a legitimate means of movement expression. SDS had not participated in the planning for the August 1968 demonstrations in Chicago against the Democratic National Convention, but at the last minute decided to support them anyway. Five hundred SDS members showed up intending to recruit disillusioned campaign workers of Senator Eugene McCarthy to the radical cause. Once on the streets, however, SDS made common cause with local youth gangs in the struggle against the police. Radicals organized "street guerrillas" into "affinity groups" to enhance their military effectiveness.[100] This alliance of radicals and hoods excited many in SDS, especially a collective of East Side street people called Up Against the Wall Motherfuckers, which had made itself conspicuous at East Lansing by waving the black flag of anarchism and threatening to punch up PL's delegates. After Chicago, Up Against the Wall hailed the birth of the "Street Left"—a new class composed of bourgeois dropouts and working-class kids, totally disaffected and itching for action. "A proletariat of Outsiders can be the only source of that class need which will make the Revolution," Up Against the Wall declared.[101] This was a manifesto for nihilism, a thinly disguised appeal for trashing in the streets, which, too soon, would become commonplace in youth ghettos from Cambridge, Massachusetts, to Berkeley, California.

Superficially, SDS appeared in robust health in the fall of 1968. Campus organizers reported students responding to their appeals in unprecedented numbers. "We're saying to kids all over the place," wrote two of them, "that if you're tired of the Vietnamese eating napalm for breakfast, if you're tired of the blacks eating tear gas for dinner, and if YOU'RE tired of eating plastic for lunch, then give it a name: Call it SDS and join us."[102] SDS claimed 100,000 campus members that fall, and poll data revealed that approximately 20 percent of all college students either strongly or partially supported the need for a mass revolutionary party.[103] But in reality SDS was beginning to fall apart. Important campus chapters were racked by internal conflicts, often occasioned by PL. And the national office was rapidly losing touch with its campus base, as evidenced by the total failure of its call for a national student strike on election day 1968. Meantime, the SDS leadership continued to churn out papers that nobody read. The National Council meeting in December 1968 endorsed one by national secretary Mike Klonsky, calling for a Revolutionary Youth Movement. Students would organize white working-class kids to fight beside blacks against capitalism.[104]

In the spring of 1969 Mark Rudd, Bernardine Dohrn, and a dozen other SDS leaders in the Chicago national office constituted themselves a national collective and imposed Leninist discipline on about two hundred allies in the regional offices and in some of the larger chapters.[105] By now repression by the government was intensifying. More members were leaving the organization than joining it. And the movement was losing its cohesion and sense of direction. But the national collective concentrated its entire attention on the approaching final showdown with PL. Hope for victory depended on a paper prepared by a clandestine committee and called "You Don't Need a Weatherman to Know Which Way the Wind Blows"—a line from Bob Dylan's "Subterranean Homesick Blues." Not by coincidence, PL hated Bob Dylan. Turgid in style, unsteady in logic, reliant on the dead language of Marxism, Weatherman was SDS's last and worst attempt to fashion an ideology for the radical movement. "Any close reading" of the Weatherman statement, wrote Carl Oglesby all too accurately, "will drive you blind."[106]

Weatherman was the culmination of the anti-imperialist tendency that had dominated the movement for two years. Most white Americans were beneficiaries of white skin privilege and lacked revolutionary potential, the paper said. When the empire fell, it would fall at the hands of Third World peoples, especially American blacks, who could destroy the monster by themselves. The sole mission of white radicals, therefore, was to assist the colonies in achieving liberation. The problem was where to find allies in white America for this task. Industrial workers would benefit in the long run from revolution but enjoyed too many temporary advantages to know their real self-interest. Only the sons and daughters of the working class—on the margin of the labor force, penned up in jails called schools, harassed by the cops and menaced by the draft—might heed SDS's call to rebel. To win over white working-class kids, SDS should organize them for self-defense against the police. The end result would be a Revolutionary Youth Movement that would give SDS a hook into the working class and advance the worldwide struggle against American imperialism.[107]

SDS held its last national convention in the dingy Chicago Coliseum June 18–23, 1969. To combat PL, Weatherman came armed not only with its ideological manifesto but with a recently concluded alliance with the Black Panther party. Weatherman acknowledged the Panthers as the vanguard of the anti-imperialist struggle in the United States, and in return the Panthers agreed to join the fight against PL, which accorded them no such distinction. Weatherman appeared to score a great coup when it actually produced Panther leaders to speak to the awed delegates—until one of the Panthers strayed from the subject to make a gratuitous sexist remark about "pussy power." Cries of "Fight male chauvinism," led by PL, drove the baffled Panthers from the platform. They were back the next day, however, to stun the convention with an ultimatum denouncing PL as "counter-revolutionary traitors" and warning SDS that it would be "judged by the company it keeps." After the Panthers departed, Rudd moved an hour's recess, but Bernardine Dohrn seized the microphone and invited all who wished to consider ousting PL from SDS to follow her out of the hall now. "Sit down, Sit down, Stay and fight, Stay and fight," PL chanted, as hundreds left to reassemble in a nearby room. After twenty-four hours of debate, the so-called SDS caucus, composed of perhaps a thousand people, made the fateful decision to expel PL. Now there were two SDSs.[108]

Soon there would be three. The Revolutionary Youth Movement was itself riven by faction. One RYM group was Weatherman, whose national secretary was Mark Rudd. The other—called RYM II and led by Mike Klonsky—accepted Weatherman's anti-imperialist framework and its desire to organize working-class youth, but looked more hopefully on the old working class and less kindly on violence. RYM II split from Weatherman in the summer and was dead a few months later. For all practical purposes, so was SDS.[109]

Weatherman, the surviving fragment, undertook the remarkable project of acting out its own fantastic program. In order to build a Red Army at home to assist anti-imperial movements abroad, some two to three hundred hardened revolutionaries formed collectives with five to twenty-five members each in a number of mid-sized American cities. Throughout the summer of 1969 these collectives labored to create the new man, revolutionary man, willing to give up possessions, bank accounts, monogamy, privacy, and, indeed, the self for the anti-imperial cause. The point was to be hard, to master the martial arts, to crush bourgeois emotions and dare to fight the pig in the streets. Hoping to attract white working-class kids with their daring, Weatherpeople that summer conducted a series of "jailbreaks" in local schools—raids in which the guerrillas took over classrooms to deliver their message of revolution. Sometimes they avoided bloody skirmishes with the police, sometimes not.[110]

Within the Weather communes, monogamy was often the paramount issue. For radical women—long relegated to making the coffee, typing manifestos, and providing sexual favors for their men —to "smash monogamy" meant to end dependency and passivity— to be taken seriously as persons and revolutionaries. For Weatherman as an organization, smashing monogamy meant liberating both men and women from sentimental bourgeois ties so they could give total loyalty to the anti-imperial cause. Couples, even married ones, were compelled to split up; heterosexuals were pressured into lovemaking with fellow communards, male and female; and group gropes were not uncommon. The goal was group marriage, in which all members of a collective would be bound in love for the armed struggle. As Susan Stern, a member of the Seattle Weather collective, recalled, "A sleeping schedule was set up. According to it, you were to have a different bed partner every night, regardless of sex. The schedule was never enforced in our collective, but its very presence testified to the seriousness with which we approached the problem of smashing monogamy."

As it turned out, monogamy and male chauvinism died hard. One day Susan Stern found Mark Rudd lounging around the filthy living room of the Seattle collective—an emissary from the Chicago Weather Bureau, which formulated the line all Weatherman had blindly to follow. Rudd had come to conduct a merciless criticism session designed to expose and purge all vestiges of individuality from the group, and his chief target was persisting monogamous relationships. That night, while Stern was trying to sleep, she heard the muffled sobs of her friend Georgia, fending off Rudd in a nearby bed. "I don't want you, I want Mike," she pleaded. "I can't help it, I love him." As Rudd prepared to take what he wanted, he whispered endearingly, "You have to put the demands of your collective above your love. Nothing comes before the collective." Lying there with her hands clamped over her ears, Susan Stern was struck by an idea she tried desperately to repress. "Perhaps," she thought, "Weatherman is wrong."[111]

Indeed, nothing worked out as Weatherman planned. In August 1969 the alliance with the Panthers fell through when Weatherman refused to endorse Panther demands for community control of the police in white neighborhoods. Striking a low blow, Panther chief of staff David Hilliard declared, "We'll beat those little sissies, those little schoolboys' ass if they don't try to straighten up their politics."[112] Weatherman's only national action that fall was the so-called Days of Rage. Hordes of white working-class kids, led by Weatherman, were supposed to gather in Chicago to trash the city, "kick ass," and "bring the war home." On the evening of October 8, 1969, the second anniversary of Che's death, eighty Weathermen, wearing black helmets and chanting "Ho, Ho, Ho Chi Minh, the NLF is gonna win," marched into Lincoln Park expecting to find ten to twenty thousand kids ready for war. No more than a few hundred were there. Nevertheless, after cheering the brave speeches of their leaders, the American Vietcong charged into the streets to smash cars and hurl bricks. Vastly outnumbered by police, most were quickly beaten and arrested.[113] Back in the park shortly after the battle ended, journalist Kirkpatrick Sale watched as "a man in coat and tie suddenly emerged from the darkness, looked around as if in bewilderment, stood a moment, and walked quickly off: it was Mark Rudd, in 'straight' disguise, a general who it seems had decided not to march with his troops."[114]

By the time Weatherman gathered in Flint, Michigan, for a National Council meeting in late December 1969, it knew that neither white students, Black Panthers, nor working-class youth would help make the revolution. Indeed, the only revolutionary force in America was Weatherman itself.[115] Death and hate obsessed Weatherman at Flint, where the latest Weather hero was Charles Manson. With his psychopathic band of followers, Manson had recently committed his ritual murders in the hills of Los Angeles. Members of the Weather Bureau saluted each other with three upraised fingers—the sign of the serving fork that had been stuck in the stomach of Manson victim Robert La Bianca. And they celebrated the death of Sharon Tate in her eighth month of pregnancy because no white baby born in the mother country of the empire deserved to live.[116]

"Dig it," Bernardine Dohrn exulted. "First they killed those pigs, then they ate dinner in the same room with them, then they even shoved a fork into a victim's stomach. Wild!"[117] After Flint, Weatherman lived out the guerrilla fantasy by going underground to set off bombs against the property of the empire.

Tom Hayden, on trial in Chicago during the Days of Rage, had showed up in Lincoln Park to tell the demonstrators before their attack that he supported any effort "to intensify the struggle to end the war."[118] He soon changed his mind. Weathermen, Hayden decided, "were not guerrillas swimming like fish among the people; they were more like commandos, fifth columnists, operating behind enemy lines. . . . They were not the conscience of their generation, but more like its id."[119]

But, like many others in the movement, Hayden could not bring himself entirely to disown Weatherman, any more than he could disown violence in the proper context. Hayden saw Weatherman not as an aberration but as "the natural final generation of SDS, the true inheritors of everything that happened from 1960 on." The Weatherpeople whom he knew had all been in SDS for years, had knocked on doors for ERAP, as had Terry Robbins, one of the three Weatherpeople who blew themselves up in a Greenwich Village townhouse in March 1970 while trying to make bombs. They had gone through the whole disillusioning experience of civil rights, Vietnam, the Democratic party, and ERAP itself. "Each one of these had ended in someone's blood, whether it was the blood in Birmingham, the blood of blacks in the northern cities, the blood of Martin Luther King, the blood of the Vietnamese, the blood of Robert Kennedy and finally our own blood in the streets of Chicago." Confronted by repression, Hayden said, they persisted in the only form of resistance that could successfully be maintained—going underground to lead the agents of the government on a perpetual goose chase. "America made them what they are," Hayden concluded, "and they are as American as can be."[120]

The death of SDS in 1969 did not immediately finish the movement. Radicals continued to paralyze campuses, blow up buildings, and trash stores. And in May 1970, in the wake of Nixon's invasion of Cambodia, a wave of strikes—unprecedented in size and militance—swept the universities, including Kent State, where National Guardsmen shot and killed four young Americans, fatalities in the new American Civil War. Protests flared intermittently for another year and then, as suddenly and unexpectedly as it had emerged, the new left was gone.

Reasons for the collapse were not hard to find: government repression, de-escalation of the Vietnam War, loss of moral authority as a consequence of movement violence, inability to find off-campus allies, commitment to revolution in a nonrevolutionary situation. More fundamental than any of these was the failure of the movement to fashion an ideology for a native American radicalism. Such an ideology would have accounted for the alienation of the new left's student base and offered a persuasive analysis of the oppressive character of American institutions. In truth, the new left never found a solution to the ideological problem because none was possible. There is no doubt that the young radicals despised mass culture, the competitive ethic, and "plastic" American civilization. But their critique was more aesthetic than political, and—Marcuse notwithstanding—few could long sustain a self-image as technology's slaves, impoverished by abundance. The young knew that they enjoyed more freedom, more privileges, more options—more Eros— by far than did poor people, peasants, their parents, or past generations of the young. Grievances they possessed, but none so crushing as to validate Marcuse's Great Refusal.

Among the sources of sixties radicalism none was more important than disillusionment with liberalism. A generation reared to believe in America as the land of the free and the home of the brave was forced by events to confront the facts of American racism, poverty, and imperialism. The same liberals who promised to abolish these evils, new leftists came to believe, played politics with race, fought a phony poverty war, and napalmed Vietnamese. Beneficiaries of a system that seemed to do evil, guilt-ridden students committed themselves to liberate those whom America oppressed. Moral outrage, then, not self-liberation, was the principal fuel of this radicalism, which went far to explain both the movement's militance and its brevity. Moral outrage could not long be sustained at high levels of intensity and eventually exhausted those whose actions depended upon it. By the early seventies, movement veterans were burned out, students entering college had heard too much too long about racism and imperialism to be shocked by either, and hard times fostered the ascendance of personal over social values. Idealists may become revolutionaries, but cynics never.

Ephemeral though it was, the movement had significant consequences. It brought the war home and so helped force de-escalation. It attacked the form and the values of the contemporary university, making it less authoritarian and more responsive to students. It helped demystify authority and contributed, therefore, to its decline. And its insistent challenge threw mainstream liberals on the defensive. Confronted by the rage of their own children, mainstream liberals moved left. Those who did not—the Johnsonian liberals of the Democratic party, the corporate liberals of new left demonology—lost their capacity to shape events. The young Americans throwing rocks at the Pentagon and chanting, "Hey, hey, LBJ. How many kids did you kill today?" were one reason why Lyndon Johnson, as he entered the election year of 1968, was staggering toward political extinction.

CHAPTER 12

Black Power

T HE history of black protest in the 1960s bore striking resemblance to the history of the new left, moving as it did from liberal hope to radical disillusionment. But there was a difference. Unlike white leftists, black protestors never doubted that they were true outcasts in America. It mattered not that progress in alleviating racial discrimination was occurring. Progress was part of the problem. As liberal accomplishment in racial reform fell short of expectations, an embittered minority of black Americans commenced the journey from civil rights to black nationalism. The quickening impulse toward racial separatism found expression at mid-decade both in the slogan "black power" and, more ambiguously, in the great ghetto riots then convulsing the cities of the nation. The task confronting nationalist spokesmen was obvious—to convert black power from slogan to ideology and thereby to harness the furies of the ghetto for a sustained social movement. How black power evolved out of the civil rights movement and then failed the ideological challenge was one of the decade's more melancholy stories.

I

It was the story, in large measure, of the Student Nonviolent Coordinating Committee, which remained through the decade on the cutting edge of the black revolution.[1] SNCC was born in the spring of 1960 when the leaders of the sit-in movement formed a body to coordinate their scattered efforts. Mostly students from southern black colleges, the original members were thoroughly imbued with liberal values and beliefs, including racial integration, nonviolence, the beneficence of the federal government, and the blessings of making it in middle-class America. Integrate the lunch counters, they said, and first-class citizenship would follow. At SNCC's founding meeting in Raleigh, May 1960, Miss Ella Baker of the Southern Christian Leadership Conference tried to warn the students that it would take "more than a hamburger," that they would have to expand their social vision. "Aw," they retorted, "ain't nothing more to it than a hamburger. If we can eat this hamburger, everything will be straight."[2] In fact, in the course of the coming years, they would put to the test each of their liberal premises and find good reasons for rejecting them all.

SNCC remained only briefly an instrument to achieve the aspirations of the black bourgeoisie. In 1961, with strong encouragement from the Kennedy administration, the organization headed into the Deep South to register black voters. No longer the extracurricular activity of college students, SNCC became an organization of sixty to eighty paid full-time staff members, working for $20 a week, mainly in southwest Georgia and Mississippi. Its purpose was to achieve political power for the black masses rather than to desegregate public facilities. Participatory democracy was SNCC's implicit goal, anarchism its intuitive philosophy. The hardships its members suffered, the unremitting terrors they endured, knit them into a close fraternity—"a band of brothers, a circle of trust."[3] Respectful of their illiterate constituents, arrogant toward outsiders, dressed in the denim overalls of the poor, SNCC learned to see the world from the bottom up, and as it did, scornfully rejected middle-class aspirations. Gradually the radical conviction took hold that a nation which tolerated Mississippi's poverty and racism was fundamentally flawed.

Among the goals that SNCC came to repudiate was racial integration. The problem was not so much the southern racists who frankly declared their hatred, but the northern whites who risked their lives to join the struggle. There had been whites in the organization from the start, but SNCC's great interracial experiment really began in the fall of 1963, when one hundred Yale and Stanford students worked for two weeks in a mock gubernatorial election that turned out eighty thousand disfranchised Mississippi blacks. SNCC leaders

were sufficiently impressed by the students' contribution to propose
inviting hundreds more into the state in 1964 for a Freedom Summer—envisioned as a massive biracial assault on the segregation
system.[4] But, when the idea came up for debate in SNCC, a substantial number of black members expressed resentment against the
growing proportion of whites in the organization (20 percent of 150
members in 1964) and the tendency of whites to take over positions
of leadership.[5] Only the personal intervention of Robert Moses, the
director of the voting project in Mississippi, rescued the proposal
from defeat.

A black Harlemite with a master's degree in philosophy from
Harvard, Moses commanded unusual respect by virtue of his courage, intelligence, and selflessness. "There was something about
him, the manner in which he carried himself, that seemed to draw
all of us to him . . ." SNCC's Cleveland Sellers wrote. "He had
emerged as the kind of person we wanted to be."[6] Moses settled the
argument over Freedom Summer by announcing, "I will not be part
of a racist organization."[7] David Dennis of CORE, who worked
closely with Moses on the summer project, admitted later that more
than idealism lay behind Moses's desire to import whites into the
state. "We knew that if we had brought in a thousand blacks, the
country would have watched them slaughtered without doing anything about it. . . . If there were gonna take some deaths to do it,
the death of a white college student would bring on more attention
to what was going on than for a black college student getting it.
. . . You see . . . we were in a war."[8]

Freedom Summer began on June 8, 1964, when seven hundred
selected students judged by a staff psychiatrist from MIT to be an
"extraordinarily healthy bunch of kids"[9] came to Oxford, Ohio, for
two week-long training sessions. From the start racial relations were
uneasy. The students, most of whom were white, expected gratitude
for having enlisted their bodies in the cause. The staff, most of
whom were black, barely masked their antagonism. Tension seethed
under the surface for some days, until one evening white students
watching a racist voting registrar on the TV news broke into derisive
laughter. Six SNCC people, infuriated by what they regarded as an
insensitive response, stalked out of the room. In the discussion that
followed, the students complained that the staff were distant and
uncommunicative and "looked down on us for not having been
through what they had." A staff member replied,

If you get mad at us for walking out, just wait until they break your head in, and see if you don't have something to get mad about. Ask Jimmy Travis over there what he thinks about the project. What does he think about Mississippi. He has six slugs in him, man, and the last one went right through the back of his neck when he was driving a car outside Greenwood. Ask Jesse here—he has been beaten so that we wouldn't recognize him time and time and time and time again. If you don't get scared, pack up and get the hell out of here because we don't need any favors of people who don't know what they are doing here in the first place.

Bitter words these, but they had a cathartic effect, and the meeting culminated in emotional singing. Said one volunteer, "The crisis is past, I think."[10]

Hardly. On June 22 Moses quietly informed the volunteers at Oxford that three project workers who had entered Neshoba County, Mississippi, the day before had not been heard from since. One was Michael Schwerner, a white social worker who operated the CORE office in Meridian; the second was James Chaney, a twenty-one-year-old black Mississippian and CORE worker; and the third was Andrew Goodman, a white college student from New York, who had just completed his orientation in Ohio. Responding to widespread public outrage, President Johnson at last took federal action in Mississippi, dispatching FBI agents, military helicopters, and two hundred sailors to hunt for the missing. What kind of a nation was it—embittered SNCC workers asked—that mourned only when a white boy died?[11]

Despite a racist reign of terror that accounted for more than one thousand arrests, eighty beatings, and thirty-seven burned churches, white volunteers and black staff stuck it out for the rest of the summer.[12] But relations between them did not improve. A woman student wrote that the staff "were automatically suspicious of us, the white volunteers; throughout the summer they put us to the test, and few, if any, could pass. . . . It humbled, if not humiliated, me to realize that *finally they will never accept me.*"[13] Meanwhile, the project sponsored Freedom Schools for 3,000 children, registered 1,600 black voters, and above all signed up 80,000 disfranchised blacks as members of the newly created Mississippi Freedom Democratic party.[14]

The Freedom Democrats bet their chips on SNCC's alliance with white liberals, particularly politicians in the Democratic party. That alliance was already under terrific strain because of the administration's steadfast refusal to furnish civil rights workers with physical protection. The Freedom Democratic party offered white liberals their last chance to prove good faith. Since the regular Mississippi Democrats excluded blacks, Moses conceived the Freedom Democrats as an extralegal alternative capable of challenging the white monopoly of political power in the state. Built by the book from the precinct up, the party held a convention early in August and selected sixty-eight delegates, four of them white, to attend the Democratic Convention in Atlantic City, there to challenge the credentials of the regulars and win recognition as the only legitimate Democratic party in the state. On the eve of the national convention SNCC had enough liberals lined up at least to get the issue out of the credentials committee and onto the convention floor. But, once Lyndon Johnson made known his opposition to the Freedom party's claims, SNCC's liberal support melted away. Angry SNCC people, refusing to compromise, got on the buses to go home, convinced that white liberals had cynically sold them out.[15] After Atlantic City, Cleveland Sellers wrote, SNCC's goal was no longer civil rights but "liberation."[16]

Along with racial integration and the alliance with liberals, SNCC also abandoned nonviolence. SNCC's commitment to nonviolence had always been more tactical than philosophical,[17] and some members had long packed guns in defiance of policy.[18] Even among believers the willingness to remain passive in the face of unrelenting terror eventually wore thin. In August 1964 the shallow graves of Schwerner, Chaney, and Goodman were discovered in Neshoba County. At their funeral in Jackson, CORE's David Dennis, who had been traveling through the state urging blacks to "Put your gun down," broke down in anger. "I'm sick and tired of going to the funerals of black men who have been murdered by white men . . ." he said, weeping. "I've got vengeance in my heart tonight. . . . If you go back home and sit down and take what these white men in Mississippi are doing to us . . . if you take it and don't do something about it . . . then God damn your souls."[19]

In the fall of 1964 SNCC underwent something akin to a collective nervous breakdown, not only because it had lost direction and was suffering battle fatigue, but because the years of nonviolence had begun to exact a high psychological toll. Alvin Poussaint, a black psychiatrist close to SNCC, listened to black civil rights workers who had been beaten by whites insist that they loved those who beat them. "Now, what do they really do with their rage?" he wondered. In time, Poussaint reported, many of those who had been "talking about being nonviolent and 'loving the sheriff' that just hit them over the head," began rampaging "around the project houses beating up each other. I frequently had to calm Negro civil-rights workers with large doses of tranquilizers for what I can describe clinically only as acute attacks of rage."[20] By 1965 the days of nonviolence in SNCC were clearly numbered, and when at last they would be gone, the long accumulated rage would find its inevitable target in the entire white race.

One symptom of the growing malaise in SNCC was the emergence after Freedom Summer, for the first time, of factional conflicts.[21] James Forman, the organization's executive secretary and the glue that kept it together, hoped to transform SNCC into a disciplined cadre devoted to building a mass-based political party. Bob Moses, truer to the original anarchist impulse, believed that SNCC should remain an informal group of community organizers who "go where the spirit say go, do what the spirit say do."[22] At a staff meeting in Atlanta in February 1965, Forman's "hardliners" took control and began to impose a modicum of order, prompting many of "the floaters" gathered around Moses subsequently to drift away from the organization. One night during the Atlanta meeting, after passing around some cheese and an empty wine bottle, Moses announced that, to relieve the pressures on him, he was changing his name to Robert Parris (his middle name). In the course of the next year, no longer speaking to whites, he gradually cut his ties with SNCC and then disappeared into Africa.[23]

Though SNCC initiated some new projects after the Atlanta meeting, Mississippi remained the major theater of struggle. In 1965, uncertain of what else to do, the organization made the curious decision to invite northern students back into the state. That summer the arrival of three hundred whites reduced SNCC's Mississippi projects to a shambles. Racial tensions caused some projects to break up and prevented serious work in others. Problems only dimly perceived a year before now assumed stark clarity. At staff meetings blacks would silence whites with such remarks as "How long have you been here?" and "How do you know what it's like being black?" and "If you don't like the way we do it, get the hell out of the state."[24] Not all the blame for the breakdown belonged to the staff, however. The questionable motivation of some white students led Alvin Poussaint to add a new neurosis to medical terminology—the white African Queen or Tarzan complex. The victim of this neurosis harbored repressed delusions of himself as an "intelligent, brave, and handsome white man or woman, leading the poor down-trodden and oppressed black men to freedom and salvation."[25]

The worst problem, not surprisingly, turned out to be sex. White women, Poussaint reported, found themselves "at the center of an emotionally shattering crossfire of racial tensions that have been nurtured for centuries."[26] A veteran worker tried to explain what happened when a Mississippi black man encountered a white woman in a civil rights project. "What you have here is a man who had no possible way of being a man in the society in which he lives, save one. And that's the problem. . . . He's just trying to find his manhood and he goes especially to the places that have robbed him of it. . . . And so in a sense, what passes itself as desire is probably a combination of hostility and resentment—because he resents what the society has done to him and he wants to take it out on somebody who symbolizes the establishment of society."[27] A white woman reported at the end of the summer, "Well, I think that the white female should be very well prepared before she comes down here to be bombarded, and she also has to be well prepared to tell them to go to hell and be prepared to have them not give up. . . . I've never met such forward men as I have in Mississippi."[28] The problem was complicated by the jealousy of black women toward their white rivals and by neurotic whites who sought to ease their guilt by permitting blacks to exploit them sexually and financially.[29] On leaving the state, a few white women told Poussaint, "I hate Negroes."[30] By the end of the summer of 1965 there was no doubt that many SNCC people reciprocated the feeling.

As its commitment to the goals of the civil rights movement dimmed, SNCC became attracted to its opposite—black nationalism —gradually placed in an anti-imperialist framework. As early as the spring of 1964 SNCC chairman John Lewis, a theology student closer to Martin Luther King's views than was any other person in the organization, noted approvingly that blacks were now identifying with people of color throughout the world. "There's been a radical change in our people since 1960," Lewis said; "the way they dress, the music they listen to, their natural hairdoes—all of them want to go to Africa."[31] In September 1964, as guest of singer Harry Belafonte, several SNCC leaders including Lewis, Moses, Forman, Julian Bond, and Fannie Lou Hamer took a trip to Guinea in "Mother Africa," as Forman called it, and rejoiced to see competent black people running their own affairs. "There were no sheriffs to dread," Forman remarked, "no Klan breathing down your neck, no climate of constant repression."[32] In February 1965 Lewis declared that whether in Angola or Harlem, Mozambique or Mississippi, "the struggle is . . . the same. . . . It is a struggle against a vicious and evil system that is controlled and kept in order for and by a few white men throughout the world."[33] That spring at an antiwar teach-in at Berkeley, Moses declared himself to be "a member of the Third World," linked the struggle of Vietnamese peasants to that of black Mississippians, and proposed the study of racial oppression in the South as the best way to learn how this country "plans and executes murders elsewhere in the world."[34] In January 1966 SNCC became the first civil rights group to speak out against the war, issuing a statement in support of draft resistance and denouncing the government for its efforts to squash "liberation movements."[35]

The man who would articulate most forcefully the emerging tendencies in SNCC and assure their dominance was Stokely Carmichael. A native of the black Caribbean island of Trinidad, who immigrated to Harlem at age eleven, Carmichael had been a self-described radical ever since his days as a student at the Bronx High School of Science, where he had read Marx and consorted with white leftists. In September 1960 he entered Howard University and immediately plunged into the civil rights movement. As a freshman he spent Christmas vacation helping evicted sharecroppers in Fayette County, Tennessee, served forty-nine days in jail for freedom riding, and spent his summer vacation working in McComb, Mississippi, registering black voters with Bob Moses. Throughout his college years Carmichael devoted nearly every weekend to demonstrating and every summer to organizing in Mississippi.[36] Much of the time he was in jail. During a 1964 confrontation with the National Guard in Cambridge, Maryland, he swallowed so much gas he almost died.[37]

Handsome, volatile, eloquent, and fearless, Carmichael became a magnet in SNCC for the militants and proto-nationalists. He was one of the first in the organization to challenge the philosophy of nonviolence, triumphantly reminding a minister during one argument, "Jesus said I come to bring the sword, not the shield, and no remission of sin without the shedding of blood."[38] When Moses proposed bringing whites into Mississippi for Freedom Summer in 1964, Carmichael opposed him. When Carmichael lost that argument, he announced that no white volunteers would be welcome in the 2nd Congressional District, where he was project leader. After he failed to recruit enough black students to do the work, Carmichael agreed to accept whites, but only on condition that they train blacks, not replace them. When SNCC decided to press the case of the Mississippi Freedom Democratic party in Atlantic City, Carmichael objected because once again blacks would be petitioning whites for redress of grievances. Blacks needed a political party that would go it alone, he insisted. After the Democrats dashed SNCC's hopes, as Carmichael knew they would, he moved to Lowndes County, Alabama, where blacks constituted 80 percent of the residents but none of the registered voters. There he founded an all-black political party—the Lowndes County Freedom Organization —which took as its symbol the black panther and had as its object control of the county government. Ironically he got nowhere until federal examiners, acting under the 1965 Voting Rights Act, entered the county and began enrolling black voters. The issue for the new voters in Lowndes was whether to join Carmichael's Panthers or the Democrats. Among those refusing to support the Panthers was SNCC's own chairman, John Lewis, an opponent of separatist tendencies, who spoke statewide over the radio during the 1966 Alabama primary election for the Democratic party. "After that," Carmichael recalled, "I wanted his blood." Enough blacks voted for the Panthers in the primary to assure the party a place on the November ballot.[39]

In May 1966, only days after his recent triumph in Lowndes, Carmichael joined 130 others in Kingston Springs, Tennessee, for SNCC's annual staff meeting. His purpose was to replace John Lewis as chairman. In truth, Lewis was little more than a figurehead, who played virtually no role in administering the organization, serving mostly as a spokesman and fundraiser. But, because Lewis was out of touch with the rising nationalist sentiment in SNCC, Carmichael felt he had to go. In the end Carmichael's faction succeeded in overturning one vote in favor of Lewis and winning the chairmanship for Carmichael himself on the next ballot.[40] SNCC then issued a statement calling among other things for "black Americans to begin building independent political, economic, and cultural institutions that they will control and use as instruments of social change in this country."[41]

A few weeks later the full import of Carmichael's election became clear to the whole nation. The occasion was the famous Meredith March through Mississippi in June 1966.[42] James Meredith, the man who integrated the University of Mississippi in 1962 with the help of the United States Army, embarked on a 220-mile walk from Memphis to Jackson to show the black people of Mississippi that they could walk to the voting booths without fear. On June 6, twenty-eight miles out of Memphis, a white man felled Meredith with buckshot. Erroneously believing that Meredith had been killed, civil rights leaders immediately flew to Mississippi to continue his walk against fear. So it was that arm in arm Martin Luther King of SCLC, Floyd McKissick of CORE, and Stokely Carmichael of SNCC marched down U.S. Highway 51.

Early efforts of the three leaders to maintain surface unity rapidly disintegrated. Significantly, the first issue that divided them was the role of white people in the Meredith march. King's workers publicly thanked northern whites for joining the procession. McKissick also thanked the northerners but announced that blacks must now lead the civil rights movement. And Carmichael mused aloud that maybe the whites should go home. As the column moved onto the back roads and southern white hostility increased, the leadership of the march failed to agree on how to respond to violence. At the Neshoba County courthouse, Dr. King, conducting a memorial service for Goodman, Chaney, and Schwerner amid three hundred jeering whites, said he believed in his heart that the murderers were "somewhere around me at this moment." Declaring that "I am not afraid of any man," he then delivered a Christian sermon.[43] But, after the service was over and local whites got rough, the marchers returned punch for punch.

The real spokesman for the march turned out to be Carmichael. In Greenwood, after spending a few hours in jail, Carmichael told the crowd, "This is the 27th time I have been arrested—I ain't going to jail no more. I ain't going to jail no more. Every courthouse in Mississippi ought to be burned down to get rid of the dirt." Carmichael then issued the cry that made him famous. Five times he shouted, "We want black power!" and, the New York Times reported, "each time the younger members of the audience shouted back, 'Black power.' "[44] Informed of this new slogan, Dr. King expressed disapproval, and SCLC workers exhorted crowds to call not for black power but for "freedom now." By the end of the march the new cry had drowned out the old.

Instantly the black power slogan—uttered in a sleepy Mississippi town by a virtual unknown—caused a national furor, mainly because fearful whites sensed the racial animosity it implied. Few who denounced it understood the concrete historical circumstances that both produced the slogan and made it explicable. SNCC had believed in integration and tried it within its own organization, but black and white together had not worked. "Integration," said Carmichael, "is a subterfuge for the maintenance of white supremacy" and "reinforces, among both black and white, the idea that 'white' is automatically better and 'black' is by definition inferior."[45] SNCC had allied with white liberals, only to discover that whenever it suited their convenience they would betray powerless blacks. In dealing with blacks, Carmichael said, white liberals "perpetuate a paternalistic, colonial relationship."[46] SNCC had tried nonviolence and found it not only ineffective but psychologically destructive. The "days of the free head-whipping are over," Carmichael wrote. "Black people should and must fight back."[47] And SNCC had shed its blood for legal equality only to conclude that the main problem for blacks was not the unfair application of the laws but economic and social inequalities embedded in society itself. But what did black power imply beyond rejection of a failed liberalism? What blueprint for the salvation of the black masses, if any, did it offer? Having proclaimed the notorious slogan, Carmichael was soon besieged by critics and constituents alike demanding elaboration of its meaning.

II

This was no easy task. Though black nationalism had been an intermittent force among American blacks for a century, none of its spokesmen had ever explained how the goal of racial separation could be accomplished practically.[48] Nationalism in general implied a historic connection between a people with a distinct culture and a nation, a homeland. But black nationalists claimed a historic link with Africa, which was a continent, not a nation, and possessed not one culture but a mélange of cultures. African cultural connections, moreover, would largely have to be fabricated, since generations in America had turned Africans into Americans. The desire of the nationalists to separate was no doubt genuine, but what could separation logically mean except returning to Africa, which, for a population of millions, was wholly impractical? As Carmichael and a host of other nationalist intellectuals wrestled with these riddles, they looked for inspiration above all to the thought and lives of two men —Malcolm X and Frantz Fanon.

Malcolm Little was a Harlem hustler who was convicted of burglary in 1946 at the age of twenty-one and then redeemed in prison by the Nation of Islam, popularly known as the Black Muslims.[49] Paroled in 1952, he became Malcolm X, a Muslim minister and protégé of the Muslim leader, Elijah Muhammad. By 1960, operating from his temple in Harlem, Malcolm had emerged as America's favorite bad nigger, a fiercely proud black man who used his oratorical gifts and razor-sharp wit to articulate ghetto rage. Malcolm's popularity among poor blacks owed little to his Muslim theology, which consisted of a fantastic description of how an evil scientist thousands of years ago used genetics to create white devils out of black people; nor was his appeal owing to his strict Muslim moral code, which condemned such pleasures as pork, alcohol, gambling, and fornication. He had no political program, radical or otherwise, and his economics were a black variant of the Protestant ethic.

Malcolm was a hero because, with no hint of fear and before almost anyone else, he dared confront the blue-eyed devils and accuse them of their crimes. To black men filled with shame, Malcolm preached race pride; for those without hope in racist America he called unequivocally for separation from the white man, either by returning to Africa or by exclusive occupation of territory within the United States. No man, white or black, was more scornful than he of the civil rights movement and its goal of racial integration. While Martin Luther King was inspiring America at the 1963 March on Washington with his dream, Malcolm X was saying,

Whoever heard of angry revolutionists all harmonizing "We Shall Overcome. . . . Suum Day . . ." while tripping and swaying along arm-in-arm with the very people they were supposed to be angrily revolting against? Who ever heard of angry revolutionists swinging their bare feet together with their oppressor in lily-pad park pools, with gospels and guitars and "I Have a Dream" speeches?[50]

While police were clubbing SNCC workers in Mississippi, Malcolm was saying, "If someone puts a hand on you send him to the cemetery."[51] While SNCC was pondering the meaning of Atlantic City, Malcolm was saying, "We *need* a Mau Mau. If they don't want to deal with the Mississippi Freedom Democratic Party, then we'll give them something else to deal with."[52]

Unfortunately for Malcolm, his growing prominence aroused jealousy among Muslim leaders, including apparently Elijah Muhammad, who silenced him late in 1963 and eased him out of the organization in the spring of 1964. Freed by necessity from Muslim dogma, Malcolm spent the last year of his life groping for a new position, exploring new ideas, even making the remarkable discovery on a pilgrimage to Mecca that not all white men were devils. But he remained an uncompromising nationalist, convinced that most white Americans were irredeemably racist and that Africa was the true homeland of his people. When an interviewer asked him in December 1964 where he was heading, Malcolm replied, "I have no idea. I can capsulize how I feel—I'm for the freedom of the 22 million Afro-Americans by any means necessary. By *any means necessary*."[53] Two months later he was gunned down in Harlem by his Muslim enemies. Every angry nationalist who came afterward acknowledged Malcolm as a model and honored him for the honest expression of his hatred.

Malcolm was not a revolutionary, though he might have become one. Frantz Fanon was.[54] A black native of the French colonial island of Martinique, then a psychiatric student in Paris, Fanon knew European racism and colonialism firsthand, which was why, when he went to Algeria to practice his profession, he eventually joined the rebels in the Algerian war for independence. In 1961 as he lay dying of leukemia in a Washington hospital, Fanon's most famous book, *The Wretched of the Earth,* was published in Paris. This was his attempt to distill the lessons of the Algerian war for anticolonial movements everywhere. In 1965 an English translation appeared in the United States, just in time to influence emergent black nationalism.

Though Fanon explicitly disavowed "negritude" as the basis for a revolutionary nationalism, black militants in America nonetheless hailed him as a prophet because *The Wretched of the Earth* offered a passionate defense of the violence to which they were increasingly drawn. The violence of colonial rule made counterviolence inevitable, Fanon argued, violence the native could turn either self-destructively inward or outward against the oppressor. Violence alone could purge the native's land of the colonial presence, even as it could transform those whom colonialism had rendered infantile into men. "At the level of individuals, violence is a cleansing force," he wrote. "It frees the native from his inferiority complex and from his despair and inaction; it makes him fearless and restores his self-respect."[55] It was a simple, if misleading, step for American nationalists to argue that ghettos were analogous to colonies and could be liberated in the same way. Thus did *The Wretched of the Earth* provide militants with an apologia for the ghetto riots. "You'd better get this book," Dan Watts of the black magazine *Liberator* told journalists during the hot summer of 1967. "Every brother on a rooftop can quote Fanon."[56]

Drawing on history, experience, and thinkers as diverse as Malcolm and Fanon, leading nationalists now attempted to develop an ideology relevant to the situation of contemporary Afro-Americans. Carmichael himself had possessed nothing approaching a real ideology when he first proclaimed black power, and during the year of his SNCC chairmanship he literally had to think out loud to manufacture one. The results of his ruminations were less than intellectually impressive, but had at least this merit: at one time or another, Carmichael advanced the three main nationalist positions—the pluralist, the cultural, and the revolutionary—despite the fact that each was incompatible with the others.

Stung by the nationwide denunciation of black power, Carmichael's initial reaction was to seek safe refuge behind the pluralist interpretation of his slogan. Just as European ethnic groups had done, he argued, blacks should turn inward and develop cohesive community institutions of their own—for example, schools, interest groups, businesses—so that when they turned outward to participate in America's pluralist society, they could do so from a position of strength. Politically, this meant avoiding unequal coalitions with whites inside the two major parties and creating instead independent freedom parties whenever possible. Once organized as a separate political force, blacks might consider allying with whites for mutually beneficial purposes. But, Carmichael emphasized, "let any ghetto group contemplating coalition be so tightly organized, so strong that . . . it is an 'indigestible body' which cannot be absorbed or swallowed up." The rhetoric all sounded reassuringly American, except that Carmichael envisioned an unlikely coalition of poor whites and poor blacks to achieve a radical reconstruction of the nation's economic and social life.[57]

At the same time that he posed as a traditional pluralist, Carmichael was also defining black power as essentially a matter of culture. It did not bother him that, while the pluralist vision assumed some ultimate common interest with whites, cultural nationalism emphasized fundamental differences in values and ways of living. Whites had maintained their dominance over blacks, Carmichael argued, by brainwashing them into accepting their own inferiority —by inculcating in them shame of race. The first task of black people, therefore, was to undertake psychological reconstruction by uncovering their cultural roots, rediscovering their African heritage, and learning from history that they were a "vibrant, valiant people."[58] Hence the vogue among blacks during the sixties of afros, Swahili, dashikis, and black-studies programs in the universities. Some cultural nationalists stressed the cultural differences between white Americans and Afro-Americans: blacks had "soul," whites did not.[59] Carmichael's cultural nationalism, on the other hand, transcended America and emphasized the common African heritage of blacks everywhere. By the end of the decade he would become a passionate Pan-Africanist who believed blacks should return to Africa and who would even go to live there himself.

But, before he embraced Pan-Africanism, Carmichael enjoyed a brief fling as a revolutionary nationalist. This was an especially odd variant of black nationalism, much influenced by Fanon and stressing not negritude but the common struggle of all Third World peoples—yellow, brown, and black—against Western capitalist imperialism. Carmichael's anti-imperialist phase emerged in the radical summer of 1967 against the backdrop of cities on fire. It was then that he affirmed the solidarity of Afro-Americans with other oppressed people and declared willingness to join the global struggle against Yankee imperialism. Though he soon moved in a different direction, his successor as SNCC chairman, H. Rap Brown, seriously advocated an anti-imperialist guerrilla war in the ghetto to free the Afro-American colony. Revolutionary nationalists dismissed cultural nationalism as "pork-chop" nationalism and its emphasis on African culture as reactionary.[60] What counted was guns. The main source of nourishment for the revolutionary hope was, of course, the ghetto riots. Were not these evidence, after all, that guerrilla warfare for liberation was not only possible in America but had already begun?

III

The archetypical ghetto riot of the 1960s was Watts, which so closely resembled most of the others that to understand its character was to understand theirs also. Most of the 300,000 residents in the ghetto of southeast Los Angeles lived in neat homes along spacious streets. But, underneath the pleasant surface, the usual depressing conditions prevailed—segregated schools, an unemployment rate twice that of the national average, inadequate transportation to decent jobs. In Watts, the neighborhood at the core of the sprawling ghetto, the social order was in the process of disintegrating—four persons in ten were poor, 38 percent of the families were headed by women, 47 percent of the children under eighteen lived in broken homes.[61] The site of the worst fury, Watts gave its name to the great riot that began on August 11, 1965, in an ordinary encounter between white policemen and the blacks who hated them.[62] Officer Lee Minikus of the California Highway Patrol stopped a car driven by Marquette Frye, a twenty-one-year-old unemployed black man, on a main thoroughfare near the Watts neighborhood. When Frye, who had been drinking, resisted arrest, a crowd gathered, forcing police to summon reinforcements. Within an hour a thousand blacks were on the street hurling rocks and bottles at the cops and shouting "Burn, Baby, Burn!" the hip slogan of a local disc jockey, the Magnificent Montague. Thus did Officer Minikus and Marquette Frye become historical personages by virtue of having caused, in the phrase of the sociologists, "the precipitating event." In 1949 the black poet Langston Hughes knew that someday Watts would come:

> Negroes,
> Sweet and docile,
> Meek, humble, and kind:
> Beware the day
> They change their minds!
>
> Wind
> In the cotton fields

> Gentle breeze
> Beware the hour
> It uproots trees.[63]

That first night along Avalon Boulevard youths attacked cars driven by whites, beat up white newsmen, and battled the police. On the next night the looting and burning began. Calmly and without shame, people smashed the windows of liquor, grocery, and department stores and helped themselves to whatever they could carry. By the third day, as rioting spread throughout southeast Los Angeles, a dull orange haze from a thousand fires hung over the city. On the streets of Watts crowds milled about amid a carnival atmosphere, exhilarated by their collective act of defiance and proud that at last they were forcing attention to be paid. With the arrival of the National Guard early in the morning of the fourth day, the authorities began to gain the upper hand, and the fire and the fury slowly burned themselves out. "Now we're on the top, and they're on the bottom," declared Police Chief William H. Parker. The toll: 34 killed, 1,072 injured, 977 buildings damaged or destroyed, 4,000 persons arrested.

The McCone Commission, appointed by the governor of California to study the riot and named after its chairman, former CIA director John McCone, explained Watts as most conservatives would explain all the other riots—as a "senseless" explosion by a handful of alienated blacks.[64] This was a thesis no knowledgeable observer endorsed. Surveys of the riot area revealed that at one time or another at least 30,000 blacks had participated in the looting, burning, and sniping, while approximately 60,000 more had been in the streets as supportive spectators. Rioters and spectators together formed a majority of the riot-age population (14–65 years old).[65] Moreover, the typical rioter was not socially on the margin —i.e., "riff-raff"—but a young man somewhat better educated than the typical nonrioter and holding a job.[66] Sociologists called the character type of which the rioter was representative "the New Ghetto Man."

Bred on the asphalt pavements of the northern cities, this new man bore scant resemblance to the stereotypical black—docile and submissive—of plantation days. Proud of his race, politically hip, savvy to discrimination, tolerant of violence, the New Ghetto Man reached maturity in the 1960s, which explained why centuries of repressed black anger erupted when it did. The riots were the new man's contribution to the black protest movement, his announcement that he would not passively submit to a life of discrimination and poverty.[67] The announcement contained clear nationalist overtones. Whites were the target of the rioters' wrath, especially whites in the ghetto who had humiliated, cheated, or exploited them. Thus rioters chased white passersby, fought white police, and meted out their version of justice to thieving white merchants. The most arresting fact about Watts—and most of the other riots—was this: Looters and arsonists moved along the streets destroying white-owned stores but ordinarily sparing stores with signs reading "Negro-owned" or "Blood." Scornful of the black middle class and the traditional black leadership, the rioters heeded no counsel except their own violent impulses. Martin Luther King was on the streets during the riot, preaching nonviolence. The rioters ignored him. Mervyn Dymally, who represented Watts in the state legislature, urged his constituents to stay cool. One New Ghetto Man handed him a bottle, saying, "If you're with the people, throw it."[68]

Black riots became such a regular feature of the decade that their annual appearance soon ceased to occasion surprise. By official count 43 racial disorders occurred in 1966 and 164 during the first nine months of 1967, the year when the insurrectionary fever peaked. Thirty-three of the 1967 disorders were serious enough to require the intervention of the state police; eight required the National Guard.[69] Two of them—Newark and Detroit—were cataclysms on the scale of Watts.

The rioters of Newark manifested remarkable discipline, looting white-owned businesses but not black, smashing windows but avoiding arson since black families usually lived above the wooden stores.[70] Newark also featured a counterriot by "peace-keeping" forces, a form of violence all too common in the decade. National Guardsmen—white, ill-trained, and terrified of snipers—proved a trigger-happy lot. "Down in the Springfield Avenue area it was so bad," reported Police Director Dominick Spina, "that, in my opinion, Guardsmen were firing upon police and police were firing back at them. . . . I really don't believe there was as much sniping as we thought." Spina watched two columns of unprovoked Guardsmen riddle a housing project with bullets. By the time they finished, three women were dead.[71] Meanwhile, police and soldiers charged down streets, shooting up black-owned stores that had been spared by the looters. Early in the morning of the fourth day, uncertain what to do, New Jersey governor Richard J. Hughes privately summoned Tom Hayden to ask his advice. Hayden, who had spent three years organizing the Newark ghetto and the past few days "looking at the streets of violence," recalled warning the governor that if he did not pull back the Guard, "the troops are gonna massacre more people, and you're going to go down in history as one of the biggest killers of all time."[72] A few hours later, Hughes withdrew the Guard, and calm returned to Newark.

Less than a week later, on July 23, 1967, the worst American riot in a century erupted in Detroit.[73] Beginning the usual way, with a police incident, it rapidly spread through fourteen square miles of black slums. But Detroit was different from the major riots that preceded it, for here disciplined violence gave way to the sheerest nihilism. Rioters looted black stores and white stores, burned down businesses and burned down homes. Middle-class Negroes in big cars joined with the poor in hauling off merchandise. Carefree kids, excited by the fires, sacked and burned for the pleasure of it, appearing to one observer to be "dancing amidst the flames."[74] Police and National Guardsmen were helpless in the face of this massive breakdown of public order—or else fed the furies of the people by their own excesses. George Romney had no choice except to become the first governor of the decade to request the intervention of federal troops. Shortly after midnight on July 25, Lieutenant General John L. Throckmorton, who had served General Westmoreland as an aide in Vietnam, began to deploy 4,700 paratroopers from Fort Bragg and Fort Campbell to pacify Detroit. The carnage of the riot, when it ended, was stunning in magnitude—43 dead, 7,000 arrested, 1,300 buildings destroyed, and 2,700 businesses looted. Surveying his city, Mayor Jerome Cavanagh grimly remarked, "It looks like Berlin in 1945."[75]

Intoxicated by the blood and fire, militant nationalists concluded in 1967 that rioters were urban guerrillas engaged in a nationalist revolution to free the black colony. Theirs was a perverse interpretation. Spontaneous uprisings against deeply felt grievances, the riots were neither revolutionary nor even consistently nationalist. Rioters harassed the white man, but even snipers did not try to kill him. Wrath was directed less against whites in general than against those whites whose presence in the ghetto had aroused local antagonism—i.e., white cops and shopkeepers. Rioters were less hostile to the National Guard than to the local police and downright friendly to federal troops. They attacked retail stores but left untouched public institutions like schools, hospitals, banks, and government buildings. They looted not in the name of socialism but because looting was one way to acquire the material possessions that they believed, in typical American fashion, would make them happy. They did not invade nearby white neighborhoods, engage in terrorism, or manifest the slightest interest in mounting a sustained struggle against the government. Torn between a desire to assert control over their own turf and the hope for full participation in America, they wanted above all to deliver a message to their white fellow citizens: progress halting, patience gone.[76] Gabriel Pope (the name was a pseudonym), one of the new ghetto men figuring prominently in Robert Conot's fine book on Watts, *Rivers of Blood, Years of Darkness,* expressed the ambivalence of the rioters and summed up their purpose:

We'll give this country a chance. We'll give 'em a chance to make up for what they've done in the past, we'll give 'em a change to say "We know we've done you wrong, and we're gonna do our best to change it!" But I'm not gonna have nobody tell me what to do. . . . I'm gonna be the master of my life, and if they try to run over me, I'm gonna demolish them! And next time, baby, let me tell you, it's not gonna be a gentle war like it was, it's not gonna be the soul people doing all the bleeding. . . . If we get pushed again, it's gonna be goodbye, baby.[77]

In perceiving the riots as nationalist revolutions, the militants were creating an inapt metaphor—a wish projection—that served to titillate the radical sensibility but otherwise did only harm. The guerrilla fantasy fed the raging ghetto fires but proved so wildly at odds with reality that in time it would discredit the nationalist impulse itself. The two leading advocates of revolutionary nationalism were Carmichael and the man who succeeded him as chairman of SNCC, Hubert Geroid Brown, known as "Rap." Born and educated in Baton Rouge, Brown had been on the fringes of SNCC for years until 1965 when he joined Carmichael full-time in Lowndes County, Alabama.[78] He was called Rap because of his ability to communicate with the brothers on the street—hardly a remarkable achievement, despite a few years of college, because in all essential respects Brown was one of them. Lean, cool, menacing, peering impassively at the world from behind his dark glasses, H. Rap Brown was white America's dreaded image of the New Ghetto Man. Curiously, the SNCC staff elected him in 1967 to replace Carmichael, who stepped down voluntarily, because it thought Brown would maintain a low profile and keep out of trouble.[79] Carmichael knew better. Introducing Brown to the press, he said, "You'll be happy to have me back when you hear from him—he's a bad man."[80]

Every step of the incendiary journey of these two across America in 1967 took them closer to the revolutionary mirage. The journey began for Carmichael in Nashville, Tennessee, in April when he exhorted the students at all-black Fisk University to "take over" the administration. One day later some of those who heard him attacked police with rocks and pellet guns. "The pellets . . . pinged off the metal helmets of the officers as cries of 'black power' rang through the area," reported the *New York Times.*[81] When Carmichael was arrested in Prattville, Alabama, early in June 1967, after shouting "black power" at a passing police car, angry snipers engaged the police in a three-hour gun battle.[82] A few days later youths in Atlanta emerged from a church where Carmichael had urged resistance to the "honky" and went on a rampage at a local shopping center.[83] ("Honky" was an ethnic epithet once reserved for Hungarian immigrants but expanded by Carmichael to include all whites.)

On July 19 as Newark was cooling down, Rap Brown was nearby in racially tense Jersey City urging blacks to "wage guerrilla war on the honkie white man."[84] A few days later, while Detroit was burning, Brown delivered a memorable summation of his credo in Cambridge, Maryland, to a night rally of three hundred blacks. "If America don't come around, we going to burn it down," he said. "The white man talks about black people looting. Hell, he the biggest looter in the world. He looted us from Africa. He looted America from the Indians . . . you can't steal from a thief." The brothers in Plainfield, New Jersey, got hold of guns and when "the peckerwood" went down there, "they stomp one of them to death. They stomp the cop to death. Good. He's dead!" The honkies own all the stores around this town, he said: "You got to own some of them stores. I don't care if you have to burn him down and run him out. . . . The streets are yours. Take 'em."[85] Police ambushed Brown a few moments later, grazing his head with a shotgun pellet. The next day ashes from the Cambridge ghetto covered the city.[86]

On August 11, the second anniversary of the Watts riot, Carmichael was in Havana, making a speech. He said,

Comrades of the third world of Asia, Africa, and Latin America, I want you to know that Afro-North Americans within the United States are fighting for their liberation. It is a struggle of total revolution in which we propose to change the imperialist, capitalist and racialist structure of the United States which oppresses you outside and us within. We have no alternative but to take up arms and struggle for our total liberation and total revolution. . . . [87]

And in Detroit, to commemorate the greatest riot of them all one month after it happened, Brown declared, "We live in the belly of the monster. So it's up to us to destroy its brain. When we do this not only will Africa be free but all people oppressed by 'the man.' "[88] By the time he made that statement, it is likely that H. Rap Brown was the most feared and hated man in America.

Ironically, as the notoriety of its leading spokesmen grew, SNCC itself was disintegrating.[89] Carmichael's status as a celebrity antagonized many on the staff who felt the controversy he aroused undercut field work and invited official repression. Stalwarts of the early years like John Lewis, Julian Bond, and Charles Sherrod became ideologically alienated and departed. Bitter quarrels over the continued presence of whites on the staff persisted until the last of them was expelled in December 1966. Field work in the South virtually ceased, and new projects in the North floundered. Widespread pot smoking and pill popping became symptoms of lax discipline and declining morale. Funds dried up as liberals recoiled from SNCC's honky baiting and its decision in 1967 to support the Arab struggle against Zionism. Local police harassed the organization, and J. Edgar Hoover made it a high-priority target for FBI counterintelligence operations. Of the remaining seventy-six staff members in mid-1967, sixteen faced legal action for draft resistance. In July Chairman Brown added to the internal turmoil by getting himself indicted for inciting a riot in Cambridge, Maryland, and in August by getting arrested for carrying a semi-automatic carbine across state lines. SNCC obviously needed an infusion of fresh energy, which was why, early in 1968, it took under consideration an offer to merge with its most likely successor, the Black Panther Party for

Self-Defense—the purest expression of the revolutionary impulse and its ultimate corruption.

IV

The sole characteristic distinguishing Huey P. Newton from a thousand other angry "brothers on the block" was audacity. It was audacious, indeed, for a twenty-four-old college dropout living off petty crime to believe he could found a new party for the liberation of blacks. And it was audacious, too, to think that he and his lone disciple, Bobby Seale, could spend one evening at an Oakland, California, antipoverty office in October 1966 and draw up a nationalist program that could say anything new.[90] Most of their platform —composed in twenty minutes—was a routine rehearsal of the prevailing nationalist line: blacks needed self-determination; whites robbed the ghetto; salvation lay in "land, bread, housing, education, clothing, justice, and peace." But point seven was in fact something different. It said, "We believe we can end police brutality in our black community by organizing black self-defense groups that are dedicated to defending our black community from racist police oppression and brutality."[91] What Newton had in mind was guns. Calling his party the Black Panthers, he recruited a handful of street brothers in the fall of 1966, dressed them in black pants, black leather jackets, and black berets and sent them into the Oakland ghetto to keep tabs on the hated police. Since California law forbade carrying concealed weapons but not weapons borne openly, the Panthers ostentatiously carried guns on patrol, an act so audacious that it intimidated the police and made Newton a neighborhood hero.

Newton attained true celebrity status in the Bay Area on February 21, 1967, when he undertook to provide an armed escort for the widow of Malcolm X on the occasion of her visit to San Francisco. While the Panthers stood guard at the office of *Ramparts* magazine, waiting for Sister Betty to conclude an appointment, the police arrived in force, obviously itching for a showdown. As one group of Panthers whisked Sister Betty away to safety, five others including Newton confronted the enemy. A beefy cop stepped forward and undid the strap holding his pistol in its holster. "O.K.," Newton shouted as he pumped a bullet into the chamber of his shotgun.

"You big fat racist pig, draw your gun!" The cop backed off and Newton walked away, laughing.[92] Newton topped himself on May 2, 1967, by sending a delegation to the state capitol in Sacramento for the purpose of protesting a proposed change in the gun laws. When 30 armed Panthers brushed past guards and walked onto the very floor of the state assembly, the new party instantly became a hot national news item.[93]

Meanwhile, Newton was revealing a useful capacity for ideological flexibility. A devoted student of Frantz Fanon,[94] he moved easily with the times in the radical summer of 1967 by adopting the imperialist hypothesis and the emerging guerrilla fantasy. Black people constituted a colony in the mother country of the American empire, he said, and like all victims of oppression, could legitimately resort to revolution—meaning guns. "Only with the power of the gun can the Black masses halt the terror and brutality perpetuated against them by the armed racist power structure," he wrote; "and in one sense only by the power of the gun can the whole world be transformed into the earthly paradise dreamed of by the people since time immemorial."[95] The task of the Black Panther party was to show the people the way.

When the Vanguard group destroys the machinery of the oppressor by dealing with him in small groups of three and four, and then escapes the might of the oppressor, the masses will be overjoyed and will adhere to this correct strategy. When the masses hear that a gestapo policeman has been executed while sipping coffee at a counter, and the revolutionary executioners fled without being traced, the masses will see the validity of this type of approach to resistance.[96]

"The heirs of Malcolm X," Newton rejoiced, "have picked up the gun. . . ."[97]

On October 28, 1967, Newton demonstrated the limitations of his teachings by getting shot in the stomach during a gun battle with police. The facts of this encounter remain in dispute. Newton claimed that two policemen stopped his car at five o'clock in the morning, ordered him unarmed into the street, and then opened fire, not only wounding him but accidentally shooting each other. One officer was killed, the other wounded. Alameda County, on the other hand, charged Newton with initiating the exchange and indicted him for murder.[98] Jailed without bond, Newton would be out of circulation for the next three years. The Panthers appeared to be doomed in any case. The active membership was down to fifteen,[99] the base of party operations remained limited to Oakland, and the state of California had passed a law in July designed to take the guns out of Panther hands, thus effectively halting the police patrols that were the only Panther program.

Enter Eldridge Cleaver, by far the brightest and most charismatic member of the small Panther circle, and the man who took control of the party after Newton's incarceration. A convict for nearly seventeen of his thirty-one years, Cleaver had found redemption in the black Muslim religion, only to abandon it upon the excommunication of his hero, Malcolm X. Cleaver had so deeply hated whites that during his criminal phase he raped white women as an "insurrectionary act" and once, while in prison, ranted against white people with such violence that he wound up in a padded cell. Yet, when Malcolm returned from Mecca in 1964 to proclaim that not all white men were devils, Cleaver felt "glad to be liberated from a doctrine of hate and racial supremacy."[100] A writer of genuine talent, he joined the staff of *Ramparts* in December 1966, after having served nine years in Soledad prison for attempted murder. Cleaver was on the steps of *Ramparts* in February 1967 when Huey Newton—"the baddest motherfucker ever to step foot inside of history,"[101] Cleaver called him—faced down the San Francisco police force. Committing himself to the Panthers on the spot, Cleaver became Panther minister of education, and after Newton's removal, the savior of the party.

Cleaver's accomplishment was truly remarkable, for after cessation of the police patrols in the summer of 1967, the Panthers never did much more to liberate the black colony than talk about it. Cleaver made the Panthers the most prominent black militant group in the country in the late 1960s by advertising Newton as a revolutionary martyr, by practicing ideological opportunism, and by seeking alliances with other radical organizations. Cleaver, for example, dreamed up the idea in late 1967 of a merger between the Panthers and SNCC, whose famous leaders he wished to enlist in a "Free Huey" crusade and whose organizational talents he desperately needed. Approaching Carmichael first, Cleaver offered not only to merge the two organizations but to make Carmichael the Panther prime minister. Carmichael, who was already well acquainted with the Panther leaders and had previously accepted a draft as an honorary Panther field marshal, appeared receptive.[102] Unfortunately, he was the wrong man to contact, since he was currently engaged in a losing struggle with James Forman and Rap Brown for control of SNCC—or what was left of SNCC. Forman had disapproved of Carmichael's 1967 foreign tour, resented his refusal to accept censure after his return and, most important, objected to his latest ideological direction, which was as unacceptable to Forman as it would be to the Panthers, once they understood it. When Cleaver got wind of the split in SNCC, he hedged his bets by adding both Forman and Rap Brown to the Panther cabinet, making one minister of foreign affairs and the other minister of justice.[103]

Cleaver's efforts to arrange the merger reached a climax at a big rally on the occasion of Huey's birthday, February 17, 1968. Five thousand people gathered at the Oakland Auditorium to hear Cleaver, Carmichael, Forman, Rap Brown, and Bobby Seale. Cleaver kicked things off with the stunning announcement that the two most famous black nationalist organizations had indeed agreed to merge. Among those stunned was James Forman, who privately feared that SNCC would be swallowed alive by these Panther upstarts and took pains in his own remarks diplomatically to explain that the arrangement was more an alliance than a merger.[104] As usual, Carmichael overshadowed all other performers with a fiery speech that incidentally revealed his latest—and final—position on the question of black liberation. Only a few months before, he had been in Havana, preaching the anti-imperialist revolution against American capitalism. But after Havana he had gone first to Hanoi, where Ho Chi Minh—of all people—asked him why black people did not return to their home in Africa; and then on to Guinea, where he fell under the spell of the exiled Ghanaian leader Kwame Nkrumah and his Pan-African ideology.[105] Now in Oakland, making his first public statement since his return, he declared, "Communism is not an ideology suited for black people, period, period. Socialism is not an ideology fitted for black people, period, period." Black people must be provided with "an African ideology which speaks to our blackness—nothing else. It's not a question of right or left, it's a question of black."[106] For the Panthers, who were becoming increasingly anti-capitalist and more friendly to white leftists, Carmichael's speech was an inauspicious beginning to the new alliance.

Indeed, the two groups took few steps during the following months to implement their alliance, finally falling out in July 1968 when a SNCC-Panther press conference at the United Nations to

promote Newton's case fell through amidst mutual recrimina-
tions.[107] In August SNCC officially severed formal ties with the
Panthers and at the same time expelled Carmichael. The Panthers
for their part ceased to regard SNCC as anything but the enemy and
eventually denounced Carmichael as an agent of the CIA.[108] The
collapse of the alliance made little practical difference, since each
group could perform the revolutionary charade just as well separately as together.

More successful was the Panther's opening to the white left, a
démarche made possible because Cleaver was one nationalist who
was not a racist as well. In December 1967 he opened negotiations
with the California Peace and Freedom party, a predominantly white
group that hoped to provide a radical alternative to the two major
parties in the next presidential election. Cleaver wanted access to
white money and administrative skills for his "Free Huey" campaign. The Peace and Freedom party needed signatures in a hurry
to qualify for a place on the state ballot, signatures Panthers could
collect for them in the ghetto. Cleaver took pains to make sure that
the terms of the alliance did not compromise his nationalist convictions. The Panthers would have exclusive responsibility for defining
the Peace and Freedom program for the black community. Whites
could define the party program for whites.[109]

By venturing to become the only nationalist group in America to
ally with whites, the Panthers emerged as the darlings of the new
left. It did not matter that they consisted of a handful of blacks with
a mimeograph machine. White radicals were so grateful to the Panthers for taking them seriously that many hailed the party as the
vanguard of the revolution, wore its "Free Huey" buttons, and took
up the unconscionable Panther cry "Off the Pig!" (i.e., kill cops).
The Peace and Freedom party ran Newton for state assembly while
he was in jail and nominated Cleaver for president at its national
convention in August 1968. Meanwhile the growing fame of the
Panthers extended into ghettos beyond Oakland. By the end of the
year, the party had attained a membership of 1,500 to 2,000 in 25
cities.[110]

Cleaver was in no position to enjoy his triumphs, including publication in March 1968 of his celebrated book, Soul On Ice. On April
6, on the way home after a day spent preventing a riot, a group of
Panthers, including Cleaver, got in a shootout with police. Who
ambushed whom was never established. Though the police quickly

captured most of the others, Cleaver and seventeen-year-old Little Bobby Hutton, the party's treasurer and its first recruit, took refuge in a basement, where gunfire pinned them down for ninety minutes. Enveloped by flames and tear gas, Cleaver finally threw Hutton's rifle out the window and staggered on a wounded foot into the street. Little Bobby, who began to run, became the first dead Panther. After spending the next two months in jail, Cleaver was released by a county judge on grounds that he was a political prisoner. But in September a higher court ordered his return to prison within two months. Rather than comply, Cleaver jumped bail, becoming an exile first in Cuba and then in Algeria, where he resumed his duties as Panther Minister of Education and lost himself in ever more violent fantasies of the imminent American revolution.[111]

During the next two years the Panthers remained highly visible. In 1969, abandoning black nationalism entirely, they declared themselves to be a Marxist-Leninist party committed to joining exploited people of all colors in a war against capitalism and imperialism. The entire white left—itself now enamored of revolution—hailed this shift as a historic departure. But the Panthers quickly became embroiled in the left's intramural quarrels, siding with Weatherman against the Progressive Labor party and then turning against Weatherman on the issue of community control of the police. By fall the Panthers had alienated virtually every organization on the white left, which nonetheless continued to use the Panthers as proof that fascist repression had come to America. Indeed, law-enforcement agencies illegally raided various local Panther headquarters, infiltrated the organization with spies and agents provocateurs, used forged letters and rumors eventually to help split Newton and Cleaver,[112] and tried its leaders in the courts at every opportunity. In Chicago, on December 4, 1969, the police conducted a predawn raid on Panther headquarters, killing the leader of the state party, Fred Hampton, in his bed.

The Panthers were hardly innocent victims. Between 1967 and 1970 the Panthers killed more police (eleven) than the police killed Panthers (five).[113] And, despite the party's effort to improve its image by sponsoring free breakfasts for the poor, many Panthers seemed more interested in crime than in social justice. Testimony by high-ranking Panthers alleged that David Hilliard, the Panther chief of staff and head man after Cleaver's exile, used the Oakland chapter to operate a burglary ring.[114] Most of the 348 Panther arrests in 1969 stemmed not from politics but from charges of rape, robbery, and burglary.[115] Meanwhile, the organization was undergoing periodic purges, its local chapters withered, and internal dissension thrived. In August 1970 an appeals court overturned Newton's conviction for murder and ordered a new trial. Back on the streets, the mythic Panther hero found little left of the organization he had served better in prison than he could ever do outside. Within a year Panthermania was no longer chic, and the Panthers themselves fell into obscurity, somehow maintaining a sleazy half-life in Oakland throughout the next decade.[116] Few lamented their decline. They had, after all, existed mainly in the demented imaginations of white leftists who insisted on mistaking their poses as the stuff of real revolution. To such an inglorious pass had the nationalist impulse come.

V

Like civil rights, the nationalist phase of the black protest movement had a run of only a few years. The last great spasm of ghetto violence occurred in Chicago, Baltimore, and Washington in the wake of Martin Luther King's assassination, April 1968. Though hundreds of other racial disorders marred the civil peace during the following three summers, there were no more Wattses and no more Detroits. As the embers of the ghetto cooled, so did the oratory of nationalist militants, whose various efforts to fashion an ideology for the black masses had so badly misfired.

The pluralist version of black nationalism actually had much to recommend it. Given the shared racial identity that bound black Americans together, it made sense to develop institutions for their collective advancement in a pluralist context. But few of those who urged this course ever bothered to think through its implications or to undertake its implementation. SNCC had acquired considerable experience helping poor blacks build institutions in the South. But on moving north it made only feeble efforts to employ its community-organizing skills. Succumbing to the lure of the media, Stokely "Starmichael,"[117] as his critics in SNCC called him, chose the lecture platform over the store front and so left behind no enduring black institution.

Cultural nationalism was also not without its merits. If it was true that black people had been brainwashed into believing that black was bad, then one remedy was to insist that black was beautiful—to emphasize the positive features of black culture and black history. Black power probably hastened the process by which the new generation of northern-bred blacks—New Ghetto Men—forged an identity based on racial self-respect. Future historians may well conclude that, for blacks, the most important event of the decade was the conquest of the conk by the afro. But racial chauvinism, however psychologically beneficial in the shortrun, could provide only the beginning of a solution of the ghetto tragedy; it could never be the solution itself. A precondition for political and economic action, perhaps; a program for political and economic reconstruction, hardly.

Nothing did more to abort the nationalist impulse than the conversion of its leading exponents to revolution. If their exhortations had been taken seriously, the black masses would have undertaken a guerrilla struggle against the greatest military machine in the history of the world. That was a prescription for suicide, which in fact emerged as a leitmotif running through nationalist rhetoric as the decade wound down. Carmichael, for example, held a press conference after King's assassination predicting a race war in which blacks would "stand up on our feet and die like men. If that's our only act of manhood, then Goddammit, we're going to die."[118] From a jail cell in New Orleans, where he had begun a hunger strike, H. Rap Brown proclaimed, "America, if it takes my death to organize my people to revolt against you . . . then, here is my Life!"[119] James Forman announced with gloomy regularity his expectation of early assassination at the hands of the authorities. And Huey Newton developed the doctrine of "revolutionary suicide" which held that blacks in America faced two choices—to acquiesce in oppression and die a spiritual death or to "oppose the forces that would drive me to self-murder" and die for humanity.[120] Newton was no doubt prepared for death; the brothers on the block were not. As a result, the main casualty of the guerrilla fantasy turned out to be the nationalist impulse itself.

But the foremost cause of the rapid decline of black nationalism was its moral weakness. However understandable its emergence, black nationalism, like all nationalisms, emphasized what divided men rather than their common humanity. Remarkably, most black Americans resisted the temptation to counter white chauvinism with black, to answer rejection with rejection. All the polls showed that blacks continued overwhelmingly to favor civil rights, racial integration, and nonviolence. In 1966 King received the approval of 88 percent of the black rank and file, Carmichael only 19 percent.[121] Among the black masses the classic liberal ideal, more important than any particular liberal failing of policy, never lost its appeal. That ideal envisioned a multi-ethnic, multiracial democracy characterized by equal justice and equal opportunity, and affording to each citizen reward according to merit. That ideal remained imperfectly realized in the late 1960s, and many blacks felt deep frustration at the slow rate of progress toward its achievement. Nevertheless, few of them ever doubted its ethical superiority over the bloody rantings of H. Rap Brown.

CHAPTER 13

The War, the Liberals, and the Overthrow of LBJ

I

IN April 1965, three months after Lyndon Johnson made his decision to bomb North Vietnam, Democratic Senator Wayne Morse of Oregon predicted that Johnson's war policy would send him "out of office the most discredited President in the history of the nation."[1] Given the popularity of both the war and the president at the time, Morse's prophecy seemed absurd on its face. But, as Vietnam dragged on month after month, it did indeed become an acid eroding Johnson's political base, until in the end it destroyed his presidency. The first constituency to be alienated by Vietnam—and the most dangerous opponent of Johnson's war policy—proved to be the liberal intellectuals.

At first glance the split between the president and the intellectuals seemed surprising. He was, after all, attempting to govern in the liberal tradition not only in his conduct of domestic policy but in foreign affairs as well. They must hate him, he came to believe, not really for anything he did but because of who he was—a crude Texas cowboy without a Harvard degree. What he failed to understand was that his liberalism and theirs—apparently so similar in 1964—thereafter rapidly diverged, his remaining rooted in the ideas of the 1950s, theirs moving far beyond.

The root of the difficulty was the breakup of the Cold War consensus. In the 1950s, of course, liberal intellectuals typically had embraced the Cold War as a holy crusade, becoming in the process staunch defenders of the American way of life. Even after Sputnik in 1957, when the intellectuals began denouncing the nation for its materialism and complacency, they did so primarily to goad the people into greater sacrifice for the struggle against world Communism. The first sign of restlessness began to appear around 1960. That was the year, for example, when Norman Podhoretz, a New York intellectual who had been a dutiful Cold War liberal but now felt the old ideas going stale, "going dead," became editor of the influential magazine *Commentary*. Daring to open his early issues to dissident voices, he discovered among the intellectuals who wrote for his magazine and read it "a hunger for something new and something radical."[2] Radicalism was hardly the term to describe the outlook of the intellectuals in the Kennedy era, but they were more open to novelty, more willing to acknowledge the flaws in American society, than they had been for years. In 1963, when Kennedy and Khrushchev moved toward détente following the Cuban missile crisis, the international tension that for so long had sustained the Cold War mentality began to dissipate, the old obsession to bore. Liberal intellectuals supported Johnson's 1964 presidential campaign because they believed he shared not only their renewed commitment to social justice but their growing willingness to reach an accommodation with the Russians.

Strains in Johnson's relations with the liberals first appeared in February 1965 when Johnson launched his air war over North Vietnam. Immediately the *New Republic,* a leading journal of liberal opinion, and the Americans for Democratic Action (ADA), the leading liberal organization, condemned the bombing and called for a negotiated settlement.[3] Johnson was perplexed by the criticism since he correctly believed that he was merely applying in Vietnam the doctrine of containment so recently espoused by the liberals themselves. He did not grasp that that doctrine had suddenly fallen from fashion. Among the prominent liberal intellectuals who attempted to account for the shifting views of their community were Hans Morgenthau, an academic specialist in foreign affairs, member of the ADA board, and an early and formidable war critic; Reinhold Niebuhr, the renowned theologian and a founder of ADA, ailing but still influential; Arthur Schlesinger, Jr., a historian, former White House aide to Kennedy and Johnson, half-hearted defender of the war in 1965, but a leading foe by 1966; John Kenneth Galbraith, the Harvard economist, Kennedy's ambassador to India, and in 1967 the ADA chairman; Richard Goodwin, a precocious speech writer for Johnson till September 1965, and a war critic by the following spring; and Richard Rovere, the prestigious political correspondent of *The New Yorker,* a late but important convert to the dove side of the war argument.[4]

The liberal intellectuals did not apologize for their past support of the Cold War. So long as Communist parties everywhere had subordinated themselves to the malign purposes of the Soviet Union, every Communist gain threatened American security. But times had changed, the liberals said. The Communist world was now "polycentric" (many-centered), a situation resulting from the Sino-Soviet split and the emergence of conflicting national aspirations among Communist states. Wrote Schlesinger, "Communism is no longer a unified, coordinated, centralized conspiracy."[5] According to Rovere, since Tito's break with Stalin in 1948, the U.S. should have known that "international Communism" was a myth, "that national interest was more powerful than ideology, and that while we might on occasion find it advisable to resist the outward thrust of certain Communist nations, it made absolutely no sense to have a foreign policy directed against an alliance that did not exist."[6] In short, it was no longer necessary to oppose every Communist initiative on every part of the globe.

With the exception of Morgenthau, who favored recognizing spheres of influence,[7] these intellectuals continued to advocate containing China. But they denied that the war in Vietnam followed logically from this policy. Secretary of State Dean Rusk's opinion to the contrary, China was not the enemy there. The war in South Vietnam, they argued, was primarily a civil war, pitting indigenous revolutionaries against the corrupt and repressive regime in Saigon. If the Communists won, Vietnam might well become a bulwark against the spread of Chinese influence in the region. As a practical matter, the U.S. could not win. Escalation on the ground in the South could easily be offset by the enemy and would do nothing to remedy the defects of the Saigon government. Bombing the North would merely strengthen the enemy's will to fight. If Johnson proceeded on the course of escalation, he would destroy the country he was trying to save or else provoke war with China.

The war, the liberals said, was not a result of American imperialism but a mistake of policy deriving from obsolete assumptions about international Communism. Unfortunately, it was a mistake not easily remedied. Liberals rejected unilateral withdrawal on the grounds that it would mean abandonment of America's friends in the South, a blow to U.S. prestige, and maybe even the rise at home of a new Joe McCarthy to exploit the frustrations attending defeat. The liberal solution was a negotiated settlement—the middle course, they called it. Stop the foolish bombing in the North, since Hanoi demanded it as a precondition for negotiations. Convince Ho Chi Minh that the U.S. could not be dislodged by force. Offer the Vietcong a seat at the conference table and a role in the postwar political life of South Vietnam. It was possible, of course, that negotiations would fail. In that event, said Galbraith, "We must be prepared to defend for the time being the limited areas that are now secure."[8] Indeed, on close inspection, it turned out that the liberals were waist deep in the Big Muddy along with LBJ and were no more certain than he of getting back to shore. The difference was that they thought the war was all a big mistake, and he was there on principle.

As opposition to the war among the intellectuals mounted, so did their impatience with the administration's response to the great racial and urban crisis that was tearing the country apart. As they never would have done during the American celebration that had characterized the heyday of the Cold War, liberals were now earnestly discussing the menace of corporate monopoly, redistribution of income, and a Marshall Plan for the cities. In its January 1967 issue *Commentary* ran both a long article by Theodore Draper attacking Johnson's foreign policy for its "willingness to use and abuse naked military power"[9] and an essay by the Keynesian economist Robert Lekachman summarizing the case of many liberal intellectuals against the president's domestic policies.[10] Lekachman wrote:

Possibly Mr. Johnson went just about as far as a conservative politician in a conservative, racist country could have gone. The Great Society has distributed the nation's income even less equally than it was distributed before 1960. It has enlarged the prestige and influence of the business community. It has lost its token bouts with racism and poverty. The Great Society, never a giant step beyond the New Deal which was President Johnson's youthful inspiration, has ground to a halt far short of a massive attack on urban blight, far short of the full integration of Negroes into American society, and far short of a genuine assault upon poverty and deprivation.

Where liberal intellectuals led, liberal politicians usually followed. But politicians skeptical of the war in Vietnam initially hesitated to tangle with a president to whom most were bound by ties of party loyalty and whose vindictive character was legend. In 1965 even senators held their tongues, excepting of course Oregon's Wayne Morse and Alaska's Ernest Gruening, the lone opponents of the 1964 Gulf of Tonkin Resolution. Among those who privately worried but publicly acquiesced in Johnson's war policy were Senators Mike Mansfield, George McGovern, Frank Church, Joseph Clark, Eugene McCarthy, and J. William Fulbright. Fulbright was the pivotal figure. If he moved into the open against Johnson, the rest would follow.

A senator from the ex-Confederate state of Arkansas, Fulbright was a gentleman of inherited wealth, excellent education, and illiberal record on matters of race and social reform. But for more than twenty years, on matters of foreign policy, Fulbright had been the leading spokesman in Congress for the views of the liberal community. Though he had had his share of arguments with presidents, he was by nature a contemplative rather than a combative man, a Senate club member who played by the rules. Fulbright's early opinions on Vietnam were hardly heretical. In March 1964, in a wide-ranging speech attacking Cold War mythology, he paused over Vietnam long enough to make a few hawkish observations. The allies were too weak militarily to obtain "the independence of a non-Communist South Vietnam" through negotiations, he said. The only "realistic options" were to hasten the buildup of the regime in the South or to expand the war, "either by the direct commitment of large numbers of American troops or by equipping the South Vietnamese Army to attack North Vietnamese territory."[11] In August 1964 Fulbright sponsored the Gulf of Tonkin Resolution, which gave Johnson authority to expand the war.

For reasons unknown, Fulbright had second thoughts about escalation once it actually began. Publicly in the spring of 1965 he backed Johnson's policy, though he called for a temporary bombing halt to induce Hanoi to negotiate. Privately, he warned his old friend in the White House against waging war on North Vietnam and tempted him with the vision of a Communist Vietnam hostile to China. Johnson seemed bored by Fulbright's conversation.[12] Fulbright gave a Senate speech in June that both criticized the bombing and praised Johnson's statesmanship.[13] In July Johnson began the massive infusion of ground troops into South Vietnam.

Fulbright's first real attack on the Johnson administration was occasioned not by Vietnam but by policy in the Dominican Republic. In April 1965 Johnson sent U.S. troops into the midst of a developing civil war, ostensibly to protect Americans but really to prevent a possible Communist takeover. Fulbright brooded over this intervention, held secret hearings on it, and finally in September delivered a powerful Senate speech attacking the administration's conduct as ruthless and lacking in candor.[14] The president promptly ended all pretense of consulting the chairman of the Foreign Relations Committee and cut him socially.

As Fulbright edged toward open rebellion on the issue of the war, so did the other Senate doves, almost all of whom were liberal Democrats. This was probably one reason why Johnson halted the bombing of North Vietnam on Christmas Eve, 1965, and launched a well-advertised peace offensive allegedly to persuade Hanoi to negotiate. The State Department moved closer to Hanoi's conditions for negotiations in early January, and both sides scaled down ground action in South Vietnam. Diplomats in several capitals worked to bring the wary antagonists together. But on January 24, 1966, Johnson hinted to a group of congressional leaders that he might soon resume the bombing. Two days later fifteen senators, all of them liberal Democrats, sent a letter to Johnson urging him to continue the pause. Fulbright and Mansfield did not sign but were on record with similar views. On January 29, Johnson ordered the air attack to recommence. The episode convinced many liberals that Johnson's talk about peace masked his private determination to win total military victory.[15]

In February 1966 Fulbright held televised hearings on the war. The scholar-diplomat George Kennan and the retired general James Gavin argued the case against it on grounds of American self-interest. Dean Rusk and General Maxwell Taylor parried the thrusts of liberal committee members now openly critical of Johnson's policy.[16] Neither side drew blood in debate, but by helping legitimize dissent, the Fulbright hearings were a net loss for Johnson. Fulbright, meantime, was reading, talking to experts, and rethinking first principles. In the spring of 1966 he took to the lecture platform to hurl thunderbolts at orthodoxy. Revised and published as a book later in the year, Fulbright's lectures were a critique of American foreign policy far more advanced than any yet produced by the liberal academicians.[17]

"Gradually but unmistakably America is showing signs of that arrogance of power which has afflicted, weakened, and in some cases destroyed great nations in the past," Fulbright said.[18] Harnessing her might to a crusading ideology, America had overextended herself abroad and was neglecting vital tasks at home. Americans meant well overseas, Fulbright conceded, but they often did more harm than good, especially in the Third World. A conservative people, Americans supported necessary social revolutions in traditional societies only if they were peaceful, that is, in "our own shining image."[19] To violent revolutions, which "seem to promise greater and faster results," Americans reacted with automatic hostility or panic.[20] Fulbright was hardly an apologist for revolutions, but neither would he oppose them, even if they were led by Communists. Fulbright dared to find much that was praiseworthy in Castro's Cuba and even extended sympathy to the aims of the Chinese revolutionaries, whose regime he would recognize de facto. In Vietnam, he said, the U.S. had blundered into a war against Communism in the only country in the world "which won freedom from colonial rule under communist leadership."[21] Fulbright favored a negotiated settlement that would provide self-determination for South Vietnam through the mechanism of a referendum.

President Johnson had expected his main trouble to come from hawks who wanted to escalate faster than he did. Stung by the sweeping attacks of Fulbright and other doves, he resorted to a scoundrel's last refuge. Before a friendly audience of Democratic politicians in Chicago mid-May 1966, Johnson defended the war as a patriotic effort to secure lasting peace by punishing aggression and then said, "There will be some 'Nervous Nellies' and some who will become frustrated and bothered and break ranks under the strain, and some will turn on their leaders, and on their country, and on our own fighting men. . . . But I have not the slightest doubt that the courage and the dedication and the good sense of the wise American people will ultimately prevail."[22] The attack failed to silence the critics. The majority of the people still backed the war, but not with the passion aroused by wars of the past. Fulbright continued to assault the premises of American foreign policy and, indirectly, the president who was acting on them. Confronted with irreconcilable views of world politics, members of the liberal public in ever-increasing numbers deserted the president and sided with the senator.

II

To make matters worse for Johnson, he faced a personal as well as an intellectual challenge to his party leadership. When Robert

Kennedy emerged from mourning in early 1964, he discovered a remarkable fact. Despite his squeaky voice, diffident public manner, private shyness, and reputation as a ruthless backroom operator, he was the sole beneficiary of his brother's political estate. In him resided the hopes of millions who believed in the myth of Camelot and longed for a Kennedy restoration. Robert Kennedy believed the myth himself and shared the longing. Lyndon Johnson, however, despised Kennedy personally and made himself the great obstacle to the younger man's ambitions. After Johnson denied him the vice-presidential nomination in 1964, Kennedy repaired to New York, where he successfully ran for the Senate. Soon there grew up around him what the political columnists called the Kennedy party —Kennedy loyalists still in the bureaucracy, some senators, New Frontiersmen out of favor, and lesser politicians, lawyers, and professors scattered around the country. Most of the Kennedy loyalists were liberals, but by no means all liberals were Kennedy loyalists. Robert Kennedy, after all, had been an ally of Joe McCarthy, an advocate of wiretapping, too zealous a pursuer of the Teamster chief Jimmy Hoffa, and a frequent offender of liberal sensibilities. But liberals unhappy with Johnson needed a popular leader, and Kennedy needed to broaden his party base. The one issue guaranteed to bring them together was Vietnam.

The issue posed problems for Kennedy. As a Cabinet officer, he had been an enthusiastic student of guerrilla warfare and strong supporter of his brother's counterinsurgency program in South Vietnam. When Johnson escalated in 1965, Kennedy questioned less the attempt to rescue South Vietnam by force of arms than the tendency to subordinate political to military considerations in fighting the war. Speaking at the graduation ceremony of the International Police Academy in July, he said, "I think the history of the last 20 years demonstrates beyond doubt that our approach to revolutionary war must be political—political first, political last, political always." To avoid offending Johnson, he excised from his prepared text the view that "victory in a revolutionary war is won not by escalation but by de-escalation."[23] Kennedy waited one whole year after escalation before putting real distance between his position and Johnson's. It bothered Kennedy that, when Fulbright asked Rusk during the televised hearings of February 1966 to state the options other than "surrender or annihilation" that he was offering the Vietcong, Rusk had replied, "They do have an alternative of quitting, of stopping being an agent of Hanoi and receiving men and arms from the North."[24] The war could go on forever if this was the American requirement for peace. So Kennedy decided to propose another option. On February 19, 1966, he became the first senator to suggest a negotiated settlement that would give the Vietcong "a share of power and responsibility"—in what he did not say.[25] Assuming he meant the government of Vietnam, the administration dismissed the idea contemptuously. Kennedy's proposal, said Vice President Humphrey, would be like putting "a fox in the chicken coop" or "an arsonist in a fire department."[26] Kennedy spent the next week clarifying and qualifying, and though he retreated some, he was clearly moving toward the peace wing of his party.[27]

Strange things were happening to Bobby Kennedy. Perhaps prolonged grief deepened his social sympathies, perhaps he was trying in his own life to vindicate his brother's legend—or outdo it. Whatever the cause, Kennedy plunged into the currents of change that were swirling through America in the mid-1960s, currents that were altering the perspective of liberalism and passing Johnson by. Kennedy opened a running dialogue with students, made a friend of Tom Hayden, felt the yearnings of the poor and the black for power and dignity, and took unnecessary political risks. Blood donations for the Vietcong? Burial for a Communist war hero in Arlington Cemetery? Why not? he asked. Kennedy went to South Africa in mid-1966 to aid the opponents of apartheid. He attacked administration witnesses at Senate hearings in August for unresponsiveness to the poor. He flew to California to stand with Cesar Chavez in his fight to unionize the grape pickers. A man who risked his life scaling mountains and defying tropical storms on the Amazon, Kennedy was becoming an existentialist in politics, defining himself in action and moving where his heart told him to go.[28]

As Kennedy and Johnson edged closer toward political combat, their personal relations worsened. In February 1967 *Newsweek* erroneously reported that Kennedy had brought back from a recent trip to Paris a peace feeler from Hanoi. The story enraged Johnson, who, believing it was planted by Kennedy, called him to the White House for a tongue lashing. According to *Time*'s colorful account, Johnson told Kennedy, "If you keep talking like this, you won't have a political future in this country within six months," warned him that "the blood of American boys will be on your hands," and concluded, "I never want to see you again." Uncowed, Kennedy called

Johnson an s.o.b. and told him, "I don't have to sit here and take that——."[29] Whether Kennedy really used vulgarity was a matter of some dispute, but there was no doubt that the gist of the conversation had been accurately reported. Less than a month later (March 2, 1967) Kennedy gave a major Senate speech calling for a halt to the bombing and a compromise settlement through negotiations.[30] A few party malcontents, especially in the liberal wing, permitted themselves a small hope that maybe the crown prince of the Democratic party would claim his inheritance sooner than expected.

III

In the summer of 1967 gloom descended on the camp of the liberals. In August Johnson sent 45,000 more troops to Vietnam and asked for higher taxes to finance the war. And, though Defense Secretary Robert McNamara himself voiced public criticism of the bombing, day after day the bombs continued to fall. Liberals who had once viewed it merely as politically stupid watched in horror as the carnage mounted and now pronounced the war morally wrong as well. Meanwhile domestic insurrectionaries were gutting great American cities, the War on Poverty was bogging down, and the long-awaited white backlash finally arrived. Among those surrendering to despair that summer was Senator Fulbright. Speaking to the American Bar Association in August, he said, "How can we commend democratic social reform to Latin America when Newark, Detroit, and Milwaukee are providing explosive evidence of our own inadequate efforts at democratic social reform? How can we commend the free enterprise system to Asians and Africans when in our own country it has produced vast, chaotic, noisy, dangerous and dirty urban complexes while poisoning the very air and land and water?" Fulbright called the war "unnecessary and immoral" and blamed it for aggravating grave domestic problems. The country "sickens for lack of moral leadership," he said, and only the idealistic young may save us from the "false and dangerous dream of an imperial destiny."[31]

Fulbright's charges about the damage done at home by the war were confirmed in the autumn. Driven by hatred of the war, new left students began acting out their guerrilla fantasies, and major campuses were threatened by chaos. No less disturbing to liberals was the fever of discontent rising in intellectual circles. Some of the nation's most brilliant writers and artists were concluding, as had their counterparts in France during the Algerian war, that they now had no choice but to resist the state.

From the beginning a minority of the nation's intellectual elite—call them radicals—saw the war as more than a blunder in judgment.[32] Most of these radicals had life histories punctuated by episodes of dissent but had stayed aloof from politics during the Cold War. Vietnam brought them back to political awareness and gave focus to their inchoate alienation. To people like the novelists Norman Mailer and Mary McCarthy, the critics Susan Sontag and Dwight Macdonald, New York Review of Books editor Robert Silvers, the linguist Noam Chomsky, the anarchist writer Paul Goodman, and the poet Robert Lowell, America appeared to be in the hands of a technological elite that was debauching the American landscape and lusting after world dominion. Morally revolted by the imperial war against the peasants of Vietnam, the radicals found traditional politics insufficient to express their opposition. The war was a matter of conscience, and good men would act accordingly.

Their first impulse was to avoid complicity with the crime. Thus when Johnson invited a group of writers and artists to participate in a White House Festival of the Arts in June 1965, Robert Lowell refused to come. Scion of a distinguished American family, perhaps the best of living American poets, and a draft resister in World War II, Lowell sent a letter to the president, saying, "Every serious artist knows that he cannot enjoy public celebration without making subtle public commitments. . . . We are in danger of imperceptibly becoming an explosive and suddenly chauvinistic nation, and we may even be drifting on our way to the last nuclear ruin. . . . At this anguished, delicate and perhaps determining moment, I feel I am serving you and our country best by not taking part."[33] Robert Silvers took the lead in circulating a statement in support of his friend Lowell and in two days attracted the signatures of twenty of the nation's most prominent writers and artists, among them Hannah Arendt, Lillian Hellman, Alfred Kazin, Dwight Macdonald, Bernard Malamud, Mary McCarthy, William Styron, and Robert Penn Warren. Johnson was so angry at "these people," these "sonsofbitches" that he almost canceled the festival.[34]

By 1967 the radicals were obsessed by the war and frustrated by their impotence to affect its course. The government was unmoved by protest, the people were uninformed and apathetic, and American technology was tearing Vietnam apart. What, then, was their responsibility? Noam Chomsky explored this problem in February 1967 in the *New York Review*, which had become the favorite journal of the radicals. By virtue of their training and leisure, intellectuals had a greater responsibility than ordinary citizens for the actions of the state, Chomsky said. It was their special responsibility "to speak the truth and to expose lies." But the "free-floating intellectual" who had performed this function in the past was being replaced by the "scholar-expert" who lied for the government or constructed "value-free technologies" to keep the existing social order functioning smoothly. Chomsky not only enjoined the intellectuals once again "to seek the truth lying behind the veil of distortion"; he concluded by quoting an essay written twenty years before by Dwight Macdonald, an essay that implied that in time of crisis exposing lies might not be enough. "Only those who are willing to resist authority themselves when it conflicts too intolerably with their personal moral code," Macdonald had written, "only they have the right to condemn." Chomsky's article was immediately recognized as án important intellectual event. Along with the radical students, radical intellectuals were moving "from protest to resistance."[35]

The move toward resistance accelerated through 1967. Chomsky announced in the *New York Review* that for the second consecutive year he was withholding half his income taxes to protest the war.[36] Paul Goodman invited federal prosecution by acknowledging his efforts to aid and abet draft resistance.[37] Mary McCarthy, back from a trip to Vietnam, said that "to be in the town jail, as Thoreau knew, can relieve any sense of imaginary imprisonment."[38] On the cover of its issue of August 24, 1967, the *New York Review* put a diagram of a Molotov cocktail, while inside Andrew Kopkind, in the midst of dismissing Martin Luther King for having failed to make a revolution, wrote, "Morality, like politics, starts at the barrel of a gun."[39] (Some intellectuals never forgave the *New York Review* for that one.) On October 12, 1967, the *New York Review* published a statement signed by 121 intellectuals and entitled "A Call to Resist Illegitimate Authority." The statement denounced the war on legal and moral grounds and pledged the signers to raise funds "to organize draft resistance unions, to supply legal defense and bail, to support families and otherwise aid resistance to the war in whatever ways may seem appropriate."[40]

A few days later Stop the Draft Week began. This was an event whose possibilities excited radical intellectuals as well as radical students. Paul Goodman kicked the week off with a speech at the State Department before an audience of big business executives. "You are the military industrial of the United States, the most dangerous body of men at the present in the world," Goodman declaimed.[41] On Friday, October 20, 1967, Lowell and Mailer spoke on the steps of the Justice Department prior to the efforts of the Reverend William Sloane Coffin to deliver to the government draft cards collected from draft resisters across the country earlier in the week. (This occasion provided evidence for later federal charges of criminal conspiracy against Coffin, Dr. Benjamin Spock, and three other antiwar activists.)[42] Saturday began with speeches at the Lincoln Memorial ("remorseless, amplified harangues for peace," Lowell called them),[43] and then the march across the bridge toward the Pentagon. Lowell, Mailer, and Macdonald, described by Mailer as "America's best poet? and best novelist??, and best critic???,"[44] walked to the battle together. Lowell wrote of the marchers that they were

> . . . like green Union recruits
> for the first Bull Run, sped by photographers,
> the notables, the girls . . . fear, glory, chaos, rout . . .
> our green army staggered out on the miles-long green fields,
> met by the other army, the Martian, the ape, the hero,
> his new-fangled rifle, his green new steel helmet.[45]

At the Pentagon Mailer was arrested, much to his satisfaction, but Lowell and Macdonald failed of their object. Noam Chomsky, also present, had not intended to participate in civil disobedience, feeling its purpose in this occasion too vague to make a point. Swept up by the events of the day, Chomsky found himself at the very walls of the fortress, making a speech. When a line of soldiers began marching toward him, he spontaneously sat down. Chomsky spent the night in jail with Mailer.[46]

In his brilliant book *The Armies of the Night*, Mailer probed for the meaning of these apocalyptic events. For him the siege of the Pentagon was a rite of passage for the student rebels, for the intellectuals, for himself. The few hundred fearful youths who sat on the Pentagon steps till dawn on Sunday were a "refrain from all the great American rites of passage when men and women manacled themselves to a lost and painful principle and survived a day, a night, a week, a month, a year." The battle at the Pentagon was a pale rite of passage, he thought, compared to that of the immigrants packed in steerage, Rogers and Clark, the Americans "at Sutter's Mill, at Gettysburg, the Alamo, the Klondike, the Argonne, Normandy, Pusan."[47] But it was a true rite of passage nonetheless, the survivors having been reborn and rededicated to great purpose. On departing from jail Sunday morning, Mailer felt as Christians must "when they spoke of Christ within them."[48] For Mailer and many other radical intellectuals, American institutions seemed so illegitimate that a moral man could find redemption only in resisting them. As for the liberals, they could only wonder what would happen to America if Lyndon Johnson was not stopped.

IV

Signs of a liberal revolt against Johnson's renomination were plentiful in the fall of 1967. Reform Democrats in New York, the liberal California Democratic Council, party factions in Minnesota, Michigan, Wisconsin, and elsewhere were preparing to oppose him. In late September the ADA national board implicitly came out against him by promising to back the candidate who offered "the best prospect for a settlement of the Vietnam conflict."[49] The *New Republic* explicitly rejected his candidacy in an editorial that same week.[50] And Allard Lowenstein, thirty-eight-year-old liberal activist and ADA vice-chairman, opened an office in Washington and began organizing a movement on campuses, in the peace movement, and among dissident Democratic politicians to "dump Johnson."[51]

Lowenstein wanted Robert Kennedy to be his candidate. And the existentialist Bobby was tempted. Kennedy worried about the frustration building up in the antiwar movement and had himself come to view the war as morally repugnant. "We're killing South Vietnamese, we're killing women, we're killing innocent people because we don't want to have the war fought on American soil, or because they're 12,000 miles away and they might get 11,000 miles away," he said on *Face the Nation* late in November 1967.[52] But Bobby the professional hated losing, and in his view he could not defeat Johnson in a fight for the nomination, and neither could anybody else. On that same TV program he stated flatly that he would not be a candidate. If he were, he said, "it would immediately become a personality struggle," and the real issues would be obscured. Asked about some other Democrat, such as Senator Eugene McCarthy of Minnesota, taking on the president, Kennedy replied, "There could be a healthy element in that." He would endorse neither Johnson nor McCarthy but support whoever was the eventual party nominee.

Eugene McCarthy had become convinced that someone would have to raise the issue of the war in the party primaries in 1968. When Kennedy and other leading doves rejected Lowenstein's pleas to be the candidate, McCarthy agreed to run. Explaining his purpose at a press conference on November 30, 1967, he said, "There is growing evidence of a deepening moral crisis in America —discontent and frustration and a disposition to take extralegal if not illegal actions to manifest protest. I am hopeful that this challenge . . . may alleviate at least in some degree this sense of political helplessness and restore to many people a belief in the processes of American politics and of American government."[53] In other words, McCarthy was offering his candidacy as an alternative to radicalism.

Only an unusual politician would undertake what no one else would dare. In truth McCarthy, who had spent eight months of his youth as a novice in a Benedictine monastery, was in the political world but not of it. He was a senator bored by the Senate, an office seeker who disdained intrigue and self-advertisement, a professional who valued honor more than influence. In recent years he had seemed more interested in Thomistic theology and writing poetry than in the business of government. His career, it appeared, would not fulfill its early promise. But the political crisis in the United States in late 1967 provided McCarthy with an opportunity perfectly suited to his self-conception. Like his hero Thomas More, he would play the martyr in a historic confrontation between conscience and power.

McCarthy's candidacy prospered beyond anyone's expectation, even his own. Though Johnson's rating on the Gallup poll was only 41 percent in November,[54] the professionals were mesmerized by the cliché that no president could be denied renomination by his own party. The war was the biggest cause of Johnson's unpopularity. Hawks and doves disagreed on how best to end the war but otherwise had much in common: both disliked the war, wanted its early termination, and tended to blame Lyndon Johnson for dragging it on.[55] It was the public's declining confidence in Johnson's ability to conclude the war that made him vulnerable to McCarthy's candidacy.

What little confidence still existed in the president's war leadership was shattered on January 31, 1968, when the Vietnamese Communists launched a massive attack in the midst of a truce called for the Tet holiday. Sixty-seven thousand enemy troops invaded more than one hundred of South Vietnam's cities and towns. The allies recaptured most urban areas after a few days and inflicted huge casualties on the attackers. But the Tet Offensive had astounded military men by its scope and daring. It showed that no place in South Vietnam was secure, not even the American embassy, whose walls had been breached in the first hours of the attack. And it temporarily derailed the pacification program in the countryside by drawing allied troops into the cities. Coming after recent administration assurances that the war was being won, the Tet Offensive dealt Johnson's credibility its crowning blow. When he and the U.S. commander in Vietnam, General William Westmoreland, issued victory statements after the offensive ended, few took them seriously, though militarily they were right. The chief political casualty of the Tet Offensive, therefore, was Lyndon Johnson.[56]

In the six weeks after Tet, such pillars of establishment opinion as Walter Cronkite, *Newsweek*, the *Wall Street Journal*, and NBC News gave way and called for de-escalation.[57] High officials in the government finally dared express their private doubts about the war to the president.[58] The Gallup poll reported a seismic shift in public opinion: in February self-described hawks had outnumbered doves 60 percent to 24 percent; in March it was hawks 41 percent, doves 42 percent.[59] And on March 10, two days before the New Hampshire primary, the *New York Times* set off waves of national anxiety by reporting a secret request from the generals to the president for 206,000 more troops for the war.

Meanwhile, in New Hampshire, the first primary state, McCarthy was proving an eccentric candidate. A lazy campaigner, he often did not return phone calls, would not court potential contributors, and avoided local politicians. His manner on the stump was uninspired, and even his references to the war were low-key. (McCarthy opposed unilateral withdrawal and advocated a negotiated settlement.) But McCarthy had an insight denied to his detractors: he mattered less in this campaign than the movement he represented. At the climax of the campaign there were so many student volunteers in the tiny state (3,000, or one for every 25 Democratic voters) that McCarthy's lieutenants begged potential workers to stay home. Scrubbed and shaven, the students ran a canvassing operation that was the envy of the professionals. Even McCarthy's peculiar style proved to be an asset. At a time when the country was fed up with politicians, shrill voices, and the hard sell, there was something reassuring in McCarthy's unhurried, dignified manner. He did not frighten people. He seemed safe.[60]

Governor John W. King, one of the inept managers of Johnson's write-in campaign in New Hampshire, said in the beginning that McCarthy would get 5 percent of the vote. McCarthy himself predicted 30 percent. On March 12, 1968, 49 percent of New Hampshire's Democratic voters wrote in the name of the president of the United States, and 42 percent marked their ballots for a senator of whom days before few had heard. Poll data showed that more McCarthy voters in New Hampshire were hawks than doves. McCarthy's remarkable showing, then, was not a victory for peace, merely proof that Lyndon Johnson, who could neither pacify the ghetto, speak the plain truth, lick inflation, nor above all end the war, was a mighty unpopular president indeed.[61]

McCarthy had done more than demonstrate Johnson's vulnerability. As he had hoped, his candidacy drained off some of the discontent flowing into illegal protest. Thousands of students who might otherwise have joined SDS got "clean for Gene." Intellectuals who had flirted with resistance a few months before became the senator's avid fans. McCarthy's traveling companion through much of New Hampshire was Robert Lowell—a symbolic relationship whose significance was probably lost on neither of these famous poets.

It had been a hard winter for Robert Kennedy. He realized after the Tet Offensive that his refusal to run had been a mistake. Throughout February 1968, while McCarthy's New Hampshire campaign was getting started, Kennedy and his advisers wrestled again with the problem of his candidacy. Kennedy was ready to go early in March and set in motion machinery for a campaign. But still he found reason to delay a public announcement. By the time he declared on March 16, 1968, the results of the New Hampshire primary had already electrified the country. Much of the constituency that would have been his now belonged to McCarthy. Lyndon Johnson, however, took Kennedy's candidacy more seriously than McCarthy's. He knew, even if the students did not, that Kennedy was the one man in the party who might beat him.[62]

McCarthy refused to step aside for Kennedy and moved on to the Wisconsin primary, whose date was April 2. Early in March the president's men in Wisconsin had been confident of victory. But McCarthy arrived with more students, money, and prestige than he had had in New Hampshire, and by mid-month the Johnson managers knew their man was in trouble. On March 28 Postmaster Larry O'Brien, an old political pro, returned from a look around the state to tell Johnson that his cause there was hopeless.[63]

While the political storms raged around them, Johnson and his advisers were deep into a momentous review of war policy. General Earl Wheeler, chairman of the Joint Chiefs of Staff, had blundered in late February when he privately requested 206,000 additional troops for Vietnam. Since General Westmoreland was in no danger of being overrun, there was never much chance that Johnson would dispatch massive reinforcements. The tax money to pay for escalation was not there, and neither was the political support. Wheeler's request had one unintended result. By asking so much, it forced policy makers to resolve the basic ambiguity that had characterized America's policy since 1965. Militarily, Johnson had been seeking victory over the Vietcong. Diplomatically, he paid lip service to a negotiated settlement, which implied compromise. Since his generals were in effect telling him that they needed more troops than he could furnish to win, Johnson had no choice now except to opt for negotiation. Accounts differ on how Johnson reached this conclusion in March 1968. But in the end those of his advisers urging some steps in the direction of de-escalation prevailed.[64] On March 31 Johnson went on television to announce that he was stopping the bombing over most of North Vietnam and would end it entirely if Hanoi demonstrated comparable restraint. Johnson called on the North Vietnamese to respond to his partial bombing halt by accepting his invitation to negotiate.[65] A few days later they did so.

Johnson announced another decision in this speech. For some time he had been dropping hints among friends and advisers that he might not run in 1968. Only at the last minute did he determine not to make his 1968 State of the Union Message the occasion for announcing his retirement.[66] But his mood seemed to change after that, and he took steps to organize a re-election campaign. Even after the ambush in New Hampshire, Johnson authorized Larry O'Brien to meet with Cabinet officers and give them marching orders for the political battle ahead.[67]

Though most Johnson intimates believed he would run, he had compelling reasons not to. Exhausted, haunted by fear of another heart attack, bitter at the vilification he had suffered, the man had had enough. "The only difference between the [John F.] Kennedy assassination and mine," he said in this period, "is that I am alive and it has been more torturous."[68] There were other reasons too. Politically he faced a Congress opposed to his programs, a public that had lost confidence in his leadership, a defeat at the hands of McCarthy in the Wisconsin primary, and an uncertain contest with Robert Kennedy. On the diplomatic front, he wished to take a step toward peace, which his opponents, domestic and foreign, would probably dismiss as insincere if he remained a potential candidate. In his speech of March 31, Johnson spoke of "division in the American house" and declared his intention to keep the presidency above partisanship in this election year. "Accordingly," he told a stunned nation, "I shall not seek, and I will not accept, the nomination of my party for another term as your President."[69] The liberals, with an assist from the peace movement, the attackers of Tet, and war-weariness, had dumped Johnson.

CHAPTER 14

Rout of the Liberals: The Election of 1968

L YNDON Johnson's withdrawal on the last day of March 1968 threw the calculations of his rivals into disarray. His policies had defined the content of debate; he had been the magnetic pole commanding the needle of the political compass. Without him, presidential politics temporarily spun directionless, its meaning uncertain. Only later did it become clear that Johnson's exit was merely an incident in a larger story—namely, the massive defection of the electorate from the liberalism that had guided the country since 1960. Liberals had once promised to manage the economy, solve the race problem, reduce poverty, and keep the peace. These promises not only remained unfulfilled; each of them would be mocked by the traumatic events of this election year. With the threads of the American fabric unraveling the electorate would turn elsewhere for leadership.

I

As T. S. Eliot wrote, doubtfully for other years but appropriately for 1968, "April is the cruelest month." Then occurred a series of shocks which exposed the vulnerability of the liberals on the very issues that they themselves had done so much to raise. Satisfy the grievances of Martin Luther King, they had said, and black violence will be forestalled. Late in March King led a demonstration supporting a strike of garbage workers in Memphis that degenerated into a minor riot. Back in the city on April 4, he intended to lead a second march, better planned than the first, to vindicate his nonviolent beliefs. He was relaxing in the early evening on the balcony of the Lorraine Motel when a white drifter and escaped convict named James Earl Ray killed him with a single rifle shot.[1] Hours later, blacks in Washington expressed their grief with unconscious irony by rampaging through their ghetto, rioting and looting. The next day federal troops ringed the White House and manned a machine-gun post on the steps of the Capitol.[2] Before the week was over, 125 more riots broke out in ghettos across America, the U.S. Army patrolled streets in Chicago and Baltimore, and 21,000 black Americans were charged with riot-related crimes.[3] Clearly the laws passed at King's insistence had not, as promised, appeased blacks. Millions of whites, preparing to call the liberals to account, applauded Mayor Daley when, after the riots, he ordered Chicago police to "shoot to kill" arsonists and "shoot to maim or cripple" looters.[4]

Meanwhile, that April, the condition of the economy was inspiring widespread anxiety, in some quarters even panic. Heed the "new economists," liberals had said, and prosperity would result. And indeed profits were rising, personal income was soaring, and unemployment had fallen below 4 percent. But at the same time the dollar was under attack abroad, the balance-of-payments deficit was worsening, and the international monetary system was approaching collapse. On April 18 the Federal Reserve Board lifted the discount rate from 5 percent to 5½ percent—the highest rate since the infamous year 1929.[5] The next day Fed chairman William McChesney Martin declared, "The nation is in the midst of the worst financial crisis since 1931."[6] Most Americans could not fathom the mysteries of the international monetary system, but one fact they understood as well as Martin. Fueled by the boom, prices were rising at an annual rate of 4 percent. Whether the cause of inflation was the Vietnam War or the ideas of J. M. Keynes did not politically much matter. As usual, the voters would blame their trouble on the party in power, the party of the liberals.

April saw, too, the shadow of the Poor People's Campaign lengthen over Washington. In December 1967 Martin Luther King had announced plans for a nonviolent spring offensive that would appeal to the conscience of America and compel the government to provide jobs and income for all who needed them.[7] In other words, poor people would demonstrate against an administration whose proudest boast was its accomplishments in their behalf. After King's assassination and the attendant riots, nobody in Washington, liberal or otherwise, could view calmly the prospect of thousands of militant poor people descending on the capital. But King's successor as head of the Southern Christian Leadership Conference, the Reverend Ralph Abernathy, decided to proceed as planned.[8]

On April 29 Abernathy kicked off the Poor People's Campaign by touring the offices of Cabinet heads and issuing demands for the alleviation of poverty.[9] Two weeks later he dedicated Resurrection City—a sixteen-acre tract in West Potomac Park, just south of the Lincoln Memorial, where A-frame plywood shacks to house three thousand poor people were being erected. Abernathy vowed to "plague the Pharaohs of this nation with plague after plague until they agree to give us meaningful jobs and a guaranteed annual income."[10] Unfortunately, it was Resurrection City which was plagued—by mud, violence, anarchy, bad planning, and poor leadership. Though fifty thousand people showed up at the Lincoln Memorial for Solidarity Day, June 9, 1968, to hear hours of turgid rhetoric,[11] no effective acts of civil disobedience were ever mounted, and few significant achievements of any kind claimed. When the Interior Department refused to extend the permit for Resurrection City on June 23, and a day later police closed it down,[12] there was near unanimous relief. The Poor People's Campaign had accomplished little except to reveal that, among those most engaged, the War on Poverty—declared and fought by liberals —stood condemned as a failure.

And then there was Vietnam, the issue which, more than any other, caused the bitter national mood of 1968—a mood whose most likely beneficiary would be the Republican party. In April unexpected diplomatic developments briefly raised hopes of a quick settlement. In his valedictory of March 31 Johnson had announced a *partial* halt of air and naval bombardment of North Vietnam, exempting from his mercy only areas north of the demilitarized zone where the continuing enemy buildup threatened allied positions. Johnson challenged the enemy to answer this act of de-escalation by agreeing to participate in peace talks. Ho Chi Minh had hitherto refused to negotiate until the United States unconditionally and completely stopped bombing his country. No one was more surprised than Johnson, therefore, when on April 3 the North Vietnamese agreed to enter negotiations. But it took three weeks of angry wrangling merely for the two nations to agree on a place to parlay. And when talks finally commenced mid-May in Paris, North Vietnam refused to discuss matters of substance until the bombing stopped totally. Fearing that the enemy would exploit a complete bombing halt by stepping up his rate of infiltration into the South, Johnson demanded a reciprocal act of de-escalation. None was promised. The war continued, therefore, coloring every aspect of the presidential campaign and threatening the dissolution of the party of the liberals, which for eight years had governed the country.

II

The Republicans stood to profit from the agony of the liberals only if they could achieve internal harmony. In 1964 the Goldwater and Rockefeller wings of the party had engaged in fratricidal warfare so deadly that it converted LBJ's inevitable victory into a landslide. Ideological divisions had not since healed and might again wreck the party. As it turned out, this did not happen in 1968, mainly because one of the Republican aspirants could command the allegience, however unenthusiastic, of both camps. Improbably, that man was Richard Nixon.[13]

In 1962, after his humiliating defeat in California's gubernatorial election, *Time* remarked, "Barring a miracle, Nixon's public career has ended."[14] None disputed this judgment, least of all Nixon himself, who despondently quit his native state in 1963 and moved to New York City to become a partner in the law firm of Nixon, Mudge, Rose, Guthrie, and Alexander.[15] According to legend lovingly cultivated by his admirers, he grew and matured in the happy years that followed, apparently finding it spiritually nourishing to make in excess of $200,000 a year, live in a Fifth Avenue apartment, dine at the 21 Club, and hold his own in competition with the best legal minds in the country. The man who emerged from this Wall Street idyll was the latest in a long line of "new" Nixons, supposedly more mellow, tolerant, and self-accepting than any of the older models. But in fundamental ways Nixon had not changed. Ambition for the presidency continued to consume him, ambition that served no higher purpose than to earn him personal vindication and lay to rest his inner doubt. Encouraged by younger members of his law firm, some of whom became his close advisers, this troubled man embarked on the most remarkable comeback in American political history.

Nixon's rehabilitation commenced in 1964 when he barnstormed the country for Goldwater while other party celebrities stayed home. And it was substantially complete in 1966, when he raised so much money and campaigned so hard in the congressional elections that he was given much of the credit for the Republican resurgence of that year. By 1967 there was no doubt that he would try for the presidency once more.

Chief among his potential rivals was Ronald Reagan, the grade-B movie actor who had achieved instant political stardom with a brilliant and frequently rebroadcast speech for Goldwater in 1964 and who had stormed to a near-million-vote victory running for governor of California in 1966. Reagan was a conservative in the Goldwater tradition but more glamorous, more politic, if anything more adored by party right wingers, especially in the South. He had only to declare, and this region was his. But he did not declare—because he had promised Californians that he would serve a full four-year term and because if pollsters pitted him in trial heats against other national candidates his lack of appeal beyond the right wing would be revealed. So throughout 1967 and into 1968 Reagan denied he was a candidate, even as F. Clifton White, the mastermind of the 1964 Goldwater coup, discreetly traveled the country promoting his nomination.

Nixon was especially fortunate in his opponents from the party's so-called moderate wing. New York governor Nelson Rockefeller was the true leader of the moderates, but as 1968 approached he apparently realized that years of antagonizing the party's professionals had virtually disqualified him from the nomination. Rockefeller's hand-picked choice to carry the standard of moderation was George Romney, the former president of American Motors and successful three-term governor of Michigan. Square-jawed and compassionate, a capitalist with a heart, Romney had everything except brains, the lack of which became all too evident in his public agonizing over Vietnam. Romney's murky pronouncements on the war required continuous and embarrassing qualifications—until he permanently destroyed his credibility in September 1967 by telling an interviewer that he had been "brainwashed" by the diplomats and soldiers who had briefed him in Vietnam two years before.[16] No one was more delighted than Nixon when, two months later, Romney formally announced his candidacy.

With Reagan immobilized and Romney self-destructing, Nixon prepared to erase his loser's image in the spring primaries. Entering the first of these in New Hampshire on February 3, he pledged to restore to America the "lift of a driving dream,"[17] a phrase whose emptiness forecast the character of his long campaign ahead. Nixon campaigned in New Hampshire primarily for television. On his second day in the state he slipped away from reporters to meet a carefully selected group of Republicans in the town hall of Hillsboro, there to answer friendly questions for a TV camera. Carefully edited to show the candidate at his relaxed and spontaneous best, tapes of this encounter were cut into five-minute segments and used to good effect not only in New Hampshire but in other primary states as well.[18]

Meanwhile, George Romney, Nixon's chief opponent, dashed energetically around the state, spending lots of Rockefeller's money and sinking steadily in the polls. Two weeks before the primary, Romney trailed Nixon so badly he quit the race. On election day, March 12, 1968, Eugene McCarthy captured more of the headlines, but Nixon, with 79 percent of the Republican vote, more of New Hampshire's voters.[19] By the time Nelson Rockefeller overcame his hesitation and became a candidate on April 30, 1968, he was too late to challenge Nixon in any of the remaining primaries. Virtually unopposed, therefore, Nixon waltzed through the primary states, rolling up huge majorities in each and apparently assuring his nomination on the first ballot at the Republican convention.

One consequence of running uncontested was that Nixon could frame the issues as he wished for the constituency he most coveted —the "decent," white, middle-class people who were growing daily more conservative and alienated. These were people who might have voted for Johnson in 1964 and might even have supported civil rights but who had been profoundly shocked by recent events—by students sneering at old values, by blacks rioting in the ghettos, by rising crime rates which made the streets a place of fear. Nixon appealed to these voters not by rousing their blood lust, as George Wallace was doing, but by posing as the experienced elder statesman and cultural square who would restore the lost American values. His goal was to align himself with the "forgotten" American without exacerbating national divisions. He wished to exploit fear but not provoke it. His intention was, in short, to capitalize on public resentments while saying as little of substance as possible. Nixon quickly embraced "law and order" as the issue best suited to his political purposes. A phrase splendid in its imprecision, law and order might intend as its targets students, blacks, criminals, or maybe all three. Let the hearer take his pick. Discussing crime, Nixon was at his demagogic worst. The solution to the problem, he argued, was not quadrupling funds for "any governmental war on poverty" but convicting more criminals. Lamenting the current low rate of convictions, he blamed both recent Supreme Court decisions safeguarding the rights of the accused and the Johnson administration, especially Attorney General Ramsey Clark, for being soft on crime. Wiretapping and more pay for police stood high on his list of remedies. Nixon's crowds were never more receptive than when he pledged, if elected, to support "the peace forces" in their struggle with the "criminal forces."[20] And who was he to deny the people what they most wanted to hear?

As for the issue of race, Nixon would have avoided it entirely if he could. But, after King's assassination, he reluctantly decided to attend the funeral and concluded that silence would no longer do. The task of writing his speech on race fell to Richard Whalen, a young intellectual on the campaign staff. For three days Whalen stared at a sheet of paper, trying to find words to express Nixon, to find "a felt presence behind the words in my typewriter." Finally admitting to himself that the essential Nixon "had eluded me," Whalen gave up.[21] The speech, written by somebody else and delivered early in May, proposed to help blacks not by breaking up the ghetto but by rebuilding it. This could be accomplished, Nixon argued, not by throwing more federal dollars at the poor but by encouraging private business to invest in black neighborhoods and to hire black workers. Let black people have "a piece of the action," let them attain ownership in black enterprises, and they would achieve black power based on black capitalism, he said.[22] This was a policy concoction which even political connoisseurs might admire. At one and the same time, Nixon expressed compassion for the oppressed, acquiesced in segregation, endorsed black power, and preached the virtues of free enterprise. This clever line on race would see him safely through the rest of the year.

A hawk among hawks for fifteen years, Nixon's biggest challenge as a candidate was the issue of the war. When the campaign began, he suffered the embarrassment of having a Vietnam position almost indistinguishable from Lyndon Johnson's. After Tet, he knew he would have to offer something different, which was why on March 5 at the American Legion Hall in Hampton, New Hampshire, he said, "I pledge to you the new leadership will end the war and win the peace in the Pacific."[23] His opponents, sensing a misstep, pounced immediately. Said Vice President Hubert Humphrey, "I think we have a right to ask: 'If you know how to end the war and bring the peace to the Pacific, Mr. Candidate, let the American people hear your formula now. Why wait until next year?' "[24] Reporters on the campaign trail were no less inquisitive and skeptical about Nixon's supposed secret plan to end the war. Nixon responded that he had no plan and, besides, it would be a mistake to give away his "bargaining positions in advance."[25] This satisfied no one. To still the clamor, he reluctantly commissioned Richard Whalen to write a major speech on Vietnam. Reviewing a draft, Nixon remarked to Whalen, "I've come to the conclusion that there's no way to win the war. But we can't say that, of course. In fact, we have to seem to say the opposite, just to keep some degree of bargaining leverage." Whalen winced, realizing that once again a presidential candidate would say one thing about Vietnam while believing quite another.[26]

Nixon scheduled his big Vietnam speech for 6:30 P.M., March 31, 1968. In it he intended to demand more reliance on political means to secure South Vietnam from subversion and to propose a path to peace leading through Moscow. If the Russians were offered "mutually advantageous cooperation," he believed, they would pressure North Vietnam into a reasonable settlement.[27] But the speech was never delivered. The day before he was to speak, he learned that Johnson also planned a speech the same night on the same subject. Johnson, of course, used that occasion to announce both his retirement and the partial bombing halt. The next day Nixon declared a two- or three-week moratorium on Vietnam to give Johnson's peace offensive time to work.[28] And later in the month he extended the moratorium for "as long as there is hope for successful negotiation."[29] To avoid undermining the American position by anything he said, he would say nothing, which was his elegant solution to the problem of how to duck entirely the year's most treacherous issue.

By the time Nixon wrapped up his last primary victory in Oregon on May 28, he had collected enough convention delegates to carry him to the threshold of the nomination—but not across it. It still remained possible that Reagan and Rockefeller, in covert and unholy alliance, could attract enough supporters between them to deny Nixon a convention majority. Everything hinged on the South. If rank-and-file delegates from the region followed their ideological inclinations and backed Reagan, Nixon would come up short.[30] But southern leaders, tired of lost causes, wanted for once to win. Nothing less than the nomination was at stake when Nixon met them for a conference in an Atlanta motel on May 31, 1968. In a three-hour meeting he said what he had to say to purchase their support—that he sympathized with their complaints against the Supreme Court, that he opposed busing to promote school desegregation, that he favored a strong national defense, and that he would divert a generous stream of patronage in their direction.

The next day South Carolina Senator Strom Thurmond flew in to join the discussions. A reactionary racist who had switched his allegiance from the Democrats to the Republicans in 1964, Thurmond was regarded by the fundamentalists of southern politics as a man of high principle. If Nixon bagged Strom, his prospects of staving off Reagan would be immeasurably improved. What Thurmond wanted was a pledge of support for an antiballistics-missile system. When Nixon gave it, Thurmond joined the team.[31] At the Republican National Convention—gaveled to order on August 5 in Miami Beach—Reagan did declare himself a candidate and did sorely tempt southern delegates; but thanks to the heroic exertions of Thurmond, abetted by Texas Senator John Tower and Goldwater himself, the South delivered enough votes to Nixon on the first ballot to secure him the prize. Indeed, Nixon's only mistake at Miami was to select as his running mate Maryland governor Spiro Agnew, a virtual unknown whose repeated gaffes during the fall campaign would acutely embarrass the ticket.

Nixon claimed to have spent two weeks writing his acceptance speech, though in fact it was merely a polished restatement of the speech he had been making all year.[32] He addressed it primarily to "the forgotten Americans—the non shouters, the non demonstrators. They're not racists or sick; they're not guilty of the crime that plagues the land. . . . They work in American factories, they run American businesses. They serve in government; they provide most of the soldiers who die to keep it free. They give drive to the spirit of America. They give lift to the American dream." He pledged to bring the war in Vietnam to an honorable end. He promised to combat crime by appointing an attorney general who would restore order and enforce the law. He resolved to pursue social justice not by "pouring billions of dollars into programs that have failed" but by enlisting "the greatest engine of progress ever developed in the history of man—American private enterprise."

Nearing his conclusion, he spoke feelingly of those American children who live a "nightmare of poverty, neglect and despair." But there was another part of America, he said, one represented by Nixon himself, a child reared in modest circumstances who had believed in the American dream and lived its vindication. "What I ask of you tonight," he declaimed, "is to help me make that dream come true for millions to whom it's an impossible dream today." It was a plea that would have been more persuasive had not Nixon so resolutely ignored the ghetto riot raging, even as he spoke, across the bay in Miami—a riot which would claim the lives of five black men who had been American children once and grown up to know the dream as a lie.

III

It improved Nixon's ultimate prospects immensely that the most likely Democratic nominee was Vice President Hubert Humphrey. As soon as Johnson withdrew, the party establishment—southern governors, big-city bosses, labor leaders, corporate contributors—rallied to Humphrey as the man best able to defend them from the insurgents gathering around the peace candidates.[33] Whether any-one else really wanted him was problematic. Once he had been a hero to the liberals—a legislator who fought with knowledge and passion for social justice and civil rights. But his stature had diminished in the vice presidency, not only because of the petty humiliations he endured at Johnson's hands, but because he became a shill for Johnson's war policies. Actually, Humphrey's views of the war were more complicated than they appeared, he having been one of the few members of the administration in 1965 privately to oppose escalation. As his reward Johnson had banished him from the inner circle and treated him with contempt.

In his relations with a president, Humphrey wrote in his memoirs, a vice president "has a choice between two relationships: acquiescence and hostility."[34] Humphrey soon chose acquiescence. In February 1966 Johnson sent him on a 43,000-mile, nine-nation trip to the Far East to promise victory over the Vietcong and a New Deal for Vietnam. Impressed by the private views of foreign heads of state that the U.S. must stay the course, Humphrey returned home to champion the war with all the fervor he had once lavished on better causes.[35] The more he defended the war, the more his erstwhile liberal friends wrote him off as a garrulous anachronism.

In November 1967 Humphrey experienced renewed doubts about Vietnam on a trip to Saigon, where he received some realistic briefings and observed first hand the extent and consequences of the war's Americanization. "I knew then," he wrote in his memoirs, "that the American people would not stand for this kind of involvement much longer."[36] But in 1968, as Johnson's legatee, how could he say so? And as a candidate for president, how could he win if he did not? He had yet to solve these riddles when on April 17, almost a month after Johnson's renunciation, he announced his candidacy before seventeen hundred cheering supporters in the ballroom of Washington's Shoreham Hotel. "Here we are, the way politics ought to be in America," he declared, "the politics of happiness, the politics of purpose and the politics of joy."[37] Spoken in a year of blood and gloom, these unfortunate words confirmed more effectively than anything his enemies could have said the inappropriateness of Hubert Humphrey. It did not matter. Even though he would enter no primaries, the party bosses still controlled enough convention votes to nominate him, and in all probability they would do so.

The only one of Humphrey's rivals with even a slight chance of stopping him was Robert F. Kennedy. Kennedy had no illusions about the task at hand. Only if he demonstrated overwhelming public support for his candidacy might he force the bosses to run him, and such support would not be easy to mobilize. It hurt Kennedy badly that he had waited until March 16—four days after McCarthy's strong showing against Johnson in the New Hampshire primary—to enter the race. Had he declared earlier, the party's peace wing would have been his. When McCarthy refused to bow out, Kennedy faced a fight not only with Johnson for control of the party but with McCarthy for control of the peace movement.

Running against Johnson in the last two weeks of March, Kennedy's campaign misfired.[38] There was no doubt that merely being a Kennedy—and one, at that, who had embraced his share of unpopular causes—he was a highly divisive figure. Now he seemed more divisive than ever. Frenzied crowds swarmed his motorcades, offering adulation ordinarily reserved for movie idols or religious prophets. Kennedy fed on the emotional energy he let loose, encouraged it, strained to match it with the intensity of his rhetoric.

At Kansas State University, speaking of Vietnam, he declared, "I am concerned that, at the end of it all, there will only be more Americans killed, more of our treasure spilled out, and because of the bitterness and hatred on every side of the war, more hundreds of thousands of Vietnamese slaughtered; so that they may say, as Tacitus said of Rome: 'They made a desert and called it peace.' " At Vanderbilt: "When we are told to forgo all dissent and division, we must ask—who is it that is truly dividing the country? It is not those who call for change, it is those who make present policy . . . who have removed themselves from the American tradition, from the enduring and generous impulses that are the soul of this nation." And in Los Angeles: "The failure of national purpose . . . is not simply the result of bad policies and lack of skill. It flows from the fact that for almost the first time the national leadership is calling upon the darker impulses of the American spirit—not, perhaps, deliberately, but through its action and the example it sets."[39] All true perhaps, but the tumult and the shouting played badly on the TV sets of those Americans, numbering in the millions, who had had their fill of emotion in the streets and impassioned political rhetoric.

Johnson's withdrawal on March 31 and the assassination of King four days later radically altered Kennedy's campaign. Overnight, black rage and white backlash replaced Johnson and Vietnam as the major national preoccupations. Kennedy immediately shifted from fist-pounding denunciation to earnest pleas for national reconciliation. After King's death, wrote journalist Jules Witcover, "the private Robert Kennedy that his closest friends professed him to be —not strident, not bombastic, but low-keyed and sensitive—increasingly emerged in his public life as a campaigner."[40] Alone among national politicians, Kennedy could walk through the streets of both white working-class and black neighborhoods and be warmly cheered in each. With these constituencies as his base, he began to reach out to the middle classes, not only by promising them "law and order," which he did, but by appealing to their conscience on behalf of the underclass. With a new tone and a new theme, he set out to defeat Eugene McCarthy in the four primaries that both had chosen to enter—Indiana, Nebraska, Oregon, and California.

Kennedy's great mistake was to underrate his opponent, for McCarthy was anything but the pushover he imagined. McCarthy had his own millions of admirers, many no less fervent in their well-bred way than Kennedy's.[41] To them, McCarthy was a man of mystery, a lonely figure who had dared to do a great deed and had done it without making deals, kissing babies, courting contributors, or compromising principle. He was the thinking man's candidate, more poet than politician, more concerned with integrity than image. Abigail McCarthy, the candidate's wife, aptly described his constituency as "academia united with the mobile society of scientists, educators, technologists and the new post-World War II college class."[42] McCarthy took pleasure in observing during the primary campaign that Kennedy was "running ahead of me among the less intelligent and less well-educated voters of the country."[43] Indeed, being for McCarthy was the latest variety of suburban chic. The campaign of no other candidate, for instance, could boast its own fashionable Manhattan boutique—McCarthy's Mart—where matrons from Westchester and Darien might purchase a 14-karat gold pin set with tiny red, white, and blue jewels and the senator's name lettered in gold—all for a mere one hundred dollars.[44]

But to know McCarthy well was not necessarily to love him. Most of his national campaign staff joined not because they were loyal to McCarthy but because they believed as he did about the issues. In time, some of them came to wonder whether he really wanted to be president, even whether he ought to be.[45] They saw the campaign as part of a movement to change America, watched in awe as the movement attained mass dimension, and hoped McCarthy's candidacy would become a vehicle to bring it to power. But the nominal leader refused to lead, even seemed bent in his perverse way on deflating his followers. He declined, except on rare occasions, to use the gift of his eloquence, discarded excellent speeches written by his writers, ignored the chaos that paralyzed his staff, and collected a retinue of sycophants who insulated him from the professional politicians and the ideologues. Jeremy Larner, one of his speech writers, later compared him to "certain athletes who would rather lose than go all-out to win. If one goes all out and loses, then one is without excuse."[46] McCarthy himself refused to throw much light on the endlessly debated topic of his motives. He said later, "What my intentions were . . . I think I knew better than some of the people who are telling what they were. And if I'm not saying what they were, why nobody knows."[47]

Though their views were similar on most issues, the two peace candidates did develop differences. And, despite Kennedy's reputation as the more radical of the two, it was McCarthy who strayed further from orthodoxy. He criticized the Cold War mentality that encouraged America to play "world judge and world policeman," attacked Kennedy for his "prominent role in formulating policies which resulted in disastrous adventures,"[48] and carried the liberal critique of the war closer to its logical conclusion. Both candidates called for a total bombing halt and for granting the National Liberation Front a role both at the peace talks and in South Vietnam's postwar political life. McCarthy was prepared to endorse in advance a coalition government including the National Liberation Front; Kennedy was not. More significantly, Kennedy was not really ready to abandon the American commitment, saying that if negotiations failed "then I think that we can take retaliatory action."[49] As the campaign proceeded, McCarthy edged closer to accepting disengagement. "I think," he said in mid-June, "the time has come when we must say we shall take our steel out of the land of thatched huts." If Saigon was unwilling to accept a coalition government as the price of peace, let her fight on alone.[50]

Even on the issue of race, it was McCarthy who took the risks. Like Nixon, Kennedy urged the reconstruction of the ghetto with the help of private enterprise. The difference was that Kennedy had for some time taken the idea seriously—so seriously that in 1966 he had induced a group of big businessmen to form an experimental corporation that channeled capital and expertise into a dilapidated Brooklyn slum called Bedford-Stuyvesant. For McCarthy, this was "apartheid." He proposed to disperse blacks out of the ghetto, not pour resources in. "I am disappointed by Senator Kennedy's overemphasis on rehabilitating the ghetto through private enterprise . . ." he said. "The ghetto may have a few more factories and a few more jobs, but it will remain a colony, it will retain its economic and political dependence." He wanted to build "new towns" on the edge of central cities so that poor people could move where the jobs were.[51] But, despite his vision of a desegregated society, McCarthy failed to shake Kennedy's hold on the black masses. The fault was partly his own. He seemed uncomfortable before black audiences, campaigned rarely in black neighborhoods, and made no effort to counter the growing impression that he lacked "compassion." Once, before a short visit to Watts, Jeremy Larner prepared a statement for the candidate on jobs and welfare. "Are you kidding?" McCarthy's valet exclaimed, "Those people can't read. They'll *eat* your press release!"[52]

The first primaries of May went as expected, Kennedy defeating McCarthy handily in Indiana and Nebraska. Said McCarthy of Indiana, "They keep talking about 'the poet' out there. I asked if they were talking about Shakespeare or even my friend Robert Lowell. But it was James Whitcomb Riley. You could hardly expect to win under those circumstances."[53] After Nebraska, where McCarthy lost to Kennedy by 21 percentage points, Kennedy's press secretary Pierre Salinger dismissed the Minnesota senator as "no longer a credible candidate."[54] But the next stop was Oregon, a state with so few blacks and poor people that it was akin to a giant suburb and resistant to Kennedy's appeal. "If I get beaten in a primary, I'm not a viable candidate . . ." Kennedy said on May 21. "I'd return to being unruthless if I lose in Oregon."[55] A week later McCarthy defeated Kennedy 45 percent to 39 percent.[56] It was the first time any Kennedy had ever lost an election.

Kennedy was so badly hurt by Oregon that he entered California for the climactic June 4th primary fighting for his political life. McCarthy's stature, on the other hand, increased so dramatically after Oregon that victory in California now seemed within grasp. Kennedy's hopes relied on a big vote from the ghettos and the *barrios*, which he stumped with the fervor of the campaign's early days.[57] McCarthy's strength resided in the thousands of volunteers working out of some 150 local headquarters, phoning, leafleting, canvassing for peace.[58] McCarthy had the momentum—until he met Kennedy for a face-to-face televised debate on the Saturday before election day. Kennedy was widely judged the winner of this dull affair, mainly because McCarthy was so bored he let Kennedy seize and hold the offensive.[59] The myth of his special powers punctured, McCarthy was denied the upset in the election he might otherwise have achieved. The margin of Kennedy's victory in California was too small for real vindication: Kennedy 46.3 percent; McCarthy 41.8 percent; Attorney General Thomas Lynch, running as a pro-administration favorite son, 11.9 percent.[60] But, by the time the tally was complete, nobody cared. Minutes after his victory statement in the ballroom of the Hotel Ambassador in Los Angeles, Robert Fitzgerald Kennedy was fatally shot in a hallway by a fanatic Arab nationalist named Sirhan Sirhan.

Of all the candidates in 1968, Kennedy would probably have made the best president. Like his last campaign, his career had not been without its flaws, but as those who knew Kennedy best could testify, he had qualities, including energy, intelligence, courage, and compassion, that might have made him an extraordinary leader. Qualification for office, however, did not assure its attainment, indeed, would not even have assured Kennedy's nomination. The narrowness of his win in California, the ambush that McCarthy's supporters were preparing for him in the upcoming New York primary, the declared preference of 70 percent of the party's county chairmen for Humphrey[61]—all these made his eventual nomination unlikely. But political emotions were unusually volatile in 1968, and the traumatic events surrounding the Democratic convention would shake the fragile foundations of Humphrey's candidacy. As those who mourned Kennedy most deeply could never forget, if he had lived, anything might have happened.

After Kennedy's death McCarthy never recovered what little zest he had had for the contest. Jeremy Larner recalled his demeanor the night before he was supposed to resume campaigning. "McCarthy was shocking: deep hollows cut under his eyes, his face ravaged and grim—as if he hadn't slept for a week." When someone asked whether he felt guilty about Kennedy, McCarthy said no. "Of course he feels guilty," Larner thought to himself. "What else would do that to him?"[62] Even the New York primary on June 18 did not improve his mood, though he won 62 delegates, compared to 30 for the martyred Kennedy, a mere 12 for Humphrey, and 19 uncommitted.[63]

McCarthy received conflicting advice from those who believed he might still win the nomination. Some urged him to spend the summer organizing grassroots support to stampede the delegates in his direction. Others advised him to seek out the delegates and assure them he was not a renegade trying to destroy the party.[64] Typically McCarthy did both, but neither with enthusiasm. He gave spiritless speeches before vast throngs in a number of cities, and he met with state delegations whom he made little effort to persuade. In truth, he knew, if his advisers did not, that the big crowds he drew and the polls showing him running much better than Humphrey against Nixon counted for nothing.[65] The party bosses would never turn to him. As the convention approached, he felt premonitions of disaster. Issuing a statement two weeks before the delegates convened in Chicago, he urged his followers to stay home lest they unintentionally increase the tension in the city and the possibilities of disorder. "This would be a tragedy," McCarthy said, "—a personal tragedy for any hurt or arrested and a tragedy for those of us who wish to give the political process a fair and peaceful test."[66] That he himself expected the test to fail he did not say.

IV

During convention week, August 25–29, 1968, armies of the right and left gathered for battle over the corpse of the Democratic party. Chicago, wrote journalist J. Anthony Lukas, was "the perfect city for the elemental clash."[67] Weened on violence, still raw and muscular, Chicago had in Richard Daley a mayor skilled in the arts of accommodation when it suited his purpose but itching to use clubs against any demonstrator who might disturb the tranquility of his convention. Daley knew that if push came to shove, the great mass of white Chicagoans who bathed, prayed, and pledged allegiance to the flag would back him all the way. Had they not backed him after the black riots in April when he implicitly rebuked his police for their forbearance by issuing his famous order to shoot looters? And a few weeks later, had they not approved when the police, taking his admonitions to heart, wantonly attacked 6,500 peace demonstrators and bystanders at the Civic Center[68]—in obvious dress rehearsal for August? Indeed, the most formidable of the armies at the Battle of Chicago was Daley's army—12,000 policemen, 5,000 National Guardsmen, and 6,000 federal troops on alert at nearby naval stations[69]—the army of the right, ready to meet protest with undisguised repression.

The left knew almost from the moment in October 1967, when the Democrats announced the convention site, that it would go to Chicago. Fresh from their successes at the Pentagon, dissident leaders envisioned hundreds of thousands of angry citizens storming the convention hall to denounce the war and the renomination of Lyndon B. Johnson. Not surprisingly, since the left by now was a many-splendored thing, the impulse to go to Chicago took a variety of forms.

There was, first of all, Yippie!, a hallucination conjured up by two anarchists named Abbie Hoffman and Jerry Rubin, soon to become national celebrities. Handsome, curly-haired, and a little bit crazy, Hoffman had cut his teeth as a radical in Berkeley and SNCC before moving into the hippie community on New York's Lower East Side, *circa* 1967. There Hoffman intended to pioneer a new type of radical —the political hippie—devoted to creating a paradise of dope and sex through revolution. This "action freak and anti-intellectual," as he described himself, turned the streets of New York into a theater for the performance of "monkey" (as opposed to guerrilla) warfare —actions so outrageous and absurd that the news media would be conned into carrying their subversive message free to the masses. Hoffman and friends exploded soot bombs in the offices of Con Edison, plastered "SEE CANADA NOW" signs on the Army Recruiting Center in Times Square, parked a giant Yellow Submarine in a tow-away zone, and sent thousands running through the streets one night to hug people, throw confetti, and shout, "The war is over!" Hoffman's guerrillas shot water pistols at tuxedoed guests arriving at the Waldorf-Astoria to hear Dean Rusk. They went to the 1967 Pentagon demonstration dressed like witches to try to levitate the evil five-sided structure. And in their most famous prank they once threw dollar bills off the balcony of the Stock Exchange, causing a near riot among the scrambling brokers below. Hoffman's antics were not infrequently tinged with menace, with the hint of violence. "Personally," he wrote later, "I always held my flower in a clenched fist."[70]

Hoffman teamed up with Rubin in the fall of 1967 when Rubin came east to help organize the Pentagon march. Rubin was already famous on the left—the *enfant terrible* who had stopped a troop train in Oakland, won 22 percent of the vote in a 1966 campaign for mayor of Berkeley, and disoriented the House Un-American Activities Committee by appearing before it dressed in the costume of an American Revolutionary War soldier.[71] "Just as Che needed Fidel and Costello needed Abbot, Jerry Rubin and I were destined to join forces," Hoffman wrote later. ". . . We both had a willingness to go beyond reason."[72] Hoffman took care of theater; Rubin supplied the political judgment. On New Year's Eve 1968, lying stoned on pillows in a Lower East Side flat, Hoffman, Rubin, *Realist* editor Paul Krassner, and girlfriends contemplated their political condition. Rubin recalled the conversation in his book *DO iT!*[73]

> It's a *youth* revolution.
> *Gimme* a "Y."
> It's an *international* revolution.
> *Gimme* an "I."
> It's people trying to have meaning, fun, ecstasy in their lives—a *party*.
> *Gimme* a "P."
> Whattayou got?
> *Youth International Party.*
> Paul Krassner jumped to his feet and shouted:
> "*YIP-pie. We're yippies!*"

What was a Yippie? "A flower child who's been busted," wrote Hoffman. "A stoned-out warrior of the Aquarian Age. 'What's a yippie?' they would ask. 'A yippie is someone going to Chicago.'"[74]

Yippie! was not a movement, just a myth of Chicago propagated by a pair of Jewish comedians with the aid of sympathetic organizers spread through the counterculture. Yippies would hold a Festival of Life in Chicago while the Democrats were holding their convention of death. Lured by a score of rock bands, hundreds of thousands of kids would flock to the convention city, nominate a pig for president, and run him on the slogan "They nominate a president and he eats the people. We nominate a president and the people eat him."[75] The Yippies threatened to float ten thousand nude bodies on Lake Michigan, pick up delegates in fake cabs and drop them off in Wisconsin, dress up as bellboys and seduce delegates' wives, wear Vietcong pajamas and give out free rice in the streets.[76] The press loved these crazies; frightened officials took their wildest fantasies literally; and the myth of Yippie grew. But within the counterculture critics began to suspect that Hoffman and Rubin would not be especially unhappy if the police transformed the festival into a riot, plunging both Chicago and the convention into chaos.

Rubin and Hoffman were not the only dissidents going to Chicago. That portion of the left still committed to linear thought and serious politics was making plans of its own. Responsibility for organizing a giant convention protest against the war and racism belonged to the National Mobilization Committee to End the War in Vietnam, popularly known as the Mobe. A coalition of some one hundred antiwar groups, the Mobe had turned out hundreds of thousands for the Spring Mobilization in April 1967, and handled the arrangements for the March on the Pentagon six months later. As early as November 1967 the Mobe had begun targeting Chicago as the site of its next great witness. To coordinate a demonstration, Mobe chairman David Dellinger, a veteran pacifist and editor of *Liberation* magazine, chose Tom Hayden and Rennie Davis. These two ex-SDS leaders based their initial planning on the premise that the Republicans would nominate Nixon, the Democrats would nominate Johnson, and the unrepresented antiwar masses would be straining by August toward higher levels of militance.[77] The problem was that by early 1968 the Mobe coalition was falling apart. Antiwar liberals merely wanted a parade, some new left groups preferred various sorts of civil disobedience, and radicals on the fringe openly espoused violence. The Mobe attempted to solve the problem of disunity by proposing decentralized movement centers where everybody coming to Chicago could do what he wanted. The climax of the demonstrations would occur on the night of Johnson's nomination, when all the protesters in the city would converge for a massive "funeral march" on the convention hall.[78]

Within the Mobe itself, the role of violence was discussed endlessly. It bothered Dellinger, a pacifist on principle, that his two coordinators seemed in a mood to tolerate it.[79] Minutes of a meeting in January 1968 reported Hayden saying that we "should have people organized who can fight the police, people who are willing to get arrested. . . . My thinking is not to leave the initiative to the police. . . . Don't want to get into the trap of violence vs. passive action."[80] In the end the Mobe decided that demonstrations should be peaceful and that acts of civil disobedience would not be designed to disrupt the convention's proceedings. Dellinger told the press, "We are not going to storm the convention with tanks and mace. But we are going to storm the hearts and minds of the American people."[81]

On March 23–24, 1968, at a retreat in Lake Villa, Illinois, two hundred representatives of the Yippies, black power organizations, and other dissident groups met at the Mobe's invitation to see if the entire left could march in Chicago under a single banner.[82] The meeting was a fiasco. Bored by the heavy political rhetoric, Rubin and Hoffman confounded the other delegates by advancing the abolition of pay toilets as a key revolutionary demand and proclaiming the slogan, "Abandon the Creeping Meatball, Come to Chicago."[83] On pulling out of the conference, they announced that Yippies would go to the convention alone. Black militant groups, for their part, regarded a convention protest as irrelevant to their concerns and eventually decided not to go at all.

Other setbacks followed Lake Villa. A week later President Johnson disappointed radical expectations by refusing to run and by commencing the process of de-escalation. The candidacies of Kennedy and McCarthy, meanwhile, had dulled the edge of radical desperation that had once made a convention demonstration seem so necessary. And from Chicago bad vibrations emanated as Daley prepared to smash heads. If Kennedy's assassination had not assured the nomination of Johnson's surrogate, Hubert Humphrey, the Yippies would probably have canceled the Festival of Life. Even so, the excitement that had charged planning for Chicago earlier in the year was never recovered.

As the convention neared, Daley kept the demonstrators off balance by dragging out negotiations for permits to legalize their protests. Without a permit the Yippies could not stay in Lincoln Park past 11 P.M., the bands would not come to the Festival of Life, and the kids would have no place to sleep. When Hoffman realized in early August that no permit would be forthcoming, he announced that the Festival would proceed anyway and the curfew would be defied. The Mobe fared no better, Chicago officials ultimately refusing it permission to march in the vicinity of the convention on the evening of the presidential nominations.[84] Not surprisingly, Dellinger would decide to march anyway. *The Chicago Seed,* a local hippie paper, warned potential demonstrators, "If you're coming to Chicago, be sure to wear some armor in your hair." The *Seed*'s advice to the peaceably inclined was to stay home.[85]

"My God!" groaned Tom Hayden on Saturday, August 24, the day when hundreds of thousands were supposed to arrive, "There's nobody here!"[86] In fact, at no time during the week were there more than five thousand out-of-town protesters on the streets and no more than ten thousand total.[87] Having intimidated the movement by his implied threats and having assembled force more than adequate to defend the city, Daley might have relented and let the disappointed few have their festivals and parades. But, out of stupidity or hate, he proceeded toward the confrontation which, more than the mass of demonstrators, he really wanted.

The week-long Battle of Chicago occurred on a seven-mile line running north-south along the shores of Lake Michigan. To the north the Yippies held their Festival of Life in Lincoln Park adjacent to the hippie community in a section called Old Town. Two miles south the Mobe held its rallies and made its speeches in elegant Grant Park across the street from the Hilton Hotel, the main head-quarters of the convention. And at the line's southern terminus the Democrats assembled in the Chicago Amphitheater, an unfortunate structure too small comfortably to hold the 6,511 delegates and alternates[88] and so close to the stockyards that foul odors per-meated its every corner.

From the outset the convention mood was gloomy. It was not merely that McCarthy's troops knew they were beaten, or that Hum-phrey's loyalists, dismayed by the latest Gallup poll showing their man trailing Nixon by sixteen points, believed he was beaten too. As much as anything, it was the depressing thoroughness of Daley's security precautions, which lent the proceedings the atmosphere of a police state. A seven-foot barbed-wire fence nearly surrounded the Amphitheater. Bulletproof panels protected the building en-trance. Manhole covers outside were sealed with tar to foil sabo-teurs. Fifteen hundred policemen were in the convention's vicinity, some with rifles stationed on nearby roofs, some in helicopters hovering overhead.[89] Inside the hall, omnipresent security men policed the aisles, frequently harassing antiwar delegations rele-gated to the far reaches of the hall. Allard Lowenstein, convention delegate from New York and candidate for Congress, was·refused entrance to one session until he surrendered his copy of the *New York Times*.[90] Alex Rosenberg, leader of Manhattan's largest Demo-cratic reform club, was dragged from the aisles when he protested an order to quit conversing. For his persistence in covering Rosen-berg's arrest, CBS reporter Mike Wallace got slugged in the jaw by a cop. "I wasn't sentenced and sent here!" Rosenberg thundered. "I was elected."[91]

Even conservative delegates were not entirely out of sympathy with the desire of the demonstrators to "Dump the Hump." A forlorn figure ignored by the convention's managers, Humphrey remained wholly dependent for his chances on the fickle mood of Lyndon Johnson. As the convention neared, Humphrey had reason to wonder whether Johnson did not, after all, want the nomination for himself. Publicly, the president said little to help Humphrey; privately, he made remarks that disparaged him. "He cries too much," Johnson told one reporter. Asked for clarification, he repeated, "That's it—he cries too much."[92] Johnson meantime was hatching a secret plan for a flight to Moscow and a summit meeting with Soviet premier Aleksei Kosygin. Presumably bearing agreements to further world peace, he would return in time to make a triumphal appearance before the convention, with what consequences no one could say. But on August 20 Russian troops invaded Czechoslovakia, bringing that wayward satellite to heel and incidentally forcing Johnson to cancel his trip.[93] Even so, southern delegates angry at Humphrey for supporting reform of the party's rules, threatened to bolt the vice president and run Johnson in his stead. It did not happen, of course. The president was so unpopular at this convention that his picture was nowhere in evidence, few speakers mentioned his name, and plans for a surprise visit to the delegates on his birthday had to be canceled for fear he would be booed off the platform.[94]

One reason the South held ranks for Humphrey was its fear of Edward "Ted" Kennedy. A few days before the convention opened, Kennedy ended two and a half months of seclusion following his brother's death with a televised speech promising to "pick up a fallen standard" and urging a quick peace in Vietnam to "extricate our men and our future from this bottomless pit."[95] It did not matter that at age thirty-six Kennedy was too inexperienced for the presidency and deeply ambivalent about seeking it. He was the heir of the Kennedy legend, and powerful men now implored him to run. Among them was—of all people—Mayor Daley, who privately wanted the U.S. out of Vietnam and feared for local Democratic candidates if Humphrey headed the ticket. On Saturday, August 24, Daley secretly phoned Kennedy and asked him to accept a draft. During the next few days Kennedy's agents worked hard to make a draft happen—in the process creating the only genuine excitement of the convention. But on Tuesday evening Kennedy called Daley and unequivocally declined to be a candidate. Kennedy acted because he did not trust a private offer from McCarthy to withdraw in his favor, because Humphrey's support stayed firm, and perhaps because, like others, he suspected that Daley might be trying to trap him into declaring for president so that he could not decline nomination for vice president. With Kennedy's exit, Humphrey became inevitable.[96]

On the whole, it was a bad week for dissidents, whether in the convention hall or on the street. For the Yippies, real trouble began on Sunday afternoon, August 25, convention eve, when the police refused to permit a flatbed truck into Lincoln Park for a scheduled rock concert. "Pig, pig, fascist pig!" the enraged young shouted. "Pigs eat shit!" By nightfall knots of dispirited demonstrators were huddled around small bonfires, bereft of direction or purpose. It was the police who saved the Festival of Life by issuing an order at 10:30 P.M. to leave the park. Hundreds of those who did charged excitedly through the streets, yelling antiwar slogans and skirmishing with policemen. Those remaining, perhaps one thousand in all, suffered the wrath of the cops, who moved in around midnight to impose their version of law and order. In addition to lots of kids, they clubbed reporters and photographers from *Newsweek*, *Life*, and the Associated Press. On Monday and Tuesday nights, while McCarthy was losing a string of credentials fights on the convention floor, police and Yippies continued the battle of Lincoln Park.[97]

Wednesday, August 28. The afternoon session of the convention featured a platform debate over Vietnam that Hubert Humphrey had hoped to avoid and believed need never have occurred.[98] Before the convention representatives of Humphrey and Ted Kennedy had painstakingly negotiated a compromise plank on the war designed to appease Senator McCarthy without antagonizing Lyndon Johnson. Though offering the peace wing less than it wanted, the compromise did satisfy its one irreducible demand by recommending a total and unconditional bombing halt. McCarthy was apparently satisfied. If Johnson acceded also, the great schism in the party might be repaired. Humphrey personally cleared the language with Secretary of State Dean Rusk and the president's hawkish national security adviser, Walt Whitman Rostow. But on the morning of the convention's first session Humphrey learned that Johnson would tolerate no deviation from his current hard line. Distraught, Humphrey called the president for an explanation. "Well," he recalled Johnson saying, "this plank just undercuts our whole policy and, by God, the Democratic party ought not to be doing that to me."[99] Humphrey acquiesced rather than risk loss of the nomination, though years later, regretting his lack of fortitude, he remarked, "I should have stood my ground."[100]

So there were two Vietnam planks, a majority plank consistent with Johnson's policies, and a minority plank that now called not only for a bombing halt but for immediate de-escalation of hostilities to permit "an early withdrawal of a significant number of our troops."[101] By a vote of 1,567 to 1,041 the Johnson-Humphrey majority plank prevailed. As the tally concluded, a priest knelt on the convention floor and prayed for peace. McCarthy delegates put on black armbands and chanted "Stop the war." And peace delegates from New York sang chorus after doleful chorus of "We Shall Overcome."[102] It was by now late afternoon. Senator McCarthy, who had declined to go to the convention to make the case for the peace plank in person, looked from his room in the Hilton at the crowd of protesters gathering below. "The worst thing about what's happening," he said, "is that it leaves these kids nowhere to go."[103]

The action on the streets had by now moved from Lincoln Park to Grant Park, from the Yippies to the Mobe. Later that evening, while Humphrey was being nominated, the Mobe was supposed to lead a mass march on the Amphitheater. Now, as the afternoon's Vietnam debate droned on in the convention hall, ten thousand demonstrators attended a rally at the bandshell in Grant Park, several blocks from the Hilton. This meeting was legal and orderly— until a kid climbed a pole to lower the American flag. Police dragging the offender away were bombarded with everything from eggs and chunks of concrete to balloons filled with paint and urine. In retaliation the cops regrouped, charged into the peaceful mass of the crowd, and flailed away.[104] Tom Hayden was so enraged at the police for opening up a three-inch gash in the head of his friend Rennie Davis that he urged the people to form small groups and go into the street "to do what they have to do."[105] Allen Ginsberg, by contrast, tried to calm the crowd by leading it in the Hindu chant of "OM," which, he said would "quell flutterings of butterflies in the belly."[106] "So as the policemen looked out in astonishment through their Plexiglass face shields," the *New York Times* reported, "the huge throng chanted . . . 'om, om,' sending deep mystic reverberations off the glass office towers along Michigan Avenue."[107]

At 4:30 P.M. David Dellinger announced that, permit or no permit, he was marching on the Amphitheater. Those who chose to accompany him should understand that his march would be nonviolent. All others, he said, ought to make their statement elsewhere. Perhaps five thousand demonstrators fell in behind him to await the outcome of the final negotiations for a parade permit. When none was granted, the police moved to break up the line of march. For an hour, demonstrators milled about, desperately seeking exit bridges unguarded by police or National Guardsmen—their destination, the section of Grant Park fronting the Hilton where two thousand other protesters were awaiting them. At last an unprotected bridge was located, and demonstrators poured across it onto Michigan Avenue, four blocks north of the Hilton. It was 7:14 P.M.[108] Gas from the park, carried by an errant breeze, drifted into the twenty-fifth floor of the hotel, bringing tears to the eyes of Hubert Humphrey on the night that was supposed to be the happiest of his life.[109]

At 7:57 P.M., this was the scene. An improbable ragtag army of 4,500 Yippies, Mobe radicals, and short-haired McCarthy supporters were crowding into the intersection of Michigan and Balbo at the northeast corner of the Hilton Hotel. One line of police blocked their path south to the Amphitheater, another cut off a possible retreat north on Michigan Avenue, and still another was moving at a rapid pace down Balbo, clubs at the ready. Though it was dusk, the glare of television lights made the streets as bright as midday. On the sidewalks people were chanting, "The whole world is watching. The whole world is watching." Safe in the hotel high above the battlefield, the liberal leadership of the Democratic party watched in helpless horror as two visions of America prepared for the physical clash. Police removed their badges and charged, swinging with bloody malice at protesters, medics, and bystanders alike, shouting, "Kill, kill, kill."[110] Norman Mailer described the scene as he saw it from his room at the Hilton: "The police attacked with tear gas, with Mace, and with clubs, they attacked like a chain saw cutting into wood, the teeth of the saw the edge of their clubs, they attacked like a scythe through grass, lines of twenty and thirty policemen striking out in an arc, their clubs beating, demonstrators fleeing. Seen from overhead, from the nineteenth floor, it was like a wind blowing dust, or the edge of waves riding foam on the shore."[111] At 8:05, as the crowd scattered down side streets with police in pursuit, the journalist Theodore White scribbled into his notebook, "The Democrats are finished."[112]

Meantime, at the Amphitheater, bored delegates listened to the nominating speeches, unaware of the carnage at the Hilton—until the first filmed reports flashed on TV monitors around the hall at 9:30 P.M. Infuriated peace delegates immediately began to shout for adjournment. On the podium to nominate George McGovern, a late-entering antiwar candidate, Connecticut Senator Abraham Ribicoff stared down at Mayor Daley not twenty feet away. "With George McGovern we wouldn't have Gestapo tactics on the streets of Chicago," the usually circumspect senator declared. There was a pause, and then the Illinois delegation leaped to its feet, booing and waving clenched fists. Purple with rage, Daley pointed a finger at Ribicoff and, in full view of the TV audience, shouted something that amateur lip readers translated as "Fuck you. You Jew son of a bitch!" Looking the mayor straight in the eye, Ribicoff retorted, "How hard it is to accept the truth. How hard it is."[113] It seemed the least important fact of the evening that Hubert Humphrey won the Democratic nomination on the first ballot.

On Thursday, the convention's last day, the delegates nominated the respected Maine Senator Edmund Muskie for vice president. In the afternoon Eugene McCarthy crossed from the Hilton into the park and spoke to the protesters, whom he called "the government in exile." He quoted them a verse of Robert Lowell's:

> Only man thinning out his kind
> sounds through the Sabbath noon, the blind
> swipe of the pruner and his knife
> busy about the tree of life. . . .

"We can turn back from that and make our nation . . . one of hope and one of trust in our fellow men . . ." he said. "I do not think many of us will remain afraid of those billion Chinese with whom we have been threatened by Dean Rusk. . . . We do not have to worry about it—not to be afraid, not to be threatened, not to live in a Kafka-like burrow in which we can always hear, if we listen closely, some kind of scratching sound. The idea of defense and of more defense, missiles and then antiballistic missiles and then antiantiballistic missiles, to infinity—this has never been the attitude or spirit of this country, when we were doing what we should do."[114] It was a better speech than the intellectually threadbare offering that Humphrey delivered that night in accepting the nomination.[115] McCarthy did not appear on the podium with the nominee or make the customary loser's pledge of support. It did nothing to diminish his bitterness that at five o'clock Friday morning, on flimsy pretext, police invaded his headquarters on the Hilton's fifteenth floor and beat up his young workers.[116]

If winners can be said to have emerged from Chicago, Rubin and Hoffman were among them. Years later Rubin confessed that he had secretly agreed with the government when in March 1969 it indicted him, along with Hoffman, Hayden, Davis, Dellinger, Bobby Seale, and two others, for conspiring to riot in Chicago. "We wanted exactly what happened," he wrote. "We wanted the tear gas to get so heavy that the reality was tear gas. We wanted to create a situation in which the Chicago police and the Daley administration and the federal government and the United States would self-destruct. We wanted to show that America wasn't a democracy, that the convention wasn't politics. The message of the week was of an America ruled by force. This was a big victory."[117]

The biggest loser at Chicago was Humphrey. A divided convention had nominated him without enthusiasm, and his performance during the week only confirmed the impression of his political irrelevance. It was time, he said two days after the convention, to "quit pretending that Mayor Daley did anything that was wrong."[118] As effervescent as always in public, privately he returned to his home in Waverly, Minnesota, more deeply depressed than at any time in his career. "I was a victim of that convention as much as a man getting the Hong Kong flu," he said. "I felt when we left that convention we were in an impossible situation. I could've beaten the Republicans any time—but it's difficult to take on the Republicans and fight a guerrilla war in your own party at the same time. Chicago was a catastrophe. My wife and I went home heartbroken, battered, and beaten."[119]

V

There was at least one man in America besides Rubin not displeased by the Battle of Chicago. He was George Corley Wallace, the wild card in a deck of the candidates, whose third-party presidential campaign in 1968 made the calculations of his two main rivals problematic. Surveying the wreckage of the Democratic convention, Wallace declared that the police had "probably showed too much restraint" and that the chaos in the streets had "put us in an excellent position" to win the election.[120] As usual, the angry little man from Alabama correctly intuited the nation's darker impulses, if not his own election prospects. Despite outraged media coverage of Daley's performance, the majority of the American people did indeed approve the thrashing his police had administered to the spoiled children of the privileged classes. A nationwide poll taken immediately after the Chicago riots revealed that 71 percent of the public regarded the city's security measures as justified, while 57 percent held that the police and national guard had not used excessive force.[121] As Wallace believed, there existed a vast public alienated by rapid racial and cultural change and edging toward political revolt. It was this alienation, this upsurge in popular illiberalism, which Wallace intended to exploit in his bid for national power.

A hero to the white South since he had physically tried to block the admission of black students into the University of Alabama in 1963, Wallace first demonstrated his appeal to northern voters in 1964 by strong showings in the Democratic primaries of Wisconsin, Indiana, and Maryland. He knew then that his true vocation was running for president. The major impediment to his ambition, as he looked forward to 1968, was an Alabama state law barring a governor from succeeding himself. He needed contributions and kickbacks from state contractors to underwrite his political expenses, and he needed state jobs for his cronies to maintain the semblance of a political organization. So in 1966 when his four-year term ended, he ran his wife Lurleen, a former dime-store clerk and political innocent for the office. Winning in a landslide, she appointed her husband as her "Number One Adviser" in the Alabama Military Department.[122] In truth, he was the de facto governor of the state. By the time George formally announced for the presidency on February 8, 1968, Lurleen was dying of cancer.[123] But by then he had been running so long and so hard nationwide that he had ceased to be solely dependent on Alabama's resources. "Governor Lurleen," as she was affectionately called in Alabama, died on May 7, 1968.[124] Four weeks later, "Governor George" was back on the hustings.

It did not much matter that Wallace's Alabama advisers were novices at the game of national politics. The real Wallace campaign existed at the grassroots level. With Klansmen, Birchers, Minutemen, and even members of the American Nazi party often playing conspicuous roles,[125] Wallace organizations sprouted spontaneously nearly everywhere, making possible the year's greatest tri-

umph for participatory democracy—the presence of Wallace electors on the ballot in every one of the fifty states. Wallace's strategy
was no more sophisticated than his organization. He knew he could
not win. But he did hope to carry so many southern and border
states that he could prevent either of the major-party candidates
from securing a majority of the "Electoral College," as he liked to
call it.[126] Then he could sit back and wait for Humphrey or Nixon
to offer a deal for his electors. If that happened, the self-proclaimed
redneck candidate would have created the Republic's worst constitutional crisis in a hundred years.

Though his presidential bid was anchored in the South, Wallace
campaigned hardest in the North, not so much to carry it as to prove
again that the redneck vote knew no regional boundaries and to lay
the groundwork for 1972. Some of his northern support came from
the middle classes—from ultra-conservative Republicans who had
backed Goldwater in 1964.[127] But Wallace pitched his appeal less
to affluent rightists than to factory workers and service employees
located toward the lower end of the status spectrum—the people he
called the "average man in the street, this man in the textile mill,
this man in the steel mill, this barber, the beautician, the policeman
on the beat."[128] The stereotypical Wallace voter was a bullet-
headed third-generation Polish steelworker in Gary, Indiana, fearful
of Negroes trying to marry his daughter and driving a pickup truck
with a bumper sticker reading, "America, love it or leave it." "I
speak better 'Polish' than any of the other candidates," Wallace
quipped.[129]

To win the northern blue-collar vote, Wallace avoided overt racism and ran as a populist voicing the social resentments of the lower
classes and defending their economic interests. "I've never made a
racist speech in my life," he brazenly asserted.[130] Though economics was peripheral to his campaign, he would point, when the need
arose, to his moderately liberal social-welfare record as governor
and to his third-party platform, which endorsed labor unions and
even contemplated a possible public-works program to provide employment for all who wanted it.[131] Mostly, of course, his appeal
rested on his naked hatred for long hair, hippies, rioters, students
flying Vietcong flags, and any citizen whose standard of patriotism
did not require whole-hearted support for our boys in Vietnam.

Wallace pursued the presidency like a traveling tent preacher,
performing the same show in a different city every night.[132] His

meetings featured the Taylor sisters (Mona and Lisa) singing Dixie, lacquered blondes taking up the collection, and a Protestant minister thanking Christ for Wallace. Then, to thunderous cheers, the great man himself would bound to his bullet-proof podium and begin to recite the best of the applause lines he had been honing for years. Head bobbing, fists chopping, he would denounce the "over-educated, ivory-tower folks with pointed heads looking down their noses at us."[133] Who were the "pseudo-intellectuals" leading the country down the wrong path? They were the "bearded professor who thinks he knows how to settle the Vietnam war when he hasn't got sense enough to park a bicycle straight."[134] They were the Washington bureaucrats who wrote guidelines forcing people to bus their little children all over creation. They were federal judges who tied the hands of the police while putting criminals back on the street. He knew how to handle all these "sissy britches,"[135] yes he did. He'd call in the bureaucrats, "take away their briefcases and throw them in the Potomac River."[136] He'd put popular checks on federal judges, and he'd stop the breakdown of "law n order" by letting the police run the country for about two years.[137] He reminded his audience that down in Alabama, if any professor advocated revolution, "he's a *fired* professor."[138] Maybe we should never have gone into Vietnam, he conceded, but if he was president, he'd ask the Joint Chiefs if the war could be won with conventional weapons, and if it could, he'd let them go in and win it quick![139] "Some scum," he would say, had tried to lie down in front of the president's car in California. "When we get to be President and some anarchist lies down in front of our car, it'll be the *last* car he'll ever lie down in front of."[140] That line or one like it could always be counted on to provoke furious chants from the hostile demonstrators who followed him everywhere. Juices flowing, TV cameras rolling, this was the moment in the show that Wallace liked best, the moment when the divisions he was trying to exploit became corporeal. "You can come up here and I'll autograph your sandals," he would sneer.[141] "These are the folks that people in our country are getting sick and tired of. You'd better have your day now because after November, I tell you, you are through."[142] Once at a rally in Madison Square Garden, the police so successfully kept out demonstrators that Wallace's aides secretly provided them a hundred tickets to guarantee a confrontation.[143] Did he get mad at the demonstrators? people would ask. Get mad at them? Wallace would reply.

"Why, they got me half a million votes!"[144]

When the political year began, Hubert Humphrey, offering the general estimate of Wallace's prospects, remarked, "I don't think he's going to rustle up many cattle."[145] But as successive traumas shook the nation's political foundation, Wallace crept upward in the polls—11 percent in February, 14 percent in May, 16 percent in July, 21 percent in late September.[146] As expected he had strong appeal in the South, where by September he was registering 38 percent in the Gallup poll, compared to 31 percent for Nixon and only 24 percent for Humphrey. The surprise was the North, where he scored 12 percent in the East and 16 percent in the Midwest.[147] Scattered but accumulating evidence showed the Confederate candidate making astonishing gains among precisely the voters he most wanted—unionized factory workers. United Auto Workers Local 326, representing four thousand in Flint, Michigan, actually endorsed Wallace. Nearby, Local 659, which was much larger, refrained from its customary endorsement of the Democratic nominee rather than offend the Wallaceites in its rank.[148] And an October survey of blue-collar workers in Gary, Indiana, revealed that 38 percent intended to vote for Wallace.[149] If the Wallace trend continued through election day, he would amass 30 percent of the national vote, with consequences potentially devastating for the major-party candidates. Wallace might conceivably win southern and border states that would otherwise go for Nixon. And he might attract enough working-class votes to cost Humphrey key states in the North. Thus did the major-party nominees have to contend not only with each other but with the emergence of a political movement that looked suspiciously like a native American fascism.

VI

Despite Wallace's strident rhetoric, the autumn campaign struck most observers as a bore. Discussion of the issues was even less edifying than usual; none of the candidates was personally popular; and until almost the last day, the contest lacked suspense. On September 15 Gallup reported the results of his first post-Chicago survey: Nixon 43 percent, Humphrey 31 percent, Wallace 19 percent.[150] A landslide of Goldwater dimensions seemed in the making —only this time it was the Democrats who would be swamped.

Running as if his election were foreordained, Nixon conceived a simple scenario for winning. With 117 electoral votes from 21 Republican states already in the bag—and needing a total of 270 to obtain a majority—he chose to concentrate primarily on the "battleground states" that had been closely contested in the past and were big enough to matter—New York, Pennsylvania, New Jersey, Ohio, Michigan, Illinois, Wisconsin, Missouri, Texas, and California. In case the anticipated near-sweep in these states failed to materialize, he developed the "peripheral strategy" to assure victory anyway. Conceding Wallace the Deep South, Nixon intended to fight him vote for vote on the region's periphery—in Florida, North Carolina, Virginia, Tennessee, and even South Carolina, where Strom Thurmond single-handedly was attempting to turn back the Wallace tide.[151] As the campaign began, Nixon's managers privately conceded Humphrey only Massachusetts and Rhode Island and gave their man a good chance to carry every one of the states he most desired.

To nurse probability into reality, Nixon could think of nothing better than to keep on doing what he had been doing since the beginning of the year. That meant blaming the unpopular Johnson-Humphrey administration for the nation's manifold ills, speaking in generalities about the issues, and exploiting the emerging conservative mood with carefully calibrated rhetoric. "The administration has struck out on keeping the peace abroad, on keeping the peace at home, on providing prosperity without inflation," he said in Kansas City. "I say three strikes are enough. Let's get a new batter up there."[152] As before, he attacked Johnson's handling of the war without offering alternatives, promised to restore law and order by appointing a new attorney general, and pledged less federal spending. Occasionally, to silence critics who accused him of speaking only in slogans, he went on the radio to give thoughtful speeches, which hardly anyone listened to, on subjects as diverse as black capitalism and the nature of the presidency.

The style of Nixon's campaign remained as consistent as the content—the pace leisurely, the details smoothly managed, the candidate safely insulated from the working press. Everything was geared for TV. Public appearances in each city were timed so that Nixon would make the evening news. Prodigious sums were spent on slick TV ads to sell the Nixon image. Carefully staged regional TV shows—live and unrehearsed—displayed the candidate competently fielding questions lobbed to him by a panel of admiring citizens.[153] The issues men who traveled with Nixon but seldom saw him complained privately about the ascendance of public-relations professionals in the campaign hierarchy. Nobody paid these grumblers any heed. Speech writer Richard Whalen quickly lost hope after Miami that Nixon would ever address the issues as a serious conservative. "I was ashamed of what I was doing," he later confessed. "I was ashamed of being in the company of mediocre merchandisers behind a façade concealing a sad mixture of cynicism, apprehension, suspicion and fear—especially fear." Early one morning, defying the orders of campaign director John Mitchell that no one leave a staff retreat in Mission Bay, California, without permission, Whalen furtively departed from his motel room and quit the campaign.[154]

Nixon's only worry in September was George Wallace. Climbing rapidly in the polls, the Alabaman threatened Nixon's southern strategy by pulling ahead in every southern state except Virginia and Texas.[155] Nixon counterattacked on the premise that about half of Wallace's supporters on the South's periphery were not racists but protest voters disturbed by hippies and bureaucrats. To win over this species of Wallaceite, Nixon refrained from attacking Wallace personally, argued that a vote for Wallace would really help Humphrey, and stated the issues with a southern inflection. Thus in an interview taped in mid-September for station WBTV in Charlotte, North Carolina, and beamed to a southern audience, Nixon affirmed the 1954 *Brown* decision but qualified his endorsement by criticizing executive efforts to enforce desegregation through withholding federal funds from dual school districts. He said, "I think that the use of that power on the part of the Federal Government to force a local community to carry out what a Federal administrator or bureaucrat may think is best for that local community—I think that it is a doctrine that is a very dangerous one."[156] He campaigned, in short, as a good ole boy with class.

Nixon's position in the campaign was actually less enviable than it appeared. The core of his constituency was white, middle class, mainly Protestant, and already Republican—some 40 to 45 percent of the electorate. By the logic of the campaign the candidate had little freedom to broaden his appeal. If he moved left to attract independents and restless northern Democrats, he would forfeit the entire South to Wallace. If he moved right to attract Wallace voters, he would alienate moderate Republicans and independents in the

North. For Nixon, then, the campaign was a holding operation—a skillful attempt to keep what he had and hope that election day would arrive before Humphrey could reassemble the fragments of the old Democratic coalition.

Rarely, if ever, did a major party candidate begin a campaign for president more inauspiciously than Hubert H. Humphrey. Party liberals pined for McCarthy. Southern Democrats in unprecedented numbers were preparing to desert the national ticket. No national organization existed to conduct a campaign, party coffers were empty, and the candidate remained tied in the public mind to Lyndon Johnson, whose Gallup rating in September stood at a dismal 35 percent.[157] Approached by Humphrey after the convention to become his campaign manager, a reluctant Larry O'Brien reportedly replied, "Look, I'm going to work my tail off for you, but as your manager I have to say to you—right now, you're dead."[158] Dead or not, Humphrey had to assume he could score an upset and devise a plan to achieve it. Expecting to carry New York, most of New England, and his native Minnesota, he could win in the Electoral College by forging pluralities in the big battleground states of New Jersey, Pennsylvania, Ohio, Michigan, Illinois, California, and Texas. The loss of three or four of these would spell defeat; the loss of all of them seemed all too likely.

Especially at the outset, many of Humphrey's problems stemmed from his own ineptitude. He formally opened his campaign on September 9 in Philadelphia, hailing a small and undemonstrative assemblage of ten thousand as "this amazing crowd, one that will live in my memory."[159] That same day he casually remarked that he could have run on the minority peace plank that had been defeated at the Chicago convention and that, regardless of the Paris peace talks, it might be possible to bring home some American troops in 1969, perhaps even before the end of 1968. A few hours later he retracted his remark about the peace plank, saying weakly that he did not know it had called for an unconditional bombing halt. Worse yet, Johnson slapped his face next day by saying that "no man can predict" when our boys can come home. Asked in Houston to reconcile the president's statement with his own, Humphrey triumphantly pointed to a headline in the Houston *Post* reporting the return of fifteen hundred marines from Vietnam. He neglected to point out that the accompanying article said no net cut in American troop strength would result.[160] By the end of the first campaign week it was clear that the war was killing his campaign.

Things did not soon improve. Through September local candidates shunned his entourage, his crowds remained sparse, and antiwar demonstrators regularly ruined his meetings. At Cleveland's Euclid Beach Amusement Park on September 22, for example, 250 leftists chanted "Stop the War," "Sieg Heil," and "Shame, shame," as he tried to speak. Hoarse from trying to outshout them, Humphrey angrily croaked, "Why don't we laugh them out of the park?" and then, according to a reporter, broke into a "loud cackle."[161] Returning from a trip to West Virginia, he asked O'Brien why he did not see any Humphrey signs or Humphrey buttons. O'Brien had to tell him, "We're broke, Hubert. We don't have any money and we can't get credit. We're not going to have the materials we wanted, and the television campaign has to be cut to the bone. The money just isn't there."[162] After three weeks on the road, Humphrey actually lost ground, Gallup now reporting Nixon at 43 percent, Humphrey 28 percent, and Wallace 21 percent.[163] Thus the vicious circle in which Humphrey was trapped—the lower the polls, the harder to raise money; the less money, the lower the polls. On a swing through the West Coast during the last week of September, Humphrey hit rock bottom—no rallies in Los Angeles; empty streets in Portland; disruptive students, shouting, "Dump the Hump," dragged by police from the galleries in Seattle.[164] By then Humphrey knew that to save his campaign—somehow, some way—he had to cut loose from Lyndon Johnson and confront the war issue as his own man.

Using the campaign's last $100,000, O'Brien bought time for Humphrey to make a nationally televised speech on the war from a studio in Salt Lake City. Long and bitter debate among his advisers attended its composition, and no one could be certain that, after delivery, Lyndon Johnson would not publicly disown its principal author. Minutes before he went on the air, Monday, September 30, Humphrey phoned Johnson and told him the speech's contents. "I gather you're not asking my advice," the president icily remarked.[165] That, of course, was precisely the point.

"I have paid for this television time this evening to tell you my story uninterrupted by noise . . . by protest . . . or by second hand interpretation," Humphrey began.[166] After rejecting unilateral withdrawal or escalation as viable options and advocating a negotiated settlement, he got to the main point, which was the bombing.

For months debate over the war had focused on the single issue of whether the enemy's demand for a total bombing halt should be met. In the only words of the campaign that commentators deemed worthy of exegesis, Humphrey now addressed this issue:[167]

As President, I would stop the bombing of the North as an acceptable risk for peace because I believe it could lead to success in the negotiations and thereby shorten the war. This would be the best protection for our troops. . . . In weighing that risk—and before taking action—I would place key importance on evidence—direct or indirect—by deed or word—of Communist willingness to restore the demilitarized zone between North and South Vietnam.

Now if the Government of North Vietnam were to show bad faith, I would reserve the right to resume the bombing.

What did these words mean? How far had Humphrey strayed from Johnson's position, or had he strayed at all? Johnson privately fumed that Humphrey had gone too far in appeasing the enemy, meaning Ho Chi Minh and Eugene McCarthy.[168] Richard Nixon, on the other hand, attacked the speech for dodging the issue altogether. "He either has to be for the bombing halt, as some of his prospective supporters and present supporters want him to be, or he has to support the negotiators in Paris. And at the present time I am not sure which side he is on," he said. The most accurate reading of the text was offered by Le Duc Tho, unofficial head of the North Vietnamese delegation in Paris. "There is absolutely nothing new in it. It's always the same demand for reciprocity which we reject."[169]

And yet Humphrey's Delphic utterance saved his campaign. In background discussions his aides told the press that the candidate had in fact committed himself to a bombing halt and that the qualifications in the speech were mere "window dressing." For liberals who wanted to come back to the party that was enough. Among those holding out for more was Eugene McCarthy, who would wait until a week before the election before offering Humphrey a weak endorsement. McCarthy or no, after Salt Lake City, antiwar demonstrators stopped dogging Humphrey's trail, money began trickling into his campaign, and most important of all, the candidate himself recovered self-respect. The polls showed barely any movement to Humphrey in the days following the speech, but political pros sensed a shift in climate. "In October," recalled Joe McGinniss, a reporter who had infiltrated Nixon's staff, "everyone suddenly got scared."[170]

Having neutralized the war issue, Humphrey was now free to concentrate on exploiting his advantage as the candidate of the majority party. In 1968, 46 percent of the electorate identified itself as Democrat, 24 percent as Republican, and 29 percent as independent.[171] To win, Humphrey had only to rekindle partisan passions sufficient to counteract the widespread urge for throwing the rascals out. This he tried to do by playing on the ancient distrust of Democrats for Richard Nixon and by reviving the memory of the Republicans as the party of hard times. "We are not about to see lines forming in front of employment offices just because Mr. Nixon thinks he'd like to play games with our economy," Humphrey warned.[172] Confronting a contingent of Wallace supporters at the Avco Lycoming plant in Stratford, Connecticut, he shouted, "Let me tell that young man with the white face down there it isn't a black man that is going to take your job, it's a Republican administration. I ask you to listen to the voice of your conscience."[173]

The appeal to conscience was crucial. Though he praised law and order like everyone else, he knew he could never successfully compete with Nixon or Wallace on this issue. He had to gamble on the idealism of his fellow Democrats and hope it was not dead. As opposed to the racist demagogue George Wallace, he said, or Wallace's "perfumed, deodorized"[174] imitator, Richard Nixon, "we can take another stand, which I take, on the principle of human equality and human opportunity . . . for every American, regardless of race, color, or creed."[175] On October 17 in Detroit, he addressed a cheering audience of black ministers. Tears rolling down his face, voice quivering with the emotion of the moment, he stated his creed: "We are the only country on the face of the earth that has ever dared to try to make what we call a biracial, a pluralistic society work. We are going to see whether we can do it in a spirit of community, whether we can do it in a spirit of unity . . . or whether or not it has to be apartheid."[176] Unlike the other candidates', Humphrey's commitment to racial amity was not in doubt.

Coincident with Humphrey's recovery was the decline of George Wallace, especially among blue-collar workers. The leaders of organized labor spared no effort to fight off the Wallace challenge and shepherd the rank and file back to their political home. By the end of October the unions had printed and distributed twenty million pieces of literature noting that Alabama had no minimum-wage laws, weak child-labor laws, union-busting state police, and niggardly welfare programs. And like Humphrey the unions appealed not only to the workers' self-interest but to their decency. In the end the propaganda blitz worked, and Wallace sympathizers by the hundreds of thousands reconsidered.[177]

Wallace bore a certain amount of responsibility for his own decline. He had achieved his fame by exploiting popular fears of violence, which he promised to repress. But there he was every night on the evening news, inciting clashes between demonstrators and police with his rhetorical excesses. As the campaign began to sap his energy, he handled hecklers less skillfully, more belligerently. "That's right, you little punk," he snarled at a protester mid-October in Los Angeles. "Why don't you come up here?"[178] More and more Americans concluded that Wallace was not the solution to violence but part of the problem. In mid-September the Harris poll reported 53 percent agreeing that "Wallace would handle law-and-order the way it ought to be handled." By the end of October the figure had skidded to 21 percent.[179]

Wallace dealt his chances their most devastating below on October 3 when he finally chose his running mate. It was former Air Force chief of staff Curtis E. LeMay,[180] best known for his remark that, if it wished, the U.S. could "bomb the North Vietnamese back to the Stone Age." After Wallace introduced him at a press conference in Pittsburgh, LeMay immediately launched into a dissertation on his favorite subject—the beauty and uses of nuclear weaponry. Wallace knew what Goldwater's loose talk about atomic bombs had cost him in 1964. He himself had been extremely careful throughout this campaign to avoid discussing these weapons or advocating their use to end the Vietnam War. Now, incredibly, here was LeMay, saying that while he did not think they were needed, he would, if necessary, drop nukes on Vietnam.

Wallace tried to interrupt him, to sit him down, to change the subject. But LeMay kept talking—about the national "phobia" of nuclear weapons, about his belief that the world would not end "if we exploded" the Bomb. Why, he said in a lyrical peroration, the U.S. had set off twenty nuclear explosions on the Bikini atoll, but nevertheless "the fish are all back in the lagoons; the coconut trees are growing coconuts; the guava bushes have fruit on them; the birds are back. As a matter of fact everything is about the same except the land crabs. They get minerals through the soil, and I guess through their shells, and the land crabs were a little bit 'hot' and there's a little doubt about whether you should eat a land crab or not." Wallace kept LeMay under wraps after that, but the damage had been done. Humphrey soon dubbed Wallace and LeMay "the bombsy twins."[181]

As Wallace faded and liberals straggled back to the party, Humphrey finally began to move up in the polls. On October 24, two weeks before the election, Gallup reported that he had nearly halved the lead that Nixon enjoyed at the beginning of the month. The latest figures: Nixon 44 percent, Humphrey 36 percent, Wallace 15 percent.[182] But Nixon remained so comfortably ahead that, in his own view, only one event might yet threaten him. That was a breakthrough at the peace talks in Paris.[183]

During the second week of October, that breakthrough seemed imminent. In a private conversation with chief U.S. negotiator Averell Harriman, North Vietnamese representatives inquired whether the United States would stop the bombing if Hanoi, in effect, accepted the participation of the Saigon government at the peace talks. One week later terms of an agreement were tentatively and secretly negotiated. The U.S. pledged a total bombing halt, and North Vietnam implicitly promised reciprocal military restraint, saying that it would "know what to do." As for future talks, North Vietnam dropped its objections to negotiating with Saigon, and the U.S. dropped its objections to negotiating with the National Liberation Front. But, on the verge of public announcement, the North raised new demands that the U.S. could not accept. On October 16, amid international rumors of a breakthrough, President Johnson dejectedly phoned the candidates and told them it was not so.[184]

But negotiations in Paris continued, finally bearing fruit two weeks later, when Hanoi agreed to accept the terms of the original bargain. Now it was Saigon's turn to balk. Johnson had hoped to announce the bombing halt in a communiqué jointly issued by the governments of the United States and South Vietnam. But on October 29, under pressure from hawks in his own government, South Vietnamese President Nguyen Van Thieu tried to sabotage the agreement by making unacceptable demands of his own. When Thieu refused to relent, Johnson decided to deny him a veto over the peace process. On October 31 at 8 P.M., Johnson made a taped television appearance to announce the bombing halt. The euphoria prompted in the United States by this first whiff of peace was considerably tempered one day later when Thieu told his National Assembly that he would not participate in the Paris talks if the NLF participated also. The legislators reacted by surging into the streets, raising the red-and-yellow flag of South Vietnam, and singing their national anthem.[185]

While the voters tried to make sense of this diplomatic melodrama, Nixon, Johnson, and Humphrey each nourished bitter thoughts about the others. "What I found difficult to accept was the timing . . ." Nixon wrote of Johnson's bombshell in his memoirs. "Announcing the halt so close to the election was utterly callous if politically calculated, and utterly naïve if sincere."[186] After Thieu publicly refused to go along, Nixon instructed his man Robert Finch to tell newsmen, "We had the impression that all the diplomatic ducks were in position. I think this will boomerang. It was hastily contrived." "Who's this guy, Fink?" Johnson angrily inquired of Nixon.[187] Nixon would blame his near-loss of the election on a late, massive shift to the Democrats resulting from Johnson's tricky diplomacy.

Humphrey harbored dark thoughts of his own against the president. He resented Johnson's lukewarm support for his candidacy,[188] and he felt that as a member of the administration he should have been briefed about the Paris developments privately rather than in a conference call with the other two candidates.[189] His relations with Johnson were so strained that a few days before the bombing accord was announced he arrived at the White House ten minutes late for a rare appointment, only to find that Johnson would not see him. The vice president recalled that he sent in a scribbled note describing "in terms that the President would understand what they could do with their meeting."[190] Indeed, in all likelihood, Johnson had pressed for an agreement before the election less because he wanted to help Humphrey than because he hoped to vindicate his presidency in its waning days with a peace agreement and felt constrained to act while he still possessed some leverage.

Johnson had complaints of his own against the two leading contenders. Both of them, he believed, bore some responsibility for Thieu's disruption of the peace process. Humphrey was guilty because he had bowed to peace sentiment in his Salt Lake City speech, provoking Thieu to help Nixon by undermining the bombing accord in the closing hours of the campaign.[191] In Johnson's view, if

Humphrey had adhered to the administration line during the campaign, Thieu would have acquiesced in the bombing halt, and Humphrey would have been elected.[192]

Johnson suspected that Nixon's role in the affair bordered on treason. Johnson had been informed by the CIA that Anna Chennault, the beautiful Chinese-born widow of General Claire Chennault and a vice chairman of the Republican National Finance Committee, not only maintained contacts with South Vietnamese officials but attempted late in October to negotiate a secret agreement whereby Nixon would offer guarantees to Saigon, and Saigon would help Nixon by torpedoing Johnson's impending peace maneuver. When on October 27 the South Vietnamese Embassy in Washington sent home an intercepted message recommending obstruction of the peace process until after the election, Johnson thought he knew why. On his orders the FBI placed Madame Chennault under surveillance and initiated phone taps at the South Vietnamese Embassy. One day after Thieu's refusal to go to Paris—November 2, 1968—Madame Chennault called the embassy urging Thieu to stand firm on grounds that the South would get a better deal from Nixon. Did Nixon know of this call? the South Vietnamese official asked. "No, but our friend in New Mexico does," she replied. Johnson, infuriated, concluded that the friend of whom she spoke was Spiro Agnew, campaigning that day in Albuquerque. It in no way diminished Johnson's suspicions that the FBI check he ordered on Agnew's outgoing phone calls from Albuquerque uncovered none to Chennault.[193] As a former high-ranking FBI official testified before Congress in 1973, the White House "felt the Republicans . . . were attempting to slow down the South Vietnamese from going to the Paris peace talks and . . . wanted to know who either Mr. Nixon or Mr. Agnew had been in touch with."[194] Humphrey too harbored suspicions of Nixon. On learning of Madame Chennault's diplomatic meddling, the candidate was tempted to discredit the Republicans in the campaign's last days by exposing it. Lacking evidence of Nixon's direct complicity, he reluctantly refrained.[195]

How much the bombing halt helped Humphrey or Thieu's recalcitrance hurt him were questions that could not be finally answered. Humphrey was coming on strong anyway. A Harris poll taken shortly *before* Johnson's bombing announcement showed Nixon leading him only 40 percent to 37 percent.[196] In the final days—hoarse, pleading, evangelical—the vice president rode the crest of a popular wave that carried him to the very brink of victory. On Sunday at the Astrodome in Houston—as Texas tilted toward the Democrats—fifty thousand people cheered Humphrey and Johnson, standing side by side for the only time of the campaign. On Monday in Los Angeles, where a month before Humphrey had passed virtually as a fugitive, hysterical crowds engulfed his motorcade. That night he won the battle of the telethons, as Nixon answered carefully laundered questions in an antiseptic atmosphere, while Humphrey took his live on a show marked by warmth, spontaneity, and moments of high emotion. The final polls caught the shifting tide of public opinion. Gallup showed Nixon leading 42 percent to 40 percent, Harris had Humphrey ahead 43 percent to 40 percent. Both agreed that in fact the election was too close to call.[197]

In the end Nixon barely stood off Humphrey's challenge. As finally tabulated, Nixon polled 43.4 percent of the popular vote, Humphrey 42.7 percent, George Wallace 13.5 percent.[198] In the Electoral College, where 270 votes were needed to win, Nixon managed to capture 301. As he expected, Nixon held on to the large bloc of strong Republican states, wrested the South's periphery from Wallace (Florida, South Carolina, North Carolina, Virginia, and Tennessee), and carried enough "battleground" states to win the presidency. But not by much. Of the big states, Nixon carried New Jersey, Ohio, Illinois, Wisconsin, and California, while Humphrey claimed New York, Pennsylvania, Michigan, Missouri, and Texas. If Humphrey and Wallace had won only thirty-four more electoral votes between them, Nixon would have been denied a majority of the electoral vote, the election would have gone to the U.S. House of Representatives, and Hubert Humphrey would have been president.

For the rest of his life Humphrey was haunted by the narrow margin of his defeat. If only he had not blundered so often in the early going, if Mayor Daley had exerted himself for the ticket in Illinois, if Eugene McCarthy had endorsed him earlier and with more enthusiasm, if he had blown the whistle on Anna Chennault, if money had been available to run a proper television campaign— if all these things had happened or any one of them, then perhaps the nation would have been spared the flawed presidency of the man who defeated him.

The most fascinating feature of the 1968 election was the candidacy of George Wallace. He entered the race hoping to become a national candidate with sufficient support to prevent either major-party candidate from winning a majority in the Electoral College. In fact, he ran well only in the South, where he polled 34 percent of the popular vote, compared to Nixon's 35 percent and Humphrey's 31 percent. The only states of the Union he carried were the Deep South states of Louisiana, Mississippi, Alabama, Georgia, and Arkansas—states where he was regarded as a conservative or "preservationist" candidate who would defend the region's peculiar racial mores from federal assault. But in the North, where he polled only 8 percent of the vote, even Wallace's supporters perceived him as a radical, and that damaged him. At the height of his campaign, 22 percent of northern manual workers (excluding blacks) considered voting for Wallace; only 9 percent finally did so. Among northern nonmanual workers—i.e., professionals, businessmen, white-collar workers—Wallace's support likewise declined, from 10 percent at its peak to 4 percent on election day.[199] Curiously, despite the 9.9 million voters he attracted, Wallace's candidacy did not much alter the election's result. A majority of Wallace supporters were nominal Democrats, some of whom would have voted for Humphrey if Wallace had not run, others of whom would have voted for Nixon. According to the most authoritative estimate, if Wallace had not run, Nixon and Humphrey would have obtained roughly the same proportion of the two-party vote that they actually received.[200]

It did not take a political scientist to grasp the meaning of the election. Four years before, perceived as a liberal, Lyndon Johnson polled 43.1 million votes. In 1968 Hubert Humphrey, running as a liberal, got only 31.2 million votes—a loss of nearly 12 million. The war, of course, did incalculable damage to the liberal candidate, but it did not do the only damage. Conditions at home hurt too. The Kennedy and Johnson administrations had appropriated the issues of full employment, poverty, and civil rights as their own. But full employment had turned into inflation, the ungrateful poor were rioting in the streets, and civil rights had become black power. The close identification of the Democratic party with the cause of racial justice did it special injury. While 97 percent of black voters went for Humphrey, less than 35 percent of white voters did so. Indeed, three of ten whites who cast ballots for Johnson in 1964 cast them in 1968 for someone other than Humphrey.[201] If not the sole cause of white defections, the backlash against black unrest was certainly high on the list. Liberals suffered too because large portions of the public believed that their idealism, which had shaped public policy for eight years, was somehow flawed, that it had delivered far less than promised in the way of social progress and social harmony. It cannot be said that this judgment was wholly false.

VII

At the time, it was possible to believe that the defeat of the liberal candidate in 1968 was owing to short-run factors—riots, assassinations, personalities, Tet. The Democrats, after all, survived the election still firmly in control of Congress, having polled 50 percent of the national vote in House elections—compared to 48.3 percent for the Republicans—and losing a net of only four House seats.[202] But it soon became clear that the presidential election was not an aberration, that a long-term trend toward conservatism had indeed set in, a trend evident in the increasingly defensive and circumspect rhetoric of liberal spokesmen and only temporarily to be obscured by Watergate. Affluence in the 1960s had fostered social optimism and undergirded liberal reform. Recessions in the 1970s fostered social pessimism and expanded the audience for conservative denunciations of Keynesians, civil rights enthusiasts, and advocates of expensive welfare programs. In 1968 Ronald Reagan had been too conservative for the Republican party. In 1980, running on a platform to repeal the cultural as well as the political legacy of the sixties, he easily won the presidency of the United States. Whether Reagan's victory made permanent the trend away from the liberalism of John F. Kennedy and Lyndon B. Johnson, whether his conservative policies could weave together the unraveled fabric of the old America, even whether the old America was something that ought to be recovered—these questions were bound to engage historians far into the nation's future.

Bibliographic Note

In addition to the books, magazine and journal articles, and published government documents cited in the footnotes, I relied on official papers, manuscript collections, and oral history interviews at the John F. Kennedy Library in Boston, Massachusetts, and the Lyndon Baines Johnson Library in Austin, Texas. For the Kennedy administration the most important collections for students of domestic policy are the President's Office Files, which were maintained rather haphazardly by the president's secretary, Evelyn Lincoln; and the papers of Theodore Sorensen, Kennedy's chief adviser on domestic matters. In general, I found the collections at the LBJ Library valuable but less rewarding than those at the JFK. Among the papers of Johnson aides, those of Bill Moyers, Douglas Cater, and Harry McPherson and Joseph Califano are most helpful.

On civil rights, the best source for the Kennedy administration is the papers of Burke Marshall, supplemented by his lengthy and informative oral history interview. Robert F. Kennedy's papers are disappointing on this subject, but his oral history contains important insights and information. Also to be consulted are the papers of the U.S. Commission on Civil Rights, on microfilm for the Kennedy years, and the papers of Harris Wofford, both at the JFK Library. For the Johnson administration, useful material on civil rights may be found in the White House Central Files, the Cater papers, and the McPherson papers at the LBJ Library.

On economic policy, the papers of Walter Heller at the JFK are indispensable for the Kennedy years and the first year of the Johnson presidency. Another excellent source, at least for 1961 and 1962, is the oral history interview, conducted in 1964 as a conversation among several of Kennedy's economic advisers. A full record of the advice and reports that

Johnson received from his economic advisers is contained in the White House Central Files at the LBJ Library.

For the origins of the war on poverty, scholars will want to consult interview summaries and copies of important documents assembled by Daniel Knapp for the book that he co-authored with Kenneth Polk, *Scouting the War on Poverty* (1971), and deposited at the JFK. Richardson White, Jr., likewise gave the library documents and interview summaries he and Beryl Radin collected for their unpublished study, "Youth and Opportunity: The Federal Anti-Delinquency Program" (1969). On administration planning for the poverty war in 1963, the CEA-Heller papers (on microfilm) are by far the best source. Several of those involved in planning the war were participants in a joint oral history interview at Brandeis University in 1973.

A collection of documents that proved especially useful was the confidential reports of OEO's Office of Inspection. With no line responsibilities, the office existed only to provide Sargent Shriver with candid, private accounts on what his agency was doing. Inspection reports on local community action agencies, though sporadic, constitute the best single source on the subject. In 1974 OEO gave me permission to examine Office of Inspection files, stored by the National Archives in Suitland, Maryland. For that permission, I am grateful.

Notes

Abbreviations

CEA	Council of Economic Advisers
Cong. Rec.	Congressional Record
JFKL	John F. Kennedy Library
LBJL	Lyndon Baines Johnson Library
NA	National Archives
PCJD	President's Council on Juvenile Delinquency
Pub. Paps.	Public Papers of the Presidents
WHCF	White House Central Files

Preface

1. W. W. Rostow, *The World Economy: History and Prospect* (1978), 247–286.

Chapter 1. The Liberals, the Candidate, and the Election of 1960

1. Robert A. Nisbet, *The Quest for Community* (1953), 215.
2. Arthur M. Schlesinger, Jr., *The Vital Center* (1949), 131.
3. *New York Times*, May 3, 1950, 7; June 27, 19; June 28, 9; June 29, 18; June 30, 6.
4. See issues of *Bulletin of Committee for Cultural Freedom;* and Christopher Lasch, *The Agony of the American Left* (1969), ch. 3.
5. John Kenneth Galbraith, *American Capitalism* (1952), 118.

6. Richard Hofstadter, "The Pseudo-Conservative Revolt," in Daniel Bell, ed., *The New American Right* (1955), 34.

7. See, for example, *ADA World*, June 1956.

8. Nisbet, *Quest for Community*, 199.

9. David Riesman and Nathan Glazer, "The Intellectuals and the Discontented Classes," in Bell, *New American Right*, 73.

10. For a discussion of pluralism in these years, Robert Booth Fowler, *Believing Skeptics: American Political Intellectuals, 1945–1964* (1978), chs. 6, 7.

11. Daniel Bell, *The End of Ideology* (1960), 110.

12. Richard Volney Chase, *The Democratic Vista* (1958), 145.

13. Arthur M. Schlesinger, Jr., "Where Does the Liberal Go from Here?," *New York Times Magazine*, Aug. 4, 1957, 7 ff. Quote on p. 7.

14. Arthur M. Schlesinger, Jr., "The Challenge of Abundance," *Reporter* (vol. 14, May 3, 1956), 8–11.

15. Quoted in *Time* (vol. 70, Oct. 14, 1957), 27.

16. John Kenneth Galbraith, *The Affluent Society* (2nd ed., 1969), xxviii.

17. Galbraith, *Affluent Society* (1st ed., 1958), 323.

18. Leon H. Keyserling, "Eggheads and Politics," *New Republic* (vol. 139, Oct. 27, 1958), 13–17.

19. James Tobin, "Defense, Dollars, and Doctrines," *Yale Review* (vol. 47, March 1958), 321–324.

20. Steinbeck quoted in *New Republic* (vol. 142, Feb. 15, 1960), 11.

21. Adlai E. Stevenson, "Extend our vision . . . to all mankind," *Life* (vol. 48, May 30, 1960), 97.

22. *Cong. Rec.* (1960), 6715–6717.

23. *Cong. Rec.* (1960), 8057.

24. *Cong. Rec.* (1960), 8053.

25. Norman Mailer, "Superman Comes to the Supermarket," *Esquire* (Nov. 1960), reprinted in Mailer, *The Presidential Papers* (1963), 25–61. Quotes on pp. 49, 38, 58.

26. Joan and Clay Blair, Jr., *The Search for J.F.K.* (1976), Preliminaries and ch. 17, 18, 44.

27. Lawrence F. O'Brien, *No Final Victories* (1974), 77.

28. O'Brien, *No Final Victories*, 58–61. Quote on p. 61. Also, Theodore Sorensen, *Kennedy* (1965), 99–106.

29. For an excellent account of the primary campaigns, Theodore H. White, *The Making of the President, 1960* (1961), ch. 4.

30. See *Con. Rec.* (1949), A 993.

31. Paul F. Healy, "The Senate's Gay Young Bachelor," *Saturday Evening Post* (vol. 225, June 13, 1953), 127.

32. Abram Chayes, Oral History Interview (May 18, 1960), JFKL.

33. Sorensen, *Kennedy*, 117–118.

34. Letter from Schlesinger to Kennedy, Aug. 30, 1960, Schlesinger file, President's Office Files, JFKL; see also Joseph Rauh, Oral History Interview (Dec. 23, 1965), JFKL; for text of ADA endorsement, *ADA World*, Sept. 1960, 1.
35. Chayes, Oral History Interview.
36. Kennedy's campaign speeches were reprinted in "Freedom of Communications," Part I, Committee on Commerce, Senate Report 994 (1961), hereafter cited as Kennedy Speeches. This quote on p. 228.
37. Kennedy Speeches, 1008.
38. Kennedy Speeches, 149.
39. Kennedy Speeches, 412
40. Kennedy Speeches, 135.
41. Memo from Samuelson to A. Cox (undated), files of the Democratic National Committee, JFKL.
42. Seymour Harris, Oral History Interview (June 16, 17, 1964), JFKL.
43. Kennedy Speeches, 1057.
44. Memo from Marjorie M. Lawson to Senator Kennedy, Robert Kennedy, Steve Smith, Ted Sorensen, June 6, 1960, Memos: Lawson file, Robert F. Kennedy papers, JFKL.
45. Harris Wofford, Oral History Interview (May 22, 1968), JFKL.
46. Kennedy Speeches, 582–583.
47. Kennedy Speeches, 576.
48. Kennedy Speeches, 192.
49. "Freedom of Communications," Part II (Nixon's Speeches), 89.
50. *New York Times*, Sept. 8, 1960, 1 and 25.
51. Kenneth P. O'Donnell and David F. Powers, *"Johnny, We Hardly Knew Ye": Memories of John Fitzgerald Kennedy* (1972), 205–207.
52. Kennedy Speeches, 208.
53. O'Donnell and Power, *"Johnny,"* 210.
54. For text of debate, "Freedom of Communications," Part III, 73–92. For accounts and reactions, *New York Times*, Sept. 27, 1960, 29; Sept. 28, 26; and Kurt Lang and Gladys Engel Lang, "Ordeal by Debate: Viewer Reaction," *Public Opinion Quarterly* (vol. 25, Summer 1961), 277–288.
55. *New York Times*, Oct. 2, 1960, 54; Oct. 23, E3.
56. White, *Making of the President*, 382–383.
57. Richard M. Nixon, *Six Crises* (1962), 309–310.
58. Kennedy Speeches, 775, 765.
59. *New York Times*, Oct. 11, 1960, 22; Dec. 13, 1.
60. Sorensen, *Kennedy*, 217.
61. Nixon Speeches, 1137.
62. *New York Times*, Oct. 13, 1960, 1.
63. *New York Times*, Oct. 27, 1960, 22.

64. Nixon, *Six Crises*, 362–363.
65. *New York Times*, Oct. 27, 1960, 22; Oct. 28, 1, 12.
66. Arthur M. Schlesinger, Jr., *A Thousand Days* (1965), 74.
67. The quote from King was reprinted in *The Case of Martin Luther King*, the brochure circulated before the election; copy in Campaign Materials, files of Democratic National Committee, JFKL; see also Sorensen, *Kennedy*, 215–216.
68. *New York Times*, Oct. 23, 1960, 10 E.
69. *Public Papers of the Presidents: Dwight David Eisenhower, 1960–61*, 838.
70. George H. Gallup, *The Gallup Poll* (vol. 3, 1972), 1688, 1690.
71. Richard M. Scammon, ed., *America Votes* (1962), 1. This volume is also the source for the returns cited in the following paragraphs.
72. Benjamin C. Bradlee, *Conversations with Kennedy* (1975), 33.
73. These charges were lovingly reported in the Chicago *Tribune* and summarized in an editorial on Dec. 11, 1960, 28. See also Earl Mazo's report in the New York *Herald Tribune*, Dec. 6, 1960. On precinct 50, Chicago *Tribune*, Dec. 1, 1960, 3.
74. For more stories reporting evidence of fraud, Chicago *Tribune*, Dec. 1, 5; Dec. 3, 1; Dec. 5, 1; Dec. 11, 1; *New York Times*, April 14, 1961, 10; May 13, 1961, 44; Nov. 30, 1960, 29.
75. This was the defense made by chairman of Illinois Democratic Central Committee, *New York Times*, Dec. 15, 1960, 39.
76. Houston *Chronicle*, Nov. 22, 1960, 1; Houston *Post*, Nov. 20, 1; Dec. 7, 1.
77. This charge was asserted most strongly in Earl Mazo, *Herald Tribune*, Dec. 4 and Dec. 5, 1960.
78. Houston *Post*, Dec. 13, 1960, 11.
79. *Statistical Abstract of the United States* (1963), 376.
80. This interpretation relies on P. E. Converse et al., "Stability and Change in 1960: A Reinstating Election," *The American Political Science Review* (vol. 55, June 1961), 269–280. See also V. O. Key, "Interpreting Election Results," in Paul T. David, ed., *The Presidential Election and Transition, 1960–61* (1961), 150–175.
81. *U.S. News and World Report* (vol. 49, Nov. 21, 1960), 69.
82. Converse et al., "Stability and Change," esp. 278.
83. This interpretation relies on findings of Russell Middleton, "The Civil Rights Issue and Presidential Voting Among Southern Negroes and Whites," *Social Forces* (vol. 40, March 1962), 209–215; and Bernard Cosman, "Presidential Republicanism in the South, 1960," *Journal of Politics* (vol. 24, May 1962), 303–322.
84. For South Carolina and Texas statistics on registered black voters, see U.S. Commission on Civil Rights, *One Nation Under God* (1959),

41; for North Carolina, same author, *The 50 States Report* (1961), 454–455.

85. *New York Times*, Nov. 8, 1960, 17.

Chapter 2. Kennedy, Keynes, and the Corporations

1. *New York Times*, Jan. 21, 1961, 9.
2. *Public Papers of the Presidents: John F. Kennedy, 1961*, 1. Hereafter cited as *Pub. Paps., JFK.*
3. *Time* (vol. 77, Jan. 27, 1961), 7.
4. Pierre Salinger, *With Kennedy* (1967), 186.
5. *Pub. Paps., JFK, 1962*, 669.
6. Quoted in *Time* (vol. 81, June 7, 1963), 19.
7. *Pub. Paps., JFK, 1962*, 347.
8. *Pub. Paps., JFK, 1961*, 429.
9. Quoted in Donald C. Lord, *John F. Kennedy: The Politics of Confrontation and Conciliation* (1977), 232.
10. Taylor Branch and George Crile III, "The Kennedy Vendetta: How the CIA Waged a Silent War against Castro," *Harper's* (vol. 251, Aug. 1975), 49–63. See also *Alleged Assassination Plots Involving Foreign Leaders*, An Interim Report of the Select Committee to Study Governmental Operations with Respect to Intelligence Activities, U.S. Senate (1976), 134–148; and Thomas Powers, *The Man Who Kept the Secret* (1979), ch. 9.
11. *Alleged Assassination Plots*, 74–85; 125–132; Judith (Campbell) Exner, *My Story* (1977).
12. This allegation is made in Victor Lasky, *It Didn't Start with Watergate* (1977), and is supported by hints in Benjamin C. Bradlee, *Conversations With Kennedy* (1975), 218; for direct supporting evidence, Memo from Mortimer Caplin, IRS Commissioner, to Robert H. Knight, May 23, 1961, reprinted in *Cong. Rec.* (1970), 12221–12222.
13. *Final Report* (Book III), Senate Select Committee to Study Governmental Operations. . . , 321–322, 328–330, 333; 345–346; 79–184.
14. *Final Report* (Book III), Senate Select Committee, 890–897.
15. James Weinstein and David W. Eakins, eds., *For a New America: Essays in History and Politics from "Studies on the Left 1959–1967"* (1970). For a history of *Studies*, see the introduction.
16. The concept "corporate liberalism" received early elaboration in an essay by the editors, "The Ultra-Right and Cold War Liberalism," *Studies on the Left* (vol. 3, 1962), 3–8.
17. Gabriel Kolko, *The Triumph of Conservatism* (1963), 2.
18. *Pub. Paps., JFK, 1961*, 87.

19. Quoted in Hobart Rowen, *The Free Enterprisers: Kennedy, Johnson, and the Business Establishment* (1964), 18.

20. Rowen, *Free Enterprisers*, ch. 4.

21. Jim F. Heath, *John F. Kennedy and the Business Community* (1969), 51, 78–80.

22. Memo from Heller to the president, Oct. 6, 1961, Memos to JFK file, Heller papers, JFKL.

23. Lee Loevinger, Oral History Interview, May 13, 1966, JFKL.

24. Quoted in Rowen, *The Free Enterprisers*, 81.

25. Lee Loevinger, "Antitrust in 1961 and 1962," *The Antitrust Bulletin* (vol. 8, May–June 1963), 349–379; Richard J. Barber, "Mergers: Threat to Free Enterprise?" *Challenge* (vol. 11, March 1963), 6–10.

26. See "President's 1961 Tax Recommendations," Committee on Ways and Means, House hearings (1961).

27. *Wall Street Journal*, July 12, 1962, 3.

28. Rowen, *Free Enterprisers*, 47.

29. *Pub. Paps., JFK, 1962*, 359.

30. *Pub. Paps., JFK, 1962*, 68–77; and Stanley D. Metzger, *Trade Agreements and the Kennedy Round* (1964).

31. Louis Banks, "What Kennedy's Free Trade Program Means to Business," *Fortune* (vol. 65, March 1962), 214. Standard Oil (New Jersey)'s views in "Trade Expansion Act of 1962," Finance Committee, Senate hearings (1962), 902–903.

32. Heath, *Kennedy and the Business Community*, 92–93.

33. For antimonopolist views, *Cong. Rec.* (1962), 10695–10701, 11027–11058, 11143–11147.

34. *New York Times*, July 11, 1962, 1; July 12, 1.

35. Michael Kinsley, *Outer Space and Inner Sanctums* (1976), 238.

36. On Kefauver's bill, "Drug Industry Antitrust Act," Committee on the Judiciary, Senate hearings (1961), 1–15, 20–35.

37. Richard Harris, *The Real Voice* (1964), 145–146.

38. *Pub. Paps., JFK, 1962*, 239–240.

39. Harris, *Real Voice*, 162–171.

40. *Cong. Rec.* (1962), 10105–10107.

41. *Washington Post*, July 15, 1962, 1 and 8.

42. *Pub. Paps., JFK, 1962*, 603.

43. *Cong. Rec.* (1962), 17415; Harris, *Real Voice*, 214.

44. For PMA position, "Drug Industry Antitrust Act," Committee on the Judiciary, Senate hearings (1961), 1993–2007. The bill as enacted contained one provision to increase competition in drug pricing. It required drug labels to bear the common as well as the trade name of the drug and its ingredients.

45. For Du Pont's view, "Taxation of Exchanges and Distributions Pur-

suant to Antitrust Decrees," Committee on Ways and Means, House hearings (1961), 64–81.

46. For antimonopolist views, "Minority Views," Senate Report 1100 (1961); *Cong. Rec.* (1962), 453–456.

47. Memo from Dillon to president, Sept. 15, 1961, Treasury file, President's Office File, JFKL.

48. *Cong. Rec.* (1961), 21042.

49. CEA, *1962 Annual Report*, 185–190. For a history of price-wage policy under Kennedy, William J. Barber, "The Kennedy Years: Purposeful Pedagogy," in Craufurd D. Goodwin, ed., *Exhortation and Controls: The Search for a Wage-Price Policy, 1945–1971* (1975), ch. 3.

50. Memo from Heller to president, Aug. 2, 1961, Steel file, Sorensen papers, JFKL.

51. Rowen, *Free Enterprisers*, 90–96; *Wall Street Journal*, April 11, 1962, 1; *New York Times*, April 11–14, 1962; Theodore C. Sorensen, *Kennedy* (1965), 443–459.

52. *Pub. Paps., JFK, 1962*, 316.

53. Roy Hoopes, *The Steel Crisis* (1963), 88–89, 94–96, 109–110.

54. Hoopes, *Steel Crisis*, ch. 7; see also Grant McConnell, *Steel and the Presidency, 1962* (1963), ch. 5.

55. Blough's text reprinted in *New York Times*, April 13, 1962, 18.

56. For economic issues in detail, "Steel Prices, Unit Costs, Profits and Foreign Competition," Joint Economic Committee, hearings (1963).

57. *New York Times*, Oct. 7, 1963, III, 1 and 7; Oct. 20, 29; Dec. 20, 9. When markets tightened in April 1963, prices went up again.

58. Bernard D. Nossiter, *The Mythmakers: An Essay on Power and Wealth* (1964), 17–23.

59. *New York Times*, May 1, 1962, 16.

60. *Wall Street Journal*, May 29, 1962, 1 and 12; and *Newsweek* (vol. 59, June 11, 1962), 19–25.

61. Report of Special Study of Securities and Exchange Commission (1963), published as House Document 95 (1963).

62. Theodore C. Sorensen, "The Kennedy Administration," June 20, 1962, Business and Administration file, Sorensen papers.

63. For a good introduction to the subject, Sidney E. Rolfe and James L. Burtle, *The Great Wheel: The World Monetary System* (1973).

64. *New York Times*, Oct. 21, 1960, 1 and 54; Oct. 22, 35.

65. *New York Times*, Oct. 31, 1960, 1 and 22.

66. "Preliminary Report of the Task Force on the Economic Outlook," JFK Pre-Presidential Papers, Economy-Samuelson file, JFKL.

67. Council of Economic Advisers, Oral History Interview (Aug. 1, 1964), 170–172, JFKL.

68. Sorensen quoted in CEA, Oral History Interview, 219–220.

69. Walter W. Heller, *New Dimensions of Political Economy* (1966), 30–38; CEA, Oral History Interview, 215.

70. *Pub. Paps., JFK, 1961*, 41–53.

71. Samuelson quoted in Hobart Rowen, "Kennedy's Economists," *Harper's* (vol. 223, Sept. 1961), 27.

72. For Heller's case, "Economic Report of the President and Economic Situation and Outlook," Joint Economic Committee, hearings (1961), 310–392; and CEA, *1962 Annual Report.*

73. Memo from Heller to President, March 17, 1961, memos to JFK file, Heller papers; for quote, memo from Heller to Tobin, Gordon and Solow, March 27, 1961, Heller Council file, same papers.

74. *Pub. Paps., JFK, 1961*, 221–227, 229–240, 396–406, 533–540.

75. Memo to Sorensen from Dillon, July 21, 1961, Tax Cut file, Sorensen papers.

76. CEA, Oral History Interview, 406–424.

77. CEA, *1962 Annual Report*, 59.

78. CEA, *1963 Annual Report*, 194.

79. Memo from Galbraith to Dillon and Heller (n.d.), Galbraith file, President's Office File.

80. Sorensen, *Kennedy*, 422–427; memo from Heller to president, June 5, 1962, Business and Administration file, Sorensen papers; CEA, "Proposals for Tax Reduction," June 5, 1962, Tax Cut file, Heller papers.

81. *Pub. Paps., JFK, 1962*, 611–617.

82. *Pub. Paps., JFK, 1962*, 460–475.

83. Arthur M. Schlesinger, Jr., *A Thousand Days* (1965), 648.

84. Dillon, "The Current Economic Situation," June 6, 1962, Tax Cut file, Sorensen papers.

85. *Pub. Paps., JFK, 1962*, 457.

86. *Pub. Paps., JFK, 1962*, 611–617. Quote on p. 616. Sorensen, *Kennedy*, 427.

87. Sorensen, *Kennedy*, 429.

88. Warren Smith to Council, Dec. 3, 1962, Tax Cut file, Heller papers.

89. Memo from Heller to president, Dec. 9, 1962, Tax Cut file, Heller papers; memo from Heller to president, Dec. 23, 1962, same file.

90. Heller, *New Dimensions*, 34.

91. Sorensen, *Kennedy*, 430.

92. *Pub. Paps., JFK, 1962*, 875–881. Quotes on pp. 877, 880.

93. *Time* (vol. 80, Dec. 21, 1962), 17.

94. Heller, *New Dimensions*, 35.

95. Herbert Stein, *The Fiscal Revolution in America* (1969), 412–417.

96. *Pub. Paps., JFK, 1963*, 13.

97. Memo from Tobin to Heller, March 27, 1963, Box 2, Tobin papers, JFKL.

98. Letter from Galbraith to president, Aug. 20, 1962, President's Office File.

99. Michael Harrington, "Reactionary Keynesianism," *Encounter* (vol. 26, March 1966), 50–52.

100. Keyserling's views in "January 1963 Economic Report of the President," Joint Economic Committee, hearings (1963), 697–765; and "Revenue Act of 1963," Committee on Finance, Senate hearings (1963), 629–715, 719–736.

101. "January 1963 Economic Report," Joint hearings, 45.

102. *New York Times*, March 6, 1963, 1.

103. *New York Times*, Feb. 18, 1963, 12.

104. *New York Times*, Sept. 10, 1963, 33.

105. See Milton Friedman, *Capitalism and Freedom* (1962), ch. 5; and Milton Friedman and Walter W. Heller, *Monetary vs. Fiscal Policy* (1969), esp. pp. 50–56.

106. Friedman's views on this question are hard to pin down precisely. In *Capitalism and Freedom,* he implies that interest rates will have a severe crowding-out effect. He seems to shift ground, without shifting his conclusion, in a difficult paper, Friedman, "Comments on the Critics," *Journal of Political Economy* (vol. 80, Sept. 1972), 906–950. For a good overview of the crowding-out problem, Keith M. Carlson and Roger W. Spencer, "Crowding Out and Its Critics," in T. H. Havrilesky and John T. Boorman, eds., *Current Issues in Monetary Theory and Policy* (1976), 128–153.

107. Milton Friedman and David Meiselman, "The Relative Stability of Monetary Velocity and the Investment Multiplier in the United States, 1897–1958," in Commission on Money and Credit, *Stabilization Policies* (1963), 165–268.

108. Memo from Heller to president, June 7, 1963, Tax Cut file, Heller papers.

109. *Cong. Rec.* (1963), 18118–18119.

110. For history and views of Business Committee, see testimony of its co-chairmen, "Revenue Act of 1963," Finance Committee, Senate hearings, 1263–1278; and its Statement of Principles, reprinted in *Cong. Rec.* (1963), 13354.

111. Memo from Joseph Fowler to president, Sept. 23, 1962, Treasury file, President's Office File.

112. Heller notes on meeting with President Johnson, Meetings with LBJ file, Heller papers.

113. Memo from Dillon to president, Nov. 25, 1963, FI 11-4, WHCF,

LBJL; and memo from Heller to president, same date, Memos to LBJ file, Heller papers.

114. Troika Meeting with President Johnson, Nov. 25, 1963, notes by Gardner Ackley, Meetings with LBJ file, Heller papers.

115. *Pub. Paps., LBJ, 1964,* 113.

116. Memo from Heller to president, Jan. 5, 1963, FI file, WHCF; James Tobin, "The Tax Cut Harvest," *New Republic* (vol. 150, March 7, 1964), 14–17.

117. Memo from Heller to president, June 2, 1964, FI 11-4 file, WHCF.

118. CEA, *1965 Annual Report,* 38.

119. Memo from Gardner Ackley to president, Dec. 13, 1964, BE 5-4 file, WHCF.

120. CEA, *1966 Annual Report,* 38 and 233.

121. *U.S. News and World Report* (vol. 58, May 17, 1965), 100.

122. *Time* (vol. 86, Dec. 31, 1965), 64.

123. Arthur M. Okun, "Measuring the Impact of the 1964 Tax Reduction," in Walter W. Heller, ed., *Perspectives on Economic Growth* (1968), 27–49. Quote on p. 29.

124. Monetarist ideas are accessible to the layman in Milton Friedman, "The Role of Monetary Policy," *The American Economic Review* (vol. 58, March 1968), 1–17; Friedman, *The Counter-Revolution in Monetary Theory* (1970); and Friedman, *Dollars and Deficits* (1968).

125. Friedman and Heller, *Monetary vs. Fiscal Policy,* 56. For an econometric study supporting the monetarist story, Richard T. Froyen, "Monetarist Econometric Models and the 1964 Tax Cut," *Economic Inquiry* (vol. 12, June 1974), 159–168.

126. Friedman's letter reprinted in his book *Dollars and Deficits,* 126–152. Quote on p. 147.

Chapter 3. Politics and Principle

1. James H. Street, *The New Revolution in the Cotton Economy: Mechanization and Its Consequences* (1957), 35–48; *Sixteenth Census of the United States: 1940, Agriculture,* vol. 3, 703; *United States Census of Agriculture, 1959,* General Report, vol. 2, ch. VII, 829.

2. *Fifteenth Census of the United States, 1940: Population,* vol. 2, part 1, 51; *Census of the Population: 1960,* vol. 1, part 1, 250.

3. U.S. Census Bureau, *Current Population Reports, Population Estimates,* Series P—25, no. 247 (April 1962), Table IV.

4. Ben J. Wattenberg and Richard M. Scammon, *This U.S.A.* (1965), 271–273.

5. "Freedom of Communications," Part I (Kennedy Speeches), Committee on Commerce, Senate Report 994 (1961), 1010–1012.

6. Donald B. Johnson and Kirk H. Porter, *National Party Platforms, 1840–1972* (1973), 599–600.

7. Roy Wilkins, Oral History Interview (Aug. 13, 1964), JFKL, 5.

8. Confidential memo from Arnold Aronson and Roy Wilkins, Feb. 6, 1961, Civil Rights file, Sorenson papers, JFKL.

9. "Summary Memorandum of Executive Action on Civil Rights" (undated), Civil Rights file, Sorensen papers.

10. *New York Times*, March 6, 1961, 1 and 21.

11. Executive Order 10925, *Federal Register* (vol. 26, March 8, 1961), 1977–1979.

12. U.S. President's Committee on Equal Employment Opportunity, *Report to the President* (Nov. 26, 1963), 39.

13. "NAACP Appraises the First Year of the President's Committee on Equal Employment Opportunity," reprinted in *Congressional Record* (1961), A3027–3028.

14. Memo from Hobart Taylor, Jr., to Stephen N. Shulman, March 29, 1962, Vice President's Papers, LBJL; see also Taylor, Oral History Interview (Jan. 6, 1969), LBJL.

15. Report of the President's Committee, 116.

16. Richard Nathan, *Jobs and Civil Rights* (prepared for U.S. Commission on Civil Rights by Brookings Institution, April 1969), 134–135.

17. Quotes from Robert F. Kennedy, Oral History Interview conducted by Anthony Lewis, Dec. 4, 1964, 706, JFKL. For RFK's views of employment committee, pp. 701–711.

18. The witness—Jack Conway—quoted in Arthur M. Schlesinger, Jr., *Robert Kennedy and His Times* (1978, Houghton Mifflin edition), 336.

19. Portion of minutes containing this quote reprinted in Schlesinger, *Robert Kennedy*, 336.

20. Quoted in Schlesinger, *Robert Kennedy*, 336–337.

21. Dept. of Justice, "A Review of Activities of the Department of Justice in Civil Rights, 1963," Burke Marshall papers, JFKL.

22. Annual Report of the Attorney General of the United States (1962), 162; Donald S. Strong, *Negroes, Ballots, and Judges: National Voting Rights Legislation in the Federal Courts* (1968); Steven F. Lawson, *Black Ballots: Voting Rights in the South, 1944–1969* (1976), ch. 9.

23. Quoted in Carl M. Brauer, *John F. Kennedy and the Second Reconstruction* (1977), 121. An invaluable study.

24. Cox quoted in Victor S. Navasky, *Kennedy Justice* (1971), 245.

25. *New York Times*, July 19, 1963, 8.

26. "Judicial Performance in the Fifth Circuit," *Yale Law Journal* (vol. 73, Nov. 1963), 90–133, esp. p. 106.

27. Memo from Clarence Ferguson to Berl Bernhard, Sept. 17, 1963,

OGS Studies—Voting file, Papers of U.S. Commission on Civil Rights (microfilm), JFKL.

28. Burke Marshall, Oral History Interview No. 1 (May 29, 1964), 64, JFKL.

29. "Literacy Tests and Voter Requirements in Federal and State Elections," Committee on the Judiciary, Senate hearings (1962), 486.

30. Martin Luther King, Jr., "Equality Now," *Nation* (vol. 192, Feb. 4, 1961), 91–95.

31. Leadership Conference on Civil Rights, *Federally Supported Discrimination*, submitted to White House, Aug. 29, 1961.

32. *New York Times*, April 21, 1962, 1; on National Guard, *Final Report of President's Committee on Equal Opportunity in the Armed Services* (1964), 16–22.

33. U.S. Dept. of Labor, *Annual Report* (1962); for critiques of Labor Dept.'s order, "Equal Employment Opportunity," Committee on Education and Labor, House hearings (1963), 140 and 470. On aid to libraries, "Nondiscrimination in Federally Assisted Education Programs," Committee on Education and Labor, House hearings (1963), 11; also Memo on Commission Viewpoint and Recommendations, Legal file, Papers of U.S. Civil Rights Commission.

34. "Integration in Public Education Programs," Committee on Education and Labor, House hearings (1962), 17.

35. Alexander M. Bickel, "Civil Rights: The Kennedy Record," *New Republic* (vol. 147, Dec. 15, 1962), 14.

36. "Freedom of Communications" (Kennedy Speeches), 12, 576, 961.

37. Theodore C. Sorensen, *Kennedy* (1965), 480–481.

38. Memo from Wofford to pres., Oct. 10, 1961, Southern Regional Council file, Sorensen papers.

39. Marshall, Oral History Interview, 53–63; Schlesinger, *Robert Kennedy*, 311.

40. Executive Order 11063, *Federal Register* (vol. 27, Nov. 24, 1962), 11527–11530.

41. This issue is thoroughly surveyed in letter from Norbert Schlei (assistant attorney general) to Lee White, Sept. 10, 1962, Civil Rights Housing Executive Order file, Lee White papers, JFKL.

42. Brauer, *John F. Kennedy and the Second Reconstruction*, 206–207.

43. For criticisms of the order, Charles Abrams, "The Housing Order and Its Limits," *Commentary* (vol. 35, Jan. 1963), 10–14; Potomac Institute, "The Federal Role in Equal Housing Opportunity," Jan. 1964, 6–11, copy kindly lent me by the Institute; and Dennis Clark, "The Housing Order: Prejudice and Property," *Commonweal* (vol. 77, Dec. 21, 1962), 331–334.

44. "Civil Rights, 1966," Committee on the Judiciary, House hearings (1966), 1350.

45. *The Crisis* (vol. 68, Aug. 1961), 388–397.

46. Clarence Mitchell, Oral History Interview (Feb. 9, 1967), JFKL; Wilkins, Oral History Interview, 10–12.

47. Letter from Wilkins to Wofford, April 5, 1961, Wilkins file, Wofford papers, JFKL.

48. Edwin Guthman, *We Band of Brothers* (1971), 156.

49. Howell Raines, *My Soul Is Rested: Movement Days in the Deep South Remembered* (1977). Both quotes on this page from Farmer interview, 111.

50. *New York Times*, May 15, 1961, 1; May 16, 1; Howard Zinn, *SNCC: The New Abolitionists* (2nd edition, 1965), 44–46.

51. Quoted in John Lewis's interview, Raines, *My Soul Is Rested*, 119.

52. Marshall, Oral History Interview, 8–9, 47–50; *New York Times*, May 20, 1961, 1; May 21, 1 and 78.

53. Doar quoted in Guthman, *We Band of Brothers*, 171.

54. *American Journey: The Times of Robert Kennedy*, interviews by Jean Stein, edited by George Plimpton (1970), 103.

55. Marshall, Oral History Interview, 21.

56. *New York Times*, May 21, 1961, 1 and 78.

57. *New York Times*, May 21, 1961, 1.

58. Farmer interview, Raines, *My Soul Is Rested*, 123.

59. RFK, Oral History Interview, 559.

60. Guthman, *We Band of Brothers*, 178.

61. *New York Times*, May 25, 1961, 1.

62. For a firsthand account by a Freedom Rider, see taped recollection of Lucretia Collins, reprinted in James Forman, *The Making of Black Revolutionaries* (1972), 150–157. She discussed the layover in Montgomery on pp. 154–156.

63. Farmer interview, Raines, *My Soul Is Rested*, 123–124.

64. RFK, Oral History Interview, 572–575.

65. *New York Times*, May 22, 1961, 26.

66. Brauer, *John Kennedy and the Second Reconstruction*, 111.

67. Press Release, "Report on Civil Rights by Robert Kennedy to the President," Jan. 24, 1963, Burke Marshall papers.

68. RFK, Oral History Interview, 396.

69. On origins of VEP, Pat Watters and Reese Cleghorn, *Climbing Jacob's Ladder: The Arrival of Negroes in Southern Politics* (1967), 44–50; Louis E. Lomax, "The Kennedys Move in on Dixie," *Harper's* (vol. 224, May 1962), 27–33; *First Annual Report of the Voter Education Project* (in files of Southern Regional Council in Atlanta); Schlesinger, *Robert Kennedy*, 301–302.

70. Interview with Jenkins and King, Raines, *My Soul Is Rested*, 228.
71. Quoted in Lawson, *Black Ballots*, 265.
72. "You Can Help Support Programs for SNCC" (undated) in files of Southern Regional Council.
73. Zinn, *SNCC*, 123–131; for full account of Albany through summer of 1962, Zinn, *Albany* (1962), published by Southern Regional Council.
74. Memo from Marshall to attorney general, Dec. 26, 1961, Civil Rights Division files, Marshall papers.
75. Howard Zinn, "Kennedy: The Reluctant Emancipator," *Nation* (vol. 195, Dec. 1, 1962), 373–376; Zinn, *Albany*.
76. Charles Sherrod, Field Report, Sept. 20, 1962, reprinted in Forman, *Making of Black Revolutionaries*, 275–277. Quote on p. 277.
77. Marshall, Oral History Interview, 70.
78. *Public Papers of the Presidents: John F. Kennedy, 1962*, 592–593.
79. Telegram from W. G. Anderson to the pres., Dec. 12, 1962. HU/2 St. 19 file, WHCF, JFKL.
80. *New York Times*, Aug. 10, 1963, 1; memo from Berl Bernhard to Clarence Ferguson, Oct. 7, 1963, OGCI Studies—Legal file, papers of Civil Rights Commission. For SNCC's account, Bay Area Friends of SNCC, *Report on Federal Prosecution of Civil Rights Workers in Albany, Georgia* (undated pamphlet); and Slater King, "The Bloody Battleground of Albany," *Freedomways* (vol. 4, Winter 1964), 100–101.
81. Zinn, *SNCC*, ch. 4; for a compilation of violence and intimidation from 1961 through March, 1963, *Cong. Rec.* (1963), 5845–5848.
82. Moses letter from Magnolia jail, Nov. 1, 1961, reprinted in Forman, *Making of Black Revolutionaries*, 233.
83. Charles Cobb interview, Raines, *My Soul Is Rested*, 247.
84. Fannie Lou Hamer interview, Raines, *My Soul Is Rested*, 233.
85. Amzie Moore interview, Raines, *My Soul Is Rested*, 237.
86. Forman, *Making of Black Revolutionaries*, 285.
87. RFK, Oral History Interview, 766.
88. Burke Marshall, *Federalism and Civil Rights* (1964), esp. 42–81.
89. Marshall, *Federalism*, 50.
90. "Discretion to Prosecute Federal Civil Rights Crimes," *The Yale Law Journal* (vol. 74, June 1965), 1297–1312.
91. Haywood Burns, "The Federal Government and Civil Rights," in Leon Friedman, ed., *Southern Justice* (1965), 228–254. Quote on pp. 238–239.
92. Arlie Schardt, "Civil Rights: Too Much, Too Late," in Pat Watters and Stephen Gillers, eds., *Investigating the FBI* (1973), ch. 7.
93. *New York Times*, Nov. 19, 1962, 21.
94. The following account is based primarily on David J. Garrow, *The FBI and Martin Luther King, Jr.: From "Solo" to Memphis* (1981). See also

"Dr. Martin Luther King, Jr.," Case Study," Staff Reports, Book III, *Final Report of the Select Committee to Study Government Operations with Respect to Intelligence Operations*, U.S. Senate (1976), 79–184; Navasky, *Kennedy Justice*, 133–155; Schlesinger, *Robert Kennedy*, 352–365.

95. Garrow, *The FBI and Martin Luther King*, 40–44.
96. Garrow, *The FBI and Martin Luther King*, 46.
97. Schlesinger, *Robert Kennedy*, 356.
98. Garrow, *The FBI and Martin Luther King*, 42–43, 59–60.
99. RFK, Oral History Interview, 682–683.
100. Garrow, *The FBI and Martin Luther King*, 61.
101. King's thought reported in Andrew Young interview, Raines, *My Soul Is Rested*, 431.
102. Garrow, *The FBI and Martin Luther King*, 62–70, 72–73.
103. Sullivan quoted in Garrow, *The FBI and Martin Luther King*, 102, 103.
104. Garrow, *The FBI and Martin Luther King*, 104–105, 106.
105. Hoover quoted in Garrow, *The FBI and Martin Luther King*, 107.
106. Excerpts of the note in Garrow, *The FBI and Martin Luther King*, 125–126.
107. Garrow, *The FBI and Martin Luther King*, 133.
108. King quoted in Garrow, *The FBI and Martin Luther King*, 134.
109. Schardt, "Civil Rights," 171.
110. Zinn, *SNCC*, 203.
111. For accounts of this crisis, see Walter Lord, *The Past That Would Not Die* (1965); and Arthur M. Schlesinger, Jr., *A Thousand Days* (1965), 940–949. Barnett quoted in *New York Times*, Sept. 14, 1962, 1 and 15.
112. Transcripts of Robert Kennedy's conversations with Barnett are reprinted in Navasky, *Kennedy Justice*, ch. 4.
113. *New York Times*, Sept. 21, 1962, 1; Sept. 26, 1.
114. Marshall Interview, 76–77.
115. This account of this conversation relies on statement prepared by Burke Marshall and reprinted in Navasky, *Kennedy Justice*, 231–234.
116. Marshall Interview, 76–77.
117. *Pub. Paps., JFK, 1962* 726–728.
118. RFK, Oral History Interview, 735.
119. Norbert Schlei, Oral History Interview (Feb. 1968), JFKL.
120. *New York Times*, Oct. 1, 1962, 1; Oct. 7, 2E.
121. "Civil Rights," Committee on the Judiciary, House hearings (1963), 908.
122. Memo from Berl Bernhard to Lee White, Feb. 21, 1963, WH/KA file, Civil Rights Commission papers, JFKL.
123. Letter from R. F. Kennedy to John Hannah, Dec. 15, 1962; letter from Hannah to Kennedy, Jan. 2, 1963, Chronological file, Burke Marshall papers.

124. Interim Report of the U.S. Commission on Civil Rights, April 15, 1963.

125. Martin Luther King, Jr., *Why We Can't Wait* (1964), 54.

126. *New York Times*, April 13, 1963, 1; April 14, 1 and 46; King, *Why We Can't Wait*, 68–75.

127. Letter reprinted in King, *Why We Can't Wait*, 76–95. Quote on p. 87.

128. Brauer, *John F. Kennedy and the Second Reconstruction*, 233–234.

129. *New York Times*, May 3, 1963, 1; May 4, 1.

130. Quoted in King, *Why We Can't Wait*, 104.

131. Schlesinger, *A Thousand Days*, 959.

132. *New York Times*, May 4, 1963, 8.

133. King, *Why We Can't Wait*, 104.

134. *New York Times*, May 12, 1963, 1 and 53; May 13, 1, 24, 25.

135. *New York Times*, May 17, 1963, 14; May 19, 2E.

136. Quoted in Navasky, *Kennedy Justice*, 99.

137. RFK, Oral History Interview, 776.

138. *New York Times*, May 19, 1963, 1 and 2E; June 2, 1 and 2E.

139. For accounts of this meeting, *New York Times*, May 26, 1963, 1; *Newsweek* (vol. 61, June 3, 1963), 19; Guthman, *We Band of Brothers*, 220–221; Schlesinger, *Robert Kennedy*, 330–335. For quote, "Kennedy and Baldwin," *New Republic* (vol. 148, June 15, 1963), 4.

140. *New York Times*, June 12, 1963, 1, 20, 21.

141. *Pub. Paps., JFK, 1963*, 467–468.

142. Sorensen, *Kennedy*, 494–495.

143. *Pub. Paps., JFK, 1963*, 468–471.

144. *New York Times*, June 12, 1963, 1.

145. *New York Times*, June 13, 1963, 1.

146. *Pub. Paps., JFK, 1963*, 483–494; for text of the bill, "Civil Rights," House hearings, 649–660.

147. See testimony of civil rights leaders in "Civil Rights," House hearings, esp. testimony of Roy Wilkins, 2141–2176.

148. Brauer, *John F. Kennedy and the Second Reconstruction*, 265–266; Marshall, Oral History Interview No. 1, 105–106.

149. Schlesinger, *Robert Kennedy*, 349–352. King quote on p. 350; RFK, Oral History Interview, 917–918.

150. *New York Times*, Aug. 28, 1963, 1.

151. *New York Times*, Aug. 29, 1963, 1, 16, 17, 19, 20. Quote on p. 17.

152. Quoted in Watters and Cleghorn, *Climbing Jacob's Ladder*, xv; RFK, Oral History Interview, 920–921.

153. King's speech reprinted in Marcus H. Boulware, *The Oratory of Negro Leaders: 1900–1968* (1969), 270–275.

154. Sorensen, *Kennedy*, 499–500; *New York Times*, Sept. 26, 1963, 28; Oct.

27, IV, 6; Oct. 30, 22; subcommittee bill summarized in *Congressional Quarterly Almanac* (vol. 19, 1963), 348.

155. *New York Times*, Oct. 18, 1963, 1; Oct. 27, 6E.
156. RFK, Oral History Interview, 854.
157. Brauer, *John F. Kennedy and the Second Reconstruction*, 303–309: House Report 914 (1963).
158. Brauer, *John F. Kennedy and the Second Reconstruction*, 282–283; RFK, Oral History Interview, 878.
159. Brauer, *John F. Kennedy and the Second Reconstruction*, 308.
160. Harris's findings reported in "How Whites Feel About Negroes: A Painful American Dilemma," *Newsweek* (vol. 62, Oct. 21, 1963), 44–57.
161. *New York Times*, Oct. 31, 1963, 1.
162. Stewart Alsop and Oliver Quayle, "What Northerners Really Think of Negroes," *Saturday Evening Post* (vol. 236, Sept. 7, 1963), 20; Harris Poll, *Newsweek* (vol. 62, Aug. 26, 1963), 25–27; Harris, "How Whites Feel," *Newsweek*.
163. Quoted in *New York Times*, Nov. 25, 1963, 8.
164. Johnson's view conveyed in memo from Norbert Schlei to attorney general, June 4, 1963, Legislative file, RFK—Civil Rights papers, JFKL.
165. *New York Times*, March 2, 1964, 12.
166. RFK, Oral History Interview, 869.
167. *New York Times*, Feb. 18, 1964, 1; May 17, 12E; also Elizabeth Brenner Drew, "The Politics of Cloture," *Reporter* (vol. 31, July 16, 1964), 19–23.
168. *Cong. Rec.* (1964), 11943.
169. *New York Times*, May 9, 1964, 1; May 14, 1; May 19, 27; and Drew, "Politics of Cloture."
170. *New York Times*, May 20, 1964, 1.
171. Hartman Turnbow interview, Raines, *My Soul Is Rested*, 26.

Chapter 4. Origins of the War on Poverty

1. *New York Times*, Dec. 21, 1960, 1. For analysis of Medicare, see ch. 8.
2. Oscar Gass, "The New Frontier Fulfilled," *Commentary* (vol. 32, Dec. 1961), 461–473. Quote on p. 473.
3. For conservative view, *The Minimum Wage: Who Pays—An Interview with Yale Brozen and Milton Friedman* (April 1966, published by the Free Society Assoc., Inc.).
4. *Pub. Paps., JFK, 1961*, 216.
5. For a colorful account of the legislative struggle, Tom Wicker, *JFK*

and LBJ: The Influence of Personality upon Politics (1968).

6. *Cong. Rec.* (1961), 4805.

7. "Freedom of Communications," Part I (Kennedy Campaign Speeches), Committee on Commerce, Senate Report No. 994 (1961), 397.

8. Statement of the American Institute of Laundering, "To Amend the Fair Labor Standards Act," Committee on Education and Labor, House hearings (1961), 466–479.

9. William J. Shkurti and Belton M. Fleisher, "Employment and Wage Rates in Retail Trade Subsequent to the 1961 Amendments of the Fair Labor Standards Act," *The Southern Economic Journal* (vol. 35, July 1968), 37–48.

10. Memo from Gardner Ackley to pres., Aug. 2, 1965, Heller papers, 6/65-12/65 file, JFKL.

11. For economics of minimum wage, Finis Welsh, "Minimum Wage Legislation in the United States," *Economic Inquiry* (vol. 12, Sept. 1974), 285–318; M. Kosters and F. Welsh, "The Effects of Minimum Wages on the Distribution of Changes in Aggregate Employment," *American Economic Review* (vol. 62, June 1972), 323–332; T. G. Moore, "The Effects of Minimum Wages on Teenage Unemployment Rates," *Journal of Political Economy* (vol. 79, July 1971), 897–902. In its 1981 *Report,* the Minimum Wage Study Commission, which was created by congressional mandate, wrestled with the issue of disemployment effects. Commission staff estimated that a 10 percent increase in the minimum wage would wipe out 120,000 (1.5 percent) of the 8 million jobs currently held by teenagers (pp. 38–39). But a study conducted for the commission by John M. Abowd and Mark R. Killingsworth estimated teen job loss from a 10 percent minimum wage increase at 525,000 to 614,000. The consequences of the minimum wage on adult employment are much less frequently studied. Figures from Abowd and Killingsworth indicate the loss of adult jobs resulting from a 10 percent increase in the minimum wage would be 2.4 to 2.8 million (p. 194).

12. Kennedy quoted in *Congressional Quarterly Almanac* (vol. 17, 1961), 249.

13. *Cong. Rec.* (1961), 3607–3618. Quote on p. 3614.

14. *Cong. Rec.* (1961), 4022–4030.

15. House Report 276 (1963), Minority Views, 33–40; *Cong. Rec.* (1963), 10694.

16. *Cong. Rec.* (1961), 10693; 11668.

17. *Cong. Rec.* (1963), 11662.

18. Sar A. Levitan, *Federal Aid to Depressed Areas* (1964), 64–66.

19. Senate Report 250 (1963), 13.

20. GAO report summarized in House Report 539 (1965), Minority Views, 54.
21. *Annual and Final Report of Area Redevelopment Administration: Creating New and Permanent Employment* (Dec. 1965), 3.
22. For background, National Commission on Urban Problems, *Building the American City* (1968); Lawrence M. Friedman, *Government and Slum Housing* (1968), 147–172.
23. Martin Anderson, *The Federal Bulldozer* (1964), ch. 2; "Federal Bulldozer's' Fallacies," *Journal of Housing* (vol. 22, April 1965), 202.
24. Edgar O. Olsen, "A Competitive Theory of the Housing Market," in Jon Pynoos, ed., *Housing Urban America* (1973), 228–238; Richard F. Muth, "The Economics of Slum Housing," in Wayland D. Gardner, ed., *America's Cities* (1970), 24–25.
25. Jane Jacobs, *The Death and Life of Great American Cities* (1961), 270–271.
26. "Housing Legislation of 1961," Committee on Banking and Currency, Senate hearings (1961), 949.
27. National Commission, *Building the American City*, 160. Estimate of persons displaced is based on number of dwelling units multiplied by 3.5 persons, the presumed average rate of occupancy per unit.
28. For popular view of automation, Walter Buckingham, *Automation: Its Impact on Business and People* (1961).
29. *Cong. Rec.* (1962), 3017.
30. Quoted in Senate Report 651 (1961), 5–6.
31. House Report 879 (1961), Minority Views, 26–27.
32. Quoted in Clyde E. Dankert, "Automation and Unemployment," in *Studies in Unemployment*, Committee Print, Special Committee on Unemployment Problems, Senate (1960), 226.
33. See James W. Knowles, "Higher Unemployment Rates, 1957–1960: Structural Transformation or Inadequate Demand," Committee Print, Joint Economic Committee (1961); and Charles E. Silberman, *The Myths of Automation* (1966).
34. *Manpower Report of the President* (March 1966), 3–5; and (April 1967), 50–51.
35. *Statistics on Manpower: A Supplement to the Manpower Report of the President* (March 1968), 86–87.
36. Department of Labor, "Earnings Mobility of MDTA Trainees" (April 1967), 1–8; "Amending the Manpower Development and Training Act of 1962," Committee on Labor and Public Welfare, Senate hearings (1965), 18–19.
37. "Employment and Training Legislation—1968," Committee on Labor and Public Welfare, Senate hearings (1968), appendix, 5.
38. Greenleigh Associates, Inc., *Opening the Doors: Job Training Programs* (Feb. 1968), reprinted in "Employment and Training Legislation—

1968," Background Information Supplement, 155.

39. Sar A. Levitan, Garth L. Mangum, Ray Marshall, *Human Resources and Labor Markets* (1972), 327–328, 333–334; Garth Mangum and John Walsh, *A Decade of Manpower Development and Training* (1973), 117, 122, 123.

40. Sar A. Levitan and Garth L. Mangum, *Federal Training and Work Programs in the Sixties* (1969), 24–27.

41. Garth L. Mangum, *MDTA: Foundations of Federal Manpower Policy* (1968), 2.

42. "Employment and Training Legislation—1968," 389.

43. For background, see James L. Sundquist, *Politics and Policy: the Eisenhower, Kennedy, and Johnson Years* (1968), 155–195; Frank J. Munger and Richard F. Fenno, Jr., *National Politics and Federal Aid to Education* (1962); and Hugh Douglas Price, "Schools, Scholarships and Congressmen: The Kennedy Aid-to-Education Program," in Alan F. Westin, ed., *The Centers of Power* (1964), ch. 2.

44. "Federal Aid to Schools," Committee on Education and Labor, House hearings (1961), 6–12.

45. *Cong. Rec.* (1961), 8663–8672; and Senate Report 255 (1961), Minority Views 18–29. From 1954 to 1959, students per classroom fell from 30.6 to 28.1. From 1954 to 1961 the number of students per teacher fell from 28.4 to 26.

46. *Standard Education Almanac: 1972,* 91.

47. *Standard Education Almanac: 1972,* 83.

48. HEW, *Digest of Educational Statistics: 1974 Edition,* 49, 51.

49. *Standard Education Almanac: 1972,* 71.

50. Richardson White, Jr., and Beryl A. Radin, "Youth and Opportunity: The Federal Anti-Delinquency Program" (unpublished study done for HEW), June 1969, 47.

51. John Knowles, *A Separate Peace* (1959), 7.

52. Kennedy's order reprinted in "Extension of the Juvenile Delinquency Act," Committee on Labor and Public Welfare, Senate hearings (1963), 413–414.

53. For legislative history, John E. Moore, "Controlling Delinquency: Executive, Congressional, and Juvenile 1961–1964," in F. N. Cleaveland and Associates, *Congress and Urban Problems* (1969), 110–139; also see "Juvenile Delinquency Control Act," Committee on Education and Labor, House hearings (1961).

54. White and Radin, "Youth and Opportunity," 48–50.

55. For a discussion of the Chicago School, Solomon Kobrin, "The Chicago Area Project—a 25-Year Assessment," *Annals of the American Academy of Political and Social Science* (vol. 322, March 1959), 19–29. See also Clifford R. Shaw and Henry D. McKay, *Juvenile Delinquency*

and Urban Areas (revised ed., 1969). On Area Projects, 322–326.

56. Richard A. Cloward and Lloyd Ohlin, *Delinquency and Opportunity: A Theory of Delinquent Gangs* (1960), 211.

57. On MFY, see White and Radin, "Youth and Opportunity," 25–29, 31–37; Daniel Knapp and Kenneth Polk, *Scouting the War on Poverty* (1971), 32–42.

58. Quoted in Knapp and Polk, *Scouting the War on Poverty,* 66.

59. Quoted in Arthur M. Schlesinger, Jr., *Robert Kennedy and His Times* (1978), 415. Schlesinger cites as source Patrick Anderson, "Robert's Character," *Esquire,* April 1965.

60. Interview of David Hackett by Richardson White, Jan. 27, 1969, notes in Richardson White papers, JFKL.

61. Memo from Hackett to R. F. Kennedy, Jan. 24, 1962, files of PCJD, National Archives.

62. *Pub. Paps., JFK, 1962,* 447–448.

63. Knapp and Polk, *Scouting the War on Poverty,* 84–87; interview with Sanford Kravitz by Knapp, Dec. 11, 1967, Knapp papers, JFKL.

64. Hackett to R. F. Kennedy, Feb. 26, 1962, copy in Knapp papers; Knapp and Polk, *Scouting the War on Poverty,* 77–79. The planning grant communities were Boston, Charleston (W. Va.), Chicago, Cleveland, Detroit, Harlem, Houston, Lane County (Ore.), Los Angeles, Minneapolis, New Haven, Philadelphia, Providence, St. Louis, Syracuse, Washington.

65. Sanford Kravitz, "The Program of the President's Committee on Juvenile Delinquency," Sept. 1963, a paper for the National Conference on Problems of Rural Youth in a Changing Environment, 12.

66. Leonard Cottrell quoted in White and Radin, "Youth and Opportunity," 184.

67. White and Radin, "Youth and Opportunity," 75.

68. Quoted in White and Radin, "Youth and Opportunity," 88.

69. Interview of Sanford Kravitz by Richardson White, Feb. 11, 1969, notes in White papers.

70. Moore, "Controlling Delinquency," 144–157. Quote on p. 150.

71. White and Radin, "Youth and Opportunity," 154–161; interview of Virginia Burns by Knapp, Nov. 28, 1967, Knapp papers; interview of Bernard Russell by Knapp, Nov. 29, 1967, Knapp papers; Knapp and Polk, *Scouting the War on Poverty,* 111–112.

72. Quoted in White and Radin, "Youth and Opportunity," 156.

73. Daniel P. Moynihan, *Maximum Feasible Misunderstanding* (1969), 76. In general, Moynihan's account is a poor guide.

74. Minutes of the Demonstration Projects Technical Advisory Panel, Nov. 30 and Dec. 1, 1962, 28–33, 36–39; and March 25–27, 1963, JFKL. Also Knapp and Polk, *Scouting the War on Poverty,* 94–105.

75. Pamela W. Reeves, "Social Planning and Political Survival: The Federal Juvenile Delinquency Project in Cleveland" (undated, unpublished manuscript), 117–127, copy in Knapp papers. Reeves was the official historian of the Cleveland project.
76. Quoted in Reeves, "Social Planning," 106.
77. See documents on Philadelphia in PCJD files, National Archives.
78. On Minneapolis, Knapp and Polk, *Scouting the War on Poverty*, 139–153.
79. Minutes of Demonstration Projects Technical Advisory Panel, June 12–13, 1963, 9–33.
80. The best study of a single planning project is Stephan Thernstrom, *Poverty, Planning and Politics in the New Boston: The Origins of ABCD* (1969).
81. For Cottrell's views, Stanton Wheeler and Leonard S. Cottrell, Jr., *Juvenile Delinquency: Its Prevention and Control* (1966); Knapp and Polk, *Scouting the War on Poverty*, 25–32; Peter Marris and Martin Rein, *Dilemmas of Social Reform* (1967), 170.
82. Interview of Lloyd Ohlin and Leonard Cottrell by Richardson White, Feb. 21, 1969, notes in White papers, JFKL.
83. Ohlin and Cottrell interview by White.
84. White and Radin, "Youth and Opportunity," 110.
85. Interview of Boone by Richardson White, Jan. 30, 1969, notes in White papers.
86. "A Proposal for a National Service Corps," Oct. 19, 1962, copy in White papers. See also White and Radin, "Youth and Opportunity," 161–164.
87. "The Federal Government and Urban Poverty," transcript of a conference sponsored by JFK Library at Brandeis University, June 16–17, 1973, 265–267, 294–297, JFKL. Boone's quote on p. 295.
88. Boone interview with White.
89. Knapp and Polk, *Scouting the War on Poverty*, 35–42, 109–111, 157–167.
90. Memo from Russell to Ivan A. Nestigen, Feb. 19, 1964, Knapp papers.
91. Memo from Hackett to AG, Aug. 5, 1963, Knapp papers.
92. Quoted in James L. Sundquist, "Origins of the War on Poverty," in Sundquist, ed., *On Fighting Poverty: Perspective for Experience* (1969), 7.
93. "Federal Government and Urban Poverty," 170–183.
94. "Federal Government and Urban Poverty," 211.
95. "Federal Government and Urban Poverty," 207.
96. Lyndon B. Johnson, *The Vantage Point* (1971), 71.
97. "Federal Government and Urban Poverty," 44.
98. Memo from Hackett to Heller, Nov. 6, 1963, Memo file, Hackett

papers, JFKL; Memo from Hackett to Heller, Dec. 1, 1963, Poverty file, CEA-Heller papers, JFKL.

99. "Federal Government and Urban Poverty," 355.
100. Knapp and Polk, *Scouting the War on Poverty*, 130–134.
101. "Federal Government and Urban Poverty," 188.
102. "Federal Government and Urban Poverty," 260.
103. "Federal Government and Urban Poverty," 260–261.
104. Memo from Heller to Sorensen, Dec. 20, 1963, Poverty file, CEA-Heller papers. To follow Hackett's proposal through the task force, see this file.
105. LBJ, *Vantage Point*, 74.
106. Memo from attorney general to pres., Jan. 16, 1964, White papers.
107. Memo from Willard Wirtz to Sorensen, Jan. 23, 1964, Poverty (Eastern Ky.) file, Sorensen papers, JFKL; Memo from Wilbur J. Cohen to Sorensen, Dec. 26, 1963, same file.
108. *Pub. Paps., LBJ, 1963–64*, 114.
109. *Pub. Paps., LBJ, 1963–64*, 182–184.
110. *Pub. Paps., LBJ, 1963–64*, 255.
111. Shriver quoted in Adam Yarmolinsky, "The Beginnings of OEO," in Sundquist, *On Fighting Poverty*, 36. See also two other useful essays on origins in this volume: Sundquist, "Origins of the War on Poverty," and Sanford Kravitz, "The Community Action Program—Past, Present, and Its Future?"
112. "Federal Government and Urban Poverty," 286.
113. Yarmolinsky, "The Beginnings," footnote, p. 51.
114. For a copy of the bill, "Economic Opportunity Act of 1964," Committee on Education and Labor, House hearings (1964), 3–18. Quote on p. 90.
115. "Federal Government and Urban Poverty," 301–302.
116. The act also created Volunteers in Service to America (VISTA) which OEO administered; the Neighborhood Youth Corps; a work-study program for poor college students; loans for low-income rural families; aid to migrant workers; a special loan fund for the Small Business Administration; and pilot projects to train unemployed heads of households on welfare.
117. "Economic Opportunity Act of 1964," 767.
118. "Economic Opportunity Act of 1964," 301–307. Quote on p. 305.
119. Knapp and Polk, *Scouting the War on Poverty*, 137.

Chapter 5. The Election of 1964

1. *Public Papers of the Presidents: Lyndon B. Johnson, 1963–1964*, 9.
2. *Pub. Paps., LBJ, 1963–64*, 721.

3. Frank Cormier, *LBJ: The Way He Was* (1977), 147.
4. Quoted in Eric F. Goldman, *The Tragedy of Lyndon Johnson* (1969), 521. For an account of Johnson's early life, which also finds him unlikeable, Robert A. Caro, *The Path to Power: The Years of Lyndon Johnson* (1982).
5. Cormier, *LBJ*, 134.
6. Cormier, *LBJ*, 206, 75, 133. On sex life of bulls, Rowland Evans and Robert Novak, *Lyndon B. Johnson: The Exercise of Power* (1966), 408.
7. Quoted in Joseph A. Califano, Jr., *A Presidential Nation* (1975), 213.
8. Quoted in Goldman, *Tragedy*, 21.
9. Barry Goldwater, *The Conscience of a Conservative* (1960), 13.
10. Barry M. Goldwater, *Why Not Victory?* (1962), 159.
11. *New York Times*, July 28, 1960, 14.
12. F. Clifton White, *Suite 3505: The Story of the Draft Goldwater Movement* (1967), chs. 3–6.
13. Robert D. Novak, *The Agony of the GOP, 1964* (1965), chs. 6, 8, 10.
14. For an early statement of the southern strategy without racist overtones, William A. Rusher, "Crossroads for the G.O.P.," *National Review* (vol. 14, Feb. 12, 1963), 109–112.
15. Quoted in Stewart Alsop, "Can Goldwater Win in '64?," *Saturday Evening Post* (vol. 236, Aug. 24, 1963).
16. *New York Times*, March 11, 1964, 1 and 18; Theodore White, *Making of the President 1964* (1965), 104, 106.
17. *New York Times*, March 15, 1964, 1E.
18. Quoted in Charles Mohr, "Close Look at a Puzzled Candidate," New *York Times Magazine*, May 17, 1964, 11.
19. Novak, *Agony of G.O.P.*, ch. 20; White, *Suite 3505*, 332, 349–350; Stephen Shadegg, *What Happened to Goldwater?* (1965), 117.
20. Novak, *Agony of G.O.P.*, ch. 21; White, *Suite 3505*, ch. 30. Richard Scammon, ed., *America Votes 6, 1964* (1966), 54.
21. Gallup cited in Nelson Polsby, "Strategic Considerations," in Milton C. Cummings, Jr., ed., *The National Election of 1964* (1966), footnote, p. 91.
22. Poll data in Irving Crespi, "The Structural Basis for Right-wing Conservatism: The Goldwater Case," *The Public Opinion Quarterly* (vol. 29, Winter 1966), 523–543.
23. Alsop, "Can Goldwater Win in '64?"
24. Norman Mailer, "In the Red Light: A History of the Republican Convention in 1964," *Esquire* (vol. 62, Nov. 1964), 83 ff. Quote on p. 87.
25. I. F. Stone, "The Collected Works of Barry Goldwater," *New York Review of Books* (vol. 3, Aug. 20, 1964), 3.
26. Quoted in Alsop, "Can Goldwater Win in '64?"

27. *New York Times*, July 15, 1964, 1 and 21.
28. White, *Making of the President 1964*, 200–201. White, *Suite 3505*, 398.
29. Text reprinted in *New York Times*, July 17, 1964, 10.
30. White, *Suite 3505*, 14–15.
31. Henry H. Wilson, Jr., to Lawrence F. O'Brien, July 8, 1964, Campaign 1964 file, Wilson papers, LBJL.
32. On Wallace, Marshall Frady, *Wallace* (1968).
33. Harold H. Martin, "George Wallace Shakes Up the Political Scene," *Saturday Evening Post* (vol. 237, May 9, 1964), 85 ff.
34. *New York Times*, April 8, 1964, 1; April 9, 19.
35. *New York Times*, May 6, 1964, 1 and 20; May 7, 20; May 21, 1 and 25.
36. Victor Hoffmann and John Strietelmeier, "Gary's Rank-and-File Reaction," *Reporter* (vol. 31, Sept. 10, 1964), 28–29.
37. Michael Rogin, "Wallace and the Middle Class: The White Backlash in Wisconsin, *The Public Opinion Quarterly* (vol. 30, Spring 1966), 98–108.
38. *New York Times*, June 8, 1964, 1; July 13, 18; July 20, 1 and 12.
39. For New York and Rochester riots, see *New York Times*, week beginning July 19, 1964; and *Time* (vol. 84, July 31, 1964), 9–11.
40. Text of leaders' statements, *New York Times*, July 30, 1964, 12.
41. *Time* (vol. 84, Sept. 4, 1964), 19a.
42. James Fallows, "Crazies by the Tail: Bay of Pigs, Diem, and Liddy," *Washington Monthly* (vol. 6, Sept. 1974), 51.
43. *Time* (vol. 84, Aug. 28, 1964), 17.
44. On SNCC, Freedom Summer, and MFDP, see Allen J. Matusow, "From Civil Rights to Black Power: The Case of SNCC," in Barton Bernstein and Matusow, eds., *Twentieth Century America: Recent Interpretations* (1969), 531–556.
45. On this episode see testimony of Cartha DeLoach in "Intelligence Activities," vol. 6, Hearings before the Select Committee to Study Governmental Operations with Respect to Intelligence Activities, U.S. Senate (1975), 174–180; see also FBI documents published in hearings as exhibits 39, 40-1, 40-2, and 41, pp. 495–510. This episode is also discussed in "Warrantless FBI Electronic Surveillance" (a staff report) in *Final Report*, Senate Select Committee, Book III, 346–349.
46. DeLoach to Mr. Mohr, Aug. 29, 1964, exhibit 39 in Senate Select Committee hearings.
47. Quoted in Matusow, "From Civil Rights to Black Power," 542.
48. On RFK-LBJ relationship see Arthur M. Schlesinger, Jr., *Robert Kennedy and His Times* (1978), ch. 27; on vice-presidential episode, ch. 28; Jackson quoted on p. 665.
49. Quoted in *Time* (vol. 84, Sept. 25, 1964), 15.

50. Goldwater's maiden speech of the campaign, "Peace Through Strength," reprinted in *Vital Speeches* (vol. 30, Oct. 1, 1964), 743–746.
51. Goldwater speech in Los Angeles, Sept. 8, 1964, Cater Box 43, LBJL.
52. Milton Friedman, "The Goldwater View of Economics," *New York Times Magazine*, Oct. 11, 1964, 136–137.
53. *New York Times*, Sept. 17, 1964, 1.
54. *New York Times*, Sept. 20, 1964, 1 and 70.
55. *New York Times*, Sept. 16, 1964, 1 and 12.
56. Goldwater campaign speech in Charleston, West Virginia, Sept. 18, 1964, Cater Box 43, LBJL.
57. *New York Times*, Oct. 12, 1964, 1 and 21.
58. *New York Times*, Sept. 30, 1964, 1 and 28.
59. *New York Times*, Oct. 10, 1964, 1 and 14.
60. Goldwater's two most important foreign-policy speeches are reprinted in *Vital Speeches* (vol. 31, Oct. 15, 1964), 5–7; (Nov. 1, 1964), 36–38.
61. Barry Goldwater, *Where I Stand* (1964), 56.
62. See Bobby Baker, with Larry L. King, *Wheeling and Dealing: Confessions of a Capitol Hill Operator* (1978).
63. Robert F. Kennedy, Oral History Interview, Dec. 4, 1964, 457–460, 645–647, 653–655. Quotes on pp. 646, 655, JFKL.
64. "Financial or Business Interests of Officers or Employees of the Senate," Committee on Rules and Administration, Part I, Senate hearings (1964); Senate Report 1175 (1964).
65. *Pub. Paps., LBJ, 1963–64*, 220–221.
66. *New York Times*, Feb. 8, 1964, 1: Baker, *Wheeling and Dealing*, 194.
67. *New York Times*, March 12, 1964, 16; March 26, 19; March 27, 9.
68. Quoted in Roger Kahn, "Goldwater's Desperate Battle," *Saturday Evening Post* (vol. 227, Oct. 24, 1964), 19–25.
69. *New York Times*, Oct. 15, 1964, 1; Oct. 18, 2E.
70. RFK, Oral History Interview, 648.
71. *New York Times*, Oct. 21, 1964, 35; Oct. 22, 1; Oct. 25, 2E.
72. *Pub. Paps., LBJ, 1963–64*, 1224.
73. *Pub. Paps., LBJ, 1963–64*, 1228, 1237, 1269.
74. *Pub. Paps., LBJ, 1963–64*, 1106.
75. *Pub. Paps., LBJ, 1963–64*, 1373.
76. For a discussion of the nuclear issue, *Time* (vol. 84, Sept. 25, 1964), 16–19; and White, *Making of the President 1964*, 296–300.
77. Pete Hamill, "When the Client Is a Candidate," *New York Times Magazine*, Oct. 25, 1964, 30–31, 136–137.
78. *Time* (vol. 84, Oct. 23, 1964), 25.
79. Hamill, "When the Client Is a Candidate," 128.
80. Goldwater, "Peace Through Strength," 744.

81. Goldwater campaign speech in Chicago, Oct. 16, 1964, Cater Box 43, LBJL.
82. *New York Times*, May 25, 1964, 1, 36; May 27, 22.
83. *New York Times*, July 18, 1964, 6.
84. Department of Defense, *United States—Vietnam Relations, 1945–1967* (1968), cited hereafter as *Pentagon Papers*, Book 3, Part IV, C .2(a), 1–40. Quote on p. 40.
85. On Gulf of Tonkin incident and its consequences, Anthony Austin, *The President's War* (1971).
86. For post-mortems see Austin, *President's War*, esp. ch. 10; and "The Gulf of Tonkin, The 1964 Incidents," Committee on Foreign Relations, U.S. Senate (1968).
87. *New York Times*, Oct. 6, 1964, 1.
88. *Pentagon Papers*, Book 4, Part IV, C .2(b), 25–26.
89. *Pub. Paps., LBJ, 1963–64*, 1126.
90. *Pub. Paps., LBJ, 1963–64*, 1267.
91. *Pub. Paps., LBJ, 1963–64*, 1165.
92. Jack Osgood Field and Ronald E. Anderson, "Ideology in the Public's Conceptualization of the 1964 Election," *The Public Opinion Quarterly* (vol. 33, Fall 1969), 380–398. Quote on p. 392.
93. On returns, *New York Times*, Nov. 5, 1964, 1 and 21; NBC analysis in *U.S. News* (vol. 57, Nov. 16, 1964), 40–41; *Congressional Quarterly Weekly Report* (vol. 22, Dec. 11, 1964), 2790–2791.
94. *New York Times*, Aug. 17, 1964, 37.
95. Herbert E. Alexander, *Financing the 1964 Election* (1968), 7–17, 84–86, 98–99.
96. *New York Times*, Sept. 4, 1964, 13; David T. Bazelan, "Big Business and the Democrats," *Commentary* (vol. 39, May 1965), 42.

Chapter 6. War, Inflation, and Farewell to Keynes

1. *Public Papers of the Presidents, LBJ, 1965*, 74.
2. For reactions to the inaugural, *Newsweek* (vol. 65, Feb. 1, 1965), 10–12, for quote p. 17.
3. Eric F. Goldman, *The Tragedy of Lyndon Johnson* (1968), 332.
4. Goldman, *Tragedy of Lyndon Johnson*, 334.
5. For Johnson's mood, Lyndon B. Johnson, *The Vantage Point* (1971), 322–324; Goldman, *Tragedy of Lyndon Johnson*, 335–337.
6. For discussions of the problem, James Deakin, *Lyndon Johnson's Credibility Gap* (1968); Hugh Sidey, *A Very Personal Presidency: Lyndon Johnson in the White House* (1968), ch. 7.
7. On bourbon, Sidey, *A Very Personal Presidency*, 173; on his operation and the Dominican intervention, Deakin, *Credibility Gap*, 45, 33–34.

8. *New York Times*, June 10, 1965, 34.
9. *The Pentagon Papers* (Gravel Edition, vol. 3), 269–275, 389–398.
10. Westmoreland's cable in *Pentagon Papers*, 438–440.
11. *Pub. Paps., LBJ, 1965*, 794, 795.
12. *Pub. Paps., LBJ, 1965*, 801.
13. *Newsweek* (vol. 65, May 31, 1965), 66.
14. Memos from Ackley to pres., May 5, 1965, and May 11, 1965, General file, Heller papers, JFKL.
15. *Pub. Paps., LBJ, 1965*, 800.
16. Memo from Ackley to pres., July 30, 1965, FG 11-3 file, WHCF, LBJL.
17. Estimates of war costs, *Pub. Paps., LBJ, 1967*, 47.
18. For discussion of Phillips Curve, Thomas M. Humphrey, "Changing Views of the Phillips Curve," in Thomas M. Havrilesky and John T. Boorman, *Current Issues in Monetary Theory and Policy* (1976), 154–176. The Council discreetly discussed the Phillips Curve in its 1962 *Annual Report*, 44–48.
19. Arthur M. Okun, *The Political Economy of Prosperity* (1970), 50; James Tobin, *The New Economics a Decade Older* (1974), 15–17.
20. For a good overview, James L. Cochrane, "The Johnson Administration: Moral Suasion Goes to War," in Craufurd D. Goodwin, ed., *Exhortation and Controls: The Search for a Wage-Price Policy, 1945–1971* (1975), 193–293.
21. Quoted in Cochrane, "The Johnson Administration," 222.
22. *New York Times*, Aug. 30, 1965, 1 and 15; Aug. 31, 1 and 24; Sept. 1, 1 and 23; Sept. 3, 1; Sept. 4, 1 and 7; and memo from Ackley to pres., Sept. 8, 1965, LA/6 Steel file, LBJL.
23. Memo from Ackley to pres., Nov. 13, 1965, BE 5 file, WHCF, LBJL.
24. Memo from Ackley to pres., Oct. 5, 1965, copy in CEA Administrative History, vol. II, part 1, LBJL.
25. Memo from Ackley to pres., Nov. 29, 1965, BE 5-2 file, WHCF, LBJL.
26. Memo from Ackley to pres., Nov. 25, 1965, BE 5 file, WHCF, LBJL.
27. Memo from Ackley to pres., Dec. 2, 1965, FI-8 file, WHCF, LBJL.
28. Okun, *Political Economy of Prosperity*, 66–69.
29. Memo from Fowler, Schultze, and Ackley to pres., Dec. 4, 1965, copy in CEA Administrative History, vol. II, part 3, LBJL.
30. *New York Times*, Jan. 28, 1966, 1 and 15.
31. Memo from Ackley to pres., Dec. 17, 1965, FI-4 file, WHCF, LBJL.
32. Memo from Schultze to pres., Dec. 17, 1965, FI-4 file, WHCF, LBJL.
33. For Johnson's version, *Vantage Point*, 439–445.
34. *Pub. Paps., LBJ, 1966*, 47–68. Quote on p. 49.
35. "Department of Defense Appropriations for 1967," Committee on Appropriations, House hearings (1966), 70.

36. CEA, *1967 Annual Report*, 282; *Pub. Paps., LBJ, 1968–69*, 97.

37. CEA, *1967 Annual Report*, 46–47.

38. *Pub. Paps., LBJ, 1966*, 376.

39. CEA, *1967 Annual Report*, 48–49.

40. Memo from Fowler, Schultze, and Ackley to pres., April 22, 1966, BE-5 file, WHCF, LBJL.

41. CEA, *1967 Annual Report*, 262.

42. The administrative budget measures expenditures and receipts of federal agencies which operate under regular congressional appropriations. The national income accounts budget includes, in addition, the transactions of the government's trust funds (social security, highway, unemployment insurance) but unlike the administrative budget, excludes transactions in financial assets.

43. CEA, *1969 Annual Report*, 301. Some scholars have questioned the view that fiscal policy was restrained in 1965–66. The national income accounts budget, in their view, underestimated the true extent of spending on the war. That budget records a government expenditure for a defense good only when it had been finished and delivered to the Defense Department. In fact, the contractor has been spending money on men and materials to produce the good long before delivery. This means that spending on war production in 1965–66 was not $6 billion, as the national income accounts budget reported, but approximately $10 billion. To put it another way, spending that showed up in the national income accounts as increased investment by defense contractors (hence a private spending) should have been recorded as direct spending by the government in the war. See testimony of Murray L. Weidenbaum, "Economic Effects of Vietnam Spending," Joint Economic Committee, hearings (1967), 193–236; and Charles E. McLure, Jr., "Fiscal Failure: Lessons of the Sixties," in Phillip Cagan, et al., *Economic Policy and Inflation in the Sixties* (1972), 42–47. Whether or not this point has merit, its force is mitigated by the fact that most of the increased spending by war contractors took place in 1966. Inflationary pressures were already building before that time.

44. See Okun, *Political Economy*, 66–69; CEA, *1967 Annual Report*, 46–47.

45. Friedman's ideas are accessible to the layman in "The Role of Monetary Policy," *American Economic Review* (vol. 58, March 1968), 1–17; *The Counter Revolution in Monetary Theory* (1970); and *Dollars and Deficits* (1968). Among other works I found helpful are Friedman, *The Optimum Quantity of Money and Other Essays* (1969); Robert J. Gordon, ed., *Milton Friedman's Monetary Framework: A Debate with His Critics* (1974); and Jerome L. Stein, *Monetarism: Studies in Monetary Economics* (1976).

46. See Milton Friedman and Anna Jacobson Schwartz, *A Monetary History*

of the United States, 1867–1960 (1963). This book is a history of business cycles, seeking to show that they are determined by changes in the rate of monetary growth.

47. Friedman, *Dollars and Deficits,* 108.

48. For critique of Friedman, James Tobin, *Essays in Economics* (vol. 1, 1971), chs. 22 and 23; Paul A. Samuelson, "Monetarism Reevaluated," in L. G. Reynolds, G. D. Green, and Dr. R. Lewis, *Current Issues of Economic Policy* (1973), 50–59; Heller's presentation in Milton Friedman and Walter W. Heller, *Monetary vs. Fiscal Policy: A Dialogue* (1969).

49. Friedman, *Dollars and Deficits,* 98.

50. Friedman's letter reprinted in *Dollars and Deficits,* 126–152. The quote is on p. 147. Friedman here used two definitions of money. M1 referred to currency plus checking accounts in commercial banks. It grew 2.8 percent annually on the historic average, compared to 3.7 percent from 1962–65. M2 included M1 plus savings accounts in commercial banks. M2 grew 4.7 percent annually on the historic average, compared to 8.3 percent from 1962–65. The disparity in growth rates between the two measures of money resulted from successive rises in interest rates in time deposits. These rises, Friedman said, "have made the rate of rise of M2 higher, and of M1 lower, than the rate of rise of an economically homogeneous monetary total" (p. 147). All subsequent references in this chapter are to M1.

51. For characterization of Martin, Sherman J. Maisel, *Managing the Dollar* (1973), 113–120.

52. Phillip Cagan, "Monetary Policy," in Cagan, et al., *Economic Policy and Inflation in the Sixties,* 96–97.

53. Maisel, *Managing the Dollar,* 69–86; *Pub. Paps., LBJ, 1965,* 1137–1138.

54. Cagan, "Monetary Policy," 96; and Friedman's letter to the Fed, June 15, 1966, reprinted in *Dollars and Deficits,* 160–161.

55. Milton Friedman, "What Price Guideposts," reprinted in *Dollars and Deficits,* 97–121, esp. pp. 100–105; see also Thomas Gale Moore, "Incomes Policy, Its Rationale and Development," in Cagan, et al., *Economic Policy and Inflation in the Sixties,* 199–239, esp. 201–202.

56. Okun, *Political Economy,* 66.

57. Milton Friedman, "Higher Taxes? No," *Newsweek,* Jan. 23, 1967, reprinted in Friedman, *An Economist's Protest* (1972), 69–70.

58. Friedman, *Dollars and Deficits,* 105.

59. CEA, *1969 Annual Report,* 301.

60. Troika to pres., July 8, 1966, BE 5 file, LBJL. (Troika consisted of Treasury Secretary, Budget Director, and chairman of CEA.)

61. Cagan, "Monetary Policy," 98–101.

62. This account of the Credit Crunch relies on Maisel, *Managing the*

Dollar, ch. 5; Albert E. Berger, "A Historical Analysis of the Credit Crunch of 1966," *Review, Federal Reserve Bank of St. Louis* (Sept. 1969), 13–30; Hyman Minsky, "The Crunch of 1966—Model for New Financial Crises?" *Trans-action* (vol. 5, March 1968), 44–51; "Recent Bank Credit and Monetary Developments," *Federal Reserve Bulletin* (vol. 53, Feb. 1967), 187–200; CEA, *1967 Annual Report*, 52–61; Alfred Hayes, "The 1966 Credit Crunch," in David P. Eastburn, ed., *Men, Money and Policy* (1970), 91–103.

63. Hayes, "The 1966 Credit Crunch," 101.

64. Letter reprinted in *Federal Reserve Bulletin* (vol. 52, Sept. 1966), 1338–1339.

65. Troika to pres., Nov. 11, 1966, BE 5 file, LBJL.

66. CEA, *1967 Annual Report*, 60.

67. "The Impact of Monetary Stringency on Business Investment," *Survey of Current Business* (vol. 47, Aug. 1967), 10–26.

68. Memo from Ackley to Califano, Sept. 9, 1966, BE 5 file, LBJL. With attachment.

69. Milton Friedman, "Inflationary Recession," *Newsweek*, Oct. 17, 1966, reprinted in Friedman, *Economist's Protest*, 40–42.

70. *Economic Report of the President, 1968*, 4; Friedman, "Current Monetary Policy," *Newsweek*, Oct. 30, 1967, reprinted in Friedman, *Economist's Protest*, 44–46.

71. "Restoration of Investment Credit and Rapid Depreciation," Committee on Ways and Means, House hearings (1967), 4 ff.

72. CEA, *1968 Annual Report*, 261, 264.

73. CEA, *1969 Annual Report*, 301.

74. Memo from Joe Califano to the Files, June 9, 1967, Economy file, Califano papers, LBJL.

75. *Pub. Paps., LBJ, 1967*, 733–740.

76. Friedman, "Current Monetary Policy," *Newsweek*, Oct. 30, 1967, reprinted in Friedman, *Economist's Protest*, 44–46; and Cagan, "Monetary Policy," 101–102.

77. "President's 1967 Tax Proposals," Committee on Ways and Means, House hearings (1967), 95.

78. Mills's suggestion conveyed in a memo from Barefoot Sanders to pres., Sept. 13, 1967, FG 110 file, LBJL.

79. Memo from Schultze to pres., Sept. 16, 1967, LE/FI 11-4 file, WHCF, LBJL.

80. Memo from Fowler to pres., Sept. 20, 1967, LE/FI 11-4 file, WHCF, LBJL (plus attachment).

81. *New York Times*, Oct. 4, 1967, 1 and 30; Mills's version in a speech reprinted in *New York Times*, Nov. 21, 1967, 1 and 74; motion to lay aside reprinted in "President's 1967 Surtax Proposal: Continuation

of Hearings—November 1967," Committee on Ways and Means, House hearings (1967), 1.

82. "President's 1967 Surtax Proposal: Continuation of Hearings—November 1967," 2–11.

83. CEA, *1969 Annual Report*, 40–41.

84. "President's Surtax Proposal: Continuation of Hearings—January 1968 (1968), 162.

85. *New York Times*, Jan. 24, 1968, 1 and 25.

86. *Cong. Rec.* (1968), 8544 ff.

87. For an account of these events, Lawrence C. Pierce, *The Politics of Fiscal Policy Formation* (1971), ch. 7, esp. 162–172.

88. Martin and Fowler quoted in Pierce, *Politics of Fiscal Policy*, 165.

89. CEA, *1969 Annual Report*, 301.

90. Memo from Barr, Zwick, and Okun to pres., Aug. 5, 1968, BE 5 file.

91. Cagan, "Monetary Policy," 103; Friedman, "The Inflationary Fed," *Newsweek*, Jan. 20, 1968, reprinted in Friedman, *Economist's Protest*, 48–49.

92. *New York Times*, Sept. 19, 1968, 71.

93. *New York Times*, Oct. 17, 1968, 69.

94. CEA, *1969 Annual Report*, ch. 1, esp. pp. 33, 45; *New York Times*, Jan. 30, 1969, 1.

95. CEA, *1971 Annual Report*, 250.

96. Arthur M. Okun, "The Personal Tax Surcharge and Consumer Demand, 1968–70," *Brookings Papers on Economic Activity* (no. 1, 1971), 167–200. Quote on p. 200. For a critique of Okun's study, claiming that the surcharge had no appreciable effect even on consumption of nondurables, William L. Springer, "Did the 1968 Surcharge Really Work?," *American Economic Review* (vol. 65, Sept. 1975), 644–659. Okun and Springer continue the debate, same journal (vol. 67, March 1977), 166–172.

97. Milton Friedman, "Taxes: The Hard Sell," *Newsweek*, May 13, 1968, reprinted in Friedman, *Economist's Protest*, 75.

98. George H. Gallup, *The Gallup Poll* (vol. III, 1972), 2086.

99. Distributional effects are discussed in Andrew F. Brimmer, "Inflation and Income Distribution in the United States," *The Review of Economics and Statistics* (vol. 53, Feb. 1971), 37–48; and Arthur M. Okun, "Inflation: The Problems and Prospects Before Us," in Okun, et al., *Inflation: The Problems It Creates and the Policies It Requires* (1970), 3–42.

100. Richard P. Oliver, "Increase in Defense-Related Employment During Viet Nam Buildup," *Monthly Labor Review* (vol. 93, Feb. 1970), 3–10.

101. Brimmer, "Inflation and Income Distribution," 45; Bureau of Census, *The Social and Economic Status of the Black Population in the United States: An Historical View, 1790–1978* (Current Population Reports, Series P-23 No. 80), 31.

102. Frank Ackerman and Arthur MacEwan, "Inflation, Recession, and Crisis, Or, Would You Buy a New Car From This Man?," *The Review of Radical Political Economics* (vol. 4, Aug. 1972), Table I, 28. Aftertax profits grew by 71 percent in 1962–65, but only 9.2 percent in 1966–69. See "Impact of the War in Southeast Asia on the U.S. Economy," Foreign Relations Committee, Senate hearings (1970), 12. Ackerman and MacEwan calculate that in constant dollars, profits actually declined.

103. "Impact of the War," Senate hearings, 15.

104. Leonard Ross, "Hurrah for Inflation," *New Republic* (vol. 163, July 4, 1970), 26–27.

105. James Tobin and Leonard Ross, "Living With Inflation," *New York Review of Books* (vol. 16, May 6, 1971), 23–26. Quote on p. 25.

106. Friedman, "The Role of Monetary Policy," 7–11.

107. A helpful exposition of the new synthesis is Robert J. Gordon, *Macroeconomics* (1978).

Chapter 7. Civil Rights

1. Harry McPherson, *A Political Education* (1972), 194–195.

2. "Voting Rights," Committee on the Judiciary, Senate hearings (1965), 9.

3. Lyndon B. Johnson, *The Vantage Point* (1971), 161; for additional evidence that Johnson had begun to explore voting-rights legislation in late 1964, David J. Garrow, *Protest at Selma: Martin Luther King, Jr., and the Voting Rights Act of 1965* (1978), 36–39.

4. *Public Papers of the Presidents, LBJ, 1965*, 5.

5. This point is developed in Garrow, *Protest at Selma*, 204, 220–231.

6. "Voting Rights," Senate hearings, 9–12.

7. Excellent narratives of events at Selma are provided in Garrow, *Protest at Selma* and Charles E. Fager, *Selma, 1965* (1974). I also used the Selma *Times-Journal*, January–March 1965, on microfilm at Harvard.

8. Interview of Wilson Baker in Howell Raines, *My Soul Is Rested* (1977), 197–203. Quote on p. 200.

9. These events are covered by Garrow, Fager, and the Selma *Times-Journal*.

10. John Lewis Interview in Raines, *My Soul Is Rested*, 212.

11. The Selma *Times-Journal*, March 8, 1965, 1 and 2; *Newsweek* (vol. 65, March 22, 1965), 18–21; Clark quoted in Fager, *Selma*, 94.

12. Garrow, *Protest at Selma*, 63, 73, and footnote 82 on p. 271.

13. Garrow, *Protest at Selma*, 78.

14. Garrow, *Protest at Selma*, 83–87; *New York Times*, March 10, 1965, 1 and 22; and March 12, 1 and 18.

15. Fager, *Selma*, 103.

16. The Selma *Times-Journal*, March 9, 1965, 1; *New York Times*, March 10, 1965, 1 and 22; March 12, 1 and 18.

17. Cleveland Sellers with Robert Terrell, *The River of No Return* (1973), 116–118.

18. James Forman, *Sammy Younge, Jr.* (1968), 75–76; and Forman, *The Making of Black Revolutionaries* (1972), 441.

19. Sellers, *River of No Return*, 123–125.

20. *Pub. Paps., LBJ, 1965*, 281; LBJ, *Vantage Point*, 165.

21. The Selma *Times-Journal*, March 21, 1961, 1.

22. King's speech excerpted in *New York Times*, March 26, 1965, 22.

23. *New York Times*, Oct. 4, 1978, 78; for a press summary of an unreleased Justice Department report on Rowe's activities in the South from 1961 through 1965, *New York Times*, Feb. 17, 1980, 1 and 16. The federal courts permanently enjoined the state from trying Rowe, for reasons not bearing on his guilt or innocence.

24. "Voting Rights," Senate hearings, 8–23.

25. "Voting Rights," Senate hearings, 31.

26. "Voting Rights," Committee on the Judiciary, House hearings (1965), 144, 154.

27. *Cong. Rec.* (1965), 6920.

28. "Voting Rights," House hearings, 367.

29. Annual Report of the Attorney General of the United States (1966), 207–210.

30. V. E. Jordan, Jr., "The Black Vote in Danger," *Civil Rights Digest* (vol. 2, Spring 1969), 2; U.S. Commission on Civil Rights, *Political Participation* (1968), 11–13; *Annual Report of the Attorney General, Fiscal Year 1968*, Table 20, 111 and 66.

31. U.S. Commission on Civil Rights. *The Voting Rights Act—The First Months* (1965), 19.

32. U.S. Commission on Civil Rights, *Political Participation* (1968), 127, 155–156, 174, 180, 185–187. Quote on p. 127.

33. U.S. Commission on Civil Rights, *Political Participation*, 177.

34. U.S. Commission on Civil Rights, *Political Participation*, 16–17.

35. Jordan, "The Black Vote," 2.

36. The indispensable book on this subject is Gary Orfield, *The Reconstruction of Southern Education: The Schools and the 1964 Civil Rights Act* (1969). On problems of school desegregation before 1964, pp. 15–22.

37. *United States v. Jefferson County Board of Education*, 372 F. 2d. 836 (1966).

38. Orfield, *Reconstruction*, 77.

39. Orfield, *Reconstruction*, 85–92.

40. Office of Education, "General Statement of Policies under Title VI of the Civil Rights Act of 1964" (April 1965), reprinted in "Guide-

lines for School Desegregation," Committee on the Judiciary, House hearings (1966), A20–A24.

41. Memo from Cater to pres., May 4, 1965, Cater papers, Title VI file, LBJL.

42. Francis Keppel, Oral History Interview (April 21, 1969), LBJL, 19.

43. "School Desegregation Statistics," *Race Relations Reporter* (vol. 2, July 6, 1971), n.p.

44. For criticisms, U.S. Commission on Civil Rights, *Survey of School Desegregation in the Southern or Border States, 1965–1966* (1966), 30–33, 50; Orfield, *Reconstruction*, 115.

45. Katzenbach to the pres., Feb. 10, 1966, Cater papers, Box 39, LBJL.

46. "Revised Statement of Policies for School Desegregation Plans," March 1966, reprinted in "Guidelines for School Desegregation," House hearings, A26–A35.

47. Letter from southern senators to Johnson, May 2, 1966, Cater papers, Box 41, LBJL.

48. *Cong. Rec.* (1966), 24543–24544.

49. Committee on Appropriations, Senate Report 1631, Sept. 22, 1966.

50. *New York Times*, Sept. 29, 1966, 1; Sept. 30, 1966, 20.

51. *Pub. Paps., LBJ, 1966*, 1121.

52. U.S. Commission on Civil Rights, *Southern School Desegregation, 1966–1967* (1967), 8, 42–45; "School Desegregation Statistics," *Race Relations Reporter.*

53. *United States v. Jefferson County Board of Education*, 372 F. 2d. 836 (1966).

54. *United States v. Jefferson County Board of Education*, 380 F. 2d. 385 (1967).

55. Quoted in *New York Times*, Sept. 24, 1967, 57.

56. Southern Regional Council, "School Desegregation 1966: The Slow Undoing," reprinted in "Guidelines on School Desegregation," House hearings, 272.

57. "Policies on Elementary and Secondary School Compliance," *Federal Register* (vol. 33, March 23, 1968), 4955–4959.

58. *Green v. County School Board of New Kent County*, 391 US 430.

59. *New York Times*, May 28, 1968, 1 and 33.

60. *Race Relations Law Survey* (vol. 1, May 1969), 19–22; Theodore A. Smedley, "Enforcement Fell Heavily on the Courts," *Southern Education Report* (vol. 4, June 1969), 30–35; "School Desegregation Statistics," *Race Relations Reporter.*

61. "School Desegregation Statistics," *Race Relations Reporter; New York Times*, May 12, 1974, 1 and 42.

62. Christine H. Rossell et al., *Assessment of Current Knowledge About the Effectiveness of School Desegregation Strategies, Vol. V. A Review of the Empirical Research on Desegregation: Community Response, Race Relations, Academic Achievement and Resegregation* (1981), 48, 183, 190–191.

63. Harold Howe II, Oral History Interview, LBJL.
64. McPherson, *A Political Education,* 153.
65. McPherson, *A Political Education,* 334.
66. Text of the report reprinted in Lee Rainwater and William L. Yancey, *The Moynihan Report and the Politics of Controversy* (1967), 39–124. Quotes on pp. 49, 51.
67. Daniel P. Moynihan, "The President and the Negro: The Lost Moment," *Commentary* (vol. 43, Feb. 1967), 31–45.
68. Rainwater and Yancey, *The Moynihan Report,* 4, 27–28.
69. *Pub. Paps., LBJ, 1965,* 635–640. Quote on p. 636.
70. Quoted in Doris Kearns, *Lyndon Johnson and the American Dream* (1976), 305.
71. James Farmer, "The Controversial Moynihan Report," reprinted in Rainwater and Yancey, *The Moynihan Report,* 409–411. Quote on p. 410.
72. Frank Riessman, "In Defense of the Negro Family," reprinted in Rainwater and Yancey, *The Moynihan Report,* 474–478.
73. William Ryan, "Savage Discovery: The Moynihan Report," reprinted in Rainwater and Yancey, *The Moynihan Report,* 457–466. Quote on p. 464.
74. Rainwater and Yancey, *The Moynihan Report,* 212.
75. Rainwater and Yancey, *The Moynihan Report,* 248.
76. *New York Times,* Nov. 25, 1965, 52.
77. Rainwater and Yancey, *The Moynihan Report,* 274; for White House strategy to keep control of the conference, memo from Clifford L. Alexander to pres., Jan. 22, 1965, LBJL.
78. *New York Times,* June 1, 1966, 1; June 2, 1.
79. McPherson, *A Political Education,* 348.
80. *New York Times,* June 3, 1966, 1.
81. Details on Bridgeport from Lois Wille, "Mayor Daley Meets the Movement," *Nation* (vol. 201, Aug. 30, 1965), 92–95.
82. Martin Luther King, "Next Stop: The North," *Saturday Review* (vol. 48, Nov. 13, 1965), 33 ff. Quotes on p. 33.
83. David L. Lewis, *King: A Critical Biography* (1970), 14.
84. For background on Chicago controversy, Wille, "Mayor Daley Meets the Movement"; *New York Times,* July 12, 1965, 20; and Orfield, *Reconstruction,* 152–163; letter from Albert A. Raby, Convener of Coordinating Council of Community Organizations, to Francis Keppel, July 4, 1965, HU 2-5 file, WHCF, LBJL.
85. *New York Times,* June 13, 1965, 65.
86. *New York Times,* June 11, 1965, 64; June 12, 16; July 12, 20.
87. "King Comes to Chicago," *The Christian Century* (vol. 82, Aug. 11, 1965), 979–980.
88. *New York Times,* July 25, 1965, 39.

89. *New York Times*, July 27, 1965, 18.
90. Letter from Raby to Keppel, July 4, 1965.
91. Orfield, *Reconstruction*, 178–179.
92. Orfield, *Reconstruction*, 180–185; and memo from Keppel to Califano, Oct. 4, 1965, HU 2-5 file, LBJL.
93. Memo from Cater to pres., Oct. 1, 1965, Cater papers, Title VI file, LBJL.
94. Washington *Post*, Oct. 10, 1965, 1; Chicago *Tribune*, Oct. 3, 1965, 1; and Orfield, *Reconstruction*, 193.
95. Memo from Marvin Watson to pres., Oct. 4, 1965, HU 2-5/ST 13 file, LBJL.
96. Orfield, *Reconstruction*, 194–195.
97. Chicago *Tribune*, Oct. 6, 1965, 1.
98. Report on Office of Education Analysis of Certain Aspects of Chicago Schools Under Title VI of the Civil Rights Act of 1964, Jan., 1967, HU 2-5/ST file, LBJL.
99. Letter from Harold Howe to James Redmond (Superintendent of Chicago schools), undated, HU 2-5/ST file.
100. U.S. Commission on Civil Rights, *Desegregation of the Nation's Public Schools: A Status Report* (1979), 20.
101. *New York Times*, Sept. 2, 1965, 20; Jan. 8, 1966, 22; March 24, 1966, 33.
102. Lewis, *King*, 331.
103. *New York Times*, July 11, 1966, 1 and 19; King quoted in *Newsweek* (vol. 68, July 25, 1966), 17.
104. Quoted in Barbara A. Reynolds, *Jesse Jackson: The Man, the Movement, the Myth* (1975), 58.
105. *New York Times*, July 13, 1966, 1; Lewis, *King*, 335–336; Coretta Scott King, *My Life with Martin Luther King, Jr.* (1969), 283–288.
106. Quoted in Merle Miller, *Lyndon: An Oral Biography* (1980), 437.
107. *New York Times*, July 30, 1966, 1.
108. *New York Times*, Aug. 1, 1966, 1 and 15; Aug. 8, 1 and 55.
109. Quoted in Lewis, *King*, 339.
110. *New York Times*, Aug. 6, 1966, 1 and 52; Lewis, *King*, 339.
111. *New York Times*, Aug. 21, 1966, 47.
112. *New York Times*, Aug. 9, 1966, 25; Aug. 22, 1.
113. *New York Times*, Aug. 25, 1965, 24.
114. *New York Times*, Aug. 27, 1966, 1; and Paul Good, "Bossism, Racism and Dr. King," *Nation* (vol. 203, Sept. 19, 1966), 237–242.
115. *New York Times*, March 26, 1967, 44.
116. Memo from Lee White to pres., Dec. 2, 1964, HU 2-2 file, LBJL.
117. Memo from Norbert A. Schlei to Lee White, Dec. 11, 1964, HU 2-2 file.
118. Memo from vice pres. to pres., May 18, 1965, HU 2-2 file.

119. *Pub. Paps., LBJ, 1966*, 5.

120. *New York Times*, Jan 24, 1966, 17.

121. This description in testimony by Attorney General Katzenbach, "Civil Rights, 1966," Committee on the Judiciary, House hearings (1966), 1069. The other sections of the bill sought to end racial discrimination in federal and state jury systems; granted authority for the Attorney General to obtain injunctive relief against interference with school desegregation; and outlawed interference by private persons with the exercise of activities protected by federal laws. This last item would satisfy the long-standing demand that the federal government protect civil rights workers in the South.

122. H. R. Report 1678 (1966); *New York Times*, May 6, 1966, 1; June 29, 1; July 20, 25.

123. *New York Times*, June 16, 1966, 21.

124. *New York Times*, Sept. 15, 1966, 1; Sept. 10, 19.

125. *New York Times*, Oct. 3, 1966, 57.

126. *Cong. Rec.* (1968), 2270–2272, 4960, 5992.

127. *New York Times*, Sept. 4, 1966, 4E.

128. Dirksen and Mondale quoted in *Congressional Quarterly Almanac* (1968), 159.

129. *Cong. Rec.* (1968), 9621.

130. U.S. Commission on Civil Rights, *The Federal Fair Housing Enforcement Effort* (1979), 70–73. Quote on p. 71.

131. U.S. Commission on Civil Rights, *Federal Fair Housing*, 82–104.

132. Edward L. Holmgren, executive director, National Committee against Discrimination in Housing, in "Fair Housing Act," Committee on the Judiciary, House hearings (1978), 106.

133. The key study is Annemette Sorensen, Karl E. Taeuber, and Leslie J. Hollingsworth, Jr., "Indexes of Racial Residential Segregation for 109 Cities in the United States, 1940–1970," Discussion Paper, Institute for Research on Poverty (1974).

134. Thomas F. Pettigrew, "Racial Change and Social Policy," *The Annals of the American Academy of Political and Social Science* (vol. 441, Jan. 1979), 122–123. Pettigrew relies on Sorensen et al., cited above.

135. HUD, "Background Information and Initial Findings of the Housing Market Practices Survey," reprinted in "Fair Housing Act," House hearings, 112–138.

136. Holmgren's testimony in "Fair Housing Act," House hearings, 106.

137. Bureau of the Census, *The Social and Economic Status of the Black Population in the United States: An Historical View, 1790–1978*, 31 and 75; and A. Philip Randolph's testimony in "Equal Employment Opportunity," Committee on Labor and Public Welfare, Senate hearings (1963), 172.

138. Herman P. Miller's testimony in "Equal Employment Opportunity," Senate hearings, 325, 238–329.

139. See, for example, Paul M. Siegel, "On the Cost of Being a Negro," *Sociological Inquiry* (vol. 35, Winter 1965), 41–57. Siegel found that even if nonwhites had achieved the same regional, educational, and occupational distribution as whites in 1959, the average nonwhite would still have earned $1,000 less on the average than a white person, a difference almost entirely attributable to discrimination.

140. The following brief history is derived from Reynolds, *Jesse Jackson*, esp. ch. 5; also, "Negroes Go National with Demands for Jobs," *Business Week* (Aug. 19, 1967), 37–38; *New York Times*, March 24, 1967, 1 and 2.

141. This was the plausible view of the civil rights lobby. See Richard P. Nathan, *Jobs and Civil Rights* (1969), 141–142.

142. Christopher Pyle and Richard Morgan, "Johnson's Civil Rights Shake-Up," *The New Leader* (vol. 48, Oct. 11, 1965), 3–6. Humphrey quoted on p. 3.

143. U.S. Commission on Civil Rights, *Federal Civil Rights Enforcement Effort* (1970), 389–390.

144. Ray Marshall, Charles B. Knapp, Malcolm H. Liggett, Robert W. Glover, *Employment Discrimination: The Impact of Legal and Administrative Remedies* (1978), 147.

145. NORC poll cited in Richard B. Freeman, "Changes in the Labor Market for Black Americans, 1948–1972," *Brookings Papers on Economic Activity* (no. 1, 1973), footnote 19, p. 94.

146. Marshall et al., *Employment Discrimination*, 17.

147. Bureau of Census, *Black Population: Historical View*, 74; figures for 1979 (November) in Bureau of Labor Statistics, *Employment and Earnings*, Dec. 1979, 35.

148. Bureau of Census, *Black Population: Historical View*, 74; figures for 1979 in Bureau of Labor Statistics, *Employment and Earnings*, 1979, 35.

149. Bureau of Census, *Black Population: Historical View*, 48; 1977 figures derived from tables in Anne McDougall Young, "Median Earnings in 1977 reported for year-round full-time workers," *Monthly Labor Review* (vol. 102, June 1979), Table 1, 36. Some erosion took place between 1974 and 1977. The ratio of black to white income for males was .74 in 1974. Figures for 1959 derived by taking figures for nonwhites and subtracting .02, the usual differential between nonwhite and black.

150. On high school diplomas, Sar A. Levitan, William B. Johnson, Robert Taggart, *Still a Dream: The Changing Status of Blacks Since 1960* (1975), 81; for 1965 college figure, Bureau of Census, *Social and Economic Status of the Black Population in the United States, 1971*, 85; for 1977

figures, Bureau of Census, *Black Population: Historical View*, 173.

151. Bureau of Census, *Social and Economic Status, 1971*, 34.

152. Moynihan, "The Negro Family," reprinted in Rainwater and Yancey, *The Moynihan Report*, 43.

153. Among scholars endorsing the view of a schism are William Julius Wilson, *The Declining Significance of Race* (1978); and Pettigrew, "Racial and Social Policy," *Annals of the American Academy*; for a discussion of the difficulties of the underclass concept, Levitan et al., *Still a Dream*, 199-204.

154. Sixty percent of black families below the poverty level received public assistance in 1974, up from 45 percent in 1969. Bureau of Census, *Black Population: Historical View*, 54.

155. Bureau of Census, *Black Population: Historical View*, 67; for 1978 figures, Scott Campbell Brown, "Educational Attainment of Workers —Some Trends from 1975 to 1978," *Monthly Labor Review* (vol. 201, Feb. 1979), Table IV, p. 58.

156. Bureau of Census, *Black Population: Historical View*, 103, 175.

157. Bureau of Census, *Black Population: Historical View*, 130; 1977 figures derived from National Center for Health Statistics, "Final Natality Statistics, 1977," *Vital Statistics Report* (Feb. 1979), Tables 1 and 13.

158. On black crime, Charles E. Silberman, *Criminal Violence, Criminal Justice* (1978); for figures on venereal disease and drug abuse for black population as a whole, Levitan et al., *Still a Dream*, 133-134.

159. Quoted in *Time* (vol. 88, Oct. 7, 1966), 30.

160. *New York Times*, Sept. 30, 1966, 39.

161. *New York Times*, Sept. 21, 1966, 1 and 33.

162. *New York Times*, Nov. 10, 1966, 30.

163. *New York Times*, Sept. 21, 1966, 1 and 33.

164. *New York Times*, Nov. 10, 1966, 1 and 28.

165. *New York Times*, Nov. 9, 1966, 29.

166. *New York Times*, Nov. 9, 1966, 31.

167. *New York Times*, Dec. 29, 1966, 14.

168. *Report of the National Advisory Commission on Civil Disorders* (1968), 113.

169. McPherson to pres., Aug. 14, 1967, HU 2 file, LBJL.

170. *Cong. Rec.* (1967), 19433-19434.

171. For Justice view, *Cong. Rec.* (1967), 19375-19376; for ACLU view, 19375-19376.

172. *Cong. Rec.* (1967), 19548-19450. A few months later the House reversed itself and passed a modified rat bill.

173. *Pub. Paps., LBJ, 1967*, 721-724.

174. McPherson, *A Political Education*, 377-379; *Pub. Paps., LBJ, 1967*, 831-836. Quote on p. 835.

Chapter 8. War on Poverty I

1. *New York Times*, Jan. 16, 1964, 1 and 21; Nov. 16, 20; April 19, 40.
2. *New York Times*, May 15, 1964, 19.
3. *Public Papers of the Presidents: LBJ, 1963–64*, 561.
4. CEA, *1964 Annual Report*, ch. 2. Quote on p. 57.
5. Robert Hunter, *Poverty* (1904), 60.
6. Paul Douglas, *Wages and the Family* (1925), ch. 1. Douglas set a poverty line for a family of five at $1,000–$1,100 but did not estimate the percent of families below it. Historian Irving Bernstein noted that over 21 percent of American families with two or more members had incomes of less than $1,000 in 1929. Bernstein, *The Lean Years: A History of the American Worker, 1920–1933* (1960), 63–65.
7. CEA, *1964 Annual Report*, 59–60.
8. Median income in current dollars for families and individuals in 1929 has been estimated at $2,340. See Table 7-1 in Christopher Jencks, *Inequality: A Reassessment of the Effect of Family and Schooling in America* (1972), 210.
9. Though the percentage of families in poverty has remained constant, there is considerable movement by individual families in and out of poverty.
10. Report of the President's Commission on Income Maintenance Programs, *Poverty Amid Plenty: The American Paradox* (1969), 37.
11. Stanley Lebergott, *Wealth and Want* (1970), 7. Lebergott is one among a great number of scholars who argues the relativity of poverty. See also S. M. Miller and Pamela A. Roby, *The Future of Inequality* (1970), ch. 1.
12. Memo from Lampman to Heller, June 10, 1963, CEA-Heller papers, Poverty file, JFKL.
13. *Time* (vol. 83, May 1, 1964), 20; *New York Times*, April 25, 1964, 1 and 10.
14. For preparation and passage of the bill, Philip Meranto, *The Politics of Federal Aid to Education in 1965* (1967); Eugene Eidenberg and Roy D. Morey, *An Act of Congress* (1969); and Julie Roy Jeffrey, *Education for Children of the Poor* (1978), ch. 3.
15. For Keppel's testimony, "Aid to Elementary and Secondary Education," Committee on Education and Labor, House hearings (1965), 82–90. Quotes on pp. 84, 85.
16. Interim Report of the Council on American Private Education (prepared for the National Institute of Education), *Summary Report: Delivery of Title I Services to Non–Public School Students* (1977), reprinted in "Part 16: Services and Student Development," Committee on Education and Labor, House hearings (1977), 556–573, esp. p. 559.

17. "Elementary and Secondary Education Act of 1965," Committee on Labor and Public Welfare, Senate hearings (1965), 511–512.

18. *Pub. Paps., LBJ, 1965,* 417; *New York Times,* April 12, 1965, 1.

19. On power in school systems, Patricia Cayo Sexton, *The American School: A Sociological Analysis* (1967), 21–23, 26–30; David Rogers, *110 Livingston Street* (1968), ch. 8.

20. Stephen K. Bailey and Edith K. Mosher, *ESEA: The Office of Education Administers a Law* (1968), 306.

21. Jeffrey, *Education for Children of the Poor,* 121, 126–128.

22. For Waukegan, Cairo, and Fresno, report by Washington Research Project of the Southern Center for Studies in Public Policy and the NAACP Legal Defense Fund, Inc., "Title I of ESEA: Is It Helping Poor Children?" (Nov. 1969), 8–14; for Camden, Jeffrey, *Education for Children of the Poor,* 127–128.

23. Bailey and Mosher, *ESEA,* 116–119. Quote on p. 119.

24. Kennedy's question in "Elementary and Secondary Education Act," Senate hearings, 500; Keppel's reply, 500–501, 510–511.

25. Decima Research, *The Participation Study: An Assessment of Who Is and Who Is Not Selected for Compensatory Education* (1977), reprinted in "Part 19: Title 1—Funds Allocation," House hearings (1977), 189–217 (esp. pp. 201, 204–205, and 220); also "Part 16: Services and Student Development," 74, 184.

26. "Aid to Elementary and Secondary Schools," House hearings, 114.

27. James S. Coleman et al., *Equality of Educational Opportunity* (1966). For data on sample survey, p. 557.

28. Coleman Report, 325. For reanalysis of Coleman Report, which gives even more pessimistic results, see Frederick Mosteller and Daniel P. Moynihan, *On Equality of Educational Opportunity* (1972), esp. chapters by David J. Armor and Marshall S. Smith.

29. Quoted in Jeffrey, *Education for Children of the Poor,* 148.

30. The best recent study indicating that schools do have an effect on student achievement independent of family background is Michael Rutter et al., *Fifteen Thousand Hours* (1979).

31. See for example U.S. Office of Education, "Education of the Disadvantaged: An Evaluative Report on Title I, Fiscal Year 1968" (1970), 126; Harry Piccariello, "Evaluation of Title I," mimeo, 1969; "An Analysis of Compensatory Education in Five School Districts" (General Electric, Aug. 1968).

32. For example, Herbert J. Kiesling, "Input and Output in California Compensatory Educational Projects" (Rand, Oct. 1971).

33. Report from National Institute of Education, *The Effects of Services on Student Development* (1977), reprinted in "Part 16: Services and Stu-

dent Development," House hearings, 471–512, esp. Table I, p. 499. Quote on p. 505.

34. Results of study conducted by SRI, summarized in testimony, "Part 19: Title I," House hearings, 493–502, esp. Table I, p. 497.

35. Lester C. Thurow, *Generating Inequality* (1975), ch. 3; also Benjamin A. Okner and Alice M. Rivlin, "Income Distribution Policy in the United States," in Paris Organization for Economic Cooperation and Development, *Education, Inequality and Life Chances* (vol. 2, 1975), 204–211; for a defense of the theory, see comment on Okner and Rivlin by Jacob Mincer, same volume, 223–226.

36. Jencks, *Inequality*, ch. 9.

37. For background on Medicare, see Richard Harris, *A Sacred Trust* (1966); Theodore R. Marmor, *The Politics of Medicare* (1970), chs. 1–3; and Peter A. Corning, *The Evolution of Medicare: From Idea to Law* (SSA Research Report No. 29, 1969), chs. 1–4. See also Robert S. Myers, *Medicare* (1970).

38. For the case for Medicare, see "Medical Care for the Aged," Committee on Ways and Means, House hearings (1963), 28–29.

39. Marmor, *Politics of Medicare*, 68–69; and Harris, *A Sacred Trust*, 186–189.

40. Eric F. Goldman, *The Tragedy of Lyndon Johnson* (1968), 290.

41. *Pub. Paps., LBJ, 1965*, 813, 814.

42. R. M. Gibson and M. S. Mueller, "National Health Expenditures, Fiscal Year 1976," *Social Security Bulletin* (vol. 40, April 1977), 8; "Data on the Medicaid Program," Committee Print, House Committee on Interstate and Foreign Commerce (1977), 26–29; and Howard West, "Five Years of Medicare—A Statistical Review," *Social Security Bulletin* (vol. 34, Dec. 1971), 18, 19.

43. Goldman, *Tragedy of Lyndon Johnson*, 291.

44. Wilbur Cohen, "From Medicare to National Health Insurance," in David C. Warner, ed., *Toward New Human Rights: The Social Policies of the Kennedy and Johnson Administrations* (1977), 146–147.

45. For the cause of medical inflation, especially in hospital prices, see Martin Feldstein and Amy Taylor, *The Rapid Rise of Hospital Costs* (Staff Report of Council on Wage and Price Stability, Jan. 1977); Martin S. Feldstein, "The Medical Economy," *Scientific American* (vol. 229, Sept. 1973), 151–159; Feldstein, "Hospital Cost Inflation: A Study of Nonprofit Price Dynamics," *American Economic Review* (vol. 61, Dec. 1971), 853–872; Stuart H. Altman and Joseph Eichenholz, "Inflation in the Health Industry" in Michael Zubkoff, ed., *Health: Victim or Cause of Inflation?* (1976), 7–30.

46. Martin S. Feldstein, "The Welfare Loss of Excess Health Insurance,"

Journal of Political Economy (vol. 83, March 1973), 252.

47. Zachary Y. Dyckman, *A Study of Physicians' Fees* (Staff Report of Council on Wage and Price Stability, 1978); also Martin S. Feldstein, "The Rising Price of Physicians' Services," *The Review of Economics and Statistics* (vol. 52, May 1970), 121–133.

48. Thirty-nine percent of Medicare reimbursements in 1967 were for services rendered to the 7.5 percent of Medicare patients with expenses of $2,000 or more. See West, "Five Years of Medicare," 27.

49. Marian Gornick, "Ten Years of Medicare: Impact on the Covered Population," *Social Security Bulletin* (vol. 39, July 1976), 19.

50. Gornick, "Ten Years of Medicare," 12–15; Karen Davis, "Health and the Great Society: Successes of the Past Decade and the Road Ahead," in Warner, *Toward New Human Rights*, 196. The figures for physician costs include supplementary insurance payments.

51. Barbara S. Cooper and Mary F. McGee, "Medical Care Outlays for Three Age Groups: Young, Intermediate and Aged," *Social Security Bulletin* (vol. 34, May 1971), 13.

52. For hospital admission rates, Theodore Marmor with James Monroe, "The Health Programs of the Kennedy-Johnson Years: An Overview," in Warner, *Toward New Human Rights*, 173; for physician visits, Karen Davis and Roger Reynolds, "The Impact of Medicare and Medicaid on Access to Medical Care," in Richard N. Rosett, ed., *The Role of Health Insurance in the Health Services Sector* (1976), 393. Using 1971 data, Davis and Reynolds define low income as $5,000 or below and high income as $10,000 or above.

53. *New York Times*, July 17, 1974, 9.

54. "Economics of Aging: Toward a Full Share of Abundance—Health Aspects," Special Committee on Aging, Senate hearings (1969), 582–583.

55. "Data on the Medicaid Program: Eligibility, Services, Expenditures, Fiscal Years 1966–1977," Committee on Interstate and Foreign Commerce, House Print (1977), 81, 57.

56. "Problems of Medicaid Fraud and Abuse," Committee on Interstate and Foreign Commerce, House hearings (1976). Cost estimate of fraud, p. 53.

57. Annual Statistical Supplement, 1975, *Social Security Bulletin*, 187.

58. Davis, "Health and the Great Society," 184–187.

59. For studies critical of value of additional health services for general population, Victor R. Fuchs, "The Contribution of Health Services to the American Economy," in Fuchs, ed., *Essays in the Economics of Health and Medical Care* (1972), esp. pp. 15–18; John H. Knowles, "The Responsibility of the Individual," in Knowles, ed., *Doing Better and Feeling Worse* (1977), 57–80; Lewis Thomas, "On the Science and

Technology of Medicine," same volume, 35–46; Victor R. Fuchs, *Who Shall Live?* (1974), esp. chs. 1 and 2.

60. Victor R. Fuchs, "Comments," in Rosett, *The Role of Health Insurance,* 389. Fuchs makes his argument in an effective refutation of a paper with different findings in the same volume.

61. Seventy-one percent of low-income pregnant women saw a doctor in the first trimester in 1970 compared to 58 percent in 1963. Davis and Reynolds, "The Impact of Medicare and Medicaid," 392.

62. Fuchs, *Who Shall Live?*, 31–37; Fuchs, "Some Economic Aspects of Mortality in Developed Countries," in Mark Perlman, ed., *The Economics of Health and Medical Care* (1974), esp. pp. 181–184.

63. This estimate on doctors' income was made by Bruce C. Stuart and Lee A. Blair, *Health Care and Income* (Research Paper No. 5, Michigan Department of Social Service, 1971), 106.

64. For a defense of Medicare and Medicaid, see Sar A. Levitan and Robert Taggart, *The Promise of Greatness* (1976), ch. 4.

65. *Pub. Paps., LBJ, 1968–69,* 248–263.

66. *Pub. Paps., LBJ, 1968–69,* 252.

67. *Pub. Paps., LBJ, 1968–69,* 866.

68. For figures, HUD, *Housing in the Seventies* (1974), 87, 95, 106, 112.

69. For favorable accounts of these programs, Anthony Downs, *Federal Housing Subsidies: How Are They Working?* (1973); Henry B. Schechter, "Critique of Housing in the Seventies," Committee Print, Senate Committee on Banking, Housing and Urban Affairs (1974).

70. Staff Report and Recommendations, "Investigation and Hearing of Abuses in Federal Low- and Moderate-Income Housing Programs," Committee Print, Committee on Banking and Currency (1970), 1; *New York Times,* Jan. 6, 1971, 1; Jan. 15, 1.

71. These events summarized in "Interim Report on HUD Investigation of Low- and Moderate-Income Housing Programs," Committee on Banking and Currency, House hearings (1971), 1–2.

72. "Investigation and Hearing of Abuses," 3–10, 11–12, 17.

73. HUD, "Audit Review of Section 235 Single Family Housing," printed in "Real Estate Settlement Costs, FHA Mortgage Foreclosures, Housing Abandonment, and Site Selection Policies," Committee on Banking and Currency, House hearings (1972), 77–150. For percentages, p. 149.

74. See for example, Gurney Breckenfeld, "Housing Subsidies are a Grand Delusion," *Fortune* (vol. 85, Feb. 1972), 136 ff.

75. Three-quarters of HUD's sample 236 projects were limited-dividend corporations; one-quarter were nonprofit projects sponsored by churches, labor unions, etc. HUD found that most nonprofit projects originated with builders and developers drumming up fees. Typical

nonprofit sponsors lacked sufficient capital to sustain a project, they lacked management skills, and their projects suffered a higher default rate than profit-making projects. See HUD, "Report on Audit of Section 236 Multi-family Housing Program" (1972), printed in "Real Estate Settlement Costs," House hearings, 151–228. See esp. pp. 216–218.

76. Financing explained in Stanley S. Surrey, *Pathways to Tax Reform* (1973), 239–241.

77. HUD, "Report on Audit of Section 236," 163–205.

78. On 20 percent forecast, HUD, *Housing in the Seventies*, 118. See also HUD, "Report on Audit of 236," 50–53; and Morton J. Schussheim, *The Modest Commitment to Cities* (1974), 70–71.

79. HUD, *Housing in the Seventies*, 107, 113.

80. HUD, *Housing in the Seventies*, 92.

81. "Real Estate Settlement Costs," House hearings, 56.

82. This analysis of filtering relies on William B. Brueggeman, "An Analysis of the Filtering Process with Special Reference to Housing Subsidies" in HUD, *Housing in the Seventies Working Papers* (vol. 2, 1976), 842–856.

83. HUD, *Abandoned Housing Research: A Compendium* (1973), 5.

84. This case is made in Arthur P. Solomon, *Housing the Urban Poor* (1974).

85. Quoted in Solomon, *Housing the Urban Poor*, 14.

86. "Economic Opportunity Act of 1964," Committee on Education and Labor, House hearings (1964), 185.

87. Christopher Weeks, *Job Corps* (1967), 186–191, 203–205.

88. Sar A. Levitan, *The Great Society's Poor Law* (1969), 278–281; Levitan and Benjamin H. Johnston, *The Job Corps: A Social Experiment That Works* (1975), 30.

89. *New York Times*, June 12, 1965, 1; Nov. 28, 87; Aug. 21, 10; July 24, 3; July 11, 48; Nov. 14, 62; Weeks, *Job Corps*, 210–216.

90. "Examination of the War on Poverty," Committee on Labor and Public Welfare, Senate hearings (1967), 3024–3025.

91. Levitan and Johnston, *The Job Corps*, 19–21.

92. Levitan, *Great Society's Poor Law*, 297; Levitan and Johnston, *The Job Corps*, 87–88.

93. Louis Harris and Associates, "A Study of August 1966 Terminations from the Job Corps," printed in "Economic Opportunity Act Amendments of 1967," Committee on Education and Labor, House hearings (1967), 412, 424; same authors, "A Study of Job Corps No-Shows," printed in same hearings, 256, 259, 296, 301. Figures for graduates taken from Harris's data in August 1966 terminations, 353, 356, 412, 424. Figure for job-related employment, 419. The General

Accounting Office supported pessimism on effects of Job Corps training in "Review of Economic Opportunity Programs" (1969), 61–65.

94. Levitan and Johnston, *The Job Corps*, 28.

95. For defense of Job Corps, see Glen G. Cain, *Benefit/Cost Estimates for Job Corps* (1967). For critique of this and other benefit-cost analyses, see Levitan and Johnston, *The Job Corps*, 98–100.

96. Daniel P. Moynihan, *Maximum Feasible Misunderstanding* (1969), 99.

97. "The Federal Government and Urban Poverty," transcript of a conference sponsored by JFK Library at Brandeis, June 16–17, 1973, 353–354.

98. Memo to Shriver from Ackley, Feb. 18, 1964, CEA-Heller Poverty file, CEA Papers, JFKL.

99. *Pub. Paps., LBJ, 1968–69*, 1061–1062; for updated figures used here, same volume, 1300.

100. Lee Rainwater, *What Money Buys* (1974), esp. pp. 149–151.

101. U.S. Bureau of the Census, Consumer Income, Series P-60, No. 114 (July 1978), cover and p. 3 for percent below half the median in 1976.

102. See Edgar K. Browning, "How Much More Equality Can We Afford?," *The Public Interest* (Spring 1976), 90–110; and Barry W. Blechman, Edward M. Gramlich, and Robert W. Hartman, *Setting National Priorities: the 1975 Budget*, 168–169.

103. This estimate is for 1978 and is derived from *The Budget of the United States Government, Fiscal Year 1980*. It includes subsidies for housing, food, and medical care. Assuming one-third of Medicare payments go to the poor and *all* housing subsidies, 72 percent of in-kind income for the poor is medical.

104. Alvin L. Schorr, "Fair Shares," in Schorr, ed., *Jubilee for Our Times* (1977), 5.

105. For precise calculation of size of transfers for various income groups under the best devised scheme (demogrants), which would have lifted 80 percent of the poor above the official poverty line, see Benjamin A. Okner, "The Role of Demogrants as an Income Maintenance Alternative," in *Studies in Public Welfare*, Committee Print, Joint Economic Committee (1973), 1–32. Okner's transfer figures for 1970 are on p. 15.

106. Testimony of Robert G. Spiegelman in "Welfare Reform Proposals," Committee on Finance, Senate hearings (1978), 1050. For report on which his testimony is based, "The Work Effort and Marital Dissolution Effects of the Seattle and Denver Income Maintenance Experiments" (May 1, 1978), reprinted in *Materials Related to Welfare Research and Experimentation*, Committee Print, Senate Committee on Finance (1978).

107. For discussion of this issue, Arthur M. Okun, *Equality and Efficiency: The Big Tradeoff* (1975), esp. pp. 98–100.

Chapter 9. War on Poverty II

1. Oral History Interview, Herbert Kramer (OEO Director of Public Affairs), March 10, 1969, LBJL.
2. Harris Wofford, *Of Kennedys and Kings: Making Sense of the Sixties* (1980), 44.
3. Richard W. Boone, "Reflections on Citizens Participation and the Economic Opportunity Act," unpublished paper (1970), 7–8.
4. Public Law 88-452, 9.
5. F. O'Reilly Hayes, "The Role of Indigenous Organizations in Community Action Programs," discussion draft, May 4, 1964, Office files of Fred Bowen, LBJL.
6. James L. Sundquist, *Making Federalism Work* (1969), 39.
7. William F. Haddad, "Mr. Shriver and the Savage Politics of Poverty," *Harper's* (vol. 231, Dec. 1965), 44.
8. Stephen M. David, "Leadership of the Poor in Poverty Programs," *The Academy of Political Science, Proceedings* (vol. 29, no. 1, 1969), 91.
9. Letter from McKeldin to pres., Jan. 10, 1965, attached to unsigned memo from Moyers to Humphrey and Shriver, Jan. 26, 1965, Office of Economic Opportunity file, Bill Moyers Office Files, LBJL.
10. OEO, *Community Action Program Guide* (Feb. 1965), 17–18.
11. Community Action Memo No. 3, May 10, 1965, N.A.
12. The *Workbook* was withdrawn from circulation by OEO, and I did not succeed in locating a copy. This summary relies on Brian Henry Smith, "The Role of the Poor in the Poverty Program: The Origin and Development of Maximum Feasible Participation" (1966), M.A. Thesis, Columbia University, 78–83.
13. Oral History Interview, Eric Tolmach (Chief of Evaluation for the Training and Technical Assistance Division, CAP), April 16, 1969, tape III, 11.
14. For a good statement of his views, Saul D. Alinsky, "The War on Poverty—Political Pornography," *Journal of Social Issues* (vol. 21, Jan. 1966), 41–47.
15. For a good account, Erwin Knoll and Jules Witcover, "Fighting Poverty—and City Hall," *Reporter* (vol. 32, June 3, 1965), 19–22; same authors, "Politics and the Poor: Shriver's Second Thoughts," *Reporter* (vol. 33, Dec. 30, 1965), 23–25.
16. Memo from Jack Williams to Bill Haddad, April 27, 1965, Syracuse file, Office of Inspection, OEO, N.A., Suitland, Maryland. Office of Inspection files contain confidential reports from the field. The

Office had no line responsibilities and reported directly to Shriver.
17. Quoted in *New York Times*, June 24, 1965, 13.
18. A good summary of Chicago developments is contained in memo from Jack Williams to Bill Haddad, June 1, 1965, Chicago file, Office of Inspection.
19. "Chronology: Office of Economic Opportunity—Chicago Committee on Urban Opportunity," April 14, 1965, Chicago file, Office of Inspection.
20. Memo from Richard Boone to Sargent Shriver, March 4, 1965, Chicago file, Office of Inspection.
21. Lois Wille, "The Payoff in Chicago," *New Republic* (vol. 153, Oct. 23, 1965), 11.
22. See Chicago *Daily News*, April 8, 1965, reprinted in "Examination of the War on Poverty," Committee on Education and Labor, House hearings (1965), 355–357.
23. Charles E. Silberman, *Crisis in Black and White* (1964), 318.
24. "Examination of the War on Poverty," House hearings, 360.
25. Marion K. Sanders, "Conversations with Saul Alinsky, part II: A Professional Radical Moves in on Rochester," *Harper's* (vol. 231, July 1965), 54.
26. "Proposed Resolution," June 1, 1965, Chicago file, Office of Inspection.
27. Memo from John J. Grunther, executive director of Conference of Mayors to members of the Special Continuing Committee on the Anti-Poverty Programs, June 8, 1965, Chicago file, Office of Inspection.
28. *New York Times*, June 8, 1965, 49; see also John C. Donovan, *Politics of Poverty* (1967), 54–57.
29. Memo from Schultze to pres., Sept. 18, 1965, OEO file, Bill Moyers Office Files.
30. Memo from Shriver to pres., Oct. 20, 1965, WE-9 file, WHCF.
31. See Robert Levine, Oral History Interview, Feb. 26, 1969, LBJL, 40.
32. Advisory Commission on Intergovernmental Relations, *Intergovernmental Relations in the Poverty Program*, April, 1966, 29–30.
33. Frank Riessman and Hermine I. Popper, "The Evolutionary Revolution," in Riessman and Popper, eds., *Up from Poverty: New Career Ladders for Nonprofessionals* (1968), 5.
34. Lillian B. Rubin, "Maximum Feasible Participation: The Origins, Implications, and Present Status," *The Annals of the American Academy of Political and Social Science* (vol. 385, Sept. 1969), 22–24.
35. *New York Times*, Dec. 7, 1965, 27.
36. *New York Times*, Dec. 9, 1965, 58.

37. Letter from Boone to Shriver, Dec. 8, 1965, Syracuse files, Office of Inspection.
38. *New York Times*, Dec. 22, 1965, 15.
39. "The National Cooperative Literacy Program," submitted by James Farmer, Aug. 16, 1965, N.A.
40. *New York Times*, Dec. 26, 1965, 1 and 53.
41. Memo from McPherson to pres., Feb. 28, 1966, Memos for the President file, McPherson papers, LBJL. In this memo, McPherson recommended approval of Farmer's grant. Instead of checking the option "yes," he checked "see me."
42. *New York Times*, Feb. 26, 1966, 11.
43. James Farmer, Oral History Interview, July 20, 1971, Tape No. 2, 2–5, 10–16, LBJL.
44. *New York Times*, July 4, 1966, 1.
45. OEO Administrative History, LBJL, 66–81. A partisan history of CDGM is Polly Greenberg, *The Devil Has Slippery Shoes* (1969).
46. The job application is reprinted in "Supplemental Appropriations for 1966," Committee on Appropriations, Senate hearings (1965), 584.
47. "Supplemental Appropriations," Senate hearings, 589.
48. Christopher Jencks, "Accommodating Whites: A New Look at Mississippi," *New Republic* (vol. 154, April 16, 1966), 21.
49. *New York Times*, Feb. 12, 1966, 56; Feb. 23, 27.
50. OEO, Administrative History, 72–73, 75, 82.
51. *New York Times*, Sept. 14, 1966, 39; Oct. 11, 39; Oct. 12, 30; Oct. 18, 23.
52. *New York Times*, Oct. 19, 1966, 35.
53. *New York Times*, Dec. 17, 1966, 17; Dec. 18, 63; OEO Administrative History, LBJL, 85–86.
54. *New York Times*, April 14, 1965, 25. Both quotes from *New York Times*, April 15, 1966, 1 and 21.
55. Moyers to pres., Dec. 19, 1966, with Shriver's handwritten resignation attached. Bill Moyers Office Files.
56. The material for this section is drawn mainly from the files of OEO's Office of Inspection, N.A. For this paragraph, memo from McKay and Krumlauf to May and Clampitt, Sept. 20, 1965; "Refunding Evaluation Visit," Aug. 11–13, 1965; memo from Krumlauf to May and Clampitt, Sept. 21, 1966, all in Atlanta file.
57. "Special Conditions—Atlanta Grant 9/65," Atlanta file, Office of Inspection.
58. Memo from Edgar May to the director, April 30, 1966, Atlanta file, Office of Inspection.
59. Memo from Crawford and Quetsch to Frank Sloan, Feb. 7, 1967, Atlanta file, Office of Inspection.

60. Memo from Bill Seward to Edgar May, April 29, 1966, Atlanta file, Office of Inspection.
61. Memo from Bob Clampitt to Bill Haddad, Feb. 13, 1965, Philadelphia file, Office of Inspection; Jack Williams, "Philadelphia: Preliminary Report," Feb. 26, 1965, same file; Arthur B. Shostak, "Promoting Participation of the Poor: Philadelphia's Antipoverty Program," Social Work (vol. 11, Jan. 1966), 64–72.
62. New York Times, May 27, 1965, 26; May 28, 30; July 24, 1966, 60.
63. Memo from Tom Kelly to Haddad and Clampitt, Aug. 19, 1965, Philadelphia file, Office of Inspection.
64. New York Times, June 26, 1967, 24.
65. New York Times, July 17, 1966, 50.
66. Memo from Tom Kelly to Ed May, March 8, 1966; memo from Kelly, Parsons, Bird to May, June 3, 1966, Philadelphia file, Office of Inspection. Quote on p. 14 of Kelly, Parsons, Bird.
67. "Philadelphia Anti-Poverty Action Committee," June 10, 1966, Philadelphia file, Office of Inspection.
68. Memo from Tom Kelly to Ed May, May 20, 1967, Philadelphia file, Office of Inspection.
69. New York Times, June 26, 1967, 24; memo from Kelly to May, May 20, 1967, Philadelphia file, Office of Inspection.
70. HARYOU's history through March 1965, is contained in a 51-page memo from Woody Klein to William Haddad, April 2, 1965, HARYOU file, Office of Inspection.
71. New York Times, June 11, 1964, 20.
72. Memo from Klein to Haddad, April 2, 1965, 6–36.
73. Woody Klein, "Defeat in Harlem," Nation (vol. 199, July 27, 1964), 27–29.
74. OEO Administrative History, 110.
75. New York Times, Oct. 13, 1965, 36.
76. New York Times, June 5, 1966, 76; and memo from George Morrison to May, Clampitt, and Williams, Sept. 27, 1965, HARYOU file, Office of Inspection.
77. Memo from Jack Williams to Ed May, Sept. 25, 1965, HARYOU file, Office of Inspection.
78. Quoted in U.S. News and World Report (vol. 59, Dec. 13, 1965), 16–17.
79. Memo from Jack Williams to Edgar May, March 3, 1966, HARYOU file, Office of Inspection.
80. Memo from Edgar May to Director, Dec. 13, 1965, HARYOU file, Office of Inspection.
81. For quote, Jack Williams to Edgar May, July 14, 1966, HARYOU file, Office of Inspection.
82. New York Times, July 3, 1968, 21.
83. New York Times, Feb. 18, 1968, 47.

84. On conflict between the mayor and civil rights groups, Ralph M. Kramer, *Participation of the Poor: Comparative Community Case Studies in the War on Poverty* (1969), 25–36.

85. Kramer, *Participation of the Poor*, 37–41. San Francisco file, Office of Inspection, *passim*.

86. Ed May to Ted Berry, Aug. 9, 1966, San Francisco file, Office of Inspection.

87. Edgar May for the Record, Sept. 28, 1966, San Francisco file, Office of Inspection.

88. Memo from Dick Fullmer to Edgar May, Jan. 5, 1967, San Francisco file, Office of Inspection.

89. Kramer, *Participation of the Poor*, 49–53.

90. Memo from Eric Biddle to Edgar May, Aug. 30, 1967, San Francisco file, Office of Inspection. This memo is a history of the summer programs.

91. Biddle to May, Aug. 30, 1967, 13–17.

92. Tom Wolfe, *Radical Chic and Mau-Mauing the Flak Catchers* (1970).

93. Biddle to May, Aug. 30, 1967, 1–2.

94. Memos from Eric Biddle to Edgar May, Sept. 6, 1967; Oct. 3, 1967; and Oct. 19, 1967, San Francisco file, Office of Inspection.

95. Betty Jo Bailey and Harold H. Weissman, "Voter Registration Campaigns," in Harold H. Weissman, ed., *Community Development in the Mobilization For Youth Experience* (1969), 83–101. The conclusion I draw from this essay is not explicitly stated but is implied throughout.

96. Harold H. Weissman, "The Housing Program 1962 to 1967," in Weissman, *Community Development*, 44–69.

97. Mary Rabagliati and Ezra Birnbaum, "Organizations of Welfare Clients," in Weissman, *Community Development*, 102–136.

98. Larry R. Jackson and William A. Johnson, *Protest by the Poor: The Welfare Rights Movement in New York City* (1974), 89–94.

99. Jackson and Johnson, *Protest by the Poor*, chs. 10 and 11. For figures, p. 122.

100. Rabagliati and Birnbaum, "Organizations of Welfare Clients," 135.

101. This discussion of MFY's 1964 crisis is based on Alfred Freid, "The Attack on Mobilization," in Weissman, *Community Development*, 137–162. Quote on p. 139.

102. Freid, "The Attack on Mobilization," 142.

103. See Bertram Beck, "Mobilization For Youth: Reflections about Its Administration," in Harold H. Weissman, ed., *Justice and the Law in the Mobilization For Youth Experience* (1969), 145–166.

104. Jackson and Johnson, *Protest by the Poor*, 59–60.

105. Joseph Helfgot, "Professional Reform Organizations and the Symbolic Representation of the Poor," *American Sociological Review* (vol. 39, Aug. 1974), 475–491.

106. Beck, "Mobilization For Youth," 160–165.

107. Sundquist, *Making Federalism Work*, 35.

108. Sar A. Levitan, *The Great Society's Poor Law* (1969), ch. 7; OEO, "Health Programs," March 1969, 43–44; OEO, *OEO Touches Your Life* (1972).

109. Levitan, *Great Society's Poor Law*, ch. 5; Government Accounting Office, "Review of Economic Opportunity Programs" (1969), 99–103.

110. Levitan, *Great Society's Poor Law*, ch. 8; OEO, "Health Programs"; "Economic Opportunity Amendments of 1971," Committee on Education and Labor, House hearings (1971), 357, 375.

111. For an exhaustive survey of Head Start's history and accomplishments, Edward Zigler and Jeanette Valentine, eds., *Project Head Start: A Legacy of the War on Poverty* (1979).

112. Westinghouse Learning Corporation—Ohio University, "The Impact of Head Start" (April 1969, preliminary draft), 0–6.

113. HEW, *Lasting Effects After Preschool* (a report by central staff of the Consortium for Longitudinal Studies, Sept. 1979).

114. Lois-ellin Datta, "Another Spring and Other Hopes: Some Findings from National Evaluations of Project Head Start," in Zigler and Valentine, *Project Head Start*, esp. 407–410.

115. Richard M. Pious, "Policy and Public Administration: The Legal Services Programs in the War on Poverty," *Politics and Society* (vol. 2, May 1971), 365–391; see also A. Kenneth Pye, "The Role of Legal Services in the Antipoverty Program," *Law and Contemporary Problems* (vol. 31, Winter 1966), 211–249.

116. Harry P. Stumpf, Bernadyne Turpen, John Culver, "The Impact of OEO Legal Services," in Dorothy Buckton James, ed., *Analyzing Poverty Policy* (1975), 191–204. Quote on p. 201.

117. Florence Heller School for Advanced Studies in Social Welfare, "Community Representation in Community Action Programs, Final Report" (March 1969). This report was mercifully summarized in David M. Austin, "Resident Participation: Political Mobilization or Organizational Cooptation?," *Public Administration Review* (vol. 32, Sept. 1972), 409–420.

118. Austin, "Resident Participation," quotes on pp. 417 and 419.

119. Barss, Reitzel and Associates, Inc., "Community Action and Urban Institutional Change: A National Evaluation of the Community Action Program," (Aug. 1970).

120. Barss, Reitzel, "Community Action," 64, 251.

121. Beck, "Mobilization For Youth," 165.

122. *New York Times*, Nov. 8, 1967, 20.

123. *New York Times*, Oct. 12, 1967, 51; Oct. 22, 3E; Dec. 25, 1 and 26.

124. *New York Times*, Oct. 12, 1967, 51.

125. GAO, "Review of Economic Opportunity Programs," 43–44.
126. Washington *Post,* Jan. 23, 1969, 1.

Chapter 10. Rise and Fall of a Counterculture

1. Statement quoted in *Berkeley Barb,* Jan. 13, 1967, 1.
2. San Francisco *Oracle,* Jan. 1967 (no. 1), 2.
3. Jane Kramer, *Allen Ginsberg in America* (1969), 25–26.
4. San Francisco *Chronicle,* Jan. 20, 1967, 11; Ginsberg's recollection to author, written April 13, 1983.
5. Quoted in Burton H. Wolfe, *The Hippies* (1968), 13.
6. San Francisco *Chronicle,* Jan. 20, 11; Ginsberg's recollection to author.
7. Quoted in *Berkeley Barb,* Jan. 13, 3.
8. Rubin quoted in *Berkeley Barb,* Jan. 13, 3.
9. Gleason's column, San Francisco *Chronicle,* Jan. 16, 1967, 41.
10. San Francisco *Oracle,* Jan. 1967 (no. 2), 9; Emmett Grogan, *Ringolevio: A Life Played for Keeps* (1972), 267.
11. Kramer, *Ginsberg,* 27.
12. San Francisco *Oracle,* Jan. 1967 (no. 2), 24; San Francisco *Chronicle,* Jan. 20, 1967, 11; Ginsberg's recollection to author.
13. *Newsweek* (vol. 69, Feb. 6, 1967), 92–95. Quote on p. 92.
14. See Sigmund Freud, *The Ego and the Id* (1927); and *Civilization and Its Discontents* (1930); for quote see Norton edition of latter, p. 98.
15. Norman O. Brown, *Life Against Death: The Psychoanalytical Meaning of History* (1959), 45.
16. Brown, *Life Against Death,* 175.
17. Norman O. Brown, *Love's Body* (1966). Quotations in this paragraph appear in order on pp. 161, 161, 83, 89, 264.
18. For a valuable first-hand account of black hipsters in Harlem in the 1930s, Milton Mezzrow and Bernard Wolfe, *Really the Blues* (1946), 206–233.
19. Quoted in Frank Tirro, *Jazz: A History* (1977), 155.
20. Marshall W. Stearns, *The Story of Jazz* (1956), ch. 18.
21. Ross Russell, *Bird Lives!* (1973), 86.
22. For a picture of hipsters in this period, see John Clellon Holmes's novel *Go* (1952); see also Russell, *Bird Lives!,* 179–180.
23. Norman Mailer, "The White Negro: Superficial Reflections on the Hipster," *Dissent* (vol. IV, Summer 1957), 276–293.
24. See interview with Huncke by John Tytell in *The Unspeakable Visions of the Individual* (vol. 3, nos. 1 and 2, 1973), 3–15. Most of this issue is devoted to Huncke.
25. John Tytell, *Naked Angels: The Lives and Literature of the Beat Generation* (1976), 5.

26. Allen Ginsberg, "On Huncke's Book," reprinted in *The Unspeakable Visions of the Individual,* 21.

27. "An Interview: Allen Ginsberg," *The Paris Review* (vol. 10, Spring 1966), 34–45. Quotes on pp. 37, 45; Ginsberg's recollection to author.

28. Bruce Cook, *The Beat Generation* (1971), chs. 3, 7.

29. Gary Snyder, "North Beach," in *The Old Ways: Six Essays* (1977), 45–48. Quote on p. 46.

30. Letter from Ginsberg to Howard Schulman, Oct. 16, 1961, reprinted in *Unspeakable Visions* (vol. 4, 1974), 75.

31. "Howl," reprinted in Gene Feldman and Max Gartenberg, eds., *The Beat Generation and the Angry Young Men* (1958), 164–174; Ginsberg's recollection to author.

32. Kramer, *Ginsberg in America,* 159.

33. "An Interview," *Paris Review,* 46; "Mescaline," in Allen Ginsberg, *Kaddish and Other Poems* (1961), 84.

34. "An Interview," *Paris Review,* 47–50. Quote on p. 50; Ginsberg's recollection to author.

35. Allen Ginsberg, *The Change* (1961).

36. Quoted in John Clellon Holmes's excellent essay on Ginsberg in *Nothing More to Declare* (1967), 58.

37. For accounts of Kerouac's life see Barry Gifford and Lawrence Lee, *Jack's Book: An Oral Biography of Jack Kerouac* (1978); and Ann Charters, *Kerouac: A Biography* (1973).

38. Jack Kerouac, "The Origins of the Beat Generation," *Playboy* (June 1959), reprinted in Thomas Parkinson, ed., *A Casebook on the Beat* (1961), 72.

39. Neal Cassady, *The First Third* (1971).

40. Charters, *Kerouac,* 128–135.

41. Kerouac, *On the Road* (Viking Compass Edition, 1959). Quotations in this paragraph appear in order on pp. 7, 194, 211, 206, 129, 206, 173, 195.

42. Charters, *Kerouac,* chs. 19, 20.

43. Alan Watts, *In My Own Way: An Autobiography, 1915–1965* (1972).

44. Alan W. Watts, *The Way of Zen* (1957), esp. chs. 3, 4; and *This Is It* (1960), esp. ch. 1.

45. Watts, *In My Own Way,* 267.

46. Gary Snyder, *The Old Ways,* 15.

47. Brief sketches of Snyder's life appear in Cook, *The Beat Generation,* 28–36; and Bob Steuding, *Gary Snyder* (1976), ch. 1.

48. Jack Kerouac, *The Dharma Bums* (1958). Quotations in this paragraph appear in order on pp. 30, 84, 86.

49. Sidney Cohen, *Drugs of Hallucination* (1965), ch. 2.

50. Albert Hoffman, "Interview," *High Times* (July, 1976), 25 ff.

51. Aldous Huxley, *The Doors of Perception* (1954). Quotations in this paragraph, in order, as they appear in the Perennial Library edition, are on pp. 16, 35–36, 56, 56, 73, 73.
52. For biographical material on Leary see John Cashman, *The LSD Story* (1966); and Timothy Leary, *High Priest* (1968).
53. Leary, *High Priest*, 283.
54. Leary, *High Priest*, 266.
55. Leary, *High Priest*, ch. 6; quotes on pp. 121, 128.
56. Leary, *High Priest*, 253.
57. Leary, *High Priest*, ch. 12; and "The Seven Tongues of God" in Timothy Leary, *Politics of Ecstasy*, ch. 1.
58. Leary, *High Priest*, 153.
59. Leary's *Playboy* interview reprinted in *Politics of Ecstasy*, 129.
60. On Leary's career at Harvard, Noah Gordon, "The Hallucinogenic Drug Cult," *Reporter* (vol. 29, Aug. 15, 1963), 35–42. On Mexico and Millbrook, Cashman, *LSD*, 58–62.
61. Timothy Leary, *Psychedelic Prayers after the Tao Te Ching* (1966). Leary discusses the process of translation in the forward. Quote on p. 3.
62. *New York Times*, Dec. 26, 1965, 53.
63. *New York Times*, Sept. 20, 1966, 33; Sept. 21, 94; Dec. 4, section 2, 5 and 9. See also "Talk of the Town," *The New Yorker* (vol. 42, Oct. 1, 1966), 42–43.
64. *Newsweek* (vol. 67, May 9, 1966); *Life* (vol. 60, March 25, 1966); *Saturday Evening Post* (vol. 239, May 21, 1966).
65. *New York Times*, April 14, 1966, 35; April 6, 1 and 25.
66. Leary, *High Priest*, 132.
67. "LSD," *Life*, 29.
68. Tom Wolfe, *The Electric Kool-Aid Acid Test* (1968).
69. Quoted in *Newsweek* (vol. 69, Feb. 6, 1967), 95.
70. Wolfe, *Electric Kool-Aid*, ch. 18.
71. On Trips Festival, see Wolfe, *Electric Kool-Aid*, ch. 19; and Ralph J. Gleason, *The Jefferson Airplane* (1969), 16–23.
72. For early history of rock and roll, Carl Belz, *The Story of Rock* (1969), ch. 2; Charlie Gillett, *The Sound of the City: The Rise and Fall of Rock and Roll* (1970), ch. 1.
73. For Beatles' early years, Hunter Davies, *The Beatles* (1968).
74. Nicholas Schaffner, *The Beatles Forever* (1977), ch. 1.
75. Quoted in Schaffner, *The Beatles Forever*, 10.
76. Quoted in Schaffner, *The Beatles Forever*, 75, 76; for Kesey at this concert, Wolfe, *Electric Kool-Aid*, ch. 15.
77. Anthony Scaduto, *Dylan: An Intimate Biography* (1973).
78. Quoted in Scaduto, *Dylan*, 204.
79. Scaduto, *Dylan*, 245–249.

80. The best discussion of Dylan's lyrics is Michael Gray, *Song and Dance Man: The Art of Bob Dylan* (1972).

81. Schaffner, *The Beatles Forever*, ch. 4.

82. Quoted in Schaffner, *The Beatles Forever*, 71.

83. Characteristics of acid rock bands discussed in Jann Wenner, "Rock and Roll Music," *Rolling Stone* (Feb. 10, 1968), 16.

84. Charles Perry, "The Sound of San Francisco," in Jim Miller, ed., *The Rolling Stones Illustrated History of Rock and Roll* (1976), 248.

85. Michael Lydon, "The Grateful Dead," *Rolling Stone* (Aug. 23, 1969), 15 ff. Quote on p. 18.

86. Ralph J. Gleason, "Perspectives: A Power to Change the World," *Rolling Stone* (June 22, 1968), 10.

87. This conversation was taped and printed in San Francisco *Oracle*, Feb. 1967 (no. 7).

88. *Berkeley Barb*, May 12, 1967, 2.

89. See interview with Thelin in Leonard Wolf, *Voices from the Love Generation* (1968), 212–231.

90. *The Haight-Ashbury Maverick* (vol. 1, no. 5, 1967), 6 ff. Quote on p. 11.

91. Timothy Leary, "God's Secret Agent," reprinted in *High Times* (Feb. 1979), 51 ff; and Mark Salditch, "Bear AKA Augustus Owsley Stanley III," same issue, 52–53.

92. San Francisco *Chronicle*, Jan. 18, 1967, 2; Jan. 27, 43; *Berkeley Barb*, April 14, 1967, 1 and 5.

93. Grogan, *Ringolevio*. Use with caution.

94. Hunter S. Thompson, *Hell's Angels: A Strange and Terrible Saga* (1967), ch. 21; Wolfe, *Electric Kool-Aid*, ch. 13.

95. Nicholas von Hoffman, *We Are the People Our Parents Warned Us Against* (1968), 112–113.

96. *Berkeley Barb*, Sept. 1, 1967, 3.

97. *Time* (vol. 90, July 7, 1967), 18 ff. Quote on p. 19.

98. Chester Anderson, "Trouble in Bohemia," *Berkeley Barb*, March 3, 1967, 7.

99. John Luce, "Haight-Ashbury Today: A Case of Terminal Euphoria," *Esquire* (vol. 72, July 1969), 68.

100. *Rolling Stone*, Nov. 9, 1967, 11; *Berkeley Barb*, Sept. 29, 1967, 3; Oct. 6, 3.

101. Brown, *Life Against Death*, 175–176.

102. Vincent Bugliosi, *Helter Skelter: The True Story of the Manson Murders* (1975), 221–223, 321–331, 635–639; the phrase "acid fascism" belongs to David Felton, ed., *Mindfuckers* (1972), 10.

103. Quoted in Robert Stephen Spitz, *Barefoot in Babylon: The Creation of the Woodstock Music Festival, 1969* (1979), 460.

104. Grogan, *Ringolevio*, 280–286; see also *Berkeley Barb*, March 3, 1967, 1 and 2.

105. This episode reported by Communication Company communiqué, reprinted in Joan Didion, *Slouching Towards Bethlehem* (1979), 101.

106. See Spitz, *Barefoot in Babylon*.

107. The following account is based on "Let It Bleed," *Rolling Stone*, Jan. 21, 1970, 18 ff.

108. Jefferson Airplane, *Volunteers* (1969).

109. Daniel Bell, *The Cultural Contradictions of Capitalism* (1976).

110. Christopher Lasch, *The Culture of Narcissism* (1979).

Chapter 11. Rise and Fall of the New Left

1. Useful books on the new left are Kirkpatrick Sale, *SDS* (1973); Irwin Unger, *The Movement: A History of the American New Left, 1959–1972* (1974); Edward J. Bacciocco, Jr., *The New Left in America: Reform or Revolution, 1956 to 1970* (1974); Nigel Young, *An Infantile Disorder? The Crisis and Decline of the New Left* (1977); Massimo Teodori, ed., *The New Left: A Documentary History* (1969), Part I, Historical and Critical Notes.

2. U.S. Census Bureau, *The Statistical History of the United States* (1976), 283.

3. Seymour Martin Lipset, *Passion and Politics: Student Activism in America*, Part I, ch. 3; Milton Mankoff and Richard Flacks, "The Changing Social Base of the American Student Movement," *The Annals of the American Academy of Political and Social Science* (vol. 395, May 1971), 54–67; Kenneth Keniston, *The Young Radicals* (1967).

4. Nathan Glazer, "The New Left and the Jews," *The Jewish Journal of Sociology* (vol. 11, Dec. 1969), 121–132; Nathan Glazer, "The Jewish Role in Student Activism," *Fortune* (Jan. 1969), 112 ff.

5. Todd Gitlin, *Student Political Action, 1960–1963: The View of a Participant* (SDS publication). See also James P. O'Brien, "The Development of a New Left in the United States" (unpublished dissertation, University of Wisconsin, 1971).

6. Abbie Hoffman, *Soon to Be Made into a Major Motion Picture* (1980), 40.

7. C. Wright Mills, "Letter to the New Left," *New Left Review* (Sept. 1960), reprinted in Paul Jacobs and Saul Landau, eds., *The New Radicals: A Report with Documents* (1966), 101–114. Quote on p. 111.

8. Thomas Hayden, "A Letter to the New (Young) Left," *The Activist* (Winter 1961), reprinted in Mitchell Cohen and Dennis Hale, eds., *The New Student Left: An Anthology* (1967), 2–9. Quote on p. 3.

9. Sale, *SDS*, 673–693. All students of the new left are indebted to this pioneering book.

10. Robert A. Haber, "From Protest to Radicalism," *Venture* (Fall 1960), reprinted in Cohen and Hale, *The New Student Left*, 34–42. Quotes on pp. 40, 42.

11. Much of the information in this paragraph is derived from Tim Findley, "Tom Hayden: Rolling Stone Interview Part 1," *Rolling Stone* (Oct. 26, 1972), 38.

12. From Hayden to SDS Friends, Dec. 11, 1961, SDS Microfilm, Series 1, no. 3.

13. SDS, *Port Huron Statement* (1964), 15.

14. SDS, *Port Huron Statement*, 10.

15. SDS, *Port Huron Statement*, 7.

16. SDS, *Port Huron Statement*, 61.

17. SDS, *Port Huron Statement*, 63.

18. Sale, *SDS*, ch. 5.

19. Dick Flacks, "Some Problems, Issues, Proposals," 1965 SDS National Convention Working Paper, SDS Microfilm, Series 2 A, no. 16.

20. SDS, *America and the New Era* (1963), quotes in order, pp. 7, 12, 15.

21. Findley, Hayden interview, 40.

22. Sale, *SDS*, ch. 7.

23. Tom Hayden, "The Politics of 'The Movement,' " in Irving Howe, ed., *The Radical Papers* (1966), 362.

24. Todd Gitlin, "Dynamics of the New Left," *Motive*, Part II (Nov. 1970), 44.

25. Carl Wittman and Thomas Hayden, "An Interracial Movement of the Poor?" reprinted in Cohen and Hale, *The New Student Left*, 175–213.

26. Sale, *SDS*, ch. 9.

27. Paul Potter, *A Name for Ourselves* (1971), 143–144.

28. Tom Hayden and Carl Wittman, "Summer Report, Newark Community Union," reprinted in Teodori, *The New Left*, 133–136. Quote on p. 134.

29. Richard Rothstein, "ERAP: Education of Organizers," *Radical America* (vol. 2, March 1968), 1–8. Quote on p. 6.

30. Hayden, "Politics of 'The Movement,' " 355.

31. The best account of the Berkeley uprising is Max Heirich, *The Beginnings: Berkeley, 1964* (1968).

32. See impressions of a participant, Michael Rossman, *The Wedding within the War* (1971), 92–120.

33. Mario Savio, "An End to History," speech reprinted in Seymour Martin Lipset and Sheldon S. Wolin, eds., *The Berkeley Student Revolt: Facts and Interpretations* (1965), 216–219. Quote on p. 216.

34. FSM, "Moral Impetus, The Factory, and the Society," reprinted in Lipset and Wolin, *Berkeley Student Revolt*, 213.

35. Jack Weinberg, "The Free Speech Movement and Civil Rights," re-

printed in Lipset and Wolin, *Berkeley Student Revolt*, 222.

36. Weinberg, "The Free Speech Movement and Civil Rights," Lipset and Wolin, *Berkeley Student Revolt*, 223.

37. Quoted in Heirich, *Beginnings*, 199–200.

38. Heirich, *Beginnings*, ch. 11.

39. Jerry Rubin, *DO iT!: Scenarios of the Revolution* (1970), 23.

40. Sale, *SDS*, ch. 11.

41. Potter's speech reprinted by SDS in a pamphlet, *March on Washington to End the War in Vietnam*, pages unnumbered.

42. Staughton Lynd, "Coalition Politics or Nonviolent Revolution," *Liberation* (vol. 10, June 1965), 21.

43. Oglesby's speech reprinted in Cohen and Hale, *The Student Left*, 312–321. Quotes in order, pp. 320, 313, 318, 316.

44. Sale, *SDS*, footnote on p. 245.

45. Sale, *SDS*, 663–664.

46. Rubin, *DO iT!*, 40–43. Quote on p. 43.

47. Sale, *SDS*, 253–263; Michael Ferber and Staughton Lynd, *The Resistance* (1971), 38–41.

48. Hayden, "The Politics of 'The Movement,'" 364.

49. Greg Calvert and Carol Neiman, *A Disrupted History: The New Left and the New Capitalism* (1971), 37.

50. Herbert Marcuse, *Eros and Civilization* (1955), 3.

51. Marcuse, *Eros and Civilization*, 44.

52. Herbert Marcuse, *One Dimensional Man* (1964), 257.

53. Calvert's speech reprinted in Teodori, *The New Left*, 412–418.

54. This paragraph relies not only on the Princeton speech but on Calvert's later elaboration of new working-class theory in Calvert and Neiman, *A Disrupted History*. This quote on p. 50 of the book.

55. Sale, *SDS*, ch. 15.

56. Carl Davidson, *Toward a Student Syndicalist Movement or University Reform Revisited* (SDS pamphlet).

57. Carl Davidson, *The New Radicals in the Multiversity* (SDS pamphlet), 16.

58. Peter Henig, "On the Manpower Channelers," *New Left Notes* (Jan. 20, 1967), 1 ff.

59. Greg Calvert, "From Protest to Resistance," *New Left Notes* (Jan. 13, 1967), 1.

60. *National Guardian*, April 8, 1967, 1 and 8.

61. Ferber and Lynd, *The Resistance*, ch. 5.

62. Robin Blackburn and Perry Anderson, "Che and Debray in Bolivia," *Ramparts* (vol. 6, Oct. 1967), 29.

63. Gitlin, "Dynamics of the New Left," *Motive*, Part II, 47.

64. Rubin, *DO iT!*, 20.

65. Che Guevara, *Guerrilla Warfare* (1961), 16.

66. *National Guardian*, Sept. 23, 1967; *New Left Notes*, Oct. 2, 1967, 1.
67. *National Guardian*, Aug. 26, 1967, 1.
68. *National Guardian*, Sept. 9, 1967, 3.
69. *National Guardian*, Aug. 19, 1967, 8.
70. Newton quoted in Sol Stern, "America's Black Guerrillas," *Ramparts* (vol. 6, Sept. 1967), 26.
71. Tom Hayden, *Rebellion in Newark: Official Violence and Ghetto Response* (1967), 70.
72. *National Guardian*, Sept. 9, 1967, 5.
73. *The Movement*, Nov. 1967, 3, 27–30.
74. *Berkeley Barb*, Sept. 15, 1967, 6; Sept. 22, 7.
75. *The Movement*, Nov. 1967; *Berkeley Barb*, Oct. 20, 1967, 2–3; Oct. 27, 3.
76. The following account of the Pentagon siege is based on reports in the Washington *Post*, Oct. 22 and 23, 1967; the Washington *Free Press* (special Pentagon edition, n.d.); Thomas Powers, *The War at Home* (1973), 238–242; *National Guardian*, Oct. 28, 1967, 1; Norman Mailer, *The Armies of the Night* (1968).
77. Rubin quoted in Mailer, *Armies of the Night*, 261.
78. Washington *Free Press*, special edition, 8.
79. Cathy Wilkerson, "Victory or Defeat," Washington *Free Press*, special edition, 9.
80. Jeff Segal, "Pop-Art Guerrilla Warfare," *The Movement*, Nov. 1967, 6.
81. Marilyn Buck, "Resistance," *New Left Notes*, Nov. 6, 1967, 3.
82. Greg Calvert, "Participatory Democracy, Collective Leadership and Political Responsibility," *New Left Notes*, Dec. 18, 1967, 1 and 7. Quote on p. 7.
83. Carl Davidson, "Toward Institutional Resistance," *New Left Notes*, Nov. 13, 1967, 1 ff. Quote on p. 4.
84. Open Letter from James Forman to New York Anti-War Conference, Feb. 3, 1968, reprinted in *New Left Notes*, March 4, 1968, 2 and 7.
85. For background on Rudd in this paragraph and next, and for quotes, see *New York Times*, May 19, 1968, 1 and 84.
86. For view that student radicals were merely acting out a generational revolt, Lewis Feuer, *The Conflict of Generations* (1969), esp. 522–523.
87. Jerry Avorn et al., *Up Against the Ivy Wall* (1969), ch. 1. Rudd's letter quoted on p. 27.
88. For description of following events, *Crisis at Columbia*, Report of the Fact-Finding Commission Appointed to Investigate the Disturbances at Columbia University (popularly called the Cox Commission), 98–113. Also Avorn, *Up Against the Ivy Wall*.
89. Sales quoted in Roger Kahn, *The Battle for Morningside Heights: Why Students Rebel* (1970), 126.

90. Quoted in Kahn, *Battle for Morningside Heights*, 127.
91. Rudd quoted in Sale, *SDS*, 440.
92. Mark Rudd, *Columbia* (SDS pamphlet), 9.
93. Avorn, *Up Against the Ivy Wall*, chs. 9–13.
94. Mark Rudd, "We Want Revolution," *Saturday Evening Post* (vol. 241, Sept. 21, 1968), 26 ff.
95. Tom Hayden, "Two, Three, Many Columbias," *Ramparts* (vol. 6, June 15, 1968), 40.
96. Sale, *SDS*, 455–456.
97. On PL, Jack Newfield, *A Prophetic Minority* (1966), 109–124.
98. *The Guardian*, June 22, 1968, 5.
99. *The Guardian*, June 22, 4.
100. Sale, *SDS*, 474–475.
101. Up Against the Wall Motherfuckers, "Respect for Lawlessness," *New Left Notes*, Sept. 16, 1968, 4–5.
102. Terry Robbins and Bill Ayers, "Give It a Name," *New Left Notes*, Oct. 7, 1968, 4.
103. Sale, *SDS*, note, p. 713.
104. Mike Klonsky, "Toward a Revolutionary Youth Movement," SDS microfilm, Series 3, no. 10.
105. Sale, *SDS*, 513–515; Milton Viorst, *Fire in the Streets: America in the 1960's* (1979), 485.
106. Carl Oglesby, "Notes on a Decade Ready for the Dustbin," *Liberation*, Aug. 1969, reprinted in Harold Jacobs, ed., *Weatherman* (1970), 119–136. Quote on p. 129.
107. Weatherman paper reprinted in Jacobs, *Weatherman*, 51–90.
108. *The Guardian*, June 28, 1969, 1 ff.; Sale, *SDS*, 557–574.
109. Mike Klonsky et al., "Revolutionary Youth Movement II," *New Left Notes*, July 8, 1969, 5 ff.; Mike Klonsky, "Why I Quit," *New Left Notes*, Aug. 29, 1969, 2 and 6.
110. On life in Weather collectives, Susan Stern, *With the Weatherman: The Personal Journey of a Revolutionary Woman* (1975); see also Jacobs, *Weatherman*, passim; Thomas Powers, *Diana: the Making of a Terrorist* (1971), esp. 118–158.
111. Stern, *With the Weatherman*. Quotes on pp. 115, 169.
112. *The Guardian*, Aug. 16, 1969, 4.
113. *The Guardian*, Oct. 18, 1969, 405; Viorst, *Fire in the Streets*, 494–500.
114. Sale, *SDS*, 608–609.
115. On Flint, *San Francisco Good Times*, Jan. 8, 1970, reprinted in Jacobs, *Weatherman*, 340–350.
116. Stern, *With the Weatherman*, 204–205.
117. Dohrn quoted in Jacobs, *Weatherman*, 347.
118. Quoted in Sale, *SDS*, 605.

119. Tom Hayden, *Trial* (1970), 94.
120. Tim Findley, "Tom Hayden: Rolling Stone Interview Part 2," *Rolling Stone* (Nov. 9, 1972), 29.

Chapter 12. Black Power

 1. For history of SNCC see, Clayborne Carson, *In Struggle: SNCC and the Black Awakening of the 1960's* (1981); Howard Zinn, *SNCC: The New Abolitionists* (1965); James Forman, *The Making of Black Revolutionaries* (1972); Cleveland Sellers with Robert Terrell, *The River of No Return* (1973); Allen J. Matusow, "From Civil Rights to Black Power: The Case of SNCC: 1960–1966," in Barton J. Bernstein and Matusow, eds., *Twentieth-Century America: Recent Interpretations* (1st edition, 1969), 531–556. Part of the following discussion is adapted from my earlier article.
 2. Sellers, *River of No Return*, 36.
 3. Forman, *Making of Black Revolutionaries*, 433.
 4. Len Holt, *The Summer That Didn't End* (1965), 35–36, 152–153.
 5. Carson, *In Struggle*, 96–100; Zinn, *SNCC*, ch. 9.
 6. Sellers, *River of No Return*, 83.
 7. Quoted in Forman, *Making of Black Revolutionaries*, 373.
 8. David Dennis Interview in Howell Raines, *My Soul Is Rested* (1977), 274.
 9. Quoted in James Atwater, "If We Can Crack Mississippi . . . ," *Saturday Evening Post* (vol. 237, July 25, 1964), 16.
10. Quotes in this paragraph from Elizabeth Sutherland, ed., *Letters from Mississippi* (1965), 5–6.
11. Carson, *In Struggle*, 114–115.
12. Pat Watters and Reese Cleghorn, *Climbing Jacob's Ladder* (1967), 139.
13. Sally Belfrage, *Freedom Summer* (1965), 80.
14. Carson, *In Struggle*, 117.
15. Carson, *In Struggle*, 123–126; Forman, *Making of Black Revolutionaries*, ch. 49; Holt, *The Summer That Didn't End*, ch. 9.
16. Sellers, *River of No Return*, 111.
17. See Moses's views in Robert Penn Warren, *Who Speaks for the Negro?* (1965), 91.
18. Sellers, *River of No Return*, 68–69; Forman, *Making of Black Revolutionaries*, 374–375.
19. Dennis in Raines, *My Soul Is Rested*, 278.
20. Alvin F. Poussaint, "A Negro Psychiatrist Explains the Negro Psyche," *New York Times Magazine* (Aug. 20, 1967), 52 ff. Quotes on p. 76.

21. Sellers, *River of No Return*, ch. 10; Forman, *Making of Black Revolutionaries*, ch. 52; Carson, *In Struggle*, ch. 10.

22. Moses quote in Gene Roberts, "From 'Freedom High' to 'Black Power,' " *New York Times Magazine* (Sept. 25, 1966), 29.

23. Moses episode described in Sellers, *River of No Return*, 137–139.

24. These quotes are from transcripts of taped interviews conducted in the South in 1965 by Stanford University students. The tapes are at Stanford.

25. Alvin F. Poussaint, "Problems of White Civil Rights Workers in the South," *Psychiatric Opinion* (vol. 3, Dec. 1966), 21.

26. Alvin F. Poussaint, "The Stresses of the White Female Worker in the Civil Rights Movement in the South," *American Journal of Psychiatry* (vol. 118, Oct. 1966), 40.

27. From Stanford tapes.

28. From Stanford tapes.

29. Poussaint, "Problems of White Civil Rights Workers," 20–21.

30. Poussaint, "Stresses of the White Female Worker," 404.

31. John Lewis, "A Trend Toward Aggressive Nonviolent Action," *Dialogue Magazine* (Spring 1964), reprinted in August Meier, Elliott Rudwick and Frances L. Broderick, *Black Protest Thought in the Twentieth Century* (2nd ed., 1971), 352–360. Quote on p. 357.

32. Forman, *Making of Black Revolutionaries*, ch. 51. Quotes on pp. 407, 408.

33. Quoted in Carson, *In Struggle*, 136.

34. Quoted in Carson, *In Struggle*, 184–185.

35. Forman, *Making of Black Revolutionaries*, 445–446.

36. Milton Viorst, *Fire in the Streets: America in the 1960's* (1979), 347–352.

37. Sellers, *River of No Return*, 72–76.

38. Quoted in Viorst, *Fire in the Streets*, 353.

39. Viorst, *Fire in the Streets*, 355–363, 367–369. Quote on p. 368.

40. Viorst, *Fire in the Streets*, 369–370; Forman, *Making of Black Revolutionaries*, ch. 54; Sellers, *River of No Return*, 155–159.

41. SNCC statement reprinted in Jack Newfield, *A Prophetic Minority* (1967), 76–77.

42. The following account is based on the *New York Times*, June 7, 1966, 1; June 8, 1 and 26; June 9, 1; June 12, 1 and 82; June 17, 1; June 21, 30.

43. *New York Times*, June 22, 1966, 25.

44. *New York Times*, June 17, 1966, 33.

45. Stokely Carmichael, "What We Want," *New York Review of Books* (Sept. 22, 1966), 6.

46. Stokely Carmichael and Charles V. Hamilton, *Black Power: The Politics of Liberation in America* (1967), 65.

47. Carmichael and Hamilton, *Black Power*, 52.

48. For an introduction to the history of black nationalism in America, see Theodore Draper, *The Rediscovery of Black Nationalism* (1969).

49. On Malcolm's life, *The Autobiography of Malcolm X* (1965).

50. *Autobiography of Malcolm X*, 284.

51. *Malcolm X Speaks: Selected Speeches and Statements* (1965), 12.

52. *Malcolm X Speaks*, 38.

53. Quoted in Peter Goldman, *The Death and Life of Malcolm X* (1973), 222.

54. On Fanon's life, Peter Geismar, *Fanon* (1971).

55. Frantz Fanon, *The Wretched of the Earth* (1965), 73.

56. Quoted in David Caute, *Frantz Fanon* (1970), 103.

57. Carmichael and Hamilton, *Black Power*, 44–49, 58–84. Quote on p. 80. See also Stokely Carmichael, "Toward Black Liberation," *The Massachusetts Review* (vol. 7, Autumn 1966), reprinted in Stokely Carmichael, *Stokely Speaks* (1971), 31–43.

58. Carmichael and Hamilton, *Black Power*, 23–32, 37–39. Quote on p. 39.

59. For example, Julius Lester, *Look Out, Whitey! Black Power's Gon' Get Your Mama!* (1968), ch. 5. Lester was a SNCC member.

60. See interview with Huey P. Newton, May 15, 1968, reprinted in G. Louis Heath, ed., *Off the Pigs: The History and Literature of the Black Panther Party* (1976), 281. For Brown's critique of cultural nationalism, H. Rap Brown, *Die Nigger Die!* (1969), 141.

61. U.S. Census Bureau, "Special Census Survey of the South and East Los Angeles Areas: November 1965," Series P-23, No. 17 (March 23, 1966), 4, 7, 9; see also "Characteristics of the South and East Los Angeles Areas: November 1965," Series P-23, No. 18 (June 28, 1966).

62. This account of the riot has been pieced together from the following: Report by the Governor's Commission on the Los Angeles Riots, *Violence in the City—An End or a Beginning?* (Dec. 1965); Robert Conot, *Rivers of Blood, Years of Darkness* (1967); and Jerry Cohen and William S. Murphy, *Burn, Baby, Burn!: The Los Angeles Race Riot, August 1965* (1966).

63. Langston Hughes, "Roland Hayes Beaten," in Hughes, *One-Way Ticket* (1949), 86.

64. Governor's Commission, *Violence in the City*, 4–5.

65. David O. Sears and John B. McConahay, "Riot Participation," in Nathan Cohen, ed., *The Los Angeles Riots: A Socio-psychological Study* (1970), 265–268, 279–280.

66. Robert M. Fogelson, "White on Black: A Critique of the McCone Commission Report on the Los Angeles Riots," *Political Science Quarterly* (vol. 82, Sept. 1967), 337–367.

67. Nathan Caplan, "The New Ghetto Man: A Review of Recent Empiri-

cal Studies," *Journal of Social Issues* (vol. 26, Winter 1970), 59–73; David O. Sears and John B. McConahay, "Racist Socialization, Comparison Levels, and the Watts Riot," same issue, 121–140; John R. Forward and Jay R. Williams, "Internal-External Control and Black Militancy," same issue, 75–92.

68. Governor's Commission, *Chronology* (vol. II), 88–89.
69. *Report of the National Advisory Commission on Civil Disorders* (1968), 38–40, 112–113.
70. This account draws on New Jersey Governor's Select Commission on Civil Disorders, *Report for Action* (1968), excerpts reprinted in David Boesel and Peter H. Rossi, eds., *Cities Under Siege: An Anatomy of the Ghetto Riots, 1964–1968* (1971), 22–66; *Report of the National Advisory Commission*, 56–69; Tom Hayden, *Rebellion in Newark* (1967); *Time* (vol. 90, July 21, 1967), 15–21.
71. *Report of National Advisory Commission*, 66–68. Spina quoted on p. 66.
72. Tim Findley, "Tom Hayden: Rolling Stone Interview Part 1," *Rolling Stone* (Oct. 26, 1972), 36 ff. Quotes on pp. 44, 46.
73. This account draws on *Report of the National Advisory Commission*, 84–108; Hubert C. Locke, *The Detroit Riot of 1967* (1969); *Time* (vol. 90, Aug. 4, 1967), 13–18; *Newsweek* (vol. 70, Aug. 7, 1967), 18–26.
74. Quoted in *Report of the National Advisory Commission*, 91.
75. *Time* (Aug. 4, 1967), 13. Contains Cavanagh quote and estimate of number of buildings burned and stores sacked.
76. This interpretation has been persuasively advanced in Robert M. Fogelson, *Violence as Protest: A Study of Riots and Ghettos* (1971), 11–13 and ch. 5.
77. Conot, *Rivers of Blood, Years of Darkness*, 363.
78. On his life, see Brown, *Die Nigger Die!*.
79. Carson, *In Struggle*, 251–253.
80. Quoted in *New York Times*, July 28, 1967, 14.
81. *New York Times*, April 9, 1967, 1 and 55.
82. *New York Times*, June 12, 1967, 88; June 13, 39.
83. *New York Times*, June 20, 1967, 23; June 25, 3E.
84. *New York Times*, July 19, 1967, 42.
85. Tape-recorded text of Brown's speech in "Antiriot Bill—1967," Committee on the Judiciary, Senate hearings (1967), 31–36. Quotes on pp. 32, 33.
86. *New York Times*, July 26, 1967, 1; Brown, *Die Nigger Die!*, 100–101.
87. *New York Times*, Aug. 18, 1967, 18.
88. Brown, *Die Nigger Die!*, 143.
89. On SNCC's disintegration, Carson, *In Struggle*, chs. 15, 16, 17; Sellers, *River of No Return*, chs. 14, 15; Forman, *Making of Black Revolutionaries*, chs. 58, 60.

90. On Newton's life and founding of the party, Huey P. Newton, *Revolutionary Suicide* (1973); on founding, see also Bobby Seale, *Seize the Time* (1970), 59–112.
91. For Panther platform, Newton, *Revolutionary Suicide*, 116–119. Quote on p. 117.
92. Eldridge Cleaver, "A Letter from Jail," *Ramparts* (vol. 6, June 15, 1968), 17–21. Quote on p. 21.
93. Seale, *Seize the Time*, 153–166.
94. Newton, *Revolutionary Suicide*, ch. 16.
95. Huey P. Newton, "In Defense of Self Defense," June 20, 1967, mimeographed leaflet reprinted in G. Louis Heath, ed., *Off the Pigs!*, 364–367. Quote on p. 367.
96. Huey P. Newton, "The Correct Handling of a Revolution," July 20, 1967, mimeographed leaflet reprinted in Heath, *Off the Pigs!*, 372–376. Quote on pp. 372–373.
97. Newton, "In Defense of Self Defense," July 3, 1967, mimeographed leaflet, reprinted in Heath, *Off the Pigs!*, 368–371. Quote on p. 371.
98. For Newton's account, *Revolutionary Suicide*, ch. 23.
99. Earl Anthony, *Picking Up the Gun: A Report on the Black Panthers* (1970), 38.
100. Autobiographical notes appear in Eldridge Cleaver, *Soul on Ice* (1968), part I. Quotes in this paragraph appear in order on pp. 14, 56.
101. Eldridge Cleaver, "Introduction" in Bobby Seale, "Selections from the Biography of Huey P. Newton," *Ramparts* (vol. 7, Oct. 26, 1968), 23.
102. Anthony, *Picking Up the Gun*, 68–69.
103. Carson, *In Struggle*, 277–282; Seale, *Seize the Time*, 218–222.
104. Forman, *Making of Black Revolutionaries*, chs. 64, esp. p. 531.
105. Carson, *In Struggle*, 276.
106. Carmichael quoted in Carson, *In Struggle*, 282.
107. Forman, *Making of Black Revolutionaries*, 534–538; Sellers, *River of No Return*, 247–249.
108. Reginald Major, *A Panther Is a Black Cat* (1971), 102.
109. Anthony, *Picking Up the Gun*, ch. 5.
110. On membership, Heath, *Off the Pigs!*, 116.
111. Gene Marine, "Getting Eldridge Cleaver," *Ramparts* (vol. 6, May 1968), 49–50; Major, *A Panther Is a Black Cat*, 185–194; Anthony, *Picking Up the Gun*, ch. 8.
112. On FBI counterintelligence against the Panthers, "The FBI's Covert Action Program to Destroy the Black Panther Party," in Supplementary Detailed Staff Reports on Intelligence Activities and the Rights of Americans, Book III, *Final Report of Select Committee to Study Govern-*

ment Operations with Respect to Intelligence Activities, U.S. Senate (1976), 185–223.

113. Heath, *Off the Pigs!*, 176–181; for circumstances of Panther deaths, Edward Jay Epstein, "The Panthers and the Police: A Pattern of Genocide?," *New Yorker* (vol. 46, Feb. 13, 1971), 45 ff.

114. "Riots, Civil and Criminal Disorders," Committee on Government Operations, U.S. Senate (1969), 3792–3798; "Gun Barrel Politics: The Black Panther Party, 1966–1971," Committee on Internal Security, House Report 470 (1971), 75–76.

115. Heath, *Off the Pigs!*, 181–182.

116. For a devastating account of Newton and the Panthers in the 1970s, Kate Coleman with Paul Avery, "The Party's Over," *High Times*, July 10, 1978, 23 ff.

117. Sellers, *River of No Return*, 184.

118. Carson, *In Struggle*, develops the suicidal theme. Carmichael quote, p. 288.

119. Brown, *Die Nigger Die!*, 115.

120. Newton, *Revolutionary Suicide*, 3–7. Quote on p. 5.

121. William Brink and Louis Harris, *Black and White: A Study of U.S. Racial Attitudes Today* (1967), 54.

Chapter 13. The War, the Liberals, and the Overthrow of LBJ

1. *New York Times*, April 27, 1965, 1.

2. Norman Podhoretz, *Breaking Ranks* (1979), 38, 81.

3. *New Republic* (vol. 152, Feb. 20, 1965), 5–6; *ADA World* (March 1965), 1.

4. For a discussion of elite intellectuals, including their views on Vietnam, see Charles Kadushin, *The American Intellectual Elite* (1974), esp. part II.

5. Arthur Schlesinger, Jr.'s contribution in "Liberal Anti-Communism Revisited: A Symposium," *Commentary* (vol. 44, Sept. 1967), 69.

6. Richard H. Rovere's contribution in "Liberal Anti-Communism Revisited," *Commentary*, 68.

7. Hans J. Morgenthau, "War with China?," *New Republic* (vol. 152, April 3, 1965), 11–14.

8. J. K. Galbraith, "The Galbraith Plan to End the War," *New York Times Magazine*, Nov. 12, 1967, 29 ff. Quote on p. 130.

9. Theodore Draper, "The American Crisis: Vietnam, Cuba, and the Dominican Republic," *Commentary* (vol. 43, Jan. 1967), 27–48. Quote on p. 45.

10. Robert Lekachman, "Death of a Slogan—The Great Society of 1967," *Commentary*, 56–61. Quote on p. 61.

11. *Cong. Rec.* (1964), 6232.
12. Haynes Johnson and Bernard M. Gwertzman, *Fulbright: The Dissenter* (1968), 202–206.
13. *Cong. Rec.* (1965), 13656–13657.
14. *Cong. Rec.* (1965), 23855–23861.
15. For this episode, see Franz Schurmann, Peter Dale Scott, Reginald Zelnik, *The Politics of Escalation in Vietnam* (1966), ch. 9.
16. "Supplemental Foreign Assistance Fiscal Year 1966—Vietnam," Committee on Foreign Relations, Senate hearings (1968).
17. J. William Fulbright, *The Arrogance of Power* (1966).
18. Fulbright, *Arrogance*, 22.
19. Fulbright, *Arrogance*, 77.
20. Fulbright, *Arrogance*, 69.
21. Fulbright, *Arrogance*, 118.
22. *Public Papers of the President, LBJ, 1966,* 519.
23. *New York Times,* July 10, 1965, 1 and 2.
24. William Vanden Heuvel and Milton Gwirtzman, *On His Own: Robert F. Kennedy, 1964–1968* (1970), 220.
25. Text of Kennedy's statement reprinted in *U.S. News and World Report* (vol. 60, March 7, 1966), 104–107.
26. *New York Times,* Feb. 21, 1966, 1.
27. *New York Times,* Feb. 27, 1966, 1E.
28. On Kennedy's senatorial career, see Arthur M. Schlesinger, Jr., *Robert Kennedy and His Times* (1978), chs. 30–36; Vanden Heuvel and Gwirtzman, *On His Own;* and William V. Shannon, *The Heir Apparent: Robert Kennedy and the Struggle for Power* (1967).
29. *Time* (vol. 89, March 17, 1967), 21.
30. *Cong. Rec.* (1967), 5279–5284.
31. Fulbright's speech reprinted in *Cong. Rec.* (1967), 22126–22129.
32. See Kadushin, *American Intellectual Elite,* ch. 6; and Sandy Vogelgesang, *The Long Dark Night of the Soul: The American Intellectual Left and the Vietnam War* (1974).
33. Lowell's letter reprinted in *New York Times,* June 3, 1965, 2.
34. Telegram to Johnson quoted and signers listed in *New York Times,* June 4, 1965, 2; for Johnson's reaction, Eric Goldman, *The Tragedy of Lyndon Johnson* (1969), 447–448.
35. Noam Chomsky, "The Responsibility of the Intellectuals," *New York Review of Books* (vol. 8, Feb. 23, 1967), 16–26. Quotes on pp. 16, 23, 26. Hereafter cited as *New York Review.*
36. See Chomsky's letter in *New York Review* (vol. 8, March 23, 1967), 28.
37. Paul Goodman, "We Won't Go," *New York Review* (vol. 8, May 18, 1967), 17–20; on Goodman's statement of complicity, see letter of Martin Jezer, *New York Review* (vol. 8, June 19, 1967), 29–30.

38. Mary McCarthy, *Vietnam* (1967), 106.
39. Andrew Kopkind, "Soul Power," *New York Review* (vol. 9, Aug. 24, 1967), 3.
40. "A Call to Resist Illegitimate Authority," *New York Review* (vol. 9, Oct. 12, 1967), 7.
41. Goodman's speech reprinted as "A Causerie at the Military-Industrial," *New York Review* (vol. 9, Nov. 23, 1967), 14–18. Quote on p. 14.
42. Jessica Mitford, *The Trial of Dr. Spock* (1969).
43. Robert Lowell's poem, "The March (for Dwight Macdonald)," was published first in the *New York Review* (vol. 9, Nov. 23, 1967), 3, and was included in slightly revised form in his collection *History* (1973), 148. I use the revised version.
44. Norman Mailer, *The Armies of the Night* (1968), 114.
45. Lowell, "The March."
46. Noam Chomsky, "On Resistance," *New York Review* (vol. 9, Dec. 7, 1967), 4–12.
47. Mailer, *Armies of the Night,* 311.
48. Mailer, *Armies of the Night,* 238.
49. *New York Times,* Sept. 25, 1967, 26.
50. "Hitched to LBJ?," *New Republic* (vol. 157, Sept. 30, 1967), 1 and 5.
51. Lewis Chester, Godfrey Hodgson, Bruce Page, *An American Melodrama: The Presidential Election of 1968* (1969), 58–65.
52. *New York Times,* Nov. 27, 1967, 1 and 15.
53. For McCarthy's account of his decision to run, see his book *The Year of the People* (1969), chs. 2–3; excerpts of his announcement were reprinted in *New York Times,* Dec. 1, 1967, 40.
54. George H. Gallup, *The Gallup Poll: Public Opinion 1935–1971* (vol. III, 1972), 2091.
55. Useful on public opinion and the war is Philip E. Converse and Howard Shuman, " 'Silent Majorities' and the Vietnam War," *Scientific American* (vol. 222, June 1970), 17–25.
56. Don Oberdorfer, *Tet!* (1971).
57. Oberdorfer, *Tet!,* ch. 7.
58. Townsend Hoopes, *The Limits of Intervention* (1969), 199–200.
59. Poll results cited in Richard M. Scammon and Ben J. Wattenberg, *The Real Majority* (1970), 91.
60. For accounts of the New Hampshire campaign, Arthur Herzog, *McCarthy for President* (1969), chs. 1 and 4; McCarthy, *Year of the People,* ch. 5; Chester et al., *American Melodrama,* 78–102; and Theodore H. White, *The Making of the President 1968* (1969), 82–90.
61. For evidence that the McCarthy showing was not a victory for doves, see Philip E. Converse et al., "Continuity and Change in American

Politics: Parties and Issues in the 1968 Election," *American Political Science Review* (vol. 63, Dec. 1969), 1092; Louis Harris in *Newsweek* (vol. 71, March 25, 1968), 26; and Scammon and Wattenberg, *The Real Majority* (1970), ch. 7.

62. On Kennedy's decision to run, Schlesinger, *Robert Kennedy*, ch. 37; Chester et al., *American Melodrama*, 105–126; Vanden Heuvel and Gwirtzman, *On His Own*, ch. 14; Jules Witcover, *85 Days: The Last Campaign of Robert Kennedy* (1969), ch. 2.

63. Chester et al., *American Melodrama*, 133–137.

64. For varying accounts see Lyndon Baines Johnson, *Vantage Point* (1971), 389–424; Hoopes, *Limits of Intervention*, chs. 8–10; Oberdorfer, *Tet!*, ch. 8; Harry McPherson, *A Political Education* (1972), ch. 12; Herbert Y. Schandler, *The Unmaking of a President: Lyndon Johnson and Vietnam* (1977), chs. 14 and 15.

65. *Pub. Pap., of the Pres., LBJ, 1968*, 469–476.

66. Lady Bird Johnson, *A White House Diary* (1970), 611–612, 615–619.

67. White, *Making of the President*, 113, 120.

68. Quoted in Oberdorfer, *Tet!*, 99; LBJ, *Vantage Point*, ch. 18.

69. *Pub. Paps. of the Pres., LBJ, 1968*, 476.

Chapter 14. Rout of the Liberals

1. *New York Times*, March 29, 1968, 1; *Time* (vol. 91, April 12, 1968), 18–19.

2. For an account of the Washington riot, Ben W. Gilbert, *Ten Blocks from the White House: Anatomy of the Washington Riots of 1968* (1968).

3. Thomas F. Parker, ed., *Violence in the U.S., Volume 2: 1968–71* (1974), 15.

4. Daley quoted in Parker, *Violence in the U.S.*, 23.

5. *New York Times*, April 19, 1968, 1.

6. *New York Times*, April 20, 1968, 1.

7. *New York Times*, Dec. 5, 1967, 1.

8. For an account, Charles Fager, *Uncertain Resurrection: Poor People's Washington Campaign* (1969). Also see issues of *Time* and *Newsweek*, April 1968.

9. *New York Times*, April 30, 1968, 1.

10. Quoted in *New York Times*, May 14, 1968, 1.

11. *New York Times*, June 20, 1968, 1.

12. *New York Times*, June 24, 1968, 1; June 25, 1.

13. The following account of Nixon's quest for the nomination relies heavily on Lewis Chester, Godfrey Hodgson, Bruce Page, *An American Melodrama: The Presidential Campaign of 1968* (1969); Jules Witcover,

The Resurrection of Richard Nixon (1970); Theodore H. White, *The Making of the President 1968* (1969).

14. Quoted in acknowledgments, Witcover, *Resurrection.*
15. Material in following paragraph covered in Witcover, *Resurrection,* chs. 2–7.
16. *New York Times,* Sept. 5, 1967, 28.
17. Speech reprinted in *Vital Speeches* (vol. 34, March 1, 1968), 299–300. Quote on p. 299.
18. Witcover, *Resurrection,* 237–239; White, *Making of the President,* 132–134.
19. *New York Times,* March 14, 1968, 31.
20. Nixon's major statement on crime excerpted in *New York Times,* May 9, 1968, 1 and 32.
21. Richard J. Whalen, *Catch the Falling Flag* (1972), 148–150.
22. Excerpts of Nixon's radio address on racial accommodation printed in *Time* (vol. 91, May 3, 1968), 21.
23. *New York Times,* March 6, 1968, 1.
24. *New York Times,* March 9, 1968, 16.
25. *New York Times,* March 11, 1968, 1.
26. Whalen, *Catch the Falling Flag,* 137–138.
27. Text of the draft reprinted in Whalen, *Catch the Falling Flag,* 283–294. Quote on p. 291.
28. *New York Times,* April 2, 1968, 1.
29. *New York Times,* April 20, 1968, 17; May 4, 11.
30. White, *Making of the President,* 236.
31. Chester et al., *American Melodrama,* 446–448; Witcover, *Resurrection,* 309–311; White, *Making of the President,* 137–138.
32. Text reprinted in *Vital Speeches* (vol. 34, Sept. 1, 1968), 674–677.
33. Chester et al., *American Melodrama,* 142–145; Hubert H. Humphrey, *Education of a Public Man* (1976), 360–361.
34. Humphrey, *Education of a Public Man,* 367.
35. For his own account of Vietnam views, Humphrey, *Education of a Public Man,* 318–353.
36. Humphrey, *Education of a Public Man,* 348.
37. *New York Times,* April 28, 1968, 1.
38. Kennedy's campaign is well covered in Jules Witcover, *85 Days: The Last Campaign of Robert Kennedy* (1969); and Arthur M. Schlesinger, Jr., *Robert Kennedy and His Times* (1978), chs. 38–41.
39. Kennedy quotes in order, Witcover, *85 Days,* 102, 109, 116.
40. Witcover, *85 Days,* 145.
41. McCarthy campaign covered in Arthur Herzog, *McCarthy for President* (1969); Jeremy Larner, *Nobody Knows: Reflections on the McCarthy Campaign of 1968* (1969); Eugene J. McCarthy, *The Year of the People* (1969).

42. Quoted in Schlesinger, *Robert Kennedy*, 892.
43. Quoted in Witcover, *85 Days*, 209.
44. *New York Times*, June 4, 1968, 50.
45. Ben Stavis, *We Were the Campaign: New Hampshire to Chicago for McCarthy* (1969), 51–53; Larner, *Nobody Knows*, passim.
46. Larner, *Nobody Knows*, 31.
47. Quoted in frontispiece of Larner, *Nobody Knows*, 13.
48. McCarthy's views on Cold War and Kennedy's complicity most forthrightly stated in a speech at the Cow Palace in San Francisco on May 22. Quotes from this speech appear in Larner, *Nobody Knows*, 94–95. See also *New York Times*, May 24, 1968, 25.
49. *New York Times*, March 17, 1968, 68.
50. *New York Times*, June 14, 1968, 1.
51. McCarthy's major speech on the urban crisis was delivered at the University of California at Davis, May 28, and is extensively quoted in Larner, *Nobody Knows*, 107–109.
52. Quoted in Larner, *Nobody Knows*, 103.
53. Quoted in Witcover, *85 Days*, 209.
54. Quoted in Herzog, *McCarthy for President*, 143.
55. Quoted in Witcover, *85 Days*, 207.
56. *New York Times*, May 30, 1968, 14.
57. Witcover, *85 Days*, 229–235.
58. Chester et al., *American Melodrama*, 330.
59. Debate excerpted in *New York Times*, June 2, 1968, 64.
60. For returns, Richard M. Scammon, ed., *American Votes 8: A Handbook of American Election Statistics* (1970), 46.
61. On county chairmen, *New York Times*, June 2, 1968, 35.
62. Larner, *Nobody Knows*, 127–129.
63. *New York Times*, June 23, 1968, IV, 1.
64. Herzog, *McCarthy for President*, 201–211.
65. Gallup poll released August 21, 1968, showed Nixon beating Humphrey 45 percent to 29 percent, and Nixon beating McCarthy 42 percent to 37 percent. George H. Gallup, *The Gallup Poll: Public Opinion 1935–1971* (vol. III, 1972), 2154–2156.
66. *New York Times*, Aug. 13, 1968, 26.
67. *New York Times*, Aug. 19, 1968, 27.
68. *Rights in Conflict: Chicago's 7 Brutal Days: A Report Submitted by Daniel Walker, Director of the Chicago Study Team, to the National Commission on the Causes and Prevention of Violence* (1968), 1.
69. *Rights in Conflict*, 60, 71, 72.
70. Abbie Hoffman, *Soon to Be a Major Motion Picture* (1980). For self-description, p. 127. Examples of monkey warfare drawn from pp. 108–110, 129–136, 101–102. For clenched fist quote, p. 99.
71. Jerry Rubin, *DO iT!: Scenarios of the Revolution* (1970), chs. 6, 9, 11.

72. Hoffman, *Soon to Be a Major Motion Picture*, 127.
73. Rubin, *DO iT!*, 81.
74. Hoffman, *Soon to Be a Major Motion Picture*, 137.
75. Hoffman, *Soon to Be a Major Motion Picture*, 144.
76. Hoffman, *Soon to Be a Major Motion Picture*, 145; *Rights in Conflict*, 49.
77. Memo from Rennie Davis and Tom Hayden to National Mobilization Staff: Chicago Organizers [undated but written in early winter, 1968], reprinted in "Subversive Involvement in Disruption of 1968 Democratic Party National Convention," Committee on Un-American Activities, House hearings (1968), 2556–2559.
78. *Rights in Conflict*, 14–19, 43.
79. Dave Dellinger, *More Power than We Know: The People's Movement toward Democracy* (1975), 121–123.
80. "Minutes of Meeting to Discuss Setting Up a Legal Committee for Chicago," Jan. 26, 1968, reprinted in "Subversive Involvement," House hearings, 2284–2289. Quote on p. 2285.
81. Dellinger quoted in *Rights in Conflict*, 11.
82. *New York Times*, March 24, 1968, 64; March 25, 46.
83. Milton Viorst, *Fire in the Streets: America in the 1960's* (1979), 446–447.
84. On permit negotiations, *Rights in Conflict*, 31–42.
85. *Chicago Seed* (vol. 2, no. 11), 23.
86. Quoted in "The Decline and Fall of the Democratic Party," *Ramparts* (vol. 7, Sept. 28, 1968), 21.
87. *Rights in Conflict*, 53.
88. On number of delegates and alternates, White, *Making of the President*, 272.
89. *New York Times*, Aug. 25, 1968, 4E.
90. *New York Times*, Aug. 28, 1968, 36.
91. *New York Times*, Aug. 29, 1968, 23. Rosenberg quoted in Chester et al., *American Melodrama*, 541.
92. Quoted in White, *Making of the President*, 278.
93. White, *Making of the President*, 277–279.
94. Chester et al., *American Melodrama*, 556–557; White, *Making of the President*, 279.
95. *New York Times*, Aug. 22, 1968, 1 and 22.
96. On movement to draft Kennedy, Chester et al., *American Melodrama*, 564–576; *Newsweek* (vol. 72, Sept. 9, 1968), 34–35.
97. On Sunday's events, *Rights in Conflict*, 87–100, 202–205.
98. For Humphrey's account, Humphrey, *Education of a Public Man*, 387–390. On pre-convention negotiations on the plank, Chester et al., *American Melodrama*, 524–537.
99. Johnson quoted in Humphrey, *Education of a Public Man*, 389.
100. Humphrey, *Education of a Public Man*, 390.

101. Text of majority plank reprinted in *New York Times*, Aug. 27, 1968, 26; minority plank quoted in *Newsweek* (Sept. 9, 1968), 33.
102. Chester et al., *American Melodrama*, 579–581; *New York Times*, Aug. 29, 1968, 1.
103. Herzog, *McCarthy for President*, 274.
104. For bandshell battle, *Rights in Conflict*, 141–150.
105. Hayden quoted in Norman Mailer, *Miami and the Siege of Chicago* (1968), 166.
106. Ginsberg quoted in Mailer, *Miami*, 167.
107. *New York Times*, Aug. 29, 1968, 1 and 23.
108. *Rights in Conflict*, 150–158.
109. White, *Making of the President*, 294; *Time* (vol. 92, Sept. 6, 1968), 16.
110. *Rights in Conflict*, 159–175. Chant quoted p. 168; police shout quoted p. 167.
111. Mailer, *Miami*, 169.
112. White, *Making of the President*, 298.
113. Chester et al., *American Melodrama*, 583–585; Mailer, *Miami*, 176–181; *Newsweek* (Sept. 9, 1968), 36; Daley's alleged remark quoted in text and note in Viorst, *Fire in the Streets*, 459. Daley denied he said it.
114. McCarthy's speech excerpted in Chester et al., *American Melodrama*, 588–589.
115. Humphrey text in *Vital Speeches* (vol. 34, Sept. 15, 1968), 706–709.
116. *Rights in Conflict*, 230–233; White, *Making of the President*, 308–310; Herzog, *McCarthy for President*, 278–281.
117. Rubin quoted in Viorst, *Fire in the Streets*, 458–459.
118. *New York Times*, Sept. 1, 1968, 1.
119. Humphrey quoted in White, *Making of the President*, 303.
120. *New York Times*, Aug. 30, 1968, 15; Sept. 3, 34.
121. *New York Times*, Aug. 31, 1968, 10.
122. Marshall Frady, *Wallace* (1976), ch. 5; Chester et al., *American Melodrama*, 272–275. Quote on p. 272.
123. *New York Times*, Feb. 9, 1968, 1.
124. *New York Times*, May 7, 1968, 1.
125. Seymour Martin Lipset and Earl Raab, *The Politics of Unreason: Right-Wing Extremism in America, 1790–1970* (1970), 351–355; *New York Times*, Oct. 6, 1968, 74; Sept. 13, 51; Sept. 18, 1 and 27.
126. *New York Times*, Aug. 25, 1968, 61.
127. Lipset and Raab, *Politics of Unreason*, 345.
128. Quoted in Chester et al., *American Melodrama*, 280–281.
129. *New York Times*, Sept. 8, 1968, 2E.
130. Quoted in Chester et al., *American Melodrama*, 279.
131. Excerpts of platform in Lipset and Raab, *Politics of Unreason*, 346–348; *New York Times*, Oct. 14, 1968, 1 and 41.

132. For description of typical Wallace meeting, Ray Jenkins, "George Wallace Figures to Win Even If He Loses," *New York Times Magazine* (April 7, 1968), 27 ff.
133. *New York Times*, Sept. 3, 1968, 34.
134. Quoted in Jenkins, "George Wallace Figures . . . ," 66.
135. Quoted in *Time* (vol. 92, Oct. 18, 1968), 18.
136. Quoted in Jenkins, "George Wallace Figures . . . ," 68.
137. *Time*, Oct. 18, 1968, 16.
138. Quoted in Jenkins, "George Wallace Figures . . . ," 69.
139. Pete Hamill, "Wallace," *Ramparts* (vol. 7, Oct. 26, 1968), 47.
140. Quoted in Jenkins, "George Wallace Figures . . . ," 68.
141. Quoted in *Time*, Oct. 18, 1968, 18.
142. *New York Times*, July 27, 1968, 1.
143. *New York Times*, Oct. 25, 1968, 1 and 32.
144. *New York Times*, July 27, 1968, 10.
145. Humphrey quoted in *Time*, Oct. 18, 1968, 15.
146. *The Gallup Poll*, 2107, 2126, 2139, 2162.
147. *The Gallup Poll*, 2162.
148. *New York Times*, Sept. 10, 1968, 32; Chester et al., *American Melodrama*, 705.
149. Thomas F. Pettigrew, *Racially Separate or Together?* (1971), ch. 10, esp. 239.
150. Gallup, *The Gallup Poll*, 2159.
151. For Nixon's strategy, Chester et al., *American Melodrama*, 620–625; and White, *Making of the President*, 330–331.
152. *New York Times*, Oct. 17, 1968, 36.
153. Joe McGinniss, *The Selling of the President 1968* (1969), ch. 5.
154. Whalen, *Catch the Falling Flag*, 210–212. Quote on p. 210.
155. *New York Times*, Sept. 8, 1968, 78.
156. *New York Times*, Sept. 13, 1968, 1 and 50.
157. Gallup, *The Gallup Poll*, 2158.
158. O'Brien quoted in Chester et al., *American Melodrama*, 632–633.
159. *New York Times*, Sept. 10, 1968, 1 and 32.
160. *New York Times*, Sept. 11, 1968, 1, 16, 28.
161. *New York Times*, Sept. 23, 1968, 1 and 30.
162. Lawrence F. O'Brien, *No Final Victories* (1974), 258.
163. Gallup, *The Gallup Poll*, 2162.
164. Chester et al., *American Melodrama*, 644–646; White, *The Making of the President*, 353; *New York Times*, Sept. 29, 1968, 74.
165. Humphrey, *Education of a Public Man*, 400–403. Quote on p. 403. See also Chester et al., *American Melodrama*, 645–650.
166. Text reprinted in *Vital Speeches* (vol. 35, Oct. 15, 1968), 8–11.
167. *Vital Speeches*, Oct. 15, 1968, 9.

168. George Christian, *The President Steps Down* (1970), 152.
169. Both Nixon and Le Duc Tho quotes in *New York Times*, Oct. 2, 1968, 27, 26.
170. McGinniss, *Selling of the President*, 126.
171. Norman N. Nie, Sidney Verba, John R. Petrocik, *The Changing American Voter* (1976), 83.
172. *New York Times*, Sept. 28, 1968, 18.
173. *New York Times*, Oct. 19, 1968, 20.
174. *New York Times*, Oct. 2, 1968, 1.
175. *New York Times*, Sept. 23, 1968, 30.
176. *New York Times*, Oct. 19, 1968, 20.
177. Chester et al., *American Melodrama*, 707–710; White, *Making of the President*, 365–366.
178. *New York Times*, Oct. 16, 1968, 31.
179. White, *Making of the President*, 364.
180. For account of LeMay press conference and the quotes in this paragraph, *New York Times*, Oct. 4, 1968, 1 and 50.
181. White, *Making of the President*, 358.
182. Gallup, *The Gallup Poll*, 2167.
183. *RN: The Memoirs of Richard Nixon* (1978), 322–323.
184. This account of the bombing-halt negotiations is based on Lyndon B. Johnson, *Vantage Point* (1971), 513–529; Christian, *The President Steps Down*, chs. 2, *New York Times*, Nov. 1, 1968, 1.
185. *New York Times*, Nov. 2, 1968, 1.
186. *Memoirs of Richard Nixon*, 323.
187. *Memoirs of Richard Nixon*, 329.
188. Humphrey, *Education of a Public Man*, 404.
189. Christian, *The President Steps Down*, 61.
190. Humphrey, *Education of a Public Man*, 404–405.
191. Johnson, *Vantage Point*, 517–518; Christian, *The President Steps Down*, 151–153.
192. Johnson offered this view of the election in a televised interview reported in *New York Times*, Dec. 27, 1969, 8.
193. Thomas Powers, *The Man Who Kept the Secrets* (1979), 197–199. Quote p. 199. See also Christian, *The President Steps Down*, 93–94; White, *Making of the President*, 380–381; William Safire, *Before the Fall* (1975), 88–91. For her own account of her role, Anna Chennault, *The Education of Anna* (1980), 170–177, 189–198. She says she acted as a conduit from Saigon to the Nixon campaign but not from the Nixon campaign to Saigon.
194. Cartha DeLoach quoted in *New York Times*, Feb. 3, 1975, 1.
195. Humphrey, *Education of a Public Man*, 8–9.
196. *New York Times*, Nov. 2, 1968, 22.

197. *New York Times,* Nov. 4, 1968, 1; White, *Making of the President,* 382.

198. For popular vote by state, with national totals and electoral vote, Scammon, *America Votes 8,* 1.

199. Lipset and Raab, *The Politics of Unreason,* 384.

200. Philip E. Converse, Warren E. Miller, Jerrold G. Rusk, Arthur C. Wolfe, "Continuity and Change in American Politics: Parties and Issues in the 1968 Election," *The American Political Science Review* (vol. 63, Dec. 1969), 1083–1105. Esp. p. 1092.

201. These estimates of black and white votes are offered on the basis of survey data in Converse et al., 1084–1085. Gallup's data placed "nonwhite vote for Humphrey at 85 percent, *New York Times,* Dec. 8, 1968, 84.

202. U.S. Bureau of the Census, *The Statistical Abstract of the United States* (1976), 1084.

INDEX

ABOUT THE AUTHOR

After receiving his Ph.D. degree from Harvard University in 1963, Allen J. Matusow went to Rice University where he is now Professor of American History and Dean of Humanities. An award-winning teacher, he has been a visiting member on the Stanford University faculty and a fellow of the Charles Warren Center of American History at Harvard. His publications include *Farm Policies and Politics in the Truman Years* (Harvard University Press, 1967); *The Truman Administration: A Documentary History* (edited with Barton Bernstein, Harper & Row, 1966); *Twentieth Century America: Recent Interpretations* (edited with Barton Bernstein, Harcourt, Brace and World, 1969 and 1972); *Joseph R. McCarthy* (edited essays and documents, Prentice-Hall, 1970). During the ten years it took him to write *The Unraveling of America: A History of Liberalism in the 1960s,* he received grants from the Lyndon Baines Johnson Library, the National Endowment for the Humanities, and the American Philosophical Society.